Cuban Cinema

Cultural Studies in the Americas

Edited by George Yúdice, Jean Franco, and Juan Flores

Cuban Cinema

Michael Chanan

Cultural Studies of the Americas, Volume 14

University of Minnesota Press
Minneapolis • London

The University of Minnesota Press gratefully acknowledges the assistance provided for the publication of this book by the McKnight Foundation.

Published by the University of Minnesota Press
111 Third Avenue South, Suite 290
Minneapolis, MN 55401-2520
http://www.upress.umn.edu

Library of Congress Cataloging-in-Publication Data

Chanan, Michael.
    [Cuban image]
    Cuban cinema / Michael Chanan.
       p.   cm. — (Cultural studies of the Americas ; 14)
    Originally published: The Cuban image. London : British Film Institute ; Bloomington, Ind. : Indiana University Press, 1985.
    Includes bibliographical references and index.
    ISBN 0-8166-3423-8 (alk. paper) — ISBN 0-8166-3424-6 (PB : alk. paper)
    1. Motion pictures—Cuba—History. 2. Motion pictures—Social aspects—Cuba. I. Title. II. Series.
PN1993.5.C8C48   2003
791.43'097291—dc22   2003020074

In memory of Luis Espinal and Miguel Cabezas,
and for Margaret and Duncan

Contents

Preface

The first edition of this book was published in 1985 and covered the history of Cuban cinema up to 1979. This new edition, which brings the story current to the turn of the twenty-first century, is separated not just by the passage of years but by a change of historical epoch. When the book first appeared, the Cold War was still in full swing, neoliberalism only in its first phase, and revolutionary Cuba had been boosted by the triumph of the Sandinistas in Nicaragua. Cuban films enjoyed a reputation around the world as the model of a cinema that conjoined political commitment and bold aesthetic novelty. At the end of the century, the Soviet bloc and the Sandinistas had both passed into history, revolutionary socialism had been discredited by an unthinkable historical reversal, and the talk was all of globalization. Yet socialist Cuba is still there, having survived the severest of peacetime economic crises without becoming a failed state. Its film industry has suffered contraction and no longer attracts the same attention abroad, but it continues to produce films that deserve to be known far more widely. I hope this new edition will contribute to such an end.

Although Cuba was almost bankrupted by the collapse of the Soviet Union, on which the island depended for three decades, nevertheless Fidel Castro and the Communist Party remain in power—widely criticized for not giving up but also admired, if sometimes grudgingly, for the very same thing, both in Latin America and beyond. This book is offered in the conviction that Cuban cinema, even in its weakened condition, provides primary evidence of the complex factors at play in this extraordinary situation, and that fulfilling this role is what nourishes its aesthetic and political fascination.

In order to reflect the distance between these two moments, I have replaced the original foreword with a new introduction, which surveys the forty years of Cuban cinema from the triumph of the Revolution in 1959 to the end of the century. This is followed by the revised text of the first edition, divided into two parts, covering the years before the Revolution and then the first twenty years after it (1959–79). Corrections have been kept to a minimum; a few paragraphs have been removed, and one or two added for clarification, but the accounts of the films have not changed. The chapters new to this edition comprise Part III, which begins with a retrospective survey of the first twenty years after the Revolution, then picks up where Part I leaves off. This gives readers, both new and previous, several possible routes through the text.

I have not amended the accounts of the films from the first edition, but I do not suppose that my readings are in any way conclusive. On the contrary, I commend the remarks of the Cuban critic Juan Antonio García Borrero on Tomás Gutiérrez Alea's *Memorias del subdesarrollo* (*Memories of Underdevelopment*, 1968) in his *Critical Guide to Cuban Fiction Cinema*. On seeing the film again, García Borrero speaks of the way it gave him the unexpected impression of never having seen it before: "I followed it conscious of the order of the scenes that would appear before me, only that now, the density of these sequences revealed new meanings, new possibilities of interpretation, readings never envisaged."[1] This is not just to say that in Cuba a film like this remains relevant many years after it was made, but that new interpretations are produced by the changing contours of history and thus the situation of the viewer.

When I first introduced this book, I wrote of my own situation as author as the function of a double movement. Having already spent time in Latin America before first going to Cuba in 1979, I knew something about the asymmetrical nature of the cultural distances contained in political geography, of the invisible divide to be crossed when traveling from the first world to the third, which only fully registered not on going but on returning. Anthropologist friends reported the same experience on returning from fieldwork. Leaving behind the smell and the taste of the country of sojourn and coming back to one's own, one felt disoriented and set apart by the encounter with the immediate reality of underdevelopment. My first visit to Cuba also taught me something else. The strange thing about that month was that because my subject of investigation was cinema, I saw both more and less than another visitor might in the same period of time. Less because most days I was sitting in a viewing theater, more because I was watching the country go by on the screen. You couldn't possibly visit so many places, meet so many people, and see so many facets of their lives in the space of a month in any other way; film transports you and condenses time. The experience taught me much about the paradoxical qualities of the medium and made me intensely aware of the space of viewing itself. I realized that the film you see depends, among other things, on where you see it. Logically speaking, the film is exactly the same wherever you watch it, but the film you seem to see depends on where that is. Film scholars have long talked about the way that film positions the viewer, but this position is also affected by the situation of viewing, the historical and geographical location of the viewer in front of the screen. The projected image is the same, but the space between the screen and the viewer's eyes is different.

I remembered a similar experience I'd had years earlier, when I saw a work of underground cinema, Carolee Schneeman's *Fuses,* first on a large screen at the ICA (Institute of Contemporary Arts) in London and then not long afterward projected on the wall of her home at a party. I had not much liked it the first time, but very much the second, and it seemed clear to me that this was because of the kind of film it was: the neutral dull space of the cinema deadened something in the image, which came alive on the domestic wall. I felt something similar in Havana: the films gave the feeling of being fully at home on these screens.

The thing struck me most vividly two weeks after arriving in Cuba. I had watched Octavio Cortázar's marvelous documentary *Hablando de punto cubano* (Speaking of typical Cuban music), which explains a song form called *controversia* (controversy), a musical competition in which singers improvise alternate verses. (I discuss the film in detail in chapter 13.) After seeing the film, I wondered to what extent the art was still alive and what kind of search was required by the filmmakers to find these obviously accomplished practitioners. The next day my hosts at the state film institute took me to Varadero for a weekend at the seaside. On the way we stopped for a drink at a beauty spot. It was midafternoon, and the only other people in the bar were a group sitting at a table in the garden at the back; judging by the number of empty beer bottles, they had been there a good while. As we sat down we heard singing, and they gestured for us to come and listen: an older man and a younger man were engaged in a *controversia*. There was a cheerful round of laughter as the older man proclaimed himself the winner, because, he sang, his opponent had slipped up and used the same word twice in the same verse. I knew at once the answer to my queries of the previous day and at the same time became aware of all sorts of other continuities between what I was seeing on the screen and what lay outside the viewing theater. This sense of contact with the immediate world from which Cuban cinema takes its image has served, I hope, to animate this book. If it hasn't, it is not the fault of the films.

The foreword to the first edition included a long list of people who gave me their help, their time, and their encouragement. I remember first those whom time has removed from us: Tomás Gutiérrez Alea (Titón), Santiago Álvarez, Manuel Octavio Gómez, Hector García Mesa, Idalia Anreus, Adolfo Llaurado, and Jesús Díaz. Then: Alfredo Guevara, Julio García Espinosa, Humberto Solás, Ambrosio Fornet, Pastor Vega, José Massip, Jorge Fraga, Sergio Giral, Enrique Pineda Barnet, Daysi Granados, Miguel Torres, Manuel Pérez, Octavio Cortázar, Juan Padrón, Gerardo Chijona, Jorge Pucheux, Eusebio Ortiz, José Antonio González, Enrique Colina, Norma Torrado, Francisco León, Sergio Núñez, the late Romualdo Santos, Mario Piedra, Manuel Pereira, Raúl Rodríguez, Roberto Roque, Jorge Sotolongo, and others. Also the composers Leo Brouwer and Harold Gramatges. For their help in organizing my activities, Olga Ríos, María Padrón, and Lola Calviño; and for their courteous assistance, the projectionists of ICAIC and the staff of the library of Cinemateca.

I also benefited from the help of many others. In Cuba (in some cases between films during successive Havana film festivals), and in other countries, they include Jorge de la Fuente, Nina Menéndez, Jean Stubbs, Pedro Sarduy, Lionel Martin, and Adrienne Hunter; Julianne Burton and Zuzana Pick; Fernando Birri, Settimio Presutto, Miguel Littín, Patricio Guzmán, the late Joris Ivens, Jorge Sanjinés, Octavio Getino, and Jorge Denti; Hector Schmucler, Ana María Nethol, the late Emilio García Riera, Jorge Ayala Blanco, and Dennis de la Roca; Lino Micciche, Peter Chappell, John King, Alastair Henessy, the late Nissa Torrents, Robin Blackburn, Angela Martin, Anne Head, Olivia Harris, Alan Fountain, Rod Stoneman, Chris Rodriguez, and people at the South West Arts Weekend

School on Cuban Cinema in 1982. Also the late Simon Hartog for drawing my attention to a number of bibliographical sources, and Ed Buscombe, Geoffrey Nowell-Smith, and others at the British Film Institute.

Material from the first edition previously appeared in the form of articles and essays in a number of places, including *Framework, Areito,* and *Third World Affairs 1985,* and in *Guerres Révolutionnaires, Histoire et cinéma,* edited by Svlvie Dallet (Paris: Éditions l'Harmattan, 1984). The bulk of the material in chapter 10 previously appeared in Santiago Álvarez, BFI Dossier 2 (1980).

For the second edition, I am indebted first to friends in England and the United States who encouraged me to take on the task. The new pages draw on conversations over the years at different times and in different countries with Titón, Julio García Espinosa, Ambrosio Fornet, and Jesús Díaz; and with Paolo Antonio Parangua, Chuck Kleinhans, Julia Lesage, John Hess, Jorge Ruffinelli, and Haim Bresheeth.

In Cuba, for once again generously contributing their time and encouragement, I thank Ambrosio Fornet, Julio García Espinosa, Pastor Vega, Fernando Pérez, Rigoberto López, Orlando Rojas, Eduardo del Llano, Humberto Solás, Rolando Díaz, Enrique Colina, Mirta Ibarra, Tomás Piard, and Enrique Pineda Barnet. I am especially indebted to Juan Antonio García Borrero for kindly giving me a prepublication copy of his excellent *Critical Dictionary of Cuban Fiction Cinema, 1910–1998,* which has made writing the new chapters so much easier. A number of people, in addition to ICAIC, gave me copies of films on video. I owe special thanks at ICAIC to Ana Busquets, Olga Outeriño, and Ivan Giroud, and thanks to Andrew Paxman of *Variety* for that photocopy.

Some of the new material in this edition had its first outing at "Latin American Cinema in the 1990s," a conference at Trinity and All Saints College, Leeds, England, in 1996; at a colloquium on Latin American cinema at Tel Aviv University in 1998; and at the Latin American Studies Association conference at the University of Liverpool in 1998. My presentation at the first of these events was published in Leeds Iberian Papers (1997).

I am grateful to the Arts and Humanities Research Board of the United Kingdom and to the University of the West of England for the funds that enabled me to carry out research on two visits to Havana, in December 1998 and December 2000.

Bristol, England, December 2003

Coppola on Cuban Film

On December 2, 1975, Robert Scheer interviewed Francis Ford Coppola in San Francisco about the filmmaker's recent trip to Cuba.

Were you able to see Cuban films down there?
Any films we wanted to see. We would just sit in the screening room and they would run anything we wanted.

What did you think of them?
I thought they were very good. I have been traveling around and I know very well the pain of a country like Australia that's a wealthy civilized place and yet has no film industry, because it's cheaper for them to buy our old television shows and our old movies. You see them struggling to have a little bit of a film thing. Yet here you have Cuba, which is a small place by comparison, and they have healthy, real, ambitious films.

Are they doing experimental things?
A person who considers himself an artist approaches a socialist society worrying about, well, the art has to be really simple and follow a certain line and make a certain point, but my impression was that there's a lot of latitude. The Cuban authority acknowledges the complexity of the human experience and their films explore that. My first impression when I saw *Memories of Underdevelopment* years ago was that it was complex and had different shades of feelings about the Revolution. They acknowledge that. They're very eloquent about it. They're not pretending

that it's just child's play to put together this new kind of society; it's really hard. And for all their many successes, they've had many failures. But they feel they're right, so it's worth pursuing it.

They know that it's hard on people: the man at the mental institution says that the incidence of neurosis is much higher than before the Revolution. They are very honest about the difficulties of creating the socialist society—people rethinking questions of property, the fact that you're not rewarded monetarily. They have a very elaborate system of competition that does reward workers materially. If you do better at your job than the next person, you get to buy the washing machine. The lowest-paid person might make $150 a month and Fidel makes $700 a month. So, I mean, there are some differences in pay. We asked most of the smart-ass questions. For example, let's say you don't want to be a street cleaner anymore. How do you get out of it? And the key word was education. If you're a street cleaner and you want to be a draftsman or an electronics engineer, you have the opportunity to study three hours a day; you don't get paid any less. The state encourages it. It's made available to them and they are not docked in pay. That, to me, is a really exciting idea.

Did you ask questions about the problem of artistic freedom?
Yes. No one is permitted to criticize the government, other than through the channels that are provided for them. If you're a worker or if you're a writer, you can do it in your various workers' groups. In a factory they get together a couple of nights a week and discuss problems—how to make things better, what's unfair, and stuff like that. So, in other words, there are channels that allow you not to criticize the idea of the society but to figure out how to make it better. I like the honesty of it. They say no, you cannot criticize the government—that freedom, no, you don't have.

Here in America you can write or say anything you want, and many people in Cuba are very impressed when you tell them this. They are surprised when they see something like *Godfather II.* They wonder, "How can you make a film that says nice things about our Revolution?" But the truth is, I believe, that the freedoms we have here are possible because they do not even come close to jeopardizing the real interests that govern our country. If there were someone who really came close to jeopardizing those interests, I believe our freedoms would vanish, one way or the other. If there were a man, a political candidate, who was elected to office and began implementing real programs that were counter to the big interests, there would be a coup or a murder or whatever was necessary.

In Cuba they don't even have the illusion of that kind of political freedom. It's as though they're saying, "Our Revolution is too fragile, it has too many enemies, it is too difficult to pull off to allow forces inside or outside to work to counter it." I understand the implications of what I'm saying, the dangers. But I put it to you: if they are right—if their society is truly beautiful and honest and worthwhile—then it is worth protecting, even with this suspension of freedom. In Chile, that newborn, elected society was not protected in this way, and so it was destroyed. Ironically, the government that replaced it is not taking any chances and is controlling the press and opposition in a way that Allende did not.

It seems that what you're saying is that in Cuba, for instance, people suddenly had the freedom to do something very positive, like create a mental institution or a school, which in some sense is a freedom we don't have. Basically our freedom is still limited freedom.

We don't have the freedom to live in a society that is healthy. *That* is real freedom. We don't have the freedom to live in a society that takes care of people.

INTRODUCTION

Forty Years On

Early in 1998, an extraordinary situation unfolded in Havana that would demonstrate that almost forty years since the Revolution of 1959 and the creation of a state film institute, Instituto Cubano de Arte e Industria Cinematográficos (ICAIC; Cuban Institute of Film Art and Industry), cinema in Cuba continued to be a highly charged political issue. Fidel Castro, in the closing speech of the February session of the National Assembly, raised a series of questions about the power of Hollywood and the huge budgets employed to ensure that Hollywood movies conquered screens throughout the world; he cited the example of *Titanic*, whose young star, Leonardo DiCaprio, had been visiting Cuba. The Cuban leader had spoken in this vein once before, at the awards ceremony of the Havana Film Festival in 1985, when he talked of the struggle of Latin American filmmakers to compete, even in their own countries. This time, however, he shifted gear, and launched into an attack on discontents in Cuba who captured international attention by making films that, instead of celebrating the positive achievements of the Revolution, proffered negative criticisms—or worse, were counterrevolutionary. He gave the example of a film that he said he'd been told about, in which a corpse was transported from Guantánamo to Havana, or the other way around, he didn't know which. His listeners were shocked to realize that he was attacking *Guantanamera,* the last film of Tomás Gutiérrez Alea, Cuba's most celebrated film director, who had died almost two years earlier. The film (codirected by Juan Carlos Tabío) is a black comedy in which an old woman from Havana dies in Guantánamo, at the other end of the island, and, because of fuel restrictions, her body is returned to Havana in a relay of hearses and bureaucratic muddles.

According to reports that circulated later, it was the minister of culture, Abel Prieto, who first approached Fidel and asked him if he realized the film in question was made by Titón—the nickname by which Alea was universally known. He did not, because he hadn't seen it, and he was taken aback to discover that he'd unwittingly slandered the memory of a man he had respected. Within a day or two he had sent a message to Alea's widow, the actress Mirta Ibarra, apologizing for his mistake, and although the speech had been broadcast as usual on television, it did not appear in the party newspaper *Granma* as it would normally have done (although it was later printed for internal party consumption).[1]

But the offense continued to rankle, raising its head again a few days later, when the Cuban leader made an unusual appearance at a meeting of the National Committee of the Union of Writers and Artists (UNEAC), which he didn't normally attend. He spoke about various issues he had recently been contemplating that also concerned UNEAC, such as the defense of national culture in the face of globalization. As the meeting was about to retire for lunch, the author Senel Paz—the scriptwriter on Alea's penultimate film *Fresa y chocolate* (*Strawberry and Chocolate*, also codirected by Tabío)—got up and asked to speak. Referring to Fidel's words a fortnight earlier, he said that he normally found he agreed with Fidel's opinions, but on the question of Alea's film, he could not do so. He was followed by a dozen or so others, some of them filmmakers, some not. All defended the film. The film director Manuel Pérez, a staunch party member, explained that *Guantanamera* invited its audience to laugh not against the Revolution, but with it. Another speaker pointed out that the film had several readings, which included Alea's own relationship to death (he was dying from cancer when he made it). Finally, Fidel asked if there was anyone who held a different opinion about the film; there was a resounding silence.

Fidel summed up. He had not realized the film was Titón's, and acknowledged that he must have been mistaken about it, since he regarded Alea as beyond reproach. However, he was concerned that so many films produced by the Film Institute, ICAIC, in recent years had the same orientation—they were too critical, and this, he said, was something that would have to be discussed with ICAIC's president, Alfredo Guevara. According to an account by the Spanish writer Manuel Vásquez Montalbán, this was part of a general complaint about the "defeatism" *(derrotismo)* that seemed to emanate from the intellectual sector in the years following the fall of communism in Eastern Europe and the Soviet Union.[2] The mood of *derrotismo* was not unique to ICAIC, nor did complaints about it originate with Fidel. The same thing was said of the leading Cuban think tank, the Centro de Estudios de América (CEA), two years earlier, when an orthodox faction within the party central committee attacked it for thinking too independently.

Alfredo Guevara was an old comrade of Castro's from student days (indeed, Castro has been known to say that it was Alfredo Guevara who introduced him to Marxism), who in 1991 had returned to the helm of ICAIC, which he founded in 1959 and then left in 1981. Guevara now held discussions with several of the directors, who came up with position papers to help him formulate the arguments to present in defense of ICAIC's policies. He also appeared in a television interview commenting publicly on the issue. The situation, he said, was a mess, and Fidel had given him the job of explaining things to him. "I think that as a result of this encounter, we Cuban cineasts will be able to prove to the Comandante en Jefe that we are the same people he's always trusted, loyal to the Revolution, critics like him, not more critical than him, capable of holding back, if it's necessary to hold back; but not to abandon our language, because the language of the cinema is either the language of the cinema or it isn't cinema, and I believe, as I've said before, that we're on the right road, the road of clarity."[3] How to read this comment is indicated by the way that one of my informants, who saw the interview on television, remembered it. Ambrosio Fornet, who is both a literary historian and a screenwriter, remembered Guevara saying that the language of cinema and the language of politics were two different things, the two did not always go hand in hand, and sometimes it was necessary to explain this to the party leaders.[4] It was as if, he added, the phoenix had risen, as if, once more—because this was a battle that had been engaged before—Guevara had won an argument on behalf of the Film Institute's autonomy, and the filmmakers' right to fulfill their artistic vocation, even when this meant taking up a critical position toward the political establishment.

This book is about the history of these arguments—about the origins of the extraordinary role that cinema has played in Cuba's Revolution, and the imperatives that led to the creation of ICAIC within three months of the seizure of power on January 1, 1959, in the first decree about cultural matters issued by the Revolutionary Government. It is about the battles engaged in the early years under Alfredo Guevara's leadership against sectarians of both right and left; about the defense of ICAIC's hard-won autonomy in the early 1970s, the period that Fornet dubbed "the five grey years" *(el quinquenio gris);* and the crisis occasioned in the early 1980s by the film *Cecilia* (directed by Humberto Solás) when Guevara was ousted. And then the resurgence that followed the appointment of Julio García Espinosa as his successor, until he too fell victim, ten years later, to attacks by the party faithful on *Alicia en el pueblo de Maravillas* (Alice in Wondertown), a biting satire by Daniel Díaz Torres, which led to Alfredo Guevara's return (until his retirement in 2000; his replacement, Omar González, is the first head of ICAIC who is not a filmmaker, but a cultural functionary, with previous experience in areas like television and publishing). Not least, it is also about the struggle to keep the film institute afloat during the economic collapse (the "Special Period") following the demise of Communism in Eastern Europe and the Soviet Union, which propelled the island into deep crisis, full of social and political tensions; and about the implications of the so-called New World Order for a tiny but hugely creative and obstinate group of Caribbean filmmakers who refuse to take the threat of their demise lying down.

It is also, of course, about the films themselves, through which these arguments and battles are projected, where politics, economics, and ideology take on aesthetic form, and enter into dialogue with public consciousness. The films made in Cuba before the cinema of the Revolution exploded onto the world's screens in the 1960s are of little aesthetic import, whatever the delights, mainly musical, they may sometimes contain. The Revolution, however, unleashed among a new generation of filmmakers a furious creative energy as they turned the cameras on the process they were living, and told the Cuban people—and anyone else who was interested—who they were and what they were doing. In 1961, in a famous speech on the eve of the Bay of Pigs invasion by an army of expatriate Cubans in the pay of the CIA, Castro told everyone that what they were doing in Cuba was called socialism. The Revolution was carried forward by mass enthusiasm and a powerful sense of direct democracy, but Cuba, rebuffed and cut off by its domineering neighbor, was rapidly thrown into the arms of the Soviet Union, which saved the country from economic collapse but enforced on the Revolution the price of Communist orthodoxy in matters of politics and economics. A series of events toward the end of the decade, beginning with the death in Bolivia of Fidel Castro's comrade-in-arms Che Guevara, shook the Cuban Revolution hard. If Che represented a powerful vision of revolutionary dedication and ethics, his departure from the scene saw a shift in the political ethos away from the force of revolutionary subjectivity to a greater sense of realpolitik, and the transition from a utopian socialism to actually existing socialism. For some commentators, a signal moment occurred in 1968 when Fidel failed to condemn the Soviet invasion of Czechoslovakia; although the Kremlin didn't much like what he said, it wasn't what everyone expected him to say. By the end of the 1960s, political events had strengthened Moscow's influence, although not without a polemic over the manuals of Marxism supplied by the Soviet Academy of Sciences, which ended with the clear-out of the philosophy department at the University of Havana and the closure of the left theoretical journal *Pensamiento Crítico*.

When it came to questions of culture, however, it was a very different story. Cuban artists and intellectuals were schooled in a highly syncretistic culture that celebrated rumba and surrealism, Yoruba gods and Catholic transcendentalism, in equal measure. Then, as the Uruguayan poet Mario Benedetti told Vásquez Montalbán, came "the splendor of those first seven, eight, nine years that produced the coincidence between ideological avant-gardism and artistic avant-gardism."[5] The Stalinist concept of socialist realism was widely considered inimical and irrelevant, except by a few "night-prowling tomcats," as Fornet once put it. The cineasts paid homage to both Eisenstein and Fellini, as well as the French New Wave and Brazilian Cinema Novo.

The first defining moment occurred in 1961, when ICAIC decided not to distribute an independent documentary called *P.M.* The resulting commotion led to a meeting where Castro, after listening to the arguments, gave the speech known as "The Words to the Intellectuals." Here he encapsulated the cultural position of the Revolution in the phrase "Within the Revolution, everything; against it, nothing," and for the moment the aesthetic conformists were caught on the hop.[6] By 1968, Cuban cinema was identified not only with anti-imperialism, but with films such as Alea's *Memorias del subdesarrollo* and *Lucía* by Solás, in which the aesthetic of the European new wave is metamorphosed through a kind of revolutionary transfiguration; and the documentaries of Santiago Álvarez (*Now, LBJ, Hasta la victoria siempre,* and many others), which seemed to reinvent Soviet agitprop of the 1920s. With films like these, the white building at the corner of 23d and 12th in Havana's Vedado district that once housed dentists' consulting rooms, threw down an exhilarating and infectious experimentalist challenge to the hegemony of the culture industry headquartered in Hollywood.

If it never reached much of an audience beyond its own shores, nevertheless, no history of world cinema can afford to ignore the Cuban transformation of the seventh art. Not just Alea, Solás, and Álvarez, but others, less well known, were infected by the same *duende,* a Cuban version of the impish spirit of creativity described by Lorca, and produced their best films under its influence in these years. They include a trio of films devised to celebrate the centenary of the wars of liberation against Spain, and to retell the history of that struggle from the perspective of a revolution that drew upon its heritage for its own legitimacy. It is a mark of the euphoric experimentalism of the 1960s that all these films transcend the merely propagandistic. Jorge Fraga's intense study of the guerrilla fighter's struggle with nature, *La odisea del General José* (The odyssey of General José, 1967), is based on an incident in 1895. Two years later, Manuel Octavio Gómez made *La primera carga al machete* (The first machete charge), a highly original documentary drama on a famous battle against the Spanish a hundred years earlier. In 1971, José Massip came up with a hallucinatory account of the last days of the Cuban national hero José Martí in 1895, in *Páginas del diario de José Martí* (Pages from the diary of José Martí, 1971). Julio García Espinosa, the director of several films, including a zany comedy called *Las aventuras de Juan Quin Quin* (The adventures of Juan Quin Quin, 1967), put forward a powerful apologia for this experimental effervescence in his manifesto of 1968, *Por un cine imperfecto* (For an imperfect cinema), in which he argued that the imperfections of a low-budget cinema of urgency, which sought to create a dialogue with its audience, were preferable to the sheen of high production values that merely reflected the audience back to itself.

Havana would become the second home of radical filmmakers throughout the continent, just as it became the champion of anti-imperialism and a leader of third-world nations. Nevertheless, economic errors were made; critics, nonconformists, and "social misfits" were victimized, and the sincere criticism of foreign friends was rejected. What most shook the cultural world, at home and abroad, were the events of 1971 when the poet Heberto Padilla was castigated for a prize-winning book of poetry, titled *Fuera del juego* (Out of the game), which went against the grain, and was then arrested. A month later, he appeared at a meeting of the writers and artists union in a public act of self-criticism seemingly reminiscent of Stalinist show trials, which led to a protest by former friends of the Revolution like Jean-Paul Sartre and Simone de Beauvoir, Italo Calvino, the Goytisolo brothers, Jorge Semprún, Carlos Franqui, and Mario Vargas Llosa—who interpreted the incident as a betrayal of the principles Fidel had so clearly enunciated ten years earlier. Notwithstanding, Fidel clearly and firmly laid down the line at a national congress on education and culture. "Our evaluation is political. There can be no aesthetic value without human content. There can be no aesthetic value against man."[7] As a matter of principle, there were some books that should not be published.

Whether or not because of Alfredo Guevara's close relations with Fidel, ICAIC, both before and after the Padilla affair, constituted a space of relative safety. It had already provided a home for long-haired young artists like the musicians who were invited to set up the Grupo Sonora Experimental in 1970, some of whom, such as Pablo Milanés, had been in work camps (the UMAP camps, or Military Units to Aid Production, which were quickly closed after protests about their excesses). When the journal *Pensamiento Crítico* was shut down, one of its editors, the writer Jesús Díaz, was invited to join ICAIC (where in due course he would make a number of notable films, both documentary and fiction, and also become secretary of the party branch). In the party at large, hard-liners, confident of Moscow's backing, held the upper hand, but their repression fell strongest on broadcasting and the press. Their influence was weaker in cultural areas like cinema, where Alfredo Guevara and others had defended the relative autonomy of artistic creativity.

Nevertheless, contemporary subjects were difficult to handle in this atmosphere, and the filmmakers turned to allegories of national identity. The black director Sergio Giral initiated a cycle of films, beginning with *El otro Francisco* (The other Francisco) in 1974, that asserted Cuba's African heritage by deconstructing and then reassembling the history of slavery (Solas's *Cecilia* belongs to this trend). Others played safe and recounted tales of revolutionary heroes in adaptations of Hollywood genres, like *El hombre de Maisinicú* (The man from Maisinicú, Manuel Pérez, 1973) and *El brigadista* (The literacy teacher, Octavio Cortázar, 1977), both of them powerful films in themselves but hardly examples of imperfect cinema. Meanwhile, the high value placed on documentaries and newsreels ensured not only that a second generation of filmmakers were brought into the Institute but that they cut their teeth on direct encounter with a constantly evolving reality. Occasionally they ran into trouble. Even Sara Gómez, an outstanding representative of the black intelligentsia, whose films deal with the essence of *cubanía* in all its manifestations, in music, popular religion, and the culture of marginal communities, was forced to abandon a projected trilogy of documentaries that touched on the excesses of machismo and the persistence of racism, although both these issues are addressed in her last and famously experimental film, *De cierta manera* (One way or another, released in 1977 after her early death). The issue of machismo then burst onto the screen in the New Wave realism of Pastor Vega's *Retrato de Teresa* (Portrait of Teresa) in 1979, one of the most successful Cuban films ever, and the stimulus for wide debate about the double oppression of Cuban women.

When the end of the 1970s saw Cuba cautiously opening up again, ICAIC played a leading role with the creation of the International Festival of New Latin American Cinema in 1979, held ever since in Havana every December. Since very few films made in Latin America, and especially not those that espoused any kind of revolutionary politics, were seen in any country other than their own—a consequence of the monopoly control of distribution by the Hollywood-based majors—Havana became the continent's capital of cinema, practically the only city where everything made in Latin America worth seeing could be seen, and a home away from home for many who, like several Chilean filmmakers after the coup of 1973, were forced into political exile.

The 1980s nonetheless began with an unexpected crisis, when Humberto Solás undertook the most ambitious film project that ICAIC had yet attempted: an epic adaptation of the nineteenth-century Cuban novel *Cecilia Valdés*. The production tied up so much of the Institute's production capacity that it caused chagrin among other filmmakers, and when Solás presented a somewhat discursive and idiosyncratic Freudian interpretation of the classic novel that, for all its visual splendors, disconcerted both traditionalists and the popular audience, disarray among the filmmakers enabled Alfredo Guevara's old adversaries to mount a rearguard attack and edge him out of power. Despite European coproduction funding, *Cecilia* was an expensive flop (and a film whose reassessment is now overdue). Castro sent Guevara to Paris as Cuba's ambassador to UNESCO. His successor, Julio García Espinosa, who for some years had been a vice minister of culture with a special interest in music, quickly brought fresh vision to ICAIC, pursuing a policy of low-budget production, democratizing the internal decision-making process, and giving a new generation of directors a chance to prove themselves. Juan Carlos Tabío scored an immediate hit with *Se permuta* (House for swap) in 1983, a satire on the intractable problem of overcrowding in Havana, and Cuban cinema now discovered a new genre, the sociocritical comedy.

Espinosa also argued successfully for funds to build up the film festival, and scored high on the international propaganda stakes by bringing to Havana sympathetic film stars and directors from Europe and especially North America; visitors over the years ranged from directors like Francis Ford Coppola, Arthur Penn, Sidney Pollack, Ermanno Olmi, and Gillo Pontecorvo to actors like Robert De Niro, Jack Lemmon, Harry Belafonte, Julie Christie, Gian Maria Volonte, and Maria Paredes. At the same time, ICAIC took advantage of the relaxation of relations with Latin America to extend coproductions with independent filmmakers throughout the region, which fortified the projection of a Latin American image on Cuban screens all year round. Meanwhile, the installation of a new regime in Moscow under Mikhail Gorbachev, and its declaration of communist renewal, with the watchwords *perestroika* (restructuring) and *glasnost* (openness), was welcomed in Havana with a mixture of relief, curiosity, and suspicion—the Cubans' relationship with the Soviets had never been an easy one. As the Cubans embarked on their own process of renovation, known as *rectificación* (rectification), there was fresh hope that the hard-liners in Havana would also have to take the lid off. ICAIC tested the water as early as 1985 by confronting the fractious issue of the split with the Cuban émigré community in the United States with a thoughtful film by Jesús Díaz called *Lejanía* (Distance). At the end of the decade, another new talent emerged with a powerful allegory on politics and generational difference in the shape of *Papeles secundarios* (Secondary roles) by Orlando Rojas.

Ironically, as Espinosa was moving from polemicist to the presidency of ICAIC, Cuban cinema was shifting its paradigmatic aesthetics. The jagged framing and fragmented montage of the 1960s, the syncopations of camera and editing, the controlled hysteria of revolutionary agitation, gave way to the composed image, the taming of the violent tropical light, a more harmonious decoupage. In place of the wild camera of Jorge Herrera *(Lucía)* and Ramón Suárez *(Memorias del subdesarrollo)*, the new visual paradigms were the chiaroscuro of Livio Delgado *(Cecilia)* and the poise of Mario García Joya ("Mayito") *(Lejanía)*. If this shift seems to suggest a withdrawal from Espinosa's ideas about imperfect cinema, this impression is superficial. For one thing, a similar change is found in independent cinema throughout Latin America, without necessarily entailing any loss in political acumen. The films continued to be shot in real locations, now in color, and increasingly using direct location sound, with the result that the sense of penetration of social reality grew more, not less, intense. Moreover, behind the surface a critical change was taking place in the script department, and a film like Tabío's *¡Plaff!* of 1988 brings back the hilarious illogic of Hollywood comedy from *Hellzapoppin'* to *Blazing Saddles,* in a new context, where self-referentiality crosses with Brechtian defamiliarization to produce a new brand of self-reflexive laughter. Is it merely coincidence, or perhaps poetic irony, that this stance is so strongly akin to the character of the carnivalesque described by the highly unconventional Russian thinker Mikhail Bakhtin, whose works were published in Cuba during the 1980s?

By the time that Daniel Díaz Torres completed the most carnivalesque of this cycle of sociopolitical comedies, *Alicia en el pueblo de Maravillas* (Alice in Wondertown) at the beginning of 1991, the Cuban Revolution had been overtaken by the fall of the Berlin Wall and the looming chaos in the Soviet Union. With the loss of its major trade partners, the Cuban economy collapsed, and rectification was replaced by the austerity measures of the Special Period in Times of Peace. Faced with an unusually scatological satire on bureaucratic mismanagement and *cavernicula* (caveman) attitudes, the party faithful reacted with fury. In the middle of the furor came an announcement about economic rationalizations designed to cope with the mounting crisis, in which it was decreed that ICAIC would merge with the state broadcasting company, ICRT (Instituto Cubano de Radio y Televisión). Ten years after the crisis provoked by *Cecilia,* the filmmakers were now faced with an even greater threat— their very disappearance as an autonomous artistic community. This time they responded with a massive show of unity. With nothing to lose, they formed an emergency committee, which one of them dubbed the "Dead Poets Society," and appealed directly to Fidel. With finely judged political acumen, they not only kept away from foreign journalists who tried to besiege them, but made their stand on their own, without calling on the support of fellow artists and intellectuals. Fidel agreed to set up a commission, and Alfredo Guevara came back from Paris to join it. ICAIC won the right to open the film in Havana, but it ran for only four days in July before demonstrations by claques of party faithful forced its withdrawal. A few weeks later, one of the meetings with the commission had to be suspended because it was interrupted by the news of the coup d'état in the Soviet Union. The commission never reported formally, but ICAIC survived: García Espinosa resigned and Guevara took back the helm.

ICAIC's future was nevertheless extremely bleak. The worsening economic crisis cut deep into the Institute's production program as it followed other entities into a new regime of self-financing operations, where the crucial factor was the need to earn the convertible currency required for its operations abroad (previously this had been provided from the state's central budgeting), and survival therefore depended on finding production finance outside the country. Although coproductions with Latin America during the 1980s, and the reputation for technical excellence ICAIC built up in the process, gave many technicians and actors the chance to earn money abroad individually, the Institute now found itself in much the same position as other Latin American film industries, thrust into a globalized cultural marketplace where they all competed for the same international coproduction funds (which in the case of Cuba excluded the United States), and where the interests of the coproducers did not by any means match the traditional priorities of Cuban cinema. If a director of the stature of Alea could ride a situation like this, for others it would become a burden, as the logic of the market began to enter the equation of a cinema that had never before regarded the market as the determining factor.

Alea's Spanish-coproduced *Fresa y chocolate* of 1993 channels a powerful plea for tolerance and a cogent defense of the autonomy of critical thinking into what was in many ways an old-fashioned film of political commitment to the socialist ideal. Its immense popularity answered to a strong collective sentiment, at the very moment that the Cuban Revolution reached its nadir, that the problem lay not in the socialist project but in the dogmatic formulations of actual socialist rule. (As Titón put it, "Socialism is a great script, but with poor directors.")[8] Here was a film that fulfilled the role of a public communicative action that voiced a critical discourse of the left, which, though Cubanologists abroad saw it as an indication of ideological thaw, was intended as a cultural intervention in a political debate. Alea's death three years later would rob Cuban cinema of its most complete representative artist, whose example now became a rallying point for Cuban filmmakers of every tendency. Significantly, he was the acknowledged inspiration for two films by young filmmakers in the late 1990s: Arturo Sotto, with his second feature, *Amor vertical* (Vertical love), produced by ICAIC in 1997, a surreal sociocritical comedy about frustrated love (which also pays explicit homage to Buñuel and Fellini); and Amanda Chávez, with an independently shot video, *Secuencias inconclusas* (Unfinished sequences) in the same year, which examines the options for Cuban cinema in the new dollarized Cuban economy, and is highly critical of ICAIC's recent policies.

The twists and turns of this history, so much of which has been played out behind closed doors and away from the public eye, have led to widely divergent interpretations being spread abroad. We need not detain ourselves with the simplistic views of the Revolution's detractors, for whom it is merely an accident if any decent films have been made in Cuba since 1959; nor with the uncritical commendation of those for whom anything Cuban is automatically praiseworthy. But if the greatest difficulty in studying Cuban cinema outside Cuba is the sparse circulation of the films, even in these days of video—which, of course, is a direct consequence of Cuba's isolation—then, at the same time, the greatest liability is the questionable problem of distinguishing the aesthetic from the political. Reactions to Cuban films are bedeviled by the viewer's incapacity to separate out aesthetic judgments from political ones in the orthodox manner once assumed by the liberal academy in the West (though nowadays questioned by critical theory). In fact, the history of Cuban cinema places in question the assumption that this is either possible, or even sensible. Politics in Cuban cinema is not a subtext that either the filmmaker or the critic can include or leave out; it is the inevitable and ever-present intertext of the aesthetic, and its constant dialogue with the political. As Armando Hart, who as minister of education at the beginning of the Revolution had overseen the literacy campaign, once formulated the problem: "To confuse art and politics is a political mistake. To separate art and politics is another mistake."[9] Every Cuban viewer sees every Cuban film with this knowledge. For the foreign viewer, however, the character of Cuban cinema as a political aesthetic presents huge hermeneutic and interpretive difficulties, not least because with limited social referents the subtexts of the films are often difficult to decipher.

The result of this situation, pointed out in a recent contribution to the debate by John Hess, is that two different scholars can use the same theoretical framework to arrive at opposing evaluations.[10] The instances he cites are accounts by Oscar Quiros and Catherine Davies in the British academic journal *Screen* in 1996 and 1997, which both use the same work by the German philosopher Jürgen Habermas (his *Philosophical Discourse of Modernity*) to argue virtually opposite positions.[11]

Davies likes the avant-garde, disjunctive, formally experimental films typified by *De cierta manera*. Quiros favors more conventional films by Solás (*Amada,* 1983), Alea (*Cartas del parque* [Letters from the park], 1988), and Enrique Pineda Barnet (*La bella del Alhambra* [The belle of the Alhambra], 1989). Davies approves of *De cierta manera* because, writing from a feminist position, she believes it challenges patriarchal socialist ideology (jokingly known as *machismo-leninismo*) "by consistently breaking down any attempt to provide a pleasurable resolution" (although other readings, which Hess thinks more accurate, consider the film to be both feminist *and* committed to the Revolution).[12] Notwithstanding, Davies perceptively considers the two main protagonists as embodying Habermas's description of communicative reason, the process of coming to a mutual understanding on the part of subjects engaged in the action of speech; in other words, this is not a love story where people use each other as objects of gratification: Mario and Yolanda are intelligent people who speak to each other and thereby achieve an interpersonal relationship that changes both of them. Their story is constantly interrupted and undercut, however, by documentary sequences explaining the sociohistorical setting, which are themselves then subject to interruption. If the result is a film that, in the words of another commentator, "offers no single internally consistent discourse," it thereby fulfills the principle of imperfect cinema, which, according to García Espinosa, is "above all to show the process which generates the problems ... to submit it to judgement without pronouncing the verdict," and thus to stimulate the audience to active involvement in the production of meaning on the screen.[13] There are critics, it is true, who consider that the commentary (completed by Alea and García Espinosa after Sara Gómez's early death from asthma) has the effect of capturing the interpretation of these multiple voices in the rigidity of an official line; on the other hand, the mix, and indeed interpenetration, of fiction and documentary (many of the secondary characters are real people playing themselves) ensures that the commentary too is only one voice among many. Gómez took the interpenetration of the imaginary and the documentary from Alea in *Memorias del subdesarrollo;* Alea, in homage to her, returned to it in *Hasta cierto punto (Up to a Point)* in 1983, in which he turns the camera on the distance between a fictional ICAIC and the real world of the dockworkers on the other side of the Bay of Havana—another unsettling and provocative film.

Quiros likes *Amada* precisely because it "does not appear to serve any particular political purpose." This freedom from political dealing is supposed to demonstrate Habermas's arguments about freedom in art, which has "the potential of indicating the existence of a set of logics independent of those of the Polity."[14] However, Solás himself considers his film to be a political metaphor, a love story set in the Havana of 1914 "through which we tried to take the temperature of a time of frustration, a moment when the popular forces had not recovered . . . after a War of Independence that had been pacified by North American intervention."[15] Quiros has simply failed to see this, just as he misses in *La bella del Alhambra,* a story of 1920s Cuban popular theater, the Brechtian quality of the film's allegory, on the impossibility of selling out and, at the same time, retaining your dignity as an artist or as a nation. Even in the case of *Cartas del parque,* which provoked critical attacks on Alea for indeed not making a political film, there is a critical subtext, for this love story, taken from a tale by Gabriel García Márquez, is a meditation on the uneven social development of early-twentieth-century Cuba, where heroes fly airplanes but resort to a professional scribe to write their love letters for them. All, in short, are political allegories in the sense indicated by Fredric Jameson when he speaks of third-world films as "necessarily allegorical," because even when narrating apparently private stories, they turn on metaphors of the inextricable links between the personal and the political, the individual and the national, the private and the historical.[16]

Altogether, Quiros's version of Cuban film history is as topsy-turvy as Díaz Torres's *Wondertown,* a black comedy about the sins of bureaucracy where wild animals roam around freely because the cages for the zoo haven't arrived yet. In the 1960s, he says, Cuban cinema labored under the heavy weight of an official Marxist-Leninist orthodoxy and the cultural bureaucracy imposed a narrow aesthetic formula called "imperfect cinema." As Hess comments, "Were he right, this would be the first time a Communist Party had imposed avant-garde forms on its artists."[17] Several of ICAIC's early members were Communists, or at least had participated in the struggle against Batista, yet ICAIC became a focus of opposition to any effort to impose aesthetic formulas like socialist realism on Cuban cultural production—but a left opposition, which operated on the principle of Fidel's famous dictum of 1961, "Within the Revolution, everything; against it, nothing." When Fidel brought the Communist old guard into power and political struggle was engaged over the definitions of cultural politics, a number of artists and intellectuals would give up and leave the country, including filmmakers like the future cinematographer of the French New Wave, Néstor Almendros, erstwhile youthful collaborator of Alea, and like Alfredo Guevara, a member of the Communist Youth in the 1950s. Departures like this were liable to be seen at ICAIC as betrayals, but the idea of imperfect cinema, which came later, was not the imposition of some kind of Marxist-Leninist orthodoxy: it was a position in a war of positions among Communists, Marxists, and fellow travelers over freedom of aesthetic expression and the rules of aesthetic engagement.

In Quiros's through-the-looking-glass history, the opposite of imperfect cinema must be perfect cinema, which supposedly arrives in the 1980s. But when he describes this as "the freedom to employ all the aesthetic possibilities the medium can offer without having to resort to particular formulae," he is simply paraphrasing García Espinosa's concept of *im*perfect cinema.[18] On the other hand, he is partly right when he says that these aesthetic qualities "suggest that the sphere of Art is not aligned with the official orthodox ideology of the Cuban Polity." That is exactly what the crisis moments of 1981, 1992, and 1998 are all about. However, you cannot understand these crises if you assume, as Quiros seems to, that "Cuban Polity" is something fixed and given, an undialectical notion that shows very little understanding of political reality.

Hess's critique of these two commentators—that they both misread the nature of ideological struggle in Cuban cinema—is a salient one. Yet Habermas may still provide a critical key for unlocking the dialectic of the Cuban image—on condition that what we ask about is the role of cinema in the structural transformation of the public sphere in Cuba, the makeover from a small, underdeveloped country to a variant of the communist state, from the status of economic and cultural neocolony to that of "actually existing socialism," where supposedly the public sphere in its classic sense no longer exists. The case of Cuban cinema suggests a different interpretation, in which the public sphere does not simply dissolve, but finds an active and vicarious surrogate on the film screen.

It is Habermas's thesis that the public sphere as a formal concept is the product of the rise of bourgeois society, the creation of a (theoretically) universal and democratic space of debate about politics and culture, which must be won from the absolutist state and the rule of the aristocracy, and then defended against encroachment by alien or illiberal forces. Initially the assertion of the rights of the propertied men of education and culture who made up the bourgeois public, encroachments come from several directions. From the left comes the need to cede democratic rights to subaltern classes, lacking in property, education, and culture, and eventually, to women. The public sphere thus becomes, in theory, all-inclusive, but in fact develops mechanisms and institutions designed to maintain a sense of social hierarchy and thus defend the body politic. Meanwhile, capitalist development produces the growth of advertising and the commercial press, which impinge on the public sphere from the right. The mass media and new communications technologies produce new forms of addressing the public, in the form of a vertical flow, wherein social dialogue is embodied in reductive genres and stereotypes (and open to manipulation by political forces who have learned how to play the game). Fascism, capitalism, and communism inherit this situation and deal with it differently. Capitalism develops practices such as public relations and news management intended to mold and bend public opinion by less than honest means, while, as Walter Benjamin put it in the closing words of his best-known essay, fascism renders politics aesthetic, and communism responds by politicizing art.[19]

The Cuban public sphere in the late nineteenth century, in spite of its colonial status under Spanish rule, was relatively well developed; indeed, thirty years of liberation wars had strengthened its instincts. North American intervention propelled the new republic into the twentieth century with a vengeance. The island became an offshore testing laboratory for U.S. penetration of Latin American media markets from the end of World War I, a bridgehead for companies like ITT and RCA—the latter took to promoting Cuban music and radio productions throughout Central America, supported by advertising agencies that trained up Cuban artists and copywriters. In one of the first Latin American countries equipped with television, the Cuban revolutionaries of the 1950s were intensely aware of the power of the media. Fernando Pérez portrays the effects in his first feature, *Clandestinos* (Clandestine, 1986), based on real incidents in which the urban underground that supported the rebels in the mountains mounted demonstrations in front of television cameras at baseball matches and audience TV shows, and even invented an advertising campaign for the Revolution under the guise of launching a new product. Meanwhile, the guerrillas in the mountains ran a free radio station that impugned the official media, and also proved highly adept at using U.S. media opportunities to their advantage. When the Revolution took power, the Rebel Army set up a film unit even before ICAIC was created, to make documentaries for the cinema explaining policies in key areas like agrarian reform (Alea and García Espinosa were among the directors). ICAIC was set up as a nonmilitarist alternative with the same political commitment, but took the form of a novel kind of public entity: an autonomous institute, not unlike what in Britain is called a quango (quasi-autonomous nongovernmental organization), but empowered to take over any part of the country's film industry that might be nationalized. While the press and broadcasting became a site of ideological confrontation where the state would soon take direct control, cinema in Cuba came to occupy a unique cultural space as a major site of public discourse that at the same time enjoyed a de facto autonomy because of a privileged relation to the source of power and authority. The result was much the same relationship to the state as the BBC in Britain, which operates according to what the British call the arm's-length principle: a major part of the cultural apparatus of the state that is nonetheless trusted to run itself, and as a result is free to experiment in the full glare of its public (which the BBC also once used to do). The conventional view is that in the communist state the political public sphere ceases to exist, and the cultural public sphere is reduced and denuded by direct censorship, the direct arm of state patronage, and sanction. In Cuba, this happened to radio, television, and the press, but not to cinema.

ICAIC's first efforts (including the Rebel Army documentaries whose production was taken over by the new institute) owed much in terms of style to the social documentary à la John Grierson, just as the first features followed the model of Italian neorealism. But these paradigms were soon surpassed by the very speed of revolutionary change, which threatened to leave the filmmakers standing on the very terrain where film and reality meet, the spatial environment. Alea was struck by the speed of change when he shot his comedy *Las doce sillas (The Twelve Chairs)* in 1962. Between going out to reconnoiter a location and coming back to film there, it would be transformed: a rich family's mansion turned into an art school, a billboard advertising a luxury hotel in Miami now declared Cuba a territory free of illiteracy. It was the volatility of spatial appearance itself that pushed the filmmakers into the exploration of new aesthetic means of capturing and expressing it, or else failing to register political reality. The problem was therefore at once aesthetic and political, and it consequently becomes impossible to understand Cuban cinema on a theoretical basis that separates politics and art, as if the artist has any choice in the matter, as if the Cuban filmmaker could choose to be political or not. But when Walter Benjamin says that communism politicizes art, in Cuban cinema there is a rider: not by diktat, but because politics and art engage in dialogue. This dialogue allows the cinema screen to become more than either propaganda or a diversionary space, but a crucial preserve of public speech, a space that engages large sectors of the population in debate about the meaning and quality of their lives; a vicarious role that is negatively reinforced by the much tighter control exercised by the party over broadcasting and the press. But as a neighbor says to me on a visit to Havana in 1998 (I am living in an apartment in Vedado), "Here people go the cinema in order to enjoy finding out what the film has to say about something relevant."

When the revolutionaries took power in 1959, cinema was at a peak of popularity. Box-office earnings in 1960 reached 22,800,000 pesos, roughly 120 million admissions; for a population of around seven million, this gives a national cinema-going average of seventeen visits annually—and this is why it mattered. ICAIC took over the production and distribution of films in Cuba in a series of steps that turned Cuban cinema into a state monopoly, but in the process opened this space up to critical expression, albeit within certain limits. Alfredo Guevara's political genius lay in persuading his personal friend and political chief to let him place art rather than propaganda at the center of the Institute's vision—in other words, to allow him the rule of artistic freedom. The results so intrigued the audience that they began to change their viewing habits. They started, for example, taking documentaries seriously, especially the films of Santiago Álvarez. In the 1970s, ICAIC researchers found that people sometimes went to the movies because they wanted to see the new Álvarez, and would then stay and watch whatever feature was put on after it—a complete inversion of normal cinema-going behavior. ICAIC responded by producing a whole series of feature documentaries for cinema distribution by Álvarez and others, a policy that affirms the screen as a site of encounter with social reality.

Álvarez himself made a cycle of films following Fidel around the world: to Chile in 1972 for *De América soy hijo... y a ella me debo*—the title is a quotation from the great Cuban patriot José Martí ("I am a son of America... and I owe myself to it"); the Soviet Union in 1973 for *Y el cielo fue tomado por asalto* (And the heavens were taken by assault, a quotation from the *Communist Manifesto*); Vietnam in 1974 for *Abril de Vietnam en el año del Gato* (April in Vietnam in the Year of the Cat). If these titles earned Álvarez the status of Fidel's poet laureate, the encomium can be misleading: to be sure, these films are full of Fidel's brand of political rhetoric, but they are also masterpieces of extended observational reportage of the Comandante in action, and sometimes relaxing, which thoroughly humanize the conventional image of the figure of the Latin American caudillo. Meanwhile, Manuel Herrera's *Girón* (Bay of Pigs, 1972) is a highly original drama-documentary of the thwarted 1961 invasion; Jorge Fraga followed a year later with an extended reportage titled *La nueva escuela* (The new school). At the end of the decade, Jesús Díaz made two films that represent the acme of the genre. The first of these, *55 Hermanos* (55 brothers and sisters), follows a group of young Cuban-Americans on a first-ever visit to the island in 1978, culminating in meeting with Fidel at his most persuasive: they should not ask to come to Cuba but remain in their new country and work on Cuba's behalf. Two years later, *En tierra de Sandino* (In Sandino's land) is a three-part portrait of the Sandinista revolution in Nicaragua, probably the most penetrating of the many films on Nicaragua at this time by filmmakers of many different countries.[20] Both are paradigms of the authored observational documentary in Latin America (not to speak of documentary art else-where) to put beside the work of Paul Leduc in Mexico (*Mesquital*, 1976), or the Colombian documentarist Ciro Durán (*Gamin*, 1978).

It was the greatest loss of Cuban cinema in the 1990s that the produc-tion of documentaries was largely curtailed. Films like these, together with the forty or more shorter documentaries that ICAIC used to pro-duce every year, fulfilled one of the prime functions that in liberal democracies is ascribed to the public-service responsibilities of the broad-casting companies, that of keeping the public informed in a manner that also educates them in the issues of the day. That ICAIC evidently did this in a manner that audiences found both more entertaining and more effective than broadcasting and the press ensured that the Insti-tute enjoyed a high reputation, which lent its filmmakers a capacity to connect with different social sectors—intellectuals and campesinos, artists and sugar-cane workers, even party bureaucrats and marginal youth—through the same films. Alea once told me that any doubts he might have had that the complex and sophisticated film language of *Memorias del subdesarrollo* was inimical to a popular audience were dispelled when he learned that a large number of people were so intrigued by the film that they would go to see it two or three times. In the early years of the Revolution, the broad acceptance of such an adventurous cinema was the result of the social cohesion generated by the revolutionary process itself, which was both symbolized and enacted in the literacy campaign of 1961, depicted by Octavio Cortázar's *El brigadista* of 1977. Teenagers from the cities taught peasants in the countryside to read and write using texts and ideas that were new to both, so that the words that expressed a new political discourse created a new set of shared values. With this extraordinary piece of social and political engineering, written language and everything that comes with it translated into access to a new sense of national culture on a mass scale from which the filmmakers were able to benefit. Aesthetically, for example, the literacy campaign is at the root of the playful way in which Santiago Álvarez replaced the con-ventional spoken commentary of the newsreel and documentary with animated words moving backwards and forwards across the screen. But the process went much further. According to the political scientist Rafael Hernández, it was as if language itself was liberated from the structures of control that previously divided the social classes into different lin-guistic communities; the traditional sociolinguistic stratification was ruptured; the most humble people took possession of linguistic territories previously veiled from them; knowledge and culture became central elements of prestige in the new social order.[21] Cuban cinema was also a celebration of this expansive popular culture, and it was in order to keep up with it, when political life gradually slid into ideological conformity, that it turned to social comedy, a genre in which it proves possible to sustain a dialogue with the audience on the basis of allusion and intimation.

The public character of the consumption of cinema, in contrast to the domestic privacy of television reception, means that even when film audiences began to decline with the spread of television (as well as competition from other forms of diversion), Cuban cinema retained its prestige. In 1984, a first feature by Rolando Díaz, the sociocritical comedy *Los pájaros tirándole a la escopeta* (Tables turned), drew an audience of two million in the first two months—nearly one-fifth of the entire population. To go to the cinema in Cuba, I am told in 1998 by the scriptwriter of *Alicia . . .*, Eduardo del Llano, who at thirty-six years of age represents the third generation of Cuban filmmakers, the generation that emerged in the 1980s, is like "what you call entering the public sphere, it depends on the public side of the thing, because going to the cinema is like an act of complicity with the public world."[22] Even today, Cuban cinema audiences not only comprise a broad mixture of every social group and age, but the darkness of the cinema is not that of silent fantasy but a constant murmur of voices, which periodically break into calls and comments on the events depicted. Cuban filmmakers strongly feel the weight of responsibility that comes with this power to address the large public, a power in many ways second only to that of the *líder máximo* (maximum leader), and naturally, as del Llano puts it, "El ICAIC por su propio autonomía tiene más ojos por encima" (ICAIC, by dint of its very autonomy, is always under scrutiny). If the filmmakers are thus engaged in a balancing act that occasionally leads them to stumble, it is not a question of simply bowing to the dictates of authority, because they sense that their privilege as filmmakers is not so much granted from above as loaned to them by the public that crowds the cinemas. In short, if Cuban cinema constitutes an aesthetic imbricated with a political spirit it is because it answers to a vicarious role in the public sphere, a calling to speak not at people, but with them, and often in their own voices.

In the crisis years of the 1990s, however, these equations started to break down and the coherence of the cultural project represented by ICAIC began to fragment. The country's economic collapse seriously curtailed ICAIC's production capacity; filmmakers and actors began to emigrate or seek short-term jobs abroad; as the institute turned its efforts to coproductions with commercial, mainly European, partners, disaffection would grow among filmmakers disoriented by the shifting ground rules. Some even wondered if the return of Alfredo Guevara represented a step forwards or backwards. Since 1993, no film has been able to achieve the same impact as *Fresa y chocolate,* but several are authentic attempts to trace a tortuous process of recovery. From 1994, *Madagascar* by Fernando Pérez is a sombre depiction of the inward journey of three generations of women; four years later in *La vida es silbar,* he turns out a surrealist comedy on three contemporary characters and their unfulfilled dreams. At the end of the decade, Juan Carlos Tabío returned to form with *Lista de espera,* a comedy in homage to Alea that allegorizes Cuba as a bus station from which no one can leave because the buses have stopped running. These and a number of other films— the portmanteau *Mujer transparente* of 1990, Julio García Espinosa's *Reina y Rey* of 1995—share a common theme identified by a recent Cuban writer, Désirée Díaz, as "The Ulysses Syndrome": the trope of the journey, found in these films in a myriad of forms, real, metaphorical, and imagined—migration, departure, return, internal exile, the impossible promise. This imagery can hardly be accidental for an island nation where successive waves of emigration over the last four decades have created the trauma of a divided community, and leaving the country becomes a dramatic act associated with feelings of rupture, repudiation, and loss. But perhaps it might be considered poetic justice that just as the coherence of ICAIC's cultural politics has been called into question, the filmmakers have responded to the crisis of Cuba's and their own isolation with an apparently shared existential tendency to allegorize the image of the nation as an imagined community.

PART I

Before the Revolution:
Cinema at the Margins

CHAPTER ONE

For the First Time

The screen comes to life. Three men wearing the working clothes of a tropical country are grouped around the front of a truck with its hood open. One of them stands more or less facing the camera, another is sitting on the fender, and the third is working on the engine. An unseen questioner is asking them about their job, and, as they speak, the picture cuts to the interior of the truck, to show us the fittings they describe, including projection gear and stowaway beds. For this is a *cine móvil*, a mobile cinema unit, and the job consists in showing films in small and isolated communities, in the schools during the day and for everyone in the evenings. Do they know of any place where movies have not yet been shown? "Yes," says one, "I know of a place that is so entangled and the road is so bad that it's almost completely cut off. It's called Los Mulos, in the Guantánamo-Baracoa mountain region."[1]

Then comes music and the title sequence, incorporating traveling shots taken from the cabin of the truck as it drives to Los Mulos, which is discovered lying in a valley. We are watching *Por primera vez* (For the first time), a prize-winning ten-minute black-and-white documentary made in 1967 and directed by Octavio Cortázar, a young Cuban director who—untypically—trained at the Prague film school.

We meet the people in the village, beginning with the children. In the schoolroom, the teacher explains about the arrival of the mobile cinema. Then a woman explains that she has lived in the village for seventeen years and they have no entertainment there. Another woman tells us, "No, I never saw films during the time of the other government, because we couldn't go to see them and neither did they come here to the country." The offscreen voice asks her, "What do you think films are?" and she replies, "They must be something very important, since you're so interested in them; they must be something very beautiful." Another woman muses, "Film is . . . well, lots of things happen in the cinema. You see snakes and you see beautiful girls and you see weddings, horses, war, and all that." "Well," says one of the others, "I've never seen a film, you know, but I think maybe you get a fiesta or a dance or something like that, but I want to see one so nobody has to describe it to me."

And then we see them watching a film—Chaplin's *Modern Times.* The sequence with the automatic lunch machine has them in tears of laughter. We see faces gazing in wide-eyed amazement and delight—the camera filming is positioned in front of them just under the screen so we see them full face. Old men and women look as if they cannot believe the cinema has really come to them, and a little girl bites her finger in excitement.

What we seem to see and hear in their conversation with the screen is what anyone must have been able to see and hear anywhere at the turn of the century, when the first teasing reports circulated about the wonders of the cinematograph machine, until finally some itinerant entertainer or adventurous small entrepreneur arrived and announced a film show. Or is it? It is said that early film viewers sometimes reacted as if the projected scene were physically before them. Maxim Gorki wrote of the Lumière film *Teasing the Gardener* that the image carried such a shock of veracity that "you think the spray is going to hit you too, and instinctively shrink back."[2] The earliest audiences, in other words, did not always see the screen as a screen, a barrier, as it were, between them and the pictured world. But they soon learned eagerly to accept the screen's power of illusion. This illusion hangs on the peculiar relationship that arose between the camera and the audience, which the development of narrative cinema came almost entirely to depend on: the camera as an invisible surrogate for the human observer that enables the audience to see without being seen, to feel that it is present but disembodied within the projected view—a condition that nowadays is largely taken for granted.

The viewer's naive identification with the camera becomes possible because paradoxically there is a sense in which the camera is outside the scene that is being filmed—in the same way that the eye, as Wittgenstein

Por primera vez (Octavio Cortázar, 1967)

mentioned, is outside the view that it sees, on the edge of it, and can never see itself except in reflection. But in another sense the camera is part of, inside the scene, occupying the same area, the same space, in which it moves around, taking up first one position and then another. The effect of film depends largely on the interaction between these two viewing conditions, for it is their fusion that gives the viewer the impression of disembodiment, being present but unseen. But this state of affairs hardly impinged on the early filmmakers, for whom the profilmic event—the scene they were filming—was still set apart like the scene within a theatrical set. The image reproduced on the screen was consequently also set apart; it was a world that at one and the same time reproduced reality and also swallowed it up and regurgitated it magically. This screen world looks the same as the one we live in, but turns out to behave according to its own logic, its own laws, which have their own form of rationality. Whether or not, however, an audience is disposed to see the screen world as a magical one or as an authentic representation of the real world is another matter, not logical but ideological and political.

To approach the question another way: just as the classical economists regarded the act of consumption of commodities as something that occurred after all the economic transactions involved were duly completed and therefore of no technical interest to them, so too the act of watching a film. The film industry regards the way in which the film makes contact with the audience exclusively under the rubric of market-ing. Reaching an audience is only a question of marketing it effectively; this is what brings the audience in. But there's entirely another way of seeing this relationship: as the reception by an audience of an aesthetic object. The film lives not through people paying money to see it, but through the sensual, sentimental, psychological, and intellectual gratifi-cation they are able to draw from it and the significance they are able to grant it.

This aesthetic relationship is supposedly the sphere of criticism, but the marketing business is so all-embracing that too often the critic be-comes merely its adjunct, a kind of glorified advertising copywriter to be quoted on the billboards (or else an oppositional and marginalized figure, whom the billboards systematically exclude). No matter that at the beginning film wasn't considered an art form. About a decade after its birth in 1895, it started to acquire the characteristics and capacities of narrative and visual expression and began to claim critical attention. But then came the big production companies that emerged after about another decade of growth, and they rapidly learned the publicity value of claiming for their product the status of art, if only to draw in past the ticket window the more respectable classes of society who were not among the early enthusiasts for the medium. In this way, old assump-tions about aesthetic consumption passed to cinema, and one of the big studios even emblazoned the formula around the head of its roaring lion: *Ars gratia artis,* art for art's sake. But it was bluff.

An Italian theorist, Antonio Banfi, has described the atomized condi-tion which the film industry imposed on its audiences, and which, in an industry that suffered substantial risks of financial loss, it reinforced above all other possible relationships with the screen, as an insurance policy against the unpredictability that, in spite of everything, audi-ences continued to manifest. The book of his from which the following passage is taken was published by the Cuban Film Institute, ICAIC, dur-ing the 1960s, as one of a series of texts on cinema and aesthetics that established the terms of reference for critical and theoretical discussion of these issues in revolutionary Cuba. Banfi describes the situation in the countries of the metropolis, and what he says is often much less true of the attitudes of audiences in underdeveloped countries where traditional popular cultures still have force and a more collective rela-tionship obtains. But then his account serves as a warning:

The cinema public is the anonymous everyday crowd of every extraction that enters with no particular social disposition or commitment, at an hour neither fixed nor anticipated, and leaves to plunge back again into the course of everyday life. As a spectator, seated among the rows, each person in the audience is enveloped in darkness, alone; there is no communication, nor reciprocal reflection. The spectator absorbs the spectacle that much more effectively and avidly as an individual.

Withdrawn from intersubjective relations, the spectator does not find the representation cathartic. Nor is there a feeling of being dominated; not only because of the impressionist and suggestive character of the representation itself and the technical artifice of which cinema avails itself with the aim of simplifying and stereotyping the action and deter-mining the meaning, but also because of the isolation and passivity that envelop the spectator in the absence of collective participation in the spectacle. First and foremost, the spectator, more in a state of fragmenta-tion than organic wholeness, accepts the elements of the spectacle just as they are served up. Rather than an integrated personality, the spectator is more often a bundle of instincts with silent, unconfessed demands, finding satisfaction in the commonplaces of rhetorical positions and solutions, the vulgar attitudes, rowdy incidents, cheap humor, and banalities that make up the pastiche of cinema . . . At the center is the fixation—sometimes obsessive—of types, gestures, tones, and values that the spectator absorbs and unconsciously imitates, seeing, or wishing to see, life refracted in them.[3]

Por primera vez marks a change in all that. Cuban cinema has done more in this film than simply capture something that evaded the first film-makers. It has produced for its audience a vision of its own self-discovery *as* an audience. These simple and least portentous of images, presented without any special tricks or cleverness, communicate to a Cuban audi-ence the most concrete possible signs of their own activity. For a non-Cuban audience too they may carry the indication of profound changes in the conditions of consumption. We see, first, that the moment of con-sumption is also a moment of production—not only the production of wonder, laughter, and all those other reactions, but the production of, precisely, an audience, subjects for the film that is the object of their at-tention. Second, we see that there is nothing private about this. The expe-rience of the audience, the excitement that enthuses them, is contagious.

At the same time, *Por primera vez* embodies a process that is hardly present in capitalist society, a circuit from consumption to production and back again to consumption *such that it raises the act of consumption onto a new level.* An audience consumes a film, a camera films them, and a film is produced; the film is then consumed by a new audience in circumstances that give them a new awareness of their own status. The circumstances in capitalist cinema generally always leave the audience in the same condition of naive consumption they began in. This is a film that may give an audience anywhere a rare experience of vicarious delight tinged with a kind of nostalgia. For the Cuban audience, it became a living analogue of the development of cinema within the Revolution, because here the audience has become, together with the filmmakers, participant observers and observant participators in the same process. It was the naive enthusiasm that people brought to the moving pictures at the first encounter that led Lenin to sign the decree of August 27, 1919, which nationalized the businesses that made up the czarist film industry. The revolutionaries recognized this naive enthusiasm as a force to be mobilized. In conversation with Commissar of Education Anatoly Lunacharsky a couple of years after the nationalization, Lenin expressed the belief that "for us, film is the most important of all the arts." The remark is often quoted in works on the history of cinema by people who have no real notion of what he meant and why he meant it. They think that Lenin, who once revealed that he was suspicious of the beauty of the music of Beethoven, was nothing but a cold propagandist. What Lenin was talking about, however, can be seen in the way early Soviet cinema responded to its mission with fantastic creative energy, bringing forward in the process the first serious theoretical considerations on the medium. Something close to this has also happened in Cuba. Cuba's leading documentarist, Santiago Álvarez, considers the parallel extremely apt. Commenting on the comparison that has been made more than once between his own work and that of Dziga Vertov, he explained in a conversation with the present author that since the comparison is obviously correct but that he didn't know Vertov's work until the early 1970s, the explanation must lie in the similarity of the situations. In other words, the discovery of cinema in both countries in and through the revolutionary process.

With the Revolution, cinema in Cuba became, in a word, highly animated. The mobilization of the audience's enthusiasm in turn enthused the filmmakers. In complete contrast, in the developed countries during the same period, the magic of cinema was wearing off. Television had invaded the home and the thrill of the discovery of the moving image that was so strong in the early years of cinema now lay as if buried in some unconscious memory. Nowadays, the child becomes accustomed to the constant presence of a miniaturized world of images constantly in motion—a very different experience from first beholding the enormous image of the cinema screen—even before it has learned to talk. It is a world it learns to recognize perhaps no later than it learns to recognize its own reflection in a mirror.

In Britain, the loss of the cinema audience was particularly steep. In 1945, thirty-five million attendances were recorded by the country's cinemas each week—in a country with a population of roughly forty-five million. By 1980, attendance had fallen to a mere 101 million for the whole year (with a further reduction of ten million over the next ten years), while the country's population had meanwhile grown by about ten million, or roughly the same as the population of Cuba.

Until the start of the 1980s, annual admission figures for Cuban cinema tell a very different story. By the late 1940s, the figure had reached about fifty-seven million; box-office earnings in 1949 were 16.69 million pesos (the Cuban peso was valued at one U.S. dollar at the time of the Revolution). It was in the late 1940s that cinema audiences in the United States began to fall, a little later in Britain. A principal cause of this fall, television, was introduced into Cuba in the early 1950s, earlier than most Latin American countries, but it made no incursion on cinema audiences because it was hardly accessible to any but the better-off classes. And indeed, cinema attendance in Cuba continued to grow until 1956, when box-office earnings reached 20.99 million pesos. A small fall in attendance in 1957 and 1958 was due to political conditions and the effects of the guerrilla war (cinemas were a target of bomb attacks). Then, the moment the Revolution took power, and its economic policies increased people's purchasing power, box-office earnings shot up again and reached 22.8 million pesos in 1960. This very high level—roughly 120 million admissions a year—represented a national average of about seventeen cinema visits per person in a year; but since a fair proportion of the population had no access to cinema, the actual attendance for those who did works out even higher. Attendance was sustained during the 1960s but fell during the 1970s to around 86.5 million, or an average of twelve annual cinema visits per person. One reason for this reduction, however, is an increase in alternative opportunities for entertainment and cultural participation. During 1977, for example, there were 46,704 professional performances in the different arts, which recorded

an attendance of 11,837,300; there were also 269,931 *aficionado* performances with an attendance of 47,874,800.[4] Taken together, these are almost three-quarters the number of paying cinema attendances. ICAIC
was not therefore too worried by the loss in the audience. But the early
1980s saw a sudden huge fall in admissions to less than half its previous
level. In fact, the cinema audience fell not only in Cuba but in a number
of other Latin American countries too, like Chile and Brazil, where
color television had now reached the mass of the audience. In Cuba, the
spread of television has been slower, but it seems to be finally catching
up on cinema there too. The reason appears to be not an improvement
in the quality of television, which is poor, so much as an increase in the
number of new films shown on television, which developments in video
have made more easily available. Yet in the cinemas, Cuban films themselves have retained their popularity. A successful Cuban film may nowadays be seen by a million people or more in the space of its first two
months. In 1984, a first feature by Rolando Díaz, the socially critical
comedy *Los pájaros tirándole a la escopeta* (Tables turned) drew an audience of two million in its first two months. It is clear that cinema in
Cuba has remained one of the most powerful instruments of both social cohesion and social debate.

   In many ways, the problem for cinema is primarily economic. Cuba
entered the 1980s with approximately five hundred 35 mm cinemas on
the island, with extremely low admission prices, which remained roughly
the same as twenty-five years earlier. A good number of these cinemas
were new, either replacing older structures or situated in new locations,
though the total number had remained more or less constant. At the
same time, the population of Cuba had grown by about three million
since the Revolution, which helped to keep the cinemas full. Addition-
ally, a part of the increased cinema audience in the early 1960s was
made up of those sections of the rural population who before 1959 had
virtually no access to cinema at all. The new regime decided to take cinema to them and the mobile cinemas were set up; their showings were
free. Nor was this a stopgap policy. They continued to operate until replaced by video salons in the 1980s. There were also a growing number
of noncommercial fixed-location 16 mm exhibition outlets, located in
cultural centers, film clubs, schools, colleges, and so forth; these too collect no box office. By the start of the 1980s, there were a total of 741 16 mm
outlets, including mobile cinemas, which held 332,700 showings between

them to an audience of 33 million. In sum, as one Latin American commentator put it, "By enormously expanding the cinema public and multiplying the opportunities of access to a variety of presentations, conditions for the diversification and enrichment of taste have been set in motion, also leading to intercommunication between regions of the country that used not to know each other, and the construction of an organic national culture."[5] If cinema is not the only medium involved in this process, it is certainly one of the main ones.

There is a related set of figures whose careful interpretation is also revealing. The number of features released annually in the 1970s was about 130. This was just over a quarter of the annual release figure at its height before the Revolution. Unsympathetic commentators would hold this reduction as evidence of the autocratic designs of the communist government. The truth is rather different. In the first place, the previous figure was primarily the result of one of the standard methods by which Hollywood ensured its control over foreign screens: by oversupplying them (the mechanisms they used are analyzed in a later chapter). Second, the lower figure of the years following the Revolution was partly a result of the nefarious designs of successive U.S. administrations in maintaining an economic blockade against Cuba, which, among other things, has made it almost impossible for the Cubans to obtain those North American movies they might want to show, and which, because of the economic constraints the country suffered as a consequence of the blockade, also required them to economize on the purchase of films from other capitalist countries. Yet these difficulties also had a positive effect: fewer films means that each film had a potentially larger share of the audience than was previously true for all but the most successful pictures. And this contributed to the role that cinema had in Cuba in nourishing social cohesion.

Indeed, there was a remarkable growth in Cuba of national consciousness of and through cinema. Another film by the same director as *Por primera vez* gives a clue as to why: *El brigadista* (The teacher, 1977), a feature movie, portrays Mario, a fifteen-year-old member of one of the 1961 literacy brigades (*brigadista* literally means "brigade member") who goes to teach in a small village in a remote part of the Zapata swamp to the south of Havana. The boy's arrival is greeted with suspicion on the part of many in the village who do not believe that a kid of his age could be a teacher—including Gonzalo, the village leader, in whose house the boy is billeted. Little by little, however, Mario's tenacity and the events of the struggle against the counterrevolutionary bandits, the *gusanos*—worms—hidden in the swamps, bring the boy and Gonzalo closer together. A profound friendship develops between them, as Mario teaches Gonzalo to read and write and Gonzalo teaches Mario to overcome his adolescent fears. The film is not without its problems. It represents Cuban cinema at its stylistically most traditional, with an orthodox narrative form that inevitably emphasizes a certain naive machismo in its young hero, which is already strong enough in the story as it is. This may even have been one of the reasons why the film was so popular, with a strong appeal across the different generations. (On the other hand, the even more popular *Retrato de Teresa* is highly critical of machismo.) However, and just as important, it was a film that had an equally strong appeal across the different generations. It stimulated the memories of both teachers and taught, bringing back to them the profound changes in their lives that the 1961 campaign had rendered, while it explained to those too young or not yet born why the literacy campaign occupied such an important position in revolutionary history. It also dealt with practically the same cultural operation, says its director, as his earlier film *Por primera vez:* the *brigadistas* brought literacy where the mobile cinemas brought the movies.[6] Both are means whereby the popular classes in Cuba have been able to discover their own reality and their own history. *El brigadista* shows a process of cultural exchange between a peasant and a boy from an urban middle-class background. The portrayal is idealized, but the film could not have been made without the very same process having taken place within the development of Cuban cinema itself. The experience of taking films to new audiences was instrumental in making Cuban cineasts responsive to the cultural needs of the popular classes. While they thrilled at their own good fortune in being able to make films for the first time, they were also enthused by the parallel thrill of an audience *seeing* films for the first time, and seeing things in them that had never previously been shown on Cuban cinema screens. One of the themes of the present study is the exploration of this process and its implications.

The birth of a new cinema with the Revolution in Cuba in 1959 was sponsored by the force that overthrew the dictatorship of Batista—the Rebel Army that grew out of the July 26th Movement. With the victory of the Revolution, the Cubans set about the construction of a new film industry even more rapidly than did the October Revolution. The Cuban Film Institute (ICAIC) was created less than three months after the Rebel Army, led by Che Guevara and Camilo Cienfuegos, entered Havana on January 1, 1959, while Fidel Castro, at the other end of the island, led the rebels' entry into Santiago de Cuba. ICAIC was set up under the first decree concerning cultural affairs passed by the Revolutionary Government, signed by Castro as prime minister and Armando Hart as minister of education (later minister of culture). Alfredo Guevara (no relation), a young activist in the urban underground that had supported the guerrillas and a *compañero* of Fidel's since student days, was appointed to head the new organization.

The new cinema that the Revolution promoted was not entirely without antecedents, either in Cuba, where the first political film dates back to the production of a newsreel by the Communist Party newspaper in 1939, or elsewhere in Latin America. The founder, in Argentina in 1956, of the Documentary Film School of Santa Fe, Fernando Birri, was one of a number of Latin Americans—others included the Cubans Tomás Gutiérrez Alea and Julio García Espinosa—who had studied film in Rome at the Centro Sperimentale in the early 1950s, and who brought back with them to Latin America the ideals and inspiration of Italian neorealism; because, as Birri has explained, neorealism was the cinema that discovered amid the clothing and rhetoric of development another Italy, the Italy of underdevelopment. It was a cinema of the humble and the offended that could be readily taken up by filmmakers in the underdeveloped countries.[7]

At the same time, especially given the limited resources available to them and the difficulty of entering the industry in those countries where a film industry existed, other influences manifested themselves as well. Birri also speaks of John Grierson, who visited the documentary and experimental film festival of the SODRE in Montevideo in 1961, of his idea of the social documentary, and of documentary as a hammer with which to mold reality—ideas that were also taught in Rome. The first film to emerge from Santa Fe, Birri's *Tire die (Throw Us a Dime)*, completed in 1958, represents a new documentary paradigm along these lines for Latin America, a film based on a lengthy investigation (which Birri called the process of "successive approximations to reality") among the shantytown dwellers with whom it deals and who were closely involved in its completion.

Cinema Novo in Brazil established a new paradigm for the feature film in Latin America, with examples such as *Rio, quarenta graus* (Rio, forty degrees) and *Rio, zona norte* (Rio, north zone), which appeared in 1955 and 1957, respectively, directed by Nelson Pereira dos Santos. While the Documentary School of Santa Fe was born, according to Birri, out of the cultural and industrial disintegration of the period—Juan Perón was deposed late in 1955—Cinema Novo in Brazil came about partly under the stimulation of the populism of João Goulart, vice president during the government of Juscelino Kubitschek and then president from 1961 to 1964, when he was overthrown by a military coup. This political atmosphere, one of the Cinema Novo directors, Ruy Guerra, has said, provided a rationale within which it was possible for a number of young directors centered in Rio de Janeiro to challenge both established Brazilian commercial cinema and the European-oriented artistic production coming out of São Paulo.[8] But these are only the most prominent examples of the beginnings of a movement that developed in a number of countries during the 1960s, in whatever way local conditions permitted, and that came together for the first time at a meeting of Latin American filmmakers in Viña del Mar in Chile in 1967.

Before the Revolution, conditions in Cuba were hardly more favorable than in most of the rest of Latin America. The film that ICAIC regards as its principal precursor, *El Megano*, dating from 1955, was made in conditions of clandestinity and was seized at its first screening by the dictator Batista's secret police. However, the decree that established ICAIC in 1959 was not, strictly speaking, a straightforward act of nationalization. It envisaged an autonomous body, empowered to "organize, establish, and develop" a national film industry, and it handed over to this body properties and facilities connected with the film business that passed into the hands of the Revolutionary Government because their owner, a certain Alonso, had been one of Batista's henchmen who fled the country after the rebels took power. The decree empowered the new body to take over other film properties that might be further confiscated from members of the dictator's entourage. Perhaps the acquisition of a studio egged the young revolutionaries on, except that they had already been egged on precisely by the fact that the thing had been in the hands of the tyranny they had been fighting. In fact, on close examination, the decree that established ICAIC cannot be mistaken for the kind of law that would be passed by a government that just happened to acquire a film studio and didn't really know what to do with it. Both the preamble and the law itself clearly show that its authors understood the character of the forces that had prevented the growth of an independent film industry in Cuba until then, and it contains an analysis of the structure needed to set up an industry that might be able in the future to escape those forces. The preamble begins by declaring cinema an art, an instrument for the creation of individual and collective consciousness, accordingly able to contribute to the deepening of the revolutionary spirit and to feeding its creative inspiration. But then it goes on clearly to speak of the need to establish an appropriate technical infrastructure and a distribution apparatus. In sum, the text tells us a good deal about the political understanding, intelligence, and intentions of its authors, members of the revolutionary vanguard that stood behind the Provisional Government. This Provisional Government was seen by the international media at the time as a novel kind of bourgeois-nationalist social-democratic grouping, which was precisely the revolutionaries' purpose. This decree, though couched in language that does not openly contradict such an impression, is, on closer examination, good evidence that whatever the appearances, there were people at work here intent on the creation of socialism.

But how far back should we go, trekking through the historical undergrowth, in order to answer the question how it was that the Cuban revolutionaries learned to place such a high value on cinema? What do we need to know about the history of cinema in Cuba before 1959? What do we need to know about the history of Cuba apart from its cinema, and about the cultural and political history of the revolutionaries who promoted the decree and set up ICAIC?

CHAPTER TWO

Back to the Beginning

In 1972, a full-length documentary appeared ironically titled *Viva la República* (Long live the republic), directed by Pastor Vega. A historical compilation juxtaposing a variety of old newsreels, photographs, political cartoons, and similar visual material, and narrated with a wit that makes the most of the very crudeness and limitations of such stuff, the film elegantly traces the history of the republic set up under U.S. tutelage at the beginning of the century, following the expulsion of the Spanish after their defeat in the Cuban-Spanish-American War in 1898. Close to the start we see two of the very earliest newsreels ("actualities," as they were then called), scenes of the war as issued by the Edison company. One of them pictures Teddy Roosevelt's Rough Riders disembarking on the island. They were among the very first films to be shot in Cuba. Like all the earliest films, they are hardly more than moving photographs.

Brief and crude as they are, these fragments should not be underestimated. However minimal they are as images—the camera remains distant from its subject and there is very little detail—they were already capable of satisfying a more than simple demand by the audience for spectacle, mere wonder at the magic of the moving image. They were made not for Cuban audiences, but for those of North America in the epoch of the robber barons, where, however naive, their interest had been carefully nurtured by the new mass press of the day—especially by the two leading newspaper chains of Pulitzer and Hearst.

William Randolph Hearst provided the model for Charles Foster Kane

Roosevelt's Rough Riders (Edison, 1898)

in Orson Welles's famous first film *Citizen Kane* of 1940. A scene early in the picture makes passing reference to the role of Hearst's New York *Journal* (Kane's *Inquirer* in the film) in fomenting popular encouragement for the Cuban war. Kane's ex-guardian Thatcher protests at a headline that reads "Galleons of Spain off Jersey Coast." "Is this really your idea of how to run a newspaper?" Thatcher asks Kane. "You know perfectly well there's not the slightest proof that this armada is off the Jersey Coast." Bernstein, Kane's general manager, interrupts with a cable from a correspondent called Wheeler whom Kane has sent to Cuba, modeled on the real Richard Harding Davis sent by Hearst. "Girls delightful in Cuba stop," reads the cable. "Could send you prose poems about scenery but don't feel right spending your money stop. There is no war in Cuba. Signed Wheeler." "Any answer?" asks Bernstein. "Yes," says Kane. "Dear Wheeler, you provide the prose poems, I'll provide the war." One of the ways Pulitzer and Hearst competed against each other was by building sensationalist press campaigns around the Cuban War of Independence.

This kind of real historical reference, and not just the film's virtuosity, is one of the elements that made *Citizen Kane* a radical movie; yet its attitude toward Cuban history—"There is no war in Cuba"—is cavalier. The newspapers of both press barons published releases by the Junta of Cuban Exiles in the United States, from the moment it was established in 1895 with the aim of winning recognition for Cuban belligerency. People certainly knew there was a war going on ninety miles from Miami— indeed, a revolution—and at that time, North Americans were not yet afraid of the word. Their own revolutionary origins were still alive in popular memory, and the Cubans attracted a good deal of sincere sympathy. But they also attracted, says the North American historian Philip Foner, "elements . . . who viewed the Revolution as an issue suited to their own purposes, such as American traders and investors who were directly connected with Cuban affairs and wished to protect their trade and investments in the island; expansionist elements who were seeking foreign markets for manufactured goods and for the investment of surplus capital; businessmen and politicians who cared nothing for the revolutionary struggle in Cuba but saw in it an opportunity to divert popular thinking away from the economic and social problems arising from the depression which had begun in 1893; and newspaper publishers who saw in the Cuban Revolution an opportunity to boost circulation."[1]

Throughout 1897 and 1898, atrocity stories flowed north from the island, both fabricated and exaggerated. Another historian: "Vivid language, striking sketches drawn by men who never left New York, lurid details composed in bars and cafes mingled with the truth about Cuba until the whole fabric dazzled millions into a stunned belief. Reporters rescued damsels in distress and upheld the American flag in filibustering expeditions. Artists furnished pictures from the palm-fringed isle and toured incognito in the devastated cane fields and sickened cities. . . . An elaborate system of spies and rumor mongers spread lies."[2]

When the USS *Maine* exploded in Havana harbor—it was moored there supposedly on a goodwill visit—on February 15, 1898, killing more than 250 officers and crew, the newspapers didn't wait for the naval report on the cause of the explosion (which might just have been an accident). A few days earlier, Hearst's *Journal* had published a photographic reproduction—another new technology—of a private letter by the Spanish ambassador in Washington insulting the American president. The

Journal now coined the slogan "Remember the *Maine,* To hell with Spain" and offered fifty thousand dollars for the "detection of the perpetrators of the *Maine* outrage." With more than eight pages devoted to the incident every day, the circulation of the *Journal* more than doubled in the space of a week. In fierce competition, Pulitzer sent deep-sea divers to the scene of the wreck, and the circulation of his *World* also rose hugely. The site of the wreck was filmed by Cuba's own film pioneer, José G. González. In France, Georges Méliès made a reconstruction of the scene, typically delightful and fantastical, fish swimming around in a glass-walled tank with a disproportionate cutout of a ship resting on the bottom.

As pressure for U.S. military intervention had mounted, wrote Albert E. Smith in his autobiography, *Two Reels and a Crank,* he and his assistant Blackton went to film the preparations for war at Hoboken, "where New York's famous old 71st National Guard Regiment was gathered to entrain for Tampa, assembly point for the invasion troops. We found the soldiers shuffling willy-nilly from ferryboat to train and called this to the attention of an officer. 'We can't take pictures of your boys straggling along this way. You wouldn't want a New York audience to see this sort of marching on the screen.' The officer assembled a hundred men in tight lines of eight, marched them briskly by our camera."[3] A revealing incident. Clearly, Smith had an eye for what constituted a "proper" picture. And evidently even the earliest filmmakers knew they were doing more than just taking moving snapshots. On the contrary, Smith was already prepared to intervene here in order to produce a certain image; he was ready to do a bit of stage managing, to work the image up in order to get what we can properly call an ideological effect. (Notice, however, that precisely the same kind of work is needed for what may also properly be termed the aesthetic labor required by the new art form.)

Nonetheless, the early filmmakers were often surprised by their own work—something that is bound to happen in any art form when the frontiers of expression are under exploration. Because they were starting from scratch, the creative conditions in which the early filmmakers worked were precisely what artists in other media engaged in the modernist revolution were themselves looking for, but for them a struggle was needed to explode the traditional parameters of expression and throw the traditional criteria of aesthetic judgment and reasoning into question. There were all sorts of things, however, that filmmakers did spontaneously and unselfconsciously that had precisely this effect, so that, in a strange way, film, which had no traditions because it was utterly new, was to become the most deeply characteristic of modern art forms.

Albert Smith was taken by surprise at the very first projection of his images of the 71st. "The film was developed in time for a special showing at Tony Pastor's that night. One factor had escaped us, and we were unprepared for the demonstration that took place. Public indignation over the *Maine* had taken on another form. Now the public was crying out its confidence in American strength; the spirit of patriotism was a rousing aria on every street corner. . . . That night at Pastor's the audience, enthralled with the idea of a war with Spain, saw their boys marching for the first time on any screen. They broke into a thunderous storm of shouting and foot stamping. Hats and coats filled the air. Never had Pastor's witnessed such a night!"

Theodore Roosevelt was assistant secretary for the navy and one of the strongest advocates of U.S. military intervention. Thanks to his great zeal for publicity, Smith and Blackton soon found themselves traveling to Cuba with the famous Rough Riders, a cavalry regiment, but on this occasion unhorsed. Once there, Smith filmed them in action in what came to be known as the "Charge up San Juan Hill." Roosevelt, who knew a thing or two about promoting his image, at one point in this charge halted and struck a pose for the camera.

An hour or two out of port as they left the island with their film in the can, Smith and Blackton heard the low distant thunder of heavy guns. In Florida, they learned that the Spanish admiral, bottled up in Santiago de Cuba by U.S. warships, had tried to make a run for it. It was the Fourth of July and the U.S. Navy had sunk the Spanish fleet. New York was buzzing with the news when they got back there. Unsure exactly what their footage was like, they at first resolved to keep mum about what they had actually filmed. But reporters hungry for information gathered round them and they were asked if they had shots of the sea battle. "At this precise moment," wrote Smith, "flushed with triumph, I think we would have taken credit for any phase of the Cuban campaign. 'Certainly, certainly,' I said, and Blackton nodded solemnly as if I had spoken a simple irrefutable truth. . . . Once in our office, we knew we were in trouble. Word had spread through New York that Vitagraph had taken pictures of the Battle of Santiago Bay."

The only way out, they decided, was to fake it. They bought large sturdy photographs of ships of the U.S. and Spanish fleets that were on sale in the streets of New York. They cut them out and stood the cutouts in water an inch deep in an inverted canvas-covered picture frame, with blue tinted cardboard painted with clouds for a background. They nailed the cutouts to small blocks of wood and placed small pinches of gunpowder on the wooden blocks. They pulled the cutouts past the camera with a fine thread and used cotton dipped in alcohol at the end of a wire, thin enough to escape the camera's vision, to set off the gunpowder charges. To complete the effect, assistants blew cigarette and cigar smoke into the picture.

The result, seen today, is clearly a model, but not then: "It would be less than the truth to say we were not wildly excited at what we saw on the screen," Smith continued. "The smoky overcast and the flashes of fire from the 'guns' gave the scene an atmosphere of remarkable realism. The film and the lenses of that day were imperfect enough to conceal the crudities of our miniature, and as the picture ran for only two minutes there wasn't time for anyone to study it critically. Deception though it was then, it was the first miniature, and the forerunner of the elaborate 'special effects' techniques of modern picturemaking. Pastor's and both Proctor houses played to capacity audience for several weeks. Jim [Blackton] and I felt less and less remorse of conscience when we saw how much excitement and enthusiasm were aroused by *The Battle of Santiago Bay* and the thirty-minute-long *Fighting with Our Boys in Cuba*. Almost every newspaper in New York carried an account of the showings, commenting on Vitagraph's remarkable feat in obtaining on-the-spot pictures of these two historical events."

Smith and Blackton were not the only people to fake a Battle of Santiago Bay. Two Cuban writers on cinema, Sara Calvo and Alejandro Armengol, mention another in a passage on the relations between politics and the newborn film business:

The principal North American companies—Edison, Biograph, and Vitagraph—exploited this war for ideological, political, and economic ends. Biograph enjoyed the financial assistance of the future President McKinley, at that time governor of Ohio. This company, under the flag of the Monroe slogan, provided the politician's personal propaganda and was to specialize in actuality and documentary material. Vitagraph was

Tearing Down the Spanish Flag in 1898, on the day hostilities between
Spain and the United States broke out. Scarcely had military operations
begun than hundreds of copies of fake documentaries on the war were
circulating through America. One of the most famous was shot in
Chicago by Edward H. Amet, using models and a bathtub to show the
naval battle. . . . Amet dealt with the problem that the battle had occurred at night by claiming very seriously that he had a film "supersensitive
to the light of the moon" and a telephoto lens capable of recording
images at a hundred kilometers' distance. It is said that the Spanish
government managed to acquire a copy of such an "important" graphic
"document" for its archives.[4]

Neither such supersensitive film nor telephoto lens existed then—they
have only been developed recently for use in surveillance satellites—but
it seems that the question didn't even occur to the press in New York.
Calvo and Armengol conclude that films like this "offered a stereotyped
image of the war, devoid of the participation of the Cubans, who suffered discrimination and not a few humiliations in the struggle."

It is not difficult to understand why audiences should have been taken
in by faked images. Smith makes it clear in what he writes that whatever
the publicity claims of the early film business about the way the cinematograph reproduced the world in all its detail and sharpness, the early filmmakers themselves were quite aware of the limitations of their apparatus. Audiences, however, had nothing effectively to compare with these
images that might reveal them as fakes, except perhaps for photographs.
But photographs were not a sufficient test. Apart from any other consideration, photographs themselves carried an ideological charge that also
contributed to the inclination of the audience to see the war uncritically.
Photographs of countries like Cuba—everywhere in the Americas south
of the Rio Grande—generally came into the category of the exotic. The
very idea of the exotic is a creation of imperialism. It expresses the point
of view of the metropolis toward its periphery. The concept of exoticism
identifies the gulf between the self-proclaimed civilization of the metropolis and ways of life beyond it: primitive societies full of strange and unfamiliar features, the stranger the more interesting—as Georg Lukács
once observed, speaking of certain nineteenth-century French novels—
like the curious use of dogs' milk and flies' feet as cosmetics.

The history of the exotic image goes back to the 1590s, when Theodore
de Bry published more than a dozen volumes of engravings of the Great
Voyages, the *Historia Americae*. Between them, de Bry and the authors

of the accounts whose drawings he copied gave visual form to the world discovered by the conquistadores, enfolding it within the mythological vision of a Europe still emerging from the Middle Ages. The fantastical images of *Historia Americae* wove spells over those who looked upon them. They evidently included Shakespeare, who doubtless found de Bry in the library of one of his patrons. Describing one of the most haunting of these images, he has Othello speak of

> travels' history:
> Wherein of antres vast and deserts idle,
> Rough quarries, rocks, and hills whose heads touch heaven
> . . . .
> And of the Cannibals that each other eat,
> The Anthropophagi, and men whose heads
> Do grow beneath their shoulders. (Act 1, scene 3)

Perhaps there is even an intimation in his last play, *The Tempest*, where he repeats the image of the "men whose heads stood in their breasts," that the strange forms and behavior of which these images tell are the projections of the colonizers—a reaction to encountering, in those they proceeded to conquer, creatures disturbingly like themselves who none-theless, like his own creation Caliban, did not fit their own ideas of what it is to be human.

The image of the exotic undergoes a transformation and intensifica-tion in the nineteenth century with the coming of photography, not just because of the new conditions for the production of images, but also because photography became a vehicle of nineteenth-century empiricism. "The view of reality as an exotic prize to be tracked down and captured by the diligent hunter-with-a-camera has informed photography from the very beginning," writes Susan Sontag. "Gazing on other people's reality with curiosity, with detachment, with professionalism, the ubiq-uitous photographer operates as if that activity transcends class inter-ests, as if its perspective is universal."[5] The camera collects the facts. A Frenchman with a daguerreotype was already roaming the Pacific in 1841, two years after the invention of photography had been announced to the world. Painters soon realized how the camera would undermine the credibility of their foreign landscapes and adopted it as an ally instead. Already in 1841 in Mexico, Frederick Catherwood took photographs in Yucatán, where he had been painting for several years. And in 1844,

From Theodore de Bry, *Historia Americae* (1590s)

Arago, the man who persuaded the French parliament to purchase the invention for the nation because of its scientific importance, promoted a daguerreotype expedition to photograph the aborigines of Brazil. The very authenticity of such images contributed to their exoticism, because of the lack of any context in which to read them. As a scientist, the early photographer was locked into the tabulating methods of empiricism, engaged in making inventories of everything, and the naturalism of the camera fitted; this was a different form of endeavor from, say, the imaginative synthesis, in Darwin, of the theoretical naturalist. The photographic intelligence in its infancy was more like that of the utilitarian minister with Bible in one hand, magnifying glass in the other (in E. P. Thompson's phrase), whose illusion of productivity in the pursuit of knowledge consisted in nothing more than the patient assembly of detail upon detail without ever being able to show their connections. In the same dissociated way, the exotic image made no connection with the immediate reality of those who looked upon it. The camera conquered geographical, but not cultural, distance.

With the coming of moving images, venturing to obtain the exotic image for the audience back home went hand in hand with opening up a market for the invention in the countries of the exotic themselves. Moving pictures were first brought to Cuba by Gabriel Veyre, agent for the French company of Lumière Frères, early in 1897. He arrived in Havana from Mexico, where he had unveiled the *cinématographe* on August 14, 1896—eight months after its Paris debut, six months after another Lumière agent, Félicien Trewey, introduced it in London. The Lumières sent a team of agents around the world on planned itineraries designed to sweep up on the fascination the new invention created everywhere, preferably in advance of competitors—the Havana debut of the *cinématographe* on January 24 was quickly followed by the arrival from the United States of Edison's version on February 13 and the rival North American Biograph on April 10. The Lumière machine served as both projector and camera and the agents were briefed to bring back scenes from the countries they visited. Since these films were developed on the spot, they were also exhibited immediately, and thus provided the first examples of local imagery in moving pictures. In Mexico, Veyre filmed at least thirty scenes, ranging from the president and his entourage to local dancing and groups of Indians. In Cuba, as a condition of being allowed into the country, he was required by the Spanish authorities to take military propaganda scenes, views of the artillery in action, and of troops on the march.[6]

The content of the images of the Cuban-Spanish-American War was, above all, the projection of the power of the state—like the content ever since of the images of U.S. landings in Latin America, from Nicaragua in the 1920s to Grenada in 1983. The spectacle of war, of the military, and of state display—coronations, state visits, imperial ceremonial—were all popular subjects in early cinema. (British filmmakers excelled at the ceremonials, but they also made effective films of the Boer War, where Smith contributed his expertise too.) For, as Thomas Hobbes once observed, power is the reputation of power. It was sufficient for early audiences to be presented with the crudest images, little more than the reputation of the reputation, and they were engaged by them. If scenes like these became a genre, an established term in the vocabulary of screen rhetoric, this is because they functioned first and foremost not on the level of information but like religious icons: they aroused the devotion of an audience to an idea.

This is the source of some of film's first ideological functions, and it comes from something more than the automatism of the camera, its mechanical capacity to record whatever it's exposed to—as Albert E. Smith, for one, realized very rapidly. Yet, although Smith's fakery was deliberate, it is not that it arose exactly from a desire to deceive, or only in a superficial sense. The "invention" of the miniature was a discovery in what the medium lent itself to, as well as an organic response to an eager audience that made the filmmakers feel they were only satisfying a "natural demand." And they were. Because, in consuming moving pictures, the audience stimulated their production not merely economically but also, through their ready surrender of self to the content of the image, on the level of symbolic exchange.

This does not, however, authorize us to say that the ideological effects of film were ingrained in the image itself, as if they were part of the chemical process. In fact, they arise in the relationship of the screen with the audience, in the space between the screen and the spectator. The ideological disposition of commercial cinema saw to it that the emerging screen vocabulary was formalized and pressed into service in ways that seemed to lock the ideological message onto the screen. Nevertheless, it would be a very undialectical approach that took the effects of film to be so fixed—and the relationship of the screen to the audience to be so mechanical—that they cannot change with different audiences and in different situations and circumstances. Pastor Vega's *Viva la República* is a film that plays on this possibility, in particular on the altered perspective of an audience that has seen the Revolution triumph and then the defeat of the invasion of the Bay of Pigs sponsored by the CIA, which left the reputation of U.S. power irretrievably tarnished.

Cuba's revolutionary cinema has sought to undermine that power further, by building on the audience's new attitude toward the screen to create both a more critical disposition in the audience and a radical film language. The experience both of guerrilla warfare and of the popular militia that the Revolution created after it took power provides the underpinning for a number of films that use experimental cinematic techniques explicitly to demystify the iconography of warfare as portrayed in conventional Hollywood cinema. Over the same years that saw the invention of film, Cuban patriots were engaged in a war of liberation against Spain, a struggle dating back to 1868. The events of that year are re-created in *La primera carga al machete* (The first machete charge), directed by Manuel Octavio Gómez, one of the films that ICAIC produced at the end of the 1960s to celebrate one hundred years of struggle. Highly experimental both visually and narratively, shot in black and white to imitate the high contrast of very early film stocks, it is constructed as if it were a piece of contemporary documentary reportage on the events, including interviews with the participants, and sections of explanatory exposition.

But it is not as if the conventional iconography of warfare was a secret. Albert E. Smith's account of his Cuban adventure includes a pertinent comment on the way the image of the Charge up San Juan Hill came to be embroidered: "Many historians have given it a Hollywood flavor, but there was vastly more bravery in the tortuous advance against this enemy who could see and not be seen." In other words, not only does the Hollywood image not correspond to reality, but it overdramatizes; intending to produce the image of superheroism, it ends up negating the quiet heroism of the real situation. (Ironically, this is often also true of the antiwar movie.) To expose these genres for what they are, the Cubans have also produced films such as Manuel Herrera's feature-length documentary reconstruction of the Bay of Pigs, *Girón,* made in 1972, a film testimonial that builds up an account of what happened through the recollections not of experts, analysts, and leaders, but of ordinary people who made their contributions on the day and then returned to their regular lives. Their testimonies are filmed in the real locations of the events, and the film reconstructs their stories behind them as they speak. A member of the militia at the time of the invasion remembers the moment when he had to throw a hand grenade for the first time: "I tried to pull the pin out with my teeth, because I thought I would try and copy what they did in the cinema, but that way I'd only have broken my jawbone. I realized that using your teeth is strictly for the movies..." And to top it off, a woman then relates how she too imitated the movies: she was on her way with a message to headquarters from her militia unit, walking along a beach, when she heard suspicious noises, which she was afraid might have been invading mercenaries. To be sure they wouldn't get the message if they captured her, she decided she'd better eat it. It was harder to chew, she says, than she expected.

Cuban cinema has not always abandoned the portrayal of war in the idealized forms of genre cinema. A number of films, like *El brigadista,* set out to use, rather than subvert, the iconography of Hollywood. They are not dishonest films, but they sometimes run into trouble, reproducing unwanted elements of genre uncritically, like *El brigadista*'s reinforcement of the individual macho hero. *La primera carga al machete* and *Girón,* however, are films of a different instinct, more central to the development of ICAIC, which is to try and relocate the point of view of the film upon the narrative that it relates, in order to find ways to communicate the popular experience of real situations without falling into the traps of populism.

The invention of cinematography had required a lengthy period of gestation, but once achieved, its basic principles were easily enough grasped by people anywhere who had moderate mechanical skills, no more than a smattering of scientific knowledge, and some acquaintance with photography. This combination existed wherever the machines of the industrial revolution had penetrated, and the task of maintaining and repairing them had produced practical knowledge. The lines of communication with the metropolis brought the rest. Local filmmakers took no longer to appear in Cuba than in most of Latin America. English machinery came into use on the sugar plantations in the 1830s, and increasing trade with the United States after the mid-century made much of the latest mechanical equipment available. A Spanish traveler found a U.S.-made sewing machine in a remote Cuban village as early as 1859. One of the men who filmed the scene of the sinking of the *Maine,* José G. González, tried his hand, like many film pioneers the world over, at many things. He constructed, for example, illuminated commercial signs. He had a competitor who apparently attempted to project signs onto clouds in the sky, an idea subsequently toned down to projection onto the facades of buildings, as was done in London in the early 1890s. A fancy anecdote, perhaps, but it shows that the principles of the magic lantern were perfectly well known in Havana—similarly, the other fashionable forms of popular visual entertainment. At the moment film made its Cuban debut there were, in the city, numerous photographic establishments and a couple of Panoramas—the Panorama Soler specialized in war scenes, and other optical illusions were on display at the Salón de variedades. There was also a range of temporary and open-air attractions.

After their intervention against Spain, the North American style of urban commercialism was transmitted rapidly to Havana. Havana had always been an open city, a busy port on the routes in and out of destinations throughout the Caribbean and the Gulf of Mexico, a cosmopolitan city open to European influences. It had suffered occupation by the British in 1762, but culturally much more important was the French presence during the nineteenth century in Louisiana and in Mexico. (There are even Hollywood movies of the 1930s and 1940s, starring such people as Nelson Eddy, in which expatriate French aristocrats roam the Caribbean from New Orleans to Martinique.) The mark of French culture survived in Cuba right into the twentieth century, but at the moment when cinema was born, Havana was poised to pass under North American influence, which, though already present, intensified greatly with the establishment of the Republic. The early years of the century saw the Havana bourgeoisie coming increasingly under the sway of North American ideas and uneasy with the revolutionary nationalism to be found particularly in the eastern parts of the island. Following the defeat of the Spanish, the United States left a military government in Cuba that tried to resist nationalist pressures but was forced, after two years, to call a constituent assembly to draw up a constitution for a new republic. This assembly was expressly instructed to make provision in the constitution for U.S.–Cuban relations, which it initially declined to do on the grounds that such provisions had no place in a constitution. But there were forces in Washington determined to curb patriotic resistance on the island and ensure that the constitution gave formal recognition to their demands. Their only concern was to give their threats and ultimatums a semblance of legality. This was contrived by means of an amendment to an army appropriation bill that carried the name of Senator Platt, and which stated the conditions the United States would require to see fulfilled before the occupation was ended. The Platt Amendment fooled nobody. There was a certain amount of doubletalk about just intentions, but the *Washington Post,* in those days a Republican and pro-administration paper, offered the truth. An editorial under the headline "Let Us Be Honest" declared:

Foolishly or wisely, we want these newly acquired territories, not for any missionary or altruistic purpose, but for the trade, the commerce, the power and the money that are in them. Why beat about the bush and promise and protest all sorts of things? Why not be honest. It will pay. Why not tell the truth and say what is the fact—that we want Cuba, Puerto Rico, Hawaii and Luzon [all acquired through the defeat of the Spanish] ... because we believe they will add to our national strength and because they will some day become purchasers at our bargain counters?[7]

The Constitutional Assembly acceded to the Platt Amendment by only a narrow majority, but it was the Havana bourgeoisie with its northward orientation that won the day with the argument that conditional independence was better than continued occupation. In Europe, Cuba was now seen as a U.S. dependency. Following official independence celebrations on May 20, 1902, the London *Saturday Review* commented:

It is true that the American troops and officials have been withdrawn, the American flag hauled down, and a republic of sorts inaugurated. But it is not true that the republic is independent even in the management of its internal affairs, while so far as foreign relations go, it is undisguisedly under the thumb of Washington. The republic has been obliged to cede naval and coaling stations to the United States; it has no power to declare war without American consent; it may not add to the Cuban debt without permission; even its control over the island treasury is subject to supervision. Moreover, the United States retains a most elastic right of intervention.[8]

That right was exercised twice in the following decade, between 1906 and 1909 and again in 1912.

This was the atmosphere in which the first filmmakers in Cuba began to work. Compared with, say, Mexican cinema, Cuba was a bit slow off the mark, but this is probably only because the market was so much smaller. Nevertheless, and despite the difference in size, the two countries show similar characteristics, most of them typical of early film activity almost anywhere, such as the links with fairground entertainment and popular comic and musical theater. They also share a trait that is frequently overlooked, a link between early cinema and advertising. The uses of film in Mexico constituted, even before the turn of the century, a catalog of initiatives in the techniques of marketing. In 1899, for example, the newspaper *El Imparcial* was offering its readers free film shows if they smoked a certain brand of cigarettes. Another paper,

El Nacional, reported in the very year film arrived in Mexico—1896—a project to set up temporary premises in the city center with free film shows of *vistas pintorescas* (picturesque views) financed by including color-slide advertisements in the program.

There is a temptation to call such examples prophetic, for the way they seem to anticipate the symbiotic relationship between program and advertisement in commercial broadcasting, but there is also something odd about them, because film wasn't destined to develop in this way. Radio and television learned to make advertisements pay for programs because they are forms of diffusion where you can't make the audience pay directly, or couldn't until pay-TV was developed. There are, of course, other methods available to pay for broadcasting—licences, sponsorship, state subsidy—and the methods each country chooses are politically significant. In the same way, it says something about conditions in Mexico that such harebrained schemes were thought up for the early film. It says that film found it difficult there for some reason to capture the audience that awaited it; and the reason must be an economic one—probably the fact that the vast majority of people had hardly any spare cash to spend on such things, and therefore needed special inducement. Conditions for working people in the metropolis, bad though they were, were already better than this: the last quarter of the nineteenth century had brought, in countries like England, a real increase in purchasing power.

Most of the desirable conditions for launching film successfully could be found in most Latin American countries, and its early development took place in similar circumstances across the continent. In Cuba, too, there was a close link, from the start, with the ideology of marketing. One of the very few early Cuban films of which records survive is *El brujo desapareciendo* (The disappearing magician)—the title suggests that it must have been a trick film of the kind that was typical of early cinema. It was made, prior to 1906, by a certain José E. Casasús. Casasús was a pioneering exhibitor who began his career traveling around the island with an Edison projector and a portable electric generator, exactly like the "town hall" showmen in Britain at the same time. This film turned out quite successfully—copies were purchased by the French Lumière company, and by Edison in the United States. But it was made with money subscribed by a beer merchant.

In 1906, to celebrate the opening of Cuba's first purpose-built cinema, the Teatro Actualidades (Theater of actualities), another pioneer, Enrique

Díaz Quesada, made a scenic film, *La Habana en agosto 1906* (Havana in August 1906), and, in the same year, *El Parque de Palatino* (Palatino Park), showing scenes of Havana's principal entertainment park. The Cuban film historian J. M. Valdés Rodríguez described this second film as a distinct achievement "that at moments conveyed irony and humor."[9] It seems, nevertheless, precisely in this film that an ideological fusion with the function of publicity took place: the film was commissioned by the entertainments park company for its publicity campaigns in the United States. Two years later, Díaz Quesada made another film in the same vein, whose title was quite explicit: *Un turista en la Habana* (A tourist in Havana). Obviously, these films presented a highly selective picture of the city, since they were meant to show it as a commodity on the tourist market.

But this would hardly have required any great effort on the part of anyone with the minimum photogenic sense of the time. The link between tourism and photography was well established. Susan Sontag calls this the predatory side of photography, and it follows upon the exploitation of the exotic. The alliance between photography and tourism, she says, becomes evident in the United States earlier than anywhere else:

> After the opening of the West in 1869 by the completion of the trans-continental railroad came the colonization through photography. The case of the American Indians is the most brutal. Discreet, serious amateurs like Vroman had been operating since the end of the Civil War. They were the vanguard of an army of tourists who arrived by the end of the century, eager for "a good shot" of Indian life. The tourists invaded the Indians' privacy, photographing holy objects and the sacred dances and places, if necessary paying the Indians to pose and getting them to revise their ceremonies to provide more photogenic material.[10]

The selective and tendentious imagery that is produced in this kind of cultural operation cannot escape having an invisible shadow, the underside of the innocuous attractions of tourism, and of the mysteries of the exotic—the menace of what these constructs render invisible, like the underworld pictured by Francis Ford Coppola at the end of *Godfather II*, where Havana is a city prostituted to the gangsterism of the brothel, the sex show, and the gambling den. It was, indeed, an ineluctable part of the city's image, which Graham Greene satirized in his spoof spy novel *Our Man in Havana*. It has also been captured by a Cuban director, Óscar Valdés, in a film made in 1973 called *El extraño caso de Rachel K.*

(The strange case of Rachel K.), a fictionalized account of an incident that occurred in 1931, when a French variety dancer was murdered during an orgy attended by politicians and prominent society leaders. A few years later, President Roosevelt was advising the Cubans to clean the city up, but the corruption only grew, until the mafiosi were able to congratulate each other (in Coppola's depiction) for finding in Cuba what they couldn't find in the United States—a government prepared to work with them as partners.

CHAPTER THREE

The Nineteenth-Century Heritage

José Casasús and Enrique Díaz Quesada were not the only Cuban film pioneers who made commissioned publicity films. In 1906, Manuel Martínez Illas made a picture about sugar manufacture called *Cine y azúcar* (Cinema and sugar). It was sponsored by the Manatí Sugar Company, which was in the process of trying to raise further capital. Now sugar was Cuba's principal crop. The island was not quite monocultural; tobacco and coffee were also important export crops. But it was above all sugar that was responsible for Cuba's economic deformation, the imbalance in its productive forces that created so much poverty and misery. It would not be possible to understand the peculiar susceptibility of the Cuban film pioneers to commercial sponsorship without considering the effects of the pursuit of sugar on ideological and cultural dispositions in nineteenth-century Cuba.

A number of films produced by the Cuban film institute during the 1970s—among them Sergio Giral's trilogy, *El otro Francisco* (The other Francisco), *Rancheador* (Slave hunter), and *Maluala,* and Tomás Gutiérrez Alea's *La última cena (The Last Supper)*—investigate the nineteenth-century Cuban social formation and the role of sugar in shaping its character, and that of the different social classes by which it was constituted. The picture these films combine to produce is of a deeply troubled colonial slave society with a class of largely Spanish-born plantation owners, grimly determined to prevent the overthrow of their rule by slave rebellion as in Haiti. Their attitudes, opinions, and political alliances were all directed to this end, with the consequence that while Bolívar and his followers brought independence from Spain on the mainland, powerful forces in Cuba preferred to keep the island under Spanish rule and maintain the institution of slavery.

A dissident group, however, began to appear within the landowning class in the 1830s, which linked up with the emerging creole bourgeoisie in the belief that slavery was holding back the island's modernization. But precisely because Cuba was still under colonial rule, the creole bourgeoisie was unable to constitute itself as a fully fledged national oligarchy; and the country was exposed to the highest levels of exploitation not only by the Spanish colonial power but increasingly by her competitors. Opposition to the Spanish grew progressively more militant, and, spearheaded by the fiercely independent coffee-growing small landowners who were largely concentrated in the eastern part of the island, a War of Independence broke out in 1868. In the first phase of this struggle, the independence movement was defeated. The Cuban historian Francisco López Segrera suggests that these circumstances encouraged the creole bourgeoisie, who owned less than a third of the riches of the oligarchy as a whole, and lacked the solid foundations for political activity, to play the role of intermediary with competing foreign capital, simply in order to defend its position.[1]

Yet, paradoxically, Cuba's historical idiosyncrasies served not so much to distinguish it from the rest of Latin America as to intensify a number of traits that could be found throughout the continent, especially in relation to cultural experience and behavior. The process of cultural development in Latin America does not fit easily into European terms of explanation. The Peruvian José Carlos Mariátegui (founder of the Peruvian Communist Party), in a seminal work published in 1928, *Siete ensayos de interpretación de la realidad peruana* (Seven essays of interpretation of Peruvian reality), puts aside both the standard bourgeois periodization of art into the Classical, the Baroque, the Romantic, and so forth, and also the orthodox Marxist classification of feudal or aristocratic, bourgeois, and then proletarian art, because neither of these systems is appropriate either to Peru itself or to Latin America as a whole. Instead, he suggests his own brilliantly simple schema: he distinguishes three periods, the colonial, the cosmopolitan, and the national. In the first, the literature of the country concerned is not that of its own people but of the conquistador. It is an already evolved literature transplanted into the colony, where it usually continues to exert an influence beyond the overthrow of the colonial power. During the second period, which is ushered in by the establishment of the independent republic, elements from various foreign literatures are assimilated simultaneously, and the unique cultural hold of the original colonial power is broken. Finally, in the third period, which implicitly only arrives with proper economic as well as political independence, a people "achieves a well-developed expression of its own personality and its own sentiments."[2]

The transition to cosmopolitanism in these new republics is clearly echoed in Cuba even though it remained a colony. The first manifestations of a new Cuban literature date from the end of the 1830s when a number of short-lived literary journals appeared and the first Cuban novels were written. Just as elsewhere in Latin America, they reveal the influence of European Romanticism—for instance, the novel *Francisco* by Anselmo Suárez y Romero, unpublished till later in the century, on which Sergio Giral's *El otro Francisco* is based.

At the same time as these cultural developments, the creole bourgeoisie in many places succumbed to the doctrines of free trade that the British were seeking to impose upon the continent. The Chilean historian Claudio Véliz has suggested that the acceptance of foreign economic principles was due primarily not to intellectual conviction but to the common sense of self-interest: payment for exports was made in foreign currency, which allowed the exporters to purchase both machinery to expand production, and manufactured and high-quality consumer goods, all at very low prices. They were advantages that favored increasing private consumption and sumptuary display. As Véliz puts it:

> They clothed their cowboys with ponchos of English flannel, rode in saddles made by the best harnessmakers of London, drank authentic champagne and lighted their mansions with Florentine lamps. At night they slept in beds made by excellent English cabinet makers, between sheets of Irish linen and covered by blankets of English wool. Their silk shirts came from Italy and their wives' jewels from London, Paris and Rome.[3]

And, of course, they sent their children to Europe to be educated, just as they nowadays send them to the United States.

The Cuban bourgeoisie was in no way deprived of similar "progress" just because it remained colonial. Of course, the cultural configuration of the island took its own form. The influence of the English was rather less than in many Latin American countries, and that of the French rather stronger, both because of the influx into Cuba of French whites fleeing the Haitian revolution and then the renewed French presence in the region during their period of rule in Mexico. But, in any case, by the 1840s, according to the Cuban literary historian Ambrosio Fornet (who became ICAIC's literary adviser and worked on a number of film scripts, both fiction and documentary), by the 1840s "social life demanded new and more sophisticated forms of consumption, similar to those of the great European capitals: the privileged classes enjoyed their leisure at soirées and operatic performances where they could show off how well informed they were, at least according to the dictates of fashion and the latest news."[4]

As the most leisured sector of the leisured classes, women played an important role in this process, making themselves socially useful in the only sphere of activity allowed them. Already in 1829 there was a Cuban journal called *La Moda o Recreo Semanal del Bello Sexo* (Fashion or the weekly amusement of the fair sex). Its pages included salon music—songs and *contradanzas*—and "pleasurable literature." From then on, says Fornet, no journal could manage without lavishing its attention on literature, which now became another item of sumptuary consumption. The success of the Romantics in Europe helped make literature fashionable in Cuba, creating a new market and a new merchandise.

Confirming the link between fashion and literature, the editor of *La Moda* was a leading literary figure, Domingo del Monte, the host in years to come of the literary circle that succored the first generation of Cuban novelists. The opening scene of *El otro Francisco* takes place in del Monte's salon. Del Monte has invited Suárez y Romero to read his new novel to a visiting Englishman by the name of Richard Madden, an agent of the British government with a commission to investigate violations of the treaty between Britain and Spain on the suppression of the slave trade. The members of del Monte's circle were liberal intellectuals opposed to slavery and in favor of social reform: *Francisco* is the first antislavery novel written in Cuba. The image of the slave that the novel presents is a romantic one—the film is called "The Other Francisco" because it sets out to show what the suffering hero, the slave Francisco, might have been like, what kind of life he would really have led, had he been a historical figure. But the members of del Monte's salon were neither unworldly nor unversed in the realities. Between the scenes in the film that narrate the novel and reconstruct it to show the contrast between romantic fiction and historical reality, we are shown the progress of Madden's investigations (the different strands come together in a brilliantly imaginative stroke, when Madden, traveling around the island, visits a plantation where he meets the characters in the novel). In one of these scenes, Madden is conversing with del Monte:

MADDEN: Tell me, del Monte, how many whites and blacks are there on the island?

DEL MONTE: 300,000 whites and 500,000 colored; 250,000 of them slaves.

MADDEN: Will abolition have an effect on the sugar industry?

DEL MONTE: Well, so far the slaves are necessary, but with the process of mechanization, importing new ones will go against progress.

MADDEN: If the problem were in your hands, what would be your solution?

DEL MONTE: In the first place, the immediate end of the slave trade. Then, the gradual elimination of slavery.

MADDEN: How do the enlightened white creoles look upon independence?

DEL MONTE: Any utterance in favor of independence involves the end of slavery. Right now it would earn us the hatred of the white population. . . . Remember that here even the poorest families have slaves.

MADDEN: Does Spain have the power to suppress the slave trade on the island?

DEL MONTE: More than sufficient.

MADDEN: And the desire to do so?

DEL MONTE: None whatsoever.

MADDEN: Then, it's fear of the blacks that holds back pro-independence feeling?

DEL MONTE: Yes, that's the fear.

Literature, in this Cuba, had become a fashionable commodity, but there was little cultural sensibility among the majority of the dominant class that made up its market, no real cultural awareness, because there was no preparedness to admit critical thinking. Only in the interstices of the growth of luxury consumption, like del Monte's literary salon, did any authentic cultural production take place within the "cultured"

El otro Francisco (Sergio Giral, 1974)

classes. For a creole bourgeoisie of this kind—and this is a trait that Cuba only reveals more starkly than elsewhere—the attitude of "vulgar" Marxists that art is nothing more than a form of luxury consumption turns out ironically to be a true description. Culture for them was indeed on a par with linen sheets and silk shirts—the very antithesis of culture as Mariátegui understands it, an active agent and expressive force within society. But this, of course, is not the kind of culture you can acquire by buying it. The culture you buy doesn't stick.

It doesn't stick because the only thing going on in such a transaction is the imitation of outward forms of behavior. The model, for example, for the sociocultural role of women was already well established in London, Paris, and other European cities. There, women exerted vigorous leadership in the bourgeois salons in a manner corresponding to the nature of the bourgeois family: the wife presided over the gathering, introduced the guests, and led the conversation. The daughters of the family were among the performers because playing an instrument was an accomplishment that demonstrated their eligibility for marriage. The discussion of fashion was a topic of the salon because different styles of dress were deemed appropriate to different types of event. The Cuban bourgeoisie simply copied all this, though rather than fashion being an extension of the salon, the salon became an extension of fashion, a place to show off dresses brought back like trophies from trips to Europe. The portrayal of a salon in the second film of Sergio Giral's trilogy, *Rancheador,* captures the style of the thing to a tee. It was the development of "cultured" musical life in Cuba after about 1810 that provided one of the principal routes of entry for European Romantic literature. Madame de Staël, Chateaubriand, and Lord Byron, Alejo Carpentier tells us, were the main authors to inspire the Cuban romances that were sung in the salons.[5]

But by the time the products of European culture had crossed the seas, they had lost the originality or polemical significance they may have started off by possessing. Indeed, very little was left except the function of being a social commodity that could be circulated and cashed in, in order to acquire social status, such as the status that went with hosting the salon. The consequences of this reduction of the symbolic values of cultural objects to the narrowest social exchange value can be seen in the fate of Cuban literature in the course of the nineteenth century. The appearance of a number of literary journals and novels at the end of the 1830s marks the beginning of a national literary renaissance that never fulfilled its promise. There is very little continuity between this brief flowering of literary sensibilities and the appearance of the *modernista* poets at the end of the century. Ambrosio Fornet tells us that the literary journals that appeared at the end of the 1830s had all disappeared by the beginning of 1841, unable to sustain their subscriptions.

The journals demonstrated the existence of a literary market, but the beneficiaries turned out to be not the publishers of journals and books, but the newspapers, which only had to concede space to literature amid the advertisements and mercantile announcements to take this market over. They began to publish novels in installments. These were not, however, auspicious conditions for literary development, as the papers found it both cheaper and safer to reprint foreign successes rather than risk publication of new and untried works by Cuban authors—safer especially ideologically. Cuban authors, like so many others throughout Latin America, tended toward radical liberalism, and there was even more of a danger in Cuba that the readership would refuse to patronize these works. It was safer, too, to avoid courting censorship. The result was that the market was de-Cubanized, and the Cuban author lost contact with the wider audience.

This situation persisted during the second half of the century and formed the background to the emergence of *modernismo*. (The movement took its name from the description by the Nicaraguan poet Rubén Darío, in 1890, of "the new spirit which today quickens a small but proud and triumphant group of writers and poets in Spanish America.")[6] The Mexican *modernista* poet Amado Nervo complained that "in general in Mexico, one writes for those who write. The literary man counts on a coterie of the selected few who read him and end up as his only public. The *gros public*, as the French say, neither pays nor understands, however simply he writes. What can be more natural than that he should write for those who, even if they don't pay, at least read him?"[7] Not surprisingly, this only increased the writers' predilection for a kind of aestheticism that was already well developed in Europe. Combining a variety of European stylistic influences, *modernismo* is a fine example of Mariátegui's cosmopolitanism, but also a highly sophisticated one.

The *modernistas* imported into Latin America the style of the bohemian, and undoubtedly they show a certain degree of dependency on their European influences. But, at the same time, in adopting bohemianism, the *modernistas* were attacking the dependency and conformism of the creole bourgeoisie, claiming the right, even if they couldn't earn a living at it, to live like writers and artists, and asserting the needs and possibilities of cultural self-determination. Moreover, they carried their project through not just with great aplomb but with imaginative originality. The manner in which they chose their paradigms and combined their features created an entirely new aesthetic synthesis that it would be appropriate to call "syncretistic." *Syncretism* is not a word that will be found in a dictionary of literary terms, though Latin American literary and cultural critics have long employed the concept. It is borrowed from anthropology, where it was applied to the process of synthesis of religious symbolism in Latin America over the period of the Conquest. The imposition of Catholicism did not succeed in simply displacing pre-Columbian cosmologies and their corresponding symbols and practices. Nor was Catholicism simply overlaid upon them. A fusion took place in which the new symbolism was interpreted through the old and acquired some of its attributes and functions, creating a new level of signification fusing elements of both. The small protective three-pronged cross that adorns peasant houses in the Andes symbolizes both the Catholic Trinity and a mythology of three that comes from the Incas.

Modernismo was the product of a similar process in aesthetic shape: more than an imitative combination of different stylistic elements, but their fusion in a poetic language with its own creative force; for the *modernistas* used the language in which they wrote with a new sense of birthright, speaking no longer with a Spanish accent but with the rhythms and lilts of real Latin American speech.

Antimaterialistic sentiments were almost a determining characteristic of the *modernista* movement. Many of its members came from the fallen bourgeoisie to be found not only in Cuba but throughout Latin America. The Cuban Julián del Casal belonged to a family that had been forced off its land by large-scale competition in sugar production following the abolition of slavery, while in Colombia José Asunción Silva spent much of his energy trying to refloat the family business that had been ruined by civil war. The parents of the Argentinian Leopoldo Lugones were forced to abandon their family estate because of financial difficulties and the Uruguayan Julio Herrera y Reissig saw his family lose their wealth and influence by the time he was twenty. Jean Franco, who compiled this list, comments that "it would be absurd to suggest that these men became poets because their families lost their money (indeed, there were also wealthy dilettantes among the modernists...) but these reversals almost certainly hardened that hatred of contemporary society which is one of the constants of their writing."[8] A figure like Julián del Casal, living the life of the bohemian aesthete, collecting Chinese and Japanese knickknacks and burning incense in front of an image of the Buddha, is indeed the very model of defiance toward material fate. And paradigmatic *modernista* writings, like Rubén Darío's story *El rey burgués* (The bourgeois king), are allegories of the fate of the artist who rejects bourgeois values and ends up forced to live the life of a beggar, which expresses, among other things, the fears of material insecurity that are never so great as among the petite bourgeoisie, especially those who are newly poor.

The *modernistas* find their antithesis in the materialism of the film pioneers, that new kind of image maker who now emerges like the poet's shadow, the double who represents exactly what the *modernistas* fear within themselves—submissiveness to the material interests of their class. And all the more so in Cuba, where it seemed to the writer Jesús Castellanos in 1910 that materialism had become the main preoccupation since the emancipation from Spanish rule; for, defenseless against the influence of North American commercialism, and exposed like nowhere else in Latin America to the penetration of the new advertising and publicity businesses, Cuba is once again the country where the reality of Latin America is least masked.

It was not long before the early film reached the stage where sustained narrative became possible, and at this point new ideological tensions appear. From the point of view of its aesthetic development, the cosmopolitanism of early Latin American cinema, if it can be called that, was inevitable. It was a function of the medium. Since film was already international at the moment of its birth, because the film trade was necessarily international—nowhere was supply equal to demand without importing films from abroad—so nowhere in the world was film immune from the most diverse range of influences. And because everyone was starting from scratch, it is impossible to imagine that it could have been otherwise. Indeed, not until the film idiom has arrived at a greater stage of elaboration and technical development is it possible to conceive of such a thing as a national style in the cinema, let alone an individual one, for that matter. The apparent exceptions, like Méliès, prove the rule. They have been inscribed in the history of film less as conscious artists with their own personal style than as ciphers of supposedly inherent possibilities within the medium—Albert E. Smith is another example. But the development of narrative introduces a new dimension.

In Europe, the development of film narrative during cinema's second decade joined with a desire to prove the respectability of the new medium to produce the first, and as yet far overstretched adaptations of the classics of stage and fiction. In Latin America, this same desire for respectability expressed itself in the choice of patriotic themes. Examples are the large-scale reconstructions *La batalla de Maipú* (The battle of Maipú) and *La revolución de mayo* (The May revolution), produced by the Italian expatriate Mario Gallo in Argentina in the centenary year of his adopted country's emancipation from Spain. In Cuba, Enrique Díaz Quesada found his subjects in the popular themes of more recent anticolonial struggle. In 1913, after several more shorts, he produced his first full-length picture, *Manuel García o el rey de los campos de Cuba* (Manuel García or the king of the Cuban countryside), based on a book by Federico Villoch concerning a bandit popularly identified with anti-Spanish nationalism. A contemporary newspaper account of the film suggests that, as one might expect, the treatment was highly melodramatic. It ended, for example, with the bandit's ghost appearing above his tomb.[9] Other nationalistic themes followed—such as, in 1914, *El capitán mambi o libertadores y guerrilleros* (The *mambi* captain or liberators and guerrilla fighters). *Mambi* was the word that identified a Cuban rebel. Derived from the name of a black Spanish officer who changed sides and joined the guerrillas in Santo Domingo in 1846, Spanish soldiers sent from Santo Domingo to Cuba in 1868 brought the term with them. Intended pejoratively to lump the white freedom fighters with the blacks, the liberation movement proudly accepted the equation.

It would seem natural to suppose that such films represented popular feeling against authority in a pseudorepublic of such obvious servility toward the neocolonialists of the north. This is the way Valdés Rodríguez describes them. "From his first film . . . to the last," wrote Valdés Rodríguez of Díaz Quesada,

> the themes and characters were firmly rooted in social reality, historical and contemporary. In some cases, such as *La zafra o sangre y azúcar* [The sugar harvest or blood and sugar], relations of property, social problems, the worker and peasant struggle for human conditions of work and of living are present in a manifest way, if rather confused, disoriented, and without deliberation. It was the innate feeling of justice, expression of the spirit of rebellion and equality, radically democratic, of the Cuban people.[10]

The films are now lost, but historical sense urges caution here. Valdés Rodríguez may be giving these films the benefit of the doubt, since there were no films anywhere at this time that were not, by later standards, confused and disoriented—even *The Birth of a Nation* and *Intolerance* are not completely free from these limitations of the early film idiom. But for the same reason, the images would have been more ideologically ambiguous—as in D. W. Griffith's films too. The evidence for this is that authority did not unequivocally condemn them as dangerous embodiments of popular feeling. On the contrary. The fact is that a regime as shaky as that of the Cuban republic had every need of the means to legitimize itself, and film was clearly a candidate for this job. Both *El capitán mambi* and Díaz Quesada's next film, *La manigua o la mujer cubana* (The countryside or the Cuban woman), were given direct assistance by the government of President Mario García Menocal. For the first, the army supplied equipment and soldiers for the battle scenes; for the second, Menocal, educated at North American universities, chief of Havana police during the military occupation, then administrative head of the Cuban American Sugar Company, and now head of a staunchly pro-imperialist government, himself intervened to allow filming to take place in the Morro Castle, the Spanish fortification—the oldest in Latin America—that overlooks Havana protecting the harbor.[11] The closing scenes of the film, which were thus vouchsafed, represented that historical moment when the Spanish flag was lowered for the last time and the Cuban flag was raised for the first. Perhaps Menocal was hoping that these images would obscure the more ambivalent memory of similar scenes when the lowered flag was the Stars and Stripes, the day the puppet republic he now headed was officially born.

CHAPTER FOUR

Melodrama and White Horses

Two Cuban investigators of early cinema in their country, Rolando Díaz Rodríguez and Lázaro Buria Pérez, have divided the years 1897–1922 into three periods. The first, 1897–1905, is the period of cinema as simple spectacle in as yet unequal competition with theater. The second, 1906–18, is the stage of the consolidation of cinema both as a spectacle and as a business, but under European domination. In the third period, 1919–22, the spectacle becomes increasingly ideological in nature, the Europeans are displaced by the North Americans, and the incipient national cinema is killed off.[1]

Early exhibition in Latin America was substantially an activity of *cómicos de la legua*, itinerant showmen, just like everywhere else. In most Latin American countries, however, the geographical spread of film was generally restricted to the reach of the railways and only a little beyond. Along the railway lines, a regular supply of new films from the capital city encouraged permanent cinemas. There was a limited hinterland where traveling showmen found places to set up in, like barns and yards, but transport and surface communication throughout Latin America were underdeveloped and there were vast remote areas that they never visited at all.

In any case, rural populations in Latin America offered very little scope for making money out of them. There is no reason to suppose that peasant communities would not have been just as receptive to films as urban workers, only they existed beyond the cash nexus and were economically marginal. (Their labor was still largely extracted by the quasi-feudal means inherited and evolved from the Spanish Conquest.) In this re-spect, Cuba stood out among Latin American countries. It had an exten-sive rural proletariat rarely found elsewhere, the workers in the *ingenios,* the sugar mills attached to the large plantations in the sugar-growing areas, which were all well served by lines of communication constructed to get the sugar out. They were also a way for film to come in.

In the years 1906 and 1907, at the start of the second period, cinemas began to spread from the center of the capital to both the popular dis-tricts and the interior of the country. Every kind of mechanism was used to attract the audience. Stores offered customers free film shows, there were free gifts and car rides home (cars were also a novelty). In these ways, and in spite of the technical and expressive limitations of the early film, cinema soon became the most widely distributed and available form of commercial entertainment in Cuba. By 1920 there were 50 cinemas in Havana and more than 300 in the rest of the country. The average number of seats in a Havana cinema was 450, with a total of 23,000 seats for a population of half a million. The total seating capacity in the country as a whole was in the region of 130,000 to 140,000 for a population of around four million.[2] There were large areas of the coun-try where people were out of reach of a cinema, but for the majority of the population the evidence is clear: the market for cinema in Cuba was not only more intensely developed than over most of Central and South America, but penetration was roughly as intense as in many regions in the metropolitan countries where film had been invented—not as in-tense as in the industrial conurbations, of course, but equal to rural dis-tricts like, in Britain, East Anglia, or to the less developed European countries like Greece, regions where cinemas were generally small but quite frequently placed.

The spread of cinema in Cuba was largely due to the overall intensity of foreign exploitation on the island and especially that of the United States, but it was accomplished through intermediaries. The emerging pattern of exploitation in the film industry did not require that the dom-inating country actually own the cinemas; it was enough for it to domi-nate the mentality of the economically dependent tribe of creole capital-ists. In Cuba, as in other Latin American countries, the cinemas came to be owned by the commercial classes, the same local businesspeople who later also set up the multitude of small commercial radio stations. Com-mercial broadcasting spread throughout Latin America during the 1930s, following the model of exploitation developed north of the Rio Grande, and again Cuba became one of the most intensely developed Latin American markets. Radio depended considerably on a supply of recorded music, for which it provided an aural shopwindow, and it grew in symbiosis with the record companies. This was a field where the North Americans supplied the technology and local producers put it to work. In Cuba, Mexico, and Argentina, recording industries took the rich national popular music and entered it in international competition, proving that they were all good pupils. In Cuba (where Andrés Segovia made his first electrical record in 1927), RCA was the first to come along with a modern electrical recording factory, and by the end of the 1930s popular Cuban recording artists like Benny Moré and the Trio Matamoros were known throughout Central America and the northern parts of South America. With cinema, where the costs of production were very much higher, local production as a result was minimal. The exhibitors were much more dependent on the U.S. distributors than radio was on North American record producers. And those distributors that were not themselves North American were still dependent on the North Americans for a regular supply of new films.

Yet in cinema the United States had been a late starter. Its entry into international competition was constrained during cinema's first twenty years or so by the ravages of the Motion Pictures Patents War, in which the companies battled viciously against each other to establish legal ownership of the industry's patents (the basis of the technological rents that formed a significant ingredient in profit rates). At one point, it seems that independents needing to flee the attacks of the would-be monopolists thought of Cuba as a possible scene of operations, before moving right out of reach to California and establishing the colony that became Hollywood. But at this time the dominant foreign film companies in Cuba were French. Although at home the Lumière company was progressively eclipsed by competitors, its careful preparations had given the French a firm foreign footing, which Pathé and Gaumont fought it out to turn to advantage. Cuba was one of the places where they competed. In 1906, Havana's Teatro Actualidades, the country's first purpose-built cinema, began to acquire films from Pathé on a regular basis. The island's first film distributors, Santos y Artiga, established in 1904, were agents for Gaumont. Around 1909, they took over the Teatro Actualidades and dropped Gaumont in favor of an exclusive contract with Pathé. The arrangement was, from Pathé's point of view, part of the fightback against the growing danger from the North Americans; back in Paris, the Kodak entrepreneur George Eastman was trying, on behalf of the Patents Company, to stymie Pathé's leadership in the manufacture of raw film stock in Europe. Gaumont's response to the North American threat was to withdraw from international markets and consolidate at home (it sold its British operations to British buyers during the same period). Pathé was able to hold its own in Cuba and other foreign territories until the First World War. But the war entailed a cutback in European production, leaving a space that the North Americans, with the Patents War now behind them, were eager to fill.

Film, a new invention, became a major branch of what the Frankfurt sociologists in the 1930s, Theodor Adorno and the others, identified as the culture industry, a segment of production financed by entertainment capital. This industry is characteristically imperialist; entertainment capital is dominated by North American interests and closely linked with the electrical industry, which for Lenin, in his 1917 pamphlet *Imperialism: The Highest Stage of Capitalism,* was the very model of capitalism in its highest stage of development. Even at the beginning, when the technology was still primitive and the expressive means still poor, the infant film business in each country was only able to satisfy demand with difficulty, and through the international character that its trading patterns even then revealed, cinema showed itself a child of late capitalism, just like the giant electric companies with their transnational structure that Lenin described. So explosively did film catch on that rates of growth were unprecedented, and for several years no country was able to produce enough for its own home market. If the colonizers of Hollywood were able to turn these conditions to their special advantage, this is because they were the first to obtain the backing of finance capital. The process upon which the North American film business then entered altered the prospects of creole capital more rapidly and radically than it affected the big European film companies. These had been seriously weakened by the war but they still had an industrial base and national roots. In the countries of the imperialized periphery, such advantages were entirely absent, and the local operators either left the business or rapidly gravitated into exhibition. Distribution concentrated on a small number of companies, principally North American subsidiaries. Production was left to a few adventurists.

José Agustín Mahieu has characterized the first period of cinema in his own country, Argentina, as one of "empirical adventurism."[3] The term could equally well be used for Cuba. In Argentina, this period lasted about fifteen years and its end was signaled, says Mahieu, in 1912, with the founding of the Sociedad General Cinematográfica, the first film dealers in the country to move from selling films to exhibitors to rental instead. In Cuba this transition had been reached five or six years earlier, with the company of Hornedo y Salas.

This changeover lays the basis for subsequent market domination by the North American distributors. They became the majors because they had understood that control of distribution was the dominant position in the industry. As the economic historian of cinema Peter Bachlin has explained:

> The distributor takes over the risks of purchasing the films while the exhibitor only has to rent them; the distributor's mediation improves economic conditions for the exhibitor by allowing a more rapid change of programs. For the producers, this development signals a growth in the market, with films able to reach consumers more rapidly and in greater number, while also constituting a kind sales guarantee for their films. In general, the distributor buys the prints of one or more films from one or more producers and rents them to numerous exhibitors; in the process, he is able to extract a sum considerably greater than his costs.[4]

The balance of power thus shifts to the distributor. But since cinemas in the capitalist system exist to provide not films for audiences, but audiences for films, so exhibitors in turn serve as fodder for the distributors, and the producers behind them.

The 1920s, in the North American film industry, became the period in which dealers-turned-distributors learned the tricks of the trade and battled for control of the exhibition market with the emerging Hollywood studios, which were trying to extend their own control over the industry. It was the period when the peculiarities of the film as a commodity first clearly emerged. The film is consumed in situ, not through the physical exchange of the object but by an act of symbolic exchange, the exchange of its projected impression. William Marston Seabury, a North American film lawyer, explained that "in the picture industry the public may be regarded as the ultimate consumer but in reality the public consumes nothing. It pays an admission price at a theatre from which it takes away nothing but a mental impression of whatever it has been permitted to see."[5] Correspondingly, the exchange value of the film is realized not through physical exchange of the object itself, but through gate money, the price of admission, in this way manifesting its affinity with various other forms of cultural production and entertainment. But if it doesn't need to pass physically into the hands of the consumer, neither does the film need to pass into the legal ownership of the exhibitor. He need only rent it.

By this means, the exhibitor becomes the prey of the ways the distributors find to manipulate the conditions of rental—"block booking" and "blind booking," for example, in which they force exhibitors to take pictures they don't want and sometimes haven't seen in order to get the ones they do want. Nonetheless, Seabury insists that film is entirely different from the commercial operation of the chain stores with which people had begun to compare the cinema. Bachlin is in agreement with this. It is, he says, "of great importance for the forms of concentration and monopoly that arise within the industry. The principles of price-fixing and ways of dominating the market will be different from those that relate to products that involve only a single act of purchase by the consumer, that is to say, products that disappear from the market in one transaction."[6] In Europe, the North American distributors found resistance to their various malpractices, and during the 1920s European countries progressively erected legal barriers to protect their own film industries, with varying degrees of success. They were barriers of which it was practically impossible to conceive in underdeveloped countries. Even had governments had the will, what should they try to protect? The only Latin American country that in those days ever tried it was revolutionary Mexico, in the early 1920s, angry at the offensive representation of their country that Mexicans began to find in the Hollywood picture. As for Cuba,

> The taste of the Cuban public is rapidly becoming more educated—the highly sensational film has had its day and interest now centres on the drama with what is called "a strong love interest." The public is now accustomed to the very best type of film, indeed to a better type than in England. Comic films are not popular and even Charles Chaplin, who combines comedy with genius, is not as popular as previously.

The action must be quick and the ending happy. Italian films have lost ground in Cuba owing to alleged slowness of action, while as an illustration of the need for a happy ending can be mentioned the *Prisoner of Zenda,* a first class film which indeed became a great success but which was shown with some trepidation and caused some criticism by its "renunciation" scene in the final act.

The market in Cuba is known as a "star" market, i.e. producers' names are rarely if ever known and advertising follows the same lines, calling the film a "Mary Pickford" film, or a "Douglas Fairbanks" film. These names are so well known to the public that it is quite sufficient to advertise the name of the star in order to fill the theatre.[7]

Just because these are the quaint observations of His Britannic Majesty's consul-general in Havana is no reason to discount this report on the taste of Cuban audiences in 1923. The consul-general's comments are concise and very much to the point:

The proximity of the United States is almost fatal to the films of other countries. Not only are all the American film stars well known to the Cuban public, but both the Spanish and American papers in Havana constantly grant publicity and a number of American cinema magazines are in circulation in Cuba. Advertising is intense. Theatre owners and others have only to run over to Florida (some 96 miles) or even up to New York (60 hours) to see the latest films and purchase them on the spot, and most of them have agents and correspondents in the United States who send particulars of all new films and report on their suitability for the Cuban market. (Ibid.)

In fact, the U.S. majors began to move in on Cuba while the First World War was in progress: Paramount was first, in 1917. By 1926, Cuba represented 1.25 percent of U.S. foreign distribution, according to the tables published in the *Film Year Book.* It is not much in comparison with Europe, where Britain commanded a huge 40 percent and Germany came a distant second with 10 percent, although several European markets were much smaller than Cuba: Switzerland, Holland, Czechoslovakia, and Poland were only 1 percent each, while Yugoslavia, Rumania, Bulgaria, Turkey, and Greece represented 1 percent between them. In Latin America, Brazil had 2.5 percent, Mexico 2 percent, Panama and Central America 0.75 percent, and Argentina, Uruguay, Paraguay, Chile, Peru, Bolivia, and Ecuador 6 percent between them.[8] None of this made it easier for Cuban producers. The director of a film made in 1925, *Entre dos amores* (Between two loves), commented that if the film failed com-

mercially while the public had applauded it, this was because of the foreign distribution companies, which were anxious to prevent the development of Cuban film production.[9] "Foreign" is a euphemism for North
American.

How did the distributors achieve this kind of market dominance,
from which they could dictate their will? They engaged not only in the
malpractices already mentioned. Seabury quotes the comments of an
independent exhibitor in the United States about the variants of the
rental system who complains that they are designed to provide the distributor with a guarantee plus a percentage, which makes the percentage "excess profit." But the bigger such excess profits, the more investment
one can attract. The industry leaders knew this perfectly well. According
to one spokesman, discussing before an audience at the Harvard Business School in 1926 the question of "how we are trying to lessen sales resistance in those countries that want to build up their own industries":

> We are trying to do that by internationalising this art, by drawing on
> old countries for the best talent that they possess in the way of artists,
> directors and technicians, and bringing these people over to our country,
> by drawing on their literary talents, taking their choicest stories and pro-
> ducing them in our own way, and sending them back into the countries
> where they are famous. In doing that, however, we must always keep in
> mind the revenue end of it. Out of every dollar received, about 75¢ still
> comes out of America and only 25¢ out of all the foreign countries
> combined. Therefore you must have in mind a picture that will first
> bring in that very necessary 75¢ and that secondly will please the other
> 25% that you want to please. If you please the 25% of foreigners to the
> detriment of your home market, you can see what happens. Of course,
> the profit is in that last 25%.[10]

Or rather, the excess, or surplus, profit. This is cardinal, because it is
not ordinary but surplus profit that attracts investment capital, and this
is ultimately how Hollywood came to dominate world cinema. Hollywood gleaned a surplus profit from the market that gave it the backing
of Wall Street, which was already fast becoming the most substantial
and modern fund of investment capital in the world.

In the 1920s, the North American film industry underwent a rapid
process of vertical integration, in which not only did the production
studios and the distributors combine, but they began to acquire their
own cinemas. This was intended to combat the formation of circuits
among independent exhibitors, where booking arrangements were pooled

in retaliation against the methods of the renters. But abroad in Latin America, the distributors faced no such organized resistance, since the exhibitors had neither the capital resources nor the bargaining power to fight, and there the distributors had no need to acquire cinemas to break the exhibitors' backs and bully them into submission. They acquired no more than a handful in each country, simply to serve as showcases. When foreign-owned cinemas were taken over in the Cuban nationalizations on the weekend of October 14, 1960, there were no more than eleven of them.

The film as a commodity has another peculiarity, which has been observed by the North American economist Thomas Guback. He points out that the cost of making prints for distribution is an extremely small fraction of the total costs of production, what the industry call the "negative costs"—the costs of getting to the finished negative of the complete film from which the prints are made. (The prints then become part of the distribution costs.) Indeed, this proportion has grown progressively smaller over the course of the history of cinema, as production budgets have grown larger and larger. It means, above all, that films can be exported without having to divert the product away from the home market (whereas with many commodities, especially in underdeveloped countries, the home market must be deprived in order to be able to export). In Guback's words, "The cost of an extra copy is the price of the raw stock, duplicating and processing—incremental costs . . . a motion picture is a commodity one can duplicate indefinitely without substantially adding to the cost of the first unit produced . . . a given film tends to be an infinitely exportable commodity; prints exported do not affect domestic supplies nor the revenue resulting from domestic exhibition. . . . We can have our film and foreigners can have it too."[11]

When you add that the United States soon developed into the largest internal film market in the world at the time, it is clear why it was irresistible. Because it was so big, U.S. producers were able to recover negative costs on the home market alone, and the distributors were therefore able to supply the foreign market at discount prices that undercut foreign producers in their own territories. They also undercut European competitors. The consul-general's 1923 report commented that "British prices are said to be too high."

However, Guback's empiricism is misleading about the shape of Hollywood's foreign policy when he suggests that the overseas offensive of the U.S. film industry dates only from after the Second World War, when the contraction of the cinema audience following the introduction of television made foreign revenue increasingly necessary for profitability. He is correct when he claims that before that, "American films were sold abroad but the resulting revenue hardly compared to what the domestic market yielded"—this is true, it was around 25 percent—but misses the point when he continues that "Foreign revenue was simply an additional increment, extra profits upon which the American film companies did not depend." It was indeed a surplus profit and therefore important in attracting investment capital. This gap in his thinking leads to his misleading conclusion that the foreign market did not warrant enough attention "to force Hollywood to modify significantly the content of its films to suit tastes abroad, nor to induce the film companies to maintain elaborate overseas organizations."[12] They didn't do this because they didn't have to—their methods were the same as those extolled by the *Washington Post* at the beginning of the century in the newspaper's declaration about wanting the overseas territories of the defeated Spanish "because they will one day become purchasers at our bargain basements." What Hollywood discovered was that in the cinema, cultural imperialism works just as well as colonialism but at less expense.

Hollywood was never entirely without international competition, however. The 1923 British consul-general's report, for instance, said that after North American pictures, the order of popularity from various countries went: Italy, Germany, France, Spain. ("The British film is unknown.... The fault lies with the British producer who has never attempted to work the market, and now there is a grave doubt whether it is worthwhile to do so.") At the end of the Second World War, things looked rather different. The main competition facing Hollywood on Cuban screens came from Mexico, and to a lesser extent Argentina.

The success of Mexican pictures in Cuba is an ambivalent phenomenon, since Mexican cinema largely consisted in the adaptation of Hollywood genres, and thereby testifies to the ideological as well as the economic effects of Hollywood domination. A U.S. government market report from 1947 informs us about the films Cuban audiences were then watching:

Film distributors and theatre owners say that Mexican movies are more popular in Cuba outside the two large cities of Havana and Santiago than the productions of any other country except fast-paced action films with a readily understood plot from the United States. Action films of this type are the only United States movies which ordinarily outrank Mexican films in popularity in theatres in cities and towns of less than 50,000 population. The preference for action pictures from Hollywood is measurably greater if their locale, stars, and supporting casts can be easily identified by patrons, as the titles suggest. An action picture in an unfamiliar setting is not as popular as a Mexican movie which does not have wave after wave of turbulent activity. . . . More than a dozen distributors, including branches of United States studios, unanimously agree that Mexican movies hold a unique, high place in the affections of the representative Cuban theatregoer. . . . Hearing Spanish instead of having to read or being unable to read Spanish subtitles of English language movies is an important but not the fundamental reason for the partiality shown Mexican movies. . . . Artistically and technically Mexican movies are not comparable with United States and European pictures. However, Mexican movies have been able to portray the national spirit, institutions, character, and social organism of Mexico, which to a large degree are similar to those in Cuba. Nearly all of the dozen or so Cuban features made to date were produced with the help of Mexican directors and stars.[13]

Or as a later commentator put it, "By the 1920s, the 'hits' produced and exported by Hollywood exerted a growing influence and even sharper competition. The Mexican film-makers fell under the cultural sway of their northern neighbor and, to the degree that they did, their filmic concern with national reality diminished"[14]—a generalization that, he adds, is by no means unique to Mexico.

The aesthetics of the adaptation of Hollywood values to Latin American cinema was analyzed by the Cuban cineasts Enrique Colina and Daniel Díaz Torres, in an essay in *Cine Cubano* in the mid-1970s titled "Ideology of Melodrama in the Old Latin American Cinema":

During the silent period . . . Hollywood fabricated and disseminated the myth of the "American Dream" by making the image of reality presented in its films conform to reflections of a falsely optimistic and promising universe. Skin-deep features of different cultures were fitted into novelettish stories that created a stereotypical image, exotic and picturesque, of the underdeveloped countries. This image showed a subworld dominated by the instincts, by a tendency toward irresponsibility and licentiousness, enveloped in a stereotyped mythical atmosphere. The primitive was counterposed to the aseptic order of civilization, and thus the screen mediated the frustrated desires of a bourgeois universe that demanded conformity and equilibrium. This discriminatory content, offered to popular consumption, opened the floodgates to a manifold process of cultural colonization that would end up resonating through-out the various "national" cinemas of the hemisphere.[15]

Colina and Díaz Torres proceed to pinpoint the leading characteristics of the Latin American film melodrama to be found in the paradigms of the Argentine and Mexican film industries in the 1930s and 1940s. "Melo-drama" is taken broadly, since the cinema of these two countries, to-gether with that of Brazil, which the language barrier kept out of Cuba, created a number of distinctive genres of their own. Their variety, how-ever, amounted to little more than different ways of treating the same basic set of conventions. The Mexican critic Jorge Ayala Blanco, who has analyzed the genres of Mexican cinema in great detail, has observed that a number of the genres thrown up in the 1930s were hybrid and artificial, and their apparent consolidation in the 1940s, in swashbuckling adventures, historical biographies, adaptations of novels of the kind that used to be serialized in the nineteenth-century newspapers, all had no other function than to substitute hurriedly for Hollywood product during the Second World War, when Hollywood was much given over to wartime propaganda that had little to do with the Mexican audience. There were other genres, however, that deserve more attention, because they elicited a more firmly based popular response: "they answered to a truly national need and can be considered as a collective expression, albeit secondhand."[16] These include the comedies of ranch life and the epics of small-town communities; the almost folkloric narratives of the Mexican Revolution and its revolutionary heroes; various films of fam-ily life; above all those films that nostalgically idealized the Porfirian *hacienda*, the semifeudal relations and paternalistic benevolence of the Mexican ranch in the years of the prerevolutionary dictator Porfirio Díaz.

There was obviously more melodrama, so to speak, in some of these genres than in others, but if they elicited a popular response it was be-cause, like the classic Victorian melodrama that dominated the London stage for much of the nineteenth century, they were just about the only dramatic forms available to the audience to deal at all with the dreams and needs of the popular classes. Inevitably, they were clumsy and emo-tionally oversimplified, and again like Victorian melodrama, thoroughly moralistic. Like the Hollywood paradigms it followed, the Mexican film melodrama was an art that proclaimed the predominance of the individual over the milieu, at the same time as it subordinated the individual to the given order. It diluted awareness of social problems by installing a Catholic-inspired "spiritual" realm in parallel to the social order. It reduced life to a single dimension, that of love and the "sentimental life"; it belittled social equality by alleging that human beings were all equal before the designs of the heart. But how did the heart behave? Entrenched in a world that was instinctively defensive and defensive about instincts, the dominant characteristic of this artless art was sentimentality, which, to give it a more precise meaning, is the disguised return of repressed feeling through the obsessive exaggeration of ordinary sentiment.

Sometimes all this took the form of the costume picture, in which case, as the Cuban writers explain, the spectator was presented with a cast of supposedly popular characters who had been reduced to caricature and given a dose of paternalistic moral chauvinism. Return to the primitive past was seen as a journey to the fountain of authenticity, and the blemishes of underdevelopment were celebrated as old popular values. True popular values were nowhere to be seen. The idea of the nation itself became completely general and empty, an ahistorical archetype that was detached from the evolution of society and real social conditions. God, Fatherland, and Home composed the inseparable triad that social equilibrium demanded and depended on.

Since morality in such a system is no more than a badge, its presence or absence can be read on the faces and in the bodies of the actors, in the iconography of villains, suffering mothers, prodigal sons, innocent girls, and women of the streets. Typecasting was taken to its extreme in the Latin American film melodrama. Sara García's long-suffering face made her the mother incarnate; María Félix and Tita Morello embodied the enigma and diabolical attraction of the female sinner, their deep voices and caressing manner the expressions of shameful amours (which never needed actually to be seen—everything was achieved by suggestion and innuendo); Carlos López Moctezuma's grim looks and disagreeable features spelled out his villainy. Cinema has always—perhaps by necessity—sought its primary iconography in the physiognomy of the actors. The actor in cinema, instead of having to project, is projected (as Stanley Cavell, the North American philosopher, has felicitously put it). This is why the nonprofessional actor, when appropriately cast, makes such important contributions to film art. But it also explains how and why the genres of Hollywood cinema were constructed to make the star system—as vehicles for the character types that the stars variously embodied. (In the process, the stars were turned into valuable pieces of property, which the studios bought and sold and rented among themselves.) The system was sophisticated enough in Hollywood and other more artistically developed cinemas to make it possible to treat films as vehicles for the stars as well as vice versa. In the imitation of the star system that developed in Latin America, however, the personality of the actor was sacrificed to the abstractions of the genre. The result—to return to the Cubans' analysis—was that relationships between the characters on the screen reduced reality to a series of artificial cause-and-effect mechanisms.

The entire semiotic system of the Latin American film melodrama is based on this. In such a world, the anecdote becomes the principal narrative form, with an oversimplified structure that makes the linearity of the average Hollywood picture into a veritable labyrinth. It typically consists of variants of no more than two or three continually repeated themes, many fewer than the basic plots available in Hollywood cinema. Whenever the film is set in the past, history remains quite alien, merely ornamental, and, of course, idealized. Past or present, the film stands outside real historical time; it is the product of a dichotomy between social and affective life. The mechanisms of cause and effect, the expression of reductive one-dimensional ethics, give a narrative form that is only apparently dynamic.

There can be no real audience identification with the complexities of character and behavior, no exploration by the film viewer of the ambiguities of intention, since there are no complexities and ambiguities in this universe except by unintended accident. (Jean Renoir once said that technique is a way of doing again deliberately what one first did by accident. But this implies a strong and highly structured artistic tradition in which ambiguity and accident are cultivated and encouraged; here it merely signifies lack of control over the medium or awareness of the complexities it can be made to yield.) Consequently, the argument of these films proceeds by a succession of climaxes that are really like escape valves that need to be decongested of accumulated emotion in order that in the end equilibrium can be restored. The imagery comes from Colina and Díaz Torres: "In this persistent correction of the level of dramatic tension," they explain, "and in the way the unusual is made to appear banal, this cinema finds its regulatory mechanisms, which prevent anything sudden revealing the undercurrent contained by their hypocritical conventions." Dramatic development—this will hardly come as a surprise—is essentially verbal, and the organization of visual elements is subordinate to the primacy of the verbal text:

> This kind of hierarchy can be explained by the fact that the suggestive value of images provokes interpretation that would go beyond the unambiguous significations of this type of filmic schema. However, a lack of aesthetic expression in the visual components of these films prevents any transcendence of the immediate, merely functional significance of locations, decor, dress, makeup, props, and so forth, which are used to reaffirm the dramatic conventions carried by the formalized gestures and standardized message.[17]

With the coming of sound also came a development that, were Guback right, would be rather strange: Hollywood began making films in Spanish. The first was actually an independent production by a successful Cuban actor, René Cardona, with the title *Sombras habañeras* (Shadows of Havana). But then the big Hollywood companies got involved and spent two or three years making Spanish-language versions of regular Hollywood movies. They were not dubbed—that was beyond the technical means the talkies started with. They were remakes in Spanish, with Spanish-speaking actors and a Spanish-speaking director, but otherwise exactly the same. *The Big House,* directed by George Hill in 1930 with Wallace Beery and John Gilbert, became *El presidio,* with Juan de Landa and Tito Davison; Tod Browning's 1931 *Dracula* with Bela Lugosi was remade under the same title with Carlos Villarías and Lupita Tovar; and there were many others.[18] They just went in and took over the sets and the shooting script and did exactly the same thing, but in Spanish.

These films did not make money directly. They were essentially a sales device for selling the talkies, for goading Latin American exhibitors to convert to sound. The talkies represented a major investment by the U.S. film industry, the product of an intricate history of competition between the studios, which was undertaken in the face of the threat of falling audiences. It was an investment that Hollywood needed to recoup as fast as possible. It was essential that exhibitors abroad were rapidly induced to spend the money necessary to convert their cinemas, otherwise the 25 percent surplus profit from the foreign market would begin to drain away. In the case of Britain, William Fox was smart enough to persuade the Gaumont circuit into it by arranging for £80 million for the purpose to be subscribed by banks in the city of London. A very large part of that was the purchase of equipment from the United States. This kind of finance was much more difficult to achieve in Latin America, but the fact that here too the cinemas were owned by local capital—though there were very few significant circuits—served the exporter's purposes. Making Spanish-language films and putting them into their showcases served to bully the local cinema owners to find the means or risk going under. They made these films for this purpose as a loss leader, and it ceased as soon as the techniques of rerecording were brought to the point, in the mid-1930s, that allowed the original production to be dubbed into any foreign language required.

One of the directors recruited to Hollywood, by Twentieth-Century Fox, to direct (supervise would be a better word) these Spanish-language versions was the Cuban Ramón Peón. Peón's career is an excellent illustration of the fate of Cuban cinema from before the talkies to the 1950s, and not only because his name crops up in connection with almost all the attempts that were made to create a basis for regular production in Cuba. Peón and the others he was involved with were optimistic opportunists. Arturo Agramonte, summing up Cuban production in the interwar years, says that it gave the impression of "photographed theater": "weak themes and deficient shooting gave the viewer the sensation that something was lacking. In fact this was due to an almost total want of close-ups, as well as an insufficient variety of angles, which made the films monotonous. It was a rude shock for the technicians and for serious investors, for whom all opportunities were closed off. This situation left the door open rather more to adventurers, who were less well intentioned than the traditional 'white horse' [caballo blanco]."[19] What in Latin America is called a "white horse" is what is called in English an angel, a theatrical backer. In Cuba, says Agramonte, they did not usually put money into films. Peón, however, managed to persuade one or two of them to do so, thus becoming the nearest thing to a professional film director in Cuba at the time. The French film historian Georges Sadoul praises his La virgen de la caridad (The Virgin of Charity, 1930), one of the last Cuban silent pictures, as almost neorealist, but this is being generous.

Peón was an energetic operator. He was associated with most of the attempts to set Cuban film production on a regular basis between 1920 and 1939. None of these businesses lasted very long. Agramonte says that apart from lack of confidence on the part of always cautious Cuban investors, the failure to establish sustained production was due above all to a total lack of support from the banks. In these conditions, the backing of *caballos blancos* was essential. Peón began his career with a trip to the United States in 1920 with the money of a stable full of them in his pocket, to purchase several thousand dollars' worth of equipment. It was duly installed in new studios belonging to a company calling itself Estudios Golden Sun Pictures, whose first production he then directed himself. He managed to make six more films over the next five years before embarking on a new collaboration in 1926 with a certain Richard Harlan, who later worked in Hollywood with Cecil B. DeMille. This was the Pan American Pictures Corporation, a grand name for a shoestring operation. Its short run of productions were mostly directed by either Harlan or Peón. Absolutely typical was Peón's *Casi varón* (Almost masculine) of 1926. It is hard to imagine a more inconsequential but thoroughly sexist absurdity: an adventuress is obligated to a villain who proposes to rob a rich mansion. She disguises herself as a chauffeur and goes along to teach the *señorito* of the house to drive. The deceit is discovered, of course, and once restored to womanhood, she is forgiven by the young gallant, and all live happily ever after.

It was in Hollywood that Peón really learned his trade, churning out the remakes. They provided a certain training, especially in speed, and when Hollywood no longer had any work to offer him, Peón went and put this training to use in Mexico, where production values were so constrained that every film had to be a quickie. A little legend grew up around Peón that his "greatest achievement" was to complete ten films in 126 days of continuous production.[20] This is doubtless an exaggeration, but García Riera confirms that he did indeed make more films than any other director working in Mexico at the time. He was the champion, says García Riera, of the melodrama.[21] The methods that were used to keep the costs of shooting down have been described by another director of Mexican quickies—they were not much different from the methods employed on similar productions in Britain in the same period: "In the first place, I reduced the use of the clapper to a minimum. Second, I didn't bother with framing up, which seemed to me unnecessary... I filmed like this: a wide shot with one camera, and when I called 'cut' I only stopped the main camera and left the lights burning; then I approached the actors with a handheld camera and took close-ups. In the third place, I never repeated a scene. If an actor made a mistake it didn't worry me. I changed the position of the camera and went on filming from the point where the mistake had been made."[22] It is not difficult to imagine the outcome. The clapper is used to mark the point of synchronization between picture and sound track—without the clapper, synchronization can be imperfect; not bothering to frame up but only pointing the camera in the right direction with an appropriate lens annihilates composition and gives the picture a sloppy look; as for handheld close-ups and only changing angles when there is a mistake, this is to discard the entire artistry of decoupage, the articulation of visual rhythm and dramatic flow. The advantage of Peón's Hollywood experience was that he could do all these things a bit more efficiently than others. He had a good line in potboilers, ranging from swashbuckling adventures set in the time of the viceroyalty, to films like *Tierra, amor y dolor* (Earth, love, and distress, 1934) and *El bastardo* (The bastard, 1937), both of them vehicles for "artistic nudity"—Jorge Ayala Blanco's nicely ironic term for one of the subgenres of 1930s Mexican cinema.[23] On the other hand, it would be unfair to deny that Peón had his pretensions: in 1933, he directed *Tiburón,* an adaptation of Ben Jonson's *Volpone,* the first such enterprise in the Mexican cinema. García Riera says of it that "in this Volpone transformed into a modern and mundane tragicomedy, Peón's timid formalist intents are shipwrecked on the verbose dialogue elaborated by a Bustillo Oro in the desire to demonstrate his culture, in homage to a cast composed of true champions of overacting."[24]

After returning to Cuba at the end of the 1930s, Peón again attempted to create a production base in Havana and succeeded in bringing together another group of backers. The resulting company, Pecusa (Películas Cubanas S.A.) installed itself in new studios in 1938, and managed to make six films before giving up the ghost before the following year was out. Some of these films—though none of the ones directed by Peón—were musical comedies, and these represent perhaps the most distinctive (but not distinguished) product of the struggling Cuban cinema of the pseudo-republic. This type of film was hardly unique to Cuba, of course. On the contrary, the coming of sound gave Latin American producers the opportunity to enlist local popular music, and employ musical artistes with a commercial track record already proven by radio and records. The answer Hollywood found to this competition was what the audience in the Harvard Business School had already learned in 1926: they poached the talent and the music. They already had Fred Astaire *Flying Down to Rio* to meet Dolores del Rio (real name: Lolita Dolores de Martínez, and not Brazilian but Mexican) in 1933. As for Pecusa, Valdés Rodríguez explained that the reason for its collapse was "undoubtedly its films, as much for their content as their form ... Pecusa had been the foremost exponent of the mistakes and lack of bearings of Cuban cinema ... [their films were] a transplant onto the screen of the Cuban *bufo* theater in its later years at a time when it was already a lesser genre, which represented the vernacular theater at its least worthy."[25]

In the 1940s and 1950s, Cuban production efforts were dominated by the Mexican film industry in the form of coproductions using Mexican directors and stars. Occasionally, there were similar efforts with Argentina. At the beginning of 1952, however, just before Batista's coup, the government of Carlos Prío set up a film finance bank and executive commission for the film industry (Patronato para el Fomento de la Industria Cinematográfica). According to a report in the U.S. trade journal *Variety,* this commission was authorized to advance producers up to 33 percent of the costs of production: "this provision, in effect, underwrites up to 33% of losses should that picture lay an egg since repayment shall only be from its earnings."[26] It added that the commission was to be financed by a national lottery (not inappropriately, one might say). Such arrangements could make no essential difference to the state of film production in Cuba. The most distinguished films made in Cuba in the years before the Revolution were North American productions on location, including one Errol Flynn movie, one Victor Mature film, and *The Old Man and the Sea,* directed to begin with by Fred Zinneman, who was replaced by Henry King, who in turn was replaced by John Sturges.

Only one other Cuban film of this period calls for special comment: *La rosa blanca* (The white rose), subtitled *Momentos de la vida de Martí* (Moments from the life of Martí). A coproduction with Mexico, it was a government-sponsored official tribute to the Cuban national hero, who was played by the Mexican actor Roberto Canedo under the direction of one of Mexico's leading directors, "El Indio" Fernández. Canedo bore not the slightest resemblance to Martí, physically or spiritually. The commission charged with supervising the production, which succeeded only in offending national dignity with its sentimentalizing, was composed of right-wing intellectuals such as Francisco Ichazo, the man who warned Julio García Espinosa a few years later about U.S. embassy concern over the clandestine *El Megano.*

In 1958, an article appeared in the Havana journal *Carteles* titled "The Possibilities of a Film Industry in Cuba: Considerations."[27] The central question the article raised was, "Is the home market sufficient to sustain a film industry?" The author, one Óscar Pino Santos, began his answer by pointing out that the average Cuban expenditure at the cinema over the years 1948–57 was 0.7 percent of the national income, as against 0.5 percent in the United States. (His figures differ from those covering the same period given in 1960 by Francisco Mota, from which an even higher average expenditure of 0.9 percent can be derived.)[28] There were fifteen people for every cinema seat in Cuba, which had no film production of its own to speak of, whereas in Mexico and Brazil, with substantial industries producing, in their best years, as many as a hundred features a year, there were eighteen and twenty-five, respectively. The fact was, said Pino Santos, the Cuban market simply wasn't big enough, even if they did spend more on cinema than in the mecca in the north. The total average income for a film exhibited in Cuba he estimated at some 26,000 pesos. Out of this sum, for a Cuban film, about 15,600 pesos went to the distributor, about 6,300 to the producer, the remaining 4,100 to the exhibitor. Was it possible to make films on this little money? No way.

Again, the figures Mota gives are a bit different, though he is talking about imported films, for which, he reported, the royalty was said to be 40 percent, although only half this sum actually left the country after various deductions. (In 1954, *Variety* reported that a new tax threatened the U.S. film industry in Cuba, a 20 percent levy on top of the existing 3 percent it had previously always managed to avoid. The article mentioned that Cuba rated as a $3-million market for the U.S. companies.)[29] Pino Santos's figures gave the exhibitors' share as 16 percent; Mota estimated 20 percent to the exhibitors. But even this difference is not material. The point is that unless a *very* much higher sum—double or even more—had gone back to the producer, not even a cheaply made film could recoup its cost. Even the 33 percent that the commission established by Prío effectively granted against losses was insufficient. It could only really serve as a subsidy to attract foreign, mainly Mexican, coproduction.

What chances, then, for ICAIC? What cheek the Cuban revolutionaries had, if they thought they could really create a film industry that would not need constant and enormous subsidy! Could an underdeveloped country afford such luxuries? The answer is that this line of reasoning only applies under capitalist conditions, in which the middlemen (the distributors) and the retailers (the exhibitors) rake off the profits before anything gets back to the producer. The provisions that are made in the decree by which ICAIC was set up envision and empower it to intervene not only as a production house but also as both a distributor and an exhibitor, in order to alter these conditions, knowing that unless indeed they were altered, films produced in Cuba would never stand a chance.

Of course, ICAIC has needed subsidy, but not because Cuban films have not taken enough at the box office. They have often done so, sometimes very rapidly. The problem is foreign exchange. The exclusion of Cuban films from many parts of the foreign market has prevented them earning enough freely exchangeable currency entirely to cover the inevitable foreign costs of the enterprise. These foreign costs are of two main kinds: first, the costs of purchasing films for distribution; and second, in order to make their own, the costs of the industry's most monopolized resource, film stock (of which there are no more than half a dozen manufacturing companies in the world). Foreign-exchange needs were reduced by trade agreements with communist-bloc countries, which supplied up to 40 percent of the new films distributed annually, and by the expedient of purchasing film stock for distribution copies of ICAIC's own films from East Germany. Even then, Cuba had to make do with no more than six or eight copies for the entire country, with the result that programming was carried out centrally, and copies had to be kept in circulation even after becoming scratched or damaged. ICAIC would prefer to shoot on Eastmancolor, which the U.S. blockade makes it difficult or expensive for it to obtain, and instead therefore often shoots on Fuji, but this is Japanese and still requires foreign exchange.

For much of its existence, ICAIC has been financed according to the system of central planning practiced by communism in power. Here profitability plays no direct role in the evaluation of the enterprise, which instead receives a prearranged sum from the state budget; any net income goes back to the treasury from which centrally budgeted funds are allocated. The system allowed social and political considerations to take precedence over market mechanisms, but could also lead to unrealistic economic judgments. In the Cuba of the 1990s, after the collapse of the communist bloc, it would become unsustainable. Before then, ICAIC's annual production budget stood at seven million pesos. In other words, its entire production program, which averaged out at around three or four feature-length movies a year (six or eight in the 1980s), more than forty documentaries, a dozen or so cartoons, and the weekly newsreel— all this has been accomplished on less than the cost of a single big-budget movie in Hollywood. Indeed, the comparison grows ever more striking as Hollywood budgets steadily increase, which they do not only because of inflation in the currency but also because of inflated production values.

In theory, as a state enterprise, ICAIC enjoyed the position of a vertically integrated monopoly, comprising production, distribution, and exhibition. In practice, its exhibition wing would consist only of the Cinemateca and a small circuit of first-run houses. After the instigation in the 1970s of the system of local government known as Popular Power, the cinemas were owned and run by the local administration also charged with running such facilities as shops and petrol stations. Box-office earnings pay for daily running costs and renting films from ICAIC's distribution wing. (This did not stop a large number of cinemas from closing down when economic crisis struck in the 1990s.)

In many respects, this economic regime was of great benefit to ICAIC and Cuban cinema, but there were two more factors that helped to keep production costs down, both of them the fruits of the Revolution in the domain of the relations of production. One is that the economics of the star system no longer exerted any influence. Because the regime established control over inflation and rationalized salaries and wages, there was no longer any pressure to keep increasing the pay of actors and specialized technical personnel—a major factor, since film production is labor-intensive, in the constantly increasing production costs in the capitalist film industries. At the same time, ICAIC's vertical integration also accomplished the elimination of the numerous small individual companies that buy and sell each other their services and facilities in every capitalist film industry, each one raking off its own profit. Under such a system, the costs tend upwards, production is risky, employment uncertain. At ICAIC, which came to employ about a thousand people in the 1980s, such uncertainty became a thing of the past (until the 1990s created uncertainties of a different order, and ICAIC would lose many of its personnel).

CHAPTER FIVE

Amateurs and Militants

"Perhaps more interesting than the professional cinema," according to an article titled "The Cinema in Cuba" in the North American magazine *Film Culture* in 1956, "is the experimental cinema in 16 mm and the intense action of the cine-clubs."[1] The author of this article, Néstor Almendros, the son of an exile from Franco's Spain, was himself a member of this movement. Like most of the *aficionados* he was writing about, he worked at the Film Institute when it was first set up, but he was also one of the first filmmakers to leave Cuba as a result of disagreement with ICAIC's policies. Meeting with success in Paris as a cinematographer with the New Wave directors, and later internationally, Almendros published his own version of these disagreements in his autobiography, *Días de una cámara (A Man with a Camera)*.[2] He rapidly became disillusioned with ICAIC, he says, because ICAIC rapidly became bureaucratic and intolerant of differences of opinion. To be fair, he was already experimenting with new styles of cinematography that were not yet appreciated, and felt frustrated that the value of his experiments was not being recognized. But there was clearly more to it than this, and to understand more fully, one needs to go back to the *aficionado* movement that ICAIC grew out of. This movement involved a whole generation of Cuban artists and intellectuals, for whom the attempt to create an independent cinema was a symbol of cultural resistance and a way of forging a sense of unity in their cultural aspirations. As the head of ICAIC, Alfredo Guevara, later wrote:

Only the cine-clubs, brave in their narrow field, denounced the apologia for violence [of the Hollywood movie] and supposed American superiority, and opened a gap for a cinema of quality, discovering for the public the significance of schools and currents, the work and value of particular directors, and the necessity, above all, of sharpening the critical spirit. But in a closed ambience, and in the face of the hostility of the distribution companies, and in some cases subject to police vigilance and pressures, there was little they could do.[3]

However little, it included laying the foundations of a future film culture. "Police vigilance and pressures" records the close links of many of these aesthetic militants with active political opposition; but whatever held the movement together, it was mainly a union of convenience, in which certain rifts opened up when the inevitable political divisions were brought out into the open after the victory of the Revolution. Not that this impugns those who were trying to use film as part of the political struggle. On the contrary, it can be argued that the artistic openness of the most militant members of the movement helped to win people over.

The movement first developed during the 1940s. In 1945, the U.S. Department of Commerce publication *Industrial Reference Service* (later *World Trade in Commodities*) reported on the development of a new market in Cuba:

> The market potentialities for the sale to amateur users in Cuba of United States motion-picture cameras and projectors are fair. It is estimated that upon termination of the war about $3,500 worth of 16mm sound projectors and $2,400 worth of silent 16mm projectors can be sold. Sales of 8mm motion picture cameras are expected to be somewhat higher.[4]

This was the last paragraph in a detailed report that examined prospects for the sale of various kinds of equipment in both the theatrical and the nontheatrical markets. Nontheatrical users included schools, the army and navy, commercial users, and amateurs. The expected sales were not particularly large, even allowing for the higher value of the dollar at the time. However, Cuba had been of interest to the United States for some time as a kind of offshore testing laboratory for trying out new technologies and techniques in the fields of media and communication.

Back in the mid-1920s, Cuba was, together with Puerto Rico, the birthplace of the now massive communications corporation ITT—the same ITT that offered the CIA $1 million to "destabilize" the Popular

Unity government in Chile in the early 1970s. ITT was set up by sugar brokers Sosthenes and Hernand Behn after they acquired a tiny Puerto Rican telephone business in settlement of a bad debt. The company was then built up on the success of the underwater cable link they laid between Havana and Miami.[5] At the same time, radio arrived; the first transmissions in Cuba took place in 1922 and Cuba quickly became one of Latin America's most intensely developed broadcasting markets.[6] By 1939, it had no less than eighty-eight radio stations and about 150,000 receivers. Mexico, by comparison, though many times larger, had only a hundred stations and no more than 300,000 receivers. Argentina had about 1.1 million receivers, but only about fifty stations. This gave Argentina the best ratio of sets to inhabitants in Latin America, approximately 1:12, but the Cuban ratio (1:30) was better than the Mexican (1:64). The ratio in the United States at the same time was 1:3.5 and in Europe between 1:6 and 1:11.[7]

Because of the inherent problems of media programming and the opportunities provided by language and national musical idioms, local capital found that it was relatively easy to enter certain parts of the culture industry, while other areas remained the prerogative of foreign capital. The two media of radio and records—which are intimately linked—were also cheaper to enter and to operate than film production after its earliest years. The Cuban commentators Rodríguez and Pérez recall that the great collapse of sugar prices in 1920 and the resulting depression that ruined many small businesses, including the foremost film business of Santos y Artiga, who only survived by returning to their earlier activity as circus proprietors; after this, local capital preferred to look to the new activity of radio. (The circus of Santos y Artiga crops up in Tomás Gutiérrez Alea's comedy *Las doce sillas [The Twelve Chairs]*, 1962.) As for records, early technology was almost artisanal and easily permitted small-scale local production, and it remained so for longer than film. Record production was already well established in Cuba before the advent of electrical recording in 1925. What electrical recording did was give the North American companies new ways of moving in on the Latin American market, but their control was still necessarily indirect. They built factories for the manufacture of records made by local musicians and produced by local companies who knew the market, and used radio stations both as their aural shopwindow and to discover new talent.

These media, taken together, are different from telephones and cables and electricity, which, at the time of the Revolution, were 90 percent in the hands of U.S. companies in Cuba, which owned and controlled them directly; in the entertainments sector, a large part of the infrastructure belonged to local capital. Electricity is a universal energy source requiring powerful and expensive generators, as well as a guaranteed constant fuel supply; telephones and cables are first and foremost, as well as being luxury items for personal use, instruments of communication for commercial and industrial intelligence and traffic. But the general availability of telephones and cables in underdeveloped countries, like that of electricity, is always restricted. The entertainments media, in contrast, are primarily directed to the exploitation of consumer leisure time, across the widest possible social spectrum. They aim in underdeveloped countries to include the people who do not have electricity and telephones in their homes—or used not to. Radio thus enjoyed a second vogue after the invention of the transistor in the 1950s, though nowadays the shantytowns that encircle the cities increasingly have electricity, and hence television, even if they still lack not only telephones, but also a water supply and drainage system.

Every communications technology and each entertainment medium manifests its own peculiarities and idiosyncrasies as a commodity, which vary with the precise conditions of the environment in which they are installed. The telephone everywhere accelerated, increased, and extended commercial intercourse, but in Cuba it also served to let North American companies run their Cuban operations not as fully fledged overseas offices, but as local branches. It made it unnecessary for them to hold large stocks of raw materials or spare parts when they could get on the phone and have them rapidly shipped or flown in from mainland depots when they were needed. The same methods are nowadays employed by transnational corporations throughout the world on the much larger scale made possible by computerization, satellite communication, and jet air transport. The advantages are not only economic: the corporations are also in this way lifted beyond the control of the countries in which their various branches are situated. Even in its simpler form in Cuba in the 1950s, this system confronted the revolutionaries with difficult problems, for the companies concerned were easily able to operate an embargo on supplies in the attempt to destabilize the new government.

Radio also has peculiarities. The first is that, for the listener who has bought a receiver, the programs themselves are not commodities—they do not have to be purchased individually. That is why radio becomes an aural shopwindow for records, but also why it is different from them; for the record that radio feeds off has the peculiarity of being linked to the phonograph on which it is played. The record cannot go where the phonograph does not go, just as the lightbulb cannot go where there is no electricity. In this way, the development of advanced technologies creates a greater and greater degree of interdependence of commodities.

But this interdependence is ideological as well as economic—the ideological and the economic are two faces of the same process. Because, in the case of radio, strictly speaking, the program is not a commodity that yields an exchange value from the consumer, other ways must be found of raising revenue to produce the programs without which the receiver is pointless. The commercial broadcasting system created in the United States and exported to Latin America does this by trading in a new commodity—the air space that is bought up by sponsors and advertisers (or the slice of the audience that it sells them). The values of the commercial publicity industry in this way invade and dominate the medium.

The development of commercial broadcasting in Latin America, however, was the result of inducement by the captains of industry in the United States. They encouraged local capital to adopt the system on its own account, to promote its own preservation and reproduction. This is not to suggest some kind of conspiracy: little capitalists naturally imitate big capitalists and big capitalists naturally encourage them to do so—though they also hedge them in to prevent real competition. But the result is still that the media become channels of ideological penetration even when the programs they carry are not themselves produced abroad. They still automatically imitate the same values. These values, however, are as foreign in Latin America and other dependent countries as the technology that carries them, and can hardly fail to deform the material that goes into the program, even if it is locally produced. The result is a central feature of the process that has been designated cultural imperialism.

We already know that cultural imperialism is not just a phenomenon of the contemporary world. Before the flooding of the market with the products of the transnational entertainments corporations, there was, for example, the colonization of literary taste, the process described by Mariátegui. The whole process started with the arrival of the conquistadores. As Alejo Carpentier explains in the opening lines of his classic historical study of music in Cuba:

> The degree of riches, vigour and power of resistance of the civilizations which the *conquistadores* discovered in the New World always determined, one way or another, the greater or lesser activity of the European invader in the construction of architectural works and musical indoctrination. When the peoples to be subjugated were already sufficiently strong, intelligent and industrious enough to build a Tenochtitlán or conceive a fortress of Allanta, the Christian bricklayer and chorister went into action with the greatest diligence, with the mission of the men of war scarcely fulfilled. Once the battle of bodies was over, there began the battle of the symbol.[8]

The power of the symbol, make no mistake, is a material power; though intangible and subject to ambiguity, it has the durability of generations. It operates frequently in the guise of myths, including the modern myths that take on their paradigmatic forms in the movies, in the genres of the western, the gangster movie, the thriller, the romance, the stories of rags to riches, and all the rest. It is possible that the situation of the Hollywood film industry gave it special insight into the ideological needs of imperialism. In any event, as the filmmakers mastered the new narrative art, it and they were pressed into telling tales that, to fulfill the function of a modern mythology, suppressed, as Roland Barthes has put it, the memory of their fabrication and origins. The control of this symbolizing, mythologizing faculty has been as much the object of the Hollywood monopolies as control of its economic functions, however unconscious and disguised their purposes become through ideological rationalizations.

But the uses of film are not limited to the commercial cinema. The *Industrial Reference Service* 1945 report speaks of the development in Cuba of the use of 16 mm "substandard" film equipment both in education and by private firms, not to mention the armed forces. It mentions with approval the example of a local cigarette manufacturer who had begun an advertising campaign using portable 16 mm equipment—an established practice in the metropolis. In Britain, for example, the cigarette manufacturer Wills showed a one-reel sound-on-disc film, *How Wood-bines Are Made,* some eight thousand times in 1934 alone around the workingmen's clubs.[9]

This 16 mm gear was classed as substandard to separate it from the 35 mm equipment intended for commercial distribution in the cinemas. Yet whatever the gauge, a camera is still a camera, a means of production of films, and the same thing happened in Cuba in the 1940s and 1950s as happened in Europe and North America in the 1930s—the emergence, alongside sponsored documentaries and amateur cine, of a political film movement on the left. The later development of portable video would similarly stimulate political responses, although in Cuba its introduction would be delayed.

If capitalism cannot resist marketing consumer versions of industrial means of cultural production, it is inevitable that from Britain to Bolivia people should conceive other purposes for its use, artistic or political, than those recognized by the market and hegemonic ideologies. Historically, the reactions to the power of cinema as an ideological institution were both aesthetic and political, and the two were not unconnected. Aesthetic experiment by modernist artists in the 1920s fed into the rise of workers' film movements in the 1930s. In revolutionary Russia, the confluence of political and artistic imperatives produced the first self-consciously revolutionary cinema, which became a mixed paradigm for political film movements in the West, an exciting, stimulating, but largely unattainable model. But its influence spread far and wide. In Latin America, for example, wherever an organized and self-educating proletarian vanguard emerged, it would typically engage in distributing Soviet films as part of its propaganda work.

In Cuba, political and artistic uses of film were born on a very small scale around the same moment, together with the appearance of amateur cine, in the 1940s. By the end of the decade, as well as the children of the nouveaux riches, there were both artists and militants among Cuban *aficionados*—sometimes the same person was both. Artistic aspirations often found common ground with progressive politics, because sycophants apart, to want to be an artist at all in Cuba was to have to struggle for the right to be heard. The merely nouveaux riches were naturally unconcerned with such problems. Film for them was pure diversion. The ICAIC director Miguel Torres has described them as "those thousands of 'white-collars' of our American countries, who launch them-

selves on Sundays into feverish filming with amateur cameras and equipment to assuage the oppression of their jobs."[10] Some of them, with the
same aesthetic attitudes, invested spare money in the shoestring companies that made local publicity films and newsreels.

The newsreel business in Cuba was quite considerable. According to
the *Industrial News Service* of 1945:

> There are six newsreel companies with laboratories which together pro-
> duce an average of one-and-a-half million feet of positive newsreel a
> year, and about 50,000 feet of commercial advertisements. The newsreel
> companies do not intend to purchase new equipment but have some
> photographic lighting equipment which they would like to dispose of.

(Perhaps someone had taken them for suckers and managed to sell
them more lighting equipment than they needed in that sunny clime.)
But what actually were all these companies doing? Two years later, in
1947, *World Trade in Commodities*, the successor to the *Industrial Reference Service*, revealed:

> Dissemination of propaganda and publicity for individuals, clubs and
> other groups, and the Government, is a chief function of Cuban news-
> reels. News as understood in the United States is only an incidental
> phase of newsreels. The propaganda arises from the fact that one or all
> persons appearing in practically all newsreels pay the producer for this
> privilege or else an organization pays for them. Fees from newsworthy
> notables are an immeasurably larger source of studio incomes than
> rental from theatres. Productora Nacional does not charge theatres
> any rental. Noticiero Nacional has a sliding scale: $5 weekly to first
> run Havana theatres to as low as $5 monthly in some other places.
>
> The father of a bride or the groom reimburses a producer for making
> a newsreel record of a wedding. A nautical club pays to have pictures
> made of some sporting event it sponsors. The official of a government
> agency will pay to have included in a newsreel shots of construction
> work on some public project. Large payments are made to newsreel
> companies by political parties during a national election campaign.
> No producers deny they are subsidized in the manner described by
> news-significant personages.[11]

The truth is that the newsreels were an ideological protection racket.
Their method was straightforward blackmail. One of ICAIC's founding
members, Tomás Gutiérrez Alea, recalls it as "a very dirty business": "if
a newsreel cameraman were to happen upon a car crash, he'd be sure to
take shots of the smashed-up car with its brand name in close-up, and

blackmail the company to pay for them not to be shown."[12] There was only one commercial producer operating in Cuba in the 1950s, says Alea, who was a serious and honorable person, the Mexican Manuel Barbachano Ponce. He had produced three Mexican pictures of some quality and importance: *Raíces* (Roots, 1954), *¡Torero!* (1955), and Buñuel's *Nazarín* (1958). *Raíces* was a four-episode film that the French film historian Sadoul calls "a striking portrait of contemporary Mexican Indian life [that] avoids the extravagant pictorial style of many previous Mexican films."[13] Directed by Benito Alazraki, it was scripted by a team that included Barbachano himself and the documentary filmmaker Carlos Velo, an exile from Franco's Spain. Velo also directed *¡Torero!*, a fictionalized documentary on the career of a well-known matador, which Sadoul regards as "a brilliant achievement." It is a formally experimental film in its use of newsreel footage, including footage of the matador Luis Procuña, regaining his fame in the last sequence, mixed with re-enacted scenes in which Procuña played himself. Future head of ICAIC Alfredo Guevara worked for a period with Barbachano in Mexico; he was assistant director on *Nazarín*. In Cuba, Barbachano produced *Cine Revista*, a ten-minute film magazine made up of brief advertisements and short items of reportage, documentary, and sketches distributed throughout the island. Alea, as well as Julio García Espinosa, gained experience through *Cine Revista* in both documentary and working with actors. (The sketches, said Alea, gave him a certain taste for comedy.) The two of them had studied film at the beginning of the 1950s in the Centro Sperimentale in Rome, when an important part of the experience lay in the political atmosphere in the country. They also both went to Eastern Europe, in different years, to attend Youth Festivals. Back in Cuba, they were both harassed and arrested, along with other cultural activists, by Batista's anticommunist squad.

The roots of the sense of protest against cultural imperialism in Cuba go back to the revolt of the Cuban intelligentsia in the 1920s, which was spearheaded by the University Reform Movement. Its mood is portrayed in Enrique Pineda Barnet's historical feature *Mella* of 1975, a dramatized biography of the student leader Julio Antonio Mella, who became one of the founders of the Cuban Communist Party. The Cuban students who held the first Revolutionary Students' Congress in 1923 shared the burgeoning consciousness of students in many places in Latin America. The University Reform Movement was born in Córdoba, Argentina, and quickly spread not only to Cuba but also to Chile, Uruguay, and Peru, rallying students in an attack on old teaching systems and the elitism of the academies. The continental character of the movement was in part an expression of generalized hostility toward the new Washington doctrine of Pan-Americanism, to which the political leaders of the day had widely succumbed in spite of some misgivings. It was also an expression of the unease of a new generation in the process of discovering what was later to be called underdevelopment. A number of emergent radical political leaders cut their teeth in the movement, including Víctor Raúl Haya de la Torre in Peru, founder of the Alianza Popular Revolucionaria Americana (APRA—American Popular Revolutionary Alliance). This was a radical party pledged to an anti-imperialist program that rejected political, economic, or social structures based on foreign models. And was Hollywood cinema, then, not to be anathema?

APRA became, through its successful populism, an obstacle to Communist politics, and was condemned by Moscow in 1928. Does this mean that Mella and the Cuban Communists surrendered their independence to the Moscow decree? Whatever the historical evidence about this from a political point of view, the Cuban Communists clearly manifested a distinctive understanding of the nature of cultural imperialism, which included cinema, and linked it with the control of information and the denial of authentic artistic expression. Mella himself wrote a review of Eisenstein's *October* in a Mexican newspaper (he was assassinated in Mexico in 1929) in which he explained:

> The public, accustomed to the bourgeois style of the yanqui film, will not be able fully to appreciate the proper value of this effort from Sovkino. It doesn't matter. It would be asking as much of them to comprehend the proletarian revolution after hearing about it through the cables of United Press, or the revolutionary movement of our own country and our national characteristics through the interpretations given them by Hollywood. However, here the ideological vanguards have the opportunity to enjoy one of the most intense pleasures the present epoch can offer in the terrain of art, through the youngest and most expressive of the modern arts: motion photography.[14]

This analysis was further developed during the 1930s by J. M. Valdés Rodríguez, who in the 1940s went on to set up a film studies department at the University of Havana, one of the earliest such departments anywhere in the world. Hollywood, he said, in an article titled "Hollywood: Sales Agent of American Imperialism" in the North American journal *Experimental Cinema*,

> presents the Latin American people as the lowest, most repulsive scoundrels on earth. A Latin, or Latin American, is always a traitor, a villain. Years ago, there was not a picture that was without a Spanish or Spanish-American villain. In *Strangers May Kiss* they present a little Mexican town: the owner of the old "posada" (inn) is a drunkard and the "mozo" (servant, waiter) is a similar character; the streets with three feet of mud; countless beggars; licentious girls.
>
> I remember, too, the picture *Under the Texas Moon*, openly offensive to Mexican women, the projection of which in a movie-house in the Latin section of New York City provoked a terrible tumult. The tumult was caused by the enraged protest of a few Mexican and Cuban students, in which one of the former . . . was killed.[15]

The whole population of Cuba, he continued, suffered drastically from the influence of Hollywood pictures: workers, peasants, and artisans, petit bourgeois and bourgeois all alike. The bourgeoisie, so complete was its identification with the American Dream, no longer accepted European films, as its better education might lead one to expect, while young people were induced to imitate the youth they saw in the North American pictures. From this there arose, said Valdés Rodríguez, a conflict, between the traditional patriarchal society of Cuba, on the one hand, and, on the other, new imported values that young—and even adult— people were beginning to adopt in matters such as family relationships and (heterosexual) love. The image of the American Dream produced only "wild parties, 'necking' orgies, licentiousness, miscomprehension of what 'free love' really means, gross sensuality, lack of control over the lower passions, and a narrow, American, utilitarian conception of life, the ardent praise of those who 'win,' no matter how." A degenerative influence on Cuban society was also to be seen in the Hollywood treatment of the black. Cuba, said Valdés Rodríguez, had not previously suffered the same terrific racial antagonisms:

> The first act of the Cuban patriots of 1868—the majority of them were slave owners—was to declare their Negroes free. So in both wars of independence . . . Negroes and whites fought for liberty, shoulder to shoulder, against the tyranny of Spain, their old enemy. . . . But things are changing, owing to the Hollywood pictures and to the Cuban youth

in America. In American films, Negroes are cowards, superstitious, dumb. . . . This depiction of their race has evidently affected the Negroes' confidence in themselves.

Intellectual and artistic rebelliousness in Cuba in the 1920s found its voice not only in the University Reform Movement but also in the Grupo Minorista, with its journal *Revista de Avance,* and in the artistic movement of Afro-Cubanism, which expressed itself most strongly in music and poetry. The Grupo Minorista met in Havana in the Hotel Lafayette, a gathering place of writers and painters, poets, sculptors, and musicians. Some of them were involved in an incident in May 1923 at the Academy of Sciences, remembered as the "Protest of the Thirteen," when the writer Rubén Martínez Villena spoke out in the presence of a cabinet minister against bureaucratic embezzlement on behalf of a group of thirteen protesters, a demonstration for which they were prosecuted. In 1927, the year in which the group's *Revista de Avance* appeared, they again linked the demand for freedom for cultural development with political protest in a roundly anti-imperialist manifesto; it condemned "the outrage of pseudodemocracy" and "the farce" of elections without effective participation, calling at the same time for "the revision of false and threadbare values," for the reform of education, and for "vernacular and modern art."[16]

Afro-Cubanism began as a quest for the roots of a Cuban national culture, and the elements that made it distinctive. Another member of the Grupo Minorista, Juan Marinello, explained that a return to the roots in Cuba, in the same way as elsewhere in Latin America in the 1920s, produced different results, because in Cuba the indigenous Indian population had not survived. Certainly, Cuba was part of Latin America—indeed, it was where Columbus first set foot in 1492. The native population, however, had been wiped out in the space of fifty years almost without the conquistadores noticing what they were doing— only the churchman Bartolomé de Las Casas observed and condemned. Consequently, where throughout most of Latin America the new artistic explorations of the 1920s became indigenist in character, in Cuba there were no indigenous roots to be found; they were African, because they lay in the culture of the population with which the slave trade replaced the missing native when workers were needed to develop the plantation economy. The same thing had happened in the English- and French-speaking Caribbean, but they had a different colonial history, and slavery there was abolished earlier. A similar phenomenon is also found in certain other Latin American countries, such as parts of Brazil and Venezuela, in regions where indigenous populations were wiped out or driven back.

In Cuba, however, being an island, the cultural consequences were particularly acute. Because of continuing Spanish rule, slaves continued to arrive in Cuba much after everywhere else except Brazil, where abolition was also delayed. Certain traits of African culture and its symbolisms remained more immediate in these two countries as a result. In Cuba, at the time of the Revolution, there were still people who had learned African languages from a grandparent, and Santería, in which Catholic saints are syncretized with African deities, was widely practiced (and since then has survived years of official disapproval).

In Cuba, declares Marinello, the black participated in the liberation struggle against Spain; in fact, black participation was decisive. General Antonio Maceo and the journalist Gualberto Gómez were two of the acknowledged leaders, and they are not the only ones. In fact, there are two respects in which the nineteenth-century Cuban independence struggle was a model—the participation of black people and its internationalist character: it attracted a number of liberation fighters from the Spanish Caribbean and beyond. Both these factors gave Cuba great advantages in subsequent stages of struggle. The political orientation of the Grupo Minorista owed a great deal to the independence movement. The movement had the support of the Federation of Cuban Workers, in which Cuban trade unionism was born, and its leaders, although not fully formed as socialists, were passionate adherents of the idea of the social republic represented for them by the Paris Commune of 1871 or the Spanish Federal Republic of 1874–75.[17]

From a cultural point of view, black participation was equally decisive. The black, said Marinello, is "the marrow and root, the breath of the people. . . . He may, in these times of change, be the touchstone of our poetry."[18] And in the poetry of Nicolás Guillén that began to appear at the end of the 1920s, the Afro-Cuban movement found a native voice. Guillén brought earlier experiments in Afro-Cubanism to flower. In imitating the rhythms of Afro-Cuban dance, and borrowing the verbal patterns and repetitions of voodoo and Santería ceremonies, this poetry is imbued with a sense of social reality and criticism, and speaks with the voices of real characters in real situations, with their argot and accents. The result was a new and shocking linguistic authenticity.

Something similar happened in music. Alejo Carpentier wrote the scenario of an Afro-Cuban ballet composed by Amadeo Roldán, *La Rebambaramba,* which they researched in visits to the ceremonies of the Abakuá, a secret religious society of African origin. It was the first of a series of works through which Roldán achieved international renown, alongside composers like Varèse, as an enfant terrible. Carpentier has recorded that one of the influences was Stravinsky:[19] the extraordinary rhythmic pulse of *The Rite of Spring*—something quite unprecedented in European art music—which they got to know from the score, showed Roldán how to "compose" the difficult cross-rhythms involved, in other words, how to notate and thereby carry into the theater and the concert hall the inflections and fusion of African rhythms with the melodic lines of the Spanish and French dance forms, which in another variant also lies at the root of jazz.

The Cuban Communist Party did not remain content with critical and theoretical observations about cinema. At the end of the 1930s, it undertook to make films of its own. The earliest political films made in Cuba date from 1939–40, when the newspaper *Hoy,* organ of the Partido Socialista Popular (PSP), as the party was then called, produced its first newsreel, to be shown at union meetings and in the open air. The cameraman was José Tabío, who twenty years later joined ICAIC.

Tabío was one of a group who set up a small production company, Cuba-Sono-Films, at the beginning of the 1940s, whose first film was another collaboration with Carpentier. According to Agramonte, the protagonists of this film, *El desahucio* (The sacking) were the workers building Route 20, and "it showed scenes of high emotion around the social theme it dealt with."[20] The list of Cuba-Sono-Films titles amounts to a catalog of party activities, though it didn't survive for long. But they took to making films again at the end of the decade, and again a future member of ICAIC was involved. Tomás Gutiérrez Alea was not a party member. He was a law student at the university with the ambition to make films. He worked on two films for the PSP, one of a May Day demonstration that had been banned but went ahead anyway, the other on the World Peace Movement.[21] His name also figures among the nonpolitical *aficionados,* those other radical intellectuals of the educated middle classes whose aspirations were mainly artistic. His first films were made on 8 mm in 1946 (*La caperucita roja* [Little Red Riding Hood]) and 1947 *(Un fakir),* when he also teamed up with Néstor Almendros, the Spanish exile's son, to make an adaptation of a Kafka story called *Una confusión cotidiana* (An everyday confusion).

The Photographic Club of Cuba held the island's first amateur cine competition in 1943. Something of its character can be gleaned from the titles of films that were shown. They included *La vida de los peces* (The life of the fish); *Varadero* (the name of one of Cuba's finest but, before the Revolution, private beaches, sited on the same promontory where the North American chemicals millionaire Du Pont built his mansion); and *Desfile gimnástico femenino* (Feminine gymnastic display), which won the gold medal! Competitions like these are part of every amateur cine movement. Similar titles with appropriate differences would be found in any ten best list of British amateur cine in the 1930s, when it was a province of the upper classes and even the aristocracy, who made up little amateur dramatics for the camera and filmed their favorite pastimes. An exception cropped up in 1943 called *Vida y triunfo de un pura sangre criollo* (Life and triumph of a pure-blood Creole—a play on words), which Valdés Rodríguez described as the only one of these films with social and economic implications.[22]

A much more reliable guide in these matters than Almendros is Valdés Rodríguez, who was the mentor of the oppositional film culture that was developing during this period: Alfredo Guevara speaks with warmth of the influence he had both on himself and others of his generation in stimulating an awareness of film. He had followed a "beg, borrow, and steal" policy, Guevara recalls, to build up an archive of films that never entered commercial distribution in Cuba.[23] Agramonte records that Valdés Rodríguez went to the United States in 1941 armed with a letter from the university to Nelson Rockefeller, as a result of which the Museum of Modern Art started sending them films. Later, he made similar arrangements with the French Cinémathèque.[24]

The University of Havana, where Valdés Rodríguez introduced film studies, had been one of the focal points of the country's political ferment since the days of Julio Antonio Mella and the University Reform Movement. In the same conversation in which he spoke of Valdés Rodríguez's influence, Alfredo Guevara also mentioned that he had only just discovered, from a book he was reading, how many of the professors when he was a student in Havana had, unbeknownst to him at the time, been active in the political struggles of the 1930s, not just the historian Raúl Roa, whom everyone knew about because he had emerged as a leader of the Revolution. The whole generation had been politicized by a revolutionary struggle in which a small vanguard of the Cuban proletariat had seized the moment to declare its own short-lived soviets: fruit of the opposition to the dictator Machado whom Batista displaced when he seized power for the first time as a young sergeant.

In the late 1940s, when Fidel Castro was a politically active law student, the university was frequently the scene of violent political confrontations between rival factions, in which gunslinging solutions to political quarrels were a constant liability, a product of the disintegration of Cuban political life. Castro once remarked that his four years at the university were more personally dangerous than the whole time he spent fighting Batista from the Sierra Maestra. Yet in 1950, the university was also the location where a group of students set up a radical cultural society with the name Nuestro Tiempo *(Our Times)*. They belonged to the students' union cultural group and included Alfredo Guevara.

Guevara—the son of a railway engineering worker who was one of the founders of the railway workers' union—began his political career as a schoolboy adherent of anarcho-syndicalism in the struggle against Batista's first government in the late 1930s. By the late 1940s, he had joined the Communist Party and it was then, while at university, that he first came into contact with Fidel Castro. They first knew each other as political rivals in Student Federation elections in which Castro failed to get elected but Guevara succeeded. The two became friends when they went to Colombia together in April 1948, as members of a small delegation to a meeting of Latin American students that was being sponsored by the Argentinian regime of Juan Perón. The Cubans were due to meet the Colombian Liberal Party leader Jorge Gaitán, to discuss his possible participation in the student congress that the meeting in Bogotá had been called to plan. On April 9, just before this meeting with Gaitán was about to take place, the Colombian politician was assassinated. The popular uprising which that sparked off in protest is known to history as the *Bogotazo*—the "Bogotá explosion." The Cuban students joined in, and took part in an attack on a police station from which rifles were taken and distributed among the people; they escaped arrest by taking refuge in the Cuban embassy, and returned to Havana in a Cuban government–chartered plane.[25] Although Castro and Guevara followed different political courses over the next few years, the *Bogotazo* constituted a shared moment in both men's political development. Their mutual firsthand knowledge of a moment of popular insurrection gave them a common point in their understanding of the political pulse of their own country. Recalling the episode in conversation, Guevara emphasized how formative an experience it was for them by comparing it with the events that took place almost exactly twenty years later in Paris in 1968, of which, this time as a representative of the victorious Cuban Revolution, he also happened to be a firsthand witness.

Nuestro Tiempo came to play a central role in the cultural politics of the Cuban Communists during the 1950s. The policy of the society included a radical program of activities both within the university and in the local community beyond its precincts—the campus was on the edge of a working-class neighborhood. These activities were such that, following Batista's coup in 1952, members of the society were considered, says Agramonte, "subversive agents."[26] José Antonio González, author of an article in *Cine Cubano* titled "Notes for the History of a Cinema without History," says of Nuestro Tiempo that "the organization of the film club and the film cycles it mounted, the pamphlets and the magazine it produced, in reality masked clandestine and semiclandestine work by the Communist Party among the intellectuals, and organized opposition to the National Institute of Culture set up by the tyranny."[27] The composer Harold Gramatges, president of Nuestro Tiempo, has explained:

> Nuestro Tiempo fulfilled a historic role during the Batista dictatorship. Formed at the beginning of 1950, [it] brought together young people who were pursuing their artistic or cultural activities in dispersal and in hostile surroundings ... in a domineering republic consisting in a regime of semicolonial exploitation and misery, the art-public relationship was limited to a privileged class ... and aided by the presence of a number of members of the Young Communists, Nuestro Tiempo embarked ... with considerable impetus on what was designated the job of a united front *[trabajo de frente-único]* ... the task of proselytising among the youthful masses.... We organized ourselves into sections: film, theater, puppetry, music, dance, plastic arts, and literature ... [we] produced publications on cinema, theater, and music, and ... the magazine *Nuestro Tiempo*.[28]

In 1953, the year of Martí's centenary and of the abortive attack on the Moncada barracks in Santiago de Cuba led by Fidel, Nuestro Tiempo was reorganized and its work extended by the party committee responsible for cultural work, which was composed of Juan Marinello, Mirta Aguirre, and Carlos Rafael Rodríguez. As the repression sharpened, the society was attacked in the press by local apologists for the United States. Its directors were interrogated by Batista's intelligence agencies, the SIM (Servicio de Inteligencia Militar [Military intelligence service]) and the BRAC (Buró para la Represión de las Actividades Comunistas [Office for repression of communist activities]). But Batista never quite dared to close Nuestro Tiempo down.

However, he entertained considerable cultural pretensions. To round off the official celebrations of the Martí centenary, he decided to bring to Havana the Bienal exhibition from Franco's Spain, adding to it the cream of Cuban plastic arts, for which he offered the incentive of large prizes. But, as José Antonio Portuondo, an intellectual of the 1930s generation, has recalled, the great majority of Cuban artists refused to collaborate in this salon and a large counterexhibition was organized. Older and younger artists all participated, not, says Portuondo, for formal reasons, but out of defiance, and a refusal to let Cuban art serve the interests of a Hispanic concept of Cuban culture. "Batista held his Bienal in January 1954 to inaugurate the Museum of Fine Arts, but the most estimable Cuban artists exhibited instead at the Lyceum, went off to the Tejada gallery in Santiago de Cuba, and returned to Havana by way of Camagüey. It was a truly rebel exhibition."[29]

Portuondo adds that this exhibition was made up predominantly "not of art with political content but essentially of abstract art, reaffirming the condition of abstract art as an expression of protest in the face of capitalist decadence." Behind the rhetorical formulation, it is significant that these views were held in the 1950s, during the Cold War, by Communist Party members, when the Moscow orthodoxy was that abstract painting was itself the very expression of capitalist decadence. Evidently, this is not quite the same orthodox and even collaborationist Communist Party that various anticommunist left-wing commentators have held it to be. The united-front approach to cultural politics made it possible to create a bond within the cultural movement of the 1950s between artists and intellectuals of different political extractions. It is hardly surprising to find that they included some who later turned out to have supported anti-imperialist objectives principally because this appeared the best route to personal artistic aims, offering the promise of liberal freedoms that did not and could not have existed under the dictatorship. Naturally, they came into conflict with those who had come to be revolutionaries first and artists second, who gave their political engagement primacy over their aesthetic ambitions because they regarded the second as impossible to achieve without fulfilling the first.

But these splits were only incipient during the 1950s, a time when official culture was on the defensive, powerless to resist the cultural penetration of North American imperialism. The work of Nuestro Tiempo and similar groups had the effect of intensifying ideological confrontation in the domain of cultural activity, and the Catholics too entered the cine-club field. The church in Cuba had set up a cinema commission just before the Second World War that afterwards became a member of the international Catholic cinema organization. The church's strategy seems to have taken a new turn in the early 1950s, when it started setting up cine-clubs of its own, in which it showed major films accompanied by cine-debates. The chronology suggests that this was at least in part a response to the initiative of the leftist militants. The Catholic cine-clubs in turn stimulated further development of the idea, spawning cine-clubs around the country that were not directly under the church's control and only loosely linked with the central organization. A report presented to the Congress of the International Catholic Office of Film, which was held in Havana in 1957, listed forty-two clubs of this kind.[30]

These were the ways in which film came to occupy its key position in radical cultural consciousness in Cuba. Because of its special nature— an industrialized art and agent of cultural imperialism, on the one hand; on the other, the indigenous art form of the twentieth century and the vehicle of a powerful new mode of perception—because of this dual nature, film readily and acutely synthesized the whole range of cultural experience for a whole generation. Cinema was at the same time an instrument of oppression and an object of aspiration. What happened was that the monopolistic practices of the Hollywood majors and their local dependents not only created a frustrated cultural hunger among aficionados of cinema in Cuba, but, combined with their own attempts at making films, this turned cinema into a battlefield of cultural politics. The cine-club movement represented a breach in the defenses of cultural imperialism, and in this battlefield lie the origins of ICAIC.

Nuestro Tiempo was one of two principal recruiting grounds for future members of ICAIC: Alfredo Guevara, Tomás Gutiérrez Alea, Julio García Espinosa, José Massip, and Santiago Álvarez were all active members; Manuel Octavio Gómez contributed short stories to the society's magazine. There was also the Cine-Club Visión, situated in a working-class district of Havana, which drew its membership not only from radical intellectuals, but also from the local people. The composer Leo Brouwer made his debut as a young guitarist under its auspices, and other members who were later to join ICAIC include the film editors Norma Torrado, Nelson Rodríguez, and Gloria Argüelles and the cameraman Luis Costales. The director Manuel Pérez recalls that through the club you could get hold of books on cinema that came from Argentina, by Sadoul, Kuleshev, Balazs, Pudovkin, and Chiarini, and it created a cultural ambience where discussion on the films was of a strongly political nature.[31]

Of the *aficionado* films of the 1950s the most significant is *El Megano*, directed by Julio García Espinosa, a documentary using neorealist reconstruction to denounce the miserable conditions of the charcoal burners in a region of the Zapata Swamps after which the film is named. García Espinosa started off in theater, rapidly moving from bourgeois melodrama to the popular vernacular stage, where he acted and directed. But then he went to work in radio, for a commercial station, producing adaptations for a program called *Misterios en la historia del mundo* (Mysteries of world history). It was in Italy, he recalls, following the debates of the Communist leader Palmiro Togliatti and talking with other Latin Americans—there was a group of them that published a small cultural magazine with anti-imperialist politics—that he first developed a proper idea of Marxism. He had gone there because some neorealist films they had shown in Cuba had excited him. He did not at that time yet have much of an idea of the relationship between politics and art. But a chance experience made him think hard about it. At an open-air meeting in Rome that Togliatti was addessing, he met the man who had played the lead in Vittorio De Sica's famous *Bicycle Thief* (1948). He learned what a miserable life this man now led, and how he had felt frustration and indignity when he was approached to figure in an advertising campaign for a bicycle firm! People talk about the aesthetics of nonprofessional screen acting, said García Espinosa, but no one ever asks what happens to these people in their real lives afterwards.[32]

El Megano became something of a cause célèbre when it was seized by Batista's police after its first screening at the University of Havana. Julio García Espinosa, as head of the group that made it, was taken away for interrogation. He was released on condition that they bring the film to the police. The group used the breathing space to look for a way of getting a copy made. Francisco Ichazo, a prominent intellectual with official contacts, warned García Espinosa that the U.S. embassy was concerned. Finally, he was interviewed by the head of the secret police. "Did you make this film?" the man asked. "Do you know this film is a piece of shit?" "Do you know," replied García Espinosa, "that it's an example of neorealism?" and proceeded to explain. The man, he remembers, listened patiently and then said, "Not only is the film a piece of shit, but you also talk a lot of shit. Stop eating shit and go and make films about Batista!" "That," he recalls, "was my first intervention as a theorist!"[33]

With music by Juan Blanco, *El Megano* had taken a year to make, shooting on location on weekends and then borrowing facilities in Havana for postproduction, including dubbing sessions for which the peasant actors in the film came up to the big city. Neorealism was a strong element in the film's style, in the shaping of the narrative, and in the use of nonprofessional actors, but the film can also be taken as belonging to a tradition of documentary denunciation incorporating reenactment that goes back both to *Borinage* of 1934, by Joris Ivens and Henri Storck, and some of the work of the British documentary movement of the 1930s.

At the same time, an understanding of the media, and how to take them into account when thinking about political strategy, had become generalized within Cuban political life in proportion to the intensity with which the Cuban market had been developed in its role as offshore testing laboratory for yanqui capital. In a book full of statistics purporting to show his achievements that he published in Mexico in 1961, Batista boasts of Cuba's leading position in Latin America in radio and television: 160 radio stations and one radio set to every five inhabitants in 1958, and twenty-three television stations and one set to every twenty.[34] Regarded by Batista as one of the indices of how advanced Cuba was and therefore how unjust the rebellion, the presence of the media in fact contributed to his downfall through the variety of uses they were put to in the unfolding of the struggle against his dictatorship. As Lionel Martin has reported:

The July 26th Movement, which had strong backing among professionals, penetrated some of Cuba's publicity agencies. Cubans still laugh about the advertisements for Tornillo Soap that followed the official newscasts. After the Batista government handouts were read, the announcer would burst in with "Don't believe in tales, woman—Tornillo Soap washes best of all." Also memorable were the Bola Roja bean advertisements that followed the news. The word *bola* as used in Cuba can be variously translated "ball" (like a round bean) or "rumor" [hence *bola roja*—"red rumor"].

Just a week before Batista fled, a two-page advertisement for Eden cigarettes showed a man with a pack of Edens in one hand and a book in the other entitled *High Fidelity.* Newspapers were ordered to stop running another advertisement showing a man with a watch on his wrist, above the caption "This is the watch that went to the Antarctic." The man's face closely resembled Fidel Castro's, complete with beard and military cap.[35]

Episodes like these inspired the plot line of a debut feature by Fernando Pérez in 1986, *Clandestinos,* about life in the urban underground. The best-known example of the revolutionaries' use of the media is the radio station, Radio Rebelde, set up by the guerrillas in the Sierra, which kept the population, friend and foe, informed of the course of the struggle from the rebels' point of view. The achievement of Radio Rebelde was that even those who rejected its propagandistic voice knew that what it said impugned Batista and his censorship.

Castro had already envisaged the use of radio at the time of the attack on the Moncada barracks in 1953. The attack was supposed to instigate a provincial uprising in which local radio stations would be taken over and used to win the support of the masses throughout the country. This was not a scheme that Castro dreamed up out of nothing. He already had firsthand experience of radio and its powers and limitations. He had broadcast a regular series of political talks on a sympathetic radio station while practicing law and trying every legal means to expose the corruption of the government. Moreover, he had been a follower of Eduardo Chibas, leader of the populist and reformist political party known as the Ortodoxos. Chibas, too, was a well-known broadcaster, who maintained that radio broadcasts were as deadly in the political sphere as weapons. He took this belief to the ultimate conclusion when he reached the end of his political tether in 1951: unable to defend unscrupulous charges that his opponents had made against him, he took out a gun at the end of a broadcast and shot himself. Castro was in the studio watching. It was a futile gesture, but after Batista seized power the following year, the media kowtowed by promising to bar "demagogues" from using them.

Nor was this the first time a politician had died on the radio. In 1947, Emilio Tró, leader of a left-wing terrorist group with which Castro was said by some to be associated, was caught by a rival group at dinner with the chief of police in a house in the Havana suburbs. A fantastic three-hour gun battle that ended in Tró's eighteen-bullet-hole death was broadcast live by an enterprising station. Television, introduced into Cuba in 1950, was also drawn into the political arena, as images of political violence inevitably began to reach the television screen. In 1955, for example, the Cuban national baseball championship was interrupted by students rushing onto the field with anti-Batista banners and being savagely beaten up by the police in full view of the cameras.[36]

Fidel's use of television after the Revolution is famous, and was certainly significant. He never had any difficulty appearing when he wanted to, although both radio and television remained, to begin with, in private hands. But then Fidel made very good TV, and he used the medium extremely creatively. Television not only extended the reach of his speeches beyond the enormous public he attracted in person, it was also a means that could be used between the big rallies. The way Fidel used television defies Marshall McLuhan's notorious slogan "the medium is the message" and its corollary, that the "message" of a medium is "the change of scale or pace or pattern that it introduces."[37] From this one would have to suppose that what mattered was not what Fidel said, but only that he used television at all. But he didn't appear on television to perform a mime act, he used it to speak to the greatest number of people, to inform about developing situations, to announce and explain decisions or make policy declarations. Obviously, some people will call this demagogy, but what Fidel actually achieved was something else. There is with television a frustration in the impossibility the viewer normally feels of participating. Fidel, in speaking on television not only to the people but also for them, performed a vital vicarious role, and his appearances became the confluence of politics and entertainment. It is a role he has repeated in a number of ICAIC's films, films that yield a great deal of insight into his relationship with the people. But that is something we shall come back to.

For their part, the leaders of North American society had emerged from the Second World War more aware than ever of the ideological as well as the commercial functions of the communications media. Things had come a long way from the earlier days of modern communications technology when the leading capitalists had first become aware of the need to take control of the channels of communication for their own intelligence purposes—for example, when the banker J. Pierpont Morgan bought into the Western Union Telegraph Company in 1882 in order to safeguard the secrecy of his cables. By the end of the Second World War, North American capital fully understood the significance for it of controlling communications on a global scale: in 1944, the business magazine *Fortune* declared that on the efficiency of U.S.-owned international communications "depends whether the United States will grow in the future, as Great Britain has in the past, as a center of world thought and trade. . . . Great Britain provides an unparalleled example of what a communications system means to a great nation standing athwart the globe."[38] The United States thus embarked on new offensives after the war, including the establishment in Mexico in 1946 of the Asociación Interamericana de Radiofusión (Inter-American radio association), with its acronym, AIR: an organization bringing radio stations across the continent under its wing, ostensibly in the name of freedom, and to combat attempts at interference in broadcasting by governments in the countries to which the member stations belonged. Behind the ideological smokescreen, AIR was an instrument of Cold War propaganda.

At the other extreme from such grandiose schemes, the Cuban rebels were adept at the imaginative use of the small-scale communications equipment available to them. What must have been the sensation of the soldiers of the dictator in the field in 1958, finding themselves addressed by Fidel Castro himself through loudspeakers?[39] The rebels knew how to take advantage of the mass media. In December 1956, shortly after the disaster that occurred when the expeditionary force on the *Granma* landed, Batista's army declared that the rebels had been defeated. A few days later, while the rebels regrouped, one of them went to Havana to contact the media and set up an interview with the rebel leader. Against the wishes of the Cuban authorities, Herbert Matthews of the *New York*

Times obliged. A week later, Castro, who had been in desperate need of publicity, was known throughout the world. Batista denied the interview had really taken place. The *Times* replied by publishing a photograph of Matthews with Castro. The regime's credibility was destroyed and its principal officials humiliated.

Che Guevara spoke about the use of the media to a meeting of Nuestro Tiempo very soon after the victory of the Revolution. Of the early days in the Sierra, he said, "At that time the presence of a foreign journalist, preferably American, was more important to us than a military victory."[40] It should not surprise us that he spoke of this to this particular audience, or that in this address he launched many of the ideas he afterwards developed into a more consistent philosophy, ideas that had a crucial influence on the development of the Revolution.

PART II

The Revolution Takes Power:
A Cinema of Euphoria

CHAPTER SIX

The Coming of Socialism

The victory of the Revolution on January 1, 1959, brought about a flurry of documentary filmmaking. Two commercial producers brought out feature-length compilation films, *De la sierra hasta hoy* (From the Sierra to today) and *De la tiranía a la libertad* (From tyranny to liberty), the latter an expanded version of a film first seen the previous year under the title *Sierra Maestra*. Shorts to celebrate the Revolution were produced by bodies such as the municipality of Havana (*A las madres cubanas* [To Cuban mothers]) and the ministry of education (*Algo más que piedra* [Something more than stone]), the former based on a letter from José Martí to his mother in 1869, the latter on a poem of the popular poet El Indio Nabori dedicated to Martí.

Meanwhile, the trade annual, in what was to be its last edition, reprinted from the newspaper *Prensa Libre* an article titled "The Second Movement," rhetorically voicing the faith of the anti-Batista business community in the new beginning. The title is a reference to what was ironically known as the "Movement of the Second of January," the grouping of established bourgeois politicians who, as a distinguished foreign visitor, Jean-Paul Sartre, later observed, "stole assistance from the victory." These people "put in a good word for themselves to the victors, letting it be known that they would accept the burden of power if it were ever so slightly offered to them." Sartre compared them with "those uniforms smelling of moth balls that one saw appear in September 1944 on the streets of Paris."[1]

The article from *Prensa Libre* roundly declared that "in this glorious and necessary hour...work is the order of the day. If there aren't sufficient technicians, bring them in, because posterity accepts no excuses." It advocated "the reintroduction of constitutional rights, not salvationism, which could degenerate into repugnant totalitarianism. And not to impede it, the leader of the revolution must turn himself into a political leader, and bring the citizen to the ballot box with the same faith as last year, when he led them into combat."[2] This from a publication that two years earlier had announced: "We have not for many years had an economic perspective as promising as that of 1957...because cinema—like few other activities—depends for its progress on the country being content and the money supply in the streets being fluid and consistent.... Thus everything seems to indicate that 1957 will be a bonanza year for the film trade."[3] In fact, most Cuban capitalists did well that year, but not the film business. The urban underground began bombing cinemas. Some of the audience was frightened away.

But the Rebel Army was not about to abandon its ideals and return the country to the anarchy that immediate elections would inevitably entail. Masses of people decidedly declared their support on the streets. They greeted the rebels with a nationwide general strike that frustrated the salvage attempts of the old order to grab back power sans Batista. And in the months that followed, as the former bourgeois opposition to the dictatorship opposed every piece of revolutionary legislation, the masses filled the squares in huge rallies to approve the Revolution.

The Rebel Army in the Sierra had done more than just fight. They had informed and encouraged the population through their radio station Radio Rebelde, and demonstrated their principles through introducing, in the areas they controlled, the first real administration of justice the Cuban campesino had ever seen. They had gained experience in how to organize both supply lines and popular campaigns. They had brought to the Cuban countryside for the first time both medical attention and education. Over the two-year campaign, they had set up thirty schools, where both the campesino and their own ranks sat down to learn at the same time. And thus they were poised to engage the political tasks created by their victory.

These tasks were formidable. The existing bureaucratic administration was riddled with Batista collaborators. The biggest fish fled immediately, followed by a growing flood of frightened rich, the incorrigibly bourgeois, and the retinue of professionals, operatives, and technical engineers who depended on them. The atmosphere is portrayed in Jesús Díaz's *Polvo rojo* (Red dust) of 1982, the story of a technician at a North American–owned nickel plant who remains in Cuba to run things when not only the other technicians and administrators but even his family leave for the States.

The Rebel Army established order, occupied radio stations, arranged for the publication of newspapers. It manifested from the outset an awareness of the importance of the means of mass communications. It brought to its tasks a zeal and an optimism, indeed a euphoria that sometimes bordered on overoptimism, which impressed every honest visitor. A North American economist, Edward Boorstein, who worked with the planning agencies set up by the Rebel Army, has recorded that the atmosphere "intoxicated almost everyone, Cubans and foreigners alike."[4]

And the Rebel Army improvised. At the Agrarian Reform Institute, says Boorstein, "there was no comprehensive, detailed and finished agricultural policy... nor could there have been. There were many ideas. And there was also the method that Napoleon explained when he was asked how he determined the tactics to be followed in a battle. '*On s'engage, et puis—on voit.*' You get into the action, and then—you see." Boorstein holds that, for all their limitations, the initial ideas were of great value because they began the process of grappling with the problems, "and 'even a poor hypothesis,' Charles Darwin said, 'is better than none at all.'"

This infectious enthusiasm was not limited to questions of economics. The Rebel Army had quickly gone in for making films. Che Guevara opened a military cultural school on January 14, 1959, at the fortress of La Cabaña in Havana, where, until a fortnight earlier, Batista had held his political prisoners. Armando Acosta, a leader of the Communist Party, headed the outfit and its predominantly young staff included Santiago Alvarez, Julio García Espinosa, and José Massip. García Espinosa was put in charge of producing two films for the Dirección de Cultura (cultural directorate) of the Rebel Army under Camilo Cienfuegos. One of them, *Esta tierra nuestra* (This land of ours), which García Espinosa scripted and Tomás Gutiérrez Alea directed, dealt with the agrarian reform and gave an explanation of the legislation to be introduced in May and why it was necessary. The other, *La vivienda* (Housing), was directed by García Espinosa himself, and dealt with urban reform.

Until the agrarian reform law was promulgated, the United States seemed ready to tolerate the new government, since its first measures caused no sharp internal divisions that could be used to try to legitimize attacks on it, though Washington was wont to launch military invasions throughout its hinterland—its "backyard"—with less excuse. The Revolution reduced the price of medicines, telephones, electricity, and rents below a hundred dollars per month. It introduced measures to root out corruption from government and business, to suppress gambling (except, at this stage, in the luxury hotels and nightclubs), to reform the tax system. It introduced, say a pair of visitors, prominent North American Marxists Leo Huberman and Paul Sweezy, "New Deal–type programs in such fields as education, housing and health. As long as legislation was confined to such matters as these, no insuperable difficulties arose, though it is clear that friction began to develop quite early between radicals and conservatives, represented chiefly by Fidel on the one side and Urrutia on the other."[5] Urrutia was a judge who had played an honorable role at the time of Moncada. When the rebels triumphed, Fidel placed him in the presidency and waited the short wait until Urrutia had no alternative but to name him prime minister. Six months later, Fidel forced him out, by resigning as prime minister in protest against his vacillation.

The agrarian reform was the turning point because it was the first piece of legislation to expropriate North American property. When Fidel went to Washington and New York in April, before the law was decreed, he was given, Huberman and Sweezy record, a friendly reception, and even received a good deal of favorable publicity in the press and on TV. There were some wary people around too, of course. "I had a three hour conference with Castro when he visited Washington, back in April 1959," wrote Richard Nixon shortly afterward, in his notorious piece of self-glorification, *Six Crises*. "After that conference, I wrote a confidential memorandum for distribution to the CIA, State Department, and White House. In it I stated flatly that I was convinced Castro was 'either incredibly naive about Communism or under Communist discipline' and that we would have to treat and deal with him accordingly."[6] But, say Huberman and Sweezy, it was not until after the agrarian reform that Fidel's stock in government and business circles declined. But now he was "assigned the role of *bête noire* (or perhaps red devil would be more accurate)," while in Cuba itself, supporters in the upper and middle classes—the Second Movement—began to fall away and moved into a posture of opposition.

Bourgeois they might have been, and only a minority of them already committed to socialist ideals, but the mood of the country's artists and intellectuals was strongly anti-imperialist, and when the Film Institute was set up by decree at the end of March, it offered those inclined toward cinema an opportunity that had never existed before. The Revolution, according to Julio García Espinosa, "represented, initially for everyone, both rupture and at the same time continuity, even for many who today are no longer with the Revolution. Everybody felt it was inseparable from their own individual history, and people put themselves at the service of the moment, which they felt as the source of creativity for the future."[7] The new institute's principal problem was to find funding. It needed all sorts of equipment in addition to what it acquired by decree if it were to function efficiently and effectively. But investment was still controlled by reactionary men sitting in banks that were controlled by the United States, who resisted them. The government, however, honored its commitment to the creation of a Cuban cinema as fully as it could. Fidel and his brother Raúl arranged for the first credits to be provided from funds controlled by the Agrarian Reform Institute, INRA, and the films begun by the group at the Rebel Army cultural school passed with them to ICAIC for completion. When Che Guevara visited Tokyo in July 1959 in search of new foreign-trade agreements, he took time to investigate the purchase of equipment for ICAIC. A letter he wrote to ICAIC's chief Alfredo Guevara gives the flavor of the time—and also of Che's inspiring personal intelligence:

> Azuba-Prince Hotel
> Honmura-cho Minato-ku Tokyo
>
> July 26, 1959
>
> My dear Alfredo,
>   Hardly had I received your letter than I made contact with a company through people here and put forward the following proposals: the installation, by Japan, of a self-sufficient studio, with a capacity of three films

a month, equipped with all apparatus except cameras, and of a cinema belonging to the studio seating 2,500, paid for in sugar. I included this last proposal myself because I consider that the institute should make itself independent of the cinemas and have its own film theater. I was struck by several surprises; first, all the studios use North American and German cameras, above all the North American Mitchell. The job of sending you all the pamphlets I've given to the ambassador, because it's large and these people work slowly; I'm sending you with the envoy a book that may be of service to you; I don't know its value because I neither speak English nor understand about cinema. On the concrete questions you gave me, I can give you the following answers: the Japanese studios are made for interior filming; they only go outside when there's no remedy and they calculate a third of the film in these conditions. Yes, it is possible to buy plans of the studios, and they offered them to me, but they haven't been back to see me again. Japanese cinema consists three-fifths in modern-day films with little scenery and low cost ($50,000); the remaining two-fifths use large sets, are generally cinemascope, and an extremely expensive film in Japan costs $250,000. According to the businessmen, they are very interested in the Latin American film market but they didn't demonstrate it, since they didn't come back to speak to us again nor send the catalogs I requested. I indicated to them the interests of the Film Institute in distributing Japanese films. I shall try again before leaving (I depart tomorrow) and will get the embassy to communicate the results to you officially. Forgive me the plainness of this letter but I haven't got enough gray matter for psychological disquisitions; yours, on the other hand, interested me greatly, but the two pages you dedicated to the analysis of Pedro Luis I can sum up in three words: *hijo de puta.*

> *Recibe un abrazo de tu amigo*
> Che[8]

If larger political developments at this time caused no dissension within ICAIC, there was nonetheless a growing rivalry between ICAIC and a group led by Carlos Franqui, one of the leaders of the July 26th Movement. During the 1950s, Franqui had been prominent in the *aficionado* film movement. He belonged to a group that included German Puig, the future ICAIC cameraman Ramón Suárez, and the writers Edmundo Desnoes and Guillermo Cabrera Infante, which revived the Cinemateca; and he had made, together with Puig, a short publicity film (*Carta a una madre* [Letter to a mother]). Puig and Desnoes made a short that was produced and edited by Suárez. Suárez and Cabrera Infante made a film together about the artist Amelia Peláez that got shown on television. Suárez and Desnoes later worked, respectively, as cinematographer and writer on Alea's renowned *Memorias del subdesarrollo,* but all except Desnoes were to leave Cuba before the end of the 1960s—and Desnoes would leave later.

Franqui was not, however, among Fidel's closest followers. In the Sierra, Franqui had been responsible for Radio Rebelde and the rebel newspaper *Revolución.* When the Revolution took power, he gave up the radio station and devoted himself fully to the paper, because, he has written, "a newspaper is a good vehicle for fights" and he "wanted to start a revolution in Cuban culture."[9] He added that, in his eyes, Fidel "looked askance at culture." However, Franqui himself looked askance at the Communists with whom he had been involved in Nuestro Tiempo—which, himself a member of the party at the time, he had helped to found—who were now embarking on the Revolution's first cultural undertakings with Fidel's support; in the case of Alfredo Guevara, there was, it seems, considerable personal animosity. Both of them, at a period during the 1950s when the Communist Party had viewed the July 26th Movement with suspicion, regarding Fidel as an adventurist, had nonetheless chosen to join. Franqui, in doing so, had gone to the Sierra and cut his political ties, while Guevara retained his party links and worked in the underground. According to Guevara, Franqui had "developed a phobia against the party, which I could understand; but it grew to the extent that when the Revolution took power, he refused to believe that Fidel was capable of developing socialism in his own way."[10] What is certainly clear from Franqui's own writings is that after the overthrow of the dictator, he saw the Communists exclusively as infiltrators into a Revolution they had done nothing to make. The situation, according to Alfredo Guevara, was that the evolution of the Revolution toward socialism was for many people a great surprise, which created many anxieties. At the beginning, many people found it easy to be progressive. The condemnation of corruption, for example, was a matter of national pride: corruption wasn't Cuban, it was something created by the gringos. That a process had been set in motion, however, leading toward socialist solutions was something relatively few comprehended, and Franqui took advantage of the situation, adopting an antagonistic stance toward the participation of Communists in this process.

Franqui certainly understood more than many the prime importance of the mass media, and determined to build a force around *Revolución* that, among other things, would rival the influence of ICAIC. In the random manner in which the process of revolutionary expropriation distributed its acquisitions, ICAIC at this time came into possession of a record factory and an advertising studio, while *Revolución* found itself with a television studio. The young *aficionado* intellectuals of the 1950s began to divide up. In particular, participants in the urban underground gravitated toward ICAIC, though its only criterion for recruits was that they should not be tainted by association with Batista. Those around *Revolución,* on the other hand, tended to be politically less experienced and correspondingly more bewildered by the course of events. Ten years later, Ambrosio Fornet recollected: "We had got hold of a terrain—that of high culture—as a piece of private property in the middle of a revolution that didn't believe in private property."[11]

Fidel soon curbed the newspaper's attacks on the Communists, whom he clearly regarded critically, but as necessary allies—some, of course, had always supported him, like Alfredo Guevara and his own brother, Raúl. But the editorship of *Revolución*—and Franqui knew this well—remained a key position on the ideological battlefield. By early 1960, printers working in the commercial press were inserting *coletillas*—"tails"—in the other papers to protest against their antagonism toward the Revolution.[12] *Revolución,* on the other hand, was a paper people knew they could trust, and Franqui attracted a group of writers, reporters, and photographers, some with more experience than others, whom he knew were hungry for the opportunity to participate.

Many, however, hardly comprehended what was happening—Guillermo Cabrera Infante, for example, an old friend of Franqui's, who now edited *Revolución*'s cultural supplement, *Lunes de Revolución.* According to Julio García Espinosa, Cabrera "was a friend, but he wasn't with us politically. We called him to become part of the directorate of ICAIC, but he chose to remain with Franqui. He was very talented but also very ingenuous: there were some among the *Lunes* group who had been associated with Batista's director of culture, even if they hadn't been closely involved. These people he kept company with were lacking in direction, while ICAIC set out from the beginning to create a communist political awareness. This was before Fidel defined the Revolution as socialist, and, not surprisingly, ICAIC soon became the target of attacks. The initial unity of the artists and intellectuals began to crumble."[13]

By the end of 1959, ICAIC had embarked on regular documentary production and had completed four films. Apart from the two already mentioned, García Espinosa also directed *Sexto aniversario* (Sixth anniversary), about the half million campesinos invited to Havana to take part in the sixth-anniversary celebrations of the attack on the Moncada barracks; this was the first great July 26 demonstration, one of the dates in the revolutionary calendar on which Fidel, in the years to come, was to make some of his major speeches. The writer Humberto Arenal, who went on to make a number of didactic films, directed the fourth film, *Construcciones rurales* (Rural construction) about improvements in conditions for the campesino through the building of houses, schools, and hospitals.

The tendency in these first few films reflected the dominant character of the Rebel Army, its orientation toward the campesino. And it was enough for these films to touch this orientation for them to evoke a response from the audience that was both demonstrative and emphatic. The audience at the premiere of *Esta tierra nuestra* gave the film a standing ovation. The following year, Alfredo Guevara wrote that "each showing of the film had the same significance as a plebiscite. . . . *Esta tierra nuestra* released a series of forces and made them explosive."[14] Not that in their style these films made any special appeal to popular culture, rural or urban. Neither did they attempt a radical aesthetic, popular or otherwise. For example, Juan Blanco's music for *Esta tierra nuestra* is simply a modern orchestral film score, and, like *El Megano* before it, the film has very much the feel of the classic documentary of social concern. In addition to well-composed if static documentary shots, it included enacted scenes, some of them picturing guerrilla warfare. Running nineteen minutes in black and white, it also uses a conventional commentary. While the film has a certain artistry and technical control, this commentary—the way it addresses its audience—tells us that this audience is still an amorphous one. Cinema attendance in Cuba in 1959 more than recovered the loss it had seen during 1957 and 1958, and this confirmed that going to the movies was the dominant form of popular entertainment; but this had little as yet to do with the efforts of ICAIC and there was very little the new filmmakers could safely assume about the audience beyond its powerful popular support for the Revolution. Nor had they sufficient experience to begin immediately to experiment. To be making films at all was experimental enough, and a dominant part of the experience of these first months.

Moreover, they had to contend with the speed of events and the state of flux they were trying to capture with their cameras. In June 1959, counter-revolutionary attacks began to take place, with small planes flying in from Florida and dropping incendiary bombs on cane fields and sugar mills. In the following months, the country found increasing difficulty in purchasing arms and in March 1960 an explosion occurred in Havana harbor aboard the Belgian vessel *La Coubre,* as an arms shipment was being unloaded, causing dozens of deaths and injuries. The British prime minister conceded in the House of Commons that the United States had been exerting international pressure to try and stop the sale of arms to Cuba. Ten years later, Octavio Cortázar reconstructed the events in his documentary *Sobre un primer combate* (On a first attack), showing that it could only have been an act of sabotage. The incident occurred during Sartre's visit to Cuba. "I discovered," he wrote, "the hidden face of all revolutions, their shaded face: the foreign menace felt in anguish."[15]

After the burial of the victims the following day, Castro called for indissoluble unity. The criminal act of the evening before, said Sartre, already united the people in rage and in the mobilization of all their energies:

If, two days before, there still remained in the depths of some soul a little laxity, a desire to rest, a lazy negligence, or a comfortable optimism, the affront swept away all those cowardly ideas: one had to fight an implacable enemy; one had to win. Castro identified himself with the people, his sole support; the people at the same time manifested their approbation and intransigence. The aggressor had taken the initiative, but the counter-blow provoked by his insensibility was the radicalization of the people through their leaders, and of the leaders through the people— that is to say, the least favored classes. At that moment I understood that the enemy, because of his tactics, had only accelerated an internal process which was developing according to its own laws. The Revolution had adapted itself to the acts of the foreign power; it was inventing its counter-thrusts. But the very situation of this country which was strangled for so long, caused its counter-blows to be always more radical, conceding more strongly each time to the just demands of the masses. By trying to crush the Revolution, the enemy allowed it to convert itself into what it was.[16]

For the time being, the Revolutionary Government allowed its ideological position to remain publicly undefined, but its socialist orientation was an open secret among groups like ICAIC, and a threatening rumor among the nationalist bourgeoisie. "What is at first suprising," Sartre wrote in *Lunes*

—especially if one has visited the countries of the East—is the apparent absence of ideology. Ideologies, however, are not what this century lacks; right here they have representatives who are offering their services from all sides. Cuban leaders do not ignore them. They simply do not make use of them. Their adversaries formulate the most contradictory reproaches. For some of them, this absence of ideas is only a deception; it hides a rigorous Marxism which does not yet dare to reveal its name: some day the Cubans will take off their mask and Communism will be implanted in the Caribbean, just a few miles from Miami. Other enemies—or, at times, the same ones—accuse them of not thinking at all: "They are improvising," I have been told, "and then after having done something they make up a theory." Some politely add, "Try to speak to the members of the government; perhaps they know what they are doing. Because as far as we are concerned, I must confess that we know absolutely nothing at all." And a few days ago at the University, a student declared, "To the extent that the Revolution has not defined its objectives, autonomy becomes all the more indispensable to us."[17]

This was the attitude among many artists and intellectuals. They entertained great concern for their own personal freedom, although nothing was threatening them. On the contrary, as Ambrosio Fornet later described it, here was a situation in which if no one could guarantee that the artists and intellectuals were revolutionaries, neither could anyone say that they weren't, "except for a quartet of night-prowling tomcats who still confused jazz with imperialism and abstract art with the devil."[18] There was, he said, a tacit agreement with the intellectuals that was later to cause problems, that allowed them to paint, exhibit, and write as they wished, disseminate their aesthetic preoccupations and polemicize with whom they wished, as long as they didn't step outside their own territory. It was, of course, a contradictory situation, because it implied that they should *not* become too politicized. Indeed, it was said in some circles that the best cultural policy was not to have one.

But this allowed many artists outside such groupings as ICAIC to get cut off, forcing them to follow the course of political development somewhat in isolation, a condition that resulted in a very uneven development of consciousness among them.

A Soviet mission arrived in Cuba in February 1960, and trade and credit agreements were signed within a few days; similar agreements with other socialist countries followed. In April, Cuba began to purchase crude oil from the USSR under the February agreements, enabling it to save foreign exchange. But Cuba's U.S.-owned refineries refused to process Soviet crude and, in the last few days of June, before a serious shortage could develop, the government took them over. Within days, President Eisenhower announced the inevitable and expected retaliation: cancellation of Cuba's sugar quota. Khrushchev immediately declared his support for Cuba and the Soviet Union undertook the purchase of the canceled quota.

The CIA had by this time already begun to deliver weapons and radio transmitters to anti-Castro agents, who, according to two U.S. journalists quoted by Boorstein, "all . . . had contact with the American embassy in Havana . . . the CIA and the United States government had thus firmly entered the conspiracy to oust Castro."[19] In this atmosphere, and demonstrating the principle described by Sartre as making the counterblows against the enemy always more radical, Fidel announced at the beginning of August the nationalization of key North American properties in Cuba: thirty-six sugar mills and their lands, the electric and telephone companies, and the refineries and other oil properties that had already been requisitioned. In September, Cuban branches of U.S. banks were nationalized, and the following month nationalization was extended to practically all other large or medium-sized industrial, commercial, and financial enterprises, railroads, port facilities, hotels, and cinemas. Nationalization of the major film distribution companies followed in May 1961. Three remaining smaller distributors were nationalized at the beginning of 1965 and the stocks of these companies, which could not be legally shown, were thereby taken over.[20]

As the nationalizations proceeded, however, and the disaffected continued to leave, trained personnel became scarcer and scarcer. Enrique Pineda Barnet, who later joined ICAIC and directed an experimental feature-length documentary, *David*, in 1967, chanced to be the first person to respond to a call by Fidel during a TV broadcast for volunteers to serve as teachers in the Sierra Maestra—because he lived close to the TV studio and was only waiting like so many others for such an opportunity. When the nationalizations came about some months later, Fidel picked eighty-two of the volunteer teachers, and they were asked to be ready to move in overnight as the new managers. Pineda Barnet found himself in charge of a sugar refinery. Recalling these events, he remarked that he not only in this way came into proper contact with workers for the first time, but he also learned a good deal about the ousted sugar bosses. He even discovered a hidden cache of soft-core porno movies.[21]

A new organism was now set up, the Bank of Foreign Commerce, to function as a government foreign-trade agency, with instructions to import large quantities of goods as rapidly as possible in order to reduce the impact of the embargo by the United States, which the Cubans now anticipated. ICAIC was thus able to acquire several crucial pieces of equipment: a Mitchell camera, an optical camera (for special-effects work), an animation table, and laboratory equipment, all from the United States. The animation table enabled it to set up a cartoon section, staffed by Jesús de Armas, Eduardo Muñoz, and the Australian Harry Reede, a Cuban resident, and the first two cartoons were completed before the end of the year. Each lasting four minutes and directed by de Armas, *El maná* (Manna) is a moral tale about a campesino who believes everything falls from the heavens like manna and ends up with nothing because his neighbors take it all; *La prensa seria* (The serious press) deals with misrepresentation by the supposedly serious newspapers.

The documentaries made during 1960 fall into three groups. The first comprises didactic films aimed mainly at the campesino, dealing with agricultural methods (films on the cultivation of rice, tobacco, and the tomato), the dangers of negligence in handling drinking water, or the advantages of the cooperatives and schools and other facilities established by the Revolutionary Government. The second group is made up of films recording the principal mass mobilizations of the year. The third group is more diverse. It includes films that record various other aspects of the revolutionary process or that deal with aspects of Cuba's social and cultural history. Manet's *El negro* is a short history of racial discrimination in Cuba from the time of slavery to the triumph of the Revolution and its prohibition (another of the Revolution's first measures). Grado's *Playas del pueblo* (The people's beaches) celebrates the opening up of the island's private beaches. Néstor Almendros made *Ritmo de Cuba* (Rhythm of Cuba) on Afro-Cuban folk music (and also, in his spare time, using, as he himself admits in his autobiography, film "short ends" that he filched from ICAIC, *Gente en la playa* [People at the beach]).[22] Some of these films are more personal than others, but for the most part the subjects and themes of the films in all three groups were chosen according to the needs of ideological struggle in the revolutionary situation. Historians of the Revolution would do well to watch these films carefully: they serve as an excellent guide to what many, if not all, of these issues were, and at the same time indicate the lines that were being drawn at each moment for the next phase; for since films take time to make, they are also evidence of how closely the leadership at ICAIC was integrated from the outset with thinking at the center of gravity within the revolutionary leadership.

Ugo Ulive, the Uruguayan filmmaker who worked at ICAIC during its early years, singles out Manet's film as "the only worthy thing accomplished by the Franco-Cuban writer during his stay in Cuba," also mentioning a film by the Puerto Rican Óscar Torres (who, like Alea and García Espinosa, had studied at the Centro Sperimentale in Rome) called *Tierra olvidada* (Forgotten land), a kind of *El Megano* revisited. The Zapata swamp is being transformed: the Revolution has come to the swamp and the wretched lives of the charcoal burners are undergoing a complete transformation. "Torres, without doubt one of the more promising directors of this initial stage, undertakes to express the change with a style that fearlessly blends a certain gratuitous grandiloquence with an occasionally moving epic scope.... In the culminating sequence, [he] juxtaposes the invasion of machinery that has come to dredge the swamp with a peasant woman giving birth in a nearby hut. The absence of false diffidence with which Torres accomplishes a sequence so full of traps as this is without doubt the mark of a director who could have been very important in the later development of ICAIC."[23] The film won second prize at the Festival of the Peoples in Florence, and an honorable mention at the Leipzig Film Festival, both in 1960—two out of five international awards achieved by Cuban films that year, the year in which (with one exception) they made their first international appearance. Torres went on to direct a feature film for ICAIC, *Realengo 18* (Plot 18), a year or two later and then returned to Puerto Rico, where he died young.

These foreign awards were hugely important to ICAIC, for international recognition of this kind vindicated the somewhat crazy project of creating a film industry and provided an answer to critics; moreover, they helped the promotion of the image of the Revolution abroad. Not that they were made with an eye to foreign approval. On the contrary, the guiding principle was that foreign recognition would follow, where it will, if the films were authentic expressions of the Revolution's own needs.

The other two films to win international distinctions in 1960 were Alea's *Esta tierra nuestra* and García Espinosa's *La vivienda*. The following year, there were collective awards for Cuban films at two German film festivals, Leipzig in the east and Oberhausen in the west. Four films were included: the film by Torres; Alea's *Asamblea general (General Assembly)*, recording the mass meeting of September 2, 1960, at which the first Declaration of Havana was proclaimed; and two films by José Massip, *Los tiempos del joven Martí (The Times of the Young Martí)* and *Por qué nació el Ejército Rebelde (Why the Rebel Army Was Born)*. The second of the Massip pair uses nonprofessional actors and runs eighteen minutes (the year's longest documentary, García Espinosa's *Un año de libertad* [A year of freedom], runs twenty-seven minutes). In terms of narrative, wrote Alfredo Guevara, "Massip found very simple solutions. He decomposes reality in order to recompose it in a succession of frescoes, some of which offer the greatest clarity."[24] But although the film was structurally uneven, he said, it was undeniably effective because of the power of the theme and the sincerity with which it was treated.

The criticism is interesting because it indicates something of the values that ICAIC was trying to develop. At the top of the list is judgment in the choice of subject matter, together with that elusive quality, sincerity. It was to give these criteria body, so to speak, that an understanding of formal aesthetic procedures was encouraged. Aesthetic experiment was felt to be thoroughly desirable, but not formalist preoccupation.

The first of Massip's films incorporates a score by Harold Gramatges, who had been president of Nuestro Tiempo and was now serving as a kind traveling ambassador based in Paris. Like Alea's *La toma de la Habana por los ingleses (The Taking of Havana by the English*—an event that occurred in 1762), this film originated before the Revolution. Using paintings, period engravings, even magazine illustrations to describe the period of Martí's youth, Massip had started making it in 1956. He was able to complete it during ICAIC's first months, and in July 1959 Héctor García Mesa took it to the World Youth Festival in Vienna, where it became the first film of the Cuban Revolution to be seen internationally. It has the distinction of being also the first film seriously and sensitively to tackle the recovery *(el rescate)* of Cuban nineteenth-century political history, a theme that was to be given great prominence in ICAIC's future output.

By the end of 1960, a number of difficulties had begun to appear in the country's economic condition. Edward Boorstein later wrote:

> The management of the Cuban economy during the first two years of the Revolution was made easier than usual by the existence of a large amount of reserves—using this word in the broad sense given to it by economists in the socialist countries. There were unutilized resources: idle land and labor and unutilized capacity in the manufacturing plants and the construction industry. There were some dollar holdings. There were over five million head of cattle. . . . The rapid progress of the Cuban economy in the early years after the Revolution took power was made possible by the reserves. The very irrationality of the prerevolutionary economy served as a springboard for advance. . . . The reserves cushioned the Cuban economy against the consequences of error. . . . The real cost to the economy of using resources that would otherwise be left idle is zero—not the costs that appear in the conventional accounting ledgers. When you raised the demands on resources to a higher level than the supply, the first consequences were not difficulties in the economy, but reductions in reserves.[25]

This was the stage that had been reached by the end of the year. Dollar expenditure was running three times as high as dollar earnings; if the deficit continued, it would wipe out the dollar reserves in about four months.

Though mistakes had been made, this situation was less a consequence of mismanagement than of the very policies of the Revolution: on the one hand, of raising the people's purchasing power, on the other, of buying in foreign goods against the likelihood of further U.S. retaliation. By spring 1961, the first shortages began to make themselves felt and the question inevitably arises of the extent to which the troubles that now occurred in the field of cultural politics were a consequence of the unequal development of political consciousness among the intellectual community, and hence among many of them a lack of preparedness for the likely developments of the Revolution's third year, which began with the United States breaking off diplomatic relations on January 3.

"We knew," says Alfredo Guevara, "through our intelligence services, that we were going to be invaded. So there were the mobilizations of the people, the creation of the militia, the military training, the civil defense. In this heroic climate there appeared a film that did not reflect any of this. It showed the Havana of the lower depths, the drunks, the small cabarets where prostitution was still going on, where there was still drug trafficking, something like the world of *On the Bowery*." (*On the Bowery* follows the ups and downs of an alcoholic through the bars, flophouses, and shelters of New York; it was made in 1956 by Lionel Rogosin and is celebrated as an early example of the new documentary.) Similarly, "*P.M.*, in only fifteen minutes, showed a world inhabited by the mainly black and mulatto lumpenproletariat. Obviously it wasn't made out of any feeling of racial discrimination, but the presentation of these images at this time was nonetheless questionable."[26] In short, it presented black people in roles associated with the state of oppression from which they were in process of liberation.

The film was made by the painter Saba Cabrera Infante, brother of Guillermo (editor of *Lunes de Revolución*) with Orlando Jiménez Leal as cinematographer, and it became a cause célèbre of the liberals of the *Lunes* group when it was banned from public exhibition at the end of May. The significance of the moment is crucial to what happened. The incident took place six weeks after the invasion of the Bay of Pigs, when U.S.-backed mercenaries were routed in the space of three days by the Rebel Army backed by the People's Militia. Not only that. The day before the invasion, at a mass rally called to protest a surprise simultaneous air attack on three Cuban cities, and in the knowledge that a CIA-sponsored invasion was on its way, Fidel publicly declared for the first time the socialist character of the Revolution. Not that this was exactly unexpected. Fidel has explained that this avowal had been anticipated by the masses and he was only acknowledging an already overwhelming mass sentiment. But the timing is significant. It is inconceivable that at a moment when the Revolution was in mortal danger Fidel would have taken this stand unless he knew it corresponded with popular conviction.[27] Indeed, it was precisely in this knowledge that Fidel chose the moment: in order to redouble the energy with which the invaders would be met. Perhaps *P.M.* was only a mildly offensive film, but in the euphoria that followed the defeat of the mercenaries the mood of the country was bound to make it seem worse. Alfredo Guevara admits, "I reacted to the film as an offended revolutionary. Today I would manage a thing like that better."

Several accounts of the affair have been published. One is Ugo Ulive's in the article already cited. Another is by a British travel writer, Nicholas Wollaston, in a dreadful (though engrossing) book called *Red Rumba*, about his visit to Cuba in the early 1960s.[28] More recently, there is a sort of version from exile, by Guillermo Cabrera Infante, the filmmaker's brother.[29] As a writer, Cabrera Infante is a kind of literary Ken Russell, the epitome of bad taste, and his article bends under the weight of so many base, bombastic, and bloated puns that it becomes a worm-eaten piece of fiction with about as much relationship to what occurred as Russell's horrific films on Tchaikovsky and Mahler to the real biography of those composers. The Cuban poet Pedro Pérez Sarduy, a culturally hungry student of literature at the University of Havana in the days when all this happened, has commented bluntly that Cabrera Infante was "one of those writers who never did know what happened," a member of "an incongruous cultural elite unable to grasp the real meaning of change."[30] Combining and adjudging these accounts, and from conversations in Cuba, what seems to have happened was this:

P.M. was a modest film, which was shot—as everyone agrees, but that's about all they agree on—in a "free cinema" style. It begins with a ferry slipping into Havana harbor from across the water. The camera then wanders into a number of crowded bars in the narrow streets behind the waterfront, where it shows people (Wollaston:) "drinking, arguing, loving, quarrelling, dreaming. . . . It falls on ecstasy and desperation, it peers blearily through the cigar smoke, singles out a glass of beer, lights for a moment on a smile, winces at a bright electric bulb [someone should tell Wollaston cameras don't wince], hovers over a shelf of bottles. A blurred negress stands in front of the lens, and the camera moves back to take in the whole jostling, sweating scene . . . the only sound is the roar of so many Cuban voices, the clink of glasses and ice from the bar, and the music. In the whole film there is not a single coherent word spoken." In the end, the "exhausted revelers" return whence they came.

Guillermo gave his brother money to complete the film, which was spent on laboratory facilities at the TV channel run by *Revolución*. Nei-

ther Alfredo Guevara nor Julio García Espinosa could remember having
seen it on television, but it was noticed by Néstor Almendros, who, having left ICAIC, now had a film column in the independent cultural weekly
Bohemia. There he praised the film as "enormously poetic" and "a veritable jewel of experimental cinema." Wollaston considers it understandable
that he should have been enthusiastic and may be excused for not having
mentioned that it was "amateurish [and] that much of the photography
was not half as good as that of his own films." But encouraged, the filmmakers offered it to the manager of one of Havana's remaining privately
owned cinemas, who told them he liked it but they would need an exhibition license from ICAIC. Assuming that this was just a formality, says
Wollaston, they were taken aback when the film was "confiscated."

But it was the Institute that was taken by surprise, since no one there
knew anything about it. The response was hostile. The film was seen, as
Pérez Sarduy puts it, as "irresponsible both to the Revolution and the
cultural tasks of those privileged to have the costly medium of cinema
at their disposal." ICAIC decided that its distribution should be delayed.
It did not expect the explosion that took place. Cabrera Infante, always
enamored, says Pérez Sarduy, of the tawdriest Hollywood movies, writes,
"We had been expecting a showdown with the Film Institute. It was to
become a shoot-out." "Guillermo," said Alfredo Guevara, "came to argue
with me, and left crying that this was Stalinism and fascism." Almendros
used his influence to rally support for the offending filmmakers. ICAIC
decided to arrange a meeting where the film would be shown and discussed. It was held at the Casa de las Américas, the revolutionary literary institute, and therefore more *Lunes*'s territory than ICAIC's. According to Wollaston, the audience supported the film as at best a piece of
original artistic work and at worst an amateurish documentary "that
was politically naive." He also reports that someone had gone down to
the waterfront and done a survey, and found that the people in the film
all supported the Revolution and some were even *milicianos* (militia
members), so how could the film be counterrevolutionary?

For ICAIC, however—only this is something beyond Wollaston's ken—
the issue was both more complicated and more serious. People at ICAIC
felt the film failed to register what was really in the air because it followed its chosen stylistic model both too closely and too uncritically.
This was not just politically but also aesthetically irresponsible. At ICAIC
they had begun to sense that the camera was not the unproblematic

kind of instrument the apologists for *P.M.* supposed, first of all because of the way they had to struggle in their films to keep abreast with the pace of revolutionary change. To paraphrase the French film theorist Serge Daney, it does not involve a single straight line from the real to the visible and thence to its reproduction on film in which a simple truth is faithfully represented. Daney says, "in a world where 'I see' is automatically said for 'I understand,' such a fantasy has probably not come about by chance. The dominant ideology that equates the real with the visible has every interest in encouraging it."[31] At ICAIC they were beginning to perceive that revolutionary change required a rupture with this equation, which meant, among other things being constantly on guard against received aesthetic formulas. The impression *P.M.* must have created at ICAIC was of a film that segmented social reality and evaded recognition that the screen belonged to the same reality as the scenes it portrayed, which thus indicted the film through its very absence.

For their part, the *Lunes* group (according to Wollaston) accused ICAIC of making "dreary socialist-realist stuff about *milicianos* and *alfabetizadores* [literacy teachers] that would convince nobody who was not already convinced." Even more cynically, it "allowed the importation of terrible Hollywood trash, Westerns and British epics about battling on the North-East Frontier that portrayed imperialists as heroes and Indians as worse than animals—a far cry from the ideals of the Cuban Revolution. Even some of the Russian and Polish films that were shown in Cuba were freer, more individualistic and subjective than *P.M.;* only the Chinese films were as dreary as the Institute's—and as Almendros said, who wanted to make films like the Chinese?"

There is never, on the part of the liberal apologists, any mention of the real problems of distribution that ICAIC faced. ICAIC, however, twice during this period conducted market investigations, and Alfredo Guevara reported their findings in *Cine Cubano:*

> During 1959, for example, 484 films were exhibited in Cuba, of which 266 were North American, 44 English, 24 French, 25 Italian, 2 Polish, 1 Brazilian, 1 Swedish, 8 Argentinian, 19 Spanish, 3 Japanese, 3 German, 79 Mexican, and 1 Soviet. The remaining 8 were Cuban, coproductions or films made in Cuba in previous years and premiered or exhibited during 1959.
>
> As can be seen, the bulk of exhibition remained in Hollywood hands and film industries under its influence....

More serious, however, is the character of the films that are shown. Out of the 484 films, 140 presented sentimental dramas and conflicts, generally of the quality of syrup and magazine serials, sometimes psychological in a visually spectacular way; 34 were war movies and 27 police, 43 westerns, and 92 action and adventure. . . . Average taste has been maltreated and certain overriding influences have created "habits" of cinema difficult to eradicate . . . the genres together with the star system predominate and their formulas amount to anticinema.[32]

The same displacement of cultural values, he continued, could be found in other media. The publishing market, for example, had its genres too: detective novels, which intellectuals delighted in; the *novela rosa* (pink novels) preferred by solitary ladies and leisured young señoritas; comics; and action novels full of Italian gangsters, Russian spies, African savages, Latin American adventurists, and treacherous Asiatics, and always, as the heroes, North Americans.

In the face of this culture of depravity, Guevara argued, the cinema needed new criteria, but they had to be realistically related to the conditions to be found among the audience. The public, he said, was divided between the popular and the exclusive. At one extreme lay the campesino masses, at the other, the extrarefined bourgeois minorities. "One was denied access to national culture and the other became estranged, indifferent, or antagonistic." But the Revolution had not only liberated campesinos and workers, he said, it had also liberated culture and the artists and intellectuals, liberated them from the prison of an exclusive and narrow public that was maimed and deformed in its taste, and from which it had sought escape in a search for eccentric originality and the repetition of all that was uttered in the great capitals of art. And indeed, the *Lunes* group, according to Ulive, was like a clan with its own enshrined idols and "an excessive urge to be up to date and if possible even ahead of the moment"; as another commentator put it, "a bit too exclusively preoccupied with beat poetry and the *nouveau roman*."[33] The divorce, says Pérez Sarduy, between them and their society had fostered a hypercritical attitude and a nonconformist intellectual rebelliousness with few roots in social reality. They were like the embodiment of the antihero of their hero Sartre—but lacking Sartre's perception. Typically unsure of their social position, too fearful to rise up yet too lucid to accept unreservedly the prevailing state of affairs, they judged their epoch while remaining outside it. Finding little outlet in the precarious and coercive world of publishing and the media under Batista, they had taken refuge in the café talk, cynicism, and satire of the déclassé intellectual, both spurned and nauseated by society. They did not see, when the Revolution came, what Sartre saw when he came to look at it, that this self-image of the intellectual is subverted by revolution—that it became, one might add, like the pterodactyl, which flew once, but was then condemned to extinction.

ICAIC, faced with disagreement at the Casa de las Américas meeting, proposed that *P.M.* be shown to an ordinary audience made up of assorted members of the revolutionary organizations, since that is what the supporters of the film argued that the people in it were. This, of course, annoyed the filmmakers even more; who asked, says Wollaston, what trade unionists or women knew about films. (One of the mass organizations was the Federation of Cuban Women.) Obviously, it said, such people would produce the verdict expected of them; and they went away to sulk and scheme again. ICAIC made a copy of the film for its archive and returned the original to the filmmakers with permission for public screening denied. (They showed it to Wollaston after all these events had taken place, privately, without legal offense, but in an atmosphere calculated to reinforce his own paranoiac suspicions.)

Rather than call this the Revolution's first act of film censorship, it is more enlightening to see it as the denouement of the incipient conflict between different political trends that lay beneath the surface during the period of the *aficionado* movement in the 1950s. The conflict brought the whole cultural sector to a boiling point, and clearly it was only resolvable through the intervention of the Revolution's maximum leader. A series of meetings was called that took place in the National Library on June 16, 23, and 30, 1961, with the participation of practically the whole intellectual and artistic community. Fidel and other revolutionary leaders attended, and his closing speech has become known as the "Words to the Intellectuals."[34] Although he had not seen the film himself, he approved the decision not to show it, for it was a question of upholding the right of a government body to exercise its function. But this was the least of what he had to say.

Carlos Franqui's account of these meetings is not a trustworthy memoir: it is scarred by general paranoia, and a marked personal hatred of Alfredo Guevara.[35] There is no denying that the meetings were highly charged, but Franqui's graphic picture of manipulation by a communist clique just does not square with a proper reading of the speech. Fidel began by apologizing for not attending to the issue sooner. Then, he identified the question at issue as fundamentally concerning "the problem of freedom for artistic creation." Distinguished visitors to Cuba, he said, including Sartre and the North American sociologist C. Wright Mills, had raised the question and he didn't doubt its importance. But the Cuban Revolution had been made in record time, it had not had time to hold its Yenan Conference, and accordingly he had a lot to learn himself; he did not presume to know more than others. Listening to the discussion, however, he had sometimes had the impression of dreaming a little because it seemed there were people there who thought the Revolution was over, it had won, and now it was going to asphyxiate them. He wanted to assure people that this fear was unfounded, the Revolution defended freedom, it had brought the country a very large sum of freedoms.

Then he went straight to the point. Everyone, he said, was in evident agreement in respecting freedom of form: "I believe there is no doubt about this problem." But over the question of content there were people who feared prohibitions, regulations, limitations, rules, and authorities. What could be the reason for this worry? It can only worry someone, he said, "who lacks confidence in his own art, who lacks confidence in his real capacity to create. And one can ask oneself if a true revolutionary, if an artist or intellectual who feels the Revolution and is confident that he is capable of serving the Revolution, can put this problem to himself; that is to say, if there is room for doubt on the part of the truly revolutionary writers and artists. I think not; the area of doubt exists for writers and artists who without being counter-revolutionaries do not feel themselves to be revolutionaries either. (Applause.)"

A remarkable formulation, politically impeccable because it outmaneuvered not only the liberals but also the revolutionary sectarians, the night-prowling tomcats mentioned by Fornet who still confused abstract art with the devil. This position of Fidel's was also ICAIC's. It also has an antecedent in the ideas of the manifesto *Towards a Free Revolutionary Art,* published in 1938 over the signatures of Diego Rivera and André Breton, which Trotsky had a hand in drafting: "True art is unable *not* to be revolutionary, *not* to aspire to a complete and radical reconstruction of society."

It was correct, said Fidel, for artists who were neither revolutionary nor counterrevolutionary to feel the Revolution as a problem. Only the dishonest and the mercenary found no problem in it and knew where their interests lay. But people who sincerely held a distinct philosophy from the Revolution, like proper Catholics, the Revolution had to respect. Its attitude toward them should be the same that it adopted toward all honest people who were not enemies of the Revolution. Thus he arrived at the much-repeated formula: "dentro de la Revolución todo; contra la Revolución, nada" (within the Revolution, everything; against it, nothing).

At the same time, Fidel defended the Consejo Nacional de Cultura (CNC—National Council of Culture), from which ICAIC was also under attack but from the left, for the CNC represented the old guard of the Communist Party whom the Young Communists of ICAIC had criticized during the Batista years. Partly addressing these Young Communists— his own comrades and contemporaries who had the unfortunate experience of having to exercise a cultural authority they did not believe ought to exist—Fidel said: "The existence of an authority in the cultural field doesn't mean there is any reason to worry about the abuse of this authority, because who is it that hopes this cultural authority should not exist? By the same count one could hope the Militia would not exist and not even the State itself, and if anyone is concerned so much that there should not exist the smallest state authority, well, there's no need to worry, have patience, the day will come when the State too will not exist. (Applause.)"

The aim of the Revolution, said Fidel, was to develop culture into the true heritage of the people; it was a struggle to create the conditions to be able to do this, but that was the CNC's job, just as it was also the job of other bodies the Revolution had created, like the Imprenta Nacional (national printing house) and ICAIC itself. Individuals had the responsibility to integrate themselves within these bodies. He did not want to propose any general rules about this: not all artistic production was of the same nature. But to do this couldn't possibly contradict anyone's artistic aspirations, as long as you suppose, said Fidel, that artists are trying to create for their own contemporaries. There can be no artists, he said, who just go around thinking about posterity, "because, in that case, without considering our judgment infallible, I think that whoever holds to this is a victim of self-delusion. (Applause.)" The same with the Revolution itself. We are not making it, he said, for the generations to come, but for now. Who would follow us otherwise? As for posterity, how would posterity judge the artist who lived through this epoch but remained outside it, did not form part of it, and did not express it?

Alluding to *Lunes* itself, Fidel allowed the need for a cultural magazine, but not that it should be in the hands of one particular group. Only one more issue of *Lunes* appeared. But arising from the discussions at these meetings, a new organization was created, the Unión de Escritores y Artistas de Cuba (UNEAC—Union of Cuban Writers and Artists). This was to be a professional-interests body rather than a trade union, and one of its first functions was to publish a journal, *La Gaceta de Cuba,* in which future cultural debates were to take place.

The confrontation over *P.M.* represents the most visible moment in the process of ideological "rupture" *(desgarramiento)* of which revolutionary intellectuals all over Latin America have spoken, "the famous 'ruptures' we intellectuals are so addicted to," as the Cuban poet and essayist Roberto Fernández Retamar once put it with affectionate irony.[36] The rupture is "an ideological conflict, a conflict of growth," which produces a crisis of self-confidence, but may be resolved in a sudden spurt of *concientización*—an untranslatable word: it derives from *conciencia,* which means both "conscience" and "consciousness"; hence, more or less, "conscience-stricken growth in consciousness or awareness."

The philosophy behind this concept has been lucidly developed by the Brazilian educationalist Paulo Freire. The rupture to which the artist or intellectual is subjected in the course of the revolutionary process is the seed of his or her translation from one social function to another, from the habits acquired under the regime of bourgeois values, through rejecting and refusing the political impotence these values imply, to a new self-image as a cultural worker. The rupture has many aspects. In the words of the Salvadoran poet Roque Dalton:

> In every rupture we intellectuals are accustomed to see first an ideological problem and then, always as a result of this, moral and sentimental problems. These resulting problems can only be resolved through the solution of the fundamental ideological conflict. In this sense, revolution is a constant challenge: its uninterrupted advance makes simple overall acceptance of its latest and most general principles insufficient, but requires permanent incorporation of its totalizing practice.[37]

The process brings on a crisis of individualism, which the whole weight of bourgeois ideology pushes the artist to defend; after all, the bourgeois myth of the artist was created around it. When this happens, those who resist the challenge are reduced to such things as making personal attacks against the conduct of those who respond to it. This is when they begin to make wild accusations of Stalinism and fascism.

Here, in Dalton's discourse, the key formulation—incorporation of a totalizing practice—corresponds to the concept of "revolution within the revolution"—not so much Trotsky's, however, as the version that Régis Debray developed around the ideas and example of Che Guevara. But let the final word on the subject go to Julio García Espinosa:

Lunes de Revolución... did not present itself as a simple alternative. It is undeniable that it ... did not represent a socialist option ... it is equally undeniable that one should not underestimate the individual talents of some of its members, and not out of unbridled admiration for artistic talent but from the firm conviction that here too was something that could contribute in some way to the the development of the Revolution. How should one struggle, then, against an opposition that at the same time should be regarded as an ally? What solution could there be? Could we think in terms of the traditional united front? But the experience we'd had of frontism was that it had been limited to bringing artists and intellectuals with an openly progressive attitude together, granted only an extremely wide and generous meaning to the concept. Besides, "revolutionary artist" and "party artist" had hardly ever meant the same thing. One could say that the only difference between a progressive artist and a party artist had been that the latter was more committed to essential party tasks and worked with more discipline at the immediate political objectives that the party defined. The difference was not owing to a more revolutionary concept of art. (And of life?) When the concept of socialist realism was raised, everyone broke out in uproar. If the united front, enmeshed in such ambiguities, was questionable under capitalism, what role could it play with a Revolution in power? Was the union of all revolutionary forces clearly and simply the unification of all progressive artists and intellectuals? The union of all revolutionary forces, yes, but under the direction of the Revolution's most advanced force. And among the progressive artists and intellectuals, who, at that moment, represented the most advanced current? The CNC, ICAIC, or *Lunes de Revolución*? If it is difficult to give a definite reply, politically we realized it was ICAIC, and fought against the tendency represented by *Lunes,* which was not directing itself toward socialism. Socialism, which in reality the Revolution had begun to define. The climax to the situation was produced by the Revolution itself. It did not deny *Lunes* members the right to continue as participants within the Revolution, but took away their opportunity of exercising cultural hegemony. The Revolution in this way established better conditions for different artistic tendencies to engage with each other on more equal terms. This was a correct, a revolutionary solution.[38]

With *Lunes* disbanded, the conditions ripened for the next episode of the cultural struggle, the struggle against sectarianism.

CHAPTER SEVEN

The First Feature Films

It was in 1960 that ICAIC made its first feature films. The first to be shown, at the end of the year, though it was completed second, was *Historias de la Revolución* (Stories of the Revolution), a film made up of three episodes directed by Tomás Gutiérrez Alea. Originally, it was intended to comprise four episodes, two by Alea and two by a director born in Spain and living in Mexico, José Miguel García Ascot, all four photographed by the Italian neorealist cinematographer Otello Martelli; Martelli's camera operator was the son of another leading Italian neorealist, Cesare Zavattini. García Ascot's episodes were later incorporated into another three-episode film, *Cuba '58*, released in 1962 with a final episode directed by Jorge Fraga, while Alea directed a third episode for the original film.

The first film to be completed by ICAIC had in fact been Julio García Espinosa's *Cuba baila* (Cuba dances). But *Cuba baila* had as its subject the prerevolutionary world of the middle bourgeoisie and it was felt that ICAIC should make its feature debut with a film about the revolutionary struggle itself. The three episodes of *Historias...* are *El herido* (The wounded man), *Rebeldes* (Rebels), and *La batalla de Santa Clara* (The battle of Santa Clara). These three stories, wrote Eduardo Heras León ten years later, offered the audience the chance of identifying with three key moments in the revolutionary struggle: the assault on the presidential palace mounted by the urban revolutionary group Directorio Revolucionario on March 13, 1957; the struggle of the guerrillas in the Sierra; and the final battle for liberation. However fragmentary the treatment, he said, the subjects themselves were enough to engage the audience. "We didn't think much at that time about the technique, about the shots, or the direction of the actors: that was secondary since the film reflected a truth, a living reality for all of us. We were anxious to relive the history that many of us had not been able to help make"—Heras León was eighteen years old when the film was first shown—"to allow the imagination fully to run its course and momentarily depersonalize us by recovering life on celluloid." "In a word," he continued,

> we wanted to feel heroes ourselves in some way—at least for an hour and a half—in order to satisfy our appetite for heroism and courage.... And naturally we were the wounded man in the first story, beaten but not defeated, as Hemingway said, and we were hurt terribly by the shot in the young rebel's leg during the assault on the palace, and suffered with him while searching for somewhere to hide ourselves; and we began to hate the petit bourgeois full of fear who ran away like a coward in order not to get involved. We felt not even a hint of sympathy for him, not even after he tried to change his attitude. Nor did we feel it was a pity when, victim of his own contradictions and fears, he fell into the hands of the police. We said, "The coward asked for it," and that was enough for us. It didn't interest us that the actors were a little artificial (sad reality about our film actors), that the characters were schematic ... that the director was clumsy in his use of the interior sets, and that, above all, the episode was lacking in what [Alejo] Carpentier calls contexts.... We were only interested in the hero and qualities of sacrifice; contexts merely rounded the story off.[1]

In the second story—which Alea based on an anecdote recounted to him by Che Guevara—they became the guerrillas in the Sierra. They decided not to abandon their wounded comrade even before the characters on the screen made the same decision. They felt the film was the clearest of lessons in the humanity of solidarity and again thought the movie was excellent. Yes, there were defects: it moved too slowly; the actors—even though they knew them to be actual rebels—were evidently self-conscious about being filmed. But these and other weaknesses did not obscure the efficacy of the message.

A viewing of the film today confirms that the original critical acclaim given in particular to the last episode was not undeserved. Shot on location in Santa Clara itself, the agile montage gives a clear overview of the course of the battle, all the more notable in that it does so with a minimum of dialogue. And again, according to Heras León, "The derailment

Filming *Historias de la Revolución*. Left to right: Tomás Gutiérrez Alea, Tomás Rodríguez, Che Guevara.

and the capture of the armed train, the scenes with the tank regiment, the fighters throwing Molotov cocktails left and right, the organization within the chaos of battle, the reception given to the heroes after the battle, and then the tragic finale—which demonstrated that the price of victory is always, above all, paid in human lives—illuminated those moments that get a little lost in legend." The tragic twist to the episode is the unfortunate death of one of these heroes, after the battle has been won, and unbeknownst to his compañera, who joins the funeral cortege amid the celebration of victory honoring the fallen fighter only to discover that the dead man is her own *compañero*.

The processes of audience identification in this film, however, continue to be basically the same as in the conventional war movie. At first sight, the final twist is no different from devices used in conventional war movies for purely sentimental effect, which, on the ideological plane, alienate the viewer's intelligence from the historical significance of the events portrayed. Normally, the film says, "This is the eternal, universal content of war," and pushes into the background the question of why *this* war, what *these* people are fighting for. And this isn't just the absence of contexts, it's the brazen rejection of context. But this is not what was happening for that audience of which Heras León was part. He says that the film seemed to them to have none of those scenes that, however full of emotion, the Cubans habitually found distant either in space or time, as in films of the Second World War, or even the assault on the Winter Palace in 1917, which was already enveloped in the fog of history. Here "it was our own image, our own history, our own day-to-day fact magnified by legend." In short, it was successful because a sense of immediacy linked the time and space on the screen with that of the audience in the cinema. This was a rare experience for the Cuban audience, and it didn't combat, but rather intensified, the regular process of naive audience identification that is associated with the kind of film ICAIC was committed to fighting against.

For the film is clearly conceived in as un-Hollywood a way as the Cubans could manage at that moment. The paradigm of Italian neorealism is present in its episodic form, a narrative structure introduced by Rossellini in *Paisà* of 1946, which was also shot by Martelli. Ironically, however, Martelli (as well as the inexperienced laboratory workers) failed to give the Cuban film the real quality of the neorealist image. By the late 1950s, Martelli's photographic style had changed, his lighting techniques had grown closer to Hollywood. The biggest problem was filming the interiors that dominate the film's first episode. They turn out rather flatly lit, perhaps the result of a misjudged compromise.

The appeal of the neorealist paradigm did not come about just because Alea and others had studied cinema in Rome in the early 1950s. There were certain parallels between the Cuban situation in 1959 and that of the birth of neorealism fifteen years earlier, though not, of course, in the political sphere. However, the Italians had needed to make a virtue of the lack of resources they suffered as they emerged from the war, just as the Cubans did in setting up a film industry in an underdeveloped country going through a revolution. And then the kind of movie both groups of filmmakers were seeking to counter was closely similar. Both had suffered the domination of Hollywood. The Italians had decided to take their cameras out into the immediate photogenic real world in order to counter the fanciful studio space of the "white telephone" film, the Italian fascist equivalent of the Latin American melodrama.

Revolutionary cinema, or a radical cinema in a critical situation, as in Italy just after the defeat of the fascists, has always involved the discovery of a new screen space to unfold in, which transcends the spatial (and sociospatial) character of whatever cinema it aims to replace. It aims to show the world changing, and the need for change; it must change the way the world looks on the screen in order to do so. One of the most strongly determining factors in the character of Italian neorealism was the starkness of the immediate photogenic world at the end of the war.

As time passed, the neorealists became committed to portraying the indifference of the republic that replaced the transitional government, and suffocated people's hopes and aspirations. If these developments created a very different situation from that of revolutionary Cuba, the ideas behind the neorealist aesthetic were far from theoretically innocent or naive. The Centro Sperimentale, founded in the mid-1930s, had been a forum for theoretical as well as practical instruction. Italian fascism was culturally more sophisticated than Nazism; futurism was as much an aesthetic of Italian fascism in the 1920s as of the Russian Revolution, and in the 1930s Italian fascism considered that there was much to learn in the art of propaganda from the communists. At the Centro Sperimentale, an independent-minded man like Umberto Barbaro was able to translate the writings on cinema of Eisenstein, Pudovkin, Béla Balázs, and others.

It was Barbaro who gave the neorealist movement its name. He used the term to evoke the realism of early, prefascist Italian cinema, not as a model to be imitated directly but to support a conviction that all humanistic art demanded realism. Barbaro and other neorealists greatly admired Soviet revolutionary cinema, but felt it was hardly an appropriate model to be adopted in attempting the renovation of Italian cinema. Its sophisticated style of montage depended on an audience, which even in revolutionary Russia had been limited, geared up to a new kind of imaginative participation in the film, a condition that certainly did not exist in Italy at the end of the war, where it had been lulled by two decades of screen escapism. They did not reject Soviet montage as nonrealist like the influential French critic André Bazin (but then Bazin was an inveterate idealist, in the mold of the French Catholic intelligentsia). They regarded it as inapplicable for conjunctural reasons: because it was culturally and historically alien. Barbaro himself argued that montage was the fundamental creative dimension of cinema—the fact that whatever the style of shooting, the film was still constructed by means of editing—and for him the neorealist idea was not intended to negate this but to constitute a particular way of providing the material upon which montage operated. By dialectical reasoning, this meant that neorealist montage could not adopt the same appearance, the same rhythms and tempi, as Soviet montage. These arguments were appealing to the Cubans, who had limited knowledge but unbounded admiration of the early Soviet classics, but, like the Italians, could not imagine, in the Cuban context, simply trying to copy them.

In addition to going out onto the forbidden streets, and into real locations and real houses, it was also part of neorealist practice to find "natural" actors instead of professionals. It was partly a matter of what might be called aesthetic opportunism. Location sound recording was still at that time physically cumbersome, and severely restricted the mobility of the camera, which the neorealists prized above all else because it enabled them not simply to picture the external reality, but also to move through it, to become part of it, as if they belonged there. "Natural" nonprofessional actors would improve the effect since they would more easily behave as if they belonged to the spaces in which the film was unfolding—because in large part (not always) that is indeed where they did belong. Professionals were too accustomed to the artificial spaces of studio and stage; nor at that time did they have the facility to represent the popular classes with conviction. The same was true in Cuba. In Italy, they were used only to dub the voices of the nonprofessionals afterwards. This was partly to provide the films with standard Italian pronunciation and avoid the difficulties of introducing regional accents. It was also a necessity imposed by the constraints of the times: to have postsynchronized the voices of the nonprofessionals themselves, as the Cubans did in *El Megano* in 1956, would have required too many expensive dubbing sessions; this was not a problem for the Cubans because *El Megano* was made clandestinely, with borrowed facilities and without commercial budgeting. But the Italian audience was, in any case, used to dubbing: the fascists had required all foreign films to be dubbed rather than subtitled—it made censorship easier and guaranteed a certain regular flow of work to the dubbing studios.

As Italian neorealism developed, the films the Italians made confirmed that certain themes have a particular affinity with certain kinds of space, and the entry of the camera into new spaces it had not previously been allowed to enter permitted new subjects to be conceived and new kinds of narrative treatment to be evolved. It became easier to break with the conventions of melodrama, with literary influences, with the specifically cinematic trickery of devices like the flashback, and the deceptions of

the techniques of suspense. Stories could be developed out of the anecdotes of everyday existence, and narrated by a camera moving with unobtrusive ease among the characters and places of the film, obeying the
natural rhythms and order of the events. When the Cubans adopted the
neorealist paradigm, there was no need for them to use it to expose continuing deprivation and official indifference, for here the government was
a revolutionary one. But the neorealist aesthetic still contained many elements that were readily transferable—above all, those that brought to
the screen the real social world outside the cinema dream palace.

Even at the beginning, however, the Cubans did not treat neorealism as
an exclusive doctrine. While employing nonprofessional actors, for example, they also searched out professionals to whom they could entrust
a good proportion of the lead parts. This wasn't just because they
weren't dogmatic, but because they were also thoroughly pragmatic. If
appropriate professionals could be found, their experience could help
others—including the crew, so many of whom were total beginners.
Moreover, in this way, ICAIC could begin to build up a team of actors, a
company of sorts, which is always in one form or another an integral
part of a thriving cinema. What chance otherwise of creating a Cuban
school of dramatic film art?

   Not only that. If *Historias de la Revolución* is clearly conceived in the
neorealist tradition, García Espinosa's *Cuba baila* is in certain respects
clearly not; for *Cuba baila* is an attempt to exorcise the Latin American
melodrama, not by seeking radical alternatives but by taking its conventions and turning them around. From this point of view, it has little
to do with neorealism except in the way certain scenes were shot. The
film was born of what is to become for García Espinosa a perennial
concern, that of using a form with which the audience is thoroughly
familiar, in order to take them through its surface illusions to the social
reality it has conventionally been used to mask. Not too didactically,
however, for, according to the criteria he later elaborated in his concept
of "imperfect cinema," a film still has to entertain. In the end, it is a
question of overcoming the opposition between notions of didacticism
and notions of entertainment.

   The main originality of *Cuba baila* lies in its treatment of music. When
he first conceived it before the Revolution, he thought of it as a kind of
Cuban musical but with a difference: where the Latin American musical

used music for purposes of evasion, here it would fulfill a dramatic function by becoming a vehicle for the class analysis of the pseudorepublic. He had not been able to find the backing for such a film before the Revolution, even after he had reworked the film with Cesare Zavattini when the neorealist master had visited Cuba. But ICAIC readily undertook its production and the script was reworked another time by García Espinosa, Alfredo Guevara, and Manuel Barbachano Ponce. Visually undistinguished, even plain, the image is nonetheless given another dimension by the music: the film works upon the characteristics of the social spaces, public, private, or semipublic, in which the different pieces of music that occur in the film are played and heard. Of course, it may well have been neorealism that made García Espinosa sensitive to this way of sensing space.

The premise of the film is that while music, of all the popular art forms, had sustained the strongest vigor, it was no less susceptible for that to the uses that bourgeois ideology found in it. The story concerns the family of a minor functionary in which the daughter is about to celebrate *los quince,* the fifteenth birthday, which is traditionally the occasion for a big family fiesta, which, the higher up the social scale you go, becomes more of a social coming-out party, a girl's launching onto the marriage market. The film moves through all the social spaces that make up the world of such a family, together or separately: from the home to the father's office, through bars and streets and other public areas and into the exclusive milieu of the fiesta hosted by the father's boss for his own daughter's fifteenth birthday.

The mother of the protagonist family is keenly aware of the importance the music at her daughter's fiesta will play. Although the cost is almost prohibitive, she wants an orchestra like the one that impresses them as minor guests among the upper bourgeoisie. Musically, such an orchestra means the Viennese waltz and North American hits, instead of the popular Cuban dances preferred by the daughter herself and her local boyfriend, whom her mother slights. To obtain a loan to pay for it, the father has to ingratiate himself with his superiors at the office by attending a political meeting in a local square. A band is employed to attract the public, but the politicians cannot hold the crowd; vociferous heckling rains down on them and, much to the petty bureaucrat's consternation, the meeting breaks up in violent disorder. In contrast, the passengers on a bus whistle together a popular tune with politically different

Cuba baila (Julio García Espinosa, 1960)

overtones. Here the film comes close to suggesting a different paradigm to neorealism, that of the French Popular Front films of the 1930s, where songs and dancing also play an important and positive role in portraying the social cohesion of the popular classes.

The parents' plan for a posh party fails to materialize. In the end, and much to the daughter's satisfaction, everyone is forced to go off and celebrate the fiesta in a popular open-air entertainment garden where, although the family's socially superior guests condescend to attend, the mother feels defrauded. The satire in this last scene is gentle but leaves no room for doubt about the hypocrisy of bourgeois values, as the camera watches the awkwardness with which the condescending guests dance to the popular music, while the daughter and her boyfriend mix unselfconsciously with the crowd.

The film has shown how the natural social functions of music—including the way it expresses and creates social cohesion—become corrupted when it is made to conform to corrupt or discreditable social ends. It offers a portrait of the prerevolutionary Cuban bourgeoisie that superficially conforms to the format of the family melodrama but, more deeply, through its careful use of music, mocks the stupidity of bourgeois convention. Perhaps the film's most surprising aspect is how much re-mains implicit, especially in comparison with the French Popular Front movies of the 1930s. It has none of the propagandizing socialist content of films like Renoir's *Le Crime de M. Lange,* even though one might ex-pect more rather than less in a film by a revolutionary filmmaker in the euphoria just after victory.

It was in his second feature, *El joven rebelde* (The young rebel), made the following year, that, as Ugo Ulive put it, García Espinosa paid his debt to neorealism. The film has an original script by Zavattini, reworked by José Massip, J. Hernández Artigas, Héctor García Mesa, and García Espinosa himself, and the story is that of a seventeen-year-old peasant boy, Pedro, who leaves his family to join the guerrillas in the Sierra.

First, however, he needs to find himself a gun of some sort, the new recruit's passport. Together with a friend, he sets off to steal a revolver from the friend's uncle. But the plan misfires, and the friend is sent home again.

Out on the open road, Pedro gets a ride from a wily old peasant who understands full well that the youngster is aiming not, as he claims, to get a job on a coffee plantation but to join *los barbudos*—the bearded fighters in the hills. At a village where soldiers are stopping and search-ing anyone they suspect of carrying supplies to the guerrillas, the old peasant covers for Pedro. On his own again, the boy enters a bar where he grabs the opportunity to steal a soldier's rifle. The soldier gives chase across the fields and corners him. Pedro fires and the soldier is wounded. The camera lingers on Pedro's face, his eyes alight with a mixture of anxiety and pride at his first unexpected shot at the enemy.

His arrival at the rebel camp, where the troop drills with pieces of wood for guns, brings with it his first set of lessons. To start with, the small girl serving as lookout who brought him into the camp turns out to be a boy. The surprise hardly has time to sink in when the rifle he brought is taken away from him because, he is told, it belongs not to him but to the Revolution. His attempt to resist the loss of what is obvi-ously the proudest possession he has ever had produces his third quick lesson in succession: a new figure appears to resolve the problem, Artemisa, a figure of evident authority—and he's black. Although feel-ing humiliated, Pedro sumbits. We soon begin to realize that the very obstinacy that brought Pedro to the Sierra is to cause him problems, as he tries to evade the guerrilla school by claiming to be able to read already. But, in a gently ironic scene following an air attack, his ignorance is exposed by his failure to read the inscription on an unexploded bomb: "Mutual Aid USA."

Then Pedro is sent on an expedition to the coast to steal salt from the salt pans. He dawdles on the way to talk with a young girl washing clothes at a pool. An understandable slackness of discipline, it is also a moment of characteristically Cuban nature symbolism: as the girl asks Pedro to bring her a seashell on the way back, the promise of the sea is associated with a sense of erotic anticipation. At the salt pans, the utmost discipline is needed in order to break cover as soon as the clouds hide the moon, reach the salt, fill the sacks, and retire again before the moon reappears. Pedro works fast and then puts down his sack and steals off to the shoreline to search for a shell. He has never seen the sea before and he pauses, looking at it with absorbed fascination. Only as the moon reemerges does he remember the need for haste, and rushes to pick up his temporarily abandoned sack. Too late, for he has been spotted, and shots ring out. His comrades watch helplessly from the wood, which he finally reaches in safety after a zigzag run pursued by machine-gun fire. The scene is directed with impressive restraint, dominated by long shots and a rhythm that corresponds to the slow tempo of the movement of the clouds across the sky. The visually arresting location—the strange dim white of the salt pans—does the rest. It enjoins us to share Pedro's feeling of magic at the seashore while also letting us sense the danger of his dalliance.

Conventional techniques of suspense reduce the conflict of contradictory perceptions to a unidimensional forward pressure with an artificial climax, because narrative convention normally assures us of the outcome in advance. But here the peculiar calmness of the scene gives rise to more complex responses. Given to experience a clash of emotions each of which is positive, we end up understanding the boy far better, and his situation more fully: the way his youthful, naive, and so far frustrated appetite for experience is precisely what gives him the self-possession he needed to join the rebels, and how it may lead at times to pride or indiscipline.

The rest of the film is devoted to showing how the guerrilla ethic knows this and is ready to tame it tenderly and constructively. During the return to the camp, just before the expedition is caught in an un-expected air attack, one of the recruits, Campechuelo, complains of hunger. In the rain the next morning, the group passes the village where the girl who asked Pedro for the seashell lives. The village has been bombed overnight, the inhabitants are leaving, and when Pedro finally finds the girl departing with her family, they are able only to exchange silent looks, as he reaches into his sack for the gift. Back at camp Pedro is still unruly enough that he has to be reprimanded for uttering a racist insult and picking a fight when he volunteers for a dangerous mule-train escort but is passed over for being too inexperienced. When the mule train arrives, it is carrying the body of the comrade Pedro fought with, who died after a fall into a ravine.

Next morning the camp is summoned to an inquiry: during the return of the salt expedition a cheese ration was stolen. The *compañero* is asked to confess but after a silent pause the comandante conducting the inquiry is forced to name him: Campechuelo. Pedro is thunderstruck. Artemisa, prosecuting, asks for punishment according to the regulations. "Within a few hours," he says, "we shall be fighting against an army equipped with tanks, heavy artillery, and planes. What do we have? We have the trust that exists among ourselves." Turning to Campechuelo, he contin-ues, "Now you're suffering, but before you lied. Everyone trusted you and you lied. Can you be trusted now? It's easy to say 'I'm with the Revo-lution' but do you know what the word means? It signifies everything changing, beginning with ourselves. You're the same as before. Cuba has a great many things . . . sugar, tobacco, coffee, it's a rich country—with a poor people, because there are thieves, big thieves. How can you judge them if you steal the ration from your comrades?" Campechuelo is duly punished, on the eve of a battle that the camp is informed Fidel has said will be decisive, by expulsion from the Rebel Army. As he is called to prepare for battle, Pedro protests to Artemisa. Artemisa's face shows that he comprehends Pedro's confusion, and he does no more than quietly order him to leave the humiliated Campechuelo and join the others. The film ends in mid-battle, with Pedro taking over the ma-chine gun at which Artemisa has been killed, and we recall Artemisa's last words to Pedro before the battle: "Now you'll earn your gun."

Heras León recalled the film's original impression; the youthful audi-ence felt themselves to be the undisciplined youth, stubborn in the face of orders, anarchic and naive, whose desire to fight justified all his actions, all his rebelliousness and incomprehension. . . . Again, the technique didn't worry us. Of course, we would have preferred the youngster to have a more expressive face, not so hard, not so withdrawn, especially in the last scene in which his consciousness is awakened and changes from a young rebel into a revolutionary soldier; we would have preferred if Isabel, the naive peasant girl, had had an attitude less like that of an underdeveloped Silvana Mangano; that García Espinosa, the director, had taken care that the photography captured the Cuban countryside with greater veracity; that Pedro had shot the drunken soldier with greater decision; and finally that the last scene hadn't been so much like *La patrulla de Bataan* by reason of its long close-up on Blas Mora's face.

"La patrulla de Bataan" was *Bataan,* starring Robert Taylor, George Murphy, and Lloyd Nolan, directed in 1943 by Tay Garnett—a Cuban favorite.

Not all these criticisms are equally valid. To criticize Pedro's indecision in shooting the soldier he stole the rifle from, for instance, betrays idealistic impatience in the viewer—it is, in fact, a scene both effectively mounted and acted. But then this idealism of the film's first viewers was an extension of Pedro's on the screen.

At the same time, there are some subtle and significant symbolic shifts and parallels in the final sections of the film that may well have escaped them. In his determination to keep his promise and bring the seashell, Pedro demonstrates an essentially generous spirit, which contrasts with Campechuelo's meanness in stealing the cheese ration—all the more so because in the midst of the destruction of the village the symbolic meaning of the seashell changes: it becomes less a sentimental gift than a metaphor for the promise of victory. But then Pedro insults a man and picks a fight and then feels irrationally guilty when the man he fought with dies an accidental death. Complexities like these give the film its most paradoxical and didactic quality: that it is a film about heroism that is antiheroic, a film about fighting that is antimilitaristic. To recall that the young rebel is a peasant, and to recognize in the film its projection of the peasant character as a paradigm of the spirit in whose name the Revolution was undertaken—the untutored appetite for experience, impetuous but generous—this is to grasp why and in what sense it has been claimed that the Cuban Revolution is not militarist, in spite of its guns and uniforms. *El joven rebelde* is not a paean to the military insti-tution, and not at all about strategies and tactics, but about the ethical education of a *guerrillero*.

The other fiction film of 1961 was Óscar Torres's *Realengo 18*, a modest picture of sixty minutes (though *El joven rebelde* is only eighty-three). The title of the film refers to one of the ownerless tracts of land that dispossessed peasants used to settle, and the film deals with an incident during the Communist-led popular rebellion of the mid-1930s. It takes place in the sierra in eastern Cuba in which the guerrillas later estab-lished their principal liberated zone. The story is one of division within a family. After his father has been shot dead, and against his mother's wishes, the son, in need of a job, joins the local guard. When a North American sugar company decides it wants the village lands, he ends up having to point a gun at the people of his own village with his staunchly defiant mother one of the leaders. The story has a Brechtian simplicity to it; the handling of the camera is unfortunately rather stiff and con-ventional. Its achievement is that it successfully applies a neorealist approach to a historical subject by using nonprofessional actors who included survivors of the events portrayed—one of Latin American cinema's first attempts to do this.

With one major exception—Alea's *Cumbite* of 1964—this is really, from a practical point of view, as far as the heritage of neorealism reaches in Cuban cinema. But this exception is a remarkable one. *Cumbite* is not only ICAIC's last neorealist picture, it is also visually the most striking: its stark black-and-white photography creates a feeling of tropical country-side better than ever before; there is an absence of background music; the narrative has the form of chronological anecdote; it is told with slow, deliberate pace to give time for the patient observation of everyday ac-tivities. Like *Realengo 18*, it employs neorealism in representing a histor-ical period, but this time the film is fictional: based on Jacques Romain's novel *Les Gouverneurs de la Rosée*, it takes place in 1942, and tells about the return of a Haitian, Manuel, to his home village after fifteen years in Cuba. It is the first of a number of Cuban films about Haiti, all of them made with the participation of the Haitian community in Cuba.

Manuel's years in Cuba have given him a knowledge of the world, enough at least to make him critical of the fatalism of the Haitian peasant, product of the fate of the Haitian Revolution, its ossification into a static society and a repressive dictatorship. Returning to his village, he finds the villagers facing the problems of drought. "If water doesn't fall from the sky," one of them tells him, "there's no water. We are wretched negroes." "It is the lack of the negro," Manuel tells his mother, "not of the good Lord." He knows they can find water and build an irrigation system. He tries to explain to the villagers, "Look, we are the earth, without us it is nothing." Many are uneasy with his challenge and regard him as an interfering outsider; they take rancor at his liaison with one of the village girls, Analaisa. This sentimental subplot Alea handles with the greatest restraint.

Manuel's scheme requires a *cumbite,* a general assembly of the village, because it requires collective labor and, moreover, Manuel wants the water to be collective property. Some of his opponents declare his proposals illegal and call him a subversive. Then he is killed in a fatal nighttime attack by his rival as Analaisa's suitor. On his deathbed he tells his mother that Analaisa knows where there's a water source—they discovered it together—and his death shocks the village into realizing the benefits the scheme will bring.

Cumbite, according to a group of Venezuelan critics in 1971, a bit harshly I think,

> is characterized by its extreme sobriety. Nothing protrudes, the story is fine, the actors well cast, the images plastic, the narrative advances in spite of everything. But perhaps it's too sober. Incorporated in the film are some sequences showing voodoo ceremonies. They are treated with an almost anthropological vision, with tremendous respect, the gratuitously picturesque is at all costs avoided, but in this way it seems to lose all its force, all intensity in the expressiveness that is worked into the material. The result is a film that is correct but removed, that succeeds neither in stirring, nor surprising, nor convincing, nor entertaining. The exploration by Cuban cinema of a world not its own remains a hybrid experience and apparently without perspective.[2]

Perhaps, since Venezuela has its own black culture, its own versions of voodoo, these critics are more sensitive to the representation of these things than a European eye, but it is still important to say that the film has its own integrity, and a sense of authenticity that is guaranteed not only by the participation of the Cuban Haitians but also by the way the camera watches their ceremonies, without any trace of voyeurism, but moving around with considerable fluidity. It is this fluidity with the camera that is to become one of Alea's distinctive capacities as a director and an important stylistic trend in Cuban cinema.

In any event, the film has several layers of significance, among them the allegorical. It is a film of solidarity with the Haitian peasant and a lesson in revolutionary ethics and the practice of collectivism. But it is also a film about the cultural complexity of underdeveloped society and its internal contradictions, for the collective spirit that Manuel seeks to mobilize is already present in the traditions of the *cumbite*—and in the form of the religious ceremonial. It is not a film that views these things schematically, or from a position of, as it were, higher revolutionary wisdom. It takes up an aspect of Fidel Castro's thinking that is both characteristic and essential to its revolutionary style: the refusal of the sectarian idea that only the purest proletarian elements in the society are capable of correct revolutionary action. This would be to deny the capacity to learn, which is common to every human being, a capacity that in Paulo Freire's idea of cultural action for freedom is recognized as a powerful social force.[3]

Finally, there is a stylistic paradox, for in *Cumbite* neorealism becomes a kind of farewell to the past. The rapid progress of the Revolution has already, by the time this film was made, created a distance from the conditions only five years earlier. As Alea has recalled:

> When we began to make films in a post-revolutionary situation the neorealist mode of approaching reality was very useful to us because in that early stage we needed little more. First of all, we were not developed enough as film-makers to posit other approaches. Secondly, our own national situation at that juncture was ... very clear. All we had to do was to set up a camera in the street and we were able to capture a reality that was spectacular in and of itself.... That kind of film-making was perfectly valid for that particular historical moment.
>
> But our revolution also began to undergo a process of change. Though certainly not the same as that which occurred in post-war Italy, the meaning of external events began to become less obvious ... more profound. That process forced us to adopt an analytical attitude towards the reality which surrounded us. A greater discipline, a much more exact theoretical criterion was then required of us in order to be able properly to analyse and interpret what we were living through.[4]

The theoretical criterion that Alea invokes here is not a particular theory of film or style, but the application to all theoretical and stylistic principles of the new way of thinking that was now established in Cuba, revolutionary Marxism—in a Cuban way, of course.

Before *Cumbite,* Alea had revealed another side of his creative personality in his first comedy, *Las doce sillas* of 1962. This is an adaptation to the Cuban Revolution of the comic novel of the early years of the Soviet Revolution by Ilf and Petrov, which was also put on the screen by Mel Brooks in the United States (*The Twelve Chairs,* 1970)—the story has that kind of crazy comedy. A masterful comedy auteur in the true Hollywood tradition that goes back to Chaplin and Mack Sennet, Brooks made a very serviceable job of it, but with the difference that he did it as a period piece, whereas Alea does it as a contemporary satire on the world immediately outside the studio. The story concerns the hunt by Hipólito, the scion of a bourgeois family, and his rascally sidekick and erstwhile servant Óscar, for a suite of English period chairs, in one of which Hipolito's dying mother-in-law has hidden the family jewels. This piece of information she delivers at the start of the tale from her deathbed, when the chairs are no longer in the family's possession, and there then follows an increasingly desperate and hopeless pursuit in which Hipólito and Óscar compete against the family priest who administered the last rites for the old woman and has hit the trail on his own. The chairs are among property confiscated by the Revolutionary Government, to be sold at auction; Óscar helps Hipólito raise the necessary money to bid—he presents him to a secret meeting as a counterrevolutionary in need of funds—but things go awry at the auction, and the chairs go to a variety of buyers. Several are sold to a circus, where one is used by a lion tamer—until the lion tears it to pieces in a typical scene, Hipólito and Óscar watching in desperate impotence for fear of the jewels falling out right there in front of the audience. When they finally track down the last chair, which was bought by the railway workers' union, they find them already celebrating the good fortune of their windfall.

Unexpectedly, Alea had the idea for this film before the Revolution, when it wasn't possible to make it. Now it was not only more apt, but the Revolution itself provided the elements of the setting, beginning with the film's Ministry of Recuperation in charge of confiscated property. Sets of initials of official organizations keep cropping up in the film— real ones, INRA, ICP, ICAP, INDER, even ICAIC itself. Then there's the whole ambience of conspiracy, the private settling of accounts within the unsettled bourgeoisie at the moment of its dissolution, the activities of the counterrevolutionaries, the treasures hidden in secret places and—as Alea himself points out—the possibility of making a film about such things. It is an imaginative adaptation, in which neorealist techniques assist the incorporation of the real environment within the inevitable stylization of the comedy form. It gives a kind of guided tour of the new society. The conspirators, at one point, unwittingly hitch a lift on a lorry taking volunteers to the fields to cut cane; at another they track down one of the chairs to a blood-donor center where they find the militiaman on duty sitting on it. Both master and servant find this new society topsy-turvy and it upturns their own relationship too. They argue about how to divide the spoils when they find the diamonds: Óscar protests that he is only trying to help his erstwhile master but if Hipólito doesn't want his help he, Óscar, will go and find the chairs by himself. Hipólito objects, "Just a moment—remember, those diamonds are mine!" To which Óscar responds: "Are you still insisting on private property?"

Alea employs a variety of techniques, including documentary insert and intertitles. He also cuts in quick shots that do not advance the narrative but simply provide additional comic sideswipes. A newspaper seller, for example, passes by announcing the latest news—the publication of *Don Quixote*. There are certain bits of satire, however, directly aimed at a rather particular target. At the beginning of the film there's an interpolated newsreel sequence—it parodies ICAIC's own newsreels, which have not yet fully escaped the old formulas: "ICAIC Social Notes... More hidden treasures found—vanity and selfishness revealed"; and the commentator intoning, "The dark interests of the past maintained our people in ignorance in order to exploit them..." At the end of the film, the target is a different branch of official art. Hipólito and Oscar arrive at the Railway Workers' Social Institute to find a mural painter describing to the workers the mural he's going to paint for them—they have commissioned him with some of the money they got for the jewels. He describes a tableau picturing the forces of the Revolution against the forces of imperialism in the style of socialist realism. The workers, listening to his highfalutin ideas, conclude that he is a bit crazy.

It was in the course of making this film that Alea and his crew discovered how rapidly the changes wrought by the Revolution were taking place: "The Revolution implies a fundamental change in the structure of society," he said, "but the appearance of things also changes from day to day. A billboard announcing a luxury hotel in Miami and inviting Cubans to spend their vacation there is substituted by another which declares Cuba a territory free of illiteracy. Suddenly, where a large mansion previously housed counts or marquesses, there is now an art school; where Cadillacs used to be sold, now they sell furniture for workers who have been given houses by the Urban Reform. When we arrived to film a lonely vantage point over a valley we found a large hotel built by the Tourist Institute full of tourists. Inside a building where we had gone to shoot a number of scenes we found walls erected and walls demolished, a new arrangement of furniture and bricklayers at work everywhere, which obliged us to change our plans and to hurry the filming through because of the danger that even during shooting they would transform the scene around us. I think that the general rhythm of the film to some extent reflects the vertigo of the Revolution."[5]

CHAPTER EIGHT

Beyond Neorealism

In an interview he gave to a Peruvian film magazine toward the end of the 1960s, Julio García Espinosa spoke of the way the rapid development of the Revolution took Cuban filmmakers beyond neorealism. Even those who had made *El Megano*, he said, who had been imprisoned and gone to work in clandestinity for the overthrow of Batista's government, had believed that they were preparing only for a multiclass government with the participation of leftists alongside the bourgeoisie, and with a national program. Nobody thought at first the outcome would actually be a socialist government—even if that is what they had dedicated themselves to work for. Neorealism they saw as the model for an appropriate cinema—a humanist and progressive aesthetic that offered a real alternative to the dominant modes of Hollywood and Latin American commercial production. An antidictatorial nationalist bourgeoisie could not have objected to it; it was a style that placed the people on the screen as historical actors, but without being too explicit about it. But the rapid radicalization of the Revolution demonstrated that there was both room and need for a cinema to go further than this: straightforward neorealist ideas could not really catch the speed and depth of revolutionary change, though what kind of cinema could do this was not yet obvious, and would not emerge for some years.

Alfredo Guevara wrote of neorealism in the first issue of ICAIC's film journal *Cine Cubano* as only one among several options.[1] There was also another film movement on the horizon that was to exert its influence in Cuba, the French New Wave. Although yet to reach its peak, it had already been named, and Alfredo Guevara was able to mention in this article the names of some of those linked to it: Molinaro, Malle, Vadim, and Chabrol, and also that Simone de Beauvoir described the New Wave directors as "anarchists of the right." Nevertheless, he suggested, they offered an interesting and valid lesson: they represented a cinema both youthful and inexpensive, a cinema without stars (substantially true at the time), a cinema that aimed to be rebellious. It was a cinema of protest, aesthetically nonconformist, innovatory and iconoclast, ready to confront "respectable" values and discard them without hesitation. There was clean, fresh air in the work of the New Wave directors. Sometimes, it was true, they played games with Hollywood formulas, transformed bedroom drama into sexual poetry, or indulged in shallow philosophy and amateur psychology, all of which amounted to little more than rebellion from the armchair or the bed. But some of their films hit the target of a genuinely new cinema: François Truffaut's *Les Quatre cents coups*, Alain Resnais's *Hiroshima, mon amour*. Most important, these were new directors who showed no fear of the technology and technicalities of cinema.

The demise of the Francophile *Lunes* group in 1961 did not mean that the influence of the French New Wave was to be curbed within ICAIC. It could be said that, on the contrary, with the establishment of new critical criteria the field was clear only now for its influence to be critically absorbed. And, in fact, we find, over the next few years, a group of short fictional films clearly influenced by the *nouvelle vague,* by a clutch of apprentice directors who were subsequently to be internationally acclaimed for their very differently styled feature films, including Humberto Solás, Manuel Octavio Gómez, Manuel Pérez, and Sergio Giral. None of these films is more than an apprentice work, but they are not without interest. Sergio Giral, reminded of *La jaula* (The cage), which he made in 1964, recalls it as "rather too much influenced by Godard."[2] It tells of a woman suffering from a paranoid psychosis. The story is told first from the husband's point of view and then from that of the patient. Tomás Gutiérrez Alea plays the psychiatrist. *Minerva traduce el mar* (Minerva interprets the sea, 1962) has the distinction of being the only film on which the poet José Lezama Lima ever collaborated, contributing the hermetic verses heard on the sound track while a pair of ballet dancers perform at the edge of the sea around a bust of Minerva.

Solás, who was barely twenty years old when he made this film with Óscar Valdés as codirector, laughs at it now as a naive experiment.[3] A year later, he and Valdés made another mysterious short, *El retrato* (The portrait), about a painter seeking inspiration by pursuing an imaginary woman whose image he finds on a portrait in an abandoned house, a tale that clearly reveals (the only thing about it that *is* clear) that good intentions are not enough to banish fascination with ancient myths about the sources of creativity. Then, in 1965, this time by himself, Solás directed *El acoso* (The pursuit). This time the subject is less obscure. An escaped mercenary from the defeated invasion of the Bay of Pigs kills a man in the countryside, takes his clothes, comes upon a cabin where he rapes the woman he finds there alone, and finally wanders lost and helpless across endless mudflats. The film is primarily a stylistic exercise, but this time by a student who has gained self-confidence in the handling of the craft. Refusing the technique of crosscutting that constitutes the conventional chase movie, and with an almost static camera, Solás still builds up an atmosphere of tension and menace, especially inside the cabin after the rape.

These fictional shorts—about a dozen were made altogether, several dealing with episodes from the guerrilla war—were originally intended to be combined into feature-length films made up of separate and unconnected episodes. Apart from *Cuba '58*, no such film was ever released. In a couple of cases, the episodes were not released at all. *Elena*, directed by Fernando Villaverde, and *El final* (The ending), directed by Fausto Canel, both proved problematic. Ugo Ulive quotes someone saying that *Elena* was "so absurd that it was unprojectable." Failures were inevitable if the policy was to let untried filmmakers experiment.

The problem, in the effort to build a film industry from scratch, was how to train the personnel. As Alea wrote about filming *Las doce sillas:*

> The main collaborators during the filming were young, without much previous experience. The director of photography, the camera operator, the focus-puller and the camera assistants were all working on a feature film for the first time. Similarly the assistant director and the continuity girl. Even the film we were using (Agfa NP20 and Ultrarapid) presented problems which hadn't been technically resolved by our cameramen.
>
> We wanted to launch out with a crew of new people in whom we had hope. Fortunately the lighting technicians, carpenters and production

team included compañeros who were old hands and highly disciplined, which gave us relative peace of mind, even though they also had apprentices engaged in this work for the first time. Perhaps not everything would go well. We had accumulated too many risks in the key positions and this at times prevented our always proceeding smoothly.[4]

Largely to help deal with this problem of training, ICAIC followed the development of the Revolution in looking toward the socialist countries for assistance, and the years 1962–64 saw three coproductions, one each with the Soviet Union, East Germany (GDR), and Czechoslovakia. In each case, the coproducing country supplied not only the director but other principal personnel too. From the GDR, Kurt Maetzig directed *Preludio 11* (Prelude 11). Wolfgang Schreyer wrote the script with José Soler Puig, a story about counterrevolutionaries in the service of the CIA making preparations for the Bay of Pigs. The director of photography and the editor were also Germans. A team of Czechs came to make *Para quién baila La Habana* (For whom Havana dances), directed by Vladimir Cech, with a script by Jan Prochazka and Onelio Jorge Cardoso, and again a Czech director of photography and editor, this time sharing credits with Cubans. The story concerned the different paths taken after the victory of the Revolution by two friends who had fought the dictatorship together, one of whom now found that his personal interests were challenged by the new social order. Finally, Mikhail Kalatozov (director of *The Cranes Are Flying*) directed *Soy Cuba* (I am Cuba) with a script by Yevgeny Yevtushenko and Enrique Pineda Barnet, and a Russian director of photography and editor. This was a film of four episodes showing different aspects of life in Cuba before the Revolution. It was the most ambitious of these coproductions, and ICAIC knew enough about Soviet production practices with their lengthy and leisurely shooting schedules to prevail upon its comrades to bring their own transport and equipment, so as not to tie up ICAIC's limited facilities and halt its other productions; by informal arrangement, the equipment was then left behind in Cuba when they finished.[5] None of these films was very successful. The Czech film grafted its plot onto a superficial and picturesque vision of Carnival in Havana; the German one was a miscalculated action movie; and the Soviet effort was a kind of "delirium for the camera" from an impossibly baroque screenplay—the description is Ulive's, but no one in Cuba thought much of these films either.

The truth is that while it made sense for ICAIC to undertake these co-productions for both artistic and material reasons, the foreign visitors didn't do their homework properly—not even Yevtushenko, who was especially enthusiastic. Still, even he was unable to get beneath the skin and go beyond the traveler's image of the island that Soviet revolutionary poetry inherited from Mayakovsky's visit in the 1920s.

The truth is that the visiting filmmakers were no better equipped to respond to the expressive needs of the Cuban Revolution than the engineers of their countries to the need for projectors to be used in a tropical climate. This was the kind of problem that cropped up continually with the aid that Cuba received from the socialist countries. Many were the disruptions caused by the wrench that the country's fixed productive forces underwent as the U.S. blockade took effect, and technicians and engineers of another breed stepped into the breach. ICAIC's experience was entirely typical. Most of the cinemas were in terrible condition, the projection gear was old and decrepit, and the previous managers had relied on the readily available supply of spare parts. As U.S. trade investigators had reported years before, most of the equipment was purchased secondhand in the first place. Now it urgently needed maintenance and replacement. The Institute conducted a technical survey and discovered that it had inherited seventy different types of projector—a real nightmare. It made a count of the most common types and sent samples of the basic set of spare parts to its East European partners so that they could make molds from them and stave off disaster. It found, when the new parts arrived and were installed, that they were not correctly engineered for tropical conditions, and they buckled in the heat.

It is true, of course, that these coproductions may also have served a political purpose by helping to take the edge off sectarian criticisms of ICAIC. Fidel himself directly addressed the problem of sectarianism in the strongest terms in the spring of 1962, when he declared in a television broadcast that "the suppression of ideas was a myopic, sectarian, stupid, and warped conception of Marxism that could change the Revolution into a tyranny. And that is not revolution!" The occasion was his denunciation of the behavior of Aníbal Escalante and others working through the Organizaciones Revolucionarias Integradas (Integrated Revolutionary Organizations [ORI]), which had been set up in 1961 with the object of integrating the old Communist Party, the July 26th Movement, and the Directorio Revolucionario (the group that carried out the attack pictured in the first episode of *Historias de la Revolución*).

García Espinosa has described the behavior of the sectarians vividly: their dogmatism, their rigidity in the face of the problem of creating socialism, their rejection of the principle of armed struggle by the national liberation movements in Latin America. These failings, he said, became well known. They also, he continues, had the effect of undermining the militancy that came from comradeship, the process of discussion with those who were still without direction, and the attempt to stick to principles and avoid personal attacks. They made popular participation, he said, almost impossible. The sectarians had an absolute distrust of artists and intellectuals, whom they regarded as an irremediable evil that they hoped would go away with time, to be controlled by means of sops and small concessions. They placed their faith in training up new generations, replacing their own tutelage for the inspiration of the revolutionary process itself. They attacked cultural policies that, through mobilizing this inspiration, aimed to raise the level of ideological struggle against inherited cultural tendencies and trends.[6]

ICAIC leveled serious arguments against sectarian ideas as they affected cultural politics, beginning with an address by Alfredo Guevara to the First National Cultural Congress in which he criticized the orthodox positions of the National Council for Culture (CNC) under Edith García Buchacha. His point of departure was Fidel's "Words to the Intellectuals" and the claim that art could not exist in Cuba outside the Revolution, which was itself a creative phenomenon of the highest order and the only possible source of artistic innovation. He insisted, however, that the endeavor of the artist was autonomous. For example, it has educational values but its purpose is not educational. ICAIC therefore believed that "if a 'revolutionary' message is required of the creator of a work of art, in the same way as of a political speech or a philosophical essay, then only one thing will be accomplished: the spiritual assassination of the creator, the asphyxiation of art in an oxygen tent." In the light of the short fiction films they were producing, he was obviously here defending the need for a space in which the young directors could freely experiment in order to find their feet.

He did more than defend, however. He launched a critique of populism. Artists were being confused, he said, by "theoretical propaganda and pseudocultural phraseology" that tried to persuade them that the way to reach the superior level of the people was to reduce the substance of the work of art. Such falsely proletarian ideas could only breed the crudest propaganda and demagogy, and then a primitive kind of art would invade the most inappropriate places, which working people would either overvalue or ridicule. "This mechanical concept of the working masses' rise to culture will thus produce not the elevation of the intellectual level but its debasement and disintegration. This is the origin of the wave of bad taste that is washing over the country and that is no way inherent in socialist development." The problem was a set of erroneous, facile, and routine ideas to be found within the cultural organizations, including the National Council of Culture, the Union of Writers and Artists (UNEAC), and ICAIC itself. "Up to now these organizations have not known how to say 'No!' publicly and openly to this ridiculous cartel, to the absurd murals that have invaded workplaces and centers of social and cultural life, to the useless papering of each wall, column, and window, many times to the concealment or deterioration of true national momuments and sites, simply in order to meet numerical goals rather than for the sake of political effectiveness."[7]

As chance would have it, ICAIC was given an opportunity to take up battle not just with images on screens but on the streets as well. The haphazard process of confiscation and nationalization gave it possession of a commercial graphics studio for making silk-screen posters. Saúl Yelín, son of an immigrant Jewish family and one of the most imaginative of ICAIC's production staff, immediately saw the possibility of ICAIC going to work to produce its own cinema posters. It would be possible in this way to invade the streets and link the battle against commercial art and the aesthetic trash of the Hollywood poster with the struggle against the cartel of bad taste. ICAIC would not only put its posters up outside the cinemas but would erect poster stands all over the city, in squares and on corners. To design the posters, it would call on individual artists who, individualistic or not, wanted to be part of the process but didn't know how, because they had too much integrity for the methods of the cartel.

In this way, ICAIC became the midwife of an unprecedented artistic explosion, and the Cuban revolutionary poster was born. Painters who until then must have wondered what their fate would be, perhaps because their style was abstract and avant-garde, were now drawn into the cultural process without having to compromise their aesthetic ideals. As a Latin American observer, Néstor García Canclini, has written:

> Artists used to painting canvases who move into this new form of production have to subordinate, but not necessarily abandon, their taste, emotional states, and desires to the collective message that is to be transmitted. Good poster art, such as the Cuban or the Polish, does not demand that the artist renounce personal style or experimentation, because the message becomes more effective when, instead of being direct and singular, it exhibits a certain tension between affirmation and suggestion, and the clarity the message must have for its reception, and the economy, condensation, and ambiguities that provoke the interest of the receiver. What the good poster requires is that the personal and formal search should be at the service of the object of communication. Instead of the narcissistic complacency over individual language that belongs to easel painting, the poster and the mural bring participation in the decoration of the urban landscape, and in the formation of popular taste and imagination.[8]

The new poster style rapidly began to drive the cartel out of business. From a formal point of view, it was sometimes reminiscent of the revolutionary Soviet poster before the institution of socialist realism. It not only introduced colorful new images, it had a playful typographical style, a direct response to the popular experience of the literacy campaign of 1961. As UNESCO was able to confirm, the campaign, in the space of a year, reduced an illiteracy rate running in the countryside at up to 43 percent, to a level of 3 or 4 percent, which is normal in developed countries. The creative effects of the campaign in expanding the print market and stimulating cultural consumption were contagious, and the new poster expressed this in the animation it seemed to impart to the written word, using imaginative plastic design combined with the utmost economy of means. The style was quickly taken up by other organizations with a need for imaginative propaganda, and gave a good number of artists much-needed economic employment. It also provided them with spiritual sustenance, linking them with the revolutionary process through their own productivity. This process brought their aesthetic ideas closer to the popular viewer so that they could return to the creation of more formal works without having to retreat into isolation. The effect that all this had on the cultural image of the Revolution is neatly captured in a story told by Ernesto Cardenal in the diary of his Cuban visit in 1970.

The painter Portocarrero showed him a photograph of the large ceramic mural of his in the presidential palace. "He told me that some delegates from Russia or one of the Eastern European countries at a reception asked Fidel, with a certain tone of sarcasm, 'And what does this mean?' (meaning 'and what does this have to do with the Revolution?'). Fidel replied, 'Nothing, it doesn't mean anything. It's just some crazy thing painted for some people who like crazy things of this kind, by a crazy person who was commissioned by the crazy men who made this Revolution.'"[9] Certainly, by all accounts, Fidel is no connoisseur of art; but he is also reported to have said to someone who demanded an end to abstract painting (Khrushchev had just publicly condemned it): "The enemy is imperialism, not abstract art."[10]

The debate was soon taken up with energy. Julio García Espinosa formulated a number of urgent questions on aesthetic matters in an article in *La Gaceta de Cuba*, the publication of the Union of Writers and Artists, in April 1963. The filmmakers then met for three days' discussion in July and published their conclusions as a document in the *Gaceta* in August. The *Gaceta* was the successor to *Lunes de Revolución*. It did not achieve the same circulation but it was not the "run-of-the-mill" publication lacking in originality claimed by K. S. Karol.[11] The same issue that carried this document also included articles on James Joyce's *Ulysses*; on Braque and the art of collage (the latter by Clement Greenberg); and an announcement that the Union's library had acquired six hundred musical scores, including contemporary works by Stockhausen, Webern, Berg, Schoenberg, Bartók, Boulez, Eisler, Nono, Birtwistle, Haubenstock-Ramati, Shostakovich, Pousseur, Messiaen, and others.

The filmmakers' manifesto had twenty-nine signatories. Not quite everyone, but the overwhelming majority. It was a forthright document that declared that while it was both the right and the duty of the state to promote cultural development, aesthetic tendencies and ideas are always in a state of conflict with each other and it is mistaken to try to impose solutions. Moreover, the relationship between bourgeois and proletarian culture is not exclusively antagonistic (as Lenin had pointed out) and "the obvious fact that a liberal bourgeois like Thomas Mann is a better writer than Marxist-Leninist Dmitir Furmanov shows that a specifically aesthetic criterion exists that cannot be reduced to the ideological position of the writers." Art cannot be reduced to its external determinants and formal categories have no class character. Therefore it is to be concluded that in the battle between aesthetic ideas, suppression on the grounds that certain forms have an undesirable class character restricts the evolution of art by restricting the struggle between the ideas themselves.

Theoretically, the argument is not without contradictions, so that when it was reprinted in *Cine Cubano* a couple of months later, Alfredo Guevara pointed out that the editors of the magazine had certain reservations about it, but they did subscribe to its conclusions and gave full support to its signatories' moral intentions.[12] For the manifesto had given rise to heated debate. Edith García Buchacha wrote a reply in the *Gaceta,* other articles appeared in *Cuba socialista* and the Communist Party newspaper *Hoy,* and the filmmakers were invited to a debate at the University of Havana. In November, the *Gaceta* published responses by Alea and García Espinosa.[13] They both emphasized that the document had achieved its purpose by stimulating all this discussion. Alea said he didn't agree with every one of its points but with its antidogmatic spirit, and he criticized certain professors who insisted that the real enemy was idealism, not dogmatism, because (they said) at least the dogmatists were on the right side. To the professors, the artists were suffering from the "original sin" of belonging to the bourgeoisie. But, as the writer Lisandro Otero had pointed out, said Alea, so did Marx, Engels, and Lenin.

García Espinosa, on the role of the party, admitted that its reaction to the threat the dogmatists represented had been too mechanical. But he went on to discuss the artist's relationship to the audience in a way that completely exposed the dogmatists' populist myths. The issue has been poorly represented in previous accounts of these episodes. The dogmatists, says Michèle Firk, in a passage that Ulive quotes as if it summed it all up perfectly well, tell the filmmakers, "The Revolution has generously given you the chance to make films. What have you given in return?" The filmmaker answers, "The Revolution has only fulfilled its duty; I am an artist." The dogmatists say, "Go to the people." The artist responds, "Let the people come to me."[14] But this is not a very intelligent way to represent the argument and has little to do with García Espinosa's position. Until now, he said, the only thing that has been insisted on is that the artist should have more contact with the people and its problems. This is correct, but it isn't enough. The people also need to have more contact with art *and with the problems of the artist.* The public is neither a monster nor an ignorant mass, as the reactionary and the decadent artist both see it, but neither is it a new species that has to be fed only with predigested foods, as the dogmatists seem to believe. It is capable of errors of judgment. It can be misled, for example, into accepting a concept of productivity in art that it is false and mechanical to attempt to apply.

This example, casually introduced, is cardinal. It puts the issue firmly in the most rigorous Marxist terms: the question is about the production and consumption of art, and in particular about the labor process of the artistic worker. The Mexican philosopher Adolfo Sánchez Vásquez has examined this question in an essay titled "Art as Concrete Labour," in which he shows that the quantification of aesthetic labor by means of its reduction to the same criteria as regular labor under normal conditions of production is of no use in evaluating the work of the artist. Why? Because the value of a work of art is determined by qualitative, not quantitative, characteristics. To apply a common quantitative denominator to artistic production can only lead in practice to a standardization of aesthetic creation, the mechanical reproduction of repetitive formulas that are totally incompatible with the creative character of the imagination.[15] This is precisely what Alfredo Guevara had spoken out against at the 1962 Cultural Congress. The disquiet of the filmmakers with the dogmatism of the sectarians was thus rather different from that of the liberals of the *Lunes* group, and went far beyond abstract notions of creative inspiration and freedom, just as it also went beyond a simple attack on socialist realism as a stylistic norm. The ICAIC critique of socialist realism was not just that it constituted a culturally alien style, but that it resulted from an inadequate conceptualization of the conditions of production in art.

For ICAIC, this was a practical, not a theoretical, issue. But in Cuban revolutionary praxis, the two were very close, and the issue was part of a theoretical debate on the nature of labor in a socialist society, a debate that invigorated the Cuban Revolution and is closely linked with the name of Che Guevara. So the filmmakers thought hard about their labor process, and the question of how the film crew should be organized in a socialist society, in order to overcome the alienation of the capitalist mode of film production, and to release not just individual, but also collective, creativity. Julio García Espinosa spoke about this in a particularly appropriate place—the Chilean cultural magazine *Primer Plano* in 1972.[16] ICAIC's advantage, he said, was having the endorsement of a revolution, that is, of knowing that it was working not for an exploiter but for the country. It was helpful to them that they were mostly young and new to the medium, although there were also a few older people, mostly technicians, accustomed to capitalist relations of production, with its overtime payments and the rest. Overtime was one of the first problems ICAIC tackled, because it induced people to work slowly to earn more money, and thereby damaged the collective. It instituted instead a system of bonus payments for completing the work schedule *(plan de trabajo)*. This indeed fostered a more collective attitude toward material reward. But it was only the first stage, because the next was the debate about moral incentives that Che stimulated.

Collective discussion produced concrete improvements to the labor process. For example, ICAIC discussed the case of the director who used time arbitrarily, who came along and asked the construction department for a wall to be built for the next day's shoot, and after they had worked all night, he used only a small part of it in the shots he devised. So, to find more effective and economical methods of working, ICAIC tried to develop a method of participation. It defended the prerogatives of creative imagination, but required discipline in its application. The result was to help overcome the problems of divided labor, because it also required the members of the different departments in the film crew to relate their specialisms to parallel problems in other departments, which in regular capitalist film production are often kept separate.

To meet the principles of collective participation, ICAIC evolved a managerial system in which, while decisions were made by a directorate whose members have various collective and individual responsibilities, these decisions were based on collective discussion. In 1983, the year after Julio García Espinosa succeeded Alfredo Guevara as head of ICAIC, one of the directorate, Jorge Fraga, for some years head of production, explained to a group of visitors from Britain some of the ways collective discussion in the Institute works: "We don't plan anything without first having a collective debate with the directors, cameramen and everyone else involved. We base our planning on their consensus. If we are increasing production, notwithstanding the kind of restrictions we have, it's because in the last year we've made an agreement to make cheaper films in order to do more."[17] In the same way, the pursuit of related themes in a series of films by different directors over the same period, like those on the hundred years of struggle that were made in the late 1960s, was the result not of some kind of directive but of collective discussion, and the consensual feeling that there is more to be gained by making films that support each other than by films that in their choice of theme remain isolated.

Individually, the selection of films is based on treatments, or scripts in the case of fiction, submitted by directors (or for first films, which are always documentaries, by members belonging to other grades) to the head of the appropriate department. Ideas are discussed, and advisers may be called in, who are drawn from among the directors or scriptwriters with most experience. Among the benefits of this system, directors are always at work and earning their salaries, a necessary provision when resources are limited and only a few films can be shot at the same time. This way, you are either working on your own script, on the basis of an agreed proposal, or else you are working with someone else on theirs. Each project goes through several stages, from synopsis to treatment to script, which aids the process of planning and organization. It also helps to stimulate discussion, Fraga said, because there is no cutting away at final results, which is the role of a censor: "If you work in the process from the start you're more constructive, you're part of it, trying to stimulate and seek solutions."[18] Alea has also spoken of the importance of the role of the adviser in this process. Trying to explain why the North American film critic Andrew Sarris was way off the mark in certain comments he'd made, he told Julianne Burton: "For me, this work is just as important as my own personal achievements. I firmly believe in our collective work. In order not to appear saintly, like some extraterrestrial being removed from all personal interest, let me explain: in order to satisfy my individual needs as a director, I need the existence of Cuban cinema. In order to discover my own concerns, I need the existence of the whole Cuban film movement. Otherwise, my work might appear as a kind of 'accident' within a certain artistic tendency. Under such circumstances, one might enjoy a certain degree of recognition, but without really achieving the level of personal realization to which you aspire. This isn't a question of personal success, but rather of the conviction that you're giving all you can in an environment where everyone, without exception, has the same possibility."[19]

Behind the introduction of a system of participation in ICAIC, there lies an undogmatic analysis of the relations of production in the film industry. Fraga again:

Well, as everybody knows, cinema is a collective art. Even in Hollywood it's a collective art, and this is based on a division of labour. So the main question is how this collective is organised and how the individualities play within this collective. We don't have a norm to determine the way that the individuals and the collective are interlinked. It is different with different directors and different people, but in general terms there is a consensus, and the consensus is that art is a very personal process, whether it is an individual or a collective art, and the collective spirit and discussion involved in the various stages of film production cannot replace the role of the personality. We are collectivists because we think that the growth of the personality needs a basic requirement: a collective sense of responsibility.

ICAIC combined collective discussion with improvisation. It had to compete with numerous other organizations for scarce resources. The national building and construction program, for instance, did not allow ICAIC as many new cinemas as it would have liked. It would quietly deliver additional architectural plans, however, in the hope that some-one else would miss the deadline. Such initiatives didn't always succeed. On one occasion, in need of specialist technicians, Alfredo Guevara enlisted the help of his brother, a psychology professor, to carry out an investigation to find the year's best technical graduates. They were in-vited to join ICAIC but failed to turn up. It turned out that the list had fallen into the hands of Fidel, who commended his friend's initiative in organizing the investigation but told him, "I'm sorry, you can't have these people, we haven't got such highly qualified applicants for the sugar industry, we need them there!"[20] It was typical of the way Fidel inter-vened in questions of the allocation of resources, human and material, about which there are many stories. (His detractors use them as evi-dence of dictatorial behavior.)

A major part of ICAIC's work during this period, however, to which resources were systematically devoted, was the organization of a new Cinemateca, which began in 1961 under Héctor García Mesa. Of the old one, nothing remained but the files with its program leaflets in them. The new Cinemateca was intended, from the outset, to be much more than an archive of Cuban and world cinema, with its own auditorium. Its activities were to extend throughout the island. It was to establish film theaters in other cities where the Havana programs could also be presented, it was to be responsible for the mobile cinema units, and it was to service and advise the film clubs. It was to succor an active film culture, from which eventually new filmmakers would emerge, just as the generation of ICAIC's founders had emerged from the film-club movement of the 1950s.

In Havana, the Cinemateca took charge of programming the new cinema that was attached to ICAIC's headquarters—an office block in the bourgeois district of Vedado, originally occupied by dentists and doctors. The Institute started out occupying the building's fifth floor but soon took over the rest, remodeled the auditorium next door, and later overflowed into other neighboring buildings. The Cinemateca opened its doors in 1961 with a season of Soviet classics of the 1920s to the 1940s, provided by its Soviet counterpart Gosfilmofond, the first time such a comprehensive retrospective had ever been shown in Cuba. There followed other national cinema seasons, from Czechoslovakia, Germany, France, and Italy, as well as a world cinema retrospective supplied by the International Federation of Film Societies.

It was an immense task the Cinemateca faced, to generate popular comprehension and preference for a completely different kind of film than audiences were used to. It was compounded by the switch that inevitably occurred when the United States imposed its blockade, and the familiar Hollywood product was replaced by a sudden influx of films from the USSR and the other socialist countries. There was, to begin with, no great liking for them. For one thing, when these countries first began to send their films to Cuba, there were no effective arrangements for their selection. No one in Cuba knew enough about the cinema of these countries to be able to make such a selection, nor did anyone in these countries know very much about Cuba and Cuban audiences. Films were sent—and they had to be shown, because new films were at a premium—that were clearly inappropriate. Perhaps it was not a rich period for socialist cinema and too many poor films got through, but they were mostly disliked because they were too different. How should an audience brought up under the narrowest Hollywood tutelage be able to respond spontaneously to films from such different cultures, with such distinct styles and symbolic systems?

ICAIC did its best to leaven the diet with films from nonsocialist Europe, where cinema in the 1960s was undergoing a true renaissance. Not that these European films were by any means always easier to access, but ICAIC believed passionately in aesthetic pluralism, in the conviction that the only way for audiences to become more discerning was to have the opportunity and encouragement to see as many different kinds of film as possible. The result of this exhibition policy was renewed attack from sectarian quarters. Early in 1964, the U.S. trade journal *Variety* (February 12, 1964) gloated ungrammatically:

"La Dolce Vita" Stirs Tain't Wholesome

Several years late, Federico Fellini's *La Dolce Vita* is stirring a number of lively debates in Castro's Cuba and adding immeasurably to the artistic excitement in that tight (control) little island. According to a report from Havana, by Maurice Halperin, published in the Jan. 9 issue of the *National Guardian* [a small-circulation left-wing weekly that was sympathetic to the Cuban Revolution] the Fellini pic started an "ideological brawl" when *Hoy,* the official organ of the United Party of the Socialist Revolution, editorialized that the pic could not be considered wholesome entertainment for the Cuban working class.

Immediately, 10 directors of the official Cinema Institute jumped to the film's defense in the newspaper *Revolución.* They charged that *Hoy's* position was like that of the Catholic Church (Ed. note: In the us, the Roman Catholic Legion of Decency gave the Fellini film a "separate classification" meaning "morally unobjectionable for adults, with reservations") and like the "Hollywood Hays Code." *Hoy's* position, reported Halperin further, "was pronounced a 'deformation of Marxist-Leninist philosophy.'"

No one in Cuba, he goes on, denies the need for the state to control the production or purchase of films because of the lack of foreign exchange. "The problem is the criteria by which the films to be bought or produced are selected, and in the socialist world, value judgments can be poles apart, as in the case of China or Poland or in different periods of Soviet cinema history...

"The current movie flare up is part of a general and continuing debate on art and society in which nearly all of the artists and writers who embraced the revolution had always had free access to the competing aesthetic currents of the whole world."

Halperin reports that the entire Cuban movie scene began perking in 1963 "after a year of movie drought during which people lined up to see beat-up American films pulled out of the archives while Bulgarian, Czech and Chinese features played in empty houses."

Last year films began coming into Cuba from Italy, France, Japan, Britain, Spain, Argentina and Mexico. "For the sophisticated moviegoer 1963 was undoubtedly a banner year in Havana. In addition to *La Dolce Vita,* films which were released included Buñuel's *Viridiana* and *The Exterminating Angel,* Wajda's *Ashes and Diamonds,* Kurosawa's *The Brave One* and Richardson's *The Loneliness of the Long Distance Runner.*"

The original piece in *Hoy* (December 12, 1963) was by a senior-ranking Communist, Blas Roca, in his regular ideological question-and-answer column. The ICAIC directors referred to by *Variety* replied in *Revolución,* where they compared Roca's position to the Hays Code and the Catholic List. Alfredo Guevara wrote his own withering reply in *Hoy* itself. "To men like you," he wrote, "the public is made up of babies in need of a wet-nurse who will feed them with ideological pap, highly sterilized, and cooked in accordance with the recipes of socialist realism" (December 17, 1963). K. S. Karol comments on the episode in a footnote: "Alfredo Guevara's use of such strong language could only mean that he enjoyed the support of Fidel Castro, his old university friend."[21] But there is nothing fishy in this: anyone can draw this conclusion from what Fidel said in the "Words to the Intellectuals"; only Blas Roca hadn't done so.

All along, ICAIC encouraged the development of every strand of promise it discovered, an attitude that entailed the Institute's tolerance toward aesthetic risk, experiment, and failure which Alfredo Guevara publicly argued for. The growing pains were only expectable. For a short period they were numerous, and the films mentioned earlier by Canel and Villaverde were not the only casualties. However, both these directors went on, like others who failed in some of their attempts, to be entrusted with full-length feature films (Eduardo Manet, for example, whose first feature project in 1961 hadn't even reached shooting). Few of these pictures were successful. Ulive modestly omits any reference in his article to his own feature, *Crónica cubana* (Cuban chronicle), made in 1963, a story that attempted to show the changes that the construction of a new society involves, which the commentators Torres and Pérez Estremera describe as simplistic. *El otro Cristóbal* (The other Christopher), directed in the same year by the Frenchman Armand Gatti, they describe as a pretentious satire on Latin American dictatorships suffering too much from a European vision of its theme.[22]

This film was never given a release in Cuba, though it was shown in France with modest success. Eduardo Manet made *Tránsito* (Traffic) in 1964; Ulive describes it as "a poor imitation of the insouciance of Godard's early films." Manet's second feature, *Un día en el solar* (A day in the tenement, 1965), he calls "a hybrid whose least disappointing moments revealed a fruitless attempt to imitate the musical comedies of

Stanley Donen"—the film added dialogue and songs to a ballet by Cuba's leading choreographer, Alberto Alonso. Fausto Canel also made two features. The first, *Desarraigo* (Uprooted, 1965), concerns an Argentinian engineer who comes to Cuba with the intention of incorporating himself into the work of constructing the new society, but his romantic and touristic idea of the Revolution impedes him. Its treatment, says Ulive, was "hasty, superficial, pseudomodern" and the film was a fiasco. Canel's second attempt, *Papeles son papeles* (Paper is paper, 1966), a comedy on the theme of dollar smuggling by counterrevolutionaries during the early years of the Revolution, was not much better. Jorge Fraga also made two features, following the episode he contributed to *Cuba 58. En días como éstos* (In days like these, 1964) was based on a novel about the life of voluntary teachers in the countryside and the effects of the experience on a girl of bourgeois extraction. He followed this in 1965 with a theatrical adaptation, *El robo* (The robbery), dealing with a provincial petit bourgeois family during the period of Batista's dictatorship. Fraga himself considers neither of these films to merit attention.[23] The first of them was pretty aggressively representative of a stylistic modernity inspired by new European "art" films that many critics found hard to take. García Espinosa later mentioned the film as an example of the pugnacity of the young directors "who were trying to find an equivalent in the cinema of the modernity that the Revolution signified politically." Raúl Molina in the *Gaceta de Cuba* compared it unfavorably with the two documentaries on closely related themes that Fraga had made previously, *La montaña nos une* (The mountains unite us) and *Me hice maestro* (I became a teacher). The feature was too schematic, he said, in comparison with the power of observation in the documentaries.[24] The criticism is highly significant.

The most unfortunate case was that of Villaverde's *El mar* (The sea). The script, says Ulive, could have been made to work in the hands of a self-confident director, but the film had to be aborted at the last moment when it only remained to make the show print—a costly mistake that was also "the most drastic measure taken against any film in the entire history of Cuba cinema." Villaverde, he says, was thrown into deep personal crisis, and shortly afterwards left Cuba with no intention of returning. Villaverde was neither the first (that was Néstor Almendros) nor the last director to leave ICAIC and Cuba. Canel, Alberto Roldán, Robert Fandiño, the cinematographer Ramón Suárez, Manet have all left. (Almendros was by far the most successful of them, though as a cinematographer, not a director.) They all made films that were not exhibited, but they were not the only ones, and others, including José Massip and Manuel Octavio Gómez, chose to remain (or rather, it didn't cross their minds to go).

Both Massip and Gómez made promising feature debuts in these years, with *La decisión* (The decision, 1965) and *La salación* (The saltings, 1966), respectively. Both films possess considerable fluidity though the control of the director is in neither case complete. Curiously, they suggest as models not the French New Wave but the English. At any rate, in spite of the different luminosity of the air south of the Straits of Florida and north of the English Channel, their black-and-white photography by Jorge Haydu and Jorge Herrerra, respectively, is reminiscent of films like *The Loneliness of the Long Distance Runner* and *A Taste of Honey*. Moreover, in both the narrative style is rather less florid than in the new French films, more calmly paced, as in the English, and the acting quieter. Both films also have this in common, that they center on young couples whose partners come from different social classes, with the consequent disapproval of both their families.

La decisión, which is set shortly before the Revolution, opens in a classroom at the University of Santiago de Cuba during a lecture on classical Greek society, a subject ironically contrasted with the tensions and political differences among the students. Daisy Granados makes her screen debut as María, an artistically rather than intellectually inclined daughter of a bourgeois family that disapproves of her liaison with Pablo, the best student in the class and a mulatto from a poor background, the nephew of a slave—"the son of a son without a father," as he describes himself. Their relationship is an awkward one, due to Pablo's pride— the pride of someone who knows that the social order is refusing to give him his due: his color bars him from getting the university teaching post his academic achievements qualify him for. Pablo is his mother's favorite, and has an uneasy relationship with his brother, who works in the factory managed by María's father, where he is active in the struggle for union recognition. In spite of his experience of racial discrimination, Pablo cannot accept his brother's militancy and the argument for revolutionary violence. Through these and other contrasts, the narrative traces a series of structural oppositions—between black and white, worker and student, bourgeois and working-class, male and female, struggle and fatalism, mother and daughter/mother and son, high culture and popular culture—by means of crosscutting between different levels of the plot in different scenes of action. Probably the thing is too schematic, but it comes to a fine, heady climax with the contrast between the popular Carnival and the masked ball of high society that Pablo gate-crashes in disguise, till his identity is discovered and he is forced to flee. Carnival in Santiago is Cuba's Mardi Gras, but it also carries political associations as the day of the attack on the Moncada barracks in Santiago in 1953, after which the July 26th Movement is named, chosen by Fidel in the first place because on this day the whole population is busy singing and dancing in the streets (or high-society masked balls). It here becomes an effective symbol for the popular forces that alone are capable of guaranteeing justice.

La salación deals with a pair of young lovers in the early years of the Revolution harassed by the prejudices of bourgeois morality on the one hand, working-class pride on the other. The girl's is a petit bourgeois family not unlike that of *Cuba baila,* the boy's is working-class. He is reluctant to get married because with his father dead he has to keep his mother and two younger brothers on a mechanic's wage. Visually stylish, a particularly memorable sequence shows the couple meeting in a large North American–style house that stands abandoned by its former owners. Evocative photography follows them entering as the rain pours down outside. Thunder and echoing footsteps intensify the atmosphere. The couple are drawn into this cavernous Freudian space where they seek refuge in order to make love, but which makes them feel distinctly uncomfortable at the same time. The tension they feel is at the heart of the film: the way in which the heritage of the physical environment, shaped by the social relations of the past, interferes with the realization of desire, and in the most immediate ways. Like García Espinosa in *Cuba baila,* Manuel Octavio Gómez has a keen sense of the social significance of different spaces. This large, empty house is contrasted with the crowded environment of the family apartment where the couple have to retreat onto the tiny balcony to gain even a minimal amount of privacy, while behind them the family argues over the volume of the radio and TV sets that different people have on in different rooms. This observation of social space—and the mapping onto it of the relationships among the family members, including mothers, cousins, aunts—lifts the rather coy love story out of the dissociation from social reality in which the cinematic genres generally leave such couples. The film shows how the personal preoccupations of young lovers do not disappear in a revolution, and what the social problems of the country look like from their point of view. It has its limitations as a first feature—its style is borrowed rather than thought out—but the intelligence of its social observation combined with its personal concerns is sufficient indication of the breadth of sympathies that ICAIC was cultivating. It is also a memorable film for another screen debut: that of Idalia Anreus in the role of the boy's mother.

CHAPTER NINE

The Documentary in the Revolution

The historical moment of the Cuban Revolution was also, by coincidence, a period of aesthetic revolution in documentary cinema. Within the space of a few years, 16 mm, previously regarded as a substandard format like 8 mm or half-inch video today, was relaunched. Technical developments, inspired by the needs of space technology as well as television, stimulated the production of high-quality 16 mm cameras light enough to be raised on the shoulder and in due course equipped with fast lenses and film stocks that reduced or even eliminated the need for lighting. They ran quietly and could be matched with portable tape recorders fitted with improved microphones, directional if need be, on which a synchronous sound track could be recorded by a sound recordist as mobile as the camera operator—though until the improvement of the system, they moved around together, since they were linked by cords. The result was that documentarists who had previously been forced to shoot with bulky 35 mm equipment completely unsuitable for flexible filming away from a studio or prepared location felt as if reborn. New-style documentary filmmakers sprang up on both sides of the Atlantic. Thus the terms *cinéma vérité* and *direct cinema* were born.

The concepts and practices of documentary go back to three developments of the 1920s: the appearance of a small film avant-garde in certain countries of Europe; the work of a maverick filmmaker of Irish descent in North America, Robert Flaherty; and the creation of a revolutionary film industry in Soviet Russia, which included the agit-prop of Dziga Vertov and the comrades of the Kino-Train. There was also, at least as far as noncommunist cinema was concerned, a catalyst in the person of a nonconformist Scottish intellectual who went to study the emerging mass-communication society in the United States. It was he who gave the term *documentary* its currency when he saw Flaherty's second film and wrote in its praise that it had the force of a living document. His name was John Grierson.

Within the group that he created in England upon returning from the States, Grierson argued for a concept of the form as didactic and social rather than poetic and individual, within which the image was to be employed for its status as plain authentic record of the actual. This aesthetic was based on a thoroughly empiricist philosophy that closely corresponded to certain practices of journalism. Although he did not say it, it could be said that Grierson wanted the documentarist to regard the nonfictional image as an authentic document of social reality (to be filmed as artistically as you like but with appropriate discretion), in rather the same way that journalists take documents like parliamentary reports or the sworn statements of witnesses as authoritative and unimpeachable versions of events. For the journalist actually to believe the authority of such documents, however, is plainly naive, and will sometimes cause problems. On similar grounds, the aesthetic that treats the authenticity of the film image uncritically can be called naive realism.

During the Second World War, the rather special conditions of official sponsorship allowed a few gifted propagandists, like Humphrey Jennings in Britain, to contribute some artistic development to the form. After the war, the ideals that inspired the first flowering of the social documentary seemed to dissolve (though they find another location in neorealism) and the best documentaries in the postwar years mostly took the shape of individual poetic essays by directors like Georges Franju and Resnais—a form in which nonfictional images provide the substrate for a more or less literary kind of reflection and self-expression. For the rest, the documentary became a merely utilitarian form serving various dominant ideological interests, including educational purposes conceived in a rather mechanical fashion. The exceptions, like Joris Ivens—of whom more later—are very few. As Karel Reisz described one typical prestige product of the genre from the 1950s:

> Song of the Clouds has some distinguished names on its credits and, the scientific film apart, represents the norm of our documentary industry. From the film-maker's point of view this is particularly disturbing because

the film represents the almost complete abdication of the creator in the film, the director. A film of this kind is planned in terms of the facts it will have to present; it is conceived in committee; it has a commentary written by another hand, which tries to give the images a weight they do not have. Under these conditions, the director's function becomes that of a technician.[1]

At the time he wrote this, Karel Reisz was a member of a new documentary movement that anticipated the appearance of cinéma vérité in a number of ways, the movement known as Free Cinema—the style of which the defenders of *P.M.* in Cuba in 1961 saw their cause célèbre as an example. Free Cinema was originally a handful of young British filmmakers of liberal disposition including Lindsay Anderson and Tony Richardson, who belonged to the generation of the so-called Angry Young Men, and whose approach to cinema was originally made through film criticism—like that of several French New Wave directors and some of the Cubans too. They presented a number of films together under this banner in London between 1956 and 1959. Stylistically, the films were rather diffuse, but they had enough in common to make the group name workable. Although the name was invented largely to attract publicity, it signaled a certain attitude of humanist commitment and sense of artistic responsibility that was real enough, and it quickly caught on among film critics and aficionados. No one in similar circles in Cuba denied that Free Cinema was an important idea. On the contrary, it was regarded as an idea to be discussed and analyzed, with arguments for and against its various features. Alea wrote about Free Cinema in an article in *Cine Cubano* at the end of 1960—before *P.M.* appeared.[2] The same issue of the journal announced the impending visit to Cuba by Tony Richardson, who at that time had just graduated to features where he caused a flurry with his radical techniques, fresh sense of style, and challengingly honest content. The Cubans saw Richardson as a representative of the same spirit of aesthetic renewal that was also to be found in the postwar cinema of several other European countries (the Free Cinema programs at London's National Film Theatre had themselves included two devoted to Poland and France), and he was one of many foreign visitors invited by ICAIC to exchange ideas and, in some more trusted cases, to work with it.

Alea's article was a polemic directed against accepting Free Cinema uncritically. One of the best assessments of Free Cinema made by anyone, its historical significance lies primarily in its implications for the whole constellation of issues about documentary that ICAIC was then debating, in which it went beyond the approach of liberal humanist commitment. Free Cinema, Alea began, had been translated into Spanish as *cine espontáneo*—spontaneous cinema. This was not, he observed, a literal translation. However, it was appropriate enough in the Cuban context, where filmmakers no longer found themselves opposing an unfree cinema compromised by its economic and political connections. Free Cinema was obviously important because it was by definition anti-conformist. Its origins lay with a group of young filmmakers faced with obstacles to their freedom of expression erected by the commercial institution of cinema: the demand for scripts, actors, lights, makeup, planned camera movements, special effects, and all the other ingredients of the "proper" movie. The Free Cinema group had offered up, in a spirit of opposition, simple fragments of daily reality, modest film essays on things close to common experience. They wanted to use film as a witness of this reality, a testimonial that brought a living document to the screen.

But Free Cinema is only one way of doing this, warned Alea. It was a certain style, characterized by great mobility and agility, in which the filmmaker took up position as a spectator and filmed fragments of reality spontaneously, as it unfolded, and without interfering in its unfolding. Afterwards, the material took shape in the editing. Its strength was in the way the film thus "liberated itself not only from various economic and political obstacles, but also largely from the dead weight that the normal processes of film production have to suffer." If, he said, a certain degree of technical perfection has to be sacrificed to achieve this, what is returned to the audience by way of the invitation to engage with what is on the screen is more important.

Here Alea is one of the first to express what soon became one of ICAIC's foremost criteria: the conviction that a filmmaker's sensitivity to the audience is more important than the achievement of technical mastery, since without it the greatest mastery is pointless. This is a different emphasis from the Free Cinema directors themselves, who were more concerned with the personal artistic aspirations of the individual director. Alea was unquestionably in favor of spontaneity and the rewards of the feeling of creative freedom, but he thought that this in itself was not enough. You must not, he said, as a filmmaker, let spontaneity allow you to forget that you are there behind a camera taking up the position of an artist or creator, and that every process of creation implies the modification of the elements it employs, which in the way that this is done gives it the filmmaker's individual stamp. Not that this is anything the Free Cinema directors would have denied. On the contrary, this individual stamp was what they were aiming for. But when cultural attitudes are translated from the great metropolis to the artists' cafés of peripheral capitals, their character changes. And what was important to emphasize in Havana at that moment was that artistic creation presupposes, as Alea put it, an attitude in the face of reality that is not impartial. Artistic creation involves judgment, and "all attempts to portray reality while avoiding judgment on it are dud. Sometimes this leads to half-truths, which can be more immoral than a complete lie." Hence Alea's conclusion—prophetic of the problem about *P.M.*—that "one should not think that Free Cinema is the new cinema. . . . Free Cinema is only a new step in a particular direction, of great value but with great dangers."

Although its example was still alive, Free Cinema as a historical phenomenon was already over when Alea wrote these lines. It was superseded by cinéma vérité and direct cinema, which in certain ways it anticipated. These movements began more or less simultaneously on both sides of the Atlantic. In France, a highly skilled camera engineer, André Coutant, introduced the enthnographic filmmaker Jean Rouch to a camera that had been developed for use in military space satellites for purposes of surveillance by the Paris company Éclair, for which Coutant worked. Coutant knew that Rouch would find more liberating uses for it, especially since it could be paired with one of the new portable tape recorders that could be swung on the shoulder. Rouch had spent ten years making remarkable documentaries in a handheld camera style he had evolved for himself, but he had been limited by the impossibility of shooting them with synchronous sound because available sound equipment, designed to meet studio needs, restricted the mobility of the camera. You needed a truck and crew to shoot sound on location. Even if this had been possible in ethnographic settings, for Rouch it defeated the purpose of making a film at all, since to show anything ethnographically authentic you had to be able to shoot *around* your subject and not do what they did in studios: move things around in a way that suited the camera (and the lights and the microphones). The new equipment allowed the development of a distinct and appropriate camera style, which is a necessary feature of direct cinema, just as the elaboration of a new sense of screen space was a necessary part of neorealism. Clearly, the two things are not unrelated.

In the United States, the English-born Richard Leacock felt a similar frustration to Rouch's. Leacock mistrusted what he called the "controlled" film, the film that re-created what a director thought a situation should be even in documentary, either because of the impossibility of shooting it as it was, or because a director like Flaherty (he had worked as Flaherty's cameraman on *Louisiana Story* in 1948) had a penchant, even a flair, for it. And it's true: this practice had come largely to negate the original idea of documentary.

It was said that the new style fetishized the camera, in the form of the unsteadiness of handheld shooting, the jerky zooms and going-in-and-out-of-focus that became its trademark—"wobblyscope," as the older generation of film cameramen in British television called it (they were all men). The truth is, of course, that it was in the studios that the camera was treated like a fetish, a veritable idol, everything laid at its feet and arranged for its convenience. Yet a certain fetishization did take place in direct cinema. At the start, you got wobblyscope because cameramen were having to relearn their craft, and to begin with they were still clumsy. Then some of them began to cultivate the effects of inexperienced handheld shooting for their own sake, because you could feel the activity of the person behind the camera in them, moving around within the same space that the image within the viewfinder is part of. But as the skills of direct filming were extended, the persistence of such features arguably became an unnecessary affectation.

Leacock has spoken, however, of how he became fascinated with effects that arose when the situations he was filming in got out of control. He began to find bits in the resulting film that he thought extraordinarily interesting: "Not because they were clever or chic or anything, but because they were true. They presented you with data to try and figure out what the hell was really going on."[3] This recalls something Walter Benjamin explained about cinema. Film, he said,

> has enriched our perception with methods which can be illustrated by
> those of Freudian theory. Fifty years ago, a slip of the tongue passed
> more or less unnoticed. Only exceptionally may such a slip have revealed
> dimensions of depth in a conversation which had seemed to be taking its

course on the surface. Since *The Psychopathology of Everyday Life* things have changed. This book isolated and made analyzable things which had heretofore floated along unnoticed in the broad stream of perception. For the entire spectrum of optical, and now also of acoustical, perception, the film has brought about a similar deepening of apperception. It is only an obverse of this fact that behavior items shown in a movie can be analyzed much more precisely and from more points of view than those presented in paintings or on the stage.[4]

To aim to work up this process of apperception has pretty clear political implications, whether the filmmaker sees them or not. For Rouch, this took on a particular form. His academic background schooled him in both philosophical and instrinsic problems about observation. He knew the observer had an effect on the observed that could never be wholly eliminated, and that was more and other than what was registered by camera wobbles. For Rouch, the whole problematic of making the film had to become a central subject for it.

The film that gave the term cinéma vérité its currency is the film that gave paradigmatic expression to this concern. Rouch used the term, a translation of Dziga Vertov's *kino-pravda* (film truth), in the subtitle of *Chronique d'un été,* which he made in 1960 with the sociologist Edgar Morin and the French-Canadian cameraman Michel Brault. Ninety minutes long, the film is a study of "the strange tribe that lives in Paris." What emerges, however, is rather different from the kind of thing Vertov meant. *Chronique d'un été* is not so much a dynamic dialectical visual inquiry as an unscripted psychodrama enacted by real persons that is called into play by the camera itself. The film proceeds in a strange way to create its own reality, which only exists because it is the result of the filmmakers' activity, the reality of a situation that the camera provokes but that isn't conventional fiction. At the end, Morin and Rouch are seen pacing the halls of the Paris anthropology museum, the Musée de l'Homme, questioning themselves about the rights and wrongs of probing someone's emotional crisis, or whether another's account of wartime deportation was not perhaps dramatized for the camera. At the door of the museum, Rouch asks Morin what he thinks. He replies, "I think we're in trouble." The films ends.

Why they were in trouble emerges from the contradiction in the appeal they made to Vertov. Vertov had not regarded even the most directly filmed scene as in itself cinematic truth. Like the other early Soviet filmmakers, he had emphasized the importance of montage, which he interpreted not simply as a process of cutting apart and putting back together, but as a fundamental principle of film art that operates on several levels: it applies to the selection of the theme, to its execution, and then to the actual editing of the film. He declared that it is not enough "to show bits of truth on the screen, separate frames of truth," but that "these frames must be thematically organized so that the whole is also truth."[5]

For the new documentarists, however, editing was a necessary evil, to be minimized not only through the greater fluidity of the camera but also by respecting the order of events as filmed, on the grounds that any other order would be "subjective." "In the discourse surrounding direct cinema," as one commentator puts it, "editing (montage) is cast as the villain of cinema's quest for the holy grail—regarded as a distortion, a formalist cul-de-sac."[6] The Cubans were highly suspicious of such dogma. They did not, at the time of the Revolution, know the work of Vertov, but they quickly rediscovered his principles. Perhaps this is not surprising. Their own explanation is that these principles come from the creative and dialectical application of Marxist thinking to cinema within the context and process of a revolution. This is surely how Alea arrived at the view he expressed in his Free Cinema article, that because reality is forever changing, it presents an infinite number of aspects with their own multiple antecedents, which must somehow be taken into account. Such thinking is also entirely congruent with criticisms that came to be made of cinéma vérité by independent Marxist thinkers in Europe, such as the remarks Lucien Goldmann directed at *Chronique d'un été*: as a sociological piece of work, he explained, *Chronique d'un été* has serious limitations, though it did, he commented, go far enough in its chosen method to imply "a justified criticism of the very large number of imaginative works which lose all contact with reality while at the same time posing as realist." However,

> the root of Morin and Rouch's preoccupations was precisely to avoid the arbitrary, to grasp actual reality, to get the truth. But precisely at this point, we fear that they have come up against a major methodological difficulty which was long since pointed out in the methodological works of Hegel and Marx: when it's a question of human realities, the truth is

never immediate, and anything which is immediate remains abstract
and, for that very reason, stained by inexactitude as long as it is not
inserted into the whole by a number of more or less large and complex
mediations.[7]

The film is really a kind of group therapy, its characters entering into
its unconventional fiction in the name of a special kind of truth, with
the self-consciousness of a very particular cultural and intellectual world.
This is where it gets the idea of self-reference from, like the incorporation
of the responses of its self-searching participants. Who were they, then?
One was a young student who began a few years later to get deeply
involved in the Cuban Revolution and the liberation struggles of Latin
America, who in the film is just called "Régis." In 1967, imprisoned in
Bolivia as an associate of Che Guevara, Régis Debray recorded his memory of those days: "With the academic year measuring out our seasons
and weeks," he wrote in his *Prison Writings,*

> we could stroll around the streets of the Latin Quarter with nothing to
> worry about except ourselves and our salvation ... we roamed about
> the Sorbonne in groups, as we met to found a magazine, or work out
> a manifesto, or drink a beer ... we were the hopeless prey of eroticism,
> little in-groups, literary journalism and the *cinémathèque.* ... We also
> learnt, for we were good pupils, that the sirens of ideological error are
> always singing, on the cinema screen, in novels and in the street, and
> that few scholars are wise enough to close their ears fully to them. So,
> to save us from ourselves, we were taught to mistrust our own credulity
> and our enthusiasms, and to lay in a supply of ear-plugs as a protection.[8]

The very achievement of *Chronique d'un été* in communicating this
world—from the professors' point of view—also made it a completely
unlikely model for the critical but enthusiastic cinema the Cubans
needed, with or without the appropriate gear, and if the techniques it
employed would only later be incorporated into the armory of Cuban
documentary style, this is because there were other matters to be worked
through first.

The preoccupations of Jean Rouch were also remote from the concerns
of the Anglo-Saxon North Americans. The year after *Chronique d'un
été,* Richard Leacock and Albert Maysles went down to Cuba—practically the first of many filmmakers from the metropolis to do so—to
shoot sequences for *Yanki No!,* a film on Latin American attitudes toward
the United States for ABC television. But they too got into trouble, and

the film they made shows how easily ideological compromise was able to swallow up the new principles. *Yanki No!* allowed people abroad to hear Fidel Castro speaking for the first time, but, bowing to the demands of television for which it was made, it overlaid a commentary that undid much of what the filmmakers intended: over shots of people on their way to a rally, the narrator intones "Now the Revolution is going to stage a show"; and about Fidel: "Fidel Castro, who looks like a raving madman to North Americans, is seen by Latin Americans as a sort of messiah. Now you will see him at his messianic best."

In fairness, Leacock was both an old Communist and a member of the Fair Play for Cuba Committee that sprang up in 1959 within the emerging New Left in the United States. (The left-wing journalist K. S. Karol shared a table with him at the Fair Play for Cuba meeting on the eve of Fidel's UN address in 1960, where they met Fidel and the rest of the Cuban delegation.[9] Henri Cartier-Bresson was there and took photographs.) But the film is caught up by the limitations of the radical liberal ideology that dominated this movement, and led the filmmakers to compromise in the interests of getting the film on television. This is not to say they necessarily knew what the effect would be—it was early days for such endeavors—but such experiences taught them to hate television.[10]

It was a Frenchman, Chris Marker, who made the film the Cubans themselves regarded at the time as the best documentary about the Revolution: *Cuba Sí!*. The title alone spells out the difference from Leacock's film. Where the latter aimed to shock the audience into realizing the way Washington policies were estranging what was previously thought to be a docile country, Marker identified completely with the Cubans and made a celebratory film. "Shot rapidly in January 1961," he wrote in the preface to the published script, "during the first period of alert (you know—at the time when the majority of French papers were hooting over Fidel's paranoia in imagining himself threatened with invasion), it aims at communicating, if not the experience, at least the vibrations, the rhythms of a revolution that will one day perhaps be held to be the decisive moment of a whole era of contemporary history."[11]

Cuba became a subject of great interest to practitioners of the new documentary because the whole circumstance of the Revolution made a great deal much more directly available to the camera than was normal elsewhere. And because it was a symbol of the throwing off of shackles, which was part of the spirit of the new documentary too. For the Cubans themselves, however, it was not primarily a matter of style or technique. Alfredo Guevara wrote in *Cine Cubano* in 1960, a couple of months before Alea's Free Cinema article, about a process of discovery that began with two films by Julio García Espinosa, *Sexto aniversario* (Sixth anniversary) and *Un año de libertad* (A year of freedom).[12] Both of them, because of the speed of change of events, had to be reelaborated during editing. The second, said Guevara, was the more difficult to make, because it used newsreel and archive footage that was very poor in narrative quality. But by reworking it, they found a narrative method for the film that took them away from the bare chronology of the old propaganda material they were using. This way they managed to construct a certain historical understanding of the events portrayed. They made their minimal resources work. How had this been possible? asked Guevara. Expertise at the editing table? The use they made of dissolves and shock cuts? No, it was the conception of events that they'd had to get right, in order to give the editing technique direction—in this case, the technique of montage.

Guevara's attitude here is the twin of Alea's and implies the same criticisms of direct cinema. This way of treating material is strictly anathema in direct cinema, not simply because of the prohibition on interfering, but because direct cinema avoids the use of found material. Guevara believes, however, that you need a critical conception of events to make a film, the kind that is summoned when you rework material, looking for a way to turn it inside out to find what was previously hidden within it. This makes you realize that appearances are liable to be both truthful and deceptive *at the same time*; and that therefore the only guarantee of cinematic truth lies beyond the lens. Better to violate aesthetic theories, felt the Cubans, in order to make the subject more intelligible, because truth is always served by its more effective communication, and communication is part of the political purpose of the film.

What is common to the approaches of Cuban documentary and direct cinema, cinéma vérité, is the aim of liberating documentary from the conventions of commercial film, such as insistent but insensitive background music, swish editing based on misplaced codes of fictional narrative, the alienation and paternalism of the commentary (not that the early ICAIC documentaries entirely avoid these ills), and the conviction that reality is not so elusive that it cannot be induced to show itself. Crucially, there was also the aim of returning documentary to the center of attention in cinema—in which by the end of the 1960s the Cubans had succeeded as no other cinema has done, with feature-length documentaries becoming regular fare in Cuban cinemas. But the way the Cubans arrived at this position strongly suggests that even if they had had the same technical resources as in the metropolis, they would still not have developed a documentary cinema substantially different from the one they did. They had good reasons for rejecting dogmatic or extreme versions of any style or aesthetic. Rouch's way of thinking was unappealing to them because with him, under the guise of objective investigation, there lurked a certain individualistic subjectivism. Rouch once expressed the notion that the best result of further technical advance would be to let the filmmaker work completely alone; but this dream of realizing what the French critic Astruc called the *caméra-stylo* (camera-pen) amounts to little more than saddling the filmmaker with the traditional role of the author. In Cuba, the whole problem was how to break down the isolation of the author, not how to bring the filmmaker to approximate to it. What does this isolation have to do with revolutionary politics and ICAIC's concern to foster collective consciousness?

Or take the idea of the camera obtruding as little as possible. Here the Cubans saw a failure in dialectical reasoning. They also suspected the need for subterfuge. They were not themselves primarily interested in people forgetting the presence of the camera in order to see them "as they really were" (even if the results could be very interesting): they wanted people to accept the presence of the camera and of the filmmakers, in order that they should open up and share their experience, through them, with others. What this needed was not better technology to make films with, but better conscience in making them.

Among the pioneers of direct cinema, those the Cubans would have found most sympathetic were the French Canadians, for their situation as members of a national minority living under the cultural as well as the political hegemony of the Anglo-Saxon empire was the closest to the situation the Cubans were beginning to leave behind. "When we try to find out what the problems of our culture mean," said Gilles Groulx, "we become aware that our uneasiness is not artistic but social: we might call it the attempt to express the man born in this country."[13] This could be a Cuban speaking.

The fact is that ICAIC was far more disposed to learn about documentary from the veteran socialist filmmaker Joris Ivens. "There is nothing surprising about Ivens's presence in Cuba," said *Cine Cubano* in November 1960 (the issue before Alea's Free Cinema piece) of Ivens's visit earlier that year. "Wherever there's a country struggling for its freedom, a people trying to liquidate the old structures and forge a sane and healthy future where man can find and reclaim his dignity, Ivens will be present. And as a creator, not a tourist."[14] Ivens, whose principal films had been prohibited in West Germany, France, and Italy, who had filmed in Spain during the civil war, in China during the war against the Japanese invader, who had voiced a cry of alarm over the Dutch government's intentions against the young Indonesian republic at the end of the Second World War and thus become an undesirable in his native country, Ivens represented an ideal the Cubans could readily identify with—the participant witness who wielded the camera with the precision of a rifle. They invited him not just to make a film about the Revolution but also, as he modestly describes it himself, to impart his experience of making films under difficult conditions.[15]

Ivens began immediately upon arrival to give talks and hold discussions with his hosts on the theory and practice of militant cinema, but it was primarily through making a pair of films with Cuban crews that his pedagogic flair took effect. The idea for the first, *Carnet de viaje* (Travel notebook), arose from discussion in the first few days of his visit about the problem of how a foreign filmmaker, however proven a militant, could possibly film "The Revolution" when he had only just arrived. (Ivens had been to Cuba once before, in 1937, with Hemingway, one of his collaborators on the Spanish civil war film, but for present purposes that didn't count.) The idea for the film was that in order to get to know the Revolution he would have to see what was going on in different places around the island; the trip would become the itinerary of the film. The simplest of ideas; perhaps only a master like Ivens could bring it off.

The second film, *Cuba pueblo armado* (Cuba, a people armed), was made in response to a request by Fidel, whom Ivens met on his second evening in Havana. When Ivens and his crew reached the region of

Escambray in the center of the island, Fidel called to ask if they could interrupt the shooting of the film that was in progress in order to make a film there of the People's Militia, who were engaged in an offensive against counterrevolutionary bands. Fidel explained, said Ivens, that the operation could have been carried out rather more quickly by the Rebel Army but it had purposely been given to the Militia. The Militia commander in the area was not too keen on having to cope with a film crew and it fell to their production manager, Saúl Yelín, to deal with the problem. Yelín, who subsequently became, until his death in 1977, what Ivens affectionately called ICAIC's foreign minister, asked the commander to call Havana. The next day his attitude had changed completely—not because he had been given some order from on high but because it had been explained to him why Ivens had been asked to make such a film. He went up to Ivens saying, "Why didn't you tell me you filmed the wars in Spain and China?"

On his second visit to Cuba the following year, while he worked at ICAIC as an adviser and assessor, helping to sort out the teething problems of the new Institute, Ivens was again called on because of his experience in filming military conflict to carry out a special task. He was approached by Osmani Cienfuegos (brother of Camilo) to undertake the training of military cameramen. With the knowledge that an invasion was due, the Cubans realized the importance of being able to film such an eventuality. They also realized it was a task beyond the capacity of ICAIC, though ICAIC would obviously contribute. A remote hacienda previously belonging to an uncle of Batista's was chosen as the site of the school, which was naturally placed under tight military security: Ivens went there in secret (it was said he'd gone elsewhere in Latin America). Faced with the problem of training fifty or sixty students, some peasants, some workers, very few of them with even an amateur photographer's knowledge, Ivens asked for six months. Impossible, said Fidel, we need you to do the job in a month: "You'll see, our people work day and night." But Ivens managed to get a concession from him and they agreed upon two.

The real difficulty was how to teach without cameras. Ivens got hold of an old Eyemo from ICAIC and found a carpenter among the students who undertook to make models of it out of wood; these were weighted so as to give the feel of the real thing. He conducted exercises with these models, and in the absence of real film to show results, each student had to recount to the others the pictures he had pretendedly taken. Ivens explained to them the way he had filmed in the Spanish civil war and the students constructed a model of the battle in question and worked out how the filming could have been improved. One result was that the Rebel Army thus reentered the arena of Cuban cinema. In subsequent years, the Cuban armed forces have not only made their own instructional films but have also made a significant contribution to Cuban documentary in collaboration with ICAIC in the shape of a number of frontline reports on liberation struggles in Africa.

Ivens spoke to *Cine Cubano* at the end of his first visit about what he had seen in Cuba. It is not difficult to see why his approach was readily appreciated:

> Among the men and women who represent the Cuban Revolution you can see the desire to manifest clearly the dignity and meaning of the idea they're defending. . . . I saw this example of dignity—and it impressed me—not only in the struggle of defense but also in places of work. In cooperatives, in industrial centers, you noticed the decision that the whole people put into constructing their own destiny. If I can be allowed to offer young Cuban filmmakers any advice, I would say that this represents the best filmic lesson for them. They should forget about the problems of technique and style. They will acquire these things with time. The important thing for now is to let life into the studios and not become bureaucrats of the camera. Film quickly and as directly as possible everything that's going on. To accumulate burning-hot direct material can be considered the best way to get to a cinema with national characteristics.[16]

Direct filming comes into this not as a normative stylistic principle— Ivens says, don't worry about questions of style—but as a way of making the filmmaker answerable to the ideals of the Revolution as they are lived out by those around them. As ICAIC developed, this idea—though doubtless Ivens wasn't its only source—became the linchpin of its system of apprenticeship in which all directors in ICAIC would be required to serve in either documentary or newsreel work.

One of the members of Ivens's film crew in Cuba wrote a diary of the filming for *Cine Cubano*. The first thing Ivens taught them was how to look afresh at their own countryside. The Cuban countryside is a great problem for the cinematographer, wrote José Massip:

> This green which is so beautiful to the human eye is not so to the mechanical eye of the photographic lens. With black-and-white film,

the different shades of green are lost in a dark and undifferentiated mass. This means, for example, that if the dramatic quality of an action is accentuated in nature by the countryside behind it, this emphasis will be considerably reduced on the screen.

The solution to this problem probably consists in finding an appropriate relationship between the landscape and the sky. Cuba's sky could be the salvation of its countryside. Ivens could not remember a sky to compare with it. Its astonishingly rich plasticity comes not only from its marvelous shade of blue, but above all from the extraordinarily varied shapes of its clouds. The sky, wisely included in the composition, can cancel the betrayal of the green.[17]

Massip goes on to recount lessons Ivens taught in how to photograph things so as to suggest the process of change; the importance of using the bottom third of the frame, the "forgotten area" in the pictorial composition of the film image; how to capture special aspects, moments, and relationships in a scene. The cameraman Ramón Suárez added a note that mentioned, among other things, the importance Ivens placed on faces. Here Ivens was passing on a lesson he himself had learned from Russian workers when he first visited the Soviet Union in 1930. When he showed them his avant-garde film *Rain*, "It seemed to them," he wrote in his autobiography,

> that I had fallen in love with reflections and textures. They said *Rain* showed too little of human reactions and concentrated too much on objects. One challenging remark was—"Why are you afraid of faces? If you could look at a face with the same frankness with which you look at a raindrop you would be wonderful." This reaction made a deeper impression on me than when audiences compared the lighting and composition in *Rain* with that in Dutch genre painting.[18]

Still, from what he taught the Cubans, Ivens had clearly not allowed himself to forget that lighting and composition were of primary importance, only as means, not ends. In a third article, Jorge Fraga noted how Ivens did not follow a rigid work schedule but instead often filmed intuitively, grasping passing moments. He reenacted things only if it was necessary not to lose a shot or because it was the only way to get the image in question, and then he always did it in the simplest way possible. Fraga also noted Ivens's constant awareness that the "phrases" of montage, the "expressive molds" of film language, are historically conditioned aesthetic categories, and that he preferred spontaneity to irrupt into the frame rather than adhering to classical rules of composition; and that he kept his camera almost always in movement.

These reports in *Cine Cubano* were one of the means adopted in ICAIC to transmit the lessons learned by those chosen to work with Ivens to the others. A later issue of the magazine includes a transcript of a round-table discussion on Ivens's work, which was another such means. ICAIC organized itself from the outset to provide an environment of a kind to facilitate the collective assimilation of experience. This work is carried on at two levels, for *Cine Cubano* and the Cinemateca reached the broad aficionado public, while there were also internal publications and ICAIC's in-house cine debates, in which all their own productions and selected foreign films were discussed among a range of production workers— directors, producers, editors, camera people, and so on. The oral history of ICAIC is in these debates, and more, for just as *Cine Cubano* is a journal not only of Cuban cinema but of the whole New Latin American Cinema movement, so too other Latin American filmmakers, both visitors and exiles to whom ICAIC gave a home, took their places in these debates as respected comrades. Even the visiting film critic researching the history of Cuban cinema would be invited to participate, to discover a dialogue that was conducted at a high and wide-ranging level, without neglect of detail and without shunning either polemic or stringent criticism. These debates, which date right back to the early years, have helped to forge the sense of collectivity in ICAIC and provide a means of mutual instruction.

Many of Ivens's practical lessons were, by these means, pretty rapidly and effectively disseminated, but it is also clear that the most important lessons ICAIC drew from Ivens were human rather than technical. The human content of Ivens's example has been well summed up by Tom Waugh in an excellent account of the veteran filmmaker's two Cuban films. He mentions the filming of a conversation between two militiamen guarding a bridge that appears in *Cuba pueblo armado*:

> At the time of the shoot, the crew were struck not only by Ivens' instinctual recognition of a good scene and of "natural actors" but also of the way in which he was able to make the two subjects feel comfortable and trustful with regard to the camera.... His ... secret for bringing out the "natural actors" in such subjects was his authentic respect for them, his involvement with them as human beings rather than as subjects.

To this effect, Jorge Fraga remembered a heated argument between Ivens and a peasant that he at first found shocking because of the obvious social disadvantage of the latter. But he suddenly realized that it was rather a total absence of paternalism and sentimentality that was responsible for Ivens' attitude, his assumption of the peasant's equality despite social and cultural barriers. Ivens' attitude was essential to the active collaboration between artist and subject in his work, which the Cubans greatly admired, a clear challenge for Havana intellectuals such as Fraga and Massip. The triumph of Ivens' approach came when he attempted to persuade captured counter-revolutionaries to re-enact their night-time surrender. . . . The prisoners, no doubt bewildered by the Communists' generous treatment, consented and can be seen in the film emerging from the jungle, hands above their heads.[19]

Historia de una batalla (Story of a battle), by a director who had no direct contact with Ivens, Manuel Octavio Gómez, shows how widespread Ivens's influence was and how much he helped ICAIC find its feet. The battle in Gómez's film is the literacy campaign. The metaphor of the title is not an invention of the film but is taken from the campaign itself, for the sheer scale of the undertaking—to eliminate in a matter of months an illiteracy rate that at its highest in the countryside approached 43 percent—required a quasi-military form of organization, though not, as we can see from the film, one that was particularly militaristic.

The political import of the campaign was established at the outset when a young volunteer teacher was assassinated by counterrevolutionaries. A few days later, Castro announced that schools would close on April 15 and "an army of one hundred thousand literacy workers" aged thirteen and over would set out to live, work, and learn with the poor and humble of the land. It is the image of these children leaving for the countryside in their brigades (while adult literacy workers took on the job in the cities) that opens the film and sets the tone. The film concentrates on the role of the children not only because it was their participation that provided the most graphic possibilities, but also because the experience that challenged them was the very stuff of revolutionary social change. The encounter of city children, mostly middle-class, with peasant life and values would be a learning experience for them as well, far beyond the immediate purpose of the campaign. It was a challenge too to their parents to let their children—girls as well as boys—leave the safety and comfort of their homes to spend weeks and months with strangers in possibly dangerous circumstances. Indeed, toward the end of the campaign there were further assassinations of *brigadistas* (brigade members) by counterrevolutionaries, to which Fidel replied by declaring that the revolutionary response to the attempt to sow terror among the families of the *brigadistas* was to refuse to call home a single one of them. But this was only the most dramatic of the dangers. The scenes in the film of mothers tearful as their children depart evoke their trepidation as they steel themselves to let the Revolution shatter the mores of the past. In fact, it was through participation in the campaign that a whole generation of children was able to join the revolutionary process with which they so eagerly wanted to identify. Richard Fagen calls the experience "a revolutionary rite of passage, their first opportunity to prove that they were fully-fledged revolutionaries."[20]

UNESCO was impressed when it made an independent evaluation of the success of the campaign the following year. (The illiteracy rate had been reduced to the level of a metropolitan country.) This film, however, is not an empirically evaluative report. The campaign was a testing ground for many of the ideas that were later to be incorporated into the revolutionary style of governance through mass participation, and it became an essential step in a process of civic education that brought about not only literacy but political awareness, a deeper understanding of national problems, a new concept of citizenship and its rights and responsibilities, a new willingness to work for the transformation of the old society. The film is a celebration of all this, which, through celebrating it, becomes part of it. Hence the interweaving in the film of mass demonstrations, the speech by Che Guevara at the UN, and the events of the Bay of Pigs, images that are presented not as background but as the expression of the play of social forces among which the literacy campaign is another.

The Peruvian critic Mario Tejada, observing that the early ICAIC documentary directors lacked sufficient dominion over filmic language to match the magnitude of the subjects they filmed, singles out this film (together with *Muerte al invasor* [Death to the invader], a report on the Bay of Pigs by Alea and Álvarez) for achieving an epic quality.[21] Yet, at the same time, Gómez personalizes his subject in the manner that was taught by Ivens, by picking out individually significant details within the overall scene in front of the camera. It isn't just the generalized anxiety of mothers as their children depart, and the joy of the reunion when they return, but the particular woman searching a parade of *brigadistas* for her child somewhere in the middle of it, or the camera following a *brigadista* home to film the doorstep embrace. The influence of Ivens is also to be felt in the lyrical-poetic commentary. Ivens has made this kind of commentary into something of a fine art, in films like *La Seine a recontré Paris* (1957), which employs a poem by Jacques Prévert, or ... *à Valparaiso* (1963) with its commentary by Chris Marker.

The rapid expansion of ICAIC's documentary output, from four films in 1959 to twenty-one the following year and forty in 1965, makes it a hopeless task, because of the sheer volume of production involved, to attempt to survey these films individually without looking for a way to categorize them. Inspection of the catalog with this aim yields half a dozen or so main thematic categories, some with internal subdivisions. The two largest groups are:

first, films on the revolutionary process, including mobilizations, struggle against the counterrevolution, social transformations, political subjects proper, and the history of the Revolution;

second, didactic films: this covers an enormous range of topics, from artificial respiration to the domestic flea, the origins of the human species, surgical operations, genetics, agricultural methods, hygiene, machine maintenance, and so on. These are followed by:

third, another large group of films dealing with cultural and artistic subjects: music and ballet, architecture, painting, handicrafts, and so on;

a fourth group comprising social history and the observation of Cuban character and social life, subjects that are frequently related to the third group;

fifth, a group of films related to the first category, which treat of the revolutionary critique of capitalism and imperialism, of international solidarity and the principles of internationalism, including coverage of liberation wars;

sixth, a group of films on the subject of women; and

seventh, sport.

A group of students in Havana, using ICAIC's own Cuban-assembled computer, analyzed the institute's documentary output over the years 1959 to 1982. Their findings were reported by Mario Piedra in *Cine Cubano*.[22] Using thirty-three thematic categories divided into nine broad groups, they found, for example, that documentaries on working-class themes, the largest group, represented 24.27 percent of the output, those on "artistic culture," 20.38 percent. The problem with this kind of approach is that it neither takes account of the stylistic variety of the films nor does it have any way of dealing with films that belong to more than one thematic category. A film like José Massip's *Historia de un ballet* (Story of a ballet, 1962) is about artistic culture but it has significant overtones of social history. Nor is it just a matter of viewing the film and deciding which is the correct emphasis. It is partly a conceptual problem. Is an instructional film on prenatal care, like *Atención prenatal* (Prenatal care) directed by Sara Gómez in 1972, to be classified as a didactic film or under the heading of women?

There is another consideration too: the themes that are less often treated are not necessarily less important. Films themselves are of different weight. A major film on a given subject may have more effect than half a dozen films with more modest intent—though also, a wholly successful modest film might go further than a botched major one. Both things have occurred in Cuba. Films dealing directly with the need to promote the equality of women and advance their position have been relatively few, but several have been substantial films that in their moment received considerable attention, like Octavio Cortázar's *Con las mujeres cubanas* (With Cuban women, 1974). At the same time, one of the most significant Cuban documentaries of all, not because it attracted attention immediately but because its reputation and influence developed over a period of years, is a six-minute montage experiment made by Santiago Álvarez in 1965, called *Now*.

And then there is the question of what a didactic film actually is. There is a sense in which, within a set of terms referring to subject areas, the category is anomalous, for it delimits not so much subject as treatment. In fact, it is an umbrella term that covers a diverse range of subjects and refers to the functional purpose of the film. It really belongs, as a category, to a different set of terms altogether, the set that identifies, rather than subject, the intention with which the film is made. There is indeed a set of terms of this kind available, it doesn't have to be invented. It does not provide a systematic scheme of classification any more than do subject headings, but it represents the way documentary is thought of in Latin America itself, because it arises directly from the conditions under which filmmakers at the receiving end of imperialism have to operate. These terms, of which didactic cinema *(cine didáctico)* is one, are far more aesthetically compelling than what has been suggested so far. Other categories include:

cine testimonio—the testimonial film;
cine denuncia—the film of denunciation;
cine encuesta—the film of inquiry, investigative documentary;
cine rescate—the film of historical recovery;
cine celebrativo—celebratory cinema;
cine ensayo—the film essay;
cine reportaje—reportage, not quite the same as investigative film but overlapping with it;
and, above all, *cine militante* or *combate*—the militant film or film of combat par excellence.

This list is not exhaustive or definitive and there is no single source from which it is drawn. They are only the most frequently used of a series of terms that occur across the whole range of Cuban and radical Latin American film writings, that is to say, the writings that belong to the same movement as the films themselves, which express its preoccupations and objectives. They can be found in film journals from several countries, including Peru, Venezuela, Chile, and Mexico, as well as Cuba: *Hablemos de Cine, Cine al día, Primer Plano, Octubre,* and *Cine Cubano,* respectively, to cite only the most important of them. The distinctive feature of all the terms listed is precisely their intentional character. They indicate a variety of purposes: to teach, to offer testimony, to denounce, to investigate, to bring history alive, to celebrate revolutionary achievement, to provide space for reflection, to report, to express solidarity, to militate for a cause. These are all needs of revolutionary struggle, both before and after the conquest of power (which only goes to show that the conquest of power doesn't divide things into before and after in the clear-cut way that is often supposed, in the mass media, in the careless thinking of daily life, and in what Sartre called "lazy Marxism"). The only difference is that after the conquest of power the conditions qualitatively change.

Quite likely all of this is what an unsympathetic critic from the metropolis would call propaganda. But then you have to understand not what propaganda is supposed to be, but what it is capable of becoming. Bourgeois ideologies have always equated propaganda with mere rhetoric, the selective use of evidence to persuade, or—as a Cambridge professor once put it—"a branch of the art of lying which consists in very nearly deceiving your friends while not quite deceiving your enemies." The purposes of propaganda are usually considered incompatible with what is supposed to be didactic and vice versa—as if the contents of formal education were sacrosanct, indubitable, and objectively true. Every revolutionary aesthetic finds this a false and mendacious antinomy. There is a tradition in revolutionary aesthetics that takes the classical concept of rhetoric as the practical art of persuasion much more seriously. (It is not for using rhetoric that advertising, commercial propaganda, is to be condemned, but for the *way* it is used, and to what ends.) Propaganda is the creative use of demonstration and example to teach revolutionary principles, and of dialectical argument to mobilize intelligence toward self-liberation (and if it isn't, it won't be effective for revolutionary purposes). It seeks, and when it hits its target it gets, an active, not a passive, response from the spectator. Revolutionary cinema, according to the Argentinian filmmakers Fernando Solanas and Octavio Getino, "does not illustrate, document or establish a situation passively; it attempts instead to intervene in that situation as a way of providing impetus towards its correction." This is one of the central assertions of the essay they wrote about the experience of making the epic *La hora de los hornos* (The hour of the furnaces) in the mid-1960s, which they called "Hacia un tercer cine" (Towards a third cinema).[23] There is obviously a didactic element in this, but there is a difference: the aim of teaching is not immediately to inspire action, but to impart the means for the acquisition of more and better knowledge upon which action may be premised. Accordingly, there is a difference in revolutionary aesthetics too, from the practical point of view, between the propaganda and the didactic film.

La hora de los hornos is a film from a radical Peronist position from which the Cubans were politically distant, but the essay in which Solanas and Getino analyzed the functions of revolutionary cinema represents a stage of thinking within the new cinema of Latin America as a movement that bears a strong relationship to where the Cubans had reached in their own development. At an earlier stage, ten years earlier, when another Argentinian, Fernando Birri, set up the film school at the University of Santa Fe, he had based the idea of the kind of cinema he was aiming for on two main sources: Italian neorealism, and the idea of the social documentary associated with John Grierson (whose teaching has sometimes had a more radical effect in underdeveloped countries, anyway in the long term, than in the country where it was born). These, however, are precedents conventionally dominated by a naive realist aesthetic, and it is not surprising to find a few years later a Colombian filmmaker, Jorge Silva, saying in an interview in the magazine *Ojo al cine*: "At the inception of the militant film movement, it was said that the essential thing was simply to capture reality and nothing more, and to make reality manifest. Afterwards, this formulation began to seem insufficient."[24]

However, it was not as if Birri or anyone else involved meant these paradigms to be accepted uncritically—after all, these models were still European. The way Birri saw it, to apply the humanistic ideas behind neorealism and the social documentary to the context of underdevelopment immediately gave them a dialectical edge. In an interview in *Cine Cubano* in 1963, he explained the function of the documentary in Latin America by means of a play on the word *underdevelopment*—in Spanish, *subdesarrollo*. In opposition to the false images of Latin American commercial cinema, documentary was called to present an image of reality, as it was and could not in all conscience otherwise be shown. It was thus to bear critical witness and show that it was a sub-reality *(sub-realidad)*, that is to say, a reality suppressed and full of misfortune. In doing this, says Birri, "*it denies it*. It disowns it, judges it, criticizes it, dissects it: because it shows things as they irrefutably are, not as we would like them to be (or how they would have us, in good or bad faith, believe that they are)." At the same time, "As a balance to this function of negation, realist cinema fulfills another, one of affirming the positive values in the society: the values of the people, their reserves of strength, their labors, their joys, their struggles, their dreams"—the same values, in fact, that Brecht saw in the working people. Hence the motivation and the consequence of the social documentary, says Birri, is knowledge of reality and the grasp of awareness of it—*toma de conciencia* in Spanish, *prise de conscience* in French—what Brecht wanted his theater to be. Birri summarizes: "Problematic. The change: from sub-life to life." In practical terms: "To place oneself in front of the reality with a camera and film this reality, film it critically, film underdevelopment with a popular optic." Otherwise, you get a cinema that becomes the accomplice of underdevelopment, which is to say, a sub-cinema *(sub-cine, like subdesarrollo)*.[25]

This is not just a play on words. Birri's thinking is informed by both the philosophy and the theology of liberation in Latin America, with their emphasis on the process of *concientización,* particularly in the work of the Brazilian educationalist Paulo Freire. Freire's philosophical arguments draw on both Hegelian philosophy and existentialism, as well as on radical Christianity, but he is thoroughly materialist in his understanding of social reality; what he proposes is a philosophy of praxis. He argues that self-knowledge is only possible because human beings are able to gain objective distance from the world in which they live, and "only beings who can reflect upon the fact that they are determined are capable of freeing themselves."[26] In consequence, they become capable of acting upon the world to transform it, and through understanding the significance of human action upon objective reality, consciousness takes on a critical and dialectical form. It is never, says Freire, "a mere reflection of, but reflection upon, material reality." In the same way, Birri wants to say that the documentary film is the production of images that are not a simple reflection of reality, but become, in the act of the film, a reflection upon it—first by the filmmakers and then for the audience. This is clearly not the position of a naive realist. But it is not the position of a simple idealist either. It can best be called *critical realism.*

A film may thus break through the *culture of silence*—Freire's term for the condition of ignorance, political powerlessness, lack of means of expression, backwardness, misery, dehumanization of the popular masses. It can promote the recognition of the condition in which the people live, and the way they are conditioned, and can sometimes even seem to give them their voice. In this way it succors *concientización,* which is only viable, says Freire, "because human consciousness, although conditioned, can recognize that it is conditioned." Hence the possibility of popular consciousness whose emergence is at least, if not an overcoming of the culture of silence, the entry of the masses into the historical process.

The power elite of the ruling classes are extremely sensitive to this. Their own form of consciousness develops to try and keep pace. There is always an intimate relationship between the ruler and the ruled (as in Hegel between master and slave). "In a structure of domination, the silence of the popular masses would not exist but for the power elites who silence them; nor would there be a power elite without the masses," says Freire. "Just as there is a moment of surprise among the masses when they begin to see what they did not see before, there is a corresponding surprise among the elites in power when they find themselves unmasked by the masses."

The conscientious documentarist is bound to serve as a witness in this process of twofold unveiling, as Freire calls it, which provokes anxieties in both the masses and the power elite, and in doing so the very idea of the social documentary is transformed; for, in this transitional process, says Freire, contradictions come to the surface, and increasingly provoke conflict. The masses become anxious to overcome the silence in which they seem always to have existed, the elites become more and more anxious to maintain the status quo. As the lines of conflict become more sharply etched, the contradictions of dependency come into focus, and "groups of intellectuals and students, who themselves belong to the privileged elite, seek to become engaged in social reality," critically rejecting imported schemata and prefabricated solutions. "The arts gradually cease to be the mere expression of the easy life of the affluent bourgeoisie and begin to find their inspiration in the hard life of the people. Poets begin to write about more than their lost loves, and even the theme of lost love becomes less maudlin, more objective and lyrical. They speak now of the field hand and the worker not as abstract and metaphysical concepts, but as concrete people with concrete lives." Since the mid-1950s, filmmakers have been in the forefront of this process in Latin America, beginning with the social documentary and moving on to explore a whole range of militant modes of filmmaking.

Take the idea of *cine testimonio,* testimonial cinema. In fact, there are two distinct strands to this idea. One of them is well represented by the Mexican documentarist Eduardo Maldonado, founder in 1969 of a group that took the term itself as its name: Grupo Cine Testimonio. *Cine testimonio,* according to Maldonado, is concerned to put cinema at the service of social groups that lack access to the means of mass communication, in order to make their point of view public. In the process, he says, the film collaborates in the *concientización* of the group concerned. At the same time, the filmmakers' awareness is directed toward the process of the film. The process of shooting becomes one of investigation and discovery, which reaches, he believes, its final and highest stage in the editing. The film thus embodies "the aesthetic approach to *concientización.*"[27]

The other strand to the idea of *cine testimonio* comes from a literary source and is particularly strong in Cuba. The earliest paradigms are found in the *literatura de campaña,* the "campaign literature" of the nineteenth-century Cuban wars of independence: the memoirs, chronicles, and diaries of Máximo Gómez, Céspedes, and others, including Martí himself. They are the accounts of participants writing in the heat of the events, with economy of style and aware of their necessarily partial but privileged perspective. These are the same imperatives that Che Guevara followed in his accounts of the Cuban revolutionary war in the 1950s and the Bolivian campaign of the 1960s in which he died. A striking thing about all these writings is that they always remain extremely personal. Hence, as the Cuban documentarist Víctor Casaus observes, the elegance and melancholy of Céspedes, the outrage and violent jottings of Gómez, the brilliance of Martí.[28]

In Cuba, Casaus continues, this literature was the origin of a genre that took shape in the 1930s, in the new and imaginative journalism of Pablo de la Torriente Brau (who died fighting in the Spanish civil war) and Raúl Roa (a historian who became one of the Revolution's distinguished elder figures). Pablo de la Torriente Brau's *Presidio modelo* (Model penitentiary), dealing with his experience as a political prisoner, was an antecedent of testimonial writings by authors throughout Latin America, including the Argentinian Rodolfo Walsh, the Salvadoran Roque Dalton, and the Uruguayan Eduardo Galeano. In Cuba itself, the genre has further flowered since the Revolution, and has produced four distinct subgenres. The first is the journalistic report or chronicle such as César Leante's *Con las milicias* (With the militias). Second are the accounts of their own experiences by nonprofessional writers, like Rafael del Pino's *Amanecer en Girón* (Dawn in Girón)—the author was a Cuban pilot during the Bay of Pigs invasion. Third, works like Miguel Barnet's *Biografía de un cimarrón (The Autobiography of a Runaway Slave)*, in which the author transcribes, as an anthropologist, the oral testimony of a man more than a hundred years old concerning the experiences of his youth. Finally, there are works like *Girón en la memoria* (Giron in the memory), by Víctor Casaus himself, which uses a filmlike montage technique to bring together a variety of materials, including interviews, documents, and press reports, around a particular theme.

These or works like them have served ICAIC directly for several documentary films, but filmmakers have also developed their own testimonial subgenres, says Casaus. The ICAIC newsreel is the first of these because its character as a week-by-week chronicle is not a simple piecemeal record of the events but, under the guidance of Santiago Álvarez, became their interpretive analysis. It is obviously essential to the idea of the testimonial that it convey a sense of lived history. This means, in cinema, that the camera is not to be a passive witness. The newsreel has learned how to insert itself, so to speak, into the events it deals with by breaking the inherited conventional structure of the newsreel form and converting itself into a laboratory for the development of filmic language. This influenced the whole field of documentary, with its already obvious affinities to testimonial literature. However, it is not, says Casaus, a matter of simply translating the written word into the filmic image or, as sometimes happens, using a first-person voice-over to narrate, and the evolution of documentary technique adequate to the re-creation of the literary genre in cinematic terms was not accomplished overnight. The vast majority of the documentaries of the early years of the Revolution, Casaus observes, are today forgotten—the proof that their method did not succeed in transforming the immediate reality into an enduring expression. This was not, according to Casaus, simply because of the inexperience of the filmmakers, but rather because of an underestimation of documentary, and consequently the persistence of techniques imported from the fiction film. The films that have survived are the ones that approached the documentary form creatively. In these films, says Casaus, a paradigmatic series of principles can be distinguished: first, rapid and flexible filming of unfolding reality without subjecting it to a preplanned narrative mise-en-scène; second, the choice of themes—the literacy campaign, military actions in defense of the Revolution, the sugar harvest, cultural processes like the mobile cinema—these are all subjects of important documentaries; third, the employment of an audacious and intuitive style of montage, of which the outstanding exponent is Santiago Álvarez; and fourth, the use of directly filmed interviews both for the narrative functions they are able to fulfill and because they provide the means of bringing popular speech to the screen. This was the last of Casaus's four principles actually to be incorporated into the Cuban documentary since the technical capacity for direct sound filming was what the Cubans to begin with lacked.

This essay by Casaus is a piece of reflective analysis of what the testimonial film had already become at the time he wrote it. The ideas behind the didactic film, on the other hand, were actively developed by ICAIC at the same time that it was experimenting in the genre itself, for it is a form that acquires particular importance when a revolution achieves power. Since militant filmmakers are no longer forced to work in clandestinity or semiclandestinity, the emphasis of their art changes, the tasks for which their films are intended qualitatively shift their focus, and nowhere is this more marked than in the scope that now opens up for a didactic cinema. As Pastor Vega explained in an article dating from 1970 titled "Didactic Cinema and Tactics," when ICAIC set up a didactic films department in 1960, dealing with a whole range of scientific and technical subjects, not all the necessary conditions for such a project existed, "but it wasn't possible to wait for them...the demands of a revolution, which alters the dynamic of history in all its dimensions, leaves no alternative."[29] ICAIC recognized that it was necessary to create a whole new batch of filmmakers without having the time to give them proper training in the shape either of lengthy apprenticeship or more formally in a film school. The films were needed. They would have to learn on the job by jumping in at the deep end. But because of this, the didactic film had to become didactic in more than one way. A film on a scientific or technical subject intended to contribute to the training of the technical cadres the Revolution needed would also serve the training of the cadres within ICAIC itself.

A film might be needed, for example, on gastroenteritis. In a similar way to Solanas and Getino's concept of militant cinema, such a documentary is conceived as an intervention into a given reality with the object of modifying it by enabling people to transform it—in this case, by learning how to combat the disease. In order to accomplish this, the film has to become a learning experience for the filmmaker first, before it can be so for the audience. In this way, both become involved in a life-and-death struggle, for in underdeveloped countries gastroenteritis is a killer. What the filmmaker has to learn takes on a double aspect—there is the subject on which the film is to be made, and at the same time, learning how to make this kind of film. Formally speaking, these are two separate functions, but in the circumstances they get completely intertwined. *Cine didáctico* then becomes a paradigm for new ways of thinking about film, and again, the original idea of the social documentary is transformed.

The new tasks of the social documentary become the essential training ground in Cuban cinema because the filmmaker has to learn to treat reality by engaging with the people the film is for. *Cine didáctico* teaches that the value of communication is of paramount concern because the film would achieve nothing if it did not succeed in its primary function, which is instruction (in the broadest sense). This theme is taken up in a paper presented jointly to the National Congress of Culture and Education in 1971 by Jorge Fraga, Estrella Pantin, and Julio García Espinosa, "Towards a Definition of the Didactic Documentary." The mood at the time of this Congress—four years after Che's death in Bolivia, a year after the Battle for the Ten Million had not quite reached its target for a ten-million-ton sugar harvest, and Fidel had made rigorous self-criticism—this is a very different mood from that of the first few years. Euphoria has now given way to pragmatic realism. The joint authors therefore begin by offering to this extremely workmanlike Congress for its consideration the old utilitarian definition of the didactic documentary as an instrument for use by a teacher in front of a class, and proceed to demonstrate the inadequacy of this concept. ICAIC's first didactic films eleven years previously, they say, even those that were not intended to be used as teaching aids, corresponded too much to the functional criteria this model required. "They were illustrations for a learning situation; it didn't matter whether that situation was real or potential."[30] This is true. Despite some notable exceptions, those early films had often been somewhat overdeliberate in their style. Flexibility and fluidity take time to learn.

But after a decade, they said, it was time to be critical. Their first concern was that the didactic film conceived this way does not provide the maximum educational efficiency even in the classroom it is intended for, as long as it remains utilitarian and takes the form of exposition by the teacher as its model and example. This is to constrain the medium unnecessarily. Film is an expensive means of cultural communication. It is impossible to make as many films as are needed. Is it legitimate to limit the scope of the films that do get made, when they could be angled to a broader synthesis of functions? Because the synthesis of functions is precisely the method of cinema.

The ICAIC team then proceeded to reconstruct for the Congress the idea of the didactic documentary according to the preoccupations that had been animating their work over the course of the whole decade. Their line of argument is itself eminently didactic. Much of what they say is philosophically grounded in the analysis of commodity fetishism and alienation, which says something about the style of Marxist thinking that had developed at ICAIC, but it is equally significant that they appeal, as professional communicators speaking to a large audience that is made up of both professionals and aficionados at all levels of culture and education in the country, to more popular concepts and ideas. This does not mean talking down, however, for in Cuba even popular ideas are a long way from being the lowest common denominators of the populism of the capitalist democracies. They first take note of the heritage of cultural imperialism. They remind their listeners of the low level of industrial development in the country, consequently of the low level of science and technology, and the inadequacy of the means of communication endowed by neocolonialism. They observe that it is no coincidence that in these conditions serious forms of cultural alienation to be found in the metropolis, such as gambling, lotteries, and astrology, make deep and extensive inroads into the consciousness of people in underdeveloped countries. This produces a way of thinking that perceives things only in a dissociated way, only as results, without grasping the processes that create them. Underdeveloped thinking comes to be ruled by a sense of contingency and fatalism, which harks back to the magical (but the magical now shorn of most of its previous cultural legitimacy). "After twelve years of revolution," they say, "we still find examples of this way of thinking even in our own communications media, mostly modelled after the tendency to exalt results and omit the process which led up to those results." But cinema possesses the very qualities needed not only to communicate knowledge and skills effectively, but also to educate for a rational, concrete, and dialectical way of thinking. Why? Because it is capable of reproducing reality in motion and therefore of demonstrating processes, and further, because it is capable of revealing relationships between items that come from the most dissimilar conditions of time and place. The utilitarian conception of the didactic documentary narrows down this field of potential (like, we can add, any kind of aesthetic prescriptivism, including that of the direct-cinema purists). What is more, the result is a dry and boring genre that is sterile and quite ahistorical. Capitalist cinema conventionally deals with the problem of the genre's dryness by adding enticements to the treatment of the film, the way that pills are sugarcoated—a technique known from advertising as "the snare." Advertising "appeals to stimuli which have nothing to do with the nature of the product in order to create more demand for it or stimulate the consumer's interest: sex, desire for recognition and prestige, fear of feelings of inferiority—anything apart from concrete demonstration of the actual properties of the object." This mentality, which thinks only in terms of selling, becomes all-pervasive, and everything, including ideas and feelings, is reduced to bundles of exchange values. To fall in with all this was obviously hardly acceptable. The didactic documentary, they said, must break once and for all with this retrogressive tradition; it must link with the urgency of its subjects and themes. The formal techniques employed "must be derived from the theme and put at its service. It's the old moral demand for unity between form and content."

Pastor Vega's account of the didactic film has exactly the same moral emphasis, and his arguments are similarly built on historical-materialist analysis. The socioeconomic transformation created by the Revolution, he explains, has propelled the newly literate peasant from the Middle Ages into the second half of the twentieth century, to become an operator of tractors and agricultural machinery. This accelerated passage through multiple stages of development, which the sudden acquisition of the products of modern science and technology involves, requires a qualitative leap in the process of mass education. In these circumstances, the mass-communications media acquire the most important functions as levers in the country's development through their catalytic action. The didactic film must be transformed accordingly, throwing off the molds of the form as it originated in the developed countries and going in search of a new originality that arises from the very different pattern of development of the Revolution. The filmmaker must acquire new perspectives and go for a different filmic language than the archetypes of the documentary tradition. The didactic film must be seen as a new aesthetic category, in which the artist and the pedagogue meet—although this only happens if certain imperatives are observed. For the work of the artist and the pedagogue, aesthetic production and teaching are not identical activities, and in the didactic film certain requirements of both must be met. This disjuncture disappears, however, when immature ideological prejudices that paralyze mental processes are no longer sustainable, as they cannot be, because "all living thought is anti-mechanistic."

Many of the principles evolved in the course of development of the social documentary in the new Latin American cinema, and especially in Cuba, have strong parallels with positions that were taken up within radical film practices in Europe and North America over the same period. The Venezuelan critic Raúl Beceyro is effectively speaking for both when he writes that "one of the initial tasks of 'new cinemas' all over the world has been to destroy certain norms of grammatical construction. . . . A cinema that aspires to establish new ties with the spectators or that intends to modify the role that spectators assign themselves could not continue to use the formal structures [of what preceded]."[31] But, in certain respects, the radical film cultures of the metropolis and of Latin America think rather differently.

Both would agree about naive realism. As the French art critic Pierre Francastel had already written in 1951:

> What appears on the screen, which our sensibility works on, is not reality but a sign. The great error that has regularly been committed is to embark upon the study of film as if the spectacle of cinema placed us in a double of reality. It should never be forgotten that film is constituted by images, that is to say, objects that are fragmentary, limited, and fleeting, like all objects. What materializes on the screen is neither reality, nor the image conceived in the brain of the filmmaker, nor the image that forms itself in our own brain, but a sign in the proper sense of the term.[32]

But what *is* a sign in the proper sense of the term? This is where the trouble begins. Following Ferdinand de Saussure, the founder of modern linguistics, as interpreted by structuralists of various disciplines, a strong current within the new radical film theory in the metropolis has come to regard the sign as a very peculiar kind of symbol. As the cultural theorist Fredric Jameson has written:

> The philosophical suggestion behind all this is that it is not so much the individual word or sentence [or image in the case of film] that "stands for" or "reflects" the individual object or event in the real world, but rather that the entire system of signs . . . lies parallel to reality itself; that it is the totality of systematic language, in other words, which is analogous to whatever organized structures exist in the world of reality, and that our understanding proceeds from one whole or Gestalt to the other, rather than on a one-to-one basis. But, of course, it is enough to present the problem in these terms, for the whole notion of reality itself to become suddenly problematical.[33]

This is quite different from the problematic nature of reality within underdevelopment, where the concept of truth follows another dialectic.

In the structuralist system, says Jameson, truth becomes a somewhat redundant idea, as it must do when there is nothing to which it can be unproblematically referred. An image in a film, therefore, is not to be thought of as truthful just because it pictures something real to which it corresponds, even though the automatic mechanism of the camera lead us to believe so. Instead, it is said to yield meaning only because it stands in a certain relationship to the other images through which it is, so to speak, refracted.

In any radical film practice in the underdeveloped world, truth remains immediate and material without falling back into transparency and naive realism. It is not a question of the accuracy or fullness of fit of the image to what it pictures, which everyone knows can never be anything like complete. More important, it lies in the relationship with the audience, because the meaning of what is shown depends as much on the viewer's position as on the system of signs within which it functions. This has also been of great concern to radical film theory in the metropolis, but the new Latin American filmmakers were worried less about the way the filmic discourse positions the spectator and rather more whether it recognizes where the spectator is already. This arguably requires a more conscientious political attitude on the part of the filmmaker.

The result is a difference in the practice of cultural politics, and the emphasis of filmic forms of intervention in the public sphere. In the metropolis, there is little to stop the film, the film as "text," and the "discourses" of cinema, from becoming dissociated objects in themselves. Whereas, according to the Colombian documentarists Jorge Silva and Marta Rodríguez, the radical filmmaker in Latin America "becomes more and more involved in the process of the masses" and "the film must become an auxiliary part of this whole formative process."[34] This is a dialectical affair that promotes a very different attitude toward both the concept of truth and the criteria of truth on the screen. Not because the masses are seen as depositories of truth in the mechanical manner of lazy Marxism, but because the filmmaker is involved in a collective process, which the philosophy of liberation holds to be an inherent potential of underdevelopment, in which truth undergoes redefinition through *concientización*.

CHAPTER TEN

The Revolution in the Documentary

We have seen how it came about that a generation of filmmakers emerged in Cuba in the early 1960s who were not only committed to the Revolution but also to the task of revolutionizing cinema. The very naïveté of the film culture they inherited became an elemental factor in their development. Through the *concientización* that the encounter with the popular audience brought about, they found themselves questioning their own naïveté, and thus became involved in questioning the production of the image. Because of the sense of urgency that the Revolution imparted, they had to do this not so much theoretically as practically. Only this would correspond to the demands of revolutionary politics; it became a priority in the program ICAIC adopted. As Alfredo Guevara later explained: "In the beginning we faced the dilemma of either teaching or doing. We lacked time for artistic introspection and decided on making films at once, without wasting time on theory. We began from scratch and filming became our school."[1] And yet, as we have also seen, the school that the Revolution itself constituted impelled the filmmakers into theoretical reflection on the nature of their practice, and even in the early years the level of theoretical discussion in ICAIC was not at all undeveloped.

With the priority of practice went a commitment to documentary. Everywhere in Latin America where filmmakers had become active, the concern for documentary was a concern to produce images that questioned reality. The critical realism that fueled the new Latin American cinema was both an outgrowth and a transformation of the tradition of the social documentary. In Cuba, the problem of creating an authentic popular film culture within the Revolution in place of the heritage of cultural colonization expressed itself in the question of how to overcome the distance of the screen from the streets that lay outside the cinemas. The key to the solution was to take the naive relationship of the audience to the screen and build on it, transforming it in the process into a collective reevaluation of the nature, content, and status of the image—a process that was to yield some extraordinary films within only a few years.

A couple of documentaries that appeared in 1965 can be seen in historical retrospect to give clear notice of something new in Cuban cinema. The two films are *Hombres del cañaveral* (Men of sugar) directed by Pastor Vega, and *Now,* directed by Santiago Álvarez.

Now is a film to a song—which had been banned in the United States where it came from—sung by the black singer Lena Horne, a militant call to the black oppressed that employs the rousing tune of the Ashkenazi-Israeli dance song "Hava Nagila." Upon this sound track Álvarez constructs a powerful collage on racial discrimination in the United States, which he had observed during a visit many years before the Revolution, on a trip from Florida, through the Deep South, and up to New York.[2] The images in the film's pretitle sequence are of racist incidents in California in August 1965 followed by a photograph of President Lyndon Johnson meeting with a group of blacks under the leadership of Martin Luther King (whom Álvarez was to eulogize in film three years later after his assassination)—a juxtaposition that establishes the film's tone of skeptical irony. This short film essay is impressive not only for the resourcefulness with which it uses its found materials, including pirated newsreel, but also for the syncopation of the editing, which intensifies the insistence of the song and leads up to its militant ending better than it would have done by slavishly following the music's surface beat.

Álvarez's film acquired within a few years the reputation of being a work of great and forceful originality. The impression made by Pastor Vega's *Hombres del cañaveral* was hardly comparable. It is difficult to judge, but this may be because stylistically the film is somewhat self-effacing, the very opposite of Álvarez's bombshell. But it is certainly a film of considerable originality, which gives it more than historical interest. The historical context, however, is crucial to its proper assessment:

it is a product of the ideological debate led by Che Guevara in the mid-1960s about the moral qualities of work in revolutionary society.

It was Che who, to begin with, propelled the Cuban economy toward central direction and control. At the same time, however, he rejected mechanical and overly schematic explanations of the economic forces involved. Some have said that Che was too idealist, or at any rate too voluntaristic, but the Revolution was attempting to transform the forces of production and Che wished to see the process of socialist economic development operate as a force for the creation of a new morality, which would itself feed and strengthen the transition to socialism. Accordingly, he argued for moral as opposed to material incentives in the struggle to relieve the island's almost unrelieved monocultural dependency on sugar.

The first few years of the Revolution saw a large migration of labor from agriculture to urban industrial and service employment, in line with the attempt to break this dependency by rapid economic diversification. The expansion of the urban sector was relatively easy because of a large pool of un- or underutilized resources, which included labor. Unemployment in 1958 had been officially rated at 17 percent[3]—a figure that disguised the truth about rural employment, because so many of those who worked in the sugar harvest actually worked only a few months in the year. The rest was known as *tiempo muerto* (dead time). Urban expansion was partly designed to take up this hidden, seasonal unemployment, but it left a problematic reduction in the labor force available for the harvest. The solution ultimately lay in the development of agricultural technology, but because of the difficulties of designing harvesters suitable for the crop, the terrain, and the climate, this was a matter for the future. Meanwhile, there was need of a system of temporary redeployment of urban labor to agricultural production during the harvest. As Bertram Silverman has explained:

> The type of labor required was the most menial and unskilled. Material incentives would have had to be unusually high to induce urban labor into these occupations. Moreover, the use of wage differentials made little sense because the transfer was frequently of workers from more skilled and productive activities to less skilled.[4]

In such circumstances, the idea of mobilizing labor through moral incentives was perfectly logical, though there were also certain contradictions, which did not escape attention. The moral incentive, if it is to operate truly, cannot be manipulated from above. It must be generated and sensed within the populace. This, says Silverman, is why many Cubans came to ask, with characteristic directness, "How can you plan voluntary work? Is this not a contradiction in terms?" Abroad, people didn't even ask; the mass media in the metropolis simply pooh-poohed the whole idea, scorning it as one more case of Communist manipulation of the population.

Clearly, this was an area where the social documentary had a crucial role to play, as potentially one of the most effective forms in which to militate for moral aims without losing sight of reality—at least if an appropriate new political language could be found. *Hombres del cañaveral* is indeed far from strident agitprop and the political tract. It is the study of a brigade of voluntary workers from the city at work in the sugar harvest, with no commentary, and a meticulously observational camera. It opens, like *Now*, with an encapsulating juxtaposition: an electric light display spelling out "Vivan la Paz y el Socialismo" (Long live peace and socialism) followed by an image of someone being shot that immediately calls to mind the sacrifice on which the Revolution is founded. Then come a set of intertitles, which inform us that the film was made with the collaboration of one of the urban voluntary work brigades; that the brigade in question, "Africa Libre" (Free Africa), held first place in the Emulación Nacional, the national emulation league table; but this was not the reason why the filmmakers had chosen this group as their subjects (though maybe it *was* the reason, after all); the real reason was (and then one by one come titles and portrait shots): The Cook; The Driver; The Cane Cutters; The Chief; and all of them. The film is a record of a day and night in the life of the brigade.

In the course of the film's seventeen minutes we see the men at work, with images of their factory in the city cut in to remind us where they've come from; we see them receiving letters from home, getting medical attention, washing off the sweat of the fields, and playing cards. They play music and listen to the radio. The style in which all these scenes is presented is curiously reminiscent of some of the wartime films of Humphrey Jennings; in other words, the product of the accumulated experience over more than ten years of the British social documentary. Although Jennings was, of course, unknown in Cuba, many of the narrative devices in Pastor Vega's film are similar to those of the British documentary, including the simple "day-in-the-life" narrative structure, although the music in the film gives it, at the same time, a rather different hue. In one respect, however, the film goes beyond the classic social documentary style, and that is in the use of expressionist devices to communicate identification with the feelings of the subjects. The film is one of the very few Cuban documentaries of the period to make direct self-reference to the artifice of filmmaking. The workers have come back from the fields, cleaned up, and started to relax. Suddenly, the mood is interrupted by a camera slate and the call of "action" and we are in the middle of a lesson in math. Eagerly attentive as they are, the men find it difficult to keep up their concentration, and through a series of changing lens effects the screen embodies their weariness.

There is also an affinity between *Hombres del cañaveral* and a film that Santiago Álvarez directed two years earlier, in 1963, *Ciclón* (Hurricane). *Ciclón* was a newsreel special of twenty-two minutes (double the usual length) using footage shot by a long list of cameramen belonging to ICAIC, the Armed Forces, and Cuban television, who recorded the devastation occasioned by Hurricane Flora in the provinces of Camagüey and Oriente, and the subsequent rescue work and clearing-up operations, which were personally directed in the field by Fidel. The film is an example of how far the ICAIC newsreel, under Álvarez's direction, had already come in the space of only four years in the creation of a new concept of the newsreel form. As Álvarez explained in an interview:

> A newsreel is essentially a product that provides information. That's clear, but it isn't all. And even though that may be its principal characteristic, this is no reason either to neglect it or to turn it into a social chronicle of socialism, following the usual linear sequence of unconnected news items. My concern has not been to separate out the news, but to join things up in such a way that they pass before the spectator as a complete entity, with a single line of argument. This concern produces a structure that aims at unity. Because of this, many people regard our newsreel as documentary.[5]

In *Ciclón,* this aim is achieved in a quite exemplary manner, not only because the film does entirely without commentary but nevertheless succeeds in constructing the clearest narrative line, but also because of the way it makes an exemplary political statement. The necessarily unplanned actuality material assembled from the multitude of cameramen in different places at the same time has, added to it, only some graphics indicating the path of the hurricane across the island. These graphics are integrated with the images to produce a political statement: at one point, we see the blades of a helicopter revolving in the same direction as the animated hurricane in the preceding graphic, so that across the cut, the helicopter becomes a symbol of command over the forces of nature in response to natural disaster. This, rather than the heroic images of Fidel, is the center of gravity in the film. Fidel, anyway, doesn't look heroic so much as businesslike. Like *Hombres del cañaveral,* the style of the film is also self-effacing, and it was not immediately picked out as innovatory. All the same, it is a film that shows remarkable mastery over what is arguably the most fundamental of the skills of filmmaking, namely, narration with mute images, here juxtaposed only with music and effects.

A year after *Now,* Álvarez made another significant advance. If *Ciclón* is a pure example of reportage, *cine reportaje,* he now extended this to produce a piece of *cine crónica,* or documentary chronicle. *Cerro Pelado* takes its title from the name of the boat that carried the Cuban sports team to the Tenth Central American and Caribbean Games, held in 1966 in San Juan, Puerto Rico, where, being a U.S. colony, the North Americans attempted to prevent Cuban participation. By now, Álvarez has developed the basic characteristics of his style. The film is constructed in the form of a chronological visual narration of the events, with minimal verbal commentary, interspersed with sections using montage and captions to expound the political background to the events. The whole is knitted together with music, which is used in place of both commentary and direct sound, not just to fill space on the sound track but to narrate the film. In order to achieve this, Álvarez not only employs humor in his choice of musical items but also draws on music's own iconography. Shots of the "Training Center for Cuba Counterrevolutionaries" in Puerto Rico (as a caption describes it), for example, are juxtaposed with the fast passage from Rossini's *William Tell* overture, which naturally recalls its use as the title music of the television western *Lone Ranger* series, which was well known in Cuba. Álvarez thus calls up the stereotypes of the idiom of cultural imperialism only to invert them, and present the counterrevolutionaries as imitation cowboys, an image at once satirical and deflating, which at the same time condemns the way these people see themselves, modeled on the propaganda myths of the United States.

To say that Álvarez uses music to narrate is therefore to say that he uses the cultural associations of his chosen music (its iconography) to orient the viewer's frame of reference. What he is doing is to politicize the representation through aesthetic means that are at once highly articulate but nondiscursive. This, for Álvarez, is a central resource of political documentary, because it is a way of mobilizing popular intelligence, which is not merely unformed by discursive intellect but, for this very reason, lies in danger of suffocation by the tricks of conventional commentary.

Various sections of the film are titled with chapter headings. "This is the boat" is followed by scenes on board of the team dancing on deck. "This is the enemy" leads into shots of warfare, and is repeated on the right-hand side of a divided screen, superimposed over a sequence of newspaper front pages, with moving images continuing screen left, to form a most complex montage between both simultaneous and successive images. The dancing on deck is replaced by the athletes warming up, cut with humor and grace to the music of "El Manisero" (The peanut vendor—a Cuban song, composed by Moisés Simons, and not, as many people think, North American). Shots of riflemen practicing are crosscut with the ever-present menace of aircraft circling overhead as the boat approaches its destination, which in turn give way to images of warfare in Vietnam and a newsreel interview with a captured U.S. Air Force pilot.

Another chapter heading introduces "The site of the Games—Puerto Rico, 'freely associated' Yanqui Colony," and captions inform us of significant statistics, interposed with images of Puerto Rican life and conditions. Within this framework, these images, which critics pretending to omniscience would regard as hackneyed, fully recover their eloquence. Then comes the response of the Cuban athletes to the coast guard's refusal to admit the boat—the Declaration of the Cerro Pelado: "The rights of Cuba are not negotiable"—which forces the North Americans to uphold the Olympic regulations that govern the games. After a section on crude North American attempts at psychological warfare, the film ends with a lighthearted portrayal of Cuban victories on the field and Fidel greeting the returning athletes.

In 1965, the same year as *Now*, Álvarez had already made another piece of *cine solidaridad*, a nine-minute report titled *Solidaridad Cuba y Vietnam* (Cuba-Vietnam solidarity). This was the first of many films to come on the struggle of the peoples in Southeast Asia. Two years later, following *Cerro Pelado*, Álvarez turned to Vietnam again to produce an eighteen-minute compilation film under the title *Escalada del chantaje*

(Escalation of blackmail), a report on increasing U.S. aggression there. Then came his first trip to Southeast Asia and *La guerra olvidada* (The forgotten war), a documentary report from Laos in which Álvarez employs avant-garde music by the Cuban Leo Brouwer and the Italian Communist composer Luigi Nono. The film is subtitled "Filmic Fragments." Apart from war footage and narrative captions at the beginning to summarize the history of Laos, Álvarez simply, and once more without commentary, shows us scenes of the activities of the Patriotic Front. Many of these scenes are taken in the caves that provided refuge and protection. In addition to such activities as newspaper printing, schooling, the manufacture of medicines, and a hospital, we also see the projection of a film of Laotian dramatic dance. This is perhaps a veiled reference to the artifice of film. At any rate, it has the effect of placing quotation marks around the doubly filmed, doubly projected image, thus emphasizing how difficult it is to reach to the heart of a reality beyond one's direct experience. Through its very restraint, the film becomes a moving call upon the viewer's ignorance. It is also a model of what can be made under the most limited conditions, while refusing to engage either in the sensationalizing tactics of the capitalist media or falling into the trap of pretending, even for laudable propaganda purposes, that the film is more than it is—an assembly of visual fragments.

Pastor Vega also made another significant film in 1967, *Canción del turista* (Song of the tourist). This film is in color and 'scope, one of the first Cuban films to use such resources, and at no more than fifteen minutes, it is a paradigm of *cine ensayo,* the film essay. The subject is the contrast between underdevelopment and revolution. The titles come up over a dancing girl in scanty costume gyrating in the style of the 1950s to sound-track music composed by Carlos Fariñas, with pressing rhythms and electronic noises that produce a menacing effect. The image here is in sepia and, still in sepia, cuts to a river and the countryside. The rhythm stops, leaving electronic noises over a series of images of underdevelopment. There is a shot of children dancing, and of a boy tapping out the rhythm on an upturned metal basin. Color begins to creep in very slowly as we watch a singer, in synchronous sound, singing about a world without love or money, in the style of a traditional ballad. Now come stills of Fidel and then shots of Fidel in action on a podium, followed by panoramic views of the demonstration he is addressing. Color continues to grow through images of industry and agriculture, women tractor drivers, the mechanization of cane cutting, new housing, new roads. Here the images are given an extra dimension, that of a wide-angle lens. The succession of images is again narrated by the music, keeping the film constantly free from every demagogic trace. We catch a glimpse of a couple kissing in the fields ("even the theme of love becomes more objective, more lyrical") and then there is traditional dancing and images of conviviality, entertainment, and sports; children doing physical training; a ballet studio. The film concludes with images of a solitary child leading back to further images of underdevelopment. A previous image of Fidel reappears and the frame closes in on a girl standing behind him. A title appears: SIN FIN (Without end). Not underdevelopment, that is, but the struggle against it. Song of the tourist? The title is clearly ironic.

Another, even shorter, film made a year earlier shows the same lucid use of montage. The portrait of a North American soldier fighting in Vietnam, *La muerte de J. J. Jones* (The death of J. J. Jones) is the work of a young black director who had spent part of his youth in New York, returning to Cuba with the victory of the Revolution—the same who made the experimental fictional short *La jaula:* Sergio Giral. Here there is no specially composed music, but a sound track put together against the black-and-white image on the editing bench to create a kind of *musique concrète* in a highly satirical key. "I am a soldier of the U.S. Army in Vietnam," the film begins. "We fight Communism because Communism wants to deny people Coca-Cola." It proceeds by deconstructing—that is, dissecting and dismembering—the imagery of consumer society, the mass media, the movies, comics, he-men of the Mr. Universe type, the army, racism, and advertising. A patriotic army advertisement is montaged with a film clip of new recruits being inducted by a sergeant who, between spitting, addresses the recruits: "You guys are going to hate the day you met me. As far as I'm concerned, you're NOT HUMAN BEINGS." The images are assembled from an ad hoc range of sources, mostly culled from the products of the North American publicity machine that sells the "American way of life." They are images of a kind by which Latin America is engulfed (the very phrase "American way of life" is regularly used by Latin American writers on media and cultural imperialism in English to indicate this ubiquitousness).

After the induction, the film comes to images of training and fighting, intercut with shots of Tarzan. Scenes of Vietnam itself are accompanied by the "Hallelujah Chorus"—"For the Lord God omnipotent reigneth." Images of German Nazism and the modern U.S. Nazi party are introduced. The film concludes with an infamous quotation from Hitler: "For the good of our country we need a war every ten or fifteen years."

The play of montage on which these films are carried is clearly and immediately reminiscent of the role that montage played in Soviet cinema in the latter part of the 1920s. In the work of Álvarez himself, as well as a number of other examples, it comes close to Dziga Vertov. The affinity is there because the two cinemas were animated by the same qualities of revolutionary thought, intelligence, and imagination. "Art is not a mirror which reflects the historical struggle, but a weapon of that struggle," Vertov declared. "Cinema," Álvarez proclaimed, "is not an extension of revolutionary action. Cinema is and must be revolutionary action in itself." "We are here," says Vertov, "to serve a specific class—workers and peasants—we are here to show the world as it is and to explain the bourgeois structure of the world to the workers." "One can only be a revolutionary artist," according to Álvarez, "by being with the people and by communicating with them."[6] The two cinemas center on the same definition of cinema as a revolutionary weapon, as a medium of communication, as a dialectical medium in which montage and the process of editing is the means of synthesis. And they both prioritize the need to offer in the film an interpretative vision according to the goals of revolutionary society.

But the Cuban montage style also reflects a purely practical problem—the lack of sufficient material and resources. "The North Americans," says Álvarez, "blockade us, so forcing us to improvize. For instance, the greatest inspiration in the photo-collage of American magazines in my films is the American government who have prevented me getting hold of live material." "Perhaps," as Miguel Orodea observes about this, "this is why there isn't a theory that holds Alvarez's work together and why he doesn't seem interested in elaborating one."[7] This indeed is something that distinguishes Álvarez from other Cuban filmmakers. Alea, García Espinosa, Alfredo Guevara, Pastor Vega, Massip, Fraga, and many others have engaged in theoretical reflection. Álvarez does not seem to have the same intellectual cast of mind, or even a bent for criticism. He expresses himself best in conversation. His written pieces are few and short and originally produced for meetings and conferences, in a terse kind of political shorthand. "Technical advances," Orodea explains, "have allowed Alvarez to experiment on a much bigger scale than Vertov could have aimed at, in the use of techniques of rostrum animation, optical re-filming, sound, colour, etc. Alvarez's visual resources vary from the use of photographic material from *Playboy* and the whole of the North American press, to extracts from Hollywood movies, Soviet classics, scientific documentaries, archive footage and television images, newspaper headlines and animated titles, put together in counterpoint with the most eclectic range of music." It is difficult, then, to speak of Álvarez's style if by style is meant anything like the conscious pursuit of a set of rationalized aesthetic aims. His style, says Orodea, "consists in adapting to the needs of the moment and using everything at his disposal. It is a style of constant evolution and change. The only constantly dominant criterion in his cinema is support for the Revolution and the anti-imperialist offensive." As Álvarez himself puts it, "My style is the style of hatred for imperialism."[8] He describes himself as "a product of 'accelerated underdevelopment'":

> The Revolution made me a film director. I learned the job fondly handling millions of feet of film. I was enabled to fulfill very old dreams, from the time of Nuestro Tiempo, when we had a film club and the aspiration to create a Cuban cinema that would be part of a different kind of society. I was restless, like every good mother's son, who goes to the cinema a lot but cannot express his restlessness. Now that I can, I do.[9]

It was not only his restlessness that he expressed. Born in Havana in 1919, Álvarez is the son of immigrant parents from Spain; his father, who earned his living as a corner shopkeeper and later a grocer's supplier, was arrested for anarchist activities when Santiago was about five or six years old. For a couple of years while he was in prison, the family had to struggle hard to survive. At the age of fifteen, Álvarez started working, as a compositor's apprentice. Before long he was participating in strikes organized by the Union of Graphic Arts. As his political involvement grew, he also decided to get himself an education. He went to night school, where he found himself setting up a students' association.[10] From these beginnings he carried forward with him a powerful sense of struggle, from which, as his creative mastery flowered in the 1960s, he drew deep poetic feeling.

The film in which this poetry is first maturely expressed is *Hanoi martes 13* (Hanoi Tuesday the 13th—the equivalent, in Latin America, of Friday the 13th), filmed in North Vietnam on the same trip as the Laos "filmic fragments." One of Álvarez's indisputable masterpieces, this is a film of the greatest sensitivity, made with the greatest integrity, and constructed with the greatest economy of means, with memorable music by Leo Brouwer.

At the beginning and the end of the film, color is used briefly for paintings and engravings by Vietnamese artists that testify to the richness of Vietnamese cultural traditions. They accompany at the beginning a striking text about the inhabitants of Southeast Asia by José Martí, from a children's book he wrote called *La edad de oro* (The golden age), which speaks of the culture of the Anamites and their age-old struggle for freedom. This opening is abruptly interrupted by an explosive montage that portrays the grotesque birth of a monster in Texas in 1908—none other than Lyndon Baines Johnson, who is treated to a rapid and satirical biography. The Vietnamese images resume peacefully, in black and white, with a visual account of their methods of fishing and agriculture. This paradigmatic structure of interruption and resumption is followed through the length of the film. Work in the fields is interrupted by the flight overhead of attacking airplanes (the film takes its title from the date of this attack, at 2:50 P.M. on December 13, 1966, shortly after Álvarez and his crew had arrived in Hanoi, and while they were out filming), and the workers in the field discard their plows and take up their guns.

These shots are unimpeachable actuality. Álvarez filmed them because he was there already filming when the attack began, and he had his wits about him. The film's title sequence, after the Johnson montage, has told us where and when: now we discover what. Because of the way Álvarez constructs the narrative, to give this information in a commentary would be redundant. And yet the scenes are not particularly dramatic, as they would be if this were conventional reportage. Álvarez knows they do not need to be, especially if the rest of the material in which they are embedded is also filmed and edited in such a way that it too gives up its information visually and without commentary.

As the workers resume, Álvarez inserts a title, not only to avoid breaking the mood of visual attention with a commentator's voice, but also the better to make his words speak for the Vietnamese rather than the filmmakers: "We turn anger into energy." Subsequently, we move to Hanoi and gradually begin to pick out from among the many activities the film observes shots that show the artisanal process of production of strange, large concrete drums. Sunk into the pavements and open spaces, they each have a lid and turn out to be air-raid shelters, just big enough for one or two people. To an educated European viewer, these drums are reminiscent of nothing so much as the dustbins or mounds of earth in which characters in the plays of Samuel Beckett become immobilized, so much so that one would be forced to regard this connotation as obligatory if this were a European film. But here they become symbols of something that, though oppressive, signals primarily defiant tenacity (which, in a sense, they do in Beckett too).

Although in this film the means are of the simplest, the editing is exceedingly subtle. True, it has a certain looseness, but the result is that the narrative line is spun out in such a way that it becomes anything but linear. It unfolds more like continuous counterpoint, which also gives you time to reflect upon the images and their rhythms. Brouwer's music encourages this, with the result that the film informs in a manner not just different, but positively alien to what documentary orthodoxy expects. Film by film, Álvarez is turning the whole mode of documentary cinema inside out.

The score for this film is one of the finest that Brouwer has written. The style has nothing to do with conventional film music, but belongs rather with isolated examples of the idiom of the contemporary concert hall brought to the screen—like, say, the music Hanns Eisler wrote in 1940 for Joris Ivens's *Rain* of 1929, in which the relationship of music to image transcends conventional associations, the two become much more independent of each other than normal, and the music far more plastic than usual. Brouwer uses a small group of instruments with contrasting tone colors, and freely juxtaposes echoes of traditional Vietnamese music, which, however, he neither merely imitates nor pastiches, together with a variety of modernist effects, in a continuously unfolding texture. What is even more remarkable are the circumstances under which this score was written. The job had to be done, Brouwer recalled, in record time, "and I even had to compose by telephone." Álvarez called him, he explained, and over the phone described the succession of shots with their timings. But this, he adds, was just the way films got made in Cuba. Instead of the usual successive stages, with the music coming almost last, everything got done practically at the same time.[11] To go by the comments of other collaborators of Álvarez, this atmosphere of creative improvisation was particularly strong in the newsreel department, which Álvarez directed, not merely for the expectable reasons but because Álvarez encourages this way of working.

In *Hasta la victoria siempre* (Always until victory), also made in 1967, Álvarez virtually reinvents *cine denuncia*, the film of denunciation, in a twenty-minute newsreel put together in the space of forty-eight hours of nonstop work in response to the traumatic news of the death of Che Guevara in Bolivia. It was made not to be shown in cinemas but, at Fidel's request, to be projected at a mass demonstration in the Plaza de la Revolución in Havana preceding Fidel's eulogy for el Che. Only the intense cooperation of Álvarez and his team made this possible. The triumph of the film is that even working at such speed, Álvarez produces a poetic and far from simple aesthetic construction, though the film is understandably very rough at the seams and edges. Beginning with a prologue that employs stills to portray the misery of life in Bolivia and signal the presence there of U.S. imperialism, the film uses fragments of archive footage of el Che during the guerrilla war in Cuba, and then after the Revolution cutting cane with others in the fields, to exemplify his creed of revolutionary selflessness, and it concludes with grainy, poorly focused, but riveting images of two of Che's last public speeches, at the UN in December 1964, and the Non-Aligned Conference of 1965.

Che had been involved since the Revolution, and especially after 1962, in an extended theoretical debate on the transition to socialism, in which his own always clearly argued position had not always been accepted. Outside Cuba, too, his theory of guerrilla struggle around a *foco* (focus) was hotly argued, and the disagreements were only highlighted by his death. Fidel would not allow such blemishes on Che's character, whom he called "the most extraordinary of our revolutionary comrades" and "our revolutionary movement's most experienced and able leader." Repudiating attempts "now after his heroic and glorious death . . . to deny the truth or value of his concepts, his guerrilla theories," he asked what was so strange about the fact that he died in combat. What was stranger was that he did not do so "on one of the innumerable occasions when he risked his life during our revolutionary struggle." He then went on to endorse the essential element in the example that Che had left behind him in Cuba: "he had a boundless faith in moral values, in human conscience . . . he saw moral resources, with absolute clarity, as the fundamental lever in the construction of communism."[12] The film is a perfect preparation for Fidel's eulogy. The excerpts from Che's speeches emphasize his anti-imperialist resolution, which he articulates in a character-istically blunt and direct fashion, in simple but forceful and graphic language. It is not that Fidel told Álvarez what he was going to say or what to put in the film—there was no time for that and, in any case, Fidel was not inclined to such artistic collaboration. He once told the Soviet documentarist Roman Karmen, who asked what he would like them to film, "Unfortunately, I understand nothing about the art of film, so I re-frain from giving advice."[13] It was rather that Fidel had seen the close-ness of Álvarez's thought to his own. And from now on, the relationship between Álvarez and Fidel is to grow closer.

Hasta la victoria siempre has left a curiously tangible imprint in the popular culture of contemporary Cuba. For his sound-track music, Álvarez uses a piece by Pérez Prado, a Cuban composer who had once been associated with one of the most popular of Cuban singers, Beny Moré. Pérez Prado had left Cuba for the United States, where he devised the transformation of the Cuban dance rhythm known as cha-cha-cha, which took Tin Pan Alley by storm in the 1950s—one of a succession of Latin American dance rhythms with which the music industry in the United States periodically injects itself. Carried to U.S. shores by the process of migration, the culture industry there pulls them out and re-processes them, and then churns them out in sterilized, safe, and predi-gested form, which, of course, it reexports. The piece that Álvarez uses here is a syrupy arrangement that on first hearing sounds oddly inappro-priate to a European ear inclined to reject—like Adorno and Eisler in their book on composing for the cinema—the devices of musical com-mercialism. A first reaction, then, is how can Álvarez be so tasteless as to use this kind of music? The piece, however, is actually a version by Pérez Prado of a work by the Brazilian Heitor Villa-Lobos, composer of the nationalist bourgeoisie, one of the few Latin American composers of art music with the originality and expertise to have commanded a reputation in Europe; and it turns out that Álvarez is doing some rearranging of his own. By using this music, Álvarez is, as it were, reclaiming it. This, at any rate, is what it must now seem, for to this day the piece is indissolubly fused in Cuban popular consciousness with Che's memory, and is regu-larly played on the radio and at gigs on the anniversary of his death.

A year later, in 1968, Álvarez produced his most biting piece of anti-imperialist satire yet, *LBJ*, which has deservedly become one of his best-known shorts. Running eighteen minutes, it is a stunning piece of visual and musical montage made entirely of found materials (except for titles), which achieves a pitch of satirical denunciation that Álvarez seems to have reserved especially for Lyndon Baines Johnson.

The film is in three main sections with a prologue and an epilogue. These sections correspond to the three letters of Johnson's initials, which are used to stand for Luther, Bob, and John (or Jack): Martin Luther King and the two Kennedys. It is a bold play on the strange coincidence that the corpses of these three men littered Johnson's ascent. Álvarez does not directly accuse Johnson of assassination, but this is beside the point. There is no commentary, no direct verbal statement, and accusations by unsympathetic critics that the film is nothing but the expression of Marxist hysteria about conspiracy say more about them than about the film. What Álvarez is doing is to portray Johnson's presidency as the culmination of a whole history of sociopolitical corruption, not of individuals—the matter of individual presidential corruption was to come with Johnson's successor—but of the "American way of life" itself. As Stuart Hood has put it, the film is "a deadly and accurately aimed attack on a political system in which assassination had become an accustomed weapon and the circumstances of the killings veiled in misinformation and mystery."[14]

The core of the satire is the image, culled from a North American newspaper cartoon, of Johnson as the incarnation of the Texas cowboy on his bucking bronco. Álvarez doubles this up with Johnson as a medieval knight in armor astride his mount, and reinforces his line of attack with clips from two types of Hollywood movie—westerns and the historical adventure. Movies of this kind are very familiar in Cuban cinemas, and Cubans, like other audiences, are still ingenuously attached to them to one degree or another. These clips are in'scope, and in refilming them on the optical camera the filmmakers have not used an anamorphic lens to unsqueeze the image—because the Cubans didn't have the appropriate lens for this particular piece of equipment. But the effect conforms entirely with the aim of the film; it puts quotation marks round the clips, as if to foreground the iconographic dimension of Hollywood mythology. And by applying this mythology to Johnson, Álvarez symbolizes one of the ideological functions of the "popular culture" of the marketplace.

The entire fabric of the film is woven out of allusions and connotations of this kind, combined in a crisscrossing montage of fine political wit. In the sequence portraying the assassination of JFK, for example, the picture crosscuts a still photo of the president's car in the fateful Dallas cavalcade, showing the scene supposedly from the assassin's point of view, gunsights superimposed, with a shot not of a rifleman but of a medieval archer aiming a crossbow. A moment later, Johnson taking over the White House is captured by a photograph of Kennedy's rocking chair being carried away by the removal men.

As the Cuban critic Manuel López Oliva put it, in the Havana newspaper *El Mundo* at the time the film appeared, Johnson becomes "an X-ray caricature of the North American 'hero.'" The image is multiplied and distorted so that "each aspect—the initials of the name, the face, the grin, Johnson's little fancies"—like his pet dogs—"his hands—come to amplify the subject's fleeting attributes, turning them into symbolic allusions that fill out the representation of the death-laden acronym."[15] This review captured the significance of the film in its moment very well. It appeared to many people in Cuba at the time as a too-personalized poetic, which broke away from Álvarez's preceding and, as it were, more classical style. It *is* highly personalized, says López Oliva, but not for that reason inferior. Several of Álvarez's films anticipated *LBJ*, like three that had gained international awards—*Ciclón, Now*, and *Hanoi martes 13*. They had used the same type of montage to create a new expressive dimension quite capable of carrying a narrative, even though the images employed were the most diverse, and sometimes even contradictory. There were some recent newsreels too, he says, especially a report on springtime sowing, where again, traditional poetics were mixed with a poetic logic of the photographic image that is taken direct from life—in other words, a kind of fusion of the individual language of the artist with the aesthetic logic of the camera, in which the primary connotation of the image is public and common.

What López Oliva is arguing for, in the Cuban context, is the recognition of an expressive need in Álvarez's idiom: in political terms, that both authority and popular opinion should reaffirm the artist's autonomy of style, which Fidel had recognized in the "Words to the Intellectuals" of 1961. By the late 1960s, the debate about the application of the principles had, if anything, intensified, and López Oliva's review is densely argued. Álvarez occupied a cetrifugal position as the head of the newsreel department and it fell to him to be, as López Oliva puts it, the first filmmaker in Cuba "to get to the point of entirely banishing classical rhetoric from the lens." To be sure, the result was a "pretty personal expressive structure," but because of the way Álvarez and his team worked, it was also collective. People around ICAIC knew that. It also constituted a "lucid collage assembly of ideas, in which historical, ideological, and didactic elements were all imaginatively deployed." In Álvarez, López Oliva concludes, art, documentary, and politics coalesce into an organic unity inseparable from the very filmstrip itself, which becomes wholly and positively suggestive from start to finish. There is no question but that the Cubans found in *LBJ* a paradigmatic expression of the defiance with which they responded to the loss of Che Guevara.

Álvarez forced the pace, but there are also other significant films of these years to be noted. In 1964, there was the first documentary by Sara Gómez, *Iré a Santiago* (I'm going to Santiago)—we shall look at all of Sara Gómez's films separately later on. Cuban and Latin American critics have singled out several others, including *El ring*, a short on boxing by Óscar Valdéz (1966), and Alejandro Saderman's *Hombres de mal tiempo* (Men of bad times, 1968), which the Peruvian Juan M. Bullitta has described as "a film about the good memory of a group of veterans from Cuba's independence struggles" and hence a fine example of *cine rescate*.[16] Then there was Octavio Cortázar's *Por primera vez* from 1967, and a year later another film of his, an inquiry into the hold still exercised on various sectors of the population by the religious beliefs of underdevelopment, a piece of *cine encuesta* called *Acerca de un personaje que unos llaman San Lázaro y otros llaman Babalú* (About a personality some call San Lázaro and others Babalú, 1968). In *El ring*, Bullitta finds a demonstration of the advantages of the compact dialectical montage of the "classic structuralist methodology" of the documentary. The film is a portrait of the world of boxing under several aspects. It juxtaposes sequences of training and interviews with both a trainer and a retired fighter from the time of Cuba's most famous boxer, Chocolatín, contrasting what the sport used to be like with what it had now become, with the commercialism removed. Bullitta singles out Saderman's film for its avoidance of the frenetic and overaudacious uses of the camera that, he says, constitute one of the notorious weaknesses of Cuban cinema. For us, the most significant of these films is the last, but that will be in another context later on.

There are also two films made in 1968 by José Massip. In *Madina-Boe,* Massip reported from the liberation struggle in Portuguese Guinea, as Álvarez did from Southeast Asia, but using a distinct approach. Massip brings to the screen a close identification with African culture, which is one of the constant features of his work. There is an affinity with Pastor Vega's *Hombres del cañaveral* in the way, using captions but no commentary, he selects individuals from the group in the guerrilla band he is filming for individual portraits: Braima, the Hunter, who performs ancestral rites before going out hunting; Indrissa, who is a Builder of Canoes; Kalunda d'Acosta, a Football Player; and Fode, the Poet. He then develops the report through parallel scenes at the camp and at a guerrilla hospital base, where a doctor from Portugal is one of the personnel, a white man whose antifascist commitment leads him to give his services to the liberation struggle. The sense of actuality is intensified by the use, a couple of times, of a simple intertitle, "At this very moment," to mark the crosscutting between the hospital and the camp in the scrub, where the guerrillas are preparing for an attack against enemy positions in the village of Madina, where some of them come from. Scenes of Braima the hunter have prepared us for the rites and rituals the fighters observe before setting out, and the film ends with shots from behind the guerrilla lines as they go into the attack; these are built up by the special-effects department back in the studios into the battle it had not proved possible to film, and the sounds of battle cross-fade into children singing, over still images of children's faces. Like *La guerra olvidada, Hanoi martes 13,* and the two films by Pastor Vega, this is a film in which revolutionary urgency is expressed reflectively, and with a strong feeling of human empathy.

Massip's *Nuestro olimpiada en la Habana* (Our Olympiad in Havana), on the other hand, is a film of idiosyncratic Cuban humor, down to the allusion in the title to Graham Greene's novel. The Olympiad in question is the international chess tournament that Havana hosted in 1968. The film is a simple nineteen-minute montage of the preparations for the tournament; the interest taken by quite large numbers of ordinary Cubans; the tournament games of the grand masters—here the camera picks out facial expressions and little unconscious nervous ticks and gestures as they concentrate; and the scene in the open air in which one of the grand masters performs his trick of playing simultaneous games against all comers, one of whom, of course, is Fidel. The shots of Fidel in this film are perhaps the most original that had yet been seen of him in Cuban cinema. They conform to none of the common images of Fidel in the old photos and newsreels as a young lawyer and then a guerrilla comandante, or those of the Revolution in power, where he becomes an orator and a TV star, the embodiment of Cuban pride and defiance. Here, following the glimpses we have had of so many different styles of concentration among players at the chessboard, Fidel is suddenly seen as just another of them, both familiar and unfamiliar at the same time. It might well be said that in this way Massip humanizes Fidel's image, except that it is not as if it were not already human.

In subsequent years, the image of Fidel on the screen is to undergo considerable elaboration, above all, but not exclusively, in the work of Álvarez, who becomes something like his poet laureate. On three occasions Álvarez traveled with Fidel on foreign trips, which he chronicled in films of length: *De América soy hijo... y a ella me debo* (Born of the Americas) of 1972, the film of Fidel's visit to Chile, is by far the longest, 195 minutes in the full version; but... *Y el cielo fue tomado por asalto* (...And heaven was taken by storm), Fidel's East European and African tour of 1972, and *El octubre de todos* (Everyone's October, 1977), of the second African tour, run 128 and 80 minutes, respectively. As Stuart Hood reflected, after a retrospective of Álvarez's work in London in 1980, we are not used to lengthy documentaries like this with their easy pace and "a certain discursive quality which can be deceptively innocent," especially *De América soy hijo...*, "loose-jointed but powerful in its cumulative effect and its insistent contextualisation of the Chilean situation."[17] They offer, nonetheless, a rich collection of glimpses of Fidel in a large variety of circumstances, both formal and informal. As an orator, Fidel comes across in these films as both jurist and actor: he commands his part as an actor like Olivier in a Shakespeare play delivering a monologue to a gripped theater. There is no denying that Fidel greeting crowds and crowds greeting Fidel can become repetitive, but such images are frequently offset by moments of individual interaction, such as an exchange he has with a working woman at a rally in Chile, or by the habit Álvarez has of leaving in the bits that many an impatient editor would wish to leave on the cutting-room floor ("untidy moments," as Hood

Images of Fidel

calls them)—Fidel fidgeting with the microphones on the podium in front of him, for instance. To these one must add the manner of his inter-action with the gathered crowds, in both individual shots and whole sequences, like a scene in which he plays basketball with students in Poland and which gave the lie to rumors in the capitalist media of a heart attack. They all add up to the image of a man who is, in fact, like the film star, larger than life.

This is tempered, however, by two other appearances he makes, in Álvarez's *Mi hermano Fidel* (My brother Fidel) of 1977, and a sequence in Jorge Fraga's 1973 feature-length documentary *La nueva escuela* (The new school). In both these films, though in rather different circum-stances, we observe Fidel in direct personal interaction with ordinary Cubans. The first is a short in which he interviews an old man who, as a child, met José Martí himself, when he landed in Cuba in 1895 to enter the war against Spain; the second is a report on Cuba's new educational system. Adjectives to describe Fidel's manner in these films trip off the tongue: spontaneous, warm, intimate, uninhibited, humorous. We rec-ognize a kind of behavior quite untypical of political leaders, which,

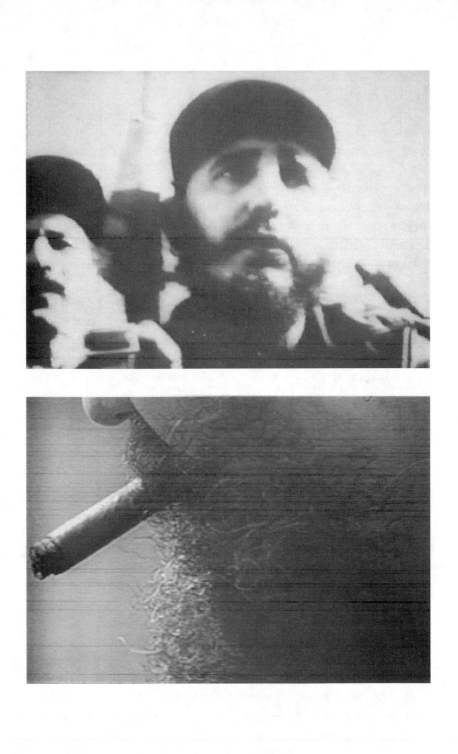

however, in the coverage of U.S. presidential campaigns, is quite calcu-latedly staged.

How can we be sure that in Fidel's case it is everything that it seems to be? There is a significant piece of evidence in each of these two films, in one case in the language, in the other in the image. Fidel's closeness to the people he meets is generally to be remarked in the mutual use of *tú,* the ordinary singular "you" in Spanish, instead of the more polite *Usted*—except that, in *Mi hermano Fidel,* Fidel throughout addresses the old man, who fails to recognize him because of his poor eyesight, as *Usted,* as a mark of respect. The evidence of the camera is equally subtle. Fidel tends fairly frequently to look at the camera (and there is no at-tempt to cut these shots out; in *Mi hermano Fidel* they even become a visual leitmotiv). When he does so, we feel the same searching eyes we observe as he listens to the old man and others with whom we see him engaged in conversation. We get the impression that he behaves toward the camera just as if it were another person. I have heard it remarked that people who treat cameras like people tend to treat people like cam-eras, but in Fidel's case the quip misfires, because we can see nothing calculating in these looks, only the signs of curiosity and attention— and the gift of entering into the moment, like the way, in *La nueva es-cuela,* he joins in with the schoolchildren in games of baseball, volley-ball, and table tennis. It is perfectly evident from this last-mentioned sequence that Fidel is a man with a highly competitive spirit; he likes to win—he was a prominent sportsman in his schooldays—he enjoys his stardom. It is also evident that there is a strong paternalistic element in his relationship to the children. But something else also comes across in this sequence, which is also strong in *De América soy hijo...,* namely, an easy familiarity, and a total absence of fear in these encounters by ordi-nary people with the leader.

In 1969, Álvarez made a film that re-created *cine militante: Despegue a las 18.00* (Takeoff at 18.00). Slow dance music and images of blood pul-sating through veins, then phrases and words appearing on the screen one by one and advancing toward the viewer: YOU ARE GOING TO SEE / A FILM THAT IS / DIDACTIC / INFORMATIVE / POLITICAL / AND... / PAMPHLETEERING... / ABOUT A PEOPLE / IN REVOLU-TION / ANXIOUS... / DESPERATE... / TO FIND A WAY OUT OF / AN AGONIZING / HERITAGE... / UNDERDEVELOPMENT. The words give way to a picture of a thatched roof and the camera zooms out to reveal a large barn being pulled down. Another title appears, the words inscribed within a circle: IF WE WERE BLOCKADED / COMPLETELY / WHAT WOULD WE DO? The camera zooms into the dot of the question mark. STOP PRODUCTION? / FOLD OUR ARMS? The image changes to an old map of the Antilles with drawings of sailing ships covering the sea—an icon of colonialism. The music changes to a Cuban *danzón* (traditional urban popular dance music) and the credits roll. (The music is again by Leo Brouwer.)

The credits end and the image cuts to a sign outside a shoe shop. The camera pans along a queue of people as the music passes into a minor key, like a blues. Then there's another queue, this time people waiting for bread. Street sounds are mixed in, and the frame freezes on a face. Faces and hands are seen in slow motion. Close-up of an old woman; again the frame freezes, and a caption is superimposed: NO HAY (There isn't any). The caption repeats itself several times, intercut with a woman gesturing with her forefinger as if to reiterate the caption. More special optical effects: the picture jumps from one freeze-frame to another of the woman's gesture and grimace. The effect is repeated with another, as if in conversational reply. Strange whistling sounds in the music interpret what they are saying. An old couple shrug their shoulders and the same caption appears again: NO HAY. Then, without warning, another image altogether: the eagle being toppled from the monument erected in Havana by the United States in the early years of the Republic, a symbolic piece of newsreel from the first years of the Revolution, a repudiation of servility to the United States. Then a strange engraving of a Chinaman lying horizontal, his clothing covered with images of various animals and objects. The captions now spell out what there isn't any of: THERE ISN'T ANY ILLITERACY—THERE ISN'T ANY PROSTITUTION—THERE ISN'T ANY UNEMPLOYMENT—THERE AREN'T ANY DESTITUTES—THERE AREN'T ANY HOMELESS—THERE ARE NO LOTTERIES—THERE'S NO POLIO—THERE'S NO MALARIA.

These opening moments of *Despegue a las 18.00* demonstrate what happens when Álvarez applies the virtuosity he has developed to the full in *LBJ* to the mobilization of workers in Oriente province in April 1968, a trial run for the kind of mobilizations that were being planned for the whole country in the battle to increase agricultural production and especially the production of sugar cane. Turning from the enemy

Despegue a las 18.00 (Santiago Álvarez, 1969)

back to the Revolution, Álvarez's restlessness takes on new energy. He first calls his audience to attention, and then teases them, almost unfairly ("If we were completely blockaded..."—as if they were not blockaded!). He coaxes and cajoles the audience with images of the daily reality of the effects of the blockade—the ration lines. It is not presented as reportage or news—everyone knows this already. Nor are these images any apology for hardship; they are the very reality of it. With his expressionist stretching of the image, Álvarez means his audience to re-experience in their cinema seats the grind of their daily lives, in order to launch from here into a piece of emblazoning agitational propaganda that reinvents the whole idea of propaganda and agitation. Not for nothing has Álvarez commented on the inventiveness of advertising techniques. But rejecting the ways, if not all the means, of advertising, his wish is not to replace the propaganda of the marketplace with some kind of socialist equivalent. He wants to engage the audience on their own territory.

Only the fainthearted will blench at the parallel the film draws between mobilization for production and mobilization for war. The film analyzes the strategy (to which, as an agitational work, it also belongs itself) needed to engage in a battle. When Fidel in a speech talks of the demanding opportunity the Revolution has created for Cuba, which asks people to work like animals so that they need no longer work like animals, and he compares this with the misery that continues in the rest of Latin America, the film takes in images of Bolivia, Brazil, Guatemala. Fidel's voice gives way to a song by Silvio Rodríguez, one of the "Nueva Trova," the Cuban New Song Movement, which takes up a theme from Fidel: "Four thousand a minute, five million a day, two thousand million a year, ten thousand million the century, for every thousand who overflow the earth one of them dies, a thousand dollars a death, four times a minute, this is life. Sharks' teeth have never come cheap." This comes from the Second Declaration of Havana, presented by Fidel for popular ratification at a mass meeting in Havana on February 4, 1962, and, like the First Declaration, an answer to the anti-Cuban pronouncements of the Organization of American States (OAS), in this case at its meeting at Punta del Este a few days earlier.

Despegue a las 18.00 is not one of the films by which Álvarez is known abroad. It is a film directed so specifically to an internal need that outside Cuba the context is lacking to grasp it properly, though it is obviously a tour de force anyway. In the same year, however, Álvarez, now at the height of his creative powers, produced another work that has justly been internationally appreciated. *79 primaveras* (79 springs) is an incomparably poetic tribute to Ho Chi Minh. A film of twenty-five minutes, the title refers to the Vietnamese leader's age at the time of his death. Its form is that of a biographical résumé of the principal dates in Ho Chi Minh's political life. The decorative titles that announce these dates are interspersed among archive footage and other intertitles, inscribed with lines of poetry elegiacally assembled. Again, the opening is beautifully constructed: first there are slow-motion shots of flowers opening, then a shot of bombs dropping almost gracefully through the sky. Then the screen goes blank and we hear the human cry of a singer. After the first credit, a negative image of the young Ho Chi Minh appears, which transforms itself into a positive image and then dissolves into close-ups. Because these close-ups are refilmed, they have become somewhat grainy— by now a familiar effect in Álvarez's language, which gives a gain in the plasticity of the image and reminds you of its material nature. We see Ho Chi Minh aging, the image returns to the negative, the screen turns a brilliant white, and the titles resume.

At the end of the credits, which incorporate moving pictures of the

Vietnamese leader, we come to a close-up of him sitting in the open air at his typewriter. A title: "They tied my legs with a rope," followed by a shot of him washing his feet. Another: "And they tied my arms," followed by a close-up of his hands rolling a cigarette. "I gave my life to my people," and a shot of Ho at a house in the jungle. An army band playing at his funeral. The simplicity of it.

When the biographical résumé reaches the victory of Dien Bien Phu, the film begins to shift gear. The "Internationale" is heard and we see the faces of international communist leaders at the funeral. We cut to a popular Cuban singer—"The era is giving birth to a heart, it is dying of pain and can stand no more"—and her audience of cheerful Vietnamese children. The scene is violently interrupted by bombs and the devastation of napalm. Over horrific images of children's burned faces and bodies the music becomes violent and discordant. A title declares: THEY BEGAN TO KILL IN ORDER TO WIN. Then, in slow motion, one of the most infamous images of the Vietnam War, a couple of North American soldiers beating a Vietnamese who has collapsed on the ground: we see feet and hands and the rifle butts of his attackers, but not their faces. Then: AND NOW THEY KILL BECAUSE THEY CANNOT WIN. No one has ever commented on Vietnam with greater economy or dignity.

The portrayal of the war continues with shots of antiwar demonstrators in the United States with placards that unequivocally establish a universalizing message: VIETNAM, WATTS, IT'S THE SAME STRUGGLE; AVENGE CHE; FUCK THE DRAFT. Then another of the most notorious media images of Vietnam, a pair of GIs taking souvenir snapshots of their victims on the battlefield, to which Álvarez appends another piece of poetry by Ho Chi Minh—and in these lines the film knits its imagery together:

> Without the glacial winter, without grief and death,
> Who can appreciate your glory, Spring?
> The pains which temper my spirit are a crucible
> And they forge my heart in pure steel.

At this point many a filmmaker would have been content to conclude. Not Álvarez, who has the nerve, or better, the cheek, to proceed with more scenes of the funeral, set to the music of Iron Butterfly. This is not simply a grand aesthetic gesture. The film was made in a period when, once again, sectarians were vocal, condemning the importation of music from the metropolis and those who were influenced by it—one

79 primaveras (Santiago Álvarez, 1969)

of those they attacked was Silvio Rodríguez. Álvarez defies them, picking one of Silvio's songs for *Despegue...*, making solidarity with the North American music of popular protest in *79 primaveras*.

And then comes the coup de grâce. A new title appears: DON'T LET DISUNITY IN THE SOCIALIST CAMP DARKEN THE FUTURE. Using animation, the title is torn apart into little pieces, which slide off the edges of the frame to leave the screen blank. The music disappears. A gunshot announces a split-screen, multi-image sequence of war footage, freeze-frames, scratches, sprocket holes, flashes, guns, planes, bombs, sounds of battle with electric keyboard noises on the sound track, in which brutal reality bursts through the limits of its portrayal on celluloid in an unrelenting and terrifying assault that ends in the annihilation of a freeze-frame, which burns up before our eyes, leaving a blank white screen. And then? The torn pieces of the title reappear and join up again. The picture cuts to rockets firing, to the accompaniment of energizing music by Bach, bursts of gunfire flash across the screen, the flowers reappear, and a final title appears: THE YANQUIS DEFEATED WE WILL CONSTRUCT A FATHERLAND TEN TIMES MORE BEAUTIFUL.

After seeing this film, Álvarez's revolutionary aesthetic comes into the clearest focus. Having banished classical rhetoric in *LBJ*—an achievement dependent on its prior mastery—and having invented agitational propaganda anew in *Despegue*..., he now explodes the cinematic image itself. Yet this is something very much more than theoretical deconstruction. For one thing, what he does is not theorized, it is the product of the aesthetic logic he has been working out from one film to the next, it answers to expressive, not theoretical needs. Álvarez cannot be called a deconstructionist filmmaker, though in his practice he seems to know more about deconstruction than the most eloquent theorist. He is, stylistically, something of an expressionist, almost the spiritual descendant of the expressionists of the first decades of the twentieth century whose revolutionary aesthetics thrust art into the modern world—but with this difference, that in Álvarez, the temper of the individual and of the collective coincide. His idiom is deeply personal, like that of any major artist of integrity, but at the same time it is a completely public form of utterance, cleansed of the shit of individualism. In Álvarez, the individual is fully submerged in history.

The result is that Álvarez also knows better than many of us who live in the belly of the monster the truth about the cinema and its place within the military-industrial culture of imperialism: that everything we hate about it, its lies, its arrogance, its preachments about what is popular, and the childish mental age it projects upon its audience, its pornographic pandering to the caprice of the marketplace, all this belongs to the same stable as the soldiers who shoot their victims with guns and then with Kodaks. Nevertheless, everything we hate about the screen to which we entrust our dreams is redeemable, but only on condition that there be openly displayed in the oppositional film what the films of the enemy try to hide: their political provenance. The most experimental techniques can then be freely explored without sacrificing communicability; indeed, the opposite. But there is a corollary: if these techniques are used, as they are by many avant-garde filmmakers, without marrying them to a clear political purpose, nothing at all can be gained. On the contrary, such films can only reinforce the breakdown of communication that they pretend to expose.

CHAPTER ELEVEN

The Current of Experimentalism

A revolutionary cinema committed to the demystification of its medium is sooner or later bound to confront the question of the image of the hero and the revolutionary leader in all its aspects. The first to explore the image of heroism was García Espinosa in *El joven rebelde,* which created an anti-militarist paradigm. The idea of heroism was to be actively deconstructed in the early 1970s by Manuel Herrera in his major documentary *Girón.* At the moment when Álvarez made *Hasta la victoria siempre* in 1967, something different was required. The film's very function was to eulogize the heroic revolutionary martyr, and the quality of Álvarez's creativity produced a way of doing this at once original and innovatory, and as vibrant with revolutionary fervor as the oratory that served as its model. The poetry of the film partly comes from the way the screen is given over to reproductions of Che's image. This succession of images of differing quality creates an effect akin to deconstruction, largely arising from the effect that refilming the images has on foregrounding their material quality as reproductions, signifiers of what is absent. Which is to say that Álvarez does not engage in this exercise for its own sake, but for its metaphorical significance, the sense of loss in the photographic imprints a man has left behind conjuring up his presence in the hour of his death; to make people realize that this is all that is left of him—his captors have secreted his body away—but it's enough because it's everything: his living example. The same theme was later treated in another documentary, made in 1981 by a Chilean filmmaker exiled in Cuba, Pedro Chaskel, which uses only the image of Che that spread around the world like wildfire in 1968, replicated on banners and posters held aloft at the countless demonstrations of that fateful year, an image taken from what is not only one of the most famous photographs of the twentieth century, but one of the few that truly deserve that much-overused epithet "iconic." A highly poetic film essay, the tone of this film is signaled by the title, *Un foto recorre al mundo,* literally, "A photo goes around the world," which in Spanish evokes the opening words of the *Communist Manifesto.*

The history of this photograph, which has only recently come to light, speaks directly of the public creation of iconic imagery of revolutionary heroism. It was taken by Alberto Korda on March 5, 1960, on assignment for the newspaper *Revolución* (later *Granma*) at the protest rally the day after the explosion of the Belgian freighter *La Coubre* in Havana harbor that killed more than a hundred dockworkers (see chapter 6). At the beginning of Chaskel's film, Korda (who for ten years was Fidel's official photographer) remembers how he took it: it was a damp, cold day, and he was panning his Leica across the figures on the dais, searching the faces with a 90 mm lens, when Che's face jumped into the viewfinder. The look in his eyes startled him so much, he said, that he instinctively lurched backwards, and immediately pressed the button. A moment later Che was gone. Another time he added, "There appears to be a mystery in those eyes, but in reality it is just blind rage at the deaths of the day before and the grief for their families."[1] The newspaper put the picture on an inside page, leaving the front page for a photo of Fidel. Seven years later, he gave a copy to the left-wing Italian publisher Giangiacomo Feltrinelli (the man who first published *Doctor Zhivago* in the West, and who died in 1972 in mysterious circumstances when he was blown up by a car bomb). A few weeks later, Che was captured and killed in Bolivia and became an instant martyr. When Castro addressed a memorial rally in the Plaza de la Revolución, Korda's photo was used to create a mural to adorn the side of a building facing the podium where Castro spoke; it is still there. Feltrinelli instantly spotted the value of the image, putting it on the cover of the publication of Che's diaries and handing it over to be used on posters, which were soon being carried through the streets in the worldwide revolutionary protest marches of 1968.

In part, this image of the noble guerrilla, with tilted beret and flowing locks, derived its potency from another: the press photo of Che's body laid out on a slab by the Bolivian military who captured him, framed and angled to imitate Mantegna's *Dead Christ*. Korda's photo seemed to constitute a reply: Che lives, defiant as ever. The image thus took on a life of its own, rapidly spreading from posters and banners to T-shirts and album covers. Supposing the photo to be in the public domain, it was soon taken up by advertisers targeting youth until it rivaled the Mona Lisa as perhaps the most replicated image ever. Korda received no royalties. Feltrinelli had used the photo without his permission, and even failed to credit him as the photographer.[2]

In the same year as Che's death appeared another film that treated the question of the image of the martyred revolutionary hero to an exhaustive and very different investigation, perhaps the most substantial it has ever had in documentary form. The product of three years' research and production, and the biggest documentary project at that time mounted by ICAIC, *David*, directed by Enrique Pineda Barnet, is a film of 135 minutes on the subject of Frank País, a leader of the July 26th Movement in Oriente province who was captured and killed on the streets of Santiago de Cuba in 1957, after an informer had told the police where he was hiding. His murder sparked off a wave of unrest and Santiago was a city in mourning when he was buried the next day in a July 26th Movement uniform with the rank of colonel.[3] "David" was Frank País's *nombre de guerra*, his clandestine name.

What they did not want to do was simply make an outsize biography. They wanted "not just to study the character of a hero but also to break the schema of the hero as a universal and infallible example. To fight the idea of the *guapo* and the *comecandela*"[4]—Latin American slang words for "tough guy." They wanted, he says, to break the fetishism of such images, demystify too the "dogmatic and melodramatic schematization of certain radio and television programs, which present young people with unachievable models of superhuman heroes." They wanted a film that would promote discussion about this, which therefore had to maintain a position of marked protest against the formulas and ritual of the stereotype, without forgetting that the traditional relation of the spectator to the screen, the ambience of cinema, the immediacy of the image, and the ease of emotional identification with it all conspired against them. This in turn they took to mean that they had to find for the film a form that was neither horizontally nor chronologically linear, but that developed a dynamic series of contradictions that would expand along the length of the film, without, however, reaching the normal closure of a passive and conservative dramaturgical method.

Method was the problem they felt themselves facing. This problem they sought to resolve by assembling, along with all their material, ideas from a wide range of sources in both cinema and theater that might serve as paradigms for the endeavor. They found them in Jean Rouch and Edgar Morin, in Chris Marker, and in the Danish documentarist Theodor Christensen, who made a film on women, *Ellas* (They [feminine]) with ICAIC in 1964, in Ivens, Kadar and Klos, Rosi, Godard, Visconti, even Preminger, as well as Brecht, Piscator, and Stanislavsky.[5]

The theatrical paradigms held a special interest for Pineda Barnet. Here he saw a solution, a reply to the conspiracy of cinema to maintain the passivity of the spectator, in the idea of using the dialectical permutation of the epic and dramatic elements of the narrative to transcend the level of anecdote. The results of this approach can be seen in the opening section of the film. At the very start, a sense of pending investigation of a mystery is communicated by shots in which the camera tracks up on objects surrounded by darkness, followed by sections of interviews from which emerges the shape of a shadowy figure to whom is attributed the words, "Nobody understands me. I'm tired of so many things. I want to go and meet other people." Some interviewees say that Frank was a churchgoing person—and a Presbyterian, not a Catholic—others that he was a man of action. A caption gives us a date: March 10, 1952. The film signals this as a time of disorder and topsy-turvydom in the form of a film clip, a musical with the singer singing in the broken English accent of a Latin American, with Spanish subtitles. An archive montage of the period ends with demonstrations at the University of Havana. Whereupon we see a blackboard, with a text written on it, from Marx's *Theses on Feuerbach,* about Feuerbach's failure to understand the social relations within which the individual lives.

For Desiderio Blanco, writing in the Peruvian film journal *Hablemos de Cine, David* is an example of *cine encuesta* incorporating the procedures of both direct cinema and classical montage, which creates a coherent universe around its absent subject more effectively than Jean Rouch created in the world of *Chronique d'un été.* The film, to be truthful, is overlong, but it is another early example in Cuban cinema of a new idiom, which in Spanish might be called *cine desmontaje*—what is known in the radical independent film movements of the metropolis as post-Brechtian deconstruction.

Experience, especially in Europe, has shown that this kind of cinema tends to inordinate length. It has also shown that while aiming to activate the audience, very often it becomes paradoxically unassertive and passive. It is therefore not surprising to find José Massip, in expressing the general response to the film in a review in *Cine Cubano,* saying:

> I do not think that *David,* aesthetically speaking, can be considered an accomplished piece of work. Its principal defect is the passivity of its structure, and even more so its language. However, this passivity is a result of the film's great virtue, which makes it the most important in our feature-length cinema at the moment: its audacious and intense approach to the revolutionary reality of Cuba. This paradox of passivity-audacity, a true example of the law of the unity of contraries, which makes up the most characteristic facet of *David* as a work, is nothing other than the expression of a contradiction between form and content.[6]

The film indeed left its audiences disoriented. Some remember that they came out of the cinemas disconcerted and a bit frustrated—they had not been given the emotional charge they had come to expect in the films of Álvarez; they had not been made to cry and laugh (in this respect, the film did not exactly live up to its Brechtian model either). But a little later, it happened that people began to talk about the personality of Frank País. Whatever its deficiencies, *David* made a strong impression, and Massip prophetically declared that it initiated a new stage in the Cuban feature-length film.

For the Cuban fictional film, the three years that Enrique Pineda Barnet spent in making *David* were transitional years. From the years 1966 and 1967 there are four films of significance: Tomás Gutiérrez Alea's *La muerte de un burócrata* (The death of a bureaucrat, 1966); Humberto Solás's *Manuela* (1966); *Tulipa* (1967), directed by Manuel Octavio Gómez; and *Las aventuras de Juan Quin Quin* (The adventures of Juan Quin Quin, 1967) by Julio García Espinosa. All are full-length and black and white, except for *Manuela,* which is only forty minutes, and was originally intended as part of a three-episode film by different directors but was judged to merit release on its own. In both *Manuela* and *Tulipa* the title role is that of a woman and the film is a drama. The other two are comedies.

La muerte de un burócrata is about a country that has made a revolution and decided to become socialist and therefore insists that its bureaucrats provide equal treatment for all, including the dead: a corpse gets
itself unburied for the sake of bureaucracy, and then finds that bureaucracy won't let it be buried again. The country where these events take
place is a hilarious mixture of revolutionary Cuba and the Hollywood
land of comedy.

The story is very simple and ingenious. A man dies and his family
buries him. Afterwards they are asked for his *carnet laboral* (labor card)
for the bureaucratic process to take its course, but unfortunately they
buried it with him as a mark of honor—he had been considered a model
worker. To recover the card, they dig up the body in the dead of night.
Unable immediately to rebury it because the cemetery keeper has been
scared and sent for the police, they take it away and return next day to
bury it afresh. The bureaucrat in charge refuses them permission to do
this on the grounds that they have nothing to show that the body is not
where it is supposed to be—in the ground. They need a certificate of
exhumation. The film pursues the efforts of the corpse's nephew to get
one. When he finally has it and returns to the cemetery, the same official,
following the same logic, still does not let him rebury the corpse because
he takes the certificate as an order to exhume it. Whereupon the exas-
perated nephew, who has already been chased through an office building by a throng of pursuers, and has balanced precariously on a parapet
above the crowds, even hanging from a clock like Harold Lloyd, loses
patience and strangles the bureaucrat. For this misdeed he is taken away
in a straitjacket while the film ends with the bureaucrat's funeral.

Alea discovered after making the film that the seminal idea had a
counterpart in reality, when a woman left a screening of the film in
tears, because her husband had, as in the film, been buried with his *carnet
laboral*.[7] In the film, the story has been elaborated to provide innumerable opportunities to parody Hollywood comedy. Whether or not Alfred
Hitchcock's *The Trouble with Harry* of 1955 was part of its inspiration,
Alea borrows liberally from practically the whole Hollywood comedy
tradition, with especially pungent plagiarism of Chaplin, Keaton, Laurel
and Hardy, and Harold Lloyd, as well as references to Jerry Lewis and
Marilyn Monroe. It is almost as if Alea felt a need to exorcise the Hollywood comedy, although since the great tradition of film comedy is itself

La muerte de un burócrata (Tomás Gutiérrez Alea, 1966)

subversive of genre, this is not a cinema that needs to be repudiated in the same way as the rest of Hollywood.

There are other comic strands to the film as well, especially a streak of black humor about death, which struck some Cuban critics as Mexican in character, though Alea himself considered it rather more Spanish.[8] Either way, there are certainly echoes of Buñuel, in small surrealist touches like the driver of the hearse with a plastic skeleton hanging in the cab, or the dog during the fight in the cemetery that runs off with a bone. Black humor is also the home key of several entire scenes that turn on the consequences that everyday problems may create for an unburied corpse. Since, for example, the family is forced to keep the corpse at home, neighbors pool their ice to keep it fresh; but ice, like other commodities in blockaded Cuba, is in short supply, and vultures circle overhead.[9]

The Cuban critics found the acts of homage to the masters of comedy truly delightful. They also found the film—not surprisingly—somewhat Kafkaesque.[10] As Alea was about to depart with the film to the Karlovy Vary Film Festival in Czechoslovakia (where it shared the Special Jury Prize with *La Vie de Crateau* by the French director Jean-Paul Rappenneau), he was asked if, perfectly lucid as it was for the Cubans, the film would be found intelligible there. "Indeed, yes," he replied, not mincing words, "the bureaucracy thing is very old. It was not invented but inherited, and in some cases enlarged, by the socialist countries, where it seems like an oppressive stage that has to be passed through. I think the mechanisms of bureaucracy as they're shown here can be understood anywhere."[11] In Cuba itself, the film was praised precisely for its implacable criticism of bureaucracy, and the very high political level it demonstrated in achieving this.

But there's another target in *La muerte de un burócrata* too. According to Alea himself, "It's a satire on rhetoric and the stereotype in art."[12] Indeed, this is how the film begins, with an animation sequence in which the uncle whose death sparks the story off is killed when he falls into a machine he has made to manufacture busts of José Martí. This machine looks as if it's been patched together in a fashion only to be expected in a country where, as Ruby Rich observes, "parts are unavailable due to the blockade and remedies left entirely to individual ingenuity."[13] It is also reminiscent of the contraptions of the "nutty professor" Jerry Lewis, and reminded one Cuban critic of the machines in Chaplin's *Modern Times*.[14] "We started," Alea explained, "with the busts of Martí because they were the order of the day—that's what I was criticizing. I went out and took a hundred photos of 'Martí corners'—the spots where the busts had been installed. Many looked cold and formal, official, a ritualistic gesture. Others, in the popular districts, were often primitively done and suggested veneration, of the same kind as popular altars to the saints. These had an authentic popular character that isn't shown in the film."[15] But this exclusion corresponds with the satire's target, for the film is a weapon in the continuing ideological battle not just against bureaucracy but also against the influence of the bureaucrats in art. The relevance of this kind of satire four years after Fidel's criticism of the political sectarians is evidence of how difficult it is to uproot uncritical thinking in relation to art and culture. Nor was this aspect of the film lost on people. The critic Bernardo Callejas, the one who saw the Martí bust machine as an echo of *Modern Times*, thought this very appropriate because it is "a satire on those who by dint of mechanistic thinking cut themselves off from the thought of great men, turning them into hollow symbols. The Martí-esque is not to be found in the repetitious bust, but in the recovery of the Apostle from absurd mystification."

Callejas ended his review of Alea's film by announcing the premiere of another new Cuban film of interest: Solás's *Manuela*. Manuela is a guerrilla, a *guajira*, a peasant woman, who demonstrates that the qualities needed to be a rebel soldier are not a monopoly of men but belong to every true Cuban. The film portrays her apprenticeship as a fighter in much the same terms as *El joven rebelde*—a process of learning to overcome the ignorance of illiteracy and to call for justice rather than revenge. At the beginning, when Batista's army razes the village where Manuela comes from, and her mother is murdered, she seeks vengeance by attacking a drunken soldier; by the end, she has become an advocate of revolutionary discipline. The plot also revolves, however, around a relationship she develops with another fighter, Mejicano, a handsome guitar player. The growth of this relationship is gently observed; she teases him, for example, for his ineptitude at washing clothes. But we never really stray far from the principal theme. After an attack on a village, Manuela joins the villagers in calling for the informer to be lynched and it is Mejicano who tells her, no, the man must be tried. Still, in between the duties of the struggle, they speculate about marrying when it is all over—though here again it falls to Mejicano to tell her how different things will then be (as we shall later learn when the same pair of actors meet again in the last part of Solás's next film, *Lucía*). In the end, Manuela is fatally wounded in combat and this time Mejicano loses his self-control, and it is she who has to remind him with her dying breath to put aside thought of personal vengeance. The message of the film could hardly be clearer.

There is a certain justice in the criticism of the film by a group of Venezuelan critics, that if *Manuela* had been made five years earlier it would have been perfect, but for 1966 it suffers from a certain lack of ideological depth, and in its moral insistence remains somewhat sentimental.[16] The image of the woman fighter is still romantic and idealized, and even in its antiheroism it makes no innovations. The dialogue is bare, deficient, though not, as far as it goes, incompetent, and the result is that all but Manuela herself remain secondary and incomplete characters, even Mejicano. What most impressed people at the time, however, was the power and assurance of the film's visual style, which is evident from the very first moments, in the judicious lensing and framing and the careful pacing, and above all in the controlled use of the hand-held camera. The music, by Tony Taño, similarly alternates between expressionism and lyricism. Compared with, say, *Historias de la Revolución, Manuela* shows the distance traveled in the stylistic evolution of Cuban cinema in only a few years. Studio and studio lighting have been abandoned and dress and makeup have become more naturalistic, even if the stylization of character remains. But then Solás was only twenty-three at the time he made this film; even so, his characters already look less like the visual stereotypes of the earlier film. In the final analysis, the strength of *Manuela* lies in Solás's having found himself an extraordinary actress, Adela Legrá, a *campesina* with no previous acting experience, to play opposite the young actor Adolfo Llauradó. At the same time, the film represented for Solás a return to public themes after the experimental shorts he had been making for a couple of years, in contrast to which, he told an interviewer, *Manuela* represented *cine rescate,* a recovery of national rather than personal values.[17]

While *Manuela* is not exactly a feminist film, *Tulipa,* a circus story of the 1930s or 1940s, is in this respect far more striking. Idalia Anreus, who would become over the years the doyenne of Cuban screen actresses, plays the title role, an aging stripper in a side act in the circus of Ruperto & Sobrino (Rupert & Nephew) who befriends a new recruit. Beba, played by Daysi Granados, has been enticed to join the circus as a "dancer" by the junior partner in the business, Cheo, the nephew, and she's an eager recruit, for the circus seems to her a way of escaping from home, which offers her no future. But she grows quickly disillusioned when she discovers what kind of act Tulipa performs and realizes that she is being groomed to take her place. "If it wasn't you," Tulipa tells her, "they'd find someone else. I've been expecting this for some time. Go on, drink. If you're going to enter show business you've got to get used to it. Don't look at me like that. You're staying, and that's it. And that's the first thing you have to learn: to sleep alone. I've been sleeping alone so long I'm practically a señorita."

The film is based on a stage work that Manuel Octavio Gómez saw in the early 1960s, by Manuel Roguera Saumell, who then collaborated on the script. The itinerant circus pictured here was a popular form of entertainment in the countryside—the early film distributors Santos y Artiga were also circus proprietors—and hence the film was predictably popular with peasant audiences. It was readily understood as an allegory of the conditions of the time, a microcosm of the pseudorepublic with its portrait gallery of the whole range of circus types, including the owner who abandons it all when some more profitable enterprise comes his way. "The film is full of social critique," wrote one reviewer, and "the profiles of the exploited circus personnel, from the bumpkin who raises the curtains to the variety star, via the master of ceremonies, are completely faithful."[18] Cheo, in the words of another, "incorporates all the primitive machismo of the Cuban man before the Revolution, his violence, his spiritual weakness."[19] For this second reviewer, "Tulipa is confronted by Beba in whom she sees her own youth and at the same time a rival." There is also the Bearded Woman Tomasa, in whom the actress Teté Vergara shows "the gentleness of the woman forced to live such a role because poverty obliges her, but who has not been contaminated." The film is thus a study of struggle by individuals in the pseudorepublic to live an authentic life, but it also goes further and becomes an examination—unique in Cuban cinema at the time—of the particular modes of exploitation that were forced upon these women, who stand for all women in the pseudorepublic, and the solidarity they create between themselves in order to survive; for, in spite of the threat that Beba represents toward Tulipa, Tulipa not only, like Tomasa, retains her dignity, but the friendship that both the older women extend to Beba is the most positive human value in this world.

At the same time, the male characters are not mere ciphers. On the contrary, *Tulipa* is perhaps generally the best-acted Cuban film up to the moment it was made. This also extends to the crowd scenes, and the honesty with which the contradictions of circus entertainment are presented—the portrayal of the sexism of the circus, for instance, which is located here quite specifically as a deformation of a kind that arises in the typical social relations of both the production and the consumption of popular entertainment to be found in the pseudorepublic. In the scene that first reveals Tulipa's act, the camera mainly holds back, at first because it is looking at the scene from Beba's point of view; but this camera position fulfills other functions too. It distances the spectator of the film from the spectacle, discouraging voyeurism and guarding our respect for Tulipa, revealing instead the way the spectacle is designed not to satisfy but merely to titillate. Finally, through the empathy the film produces for the three women, it also becomes an allegory on the frustrations forced upon any artist in the circumstances. By using these women as the vehicle of this allegory, Gómez marks the changing consciousness of the artist within the Revolution in some important respects.

In a way, *Tulipa* stands halfway between Alea's *La muerte de un burócrata* and García Espinosa's *Las aventuras de Juan Quin Quin,* Cuban cinema's first fully accomplished experimental feature film, and significantly a comedy. This is a film that was conceived in direct relation to the problem of a growing crisis in communication, in which experimentation seemed to be becoming more and more urgent. Before the Revolution, García Espinosa explained in 1969, cinema entertainment was regarded by many people as escapism, but now the filmmakers could not afford to think that way. However, a crisis of communication had developed because the serious filmmaker could hardly continue to employ the traditional concept of art, a concept premised upon a split between "serious" and "popular" in which the artist was left isolated in a self-protective cocoon of elitism. The Revolution had made the need for such self-protection an anachronism (as Fidel had argued in the "Words to the Intellectuals"). But simply to try and exchange elitism for populism was equally unacceptable. An entirely new mode of addressing the audience was needed, combining entertainment with the critique of the old forms of entertainment. This, for García Espinosa, was connected with another challenge, that of learning how to avoid the tendency of the Revolution to treat itself too solemnly: "Which is not to say that the processes of the Revolution are not dramatic; they are very serious, but they don't have to be treated in a formalist way, which is when stupidity begins."[20] *Juan Quin Quin* was an attempt to confront these problems.

Like *Tulipa, Las aventuras de Juan Quin Quin* was based on a recent literary work, in this case a novel by Samuel Feijóo titled *Juan Quin Quin en Pueblo Mocho.* It was a novel in many ways suited to the task in hand, evoking the popular Hispanic tradition of the picaresque, in which the romantic hero is replaced by the rascal who lives off his wits. Yet, in spite of the typically episodic structure of the picaresque novel, the filmmakers felt it had too linear a structure for their purposes:[21] a pair of peasant woodcutters, Juan and his friend, pass through a series of adventures that spur them to a *toma de conciencia,* a moment of enlightenment, that leads them to take up arms against an intractable reality. The original adaptation proposed a familiar world in which the picaresque aspect appeared as a cross between a western and a classical adventure. This treatment was rejected, partly on grounds of length, and they began to rework it, both eliminating characters and combining them. In the process, they discovered a way of giving it a highly original nonlinear structure.

The film begins with a brief sequence that shows Juan Quin Quin at war, burning cane fields, and being cornered by soldiers commanded by a caricature mayor. This immediately gives way to Juan Quin Quin in times of peace, in which our hero advances from being a rather too-worldly acolyte in the service of a self-righteous priest, to becoming a bullfighter. But then we see him at war again, among a band of fighters trying to break an encirclement by the enemy; Juan's friend Jachero escapes to try and bring help but meets with unexpected and gratu-itous death—though since the narrative is not linear, this does not stop him reappearing during the rest of the film. Next, it is revealed how our hero met his sweetheart Teresa—while appearing in a circus act as Jesus on the cross—and also how he begins to rebel against the estab-lished order, which he confronts in the shape of the manager of a sugar mill and his North American paymaster. In the final section, we learn how Juan and his comrades form a small guerrilla band.

Not only is the narrative structure thus shaken apart and reassem-bled in an apparently haphazard way, but in the process, each different sequence has come to be treated as if it belonged to a different kind of film. Juan's adventures thus become, as Anna Marie Taylor observed in an article in *Jump Cut*, a series of escapades through different cinematic genres.[22] The film begins like a cinemascope western; there are parodies of the war movie and the detective picture with its wealthy oriental vil-lain, and always there is the handsome hero, the beautiful heroine, and the excitement of adventure. The parody even moves outside cinema proper: Jachero meets his untimely end in a skit on the *fotonovela,* or photonovel (a cross between the comic-book and the magazine love story in which drawings are replaced by photographs staged to look like film stills, a cheap printed format that first appeared just after the Second World War in Italy and then found a market in Latin America).[23] The "elaborate inappropriateness," as Anna Marie Taylor puts it, "of the paro-dies in *Juan Quin Quin,* succeeds in effectively calling attention to the artificiality and formulaic quality of the cinematic codes at work in each case.... Distanciation effects used in the film's long series of adventures require the viewer to be constantly aware of cinematic illusion as pat-terned convention."

There are other purposes in this treatment too. As well as "demon-strating to the spectator that this is a film and not reality," as García Espinosa himself puts it, there was also the problem of how "to ridicule a number of typical elements of the adventure film without being led to satirize our own reality."[24] So the film foregrounds the trickery of edit-ing and special effects in order to frustrate narrative expectation, to subvert narrative logic, and to satirize genre by means of exaggeration. A lion turns miraculously into a bull; character types from one genre interpose themselves in another; Juan jumps off a roof to land ever so conveniently on his horse. At the same time, there are interpolations on the nature of underdevelopment. Among captions that come up like chapter headings, such as "Juan Quin Quin in Peacetime," "How Juan Quin Quin met Teresa," and so forth, are a couple that break the frame-work: "Here we could insert a number of scenes of daily life in Latin America" and "We could equally show any one of the useless meetings of the United Nations."

For Anna Marie Taylor, there is, however, an area of the reality of underdevelopment that the film still evades: "Juan's handsome demeanor and cool, understated, Hollywood-style acting . . . hardly confront, let alone undercut . . . audience identification, even with a comic hero . . . the women are still dressed and act as exploited sex objects and García Espinosa's intent to satirize such roles cannot compensate for his more or less straight reproduction of these sexist codes." And it is true that in this respect *Juan Quin Quin* is less advanced than *Tulipa*.

However, the film's treatment of the idea of the hero has other com-plexities. The problem as García Espinosa saw it was the antagonism that exists between the dramatic idea of the positive hero (who is finally, he observes, less interesting than the "baddies") and the superficiality of the hero in the adventure genre. They belong to different aesthetic tra-ditions. He wanted not to combine them, elide the one into the other, but to expose the contradiction—not an easy thing, since "questioning genre isn't a pure, clean, abstract matter"[25] (which Anna Marie Taylor's criticism, of course, confirms). The problem revolved around the con-cept of the *toma de conciencia,* the hero's moment of enlightenment, when the truth is revealed and his duty becomes clear. In both cinema and literature this moment is always carefully constructed, and is cen-tral to the ideological function of the work. It normally comes after the hero has suffered a series of defeats and disillusioning experiences—

which the mechanisms of the genre are designed to provide—and is given the force of a psychological breakthrough. Indeed, the entire genre philosophy of the good, the bad, and the ugly is based on a hypostatized psychology—a notion, that is, of psychological types and processes as causes instead of effects. In this way, the realities of social history and class struggle drop out of the picture; instead of the hero's *concientización,* a process of critical reflection on the world that surrounds him, genre cinema treats the hero to a sudden moment of revelation, not unlike the decongestion of accumulated tension that Enrique Colina and Daniel Díaz Torres speak of in their analysis of the Latin American melodrama.

The scene in which this comes to the surface is at the end of the film's penultimate section, where Juan is being inspected by the North American paymaster of the sugar mill like a piece of livestock. A caption interrupts the image, inscribed with a ridiculous sentence from a play well known in Cuba and Latin America, *Don Juan Tenorio,* written by a Spanish romantic poet, José Zorrilla, in 1844. It reads: "Llamé al cielo y no me oyó" (I called upon heaven and it did not hear me). Our hero has lost his patience. He lunges at everyone in sight, and, jumping through the window, departs to join the struggle. A second caption drives the message home: "y pues sus puertas me cerró" (and it closed its doors against me), after which it only remains for a third caption to state: "etc. etc." The rationale behind the choice of these lines is quite simple: it clinches the preceding religious satire—from Juan the acolyte to Juan on the cross. For the film is militantly atheistic. The sequence concludes with a transitional caption to the final section, quoting Fidel: "There is always armed struggle, but sometimes they're the ones with the arms, and it's necessary that we have arms too." Evidently, this includes films.

The experimentalism of *Juan Quin Quin* is an expression of currents already found in various documentaries by Santiago Álvarez and the example of Pineda Barnet's *David.* It also anticipated a series of major fiction films of 1968 and 1969: Jorge Fraga's *La odisea de General José* (The odyssey of General José), Alea's *Memorias del subdesarrollo (Memories of Underdevelopment), Lucía* of Humberto Solás, and *La primera carga al machete* (The first machete charge) by Manuel Octavio Gómez, as well as others that came later, like José Massip's *Páginas del diario de José Martí* (Pages from the diary of José Martí) and another film by

Alea, *Una pelea cubana contra los demonios* (A Cuban battle against the demons), both dating from 1971. The sheer exuberance of all these films fuels an attack on stable and established filmic vision that has very few precedents in the history of cinema. The attack takes shape most strikingly, but by no means exclusively, in the matter of camera style and cutting, especially in the first part of *Lucía*, in *Una pelea cubana...* or in sections of the film by Massip. In *La primera carga al machete*, Jorge Herrera's handheld camera combines with high-contrast black-and-white photography in a swirling battle scene that takes place in a forest, in which the battle consequently becomes an abstract image of pure energy that reveals a high degree of tolerance for controlled visual chaos, or, to put it more positively, for Gestalt-free form. According to the teachings of Gestalt theory, the artist is primarily concerned with organizing perception into stable forms according to the laws of unity, segregation, and balance, which reveal harmony and order, and stigmatize discord and disorder. Ironically, this theory was being elaborated at the very same moment that the modernist movement was engaged in dramatically changing the rules, breaking down the traditional surface structures of art to reveal complex relationships that refuse to be caught in the stable and neat grid of orderly perception. Instead, according to psychoanalysis, "incompatible outlines and surfaces permeate and try to crowd themselves into the same point in time and space."[26] In this way, traditional artistic languages, especially those of the plastic arts and music, were revolutionized; similar experiments in the disruption of the rational surface followed in every other art form. In cinema, however, this kind of avant-gardism found itself restricted to the margins by the aesthetic intolerance of big money, or, in the Soviet Union, after the experimentation of the 1920s, by the orthodoxy of socialist realism. The fears that motivated this refusal of filmic experimentalism were not just of the destruction of the naturalistic illusion and the realism effect, but of the rupture of the exemplary nature of narrative. And indeed, the subversion of traditional narrative is another major feature of this extraordinary period in revolutionary Cuban cinema, which made a lot of otherwise good-natured people very uncomfortable.

This experimentalism was by no means limited to cinema. There was an experimental current alive around this moment in other art forms too. Indeed, in painting it was the tradition—and it was already a few

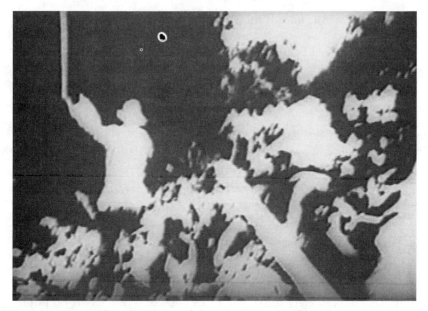

La primera carga al machete (Manuel Octavio Gómez, 1969)

years since Fidel had said, "Our fight is with the imperialists, not with abstract painters." In literature, there are various examples; 1967, for instance, saw the publication by the writer Pablo Armando Fernández—once assistant editor of *Lunes*—of his best-known novel, *Los niños se despiden* (The children say good-bye), which received a Casa de las Américas prize the following year. As one foreign commentator said of it: "With its kaleidoscopic treatment of time, its promiscuous blend of the rhetorics of dream and technology, its characters that merge and separate, its disembodied voices, *Los niños se despiden* is a modern classic."[27] Other less spectacular kinds of literary experiment can be found in testimonial literature like Miguel Barnet's *Biografía de un cimarrón* (The autobiography of a runaway slave) of 1968, where the author, recording as an anthropologist the memories of a man of 108 years of age, has turned them into a unique first-person literary narrative of the experience of slavery, escape, and participation in the Cuban Wars of Independence, redolent of the cultural heritage, including their roots in African religion, of the Cuban slave in the nineteenth century.

In music, too, there was more than one kind of experimentation going on. Indeed, nothing symbolizes the spirit of the moment better than an orchestral work in an advanced avant-garde style that Leo Brouwer wrote for a modern music festival in Colombia, called *La tradición se rompe... pero cuesta trabajo* (Tradition is breakable, but it's hard work). It was also hard work breaking the hold of the contemporary musical environment. Music was probably, except for cinema, the area of cultural production most deeply affected by the processes of cultural imperialism and the unstoppable invasion of the products of the culture industry of the metropolis. In 1967, Joseph Klapper of CBS told a congressional committee in Washington inquiring into "Modern Communications and Foreign Policy" that "the broadcasting of popular music is not likely to have any immediate effect on the audience's political attitude, but this kind of communication nevertheless provides a sort of entryway of Western ideas and Western concepts, even though these concepts may not be explicitly and completely stated at any one particular moment in the communication."[28] Certainly, the Miami radio stations that poured their ephemera into Cuba threatened to wreak havoc on popular musical sensibility, and, in 1968, in an excess of revolutionary fervor of the moment, a ban was issued against rock music on Cuban radio and television. The year was one of great revolutionary upheaval. Fidel had launched a campaign to eliminate petty profiteering, which swept away the remnants of private trading such as stalls, bars, shops, and private servicing; some of it was illegal, and among its effects there was hoarding. A war was declared on "indulgence, selfishness, individualism, parasitism, vice." In the course of events, the cabarets—there were dozens and dozens of them across the country—were closed, and many musicians found themselves without the usual places to play. For the younger ones, experimenting with new styles, there were real problems.

Those at ICAIC, among others, felt that the ban on rock music was misconceived, because it failed to comprehend the complexities of the problem. For one thing, the moment was one of rejuvenation of popular music in the metropolis itself, with groups and singers like the Beatles, Bob Dylan, and many others. Much of the most interesting of this music was known in Cuba not from the transmissions of U.S. radio stations, from which a lot of it was excluded, nor even from records, which were very difficult to get hold of, but from the circulation of cassettes, which were just beginning to become available. Many people in Cuba found this music appealing not only for its musical originality but also for its voice of protest, against the war in Vietnam and the inhuman and aggressive society that was conducting it; and a group of young musicians emerged who began to take up the various styles of this music. ICAIC, which until that time had mainly worked with classically trained musicians, responded to the situation with the creation of the Grupo Sonora Experimental (Experimental Sound Group), which brought the best of the young popular musicians together—including Pablo Milanés, Silvio Rodríguez, Noel Nicola—alongside instrumentalists like Leo Brouwer, Sergio Vitier, and Emilio Salvador. Two workshops were formed, one devoted to instrumental music and the other to the transformation of popular song; and it was out of this initiative that the Nueva Trova, the New Song movement, was born. A distinct and important ingredient was the discovery of a different popular music of the moment in Brazil—which came about, according to Alfredo Guevara, partly through clandestine contacts with Brazilian revolutionaries.[29] With its Afro-Brazilian provenance and the closeness to Cuban culture of its rhythmic and melodic subtleties, the Cubans immediately understood its mobilizing power.

There were, at this time, a couple of cultural events of the greatest importance that also gave expression to the militant desire for an experimental aesthetic. In July 1967, the Cuban government invited to Havana the modernist *Salon de Mai* from Paris, an exhibition of European avant-garde painting and sculpture, and a good number of writers and artists with it. Then, at the beginning of 1968 came the momentous Havana Cultural Congress on the theme "The Intellectual and the Liberation Struggle of the Peoples of the Third World," which brought together about five hundred revolutionary and progressive artists and intellectuals from as many as seventy countries in a great act of affirmation. They were, in the words of the Mexican Alonso Águilar, "intellectuals in the broadest Gramscian sense": "poets and dramatists, physicists and doctors, actors and economists; old party militants and young people just entering the revolutionary struggle; blacks and whites; Europeans, Asians, Africans, delegates from Vietnam, India, Mexico, Algeria and Laos."[30]

The atmosphere of the Congress is vividly conveyed by Andrew Salkey, in his book-length account *Havana Journal*. Participants joined one of five working parties on different aspects of the problems of culture, underdevelopment, national independence, and the mass media. Salkey joined the group discussing intellectual responsibility in the underdeveloped world and gives a very detailed report of its sessions. The Cuban Federico Álvarez read the opening paper, on the theme that "One kind of man is dying and a new kind is being born, and the intellectual must assist in his birth":

> Alvarez suggested that we must own up to Julio Cortázar's dictum: "*Every* intellectual belongs to the Third World!"
>
> In reply, C. L. R. [James] objected to one of Alvarez's statements which included the fact that Albert Schweitzer had contributed to the emancipation and development of the Third World. C. L. R. also proposed that all intellectuals, those from the developed world and those from the underdeveloped, should be firmly discouraged, and in fact abolished as a force.
>
> Salon dead still. Consternation. Bewildered, silent delegates everywhere.
>
> Alvarez disagreed vehemently. He counter-proposed by saying that the Third World has the right to make use of the finest intellectual energy and benefits which it can pluck from the developed world. He said that the Third World does have to depend on the help, cultural development, technology, wealth, good will, troubled conscience and proved sincerity of the few countries of its choosing in the developed world. It is vitally important, he advised, that the Third World learned to pick and choose with great care and with enlightened self-interest.
>
> Julio Cortázar of Argentina explained, succinctly, that the ivory tower intellectual is dead.[31]

Thus the Congress proceeded through its eight days, with the Cubans presiding over the thorniest sessions and acting as peacemakers with great skill and tact.

C. L. R. James's call for the disappearance of the intellectual may have struck his audience as shocking because it seemed out of step with what might be called the tone of revolutionary existentialism of the Latin American intellectual that dominated the intellectual style of the Congress. The concept of the intellectual with which this philosophy operated was well articulated by the Uruguayan writer Mario Benedetti.[32] To begin with, the intellectual is seen as a nonconforming social critic, a witness with an implacable memory. The type stands opposed to another familiar Latin American, the man of action, the primary category of machismo. The motivation of the man of action, whether political caudillo or entrepreneur, army officer or advertising agent, is "the search for a dynamic style in his way of life." Most of them, however, says

Benedetti, "are the typical exponents of a dissolute conformism before the most abject exigencies of the empire. To such a man of action, the intellectual begins to acquire a certain ignominious reputation as the passive observer, or the static being." But in fact, within the revolution, the intellectual may fulfill a new kind of activity: the anthropologist, the linguist, or the ethnologist, for example, may play a decisive role in providing the guerrilla with real knowledge of the population in which a *foco* is to be established. (One can also think of the role of the revolutionary priest in a number of revolutionary movements across Latin America.)

Also, of course, it falls to intellectuals to become guardians of truth. If this is a somewhat unfashionable idea for postwar generations in Europe, it was nevertheless a European, Régis Debray, who said, as quoted by Benedetti: "Militant is also he who in his own intellectual work ideologically combats the class enemy, he who in his work as an artist roots out the privilege of beauty from the ruling class." Explains Benedetti: "The truth is that neither beauty nor art is to be blamed for having been monopolised for centuries by the social strata which had easy access to culture. At the same time as it liberates the soil and the subsoil, the Revolution also tends to put an end to the latifundists of culture, to restore to the people its well-earned right of having access to beauty, of ascending to good taste, of producing its own art."

Finally, the intellectual becomes, within the revolution, its vigilant conscience, its imaginative interpreter, and its critic. But this word *critic* is problematic, too ambiguous. There is a crucial difference from bourgeois society, where the critic, to be more than either apologist or mere journalist and reviewer, is forced to take up an antagonistic stance. In revolutionary Cuba, such a stance was by now liable to seem sectarian and divisive—and this was something that worried not the functionaries with their own sectarian susceptibilities, but other intellectuals, with a better grasp of the movement of history. Alea's film of the same year as the Congress, *Memorias del subdesarrollo,* with its incapacitated and unfulfilled writer as its antihero, and its self-enclosed roundtable discussion of intellectuals and artists, is very much about this struggle for redefinition by the intellectual, the struggle to pass successfully through the *desgarramiento,* the "rupture," that was spoken of by Roque Dalton and Roberto Fernández Retamar.[33]

Still, it is clear enough what Benedetti envisages as the role of the intellectual within the revolution. The dichotomy between the intellectual and the man of action is not to find its solution in the intellectual becoming the amanuensis of the revolutionary, a coarse puppet of the kind the bourgeois media love to ridicule. "'We must not create wage-earners, docile to official thought,' Che Guevara warned us," says Benedetti. Nevertheless, the intellectual is to take on a certain role, like that of the technician, the teacher, or even the athlete: a person with particular skills, all of which are needed in the effort to create a new kind of human being, a job just like any other.

Not that this really contradicts C. L. R. James. It is only a less shocking way of putting things; for James is not talking of the intellectual abdicating responsibilities but rather of a kind of self-propelled dissolution of the intellectual's privileges—which is also what ought to happen in Benedetti's scheme of things. Besides, what James has to say about the Caribbean intellectual is very relevant. The West Indian intellectual, for James, means such names as Marcus Garvey, George Padmore, Frantz Fanon; Bellay, Dumas père, Leconte de Lisle, José de Heredia, Saint-John Perse, Aimé Césaire; the West Indian novelists, including Alejo Carpentier and Wilson Harris; "and the American revolutionary leader Stokely Carmichael who was born in Trinidad." In the brief discussion paper James presented to the Congress, which Salkey quotes in full, he explains:

> This unprecedented role of West Indian intellectuals is due to the fact that the population of an underdeveloped area uses highly developed modern languages and, although many of us live at a level little above that of slavery, the structure of life is essentially European. . . . That situation has produced this tremendous body of intellectuals both in politics and in literature whose climax has been attained in the Cuban Revolution, embodied, for our purposes, in the work and personality of Fidel Castro. . . . The Cuban Revolution tells us that the remarkable contributions which the West Indian type of intellectual has made to the emancipation of Africa and to the development of Western civilization have now come to an end. This unprecedented capacity for creative contributions to civilizations must not now be primarily applied abroad, as formerly in regard to Africa, or to the development of French or British literature; but it is in the application of this capacity to the life of the Americas that the West Indian intellectual will find the necessary elements for the development of culture in the underdeveloped countries, and this must not be forgotten in the developed countries as well.

For the artist of the metropolis, however, various difficulties stood in the way of a proper comprehension of the conditions of underdevelopment. The whole historical situation seemed to go against it, as the Mexican philosopher Adolfo Sánchez Vásquez explained.[34] There is a powerful link, the philosopher argued, between revolutionary idealism and aesthetic experiment. Artistic creation has long revealed a tendency toward rupture and innovation whenever creative possibilities have fallen into decadence and been exhausted. An artistic vanguard arises in opposition to the dominant aesthetic order, in order to ensure the continuity of innovation and creative movement. The notion of a decadent avant-garde is in this sense a contradiction in terms: there is, in fact, a definite incompatibility in capitalist society between the artistic vanguard and the social decadence that surrounds it. But the manner in which an artist responds to this situation, and to the nature of the ideological machinery that is brought into action against the avant-garde, is crucial. Several historical phases can be distinguished. Surrealism, for instance, marks the limits of protest of an artistic vanguard that, not wishing to accept such conditions, attempts to draw closer to the political vanguard. (Doubtless Sánchez Vásquez is thinking here of the manifesto *Towards a Free Revolutionary Art* written by his compatriot, the muralist Diego Rivera, with the French surrealist André Breton, and Leon Trotsky as their collaborator.) The ruling echelons, however, discovering that artistic revolutions do not really endanger the body politic, learn to modify their initial hostility toward the avant-garde. The rebellious artist is no longer proscribed, but tempted instead, and provisions are made for the avant-garde's incorporation—but only on condition that it remain isolated from the broad populace. (This, one might add, is not too difficult, since the institutions of art, the galleries and museums, the dealers and auctioneers have already isolated high art, allowing access only through a protective and mythmaking grid that removes it from living experience.) If the artist gives in, artistic rebellion is contained by social conformism, and becomes the accomplice of the bourgeois order.

It would be false, says Sánchez Vásquez, to reply to these conditions with utopianism or voluntarism. Artistic revolutions *cannot* change society. But nor should the endeavor be put aside or renounced in favor of a search for lost communication by means of simplification or vulgarization. This way the vanguard can only negate itself. To remain true to the drives that produce artistic revolutions, the artist is obliged to find ways of relating his or her work to the diverse currents of struggle for social transformation; in fact, the artist's revolutionary needs are double: to dissolve the illusion that aesthetic revolution can be self-sufficient, and to show that political and social conformism are incompatible with artistic creativity. Unfortunately, orthodox Marxist-Leninist politics, both within and beyond the socialist camp, has contributed to the split through a failure to think through properly the categories of "progressive" and "reactionary," and through a failure of imagination concerning the possible meeting between aesthetics and politics. (Here one might add: in spite of the successful work of Rivera, of Eisenstein and Vertov, of John Heartfield, of Bertolt Brecht and Kurt Weill, and quite a few more.) Bourgeois ideologies have been able to exploit this situation by encouraging the avant-gardes to try and preserve themselves from contagion by politics, with the result that many artists close their eyes to the real significance and magnitude of the modernist revolution, and turn instead to formalist and decadent preoccupations (whereupon they cease to be a real avant-garde at all).

If this scheme sounds oversimplified, we need only remember that Latin American society allows many fewer subtleties, and the characteristics of the social formation are more starkly and clearly seen—in the same way that the very sight of rich and poor is starkly contrasted in cities where mansions are overshadowed by shantytowns, and poverty invades every street. In this kind of world, the Cuban Revolution had brought about, said Sánchez Vásquez, the modest beginnings of a profound change, for it created the first real experience in Latin America of a revolution in an underdeveloped country, where the springs of popular culture have not yet been alienated to anything like the degree of their alienation and destruction in the metropolis. The Revolution opened up a field of action for the artist and intellectual, a potential influence in the creation of new cultural values of a kind no longer within reach in the metropolis—not in the same way that the artist and intellectual had a formative influence a century and more ago. For Sánchez Vásquez, the Cuban Revolution was not only a creative act in itself, it also established the conditions for art to become a social birthright, through creating a new base from which the dichotomies and antinomies of bourgeois society could be overcome.

It also, he believes, showed that vital questions of art, such as freedom of expression, are *political* problems that require of the artist a revolutionary political commitment—but again, of a kind that does not imply a servile relationship to politics. Clearly, the function of the artistic vanguard changes. In the first place, the sudden acceleration that the Revolution engenders places many traditional values in crisis through the exertion of a new reality that demands novel forms of expression. At the same time, the inertia of traditional forms intervenes, and to attack this resistance, a new spirit of experimentalism is also needed. Inevitably, there are problems. The new reality creates a new audience that is still naive because only newly literate. The artistic vanguard therefore begins to split into two again: some remain attached to experiment for experiment's sake, and take advantage of the revolutionary principles that vouchsafe stylistic freedom; others, however, look to the application of a critical consciousness for the creation of new forms, in which the traditions of the avant-garde can be preserved, only modified by the demands of the new audience.

This whole argument is clearly allied to the position at ICAIC. It also finds force in the connection to be found between this upsurge of experimentalism in Cuba in the late 1960s and the wider political events of the period, in particular the intensification of international struggle. For the difference between the two avant-gardes—and not only in Cuba—or between what perhaps should be called the traditional avant-garde and a new political-artistic vanguard, is nowhere more clearly to be seen than in the response of the latter to international events, which is usually entirely lacking in the former. There can rarely be found in history as direct an artistic expression of political affairs—on the contrary, such connections are usually indirect and often delayed. But the 1960s were an exceptional decade, exploding in 1968 into months of intense and violent agitation, protest, confrontation, and rebelliousness right across the globe. In Europe, many intellectuals solemnly declared their decision to commit suicide as a class. In Cuba, in April 1967, the revolutionary body OSPAAAL (Organization for Solidarity among the Peoples of Africa, Asia, and Latin America) published the text of a message from Che Guevara calling upon Latin American revolutionaries to declare their solidarity with Vietnam, and to create "two, three, many Vietnams" in their own continent.[35] Four months later, the Latin American

Solidarity Organization, OLAS, held a widely publicized conference in Havana that declared the political, economic, and social unity of Latin America to be far more significant than the political divisions and antagonisms in the continent.

Cuba had been gripped with an intense spirit of internationalism ever since Che had departed the island in 1965 "for new fields of battle," as Fidel informed the people. Fidel, after Che's departure, gave continued support to his ideas and their moral emphasis. It was, in any case, a constant element in Fidel's own thinking that "the duty of a revolutionary is to make a revolution"[36] and that revolutionaries are not to be distinguished by adherence to scholarly principles, but rather, "the best textbook in matters of revolution [is] the revolutionary process itself."[37] There were plenty, and not only on the right, who when Che was killed in Bolivia accused the Cubans of the invention of a new revolutionary dogma of guerrilla struggle. The Cultural Congress had already been called when the event took place, and when the intellectuals gathered in Havana, the spirit of defiance was high. Fulfilling expectation, Fidel took the opportunity in his address to the closing session—which some interpreted as a defiant reply to critics—to praise the assembled company for the way the intellectuals had carried Che's banner to the rest of the world after his death, when politicians and political organizations of the left had failed to respond. And to the delight of the audience, he repeated his conviction that "Marxism needs to develop, to break away from a certain rigidity, to interpret today's reality from an objective, scientific viewpoint, to conduct itself as a revolutionary force and not as a pseudo-revolutionary church."[38] The debates didn't cease after this, any more than after the "Words to the Intellectuals." A series of articles appeared in *Verde Olivo*, the journal of the Cuban armed forces, directed against refractory intellectuals. There was even, among some of them (if they hadn't left), a stiffening of attitude that was to cause further trouble. But at ICAIC, the euphoria of experimentalism was in full flood.

CHAPTER TWELVE

Four Films

Of the fiction films released by ICAIC in 1968, the most closely related to the figure of Che Guevara himself is Jorge Fraga's *La odisea de General José*. Premiered at the end of February, it was one of the first of a group of films around the theme of the hundred-years' struggle for independence, which also included *Lucía* and *La primera carga al machete*, the short fiction *El desertor* (The deserter) by Manuel Pérez, and two documentaries, Saderman's *Hombres del mal tiempo* and *1868–1968* by Bernabé Hernández. These films were more than a celebration of the anniversary of the start of the Cuban Wars of Independence: they constituted an extended essay in *cine rescate*, the recovery of history from the suppression, distortion, and falsification to which it had been subjected by bourgeois ideology. As Manuel Octavio Gómez expressed it, they were films that corresponded to a historical necessity to discover the sources of Cuban nationhood, and the continuity between the birth of the independence struggle and the final achievement of national liberation with the victory of the Revolution.[1]

Internationalism is a theme that repeats itself in several of these films. In *General José*, José Maceo and his brother Antonio are Dominicans, not Cubans; nor were they the only foreigners to take part in the Cuban struggle at one stage or another. The same is true of Che Guevara himself, of course, an Argentinian who was engaged in his last internationalist endeavor in Bolivia at the same time this film was being shot. The film is based on an incident recounted in a letter by another independence leader, Máximo Gómez, and further informed by a careful study of Gómez's campaign diary.[2] The incident in question occurred in 1895, when José and Antonio landed in Oriente province with some twenty comrades, to join the freedom fighters engaged in the new campaign against the Spanish that had just been launched. A few days after the landing, the group is surprised by an enemy ambush from which they only just manage to escape, becoming dispersed in the process. José seeks refuge with two or three others in the mountain forests where the film opens, hiding behind trees, using the undergrowth for camouflage, to escape the Spanish soldiers pursuing them.[3]

The identification of the camera with the pursued permeates and pervades the entire film, but without any of the tricks that genre cinema plays in such situations. Suspense is an alien posture to this film. The bond between the camera and the subject is of a completely different order. After an exemplary scene in which the General shares with a *compañero* an edible snail plucked from a bush, the group is once more attacked; he himself makes an escape by jumping a precipice, but his companions are either killed or captured. The camera now indissolubly attached to a single man, it transfixes him and becomes a wholly objective scrutineer of his struggle against nature to survive. The intensity the film takes on in this portrayal invokes memories of King Lear shorn of all pretense in the face of the tempest, or invites comparison with Kurosawa's *Dersu Uzala* and the solitary individual battling for survival against the full force of nature's might in the Siberian winter: here it's a tropical forest. For the Cubans, there was also shortly to be a more immediate source of comparison. "We had walked a kilometre," wrote Che Guevara in his Bolivian diary (entry for June 16, 1967),

when we saw the men of the vanguard on the other side. Pancho had found the ford and had crossed it while exploring. We crossed with the icy water up to our waists and with some current—without mishap. We arrived at the Rosita an hour later, where we noticed some old footprints, apparently the army's. We then became aware that the Rosita was deeper than we had foreseen and that there are no traces of the trail marked on the map. We walked for an hour in the icy water and then decided to camp so as to take advantage of the *palmito de totai* [edible top of the palm tree, usually considered a delicacy] and to try and find a beehive that Miguel had seen while exploring yesterday; we did not find it, and ate only *mote* [dried corn kernels boiled without salt] and *palmito* with lard. There is still food for tomorrow and the day after *(mote)*. We walked for three kilometres down the Rosita and another three down the Rio Grande. Height: 610 metres.[4]

Miguel Benavides turns in a carefully measured performance as the General, holding the screen alone for a large part of the film, displaying, as he confronts the hostile environment, the steel will and tenacity that Fidel recalled in Che. When a cold wind begins to blow, he starts to perform a weird kind of dance, running backwards and forwards and beating his arms across his chest to keep warm; when it starts raining, he crouches down to keep his bag and rifle covered. In all of this, the most memorable aspect of the film, the camera is the actor's most intimate partner, counterpointed by the chatter of the forest on the sound track, until, hungry and fevered, Maceo begins to hallucinate and meets a corpse. The moment is one of highly charged ambiguity: is this his tormented imagining or the real remains of another fleeing *guerrillero?* The Peruvian critic Nelson García Miranda finds this the first occasion in Cuban cinema in which the movement from the conscious to the unconscious—attempted by several directors—is accomplished with the same conviction as in (his example) Mizoguchi's *Ugetsu monogatari.*[5] Humberto Solás will achieve something similar even more effectively in the first part of *Lucía.*

In *Lucía,* Humberto Solás has interpreted the theme of the hundred-years' struggle in an entirely novel way to create an epic in three separate episodes: each centers on a woman called Lucía and takes place in a different period of Cuban history, corresponding to the three stages of colonialism, neocolonialism, and socialist revolution; the three episodes also present us with Lucías of different social classes. In the first, the year is 1895, approaching the climax of the Wars of Independence, and the milieu is that of the landed creole aristocracy. The second episode takes place in 1933 at the moment of the abortive revolution in which the dictator Machado was overthrown; this time Lucía is a member of the bourgeoisie. Finally, the Revolution, 196–, and Lucía is a rural peasant girl, a member of a new agricultural collective.

A love story provides the basic plot for each episode: the first is tragic, the second melodramatic, the third a comedy. The first and last are of a richness that can only be called Shakespearean. This, and the film's length (160 minutes) make it by far the most ambitious movie that ICAIC had yet attempted, and the most expensive. Solás chose to make women his principal protagonists, as in *Manuela*, because, he explained, "The woman's role always lays bare the contradictions of a period and makes them explicit.... *Lucía* is not a film about women; it's a film about society. But within that society, I chose the most vulnerable character, the one who is most transparently affected at any given moment by contradictions and changes."[6] This, he says, has nothing to do with feminism per se. Nonetheless, the final episode is directly concerned with "the problem of *machismo*... which undermines a woman's chances of self-fulfilment and at the same time feeds a whole subculture of underdevelopment."

On another occasion, Solás explained the germination of the film. "I began to prepare *Lucía* rapidly following the premiere of *Manuela*. The present group of stories is not what originally appeared in the first project. Only the first remains. The second and third (those concerning the republic and the Revolution) were not accepted. In truth, it was a very different film from the present one. And I'm really happy that the project as a whole was not approved. Neither of the rejected stories has ceased to interest me: a satire on the republic seen through a couple trying to find a place to make love one day in Santiago de Cuba, and a dramatic story on the difficulties of a pair of lovers (him married, her single) who work in the same firm. But with the passage of time, I feel that the stories that have been substituted for these give the film a much richer and more harmonious structure."[7] Aesthetically, the most interesting thing about the alteration is that not only have the stories been changed but the positions of the melodramatic and the humorous episodes have been swapped around. At the same time, the changes are a positive result of the production system at ICAIC, where scripts are able to evolve through criticism, which unsympathetic commentators describe as regimentation and censorship.

"Lucía 1895" begins—like the other episodes—with a paradigmatic shot that presents the historical period in a dominant aspect, in this case a town square framed to show its colonial architecture weighing down upon the inhabitants. We are introduced to the daughters of the aristocracy, lavishly dressed and parasoled, living a life of opulence, leisure, gossip, and superficiality. Several of the many accounts of the film— *Lucía* has been written about more than any other Cuban film except *Memorias del subdesarrollo*—emphasize the European appearance of

Lucía I, 1895, from *Lucía* (Humberto Solás, 1968)

this group "with its imported furniture, sculptures, photographs and drapes" and "the envy displayed towards the new Parisian husband and hat of a returning acquaintance."[8] Lucía herself, according to the most substantial of these accounts, by the North American critic Stephen Kovacs, is "a spinster who stands at that delicate age where she is still capable of falling in love but is already on the road to settling in to a carefully circumscribed world of maidenhood . . . her company consists only of her family and of other women of her class . . . while her friends bubble with excitement at afternoon tea parties, she remains sedate, smiling, accommodating."[9] Playing the part, Raquel Revuelta, one of Cuba's leading stage actresses, displays, in Kovacs's eyes, the linear features of a classic Spanish profile. For the Peruvian critic Isaac León Frias, the similarity of her appearance to that of Dolores del Río or María Félix is not accidental, for we are in the world of 1940s Mexican melodrama crossed with Emily Brontë's *Wuthering Heights*.[10] Solás himself has mentioned the influence of the novels of Flaubert.[11]

Suddenly, in stark contrast to the comforts of the aristocratic setting, there is a cut to a cart full of bloody, ragged bodies of soldiers making its way through the streets, and the character of Fernandina—a bravura performance by Idalia Anreus as the mad nun whose story parallels Lucía's as Gloucester's does King Lear's. The tale of her brutal rape by Spanish soldiers, which drove her mad, is told with morbid excitement by one of Lucía's companions, and we see it on the screen in surrealistic, over-exposed shots, which Anna Marie Taylor describes as a "dream-like allegory, the rape of Cuba by Spain."[12]

As a virgin approaching middle age, anxiously hoping for a man to appear to complete her social existence, Lucía's life changes when she meets Rafael, a Spanish dandy who professes love to her. The last flower of an effete and doomed colonial culture, explains another commentator on the film, Peter Biskind, Lucía breaks away into the only alternative available to a woman of her class and time: "She abandons herself to a grand passion, to a myth of self-fulfilment . . . which is as derivative in its way of a bygone Byronism as the finery of her class is imitative of Paris fashions."[13] Her happiness is shattered, however, by the rumor that Rafael is a married man. She goes to meet him at an abandoned sugar mill—an ambiguous location: Kovacs calls it "a desolate monastery," a Venezuelan critic "a small abandoned fort."[14] As Kovacs describes the scene, Rafael "tries to insist on his love for her. The genteel mood of courtship is past. He looks darker, more menacing, desperate, as he chases her amidst sombre stone walls. He throws himself upon her, attempting to possess her at once. His energy spent, he retreats into a corner, like a beaten animal, sobbing in the dark. Lucía herself has changed: her disheveled clothes and her hair in disarray indicate that she has come closer than ever before to her own sexuality . . . she approaches resolutely, tears his shirt and embraces him." Several critics have found this an extraordinary scene, but too extended. For the Venezuelans, the way the camera hugs the walls with Lucía as she retreats before Rafael—the subjective camera in full flood again—is an image of beauty as long as its signification is fresh, but once exhausted it becomes precious. For Daniel Díaz Torres, the scene is "one of the most beautifully achieved moments of all, containing an almost perfect blending of the sentimental and the visual, or of the sentimental-aesthetic—some other ambiguous term might do just as well," but again, it should have been shorter.[15] What is certainly true is that there is something very uncomfortable about this scene. Biskind remarks that "in the fragile world of colonial Cuba, far from Europe, [Lucía's] gestures of passion become a strained and unnatural parody of borrowed forms, a feverish mimicry of Continental literary romances." This could also be said of the very style of the film, except that it is perfectly deliberate in its feverish mimicry of the grand style of directors like Visconti or Fellini.

Lucía's passion is shattered, however, in a collision with historical reality (as Biskind neatly puts it). Gradually, the political conflict that surrounds them inserts itself. As a guest at her house, Rafael purports to have no interest in taking sides in the war, while she, on the other hand, is a tacit supporter of the revolutionaries through her love for her brother Felipe, who is organizing guerrillas on the family plantation. When Rafael entreats her to take him to the estate, the full political drama unfolds. As they approach their destination, the Spanish cavalry suddenly emerges to wage battle on the guerrillas. As Rafael dumps her in the middle of the Spanish troops he has led to the site, Lucía realizes that he has been using her to accomplish his task as a Spanish agent. The battle claims her brother as a victim and, back in the city, driven mad with shame and sorrow, she finds Rafael, dressed in Spanish uniform, and publicly stabs him to death. The critics are generally agreed that this is not just a murder for revenge, but the execution of the oppressor.

Solás has acknowledged Visconti as an influence; the critics concur. Biskind pins the model down to *Senso*, the tale of a high-born Italian woman compromised by a desperate passion for an Austrian officer that leads her to betray her patriotic cousin and her country during the war of Italian unification (though in Solás, Lucía is more the victim than Visconti's Livia, more a pawn of forces beyond her comprehension). But if, says Biskind, the affair between the lovers is "orchestrated to a score of sighs, flutters, fixed stares, and throbbing music characteristic of the later, operatic Visconti," for the trip to the plantation—lush, mist-shrouded tropical rain forest—Solás has adopted the look of Kurosawa, while the stark landscape of battle he finds reminiscent of Has's *Saragossa Manuscript*: "In fact, this entire section of Lucía is strongly flavored with a feverish romanticism characteristic of the Polish school in some of its wilder moments." This is not such an unlikely comparison: the Cuban critic Puri Faget refers to the influence of the Polish director Jerzy Kawalerowicz's *Mother Joan of the Angels*, a film that seems to have made a deep impression in Cuba.[16] One thing is certain. *Lucía* is just the kind of film that inspires critics to the heights of speculation about its sources and influences. The names of Buñuel, Godard, Antonioni, Resnais, and Bergman have all been mentioned. For Díaz Torres, the battle recalls the extraordinary battle sequence in Orson Welles's *Chimes at Midnight*. Solás himself outdoes his critics by bringing in Pasolini as well. He also mentions the Brazilian Cinema Novo directors, and Faget believes that Glauber Rocha's concept of the "Aesthetics of Violence" is more important than the Italian or Polish influences. Cinema Novo, Rocha wrote, "teaches that the aesthetics of violence are revolutionary rather than primitive. The moment of violence is the moment when the coloniser becomes aware of the existence of the colonised. Only when he is confronted with violence can the coloniser understand, through horror, the strength of the culture he exploits."[17]

As for the role of Fernandina, there is a crucial moment halfway through the tale, when Lucía decides to ride off with Rafael, when their paths cross. She steps out onto the street and immediately Fernandina throws herself on her, pleading with her not to go. They meet again at the end, after Lucía has executed her lover, Fernandina following her as she is led away. Lucía is a daughter of the upper classes with fine Castilian features; Fernandina a *mestiza* with dark skin and the hooked nose of her ancestors. Lucía we first meet surrounded by her friends in a tranquil environment, and situated within a stationary framing; Fernandina we encounter crazed and alone in the streets, pictured with a jerking, shifting handheld camera. This scheme of binary oppositions is every bit as poetic and resonant as it would be in a Shakespeare play. The coming together of these two women at the end, Kovacs observes, produces "not only a moment of human recognition and solidarity, but a confluence of mythical forces as well."

These mythical forces find their most luminous symbolic expression in the battle scene, which for Kovacs is "one of the most striking ever to appear on the screen. Naked black men ride out on horses to meet the Spanish cavalry: they are man and horse combined, human flesh joined to animal, modern centaurs bringing horror to the uniformed Spanish." The image is not invented by Solás. A troop like this rode in the Wars of Independence at night, naked because it made their black bodies almost invisible. With the cry they let out as they rode into battle, they had a terrifying effect on the enemy.[18] That image, says Kovacs, "seems so modern, yet its modernity is merely an affirmation of its mythic, timeless verity." At first, he says, we are aware only of the massive, choreographed battle scenes in the manner of Hollywood and Soviet spectaculars. Soon the men are on the ground and we recognize the hand-to-hand combat implanted in our memories by countless fist-fights in Western saloons. Then suddenly a new sensation overtakes us as we experience the physical agitation of the hand-held camera running after the soldiers. The unwritten but strictly observed rule requiring a relatively stable image on the screen is flung to the past as our eyes ricochet off one body, then another, our balance upset, our senses jerked to attention. Yes, the hand-held camera has been used before by New Wave directors, but they sought to create a casual, personal—at the most extreme—disjointed style. Solás, on the other hand, infuses the image with a kinetic tension unknown to his Parisian predecessors, almost as if the storm of the battle engulfed the camera in one of its powerful waves. Even in its agitated state the camera responds to his command to focus in close-up, if only momentarily, upon distorted faces, distended limbs. [This is where *Chimes at Midnight* is evoked.] He used the hand-held camera and extreme close-up before, when he wanted to depict the rape of Fernandina and her harassment on the streets, and he uses them again in the final scene of Lucía's revenge and emotional collapse.

This technique of handheld close-ups keeps recurring, Kovacs speculates, because it faithfully expresses both individual anguish and mass violence, two succeeding stages in the struggle against oppression.

The cameraman who accomplished this, one of the most creative cinematographers not only in Cuba but throughout Latin America, was Jorge Herrera. From now on, the increasingly fluid use of the handheld camera will recur in a number of Cuban films, reaching its apogee in the work of its most sensitive and creative practitioner, Mario García Joya (Mayito), in the films of Tomás Gutiérrez Alea in the 1970s. Indeed, Mayito built his own blimps—the soundproof casing that masks the noise of the camera motor from the microphone—specially designed to make it easier to carry the weight of a fully loaded 35 mm movie camera. The aesthetic effects of the technique will vary, of course, and the associations and connotations of the style will not remain fixed. What Solás and Herrera achieve in *Lucía* is not to provide the language of Cuban cinema with new terms of vocabulary, but the elaboration, in flinging the rule of the relatively stable image away, of a startling new tone of voice, an uncompromising new accent. Manuel Octavio Gómez and Herrera in *La primera carga al machete* and Alea and Mayito in *Una pelea cubana contra los demonios* (A Cuban battle against the demons,

1971) will adapt this new accent to their own expressive needs. Both of them also exceptional films, a number of critics have found them physically straining to watch. Indeed, they strain at the very fabric of vision, pressing against the limits of visual comprehension as they wrench at traditional patterns of perception in giving birth to the new.

After the heightened bravura of "Lucía 1895," "Lucía 1933" is more controlled and gentler on the eyes. It is also the most personal of the three stories. In "Lucía 1933," Solás explained in the *Jump Cut* interview,

> I'm reflecting a family experience, particularly the story of my father—a man who participated in the insurrection against the dictatorship of Gerardo Machado. He didn't die a violent death then, as the character Aldo does, but he "died" as a vital human being—a sort of death by frustration. When I was born, I was surrounded by all those ghosts, by a failed revolution, by a man whose course in life was interrupted by this collective failure.
>
> That segment of the film grows in part out of the need to express this experience which, though not directly mine, touched me deeply. The fact that I joined the revolutionary insurrection against Batista when I was very young, given my lack of ideological orientation at the time and the spontaneous nature of my actions, must have had a lot to do with my desire to resume my father's interrupted trajectory.

Where "Lucía 1895" is Europeanized, "Lucía 1933" is already closer to North American culture, and belongs to the commercial middle class. The establishing shot, however, which opens the episode (like the colonial town square previously) is this time of a factory interior, the camera looking down toward its women workers with Lucía among them, and the story is then told in flashback. The flashback begins with Lucía and her imposing mother arriving by ferry at one of the offshore keys for a vacation in their summer house away from the city. (We later find out that they have been sent there early in the season by Lucía's father to allow him more time with his mistress in Havana.) Lucía observes the clandestine arrival, after a gun battle in the streets of Havana, of the wounded Aldo, and she becomes involved with him. Kovacs observes that the contrast between the spacious summer house and Aldo's single room succinctly spells out the contrast of lifestyles that Lucía now begins to cross. Her mother posing in front of an ornate mirror is contrasted with Lucía in long shot sitting up in bed in Aldo's bare room. Their love is very gentle. Aldo confesses, "You are my first love; I'm not sorry to say, you're my first woman." Obviously, he is her first love too.

The mirror shot of her mother is particularly significant. There have already been mirror shots in "Lucía 1895," especially a shot of Lucía preparing herself to meet Rafael, with the camera watching the mirror image over her shoulder so that the social stereotype of her mirrored self is at the center of attention. The image of the mother in 1933, however, is shown from a camera position that is quite clearly her daughter's point of view. According to the detailed visual analysis in a second essay on the film by John Mraz, this shot captures "the neocolonial deformities of Cuban culture [that] are expressed in her imitation of Jean Harlow."[19] Then, "after seeing her mother serve as a model of colonized femininity, Lucía enters the room and is forced by her mother to sit in front of the mirror in order to be molded into the same alienated patterns." The different relationship mother and daughter each has to her mirror image is given expression in the different composition of the two shots, in particular the way the segmented reflection of the daughter cuts across the film frame. It is clearly to escape from this alienation that Lucía joins Aldo; the equality of their relationship is based on this knowledge she already has of the nature of the world she comes from. With him, she is able to learn about the world she has been guarded from.

Back in Havana, Lucía goes to work. And while the menfolk carry out an ambush on a bunch of policemen enjoying a rehearsal for a "girlie show," Lucía is organizing the women in the factory. Parallel editing between the two compares and contrasts the two modes of exploitation of women in the pseudorepublic, the rampantly sexified as opposed to the artificially demure, as Lucía also discovers that mirrors can be put to new purposes: for scrawling political slogans on them with lipstick.

There are demonstrations on the streets in which the women participate, which are violently suppressed. Still, Machado falls. The Revolution, however, is abortive and produces no fundamental change. What transpires is well described by Mraz in his earlier article: "The disillusionment of Lucía and Aldo with the new situation contrasts sharply with the opportunism shown by their counterparts and former co-revolutionaries, Antonio and Flora. While the latter move quickly to ensure themselves an advantageous position in the regime, Aldo and Lucía remain true to the ideas that guided them in the struggle against Machado. Sickened by the decadence and debauchery which characterize the new political arrangements . . . Aldo returns to terrorist activity. He is killed and Lucía is left alone, as indeed the superficiality of the relationship with Flora,

Lucía II, 1933, from *Lucía*

her only friend, had shown her to be almost throughout."It almost goes without saying that there is also a mirror shot of Flora and Lucía together: it shows Lucía's face and Flora's back and Flora's mirror image between them.

For Peter Biskind, Aldo, "with his troubled student's face, his straw hat and tommy gun, is a militant Michael Corleone, a tupamaro of the thirties." And it is true, Aldo is given a highly romantic image, the most idealized in the whole film; the odd mixture of Biskind's references shows that this is one of the film's weakest elements. He operates, Biskind continues, "in a seemingly isolated guerrilla band without apparent contact with the other such groups we assume must exist"; and thus, with the virtues and limitations of the bourgeois urban revolutionary, he gets gunned down amid what another commentator calls "the general political chaos of the street fighting of the time."

Like the first Lucía, the second Lucía goes through dramatic changes brought about by personal and historical circumstances. But her liberation as a woman is inevitably constrained. Biskind again: "It is Aldo who talks, fights and dies; it is Lucía who sticks loyally to him ('I'll follow you; I'm your wife, Aldo'), carries his baby, and endures, alone, after his death." Anna Marie Taylor notices that "several cuts to the figure of Lucía, pregnant and alone in their room in Havana during Aldo's long absences, dramatize the marginality of women to the events of this period. Even her political involvement at the factory can be seen as merely an adjunct to Aldo's activities. Nevertheless," she concludes, "the moments of solidarity among the women of the factory show more promise for the future than do Aldo's individualistic and ultimately nihilistic acts." There is a lot to be said for this reading of the episode, though it ends nonetheless in a mood of desolation.

There are various symbolic moments in this episode too, especially in the music. In the first episode, the composer Leo Brouwer uses a theme from Schumann to create a musical icon of the period. In the second, the dominant mood is conveyed by the use of themes from Chopin and Dvořák, and he also uses "Poor Butterfly" to depict the American penetration of Cuba in the scene of a debauched victory party. This is like the way Álvarez uses music. Overall, the style of the episode remains quiet and muted. Biskind likens it to Truffaut's *Jules et Jim* and Franju's *Thérèse* in its employment of slow, deliberate pans, tracks, and zooms. On the other hand, another writer, Michael Myerson, finds in its muted tones a pastiche suggestive of Hollywood of the period portrayed, and Mraz agrees with this, speaking (in his earlier article) of "long, slow, soft shots in which foreground focus and lighting are used to convey a 'portrait image' closely resembling that of Hollywood productions during the golden age."[20]

The Peruvian critic Isaac León Frias finds "Lucía 1933" close to Hollywood models of the 1930s such as Cukor or Kazan. Among the Cuban critics, Elena Díaz likes the sobriety of the episode, which she thinks the most mature of the three. The ending, however, she finds stereotyped. Evidently, the inadequacies in the portrayal of Aldo's character become too much for her. But it is a minor deficiency, she believes, commending the accuracy of observation of the women in the tobacco factory, the demeanor of women in a certain way imitating men, which was characteristic, she says, of (Cuban) feminism in the 1930s.

In the final episode, Solás emerges, as Kovacs felicitously puts it, from the haunted past, and steps into the sunshine of the present. He also moves out of the close and seething city of 1933 to the brilliant light of the Cuban countryside, for "Lucía 196–" is set in a new agricultural cooperative. It opens with an early-morning shot of two peasant women chatting on a roadside as a noisy truckload of their fellow workers comes to pick them up. We find ourselves immediately in a highly particularized scene as the truck stops outside a row of small houses. The driver honks the horn and says "Let's see how long it takes her today. Since she's got a boyfriend we have to wake her up in the morning!" The boisterous characteristics of a fast-paced farcical comedy are thus immediately established, and never let up. There is an enormous sense of exhilaration in this last episode, exuberance and optimism. This is also carried by the music, which employs the traditional "Guantanamera" (its roots, according to Alejo Carpentier, are the Spanish sixteenth century), to which Brouwer gives a brilliant and jazzy orchestration not unlike the Leonard Bernstein of *West Side Story*—though the Mexican composers Chávez and Revueltas are present in this music too—and to which Joseito Fernández, on the sound track, sings humorous and moralistic verses the way he did on the radio in the 1930s.

Adela Legrá (of *Manuela*) as Lucía 196– emerges to join the women on the truck, and they all talk animatedly about changing social mores as she tells the *compañeras* that her new boyfriend, Tomás (Adolfo Llaurado from *Manuela*), doesn't want to let her work after their marriage. We meet him waiting for Lucía after work as the first of the "Guantanamera" verses is heard:

> My divine country girl, girl from Guantánamo,
> The country is a source of innumerable riches . . .
> Men and women alike must gather its bounty.

The sequence stands in for their wedding, which we hear about in the next scene from two old peasant women. "He spends the whole day on top of her," says one, "he doesn't even let her up for air." This is what the other calls the "steamroller treatment." Tomás is shown through their joking as oversexed—and from a woman's, not a man's, point of view. Then the film moves from the public world in which it began into the private interior space of the married couple, where we now see them playfully running around the house, Lucía hiding, Tomás seeking, till they end up on the bed, Lucía shrieking (as the published script describes it) both delighted and terrified. The entire scene inevitably recalls Lucía 1895 with Rafael in the abandoned outhouse of the sugar mill.

The couple are then summoned to a birthday party at the community center. The scene is crowded and eventful, in the greatest contrast to the party in "Lucía 1933." Lucía discusses with an older woman from the truck, Angelina, Tomás's refusal to let her go to work. Lucía seeks sisterly advice from her: "He says that the Revo . . . that *he's* the Revolution! I love him a lot, Angelina, what am I going to do?" We catch a glimpse of a group of foreigners—evidently Russians or East Europeans—whose appearance is so distinctive that they create quite a stir among the campesinos. Some critics have made rather too much of this, supposing it to be a deliberate jibe. But although the campesinos are bemused, and, when one of the women attempts to dance like a Cuban, amused as well, it is not certain that the symbolic significance of their presence, as Mraz thought in the first of his articles, is to compare Soviet imperialism with the North American variety, as if they were equivalents, but something much less devious, simply an ironic comment on cultural distance.

Their appearance is, in any case, brief. A moment later, Tomás, consumed by clearly irrational jealousy, picks a fight with someone who is dancing with Lucía while he talks with Flavio, Angelina's husband. Immediately we are back with the couple in their small house, Tomás, possessed, nailing the windows shut to turn the house into a prison, shouting at Lucía: "What did you expect? That you could go around dancing to crazy music with every pair of balls that comes along? I want you to obey me, you hear? That's what you're my wife for!" For the second time comes the "Guantanamera" commentary: "The scourge of jealousy . . . causes a ton of grief . . . such behavior in our new life / Today is out of place." The interpolation of the song is more Brechtian than Shakespearean, but the unfolding of the story is very much like Shakespearean comedy—one that deals with the public and private lives of a warring couple.

The community breaches Tomás's defenses by means of the literacy campaign. Tomás is, of course, intensely suspicious of the young teacher ascribed to Lucía, but in the end Lucía's education must take its course. To cut a long and subtly narrated story short, Lucía finally escapes from the house, leaving Tomás a note that reads "I'm going. I'm not a slave." She moves in with Angelina. When Tomás comes searching her out on the salt flats where she is working, her *compañeras* energetically restrain him. He has been weakened, "morally destroyed," as Joseito Fernández sings, "a laughingstock . . . a product of that jealousy which comes of poor imagination." As the film closes, Tomás and Lucía are still fighting,

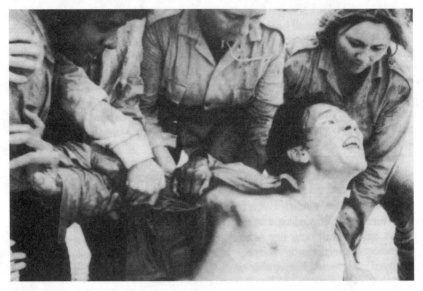

Lucía III, 196–, from *Lucía*

but the final image is that of a little girl who laughs at them and then goes off, as if turning away toward the future.

The camera work in "Lucía 196–" is mostly in a rough and fluid, hand-held, eye-level mid-shot with a good proportion of close-ups, which, as Anna Marie Taylor has noticed, brings the viewer into intimate contact with the people of this small country community. Mraz, in his second article, observes that there is also a recall of the mirror shots of the previous episodes, in which Lucía is seen making up, but this time flinching from the mirror image for its reflection of behavior so obviously inappropriate. The shot in question comes just as Joseito Fernández is singing "But such behavior in our new life / Today is out of place." It combines with the sung commentary to create a perfect instance of Brechtian cinema—an effect of distantiation combined with the gesture of an actor stepping out of one role and into another. This is contrasted with Tomás at the mirror too—proudly preening himself. It makes a powerful critique of machismo.

In *Memorias del subdesarrollo* the Cuban intelligentsia, the artistic and intellectual community Fidel spoke to in the "Words to the Intellectuals," confronts itself. It discovers itself in the act of breaking down the vocabulary of its own existence. Tomás Gutiérrez Alea's film, based on a novel by

Edmundo Desnoes, is an exercise in the fragmentation and dissociation of imagery and representation, as the prerevolutionary world is dismembered while the cultural shapes of the new have not yet emerged. Of all Cuban films of the 1960s it is in certain ways the closest to the ethos of the metropolitan intellectual, a film that portrays the subjective condition of its central character, a kind of intellectual antihero in a state of paralyzed perceptiveness. But although metropolitan critics have compared this film to Antonioni, and its lead actor Sergio Corrieri to the young Mastroianni, seeing the film as a portrayal of middle-class angst in the midst of a vapid society, there is none of Antonioni's nihilism here and, as Michael Myerson has said, "revolutionary Cuba is not capitalist Italy, and the milieu in which Corrieri's Sergio operates (or rather, cannot operate) is far different from that pictured by Antonioni."[21]

Sergio is neither a revolutionary nor a counterrevolutionary. He would like to be a writer, which he perceives as a vocation outside the realms of the political imperative. Before the Revolution he owned a furniture store, which his father gave him to set him up in business. Now he lives off the payments made to him by the state as an allowance for the confiscation of his property as a landlord, for he also owned a block of flats in the well-appointed Havana district of Vedado, one of the city's tallest buildings, at the top of which he now lives alone. His wife, from whom he is divorced, left with his parents for the United States during 1961 in the mass exodus of the bourgeoisie. This is the point in Sergio's tale of woe at which the film opens.

Except for the title sequence, that is. The titles are superimposed over a nighttime carnival scene filmed from within the midst of a dancing, jostling crowd by a handheld camera. A disturbance takes place, we catch a glimpse of a body lying amid the feet on the ground in a pool of blood, then lifted up and carried away through the throng. The last credit appears and the picture cuts to the airport, where we discover Sergio, in a different crowd, with his wife and parents, making their farewells. As the images of the title sequence recede into the antechamber of our attention, they leave behind the feel of enigma, an unresolved tension that pervades everything that proceeds to unfold (until eventually, much later in the film, the scene is repeated, only from a different point of view), while the cut to the airport establishes a paradigm for the oblique montage and narrative style of the film, which sets up many an enigma as it unfolds through the surprise juxtaposition of some new scene of contrasting aspect. One of the modes the film adopts for its fragmentation of imagery and representation, this is, of course, a characteristic form of expression of the modernist aesthetic.

The look in Sergio's eyes as he separates himself from the parting embrace of his family shapes another paradigm that will be constantly evoked throughout the film. It is the look of distantiation, which is immediately reinforced here by the not quite invisible wall of plate glass—visible only in the reflections cast upon it—that separates the travelers from their homeland as they go through the partition into the departure lounge, a wall of silence that the camera places us alternately on either side of.

On the balcony of his flat, after returning from the airport, Sergio surveys the scene below him through a telescope, obviously a habitual occupation since the telescope is mounted on the parapet, and at the same time a metaphorical extension of the distant look in Sergio's eyes, because the telescope fragments, breaking vision up into an infinity of rounded images, each of which is a separate little scene in itself. What Sergio does not seem able to discover as his story unfolds, but which the film itself exemplifies as it does so, is the synthesis of perception through creative montage. This is not so much an interpretation of the film as a statement of its method. In a set of working notes on the film, the director explains: Sergio is a person unable to enter into the new reality that the Revolution forces upon him, which is so much vaster than his previous world. Why, then, did he not leave too? Because "for him everything has come either too early or too late and he is incapable of making decisions." Yet "through this personage who in almost all respects we are inclined to reject, we can discover new aspects of the reality that surrounds us. Sometimes through him, sometimes by contrast. His attitude as a spectator with a minimum of lucidity keeps the critical spirit awake in us ... the confrontation of his own world with the 'documentary' world that we show (the world of our subjectivity, not his) becomes rich in suggestion."[22]

They accordingly set out, says Alea, with the basic intention of making a kind of documentary about a man who ended up alone, and the idea that the vision of reality offered by documentary inserts would strike against the subjective vision of the protagonist. Direct documentary filming, bits of newsreel, photographs, recordings of speeches, filming in the streets with a hidden camera—these were the resources that would be brought to bear. Some things in the novel would be dropped, new sequences introduced, Sergio's voice-over would speak its testimony, but the film's open and "seemingly disarticulated" language would give the effect of a plastic montage more than a literary narration. The multiplicity of means would make the idiom of the film not only more open but also richer in its signifiers. Ultimately, the intention was not to reflect reality but to detect a problem, not to soften reality but to bring it alive, even aggressively, even, so to speak, to disturb the peace. Not, one should add, that things in Cuba were exactly peaceful at that moment: there was great revolutionary energy and ideological struggle going on. But there were always people, says Alea, who thought certain things would look after themselves, and these were the same people who tended to believe themselves depositaries of the revolutionary bequest, who spoke of the people as a promising child and tried to tell others how this child should be spoken to. These people the film, among other things, proposed to aggravate and provoke.

Surveying what he can see of Havana from his balcony, Sergio's voice is heard over the images speaking to himself: "Everything remains the same," he says, seeing lovers by the swimming pool of an adjacent hotel; "Cuba free and independent," over scenes of defense preparations, "who would have thought that this can happen?" And over a shot of the plinth from which the imperial eagle of the United States has been removed (one of the established icons of Cuban cinema—the scene of the demonstration in which it was pulled down crops up in several ICAIC documentaries) he wonders, "Where is the dove that Picasso was going to send?" adding that "it's very comfortable being a communist millionaire in Paris." Loaded with the ambiguity of innuendo, these are significant words, which spell out several things about the person who speaks them: the European axis of his thinking, his sense of frustration, his feelings of passive belligerence toward the world, his resentment. No, he is not an attractive character.

Especially as he goes on to enact his own unattractiveness to himself in a grotesque orgy of self-abuse. He rummages through the belongings his wife Laura has been forced to leave behind, trying on her furs and manhandling, so to speak, the icons of her femininity—a powder puff, pearls, lipstick. Twisting the lipstick up and down obviously seems a classic Freudian symbol, and Alea is not the kind of director to overlook this. On the contrary, he means to advise us of Sergio's phallocentricity,

Memorias del subdesarrollo (Tomás Gutiérrez Alea, 1968)

which the film will develop. And for once, because of corresponding symbols in the film concerning vision—like the telescope—the film itself licenses the finding of the relationship that psychoanalytic film theory posits between phallocentrism and the camera.

Sergio then sits down with the lipstick in front of a mirror and proceeds to doodle with it. If the image reminds us of "Lucía 1933," it should also be observed how differently the same idea is used here. Sergio scribbles on the mirror not so much to interfere with its hated reflection, but rather more narcissistically, like an artist putting the finishing touches to a self-portrait. Finally, he takes one of Laura's stockings and pulls it over his head, distorting his features, as he listens to a tape recording he made of a conversation in which he and Laura are arguing, first about a movie they have seen, then, as he taunts her, about herself and what he calls her "struggle between elegance and vulgarity," her use, to disguise her vulgar origins, of all the commodities women are offered to construct their image with. "You get more attractive each day," Sergio mocks her, "you're more artificial, I don't like natural beauty." At the climax of the row, he tells her he has recorded the whole thing on tape, "everything, word for word, it'll be fun later on, when you hear it."

The nature of Sergio's attitude toward women is developed out on the streets of Havana where he scrutinizes them. He enters a bookshop, where the shelves are stocked with the classic works of Marxism, cheap editions of novels, and clearly situated behind his shoulder, drawing our attention away from his observing eye, a book called *The Hero of Our Times*. Voice-over, he is saying, "Here women look into your eyes as if they want to be touched by your look. That only happens here." Out on the streets again, Sergio passes a bust of Martí—Alea has not forgotten, as a good modernist artist, to allude to himself—with an inscription, "Nuestro vino es agrio, pero es nuestro vino" (Our wine is sour, but it's our wine). But Sergio evidently does not share the feeling of combativity that surrounds him.

A title appears, the single word "Pablo," and the film changes pace as we cut to Sergio driving with a friend along the Malecón, Havana's seafront drive. Over a flashback to the two men with their wives at a nightclub, Pablo spills out his cynicism—"I never got involved with politics, I have a clear conscience"—but Sergio is completely uninterested. More than uninterested. Something in him is incensed by his erstwhile friend's insensitivity, and, as he stares ahead of him (the absent look in his eyes we've seen before), the picture cuts to a montage of stills of scenes of poverty in Latin America, as he muses: "He says the only thing a Cuban can't stand is hunger. All the starvation we've gone through since the Spanish came! In Latin America four children die every minute due to illnesses caused by malnutrition." The statistic comes from the Second Declaration of Havana. A moment later, up in Pablo's apartment, the conversation turns to the subject of the prisoners captured at the Bay of Pigs, a topic Sergio introduces to taunt Pablo. In a most extraordinary and spectacular event, forty of these prisoners were interrogated by a panel of journalists before a packed audience in a Havana theater just a few days after their defeat. The whole event, which lasted four days, was televised, published verbatim in the press, and later in book form. The sequence begins with a newsreel of the invasion and the captured mercenaries being marched along hands on head. A title appears: "The Truth of the Group is in the Murderer." Sergio, reading from the book, narrates: "We found beneath the military organization of the invaders an order in their social duties that summarizes the division of the moral and social functions of the bourgeoisie: priest, businessman, official, philosopher, politician, torturer, and the innumerable sons of good families." Alea's procedure here in putting Sergio's voice-over to work like a newsreel commentator is a bold one, which allows the film to elaborate the sense of social anatomy through which Sergio himself is refracted. One of the prisoners on trial declares, like Pablo, that he is not a political person. A moment later, Sergio's voice-over appears to be holding a dialogue with another. We surmise that Sergio understands perfectly well what these claims about being nonpolitical amount to. At the end of the sequence, he comments that "in none of the cases considered was there a recovery of the true dialectical relationship between individual and group"; we are left reflecting not only that this is true of his own situation, but that he knows it.

Another title, "Noemí," introduces us to the girl who cleans his apartment (played by Eslinda Núñez of "Lucía 1933"), about whom he fantasizes vividly. Then another title, *Elena* comes up and we are on La Rampa, Havana's nightlife strip of yore. Elena (played by Daysi Granados) is a pretty Havana girl whom he spies and picks up. His opening words, "You have beautiful knees, do you want to have dinner with me?" are spoken with the self-assurance of a man of social advantage who knows that women find him attractive, especially since he is taller and his features are more European than those of most Cuban men. His whole demeanor hides his internal angst.

The film enters a new phase, for each new name title also brings a new theme. Elena is waiting, she tells Sergio, for someone from ICAIC about a possible job, but he hasn't turned up. Sergio tells her, as they eat dinner, that he has a friend who is a director there, and then asks her why she wants to be an actress. "Because," she says, "I'm tired of always being the same. That way I can be someone else without people thinking I'm crazy. I want," she adds, speaking the words like a line she's learned, "to unfold my personality." She thus enters the film and Sergio's life like his shadow, his double, another lens through which his own identity crisis is refracted, which he himself undoubtedly recognizes since he is too intelligent not to see it, and which he decides to humor: "But all those characters are like scratched records." No one by this stage in the film will be wholly surprised when this scene cuts to a montage of clips of scenes from movies. But Alea still has plenty of surprises up his sleeve and the clips arrest us by repeating themselves—images of couples in the clasp of lovemaking, of a woman stepping into a shower, of a stripper. Abruptly the images stop and lights go up and we are in a viewing theater. Sergio, sitting next to Elena, turns to someone behind them and asks, "Where did you get them?" This is evidently his friend the director. In fact, it is Alea, though as a character in his own film he remains unnamed. "They showed up one day," he replies, "they're the cuts Batista's censors made, they said they were offensive to morals and good breeding." "What are you going to do with them?" asks Sergio. The director explains that he's going to put them into a film. "It'll be a collage with a little bit of everything." Obviously, it is the film we are watching. "Will they release it?" asks Sergio. The scene is a kind of conceit, but it is much more than a clever way of suggesting, as a number of metropolitan critics thought, that the new regime was not as mindless as its predecessors.

Actually, the scene is a step in the translation of the novel to the screen. The adaptation of the novel involves certain problems, because the whole thing is a conceit: it is written in the first person by a character with the ambition to be a writer who has the same name as the author, of the novel. This is a kind of play upon the identity of the author, which is another typical trait of modernism. In the work of a Borges, for example, such conceits are used to set up metaphysical conundrums about the human condition. Here the purpose is to capture, in the spider's web of language, certain elusive aspects of the identity crisis of the artist within the revolutionary process, the problem of the *desgarramiento*, the ideological rupture with the past. But how can you translate the novel's first person to the screen? There is no direct or logical equivalent in film of the persona of the first-person narrator in literature except a voice on the sound track, which is not the same. As an analogue of the writer's pen the camera is impersonal; it cannot say "I," it always says "there is," "here is." This is why the filmmakers chose to oppose the camera to the pen as instruments through which to record the world, by contrasting Sergio's subjectivity with the documentary quality of the camera image. In fact, the film invites us alternately to identify the camera with Sergio and to separate them, and it does this in odd and irregular ways, like making his voice the commentary to a piece of newsreel.

Sergio takes Elena back to his apartment. She is awkward and embarrassed. Sergio tries to win her over by giving her some of his wife's discarded clothing to try on. A classic game of seduction takes place, filmed with a nervous handheld camera, as she alternately lures him on and repulses him until he forcefully pins her down on the bed and she gives in to him. Afterwards she cries, protests that he has ruined her, and leaves.

With Sergio alone again, the camera pans around the room until it lands on Sergio together with Laura, in the middle of the argument on the tape recording we heard earlier.

Pablo is leaving. Sergio goes to see him off at the airport. His departure occasions in Sergio another bout of self-reflection, in which a certain self-honesty is mixed up with his self-delusion. "Although it may destroy me," he says, "this Revolution is my revenge against the stupid Cuban bourgeoisie. Against idiots like Pablo . . . everything I don't want to be." The trouble is not only that he has forgotten how his wife left Cuba to escape him as much as the Revolution, but that he has also conflated the personal and the political without properly understanding either. His only solution is to try and hold himself apart, even though he knows what it costs him to do so: "I keep my mind clear. It's a disagreeable clarity, empty. I know what's happening to me but I can't avoid it." In a flashback to his childhood, he associates his present self-paralysis with the subjugation of the schoolboy to the power of the priests at his Catholic school, which taught him the relationship, he says, between justice and power. But the flashback is paired with another, his induction into the mysteries of sex in a whorehouse, and as the image cuts back to the present, with Sergio reflecting upon Elena and his discovery that she wasn't as "complex and interesting" as he first thought, it is not so certain that he really understood the relationship between justice and power after all, at least insofar as it concerns the power men wield over women. That he has power over Elena he is perfectly aware, but he conceives of himself wielding it benevolently as he decides to educate her. As they visit an art gallery, his voice-over explains, "I always try to live like a European, and Elena forces me to feel underdeveloped at every step."

The sequence that follows is not in the original version of the novel, only in the rewrite Desnoes produced after collaborating on the film. Julianne Burton records that in the view of Desnoes, Alea "betrayed" the novel, but in a creative and illuminating way, objectivizing a world that was still abstract in the book and giving it social density; the interpolation of this new sequence goes even further, expanding the commentary on the social role of the artist. It is also another step in transposing the novel to the screen. Following a title, "A Tropical Adventure," we find ourselves in Ernest Hemingway's house near Havana, which is now the Hemingway Museum. Sergio has taken Elena there in the interests of her education. She is predictably unimpressed ("Is this where Mr. Way used to live? I don't see anything so special. Books and dead animals.") and she quickly becomes bored, wandering off and posing for photographs for some foreign tourists. Sergio hides from her and watches as she gives up searching and hitches a ride back to town. There is much more to the sequence, however, which is a long one, than Sergio ditching Elena. It amounts to a disquisition on the social and historical relations of the writer and is in many ways the pivot of the entire film, the confluence of Sergio's most objective reflections on the topic and the analysis of the filmmakers, in which, by uniting the two, the filmmakers at once pay not uncritical homage to the tradition of the writer as the embodiment of social conscience and reflect upon the revolutionary transformation that this conscience must now undergo. The sequence begins with the commentary of the museum guide, about whom we learn from Sergio's voice-over: "Hemingway found him when he was a little boy playing in the streets.... He molded him to his needs. The faithful servant and the great lord. The colonialist and Gunga Din. Hemingway must have been unbearable." The guide, however, describes him as a good man, a humane man, a war correspondent in the Spanish civil war who joined the International Brigade, by implication a friend of the Revolution even though not a revolutionary himself. It is clear, never-theless, that he was not only a good writer, he was a rich one too. As Sergio explains: "This was his refuge, his tower, his island in the trop-ics.... Boots for hunting in Africa, American furniture, Spanish photo-graphs, magazines and books in English, a bullfight poster. Cuba never really interested him. Here he could find refuge, entertain his friends, write in English, and fish in the Gulf Stream." But if we conclude that he came here to solve his problems, we are not slow to think of his last problem, whose solution he found elsewhere, at his Idaho ranch. (It was after his suicide that his wife gave his Cuban house to the Revolution.)

From Sergio's commentary on the commentary of the guide, two things emerge. One is the question of "official" museum versions of culture; this belongs to the critique the film directs toward the paternalists within the Revolution. But second, from the position of the sequence within the unfolding argument of the film, it becomes symbolic of the inevitable death, indeed, the necessary spiritual suicide, of the old kind of writer in the face of the new society. And yet, although Sergio realizes this perfectly well, he is unable to tear himself away from the relics in the museum in the same way that he cannot kick over the traces within himself of the anachronistic social model that Hemingway represents.

The problem is not only Sergio's. Another screen title announces: "Round Table—Literature and Underdevelopment." Like the guide at the Hemingway Museum, the participants are real people: the Haitian poet René Depestre, the Italian novelist Gianni Toti, the Argentinian novelist David Viñas, and, significantly, the author of *Memorias del sub-desarrollo* the novel—Edmundo Desnoes. The panel discusses the topic while Sergio, in the audience, tries to follow the argument, but like everyone else becomes restless. When the discussion is thrown open, someone requests permission to speak in English. He is the North American playwright Jack Gelber, translator of the English edition of Desnoes's novel. "Why is it," he asks, "that if the Cuban Revolution is a total revolution, they have to resort to an archaic form of discussion such as a roundtable and treat us to an impotent discussion of issues that I'm well informed about and most of the public here is well informed about, when there could be another more revolutionary way to reach an audience like this?" The picture cuts away to a long shot of Sergio walking the streets again. The camera zooms in very slowly toward him, into bigger and bigger close-up, until finally the image loses focus and he disappears into a blur, while his voice-over reflects: "I don't understand. The American was right. Words devour words and they leave you in the clouds. . . . How does one get rid of underdevelopment? It marks everything. What are you doing there, Sergio? You have nothing to do with them. You're alone. . . . You're nothing, you're dead. Now it begins, Sergio, your final destruction."

Another title, "Hanna," another flashback, girls emerging from a school. Hanna was a Jewish refugee from Hitler; they were going to get married but her parents took her off to New York; she had all the poise he finds lacking in his other women, especially Elena, who, back in the present, is waiting for him outside his flat. He avoids her, but then it turns out she's told her family he has ruined her. They demand that he marry her and when he refuses they decide to press charges against him for rape. Is this, then, to be his final undoing? He fully expects so, and as the courtroom scene unfolds, so do we. But the court finds the charges against him unproven. He is left to wonder: "It was a happy ending, as they say. For once justice triumphed. But was it really like that? There is something that leaves me in a bad position. I've seen too much to be innocent. They have too much darkness inside their heads to be guilty."

The closing section of the film shows Sergio's ultimate self-paralysis as the city around him engages in defense preparations during the un-folding of the so-called Cuban missile crisis. If the confrontation be-tween the United States and the Soviet Union in October 1962 over the placing of Soviet missiles in Cuba was experienced throughout the world as a moment of reckoning, the place it occupies within collective and individual memory in Cuba itself is saturated with peculiar significance. It was another of the experiences of the Revolution's early years that played a definitive role in forging social cohesion and bonding the is-land's unity, like the experiences of the literacy campaign and the Bay of Pigs invasion. In the popular experience, the way people remember it, it was a moment in which individual fears were submerged in the collec-tive, and national consciousness took on a peculiarly tangible form, as of a people that finds itself condemned to a historical test in the defense of self-determination. A junior member of ICAIC, in his early teens at the time, remembered in a conversation with the present author the sensation of knowing they were targets for a kind of attack that no one, if it came, would be able to escape, and that therefore called up a unique shared resoluteness. The sensation gripped them with special intensity because while the world was holding its breath because of Cuba, the Cubans themselves were powerless. As Sergio puts it, in his final voice-over, sandwiched between speeches on television by Kennedy and by Fidel, "And if it started right now? It's no use protesting. I'll die like the rest. This island is a trap. We're very small, and too poor. It's an expen-sive dignity."

I believe it must have been this last sequence as much as anything that was responsible for the initial misreading of the film that occurred in the metropolis, where a number of critics were so surprised to find a Cuban picture handling the theme of bourgeois alienation that they failed to perceive the critique it leveled not merely at Sergio but by im-plication at anyone identifying too closely with him. These critics, insen-sible to the nature of Sergio's narcissism but narcissistically sharing his all-consuming sense of resentment, instead felt flattered at seeing such an accurate portrayal of their own reflection. And the epilogue is con-structed with such understatement that it must have allowed them to identify completely with his own sentiments in the face of the threat of nuclear annihilation. Since they could hardly, as alienated intellectuals, conceive of any other sentiment in the face of the missile crisis—for example, that national dignity is not negotiable—so they imagined that the film was meant to be critical of the political process that led up to it. They assumed that the director of such a film could only be a fellow spirit, that he couldn't possibly be an enthusiastic supporter of such a state as they took Cuba to be. They saw the film's critique of under-development as a criticism of the stupidity of the common people, as if individuals and not the social heritage were responsible. Many critics, to be sure, escape these strictures—Vincent Canby, for instance, who cited Antonioni in order to contrast the Italian and the Cuban.[23] But if there was a Vincent Canby, there was also an Andrew Sarris, who as president of the U.S. National Society of Film Critics, tried to turn Alea into a dissident of the type the capitalist media loved to find in the Soviet Union.[24]

That was when the U.S. State Department refused to grant Alea a visa to attend the society's awards ceremony at which he was due to receive a special prize for the film. This was not the first time a Cuban filmmaker had been refused a U.S. visa. The same thing happened a short while earlier in 1972, to a delegation from ICAIC intending to visit the United States for a Cuban film festival planned by an independent distributor, ADF (American Documentary Films), in New York and other cities. Not only were they refused visas but anti-Castro émigré terrorist groups threatened violence if the festival were allowed to go ahead, and there were indeed attacks on the Olympia Theater in New York where the films were to be shown. But the biggest attack on the festival was that of the U.S. government, which seized one of the films from the cinema and raided the ADF offices, thus bringing the festival to a halt. The grounds the government used for these actions were that the films had been ille-gally imported. As Michael Myerson has explained: "A meeting between a Festival spokesman and Stanley Sommerfield, Acting Head of Foreign Assets Control in Washington, was straight out of *Catch-22*. Sure, said Sommerfield, the government exempts the news media and universities from the Cuban embargo statutes because news gathering and a body of scholarship are in the national interest. But no, he continued, in answer to a question, it would not be in the national interest if the population as a whole had direct access to the materials instead of having selected elites act as middlemen in deciphering them."[25] Protests were made, of course, on both occasions, and they involved a large number of distinguished persons. When the ICAIC delegation were refused their visas at the very same moment Nixon was visiting China, Senator William Fulbright asked why the U.S. government should consider four Cuban filmmakers a security threat and not Mao Tse-tung and the People's Republic. When Alea was banned, he declared in Congress: "I find it passing strange that the Treasury Department would be so terrified of the impact of Cuban films on the American people, while the State Department is encouraging such exchanges with the Soviet Union."[26] *Washington Post* columnist Nicholas von Hoffman, criticizing the aforementioned Treasury official, pointed to a more insidious anomaly: "Go every morning to your hutch in the Treasury Department, Mr. Sommerfield," he wrote, "drink your coffee, read your paper, and daily bring a full measure of aggravation into the lives of people who don't yet know your name. Keep out the movies.... The rest of the Treasury Department will let the heroin flow in."[27]

ADF was forced by these attacks into bankruptcy, though *Memorias del subdesarrollo* was finally able to open commercially in New York in May 1973, to be selected early in 1974 by the *New York Times* as one of the year's ten best movies. The same newspaper, when Alea's visa was refused, again criticized the ridiculous behavior of the officials and declared it irrational to treat the offer of a prize to a film as a subversive act.[28] The Cubans took the whole affair stoically. It did not escape their attention that these responses did not all square up. As Alea made plain in the statement he sent to be read at the awards ceremony, the Cubans were not surprised by any of it, for the film itself, the subject of the whole to-do, reflected the aggressions directed by the U.S. government against the Cubans from the beginning, including the blockade, the disinformation, and the gamut of actions intended to impede contact between the two peoples, which kept the North Americans in a state of ignorance about Cuba and what was really going on there.[29] It was precisely this kind of ignorance that allowed Andrew Sarris to utter his misinterpretation of Alea's position. As the Cuban director put it when Julianne Burton asked him for his comments on Sarris: "His lack of information was such that one suspects a kind of tendentious ignorance, if such a thing is possible. It's hard to know in such cases where ignorance leaves off and stupidity or malice begins."[30]

In Cuba itself, *Memorias,* because of its sophistication of style, proved a difficult film for many of the audience. But Alea recalled later that it produced the very positive effect of sending many people back to the cinema to see it a second and even a third time.[31] Here was evidence that ICAIC's policies were really beginning to bite.

From *Memorias del subdesarrollo* on, the interpenetration of fiction and documentary becomes a distinctive preoccupation in a number of Cuban films. In particular, it is next pursued with great originality and virtuosity, a year after *Memorias,* by Manuel Octavio Gómez in *La primera carga al machete.* A shortish film of eighty-four minutes in black and white and using a wide screen, *La primera carga al machete* is another of the films on the theme of the hundred years' war. It deals with the events that opened the war against the Spanish in 1868 when independence fighters under the generalship of the Dominican Máximo Gómez began the rebellion in the east of the island, where they succeeded in taking the important city of Bayamo. The Spanish captain general sends two strong columns of the colonial army to recapture Bayamo and put down the rebellion. The rebels force one of the columns to retreat by means not of direct confrontation but of a strategy of deception, while the second column is destroyed at the very entrance to Bayamo by the attack after which the film is named.

Gómez said that he found the historical movie, the grandiloquent kind of film the term is usually identified with, insupportable, and for this reason a documentary method seemed to him the logical way to approach the subject. But how exactly to apply this to a historical subject? "From the beginning we set about trying to give the idea that we were developing the story as if it were being filmed at that very moment, as if it had been possible at that time to use a camera and recorder to collect the facts."[32] They applied this idea visually by using high-contrast photography to give the impression of very early film stock. This is combined with a handheld camera and direct sound (which Alea had used extensively for the first time in Cuba in *Memorias*). At the same time, the film employs a number of documentary procedures, especially the interview carried out in the manner of television reportage, interviewee on camera speaking to an interviewer offscreen. There is also a discussion among a patriotic group commenting on the events, who begin by introducing themselves to camera one by one, and a sequence in which

an agitator, a kind of accomplice of the camera, accosts people in a public square in Havana and obliges them to give their opinions about the
independence issue, until Spanish soldiers appear on the scene to break
up the disturbance that has thus been created. Other interviewees, at the
scene of battle, include Spanish soldiers who have survived the machete
charge and describe the terror of having to face such a deadly weapon;
Spanish functionaries—including both the island's governor and the
commander of the troops; patriotic inhabitants of Bayamo, victims of
Spanish repression; and rebel soldiers. The documentary techniques
allow considerable fluidity in the structuring of the film. Indeed, the film
opens after the machete charge, with Spanish soldiers who have survived it and the patriots discussing its significance, before going back to
reconstruct the events, by way of a documentary sequence on the machete itself, its origins and uses, which is thus presented as a character in
the film in its own right, so to speak. Finally, the film is punctuated by
the figure of a singer (Pablo Milanés), a roving troubador who sings a
ballad that provides a further commentary on the events.

   The net result of these techniques is not so much to transport the
viewer into the past as to bring the past into the present. This is the very
opposite of the conventional historical movie, which aims, in its crass-
est examples, through creating an illusion of distant times, to provide a
vehicle of escapism. Such films misconstrue the past in order to shore
up the present status quo through the back-projection, as it were, of the
supposedly universal and eternal values of the dominant bourgeois ideology. This film, as the Venezuelan critics put it, changes the habitual
perspective of such historiography, and thereby displays the continuity
of struggle between past and present with incomparable urgency. One
indication of this is the parallel the filmmakers found to emerge while
they were making the film between the figure of Máximo Gómez and
that of Che Guevara, which they had not originally thought of. At the
same time, this transportation of the past achieves, once again, distinctly Brechtian results, for, as the Venezuelan critics also observe, the
mummification of the past in the scholarly texts is substituted by a
form of representation that eliminates conventional emotional identification with the characters in the drama, and stimulates instead a process
of reflection that inserts the contemporary viewer into the problematic
of the past just as much as it inserts the heritage of the past into the
problematic of the present.

If this film had been made for British television, it would doubtless have been called a drama-documentary in the manner of Peter Watkins's not dissimilar *Culloden*. For Latin American critics, it is an example both of *cine rescate*, the recovery of history, and of the application of *cine encuesta*, the film of inquiry, to a historical subject. This again is to place the emphasis on the film's affinity with documentary. It is more than affinity, really: the entire conception of the film is that of documentary, with the consequence that while *Lucía*, with which it shares a great deal stylistically, especially in the way the camera is used, remains firmly within the fictional mode, *La primera carga al machete* does not. On the contrary, it represents a high point in the attack on conventional narrative with which several Cuban filmmakers now engaged, and which is one of the themes behind Julio García Espinosa's concept of imperfect cinema.

CHAPTER THIRTEEN

Imperfect Cinema and the Seventies

It was at the end of the 1960s, arising from the experience of *Juan Quin Quin*, that García Espinosa wrote the essay *Por un cine imperfecto (For an Imperfect Cinema)*, a polemical reflection on the whole practice of revolutionary film, which is not only a powerful credo for Cuban cinema but one of the major theoretical statements defining the scope of the New Cinema of Latin America.[1] Much misunderstood, the essay starts off as a warning against the technical perfection that, after ten years, now began to lie within the reach of the Cuban filmmakers. Its argument, however, is more widely applicable, and its implications for revolutionary film practice outside Cuba were the subject of heated debate. The thesis is not that technical and artistic perfection necessarily prevent a film being politically effective—that would be absurd—but that in the underdeveloped world these cannot be aims in themselves. Not only because to attempt to match the production values of the big commercial movie is a waste of resources, but also because in the commercial cinema of the metropolis these values become irredeemably superficial, the beautifully controlled surface becomes a way of lulling the audience into passive consumption. This is contrary to the needs of an authentically modern cinema that seeks to engage with its audience by imaginatively inserting itself and them into social reality, to film the world around it without makeup, to make the kind of film that remains incomplete without an actively responsive audience taking it up. This sense of incompleteness without the audience is part of what García Espinosa means by imperfection. Fifteen years after the original essay,

García Espinosa admitted that the term *imperfect* was confusing, and explained it this way: art is essentially (or traditionally) "a disinterested activity, but if we're in a phase when we have to express interests, then let's do it openly and not continue to camouflage it. And therefore, if art is substantially a disinterested activity and we're obliged to do it in an interested way, it becomes an imperfect art. In essence, this is how I used the word imperfect. And this . . . isn't just an ethical matter, but also aesthetic."[2] Sara Gómez, the director in the early 1970s of *De cierta manera,* summed up imperfect cinema in her own way in the same year as García Espinosa's essay, when she said in an interview about her work as a documentarist, "Cinema, for us, is inevitably partial, determined by a *toma de conciencia,* the result of a definite attitude in the face of the problems that confront us, of the necessity of decolonizing ourselves politically and ideologically, and of breaking with traditional values, be they economic, ethical, or aesthetic."[3]

On the face of it, the concept of imperfect cinema has a number of similarities with ideas that have been developed within radical film culture in the metropolis since the late 1960s, which often invoke the name of Brecht, are theoretically based in the intellectual techniques of structuralism, and are concerned with the business of deconstruction. For instance, speaking of the production of the news in the media, it is necessary, according to García Espinosa, "above all to show the process which generates the problems . . . to submit it to judgment without pronouncing the verdict," so as to enable the audience to evaluate it for themselves instead of passively submitting to the commentator's analysis, permeated as it is with a priori assumptions that block the viewer's intelligence. There are differences, however. For one thing, imperfect cinema is less dogmatic and sectarian than you frequently find within radical film culture in the metropolis about how to achieve its aims: "It can use whatever genre or all genres. It can use cinema as a pluralistic art form, or as a specialised form of expression. These questions are indifferent to it, since they do not represent its real problems or alternatives, still less its real goals. These are not the battles or polemics it is interested in sparking." The core of imperfect cinema is the call that García Espinosa shares with other key polemicists of third-world struggle, like Frantz Fanon and Paulo Freire, for cultural decolonization. It therefore asks for something much more than deconstruction, which instead it subsumes as one of its possible methods; and this also gives it a critical stance toward the radical cinema of the metropolis.

It is also more visionary. There is, says García Espinosa, a dangerous trap, a contradiction, liable to beset even the most revolutionary artist as long as resources and opportunity remain scarce. In ideal conditions, where the means of production were equally available, this would not only be socially just, but would also liberate artistic culture: it would mean "the possibility of recovering, without any kind of complex or guilt feeling, the true meaning of artistic activity," namely, "that art is not work and that the artist is not in the strict sense a worker." Here, it must be said, the hardheaded Cuban revolutionary seems every bit as idealist as the student on the barricades in Paris in 1968, except that he does not fall for thinking that this utopian state of affairs is just around the corner. He therefore sees that, until such time, there remains a difficulty: "The feeling that this is so, and the impossibility of translating it into practice, constitutes the agony and at the same time the pharisaism of all contemporary art." What is needed in this situation, says García Espinosa, is not so much a new cultural policy as a new poetics, based on an openly partisan belief in the Revolution as itself the highest expression of culture, because its purpose is to rescue artistic activity from being just a fragment of the wider human culture. When that has happened, he says, the old idea of art as a disinterested activity will again be possible. But for any such thing to come about, what is needed is, paradoxically, a poetics "whose true goal will be to commit suicide, to disappear as such" (curious echo of C. L. R. James at the 1968 Cultural Congress); and to achieve this, the artist must resolutely turn outwards, to the demands of the revolutionary process, the demands of the construction of a new culture. "The Revolution has liberated us as an artistic sector. It is only logical that we contribute to the liberation of the private means of artistic production." To do this, the way García Espinosa means it, is to challenge, of course, precisely those complexes and guilt feelings that constitute the agony of contemporary art, whose effect has been to turn the artist's individual neurosis into the central subject of his or her work; but "the narcissistic posture has nothing to do with those who struggle."

Born of the disquiet that produced *Las aventuras de Juan Quin Quin*, García Espinosa tried to develop some of the ideas of imperfect cinema in practice in a feature-length documentary about Vietnam, *Tercer mundo, tercera guerra mundial* (Third world, third world war). The film was shot during the period following the cease-fire at the end of March 1968. Its purpose is, on the one hand, to analyze the policies and strategies of the United States in the conduct of the war, and, on the other, to demonstrate the essential creativity of the response of North Vietnam. Its manner is both didactic and demonstrative. It employs a range of documentary devices, techniques, and styles to show up Washington's behavior, contrasting the inhumanity of the North American war machine with the very simple but very real humanity of the Vietnamese peasants forced to take up armed struggle in order to survive. Among key scenes are those of a carpenter experimenting with an unexploded antipersonnel bomb to find out how it works; peasants learning to shoot down enemy aircraft with mere rifles; and, above all, an encounter in which the Cuban crew hand their camera over to a young Vietnamese woman of eighteen so she can then direct a short sequence of the film herself; García Espinosa had argued in his essay for a cinema that would, among other things, demystify itself. The rough-edged but hardheaded manner in which this film delivers its analysis ensures that these lyrical moments do not get lost in sentimentalism or romanticism. García Espinosa's thesis is that the third world = third world war = anticolonial war = war against an imperialist enemy that can only be vanquished on condition that the inhuman machinery of its warfare is countered by the simple human resourcefulness and creativity that are all the third world has to fight with.

The theme of internationalism in *Tercer guerra, tercer guerra mundial* is pursued by ICAIC in a long series of major documentaries during the 1970s: in the same year comes Álvarez's *Piedra sobre piedra* (Stone upon stone) about Peru, and in 1972 his film of Fidel's tour of Chile, *De América soy hijo . . . y a ella me debo.* Pastor Vega follows his *Viva la República* of 1972 with a film on Panama, *La quinta frontera* (The fifth frontier) in 1974. Álvarez returns to Vietnam to produce *Abril de Vietnam* (April in Vietnam) in 1975, and in 1976 come two films on Angola, José Massip's *Angola, victoria de la esperanza* (Angola, victory of hope), and *La guerra en Angola* (The war in Angola) by Miguel Fleitas, made in cooperation with the film department of the Cuban Armed Forces.

Piedra sobre piedra, in the country where it was shot, was a controversial film. Some Peruvian critics felt it was awkwardly structured. The first half was too general, and the second half, which reported the devastation of the Peruvian earthquake of May 31, 1970, was too disconnected. According to Isaac León Frias, Álvarez was proposing an equation between the sixty seconds of the earthquake and the earthquake of underdevelopment that lasted 365 days a year, to which Juan M. Bullitta responded that if you were not already familiar with Álvarez's style, or were not familiar with the political concepts he dealt in, then it did not come across very clearly. Behind these doubts was the key question about what stance the film adopted toward the country's new military regime, headed by Juan Velasco Alvarado, which claimed to be revolutionary, held anti-imperialist attitudes, enacted an agrarian reform, reopened diplomatic relations with Cuba, but declared that it was itself neither capitalist nor communist.[4]

Álvarez himself had provoked these doubts by his oddball approach to the subject. Faced with the problem of being an official filmmaker, in other words, the difficulties of what to film and what not to film and of whom, the atheistic Cuban chose to structure the entire documentary, all seventy minutes, around an interview with an army chaplain. In the circumstances, this was an astute thing to do. You are faced with the problem of representing to an audience, most of whom have never been abroad, a picture of a co-lingual country that you yourself have never visited before. Captain García was working-class. "As a boy I worked as an agricultural laborer," he tells the interviewer. He became a priest, he explains, and then joined the army, because he felt too distant from the people he preached to. At the end of the film, when we watch him talking with a crowd of people, trying to win over his listeners, some of whom display a noticeable degree of recalcitrance, to believe in Velasco's goodwill, we see him clearly as one of the radicals of the junior officer ranks in the Peruvian army whose backing Velasco depended on, but who were more radical than the leader, for this Velasco was no Fidel. Nevertheless, the chaplain—who does not actually look like one—sees the army, with its obligatory military service, as a school available to the abandoned classes for their betterment. There was a lot that a Cuban audience could identify with in such a character, for various and even contradictory reasons: the familiarity of his way of speaking, and a certain attitude toward the army as a body that got things done, but also the oddity of seeing this in a priest for the people of a country where religion was weak. This was like a signal to the Cubans to remember that revolutionaries could well be religious. In this respect, it is a film prophetic of the growing militancy of the radical priesthood throughout Latin America since the Cuban Revolution, from the actions of individual priests such as Camilo Torres, through the theology of liberation, to the integral role of popular religion in the revolutionary movements of Central America in the 1980s.

The following year, 1971, Álvarez made the first of three films about Chile: *¿Cómo, por qué y para qué se asesina un general?* (How, why, and wherefore is a general assassinated?). This is an extended newsreel of thirty-six minutes on the assassination of General René Schneider on October 22, 1970, with which the right wing attempted, with CIA backing, to destabilize the Popular Unity Government of Salvador Allende at the very outset, two days before the Chilean parliament was due to ratify his electoral victory. The last of the group is a shorter extended newsreel, fifteen minutes, Álvarez's response to Popular Unity's overthrow three years later, *El tigre saltó y mató, pero morirá... morirá* (The tiger pounced and killed, but he'll die, he'll die). As entirely unorthodox a newsreel as such a title suggests, the film is named after a phrase of Martí's; its sound is that of three Chilean songs sung by Víctor Jara, who died among the numberless victims of the coup who passed through Santiago's football stadium; the tragedy and horror are expressed to this accompaniment in a varied montage of visuals combined in chunks from a number of sources, including evocative animated titles. Very rapidly made, it incorporates sections of material lifted bodily from the second of Álvarez's films on Chile, *De América soy hijo... y a ella me debo,* a title drawn, again, from the writings of Martí.

Subtitled "Film record of a journey that transcends seas and mountains and unites the Sierra Maestra in the Antilles with the Andean Sierra in the South," this is a chronicle, running three and a quarter hours in its full version, of Fidel's visit to Chile at the end of 1971: Álvarez at the height of his powers deliberately laying down a challenge to the habits and theories of commercial cinema—as he himself announced to the Cuban press in an interview for the film's launching.[5]

Álvarez takes his strategy for holding a film of such length together from a unique source: Fidel's speeches. A growing influence on Álvarez's filmmaking, they are paradigmatic in various respects. First, Álvarez derives the paradigmatic structure of the film from the speeches Fidel made during the trip. He uses them to provide entry points to sequences that narrate a key series of moments and aspects of Latin American history, contrasting them with critical features of the experience of the Cuban Revolution. The film alternates between reportage, which is gently paced, full of relaxed observation of Fidel's encounters with the people of Chile as well as picturesque images of the country, even of a meeting between Fidel and a llama, and the interpolated sequences with their maps and engravings and animated textual graphics, which are sometimes even accompanied by a different spoken text. The result of the whole procedure, which is described by Stuart Hood as "deceptively loose-jointed but powerful in its cumulative effect,"[6] is exactly, from the point of view of rhetoric, that of Fidel's style of speaking. To examine the published texts of these speeches shows why: while his form of argument owes everything to his legal training, the listener is also guided by a series of metaphors and images, often aphoristically expressed, which Álvarez translates onto the screen through his instinct for montage.

From an economic point of view, 1970 in Cuba was a year of trial. The attempt during the 1960s to diversify production and reduce the country's dependence on sugar was less than successful. There was a certain distance between hopes and realities. Economically, the Revolution had not yet succeeded in breaking the vicious circle of underdevelopment, despite Che Guevara's energetic optimism. How could industrial development be achieved in a small island under a blockade, cut off from the continent that forms its natural geographical and economic sphere? The emphasis on industrial development left a falling sugar harvest and a reduction in foreign earnings, exacerbated by the fact that most of the sugar produced went to the Soviet Union, which, even though it paid preferential prices, did so mostly in nonconvertible currency and was unable to satisfy the variety of Cuba's developmental needs. The year known as the Year of the Decisive Effort, 1969, was to be devoted to the reinvigoration of agricultural, and especially sugar, production. The aim was a ten-million-ton sugar harvest in 1970. The media in all their forms—newspapers, radio, television, cinema, posters—and the political organizations, the trade unions, the Committees for the Defense of the Revolution (Los CDRs) were all enlisted to mobilize the people for the effort. Resources were diverted, and their diversion caused privations. ICAIC's production program was reduced: in 1970, twenty-four documentaries, only one short fiction film of half an hour, and one animation.

Even fewer documentaries were made in 1971, as the limited resources were diverted to make up for the lack of new fiction. Five new fiction films were produced, one of them a half-hour short, one of them a ballet film; the other three were Massip's *Páginas del diario de José Martí* (Pages from the diary of José Martí), *Los días de agua* (Days of water) of Manuel Octavio Gómez, and Alea's *Una pelea cubana contra los demonios* (A cuban struggle against the demons)—all of them (as we shall see) very considerable achievements that significantly develop the thematics of Cuban cinema.

In the event, the 1970 harvest fell somewhat short of the target at 8.5 million tons, and Fidel made a momentous speech of self-criticism. It was still the largest-ever sugar harvest in Cuba's history and 18 percent higher than the previous largest, but the mood was less than celebratory.[7] Above all, what the episode revealed was Cuba's continuing economic dependence on sugar and tobacco, and the implication that its growing reliance on the Soviet Union was no recipe for lifting itself out of the condition of economic underdevelopment. The mood was not auspicious. The euphoria of the late 1960s evaporated. Then, in 1971, unfortunate events concerning the poet Heberto Padilla created a new crisis in cultural politics, when his arrest and detention for twenty-eight days produced an international protest; signatories who included visitors to the Cultural Congress in 1968 interpreted the incident as a betrayal of the principles Fidel had so clearly enunciated ten years earlier, and a sign that Cuba was falling under Soviet influence culturally as well as economically.

There is no denying that Padilla was a marked man, for he had attacked the respectable revolutionary writer Lisandro Otero and defended a book by Guillermo Cabrera Infante, who had finally parted company with his country with a certain amount of self-publicity in 1965. In 1968, Padilla won the UNEAC international jury prize with a book of poems provocatively entitled *Fuera del juego* (Out of the game). Some of these poems were skeptical about the Soviet Union and others expressed disenchantment with things in Cuba. They had a cynical tone to them, and it is easy to see why they produced offense. They were attacked in the armed forces' journal *Verde Olivo*, and when the book was published it carried an introduction by the artists' and writers' union in the form of a disclaimer. Padilla, however, did not want to leave the country, like the sorry rump of liberals who departed one by one during the late 1960s (including the filmmakers Fausto Canel, Alberto Roldán, Roberto Fandiño, and Fernando Villaverde).

What happened in 1971 has been recorded by the Chilean writer Jorge Edwards, who served in Cuba as chargé d'affaires when diplomatic relations between the two countries were restored under Allende. Edwards, a Chilean liberal intellectual who kept company with Padilla, is not a sympathetic observer of the Cuban process, but he recounts the cause of the poet's arrest as a consequence of his unstable mental condition. Padilla, writes Edwards, began to behave in a somewhat paranoid fashion, carrying the manuscript of a novel around with him wherever he went. He was "over-excited . . . half-crazed," full of "indiscretion and egomania." "The truth is that Padilla was very fond of hinting at the existence of mysterious links between him and some secret powers. He had given me to understand on more than one occasion that he managed to stay successfully afloat thanks to the conflicting currents inside the Government. These hints, which were figments of his passion for inventing myths, would be accompanied by bellows of self satisfied laughter."[8] These are the sad facts. Padilla was detained, and doubtless had to confront an angry Fidel. Then he was released and made a public self-criticism at a meeting at the artists' and writers' union. Not a procedure to appeal to the foreign critics, who had previously looked to Cuba as a bulwark against Stalinism.

The most lamentable aspect of the Padilla affair, according to Ambrosio Fornet, was that it confirmed the positions of extremists on both sides. Each believed they had found an authentic dissident. Abroad, the Cold War Cubanologists and the press declared an end to the mystique of the Cuban Revolution that had attracted so many fellow travelers among the artists and intellectuals of the first world. Inside Cuba, the party dogmatists considered their position vindicated, and the National Council of Culture (Consejo Nacional de la Cultura) responded with a shortsighted policy that twinned its aim of hatching a "new" intelligentsia by promoting the youngest writers and artists with a populist rhetoric about the cultural value of amateurism.[9]

The affair, which did not, says Fornet, involve ICAIC directly, marks the beginning of what he has called the *quinquenio gris,* or "five gray years," when "a vain attempt was made to implement, along with the Soviet economic model, a sort of criollo socialist realism."[10] For two Cuban film critics, Rufo Caballero and Joel del Río, writing in 1995, the country's economic situation and the revival of intolerance produced a conjunctural belief that only monolithic unity of thinking could guarantee the historical continuation of the revolutionary project.[11] The ranks of artists were filled in the 1970s, they say, by apologists adept at schematic and saccharine simplifications. Literary production descended to the lowest levels of stolid conformism, and the plastic arts, despite the renewal that might have emerged from photorealism, neoexpressionism, and the turn to figurative painting, failed to break free of this regression. Only in cinema and music—with the Nueva Trova—did a spirit of renovation survive, and in the case of cinema this was largely due, they believe, to the temporal lag between the conception of a film and the moment it reaches the screen, thanks to which ICAIC was able to influence cultural politics rather than become merely its tool.

This was certainly true of the films released in 1971, although the following year there was a casualty in a highly personal film by Humberto Solás, *Un día de noviembre* (A day in November). This film was certainly an oddity, the contemporary tale of a young Cuban revolutionary who discovers he has a fatal illness and is forced to reassess his life, doing so with such a degree of honesty that in the conformist attitude of the moment, ICAIC decided it was best to delay the film's release. When it was premiered a year and half later, the decision was also ICAIC's. Solás himself, as he told the present writer years later, now felt the film was too weak, and would not have minded if nobody saw it.

The three fiction films released in 1971 all in one way or another develop the principles of "imperfect cinema." Massip's *Páginas del diario de José Martí* uses almost every imaginable resource—fictional, documentary, realist, surrealist, ballet, cantata, theatrical—to create a mobile tapestry that moves impressionistically through the events the diary obliquely narrates. It opens with a spoken delivery of the film credits by a chorus of simultaneous and overlapping voices, which very much sets the tone for the film's idiosyncratic form of narration. Images pass rapidly. An old man carrying a naked baby enters a group of peasants singing unaccompanied in prayer. Ballet dancers mime a fertility rite. Period engravings of scenes from the late nineteenth century appear. The voices evoke a time "a hundred years ago [when] the nation was born in war." Color is used expressionistically, with filtered reds and greens, as the voice of an old man remembers Martí stopping at his house just after his clandestine return to Cuba's shores. The film proceeds in episodic fashion, through scenes of peasants at work, and of Martí and Máximo Gómez preparing their campaign, and the violence and brutality of raids by Spanish soldiers in the countryside, always interspersed with the voice of the diary, until we come to the day of battle and the death of the Apostle from a stray bullet, shown in mute sepia accompanied by an avant-garde orchestral score by the composer Roberto Valera. A reflective epilogue concludes the film with images of Martí in a mural in an artist's studio. A truly hallucinatory film.

Alea's *Una pelea cubana contra los demonios* is the farthest back Cuban cinema has gone in historical reconstruction, a film about priests and pirates and demons at the time of the Spanish Inquisition, based on a work of the same name by the cultural anthropologist Fernando Ortiz, a leading figure of the rebellious intellectual generation of the 1920s. It enacts a documented story of the year 1672 (given as 1659 in the film) in which the priest of a coastal township, fueled by religious fanaticism, attempts to remove the entire community to an interior site, out of reach of pirates and heretics—the latter a euphemism for Protestant privateers trading illegally along the coast. He has to contend, not surprisingly, with the opposition of practically all of the landowners he is seeking to prevail over, among them the distinctive figure of Juan Contreras, hedonist, skeptic, and a bitter ideological enemy of the church. Against Contreras and his ilk, Padre Manuel (marvelously acted by José Rodríguez) calls upon the same methods that the Inquisition uses against the fearful forces of witchcraft and black magic, superstition and demons, which it everywhere sees, of course, in the pagan religion of the illiterate. In order to enlist the support of the authorities from Havana, he concocts a testimony about calamities that have overtaken the community, in which he claims to have exorcised hundreds of evil spirits. The authorities order the community to remove itself to another site, though some of the townspeople refuse to leave.

This is a film that in its narrative style rejects all conventions of genre, and again, as in *Memorias*, Alea refuses us the chance to identify in the familiar way with a positive hero. The first of Alea's films to be photographed by Mario García Joya, who collaborated on all his subsequent films except the last, the fluid camera style involves long takes with an almost constantly moving handheld camera, which allows few of the syntactical devices of genre film language—point-of-view shots, reaction shots, strategic close-ups—by which such identification is normally established. (In general, of course, it is not a question of these devices being totally eliminated, but of their not being used in the form of the articulated system of orthodox narrative découpage.) Instead, Alea creates the loaded atmosphere of a world half real and half mythical, of brazen individuals and collective hysteria. The film's extraordinary visual fluidity, together with its striking black-and-white photography, leads it to depart from the straightforward narration of historical facts, but it also turns the film into a corrective interpretation of history, a study of the social and economic forces of seventeenth-century Cuba, with their demons both spiritual and physical: the theology of the Inquisition, and the smugglers and pirates who came in the wake of the Spanish colonists.

The film is rich in the parallels and oppositions contained in its metaphors and symbols, especially those built around the similarities and contrasts, visual and symbolic, between the rituals and ceremonies of the church and the shamanism of the slaves. This is a tendency toward the structural organization of symbolic language to be found in several Cuban films, like *Lucía* by Humberto Solás and *De cierta manera* of Sara Gómez. A raid by pirates, who pillage and rape, is followed with an attack by invisible predators: during a hellfire sermon, a woman is seized with convulsions—her body twisting as if once again struggling against the rapist's attack. The preaching priest himself seems to be possessed, the camera moving in on him in close-up, as he cries out that the devil is always among them, chaos rules over them. It is the island's economic and political structure that is in chaos. Sugar exports are threatened by smugglers who prey on shipping and then undercut the market price, while desperate slaves commit suicide to escape their misery, in the hope that their bodies will return with their souls to Africa.

The film serves as an oblique allegory on the situation of contemporary Cuba, centered on the contradiction personified in the contrast between the skepticism of Contreras, the populism of Padre Manuel, and the opportunism of Evaristo. To try to dissuade their workforce from abandoning them, Contreras warns the people of the town against Padre Manuel's promise to lead his followers to a land free of demons, while Evaristo advises the authorities from Havana of the impending arrival of a smugglers' ship, with which Contreras is involved in doing business. But if we see in the figure of Contreras elements of a critique of the church, he is also refracted by his position outside not one, but two religious systems. The other, which he is voyeuristically drawn to, leads him to visit a shaman woman who lives in a cave and goes into a trance in which she speaks of the river of native blood to come. Her voice is heard over a blank screen while tachistoscopic images flit by, a frame or two at a time—the faces of Martí, Fidel, el Che. He understands from her vision that the rebellion of the people is inevitable.

Los días de agua, scripted by Manual Octavio Gómez with Bernabé Hernández and Julio García Espinosa, is about the same themes in more recent times, a story of the political manipulation of religious hysteria in the 1930s, based on real events in the province of Piñar del Río in 1936. A local woman, Antoñica Izquierdo, has become known as a saintly healer. Long processions of the sick come to her house to receive the healing she administers with holy waters. With them comes a journalist after a story, and an opportunist businessman who sets up food stalls. The place becomes both a sanctuary and a fair. The local doctors, drugstores, and priests, seeing their interests threatened, conspire to get rid of the healer and her followers. There is a death among the sick, and Antoñica is accused of murder. A lawyer seeking the governorship of the province comes to her defense and wins her freedom, his consequent popularity winning him election. Once in power, he decides that her activities now hurt his interests. The army mounts an attack, Antoñica tries to defend herself with holy water, while among her followers, violence provokes them to respond with violence. But this open act of rebellion is doomed before it begins, for the journalist has been right about one thing: "What a waste of power! What a stupid woman! People believe in her and she doesn't know how to lead them!"

On one level, the film is about who pays the costs of sickness in a sick society. Antoñica declares her powers a free gift, an act of social rebellion against the cartel of the priests and medics. But she also declares that there are diseases that cannot be seen. Like *Una pelea cubana...,* this narrative is offered not in the form of a cold and considered historical reconstruction, but in the shape of a hallucinatory allegory. The story is told inside out, as it were, and from a series of different angles, like a written narrative that shifts the point of view of the narration between the different characters: Antoñica herself, the journalist, the opportunist, the fanatic, the politician Navarro, the priest, the municipal sanitation officer, the chief of the rural guard. The film is particularly memorable for the manner in which the various episodes are plastically

expressed in the treatment of color, from the early sequence which narrates the origins of Antoñica's powers—a vision in which the Virgin saves
her child—where color is rendered dreamlike through underexposure,
to the wild activity of the scene of the rebellion, which the handheld
camera pictures from within as a participant, with the result that the surface smoothness of orthodox color photography is broken up, not unlike
the rupture of the image in the battle scene of *La primera carga*. . . .

These two films about religious and magical beliefs, and the hierarchy of repression that is built upon them, share important features with
a number of the most distinctive Brazilian films of the previous decade,
belonging not to the neorealist tendency pioneered by Nelson Pereira
dos Santos, but to the very different stylistic impulses, much more baroque and emotional, identified with Glauber Rocha and dubbed "tropicalism." Thematically, these films include *Ganga Zumba* of 1963 by
Carlos Diegues, about the search of escaping slaves for the mythical
black kingdom of their kind; but the main paradigms are two films by
Rocha, *Deus e o Diablo na terra del sol* (Black god, white devil—literally
"God and the devil in the land of the sun," 1963) and *Antonio das Mortes*
(1968). Here is a world in which emblematic characters perform stylized
actions in a dreamlike amalgamation of history and legend, epic and
lyric. For Rocha, the mysticism of popular religion in the Brazilian
northeast is a fusion of Catholicism and the motifs of African religion
transplanted with the slave trade, which produces the authentic voice of
the people of these lands, the expression of a permanent spirit of rebellion against constant oppression, a rejection and refusal of the condition in which they had been condemned to live for centuries. The
Cuban films are less schematic, less formalist, but the style is in many
respects, visually and in other ways, closely similar. Fundamentally, they
have the same feel for that process, known as syncretism, by which the
symbolic systems of different religions are conjoined by a kind of osmo-
sis. In a key scene in *Los días de agua*, two religious processions, one
Christian, the other Yoruba, meet and fuse: a paradigmatic rendering of
the simultaneous presence in the syncretistic culture, in its practices and
its products, of symbolic elements from historically separate origins,
which have been brought into confrontation and have interpenetrated.

Several documentaries on themes of religion and syncretism were
made during the 1960s, including two films by Bernabé Hernández on
the Abakuá religious society and aboriginal culture in 1963 (*Abakuá* and

Cultura aborigen). Octavio Cortázar, after making *Por primera vez,* investigated the question of syncretism in a twenty-minute documentary from 1968 with the intriguing title *Acerca de un personaje que unos llaman San Lázaro y otros llaman Babalú* (About a character some people call Saint Lazarus and others call Babalú). The object of investigation is an annual religious saint's-day celebration in which the worshipers approach the shrine crawling on their knees to give thanks or to pray for recuperation from illness. Interspersed with the scenes of the pilgrimage and festivities are a series of interviews with both participants and commentators, either specialists or just people in the streets. It emerges that there is considerable confusion about who this Lazarus is. A Catholic priest maintains that he is a separate person from the Lazarus raised from the dead, a lay leader of the procession holds the opposite. (Cortázar playfully intercuts an old film clip of the raising of Lazarus.) The provenance of the icons of Lazarus to be found in Cuban churches is traced— three of these images come from different parts of the Christian world and suggest different associations. But whichever, Lazarus has an alter ego in Babalú, the African god with whom he shares a number of characteristics, most importantly his healing powers. There is some disagreement, too, between people who hold these beliefs to be incompatible with the Revolution, and others who consider them harmless enough. And there is also the analysis of the cultural historian who sees the phenomenon as a paradigm of syncretism, for Lazarus and Babalú are not separate, the one identified with the other merely for convenience, they are one and the same, Christian and African at the same time—or in short, Afro-Cuban.

Another area where Cuban filmmakers have drawn attention to a closely similar phenomenon is music. A number of documentaries from the late 1960s on, dealing with different aspects of Cuban popular music, have celebrated its diversity and riches, showing that much of it is a result of syncretistic processes. *Y... tenemos sabor* (And... we've got taste, 1968) by Sara Gómez, who was a trained musician, is a guide to its exotic range of percussion instruments—claves, spoons, maracas, bongos, the güiro (made from gourds), cowbells, horse's jawbone, and so on—and their origins, some primitive, some mixed (mulatto).

Musicologists have shown that the evolution of musical forms is also a long and complicated affair. The *habañera,* for example—like the one

Bizet included in *Carmen*—can be traced back to the early English country dance and the French *contredanse,* transmitted largely through the Spanish *contradanza*. However, while Cuba was a Spanish colony, it also received French musical influences more directly, as a neighbor of Saint-Domingue (Haiti) and French Louisiana. Havana itself was a point at which many cultural influences coalesced, carried by sailors and their passengers across the seas. It was a city of sojourn for long-distance travelers, like the emigrants to Veracruz in Mexico who left a dance on their way through known in Havana as the *chuchumbá,* which was banned by the Tribunal of the Sacred Inquisition for the indecency of its forms and rhythms. This is a constant theme, and all sorts of excuses will do. In 1809, the journal *Aviso de la Habana* condemned the French *contredanse* simply on the grounds of its national origins: "Why have we not disposed of the waltz and the contradanza, those always indecent fabrications introduced to us by the diabolical French? They are diametrically opposed in their essence to Christianity. Lascivious gestures and an impudent vulgarity are their constituents, which, from the fatigue and the heat with which the body suffers, provoke concupiscence."[12] But music defies edict, and the dance continued to evolve, crossing backwards and forwards from Cuba to Spain and back to Latin America, to produce the inimitable lilt of the *habanera,* which got its name in Spain, and the *danzón,* as the Cubans called their own version, and, in Buenos Aires, the tango (which, when it took New York by storm in the 1920s, was again subjected to pious protests).

As with instruments and dances, so with song forms, which are often particularly responsive to social and political currents. *¿De dónde son los cantantes...?* (Where do the singers come from?, dir. Luis Felipe Bernaza, 1976) recalls the career of the Trio Matamoros, three brothers from Oriente who started playing together in 1925, singing serenades under balconies at night. They based their music on a version of a traditional song form called the *son* (as in García Espinosa's *Son o no son*), which took shape, the commentary tells us, in the Sierra Maestra in the last years of the nineteenth century, among singers who were engaged in the independence struggles and composed satirical verses against the Spanish and North Americans alike. The style took a couple of decades to reach Havana, where, like the equally satirical *decimas,* it enjoyed great popularity during the so-called golden period of Cuban music in the

1930s—the decade following the arrival of RCA Victor and Columbia and the stimulus they gave to commercial music production in Cuba.

The film celebrates the survival in this music of certain authentic popular values—those that E. P. Thompson describes as the Brechtian values of irony in the face of moralism and the tenacity of self-preservation—in the midst of all the commercialism, when singers were promoted under such tags as "el tenor de la voz de seda" (the tenor with the voice of silk) and "la estrella de la canción" (the star [female] of the song). Cinema itself, of course, with the coming of sound, contributed to the process, a succession of films from different countries helping to create fashions and crazes—tap dancing after *Piccolino,* tangos with *Boliche,* both in 1935; Spanish music with *Nobleza baturra* and *Morena clara* in 1936 and 1937; Mexican music with *Allá en el Rancho Grande* and *Jalisco nunca pierde* in 1937. But not all the music documentaries of the 1970s are equally successful in dealing with the problems of this history. *Qué buena canta Ud.* (How well you sing, dir. Sergio Giral, 1973) is a homage to the singer Beny Moré, which interweaves memorabilia and interviews with his family and colleagues, but says very little about the manner of his commercial promotion—he was one of the biggest of Cuban musical stars, whose records captured markets throughout Central America and the northern shores of South America, the hinterland of the Cuban commercial music business. "Vox pop" interviews, which generally follow the line "Beny is dead but he lives; his music is neither old nor modern," testify to his genuine popularity, but their effect, when the film is viewed outside its original context as obituary, is to leave an otherwise highly delightful film with an excessively populist evaluation of the music. Yes, his music is very vibrant, but all those prerevolutionary film clips of him, where do *they* come from? There is rather little in this film of the approach of imperfect cinema, no questioning of the construction of the imagery, or of the ideological uses of its musical clothing, no interrogation of the mythology of "popular" music (of which Colina and Díaz Torres wrote, speaking of the use of music in the melodrama and the musical comedy of the time: "the melodic motifs of tangos, rancheros and boleros fulfil a double function: they enhance the spectacle, channelling it towards the popular classes, and they serve, in their own right, to reduce the essential content of the film to that of contagious tunes").[13]

One of these films, however, from the late 1970s, *La rumba,* directed by Óscar Valdés with a script by Julio García Espinosa, confronts the question head-on. The opening images are of two contrasting snatches of dance. "For the people of Cuba," says a narrator over the first, "this is a commercial manifestation of the rumba, a commodity, and false." "This," continues the voice over the second, "is an authentic rumba. But there are still lots of Cubans who don't feel it belongs to them. The rumba is one of this people's most legitimate artistic creations. What is the prejudice they hold against it?" In the course of forty-five minutes, the film proceeds to trace its historical origins. The word itself comes from Spain, where it was not originally the name of a dance, but described a certain kind of woman, who lives what is called a "happy life," a certain kind of frivolity; in other words, the very name of the dance involves a prejudice. This is amplified later in the film: such a prejudice is typically *machista,* and the rumba has developed an erotic narrative version, danced by a couple, which evolved from African fertility ritual and enacts the possession of the woman by the man. What happened was that a Spanish word gave a name and an identity to a dance and a rhythm whose origins were completely African (and in which the eroticism doubtless had different cultural meanings). To confirm this thesis, we learn that there were musical clubs in Cuba, particularly among the petite bourgeoisie, which, for respectability's sake, never danced the rumba, but took to the *danzón* instead.

Another film that deals directly with the African roots of a large part of Cuba's musical heritage is *Miriam Makeba,* a portrait of the African singer by Juan Carlos Tabío, made during her tour of Cuba in 1973. There is a sequence in which she and her band meet with a group of Cuban musicians and compare notes. Makeba's is by no means the purest of African song; she has adopted harmonies and other elements that are of modern Western origin and originally alien to the African idiom. Nor, as she tells her hosts, is she a "learned musician." But listening and watching attentively with growing delight to black Cuban drummers, she declares that "If Cuban drummers play, unless they start singing in Spanish, I can't tell whether they're Cuban or African!"

Of these films, only the one by Sara Gómez is filmically remarkable in any special way. The others are all more or less conventional in their various uses of commentary, interviews, historical footage, and the filming of historical relics. The first impression that *Y... tenemos sabor* makes on the viewer is the way its jagged and syncopated cutting captures and expresses the rhythms of the music it is describing. It is also an excellent example of imperfect cinema. Toward the end of the film, the musician showing us the instruments remarks, "But we don't *need* all these instruments, we can just as well make music with bits of iron and sticks." "This," Tomás Gutiérrez Alea remarks, "was Sarita's attitude to making films."[14]

There is another musical documentary, however, *Hablando del punto cubano* (Speaking of typical Cuban music, dir. Octavio Cortázar, 1972), which is an altogether exceptional film, the effect of a truly delightful paradox built into its commentary, which is sung instead of spoken. The word *punto* in the title cannot really be rendered into English; it refers to the art of the verbal improvisation in song form, either by an individual singer or by a pair of singers engaged in what is called a *controversia,* or controversy. Again we are given historical information: the *punto* has a Spanish heritage. It became an art of itinerant campesino singers, who in this way carried news and comment around the countryside. But instead of dying out, a new generation of professional campesino musicians grew up in the 1930s with the opportunities provided by the radio. Later, many of these artistes suffered eclipse, but one of them is featured through the length of the film, the incomparable Joseito Fernández. His is a name inseparable in Cuba from one of the Cuban songs best known internationally, "Guantanamera." The form in which it is known abroad, appropriately enough set to verses by José Martí, is a recent adaptation, popularized in the early 1960s in solidarity with the Cuban Revolution by the North American folk protest singer Pete Seeger, who learned it from a student. According to Alejo Carpentier, the tune of the song's opening phrases is none other than the old Spanish romance "Gerineldo," preserved through the centuries by the most authentic peasant singers.[15] In the 1930s, it became Joseito Fernández's theme tune, when he had a weekly radio program and used it to improvise a popular commentary on politics and current events. Here in this film it turns up in a new guise: this is its commentary.

The whole film plays on the paradox of using film, whose personae are not physically present to the audience but only projected, and can therefore have been manipulated this way and that, to portray an improvised art form. In fact, it takes the bull by the horns. "Lots of people," sings Joseito, "would like to know if this stuff's improvised or not"; and

Hablando del punto cubano (Octavio Cortázar, 1972)

there is a spontaneous discussion—one of those discussions that is provoked by bringing a group of people round a camera and asking them
certain questions—among a group of workers outside a bus factory,
arguing about the kind of artistry involved in the practice of the *punto*.
One speaker accuses another of credulity at the idea that a *controversia*
is really improvised. The singers, he says, have so much practice and
preparation that it isn't really improvisation, it is virtually prepared, they
don't really have to improvise because they've got it all stored up in
their heads. It clearly, however, looks very different from that in the example of a *controversia* we see on camera.

Cleverly, the camera operator has kept the camera trained part of the
time on the singer in the pair who is not at that moment singing, and
the editor has left the shot to pan backwards and forwards without
cutting so we know they have not cheated: the look of concentration
on the silent singer's listening face reveals all: the moment, listening
to his rival, when he slowly tilts his head and breaks into a broad and
very special smile of anticipation, as he discovers how to couch his
reply. Other singers show similar evidence—it is impossible not to recall the passage of Walter Benjamin's in which he talks about the way film
makes it possible to analyze minutiae of behavior that were previously

too fleeting sometimes even to be noticed. And carrying it all along, is the masterly Joseito himself, a graceful, thin, tall mustachioed figure, who wanders through gates, gardens, and down streets, a floating presence, teasing us with his improvised singing commentary, challenging us, it seems, to challenge him over it, knowing, of course, we cannot, and even if we could, it would have to be on his terms, and he would win.

In 1971, Roberto Fernández Retamar published another key essay of Cuban revolutionary aesthetics, called "Caliban." The old Caliban, he said, the base, deformed half-man half-fish of Shakespeare's last play, was dead; a new one was being born. He is not the only Caribbean intellectual to see Caliban this way. He refers himself in his essay to a number of others, including George Lamming, Edward Braithwaite, and Aimé Césaire.

Why Caliban? Who is he? His name, as numerous scholars tell, is an anagram of "canibal," which derives from *caríbal*, carib, Caribbean. All sorts of historical evidence reveals that *The Tempest* alludes to the "discovery" of the Americas: Shakespeare's island is the poetic symbol of the islands where Columbus first landed and where an English ship was wrecked in 1609, providing the Elizabethan playwright with a firsthand

Joseito Fernández in *Hablando del punto cubano*

account upon which to draw. It was, moreover, a topical play, for the conquest of the New World, and in England especially the renewed project for the colonization of Virginia, was a burning question of the day.

The central theme of the play, to modern Caribbean eyes, is the utter opposition between master and slave, colonizer and colonized. Implacable realist that he was, says Fernández Retamar, Shakespeare created in the figure of Caliban the other face of the nascent bourgeois world. He takes the noble savage from his contemporary Montaigne and turns him into the pathetic figure that the European colonizers produced in those they conquered and brutally exploited. The attitude of the colonizer is roundly represented in Prospero:

> I pitied thee,
> Took pains to make thee speak, taught thee each hour
> One thing or other: when thou didst not, savage,
> Know thine own meaning, but wouldst gabble like
> A thing most brutish, I endow'd thy purposes
> With words that made them known.

And the attitude of the rebellious slave in Caliban's reply:

> You taught me language; and my profit on't
> Is, I know how to curse. The red plague rid you
> For learning me your language! (Act 1, scene 2)

The Tempest has exerted particular fascination in Latin America ever since the Argentinian Juan Rodó wrote an essay at the turn of the nineteenth century on the nature of Latin American culture, called "Ariel." His interpretation of the play followed traditional lines: Caliban was base, Ariel was the imprisoned spirit of creativity. The twist in the tale was that Rodó identified Caliban with the United States of America, the imperialist power in the north that, as his contemporary Martí explained, had come to represent the major threat to the integrity of Latin America. In the second half of the century, Rodó's version was overturned. The imperialists became Prospero, the tyrannical and sadistic foreign duke who exercises power through magic. Caliban was his militant anticolonialist opponent.

Ariel also changes—Prospero's other slave, his houseboy, who, just as Caliban performs Prospero's physical labor, carries out his spiritual desires. Previously, Ariel, who openly demands his liberty from Prospero, was seen as the symbol of the enslaved creative spirit, the symbol of everything aspiring, in contrast to Caliban's baseness. But now the Caribbean novelist George Lamming calls him Prospero's intelligence agent: "the archetypal spy, the embodiment—when and if made flesh—of the perfect and unspeakable secret police."[16] In the version of the play that the Martinique poet Aimé Césaire wrote for a black theater company in 1969, Ariel becomes a mulatto; and having carried out Prospero's wishes against his own better judgment and defiantly made his scruples known, Prospero replies, "Here we go! Your crisis! It's always the same with you intellectuals!" But at least Ariel now has a choice: either to continue serving Prospero, or to turn his back on him and join with Caliban in the real liberation struggle.

Aspects of the Caliban theme found expression in Cuban cinema during the 1970s in a series of films about slavery in which the image of the slave is powerfully deconstructed: Sergio Giral's trilogy, *El otro Francisco, Rancheador,* and *Maluala,* Alea's *La última cena,* plus an assortment of documentaries. They are films in which the figure and historical personage of the slave is seen in an entirely new light.

El otro Francisco, on which Alea and García Espinosa collaborated with the director and Héctor Veitía in writing the script, is (as we saw earlier) a piece of deconstruction that has been worked upon its source, a romantic abolitionist novel of 1839, not a free adaptation but the product of a careful critical operation. The North American film theorist

Julianne Burton puts this film forward, along with *Girón* and *De cierta manera,* as a paradigm of the subversion of the dominant phenomenon of cinema as spectacle. *Girón* "simultaneously imitates and subverts the blood-and-guts war movie"; *De cierta manera* "subverts the Hollywood romance"; and *El otro Francisco* "critiques the historical melodrama."[17] *Rancheador* is similarly based on a literary source, *Diario de un rancheador* (Diary of a rancher) by Cirilo Villaverde (who also wrote the much better known *Cecilia Valdés* on which Humberto Solás based his epic, but less than successful, *Cecilia* of 1983). Villaverde, in turn, based his novel on the diary of a certain Francisco Estévez, a hunter of runaway slaves in the pay of the landowners. The film adopts a different aesthetic strategy. Cast in the form of an orthodox but ingeniously crafted narrative, *Rancheador* pictures Estévez as one of the bloodiest and most ambitious of mercenaries. He not only hunts down slaves in their *palenques,* hidden communities in the hills, but he employs his henchmen in repressing outbursts of rebellion, black or white, slave or free. His behavior threatens to expose the maneuvers of the sugar landowners who employ him, in their factional conflicts with the smallholding coffee growers. He tries to vindicate himself by setting out to hunt for the legendary woman leader of the runaway slaves, Melchora. But Melchora is a mythological personage, a symbol to the slaves of their freedom, a psychological weapon of combat. In his blind and obsessional fury, Estévez commits a series of crimes that begin to contradict the class interests he serves, and his employers, ever ready to sacrifice their bloodiest servants when necessary, abandon him to his destruction. Although it undoubtedly has elements in it of an epic western, this is actually much less of a genre movie than this description makes it sound, first because of the dialectical analysis of the historical forces involved, and second because of the potent Afro-Cuban symbolism of the myth of Melchora and its effect, among other things, in dissolving the individualism of the story's heroes into the collective.

This is also a strategy adopted in *Maluala,* which deals with the least documented area of the history of slavery. The film's title is the name of a *palenque,* or settlement of escaped slaves, one of a group of such settlements somewhere in the eastern, mountainous part of the island, though exact time and place remain unspecified. The story describes how the Spanish set out to divide the leaders of the *palenques* against each other, with considerable but not total success. The three films of the trilogy taken together show a development of consciousness from singular to collective, from individual resistance to collective struggle, from suicide to battle. Combining professional and nonprofessional actors, and with music by Sergio Vitier, *Maluala* shared the top prize for fiction at the first Havana international film festival in 1979 with the Brazilian Geraldo Sarno's *Coronel Delmiro Gouveia.*

Alea's film *La última cena (The Last Supper)* is a subtle, ironic fable, an allegory of the religious hypocrisy of a plantation owner toward his slaves, set in a time just after the Haitian Revolution of 1795. The Cuban landowners are suddenly instilled with the fear of slave rebellion at the same time that the disruption of agriculture in Haiti offers them the chance to improve their position in the international market, but only on condition that they buy more slaves and intensify their exploitation, which only increases, of course, the dangers of rebellion. The Count of Casa Bayona, brilliantly played by Nelson Villagra, is a sensitive man, whose stomach turns at the sight of the treatment his overseer metes out to a runaway slave, Sebastián, when he is punished by having his ear cut off. The count, who sees himself as a source of protective Christian love toward his slaves, would rather they accepted their lot with humility. Accordingly, he selects twelve of them, including the runaway, for an Easter ritual: first he symbolically washes their feet—very symbolically, for touching the black men's feet offends his delicate constitution—and then he wines and dines them the evening before Good Friday.

What follows is a tour de force of black comedy. As Philip French reports, "At the centre of the movie is a modern re-creation of the Last Supper that inevitably brings to mind the beggars' blasphemous celebration of the Eucharist in *Viridiana.* But Alea's mentor, Buñuel, contrived that scene to produce a brief shocking frisson. Here it is the occasion for an extended, sinuous debate on the human condition in which the pious Christian, not his insulted and injured guests, brings the precepts of his religion into question. . . . He has a little trouble in explaining to some of his guests the difference between transubstantiation and cannibalism, and not all of his temporary disciples understand his Franciscan sermon about the need to embrace their misery joyfully. But they think he's a grand, generous fellow, and when he frees an aged bondslave (who immediately asks if he can stay on anyway), they're convinced of his good faith. However, after the Count slumps on the table asleep, the supper's Judas-figure comes into his own. He is, of course, the slave

Sebastian who regales the company with a forceful parable of his own about Truth and Dishonesty, and how decapitated Truth put on the head of Lies and went around the world deceiving people."[18]

This parable of Sebastián's is his African reply to the Christian myth of Genesis and the Fall. "When Olofi made the world he made it complete with day and night, good and bad, Truth and Lie. Olofi was sorry for Lie, who was ugly, and gave him a machete to defend himself. One day Truth and Lie met and had a fight. Lie cut off Truth's head. Headless, Truth took Lie's head. Now Truth goes around with the body of Truth and the head of Lie." The count's explanation of transubstantiation is similarly translated by his listeners, one of whom acts out the tale of an African family fallen on bad times. In order to get money to buy food, a father sets out to sell his son into slavery, but his son turns on him and sells him in place of himself. Whereupon the family turns on the son and delivers him up to the authorities, who sell him in turn into slavery, and they end up that way eating twice as much. What we get in this long scene is a dialogue between master and slave—an extraordinary achievement by the scriptwriters, Tomás González and María Eugenia Haya, as well as Alea himself—a metadialogue of symbolic meanings, which, the North American critic Dennis West observes, enacts "the profound and intricate Hegelian dialectic of lordship and servitude traced in *The Phenomenology of Mind*."[19]

This dialogue is prepared by the early scenes of the film, and especially the relationships between the three men who administer the count's estate: the overseer, the priest, and the sugarmaster. The clergyman preaches moral platitudes to the slaves while grumbling about the godlessness of the overseer. The overseer, however, is much more the count's alter ego, which some of the slaves realize perfectly well. (The ones who don't are those who, around his table, continue to believe in the count's good faith.) The most equivocal of the three is the sugarmaster, an educated Frenchman with a scientific mind, analyzing and improving the methods of refining sugar. He develops a system of burning cane waste for fuel to replace the depleted forests. He explains to the count that a nice new piece of English machinery would only be worth purchasing if he also got more slaves to increase production. Sympathetic to the suffering of the slaves—he later conceals the fugitive Sebastián from the slave hunter—the sugarmaster teases the priest about the secrets of his art, which, he says, come from the mysteries of nature herself. To the priest's cautious inquiry if such beliefs are not a little like witchcraft, he responds with the question whether the church is not also witchcraft, and dangles a little bag containing the substances needed for the transmutation of raw cane juice into refined sugar, taunting him with its mystery: "It seems that what is to become white must first be black." But there is no magic in the substance: it's *caca de poule,* chicken shit. It's all up here, he says, tapping his head. He shows off the products: decreasing shades of brown and finally pristine white. But not all of it, he says, is capable of being purified, just like souls in purgatory.

And then it is that we come to the grotesque comedy of the supper, and at its center, a key symbolic gesture: "Hegel's notion of recognition," writes West, "means that the master depends on his bondsman for acknowledgement of his power, indeed for assurance of his very selfhood. As the count reiterates his order that Sebastian recognize him [the Judas parallel] the camera emphatically dollies in on their juxtaposed faces, and a tense silence reigns. The slave's eventual answer is to spit in the master's face—a brutal refusal to recognize the other's lordship and the graphic expression of the bondsman's true self-consciousness: in spite of his actual bondage, the slave's mind is his own."

CHAPTER FOURTEEN

One Way or Another

In 1974, Julio García Espinosa got involved with the Italian film critic Guido Aristarco in an altercation about what was going on in Cuban cinema. The occasion was the Rencontres Internationales pour un Nouveau Cinéma in Montreal, a gathering of some seventy-five radical filmmakers from all over the world, together with critics, distributors, and political activists given to using film. There were, reported John Hess in the North American film journal *Jump Cut*, several areas of awkward political disagreement that came to light during the course of the event, especially a series of misunderstandings between European and Latin American participants that reflected, he said, their very different relationships to the institutional structures of both film industry and state in the two continents. It was clearly a variation on this theme when the Italian criticized Cuban cinema for the peril of allowing the portrayal of triumphalist heroes rather too much like those of socialist realism. It is not to deny that the nature of the heroic icon may well be a barometer of certain critical aspects of a society to say that Aristarco's criticism seemed not only to the Cubans but to other Latin Americans present to be schematic and unjust. To be sure, it was true of some of the early Cuban films like *El joven rebelde,* but it could hardly be said to apply to the astonishing output of the late 1960s—*Memorias del subdesarrollo, Lucía,* and others, though it is also the case that in one or two of the very latest films at the time, like *El hombre de Maisinicú* (*The Man from Maisinicú,* dir. Manuel Pérez, 1973), the problem was beginning to crop up again. There was some general discussion about the question, but

García Espinosa provided a more considered reply in his own paper to the meeting, where he stepped back to look at the whole problem of militant cinema in the particular situation of a third-world revolution in power.

"We controlled the means of production and the cinemas," he began, "but after ten years we had to recognize that we weren't yet the masters of these cinemas because, quite simply, one cannot show only revolutionary films in them."[1] It was necessary, he explained, to undertake first a preliminary stage in the decolonization of the screens in terms of the concrete choice of films available on the international market, and the first step was that Cuban audiences were able to see films from everywhere, not just North American films as before the Revolution. But there was a problem: the majority of films they found themselves showing left a great deal to be desired ideologically speaking. The situation, he admitted, led to absurdities, such as showing Japanese films just because the faces of the heroes weren't white. He was saying implicitly that whatever it was in Cuban cinema Aristarco found to be suspicious, it didn't come, as the Italian was arguing, from some kind of mythical leftist aesthetic orthodoxy, it was a material consequence of the colonization of the screens by the capitalist metropolis. Jorge Fraga thought the problem was getting worse: there were many films in the 1960s that were ideologically acceptable. In the 1980s, mainstream cinema came to be more and more dominated by violence and pornography.[2]

The Cubans had been able, said García Espinosa, to resolve the problem of informing people more adequately about the society they lived in. But a cinema, he suggested, that provides its audience with more authentic and relevant information is relatively easy to accomplish. What remains the greater challenge is entertainment. The explosion of the technologies of mass communications in the 1960s, he said, had produced a highly paradoxical situation in Cuba. All over the world, people were seeing—mostly on the small screen—a growing range of highly informative documentary images. Although there was much in their form of presentation and contextualization that needed to be questioned, the problem in Cuba, because of the isolation forced upon it, was that the images that reached them from abroad were virtually all fictional. Cuban filmmakers were consequently confronted with a battle between two kinds of image, two types of cinema, documentary and fiction, which appeared fundamentally like a struggle between authenticity and falsehood. The audience continued, however—and why not?—to reach for the fictional image, to satisfy what are, after all, perfectly real needs for the dramatization of experience, which there have always been aesthetic forms to satisfy. This, said García Espinosa, was a most difficult and delicate problem for them.

The truth is that a number of Cuban features during the 1970s could be said to have succumbed before this problem by adopting the weak solution. In a way, this is because the very thing García Espinosa had warned about in introducing the idea of *cine imperfecto* had come to pass. Cuban filmmakers had grown so much more confident in their control over the medium that they now took the very codes of Hollywood narrative and started playing around with them. The result was a series of films that included, in 1973, *El extraño caso de Rachel K.* (The strange case of Rachel K., dir. Óscar Valdés) and *El hombre de Maisinicú* and *Patty-Candela* (dir. Rogelio París) in 1976; and a year later, Cortázar's *El brigadista* and another film by Manuel Pérez, *Río Negro*. To put it crudely, these are all films that swap around the baddies and the goodies and play a few narrative tricks, and end up as Cuban versions of genre movies. Because—except for *Río Negro*—they are all based on real people and events, this has an effect of mythologizing recent Cuban history.

El extraño caso de Rachel K. is a film noir, following the lines of a newspaper investigation, which tries rather too self-consciously to use the iconography of the genre as a kind of pathetic fallacy for the doom-laden mood of the time. It is set in 1931, a year before the fall of the dictator Machado. Ignoring a police raid on a meeting of tobacco workers, the press becomes obsessed with the sordid murder of a French nightclub dancer. While the workers' leader is assassinated in prison, the murder investigation threatens to reveal corruption in high places, and Machado is forced to silence the newspapers. *El hombre de Maisinicú* is also based on real events, concerning an undercover agent, played by Sergio Corrieri, in the Escambray mountains in the early 1960s who infiltrates and destroys a band of counterrevolutionaries supported by the CIA. A homage to the secret hero of the Revolution, here the genre is a mélange of western and thriller, transposed to a Cuban rural setting that gives the film the frisson of using the mythology of the western to implicitly critique the ideology of the western. According to Fornet, it was entirely expectable that a movie like this, with all the right elements—a popular

subject, full of action and violence, a hero played by a charismatic actor—would find a large audience, but no one, he says, could have pre-
dicted the overnight success it became at the box office, which turned it
into a model much imitated both in subsequent films and in serialized
form on Cuban television. If foreign critics expressed alarm at what
appeared an unpardonable concession to the populism of Hollywood-
style narrative, Fornet sees this response as a prime instance of the
difference that is made by the space in which a film is viewed, a result of
the different sociocultural codes that are called into play by different
viewers in different places. The Cuban audience, with its own concrete
knowledge of the events depicted, is less interested in the authenticity of
the discourse than in that of its referent.[3]

In a similar vein, *Patty Candela* is an espionage movie about operations against the CIA in 1961 that shifts its point of view from that of the
conspirators to that of the Cuban security forces, but then finds it necessary to tack on an epilogue. *Río Negro,* Manuel Pérez's second feature, is a Cuban western set on a ranch in the Escambray at the time of
the Bay of Pigs, in which Tirso, a revolutionary militiaman, son of a
peasant whose land was seized in the bad years before the Revolution,
slugs it out with Chano, a counterrevolutionary who had been involved
in the land seizure. The greatest delights in this last film are the superb
performances of Sergio Corrieri as the self-searching Tirso and the
Chilean actor Nelson Villagra as the thwarted Chano, but the genre format—and especially the spectacular shoot-out with which the film
ends—overwhelms the attempt that had been made to mold the character of Tirso differently from the conventional genre hero, above all by
introducing contradictions in his personality and a level of political discourse that Hollywood would never permit. As for Sergio Corrieri, after
Maisinicú and *Río Negro* he withdrew from screen acting in order, he
said, to avoid getting typecast as Cuba's principal male lead, and went to
work instead in community theater.

Mention should be made of a visual feature in several of these films
that may be judged as symptomatic: the rather frequent and often ragged
use of the zoom. A predilection for the zoom is found in a good deal of
Cuban cinema, including the style developed by Álvarez's principal cameraman, Iván Napoles, where it expresses the rough spontaneity of many
of the best Cuban documentaries. In the case of fiction, however, at least

in films like these that are stylistically imitative of Hollywood, the use of the zoom is more intrusive than the smoother and more facile zooming that became something of a Hollywood trademark of the period.

However, the fundamental difficulty in these films (except perhaps for *Rachel K.*) is that of trying to portray the very real anonymous heroism that many people showed during the course of the Revolution in a form inseparable from the traditional imagery of machismo. *El brigadista* shows perhaps most clearly what the dangers are of this approach, because it is a film of adolescent adventure and initiation, on a model whose original, perhaps, is Tom Sawyer. The crux of the difficulty is contained in a pair of incidents that reveal the obverse of machismo: the implications it has for the imagery of women. In the first, our young hero Mario meets with a girl by chance at night; they are carried off by adolescent dreams of first love, and Mario pledges himself to her with the gift of his watch—it doesn't work, but he tells her "it's like a ring." In the second, he is almost seduced by the wife of a *gusano* whom he visits in her house quite legitimately as the village teacher, while her husband is in the swamps with an armed band of counterrevolutionaries. There is a clear and unfortunate equation at work here, in which revolutionary *brigadista* equals romantic idealism equals the danger of corruption, which can only come as an act of treachery on the part of a woman tainted by sharing her bed with a traitor to the Revolution. Both these women, the virgin and the adulteress, have virtually no other presence in the film than this, and both are the crudest of misogynist stereotypes.

These were all successful films with the audience—some more than others—and how they came to be made is not difficult to understand. On the one hand, the political climate of the 1970s encouraged a greater degree of populism; on the other, ICAIC frowned on aesthetic conformism and did not consider that there was any a priori reason why such approaches should not be tried. At the same time, there are other films that, though not as immediately arresting as those which immediately preceded, still attempt to come to terms more critically with the problems of narrative and representation. Manuel Octavio Gómez, for example, did so twice in the mid-1970s, in *Ustedes tienen la palabra* (Now it's up to you, 1974) and *Una mujer, un hombre, una ciudad* (A man, a woman, a city, 1977). These two films, both highly accomplished, are concerned with issues that, although of universal concern, are also subjects of particular political debate within the Cuban revolutionary process: the administration of justice and the problems of urban renewal. This makes for certain difficulties in assessing them. A lot of our recent film theory, as John Hess points out in discussing these films in *Jump Cut*, condemns conventional narrative means as hopelessly tainted by bourgeois ideology, which the imperfect cinema thesis largely seems to confirm. It is consequently pretty easy to pick out various films that offend from both points of view. But with these two films we find ourselves in an uncertain position to judge how effectively they may conduct a political dialogue with the audience, which in Hess's opinion suggests that they raise questions about the universal applicability of antinarrative theories. At any rate, if bourgeois films, he says, "include politics and social issues at all, it is usually as a background theme which the film-maker soon abandons in order to concentrate on the moral and romantic concerns of a few central characters. Manuel Octavio Gómez's two films, however, move in the opposite direction. They open with moral questions and move out to the underlying historical and political questions."[4]

Ustedes tienen la palabra deals with fictional events seven years earlier than the year of its release. Eight years have passed since the overthrow of Batista. The heroic struggle against imperialist military intervention is past, the October crisis is history, the remaining counterrevolutionary bandits have been routed. The Revolution has entered resolutely on the tasks of reconstruction. The institutionalization of the new Communist Party has begun. But the new society is still only in process of formation and old attitudes persist.

The film opens with one of those pre-title sequences that have become a hallmark of Cuban cinema: A fire rages at night in a wood, a large thatched building burns. People rush around trying to put it out. Following the titles, we find ourselves among the ruins of the building: it has been turned into a court of law and a trial is in progress of a group of people accused of arson—counterrevolutionary sabotage. The camera roams across the shell of the building, a warehouse in the Río Palmas Forestry Collective, and as it emerges how the arsonists had tried to do their dirty work elsewhere and failed, the trial broadens out to become a general investigation by the community of itself. The first of the accused was, before the revolution, a manager for the previous owner of the land, who now lives in the United States. The second was the same man's chauffeur. They deny their guilt, and, as the trial proceeds to uncover an intricate story, it becomes clear that in a way their particular guilt is not the main issue; for the film becomes a Brechtian demonstration of the real concerns of popular justice—it brings to mind the atmosphere of the prologue to *The Caucasian Chalk Circle*—which is not so much a matter of facts and sworn evidence as the investigation of the state of consciousness in the community, as well as the circumstances of the crime and the political nature of another kind of guilt—the guilt of those whose lack of consciousness allowed the crime to happen in the first place. As the story is pieced together through flashbacks corresponding to the successive stories told by defendants and witnesses, the investigation takes in the lack of proper planning and economic controls in the collective, the disorganization of the labor process, the improper use of resources, and poor communication between the union and the administration. A central fact, immediately obvious to the Cuban viewer, is the absence in the collective of a party caucus. According to Leopoldo Perdomo reviewing the film in *Juventud Rebelde* (April 1, 1974), the film reveals five kinds of deficiency, which also include the persistence of certain negative religious attitudes.

But this makes the film sound schematic and even doctrinaire, which it certainly is not. In fact, every effort was taken to avoid it being so. It was shot on location with the active participation of local people who contributed to the script, especially, according to the assistant director Fernando Pérez (*Granma*, March 15, 1974), in the scenes of the assembly and in the staging of the fire. To achieve greater authenticity, the film was shot in 16 mm and then blown up to 35 for cinema release, like *De cierta manera* by Sara Gómez, which allowed the cameraman, Pablo Martínez, a more than usually flexible and fluid, and hence intimate, style of filming. It is true that the narrative is linear, but as Manuel Octavio Gómez himself explained, in *La primera carga...*, the interviews and the reportage themselves produced the analysis; in *Los días de agua*, the successive subjective visions of each character provided more and more information for an understanding of certain facts; in this film, the narrative simply follows the lines of the judicial inquiry.[5] Yet the flashbacks are not as simple in their internal structure as this implies. They are a means of fusing the incompleteness of the various individual points of view of the protagonists; on occasion they even begin with one character and end with another. The result is that while the film foregrounds individual behavior, it does not psychologize it. At the same time, instead of the mechanical notion that people's behavior will change as a result of improvements in economic planning and efficiency and material improvement in their conditions of life, the film poses the question exactly the other way around: how are these improvements to come about if the imperfect state of people's consciousness impedes the achievement of the more rational organization of production?

The plot of *Una mujer, un hombre, una ciudad* is somewhat more complex and diffuse. Gómez takes up material he filmed nine years earlier in 1968 for a documentary on the rapidly growing port and industrial town of Nuevitas in the province of Camagüey—the city of the title—and uses it as the context for two parallel biographies. Marisa, the town's director of housing, has been killed in a car accident. Miguel, a young Havana-trained sociologist, reluctantly returns to his native city to replace her, he believes, temporarily. He becomes increasingly obsessed, however, with finding out who Marisa was, and, as he talks to the people who knew her—family, friends, and colleagues—the film develops, as John Hess points out, a format of flashbacks over her life resembling that of *Citizen Kane*. He starts out, Hess observes, with very personal reasons for conducting this investigation. The ghost of Marisa's exemplary political life suffocates him. Everyone he talks to describes Marisa in glowing terms and he feels himself unfavorably compared with her. But he cannot comprehend the records she has left behind, cannot figure out the basis on which she allocated housing, and thinks she did it subjectively, with none of the scientific methods and rigor he has learned at the university in Havana: and "he wants to prove her wrong to validate himself."

As he discovers more and more about Marisa, however, and at the same time becomes increasingly involved with the city and its people, he begins to change. He becomes uncomfortable with his Havana friends, including his architect wife, whose lack of relationship, personal or political, with the people for whom her apartments are intended, utterly contrasts with Marisa. In the end, he decides to abandon Havana and his wife and stay in Nuevitas. The critique of the postrevolutionary Havana intelligentsia that the film thus elaborates makes it a successor to the concerns of *Memorias del subdesarrollo*. It is also directed toward the difference between the theory that is taught in the academy, including the misconceptions of various new administrative practices, and the reality to which they have to be applied.

Moreover, in contrast to the stereotypical portrayal of women in the genre films, Gómez clearly takes the question of women in the Revolution very seriously—and has found in Idalia Anreus an ideal actress for the character of Marisa, full of nervous energy and determination, just as she had so marvelously accomplished the role of Tulipa ten years earlier. We find her, immediately after the Revolution, arguing for the right of women to work in the docks. Her husband supports her in finding another job when the male dockworkers force the women to quit, but, as Hess remarks, when she becomes increasingly involved with her work and starts attending long meetings after hours, her husband rebels and asks her to quit. She refuses and the marriage ends. Although she then finds herself unable to handle an involvement with another man, Hess is substantially right (he exaggerates a bit) that Gómez has somewhat idealized her character: "Since she basically serves . . . as a symbol of the revolutionary woman, of the New Woman, he portrays her as morally superior to everyone else. She exhibits the greatest sensitivity to the problems of ordinary people and the greatest possible commitment to the Revolution. She can stand up to men with a great deal of strength . . . and can articulate the needs of . . . other women, children, the sick, the uneducated peasants and workers. Nonetheless, her basic role . . . is passive; she becomes an example, a symbol. She does not propel the plot forward but serves as the locus of moral values . . . the model revolutionary woman as imagined by men."

Hess concludes his account of these two films by observing that, in contrast, *De cierta manera* (One way or another) by Sara Gómez is a unique example of a Cuban film in which the female lead is an ordinary person with no symbolic baggage to carry around with her. By tragic mischance, Sara Gómez became the first Cuban director whose work could be seen as a whole—but an imperfect whole, like the imperfect cinema she practiced: she died, from asthma, as *De cierta manera*, her first feature, was being edited; it was completed under the supervision of Alea and García Espinosa.

The editing, at the moment of her death, was well advanced. Most sequences were already cut, and the commentary had been planned, though not all of it written. However, her death obviously delayed completion, which was further held up by technical problems in the laboratory, including damage suffered by the negative. In the end, the negative had to be sent to Sweden to be treated and then blown up to 35 mm, and the result was that the film was not released for a couple of years.[6] Some observers find it difficult to believe that there wasn't something deliberate in this delay, and that ICAIC was uncomfortable about the film's critique of macho values. This could well be true, but it doesn't have to enter into any explanation of the delay. Cuba is a Latin American country, and in the experience of the present writer more efficient to film in than any other; but people in Cuba still have a quite different, less anxious, sense of time to that of the overprogramed metropolis. It does not require sinister motives to explain how the technical problems alone that the film encountered could have taken two years to solve.

Sara Gómez trained as a musician, but after six years at the Havana Conservatory she decided, she said, that she didn't want to be "a middle-class black woman who played the piano."[7] She got a job as a journalist and then joined ICAIC as an assistant director, working with Alea, Fraga, and, on a visit to Cuba, Agnès Varda. Then, between 1964 and *De cierta manera* in 1974, she made ten documentaries, most of them no longer than ten minutes' duration, on a range of subjects that included popular culture and traditions, the mechanization of tobacco production, music, civic education, traffic accidents, child care, prenatal attention, popular democracy, and labor relations. What emerges is a body of work largely concerned with the same kinds of theme as her final film. It also demonstrates the acquisition of an exceptional economy of means in communication.

Iré a Santiago (1964), which takes its title from a poem by Federico García Lorca, is a fond and gentle portrait of Santiago de Cuba and its people. Its style of shooting (the photography is by Mario García Joya), editing, and informal voice-over commentary make it perhaps the most striking "free cinema" documentary ever produced in Cuba. It has a very personal quality, which is reflected in the credits: as in one or two other films, Mario García Joya is listed under his nickname Mayito, and the director lists herself as "Sarita," the name by which she was known in ICAIC. A year later came *Excursión a Vuelta Abajo* (Trip to Vuelta Abajo), which describes tobacco culture in a village in the province of Pinar del Río and the changes brought about by the Revolution. Curiously, it is more of an apprentice work than the first film, but it is notable for including in the focus of its social observation aspects that are unusual for the emerging pattern of the Cuban documentary—for example, the way it foregrounds the image of women workers in the fields, at a time when the subject had not yet drawn the attention of historians. It is true of all of Sara Gómez's films that she gives a stronger presence to women and black people than you get with a number of less conscientious directors within ICAIC.

Her third film was *Y... tenemos sabor,* which has already been discussed, and is one of the most delightful Cuban music documentaries in a quarter century. Then came a trio of films on the Isle of Pines, which the Revolution renamed the Isle of Youth when it decided to turn it over to youth and education. The last of the three, *Isla de Tesoro* (Treasure Island, 1969) is a short, poetic, celebratory film essay, which simply crosscuts between shots of the Model Penitentiary of the pseudorepublic years, where Fidel was imprisoned by Batista, and the production of citrus fruit, which ends up being packed and labeled as "Treasure Island Grapefruit Produce of Cuba." The two films that precede it, *En la otra isla* (On the other island, 1967) and *Una isla para Miguel* (An island for Miguel, 1968), are among the most extraordinary documentaries by any Cuban director.

The first and longer of them (at forty minutes) is a loose collection of individual portraits of people in the island: a seventeen-year-old girl who wants to be a hairdresser; a man of the theater who works as a cowboy during the day and runs a theater group in the evenings; another agricultural worker who used to be a tenor in Havana; an ex-seminarian; a girl at the reformatory; the woman at the reformatory responsible for her. The interviews—and as a result the structure of the film—have unusual qualities. Cubans are people who, from the evidence of Cuban cinema, are always eager to talk to cameras and microphones, but rarely in the manner we see here. Sara Gómez clearly had a remarkable way of gaining the trust of her subjects, and drawing out of them stories and reflections that go far beyond most other documentaries. The tenor, for example, speaks of the experience of racism he had in Havana as a black singer wanting to sing leading operatic roles. The interview, which is a two-shot of the both of them, sitting very informally in the open air, ends with him asking his interviewer, "Sara, do you think one day I'll sing *Traviata*?" Other interviews touch further awkward subjects, above all questions of delinquency and reeducation, and the difficulties of life for children in a reformatory or reeducation camp. The girl, Manuela, whose father has been imprisoned as a CIA agent, while her mother has gone to the States, describes her own experience, and Cacha, her supervisor, answers questions very frankly about the need to treat inmates as adults, especially in the matter of sexual relations. This is also one of the handful of Cuban films that make self-reference to the camera and the business of filming, along the lines of García Espinosa's call in "Imperfect Cinema." Clapper boards are seen, the film has captions that say what comes next. The most striking moment of this kind tells us that Cacha, the supervisor, is going to comment on the interview with Manuela afterwards. The effect is to have us see the subjects in the film as integral human beings and representatives of particular social roles at the same time, and in a mutually illuminating way: it helps the viewer to make a judgment about the dialectic between the individual and the social. The same is true of *Una isla para Miguel*, which, beginning with a hearing before the disciplinary assembly at one of the reeducation camps, is a case study of the boy being disciplined. It includes memorable interviews with Miguel's mother—in their poorest of homes, she and her countless children abandoned by her husband— and with his best buddy. A supervisor comments dramatically, "They are rebels without a cause, our task is to give them the cause." Although in our own countries we are nowadays used to television reports that probe similar topics about reformatories and their inmates, this is somewhat rare footage for Cuba—which is a great pity. These reformatories are not the same as the UMAP (Military Units to Aid Production) camps in the two years 1965 to 1967, which were set up in a wave of sectarian fervor to rehabilitate those who were deemed social misfits: drug users, Jehovah's Witnesses, hippies, and homosexuals—people thought to be easy marks for CIA activity. What these films show is very far from the exploitation of fears inflamed by the constant threat of external attack, but a serious, humane approach to the real problems of socially marginal individuals. If there had been more films of this kind, the Revolution would have been less susceptible to attacks abroad on the grounds of irrational inhumanity toward social dissidents.

The next two films deal with public subjects. *Poder local, poder popular* (Local power, popular power, 1970) and *Un documental a propósito del tránsito* (A documentary about traffic, 1971). The first is political and expository, and the only film of hers that is both too long and, in its structure, unwieldy; the second is a sociological and technical investigation of the problems of city traffic, inevitably somewhat prosaic. The next two, *Atención pre-natal* and *Año Uno* (Prenatal attention and First year, both 1972, each ten minutes), are most remarkable, from the point of view of a masculine viewer, for the way they address themselves directly to women, about preparing to give birth and about lactation during the baby's first year of life, ignoring the presence of any chance male viewer, although they were made for general screening. *Sobre horas extras y trabajo voluntario* (On overtime and voluntary work, 1973) addresses everyone. Also a very short film, it is politically more effective than the longer essay on popular power. The theme, of course, needs far less exposition—it goes back to Che Guevara in the 1960s. Together with *Isla de Tesoro* the film of Sara Gómez that is closest in style to Santiago Álvarez, its stance is boldly agitational: there must be a struggle against the unnecessary use of overtime, but also, at the same time, against wasteful voluntary work that is not properly organized.

Nearly all her films, then, were—as imperfect cinema requires—socially and politically functional: we find that the style and idiom of the film are subordinate to its purpose, never the other way around. Whenever possible, a radical aesthetic is explored, but emerges from within, so that the film can be readily grasped and still communicate on a popular level. Gómez's last work, *De cierta manera* is nothing if not an aesthetically radical film in this manner. Above all, it mixes different modes of filmic discourse, fiction and documentary, in the most original way, not merely by alternating them but by using real people to play themselves alongside professional actors. Moreover, these real people appear both as themselves—documentary material about them tells us who they are—and as characters within the story. None of this is at all forced; it arises from the familiarity both of Gómez herself and of Cuban audiences, with a whole range of forms in both documentary and fiction.

Two things can be said about this. First, it is an answer to the problem of the battle between the two forms of fiction and documentary of which García Espinosa spoke in Montreal. In fact, to find a way of integrating them was an endeavor of Cuban filmmakers that first clearly surfaced in the late 1960s with films like *Memorias del subdesarrollo* and *La primera carga al machete*. Manuel Octavio Gómez pursued the attempt in *Una mujer, un hombre, una ciudad* through incorporating his own documentary material of a few years earlier. There are yet other examples, such as Manuel Herrera's *Girón* of 1972, which adopts the format of a wide-screen war movie to present the results of an exhaustive documentary investigation of the events. The second comment is that what *De cierta manera* achieves is a veritable interpenetration of the two forms of address, a teasing synthesis, which makes it a prime example of the process of syncretism. The only problem of the film as finished is a miscalculation over the commentary, which imitates the didactic documentary in its use of a certain kind of formal sociological language. It is intended, according to Rigoberto López, "as an element of distantiation, and, at the same time, to amplify the analysis."[8] But, as Julia Lesage remarks in her perceptive piece on the film in *Jump Cut,* it has a tendency to sound pompous and grating.[9] (I don't think this is reducible, however, to insensitivity on the part of Alea and García Espinosa in the course of finishing the film: the commentary, Alea told me, was what Sara Gómez herself intended—though one would like to think that, had she lived, she might have had second thoughts, at least as far as the tone of its delivery is concerned.)

Another feminist commentator on the film, Annette Kuhn, finds that the way the film takes up and in various ways combines the two different conventions of film realism undercuts the normal relationship a viewer has with either on its own. It is a form of deconstruction, she says, that works by setting up expectations and then cutting them off, leaving the film with "no single internally consistent discourse."[10] I think this is only partly true. It is demonstrable that while the film is deconstructional in the way she describes, its internal discourse is quite consistent—it speaks to us from within the quite particular experience of the Cuban Revolution. For a third commentator, E. Ann Kaplan, the "juxtaposition of two cinematic strategies forces the spectator to become aware of his/her need for narrative. For as one watches, one becomes impatient with the documentary sections; one always wants to get back to the story."[11] I think probably this effect is in certain respects less acute with the Cuban audience, because of its considerable familiarity with the range of documentary styles that have been discussed in this book. But it is true, as she says, that the question of the power of narrative film preoccupies Cuban filmmakers and critics; that this is because Cuban audiences continue to respond strongly to classical Hollywood cinema; and that what Sara Gómez is attempting in this film is to give a moral lesson in a pleasurable way. The film in fact is hugely pleasurable, and zips along (it runs only seventy-two minutes), brimming with lightness and good humor, however jarring the jumps. On the contrary, the jar of the jumps becomes part of the pleasure.

For *De cierta manera* is a revolutionary love story, which means a film about the growing relationship between a man and a woman that refuses to isolate their elective affinity from the social determinants that have not only made them what they are, but continue to affect them as they get to know each other. Nor does their relationship follow a smooth course, but pride and conflict interrupt it, the result not of the mysterious qualities of the irreducible personality but the expression in the individual of class background, cultural inheritance, and personal history, refracted through the impact of the Revolution. The central protagonists are Mario (played by Mario Balmaceda, who also played Miguel in *Una mujer, un hombre, una ciudad*), a worker at a bus factory, and Yolanda (Yolanda Cueller), a primary-school teacher from a lower middle-class background.

The setting of the film is Mario's beat. In 1961, in one of the Revolution's first major projects to tackle the country's enormous housing problem, five new neighborhoods were built for people living in Las Yaguas, a Havana slum that was one of the worst. The new neighborhoods were constructed by the same people who were to live in them, who belonged to the dominantly black lumpen classes. One of these districts is Miraflores, where our two protagonists live and work. For Yolanda, it's a confusing place: "How do I feel?" she asks in a Godardian testimony to camera. "Well, not very good. I graduated from different schools. Then I came here, and all this was a different world, one I thought no longer existed."

All of this we learn early in the film, amid a sequence of commentary over documentary images, which begin with a dramatic shot of demolition that serves as a thematic image for the whole picture. Here and in subsequent commentaries, the film develops the thesis that rehousing is only a start. By itself it can do little to improve the life of people previously consigned to subsistence in the belts of squalor and poverty that still surround all other major cities throughout Latin America. With rehousing must come the provision of employment, education, and health care. Even these things only make up the groundwork. Revolutionary change involves cultural regeneration, but this is not an automatic process. It requires a struggle to overcome the habits, customs, beliefs, and values of the old society. And in the case of the marginal classes, without even a tradition of participation in trade-union and political activity, their hermetic culture contains a high degree of resistance and

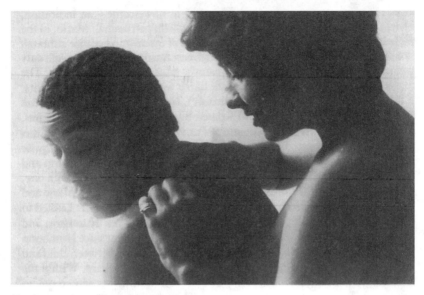

De cierta manera (Sara Gómez, 1974)

inertia toward such changes; hence the persistence of certain antisocial attitudes within the Revolution.

To focus the problems, the film investigates the Abacuá religious society (a phenomenon that has also been examined in a number of Cuban documentaries on various subjects where the Abacuá influence can be felt, like music, such as the Óscar Valdés film *La rumba*). Mario and Yolanda are conversing on a hillside, talking about Mario's background and adolescence. He was lucky, he says, to have been conscripted into the army, because military service saved him at the moment he was thinking of "going." "Leaving the country?" asks Yolanda. "No, no, what for? 'Going' means taking the oath." "What oath?" "When I was a kid I wanted to be a *ñáñigo*." "A *ñáñigo!*" Yolanda repeats in horror, to which Mario responds, "You think they eat babies on Santa Bárbara's Day, right?" and the film shifts to a documentary sequence on the Abacuá to which the *ñáñigo* belongs. The Abacuá is a secret society, a heritage of the religious practices and beliefs conserved in the legends, rites, symbols, and language of the slaves. The society took form during the nineteenth century in the marginal population of the ports of Havana and Matanzas, where it not only fulfilled religious functions but also became a mutual help association that defended the rights of its members (white as well as black). However, as an exclusively male domain, it "epitomizes the social aspirations, norms, and values of male chauvinism in Cuban society." The sequence that informs us of all this is not merely a convenient way of instructing us about it. It also serves to teach us that Yolanda's horror has elements of social prejudice in it, and that Mario is a man aware of the need to fight free of its influence.

Male chauvinism takes its toll in the problems that Yolanda encounters in her workplace. She is criticized by fellow teachers for her lack of sympathy in her dealings with "La Mejicana," the mother of one of her pupils, Lázaro, a somewhat delinquent child. La Mejicana and Lázaro are real people; Lázaro is the eldest of five children in a fatherless family. As La Mejicana explains to Yolanda, she had a fight with her husband in 1962 and has not heard from him since. A narration in the film tells us that "Around 53 percent of the family units in a group of 341 people were headed by women, a characteristic of marginal families whose marital-instability indexes are high."

Machismo takes another form where Mario works. In fact, the film opens—and apart from an epilogue, closes—with a workers' assembly at Mario's factory that is called upon to examine the case of a buddy of Mario's, Humberto. Humberto has been missing from work—he skipped work in order to go and get laid, though only Mario knows this. Humberto tells the assembly that he went to visit his dying mother at the other end of the island. Humberto is in many ways Mario's alter ego. Different aspects of the old marginal culture survive in each of them, but more rigidly and individualistically in Humberto, for whom the pursuit of personal whim justifies the evasion of social responsibility toward his fellow workers and dissimulation in the interests of private gratification. In Mario's case, the predominant survival of marginalism is found in his adherence to the code of loyalty—not giving Humberto away. But in the assembly, Mario feels provoked by Humberto's behavior and spills the beans, which we witness in the opening sequence and then finally come to understand at the end when we see it again in context. When this happens, we recognize one of the members of the workers' council that presides over the assembly as Mario's father, Candito, whom we know to be a good revolutionary and critical of Humberto because he has been before the council three times already. And what we have learned from Candito makes it clear that Mario has exploded because he is confused by a conflict of loyalties, the old code of loyalty to his buddy and the new social code of the Revolution and loyalty among *compañeros.*

The film opens and leads back to this explosive moment of rupture, and the love story is contained within this trajectory. The two strands stand in opposition to each other: an old friendship and an old code of behavior is shattered, while a new relationship is formed on the basis of new codes of behavior, antagonistic to the first. For his part, Humberto is clear about this. At one point he tells Mario, "The teacher's brain-washed you, made you a Komsomol!" Mario, however, remains confused. In the epilogue, after he has turned against his former buddy, he says, "I acted like a woman, turning him in." Here the film not only refuses to idealize its "hero" but quite the opposite: it wants to be sure we know he has done the right thing for totally the wrong reason—not because he *has* acted "like a woman," but because that's what he tells himself. This judgment upon him to which the whole course of the film has brought us is reinforced by remarks in the epilogue, in the scene in which work-ers from the assembly discuss what has happened. These are real workers from the bus factory where the film was made, and this unscripted dis-cussion is another index of imperfect cinema in practice, for these are no longer simply actors in a story, but representatives of the audience watching the film, who show the audience what it is to be, as in Cortázar's *Por primera vez,* at the same time participant observers and observant participators in the dramas of daily life.

De cierta manera is seen, with great justification, by critics in the me-tropolis as a feminist film, but in Cuba the term *feminism* was not part of the revolutionary vocabulary because of overtones of antagonistic confrontation between men and women that were regarded as unwel-come—perhaps an indication of the degree to which Cuban society re-mained patriarchal. Mario, in the film, has not yet escaped the thought structures of machismo because, although he knows he has been in their grip and is fighting against them, he can still only imagine that to break them is to be womanish rather than revolutionary. The struggle for women's equality in Cuba, the film is telling us (not women's rights: the Revolution has given them these already), is a struggle against machismo, which has to be joined by men and women together, within the Revolu-tion, because machismo is one of the symptoms of underdevelopment. We can see this more clearly if we map out the way a whole series of ele-ments in the film comprise a surprisingly symmetrical set of structural oppositions. First, Humberto and Lázaro are the film's two delinquents; an absent mother is associated with one, an absent father with the other. Second, there are conflicts between Mario and Humberto, on the one hand, and Yolanda and Lázaro, on the other. Linked to these two conflicts is a further pair of antagonisms, between Humberto and Candito, and between Lázaro and his mother La Mejicana. But since Humberto is Mario's alter ego, what you get symbolically are two conflicts between child and parent, one in Mario's sphere, one in Yolanda's, making a square. Within the square are various other parallels, especially between the factory and the school, as the two central protagonists' places of work, and between the workers' assembly in the one, and, in the other, Yolanda's meeting with her fellow teachers:

```
HUMBERTO ◄----------------------------► LAZARO
[absent mother]                         [absent father]

          MARIO ◄-----► YOLANDA
  |       factory  -------  school         |
  |       workers'  ------  teachers'      |
  |       assembly          meeting        |

[father]                                [mother]
CANDITO - - - - - - - - - - - - - - - - - - - LA MEJICANA
```

Certain other features fall within this pattern too, such as relations of authority: Candito's authority over Humberto, and Yolanda's over Lázaro, arise from their positions within the institutions they belong to, factory and school, in Candito's case as an elected representative, in Yolanda's because teachers are expected to concern themselves with their pupils' well-being.

These institutional settings are important elements in the sociospatial discourse of the film—the way the film maps the social relationships it portrays onto the spaces, physical and institutional, in which they occur: the factory, the school, the street, the home, and other places where the film unfolds. Each location corresponds to a different kind of social encounter, and each kind of social encounter involves a different aspect of a character's social existence, and therefore calls forth different behavior. The way the film handles these differences and contrasts is manifold and paradigmatic, exposing the poverty of traditional narrative plotting that ignores everything about its characters that falls outside the particular set of motivations concentrated in the conventional plot and its linear trajectory. The sociospatial discourse of a conventional narrative movie, though it always exists—actions always *take place,* every scene has a setting—is subordinate to the designs of the plot, and location is a coloring rather than part of the film's very fabric. But not here. Just as Miraflores, the district, is almost a character in the film in its own right, so too the individual locations contribute their own character to the dialectic of action and interaction. The narrative system of the film is thus a constant movement of many points, not a single unfolding line, and the character of each protagonist is not a predefined entity that can only change according to the exigencies of the plot, but a living field of possibilities arising from the constraints and sanctions of the different social spaces these people inhabit. This is why Sara Gómez is able so successfully to introduce real persons alongside fictional ones, not as nonprofessional actors but as themselves, people "with their own name and surname," to borrow a phrase from the neorealist Zavattini.

Only two locations in *De cierta manera* require special comment because they carry specific local connotations. The first is the bedroom where Mario and Yolanda have been making love, which probably only a Cuban audience would instantly recognize as a room in one of the *posadas* or *albergues* that the government erected after the Revolution to alleviate one of the problems of the housing shortage: these are hostels where couples can hire rooms by the hour. The conversation in this scene is a function of the fact that the room is neutral territory in which couples meet as equals, at least to an extent that might not be possible in their own rooms in an overcrowded house where privacy is elusive.

In the second, the scene acquires a crucial dimension of irony if you know the location's symbolic connotations. At the end of the film, when Mario makes his remark about behaving like a woman, he is talking with a workmate in a public garden, underneath a statue of General Maceo. The general sits astride a horse with enormous balls. The irony arises because to say in Cuba that someone has the balls of Maceo's horse is to say that he's more macho than everyone else. "After all, it's men who made the Revolution," says Mario, and the location silently asks, "What kind of boast is that?"[12]

The particular significance within this scheme of the institutional settings is twofold. On the one hand, this is where the ethics of the Revolution establish the standards against which other forms of behavior must be measured. It is as if the film is an inquiry into the extent to which revolutionary ethics have become generalized, entering even the more informal, more enclosed, less public spaces in which people live out their private lives, spaces where it is much more difficult to root out the old values. At the same time, the different worlds of factory and school are contrasted in the film as the different realms of the central pair, Mario and Yolanda. They seem therefore to represent the two realms of male and female. The division is a symbolic arrangement that reveals a pattern of interdependence, fractured moieties that seek completion in each other, symbolized by the elective affinity between Mario and Yolanda. The difficulty, revealed by the parallel conflicts in the story, is that the forms of bonding in which people either find themselves or engage—family, friendship, sexual love—can become either wholesome or, when social codes conflict, antagonistic. In the case of the love bond, antagonism usually comes less from determinate differences of class background, cultural inheritance, and personal history than when one partner refuses to accept the challenge of the other to change. But in the film and in Cuban society, the major force for change comes from beyond either partner: it comes from the dynamics of the Revolution. Marginalism, underdevelopment, machismo are forms of disruption inherited from the past. And if the Revolution can hardly tolerate them, neither can it accept any solution to the problems they create that only intensifies antagonism. No society can be totally free from coercion, but coercion must be tempered by collective responsibility, for otherwise the Revolution would be denying its own character. It must therefore be part of the character of revolutionary ethics—and De cierta manera is above all a film about revolutionary ethics—that it recognizes conflict and negation as productive, according to the laws of dialectical logic. But although this is a perfectly consistent and cogent position, it leaves open the question of whether the Revolution in reality can live up to the Revolution as depicted on the screen.

PART III

New Generations:
A Cinema of Readjustment

CHAPTER FIFTEEN

Reconnecting

Despite the alteration of the political climate in Cuba in the 1970s, the lessons of the Revolution's first decade remained vigilant. According to Ambrosio Fornet, literary historian turned screenwriter:

> At the triumph of the Revolution, the first thing we found was that for the first time we had the means of disseminating our culture, that is to say, we had publishers, a Film Institute, centers of investigation—but the question was, Now that we've got these resources; what culture shall we disseminate? What concept of culture, what concept of the relationship between the writer, the intellectual, and the people? Because we had been formed—the majority of intellectuals—in a tradition that was based in European and North American culture, which means, in social terms, in a bourgeois cultural tradition. Few of us were Marxists. So the first question we had to pose was, What concept of culture are we going to defend? We didn't have the answer, it wasn't written anywhere, no angel descended with it from heaven. We had to find the answer in practice, in the revolutionary process itself. Obviously, this produced clashes and conflicts between those who in some way continued defending the old concept of culture and the position of the intellectual in society, and those who wanted to defend a new sense and concept of culture. For the first time, the people, through the Revolution, had come into close-up, so to speak, in the scenario of history and were transforming the bases of society. It seemed impossible to many of us in a situation like this that the traditional concept of culture should remain untouchable. A large group of us thought, We cannot simply defend what in Occidental culture are called the eternal values, because we had discovered that eternal values didn't exist. Eternal values are historical values, and they were changing. And obviously, in contact with this changing reality, we also changed our conceptions.[1]

If this describes the years in which the cultural politics of the Revolution were forged, ICAIC played a leading role throughout this period in the ideological confrontations through which the new cultural politics was defined. The Film Institute developed and defended positions more lucidly than any comparable institution against both the sometimes near-hysterical attacks of liberals who feared the encroachment of the state, and the mechanical application of schemes for socialist realism on the part of more orthodox and traditional Marxists associated with the old guard of the Communist Party. Defending the right of its members to experiment in the most varied styles and techniques, ICAIC argued that economic criteria of productivity could not be applied to artistic work, which could not be reduced either to purely didactic functions or to propaganda. Nor, it said, should the audience be refused the right to see the work of aesthetically progressive European filmmakers because they supposedly dealt in the portrayal of bourgeois decadence. Instead of such communist orthodoxies, ICAIC's filmmakers wanted to undermine the adverse powers of the dream screen of commercial entertainment cinema by building on what started as the audience's spontaneous change of perspective in order to create both a more critical disposition in the viewer and a radical film language. The result was a series of exhilarating, experimental films by Tomás Gutiérrez Alea, Julio García Espinosa, Humberto Solás, Manuel Octavio Gómez, Santiago Álvarez, and others in the late 1960s that were recognized on every continent of the globe as a major new presence in world cinema—a moment it would prove hard to maintain.

During the 1960s, at a time when filmgoing in countries like the United States and Britain had begun to fall in the face of the spread of television, there was huge growth in the Cuban cinema audience, which almost doubled, from just over 54 million admissions in 1962, to almost 100 million in 1972.[2] There were also, in that year, an estimated 25 million mobile cinema spectators, an audience that didn't exist before 1959. There is no better general indicator of ICAIC's overall success, unless the fact that by 1972 nine Cuban feature films had achieved a spectatorship of more than one million each. They included three films by Alea and three by García Espinosa (Table 1). These are huge figures for a country with a population of around ten million. In Britain, a country five times the size, the cinema audience was only slightly higher (119 million in 1978).

Table 1. Top Cuban films by admission, 1960–71 (Cuba)

Film	Director	Year	Admissions (in millions)
Historias de la Revolución	Tomás Gutiérrez Alea	1960	1
Cuba baila	Julio García Espinosa	1960	1.2
El joven rebelde	Julio García Espinosa	1961	1
Las doce sillas	Tomás Gutiérrez Alea	1962	1.7
Cuba 58	Jorge Fraga and José Miguel García Ascot	1962	1.3
La muerte de una burócrata	Tomás Gutiérrez Alea	1966	1.4
Las aventuras de Juan Quin Quin	Julio García Espinosa	1967	3.2
Lucía	Humberto Solás	1968	1.2
Los días de agua	Manuel Octavio Gómez	1971	1

The Cuban figures therefore indicate both a high frequency of attendance and the huge social reach of the successful individual film.

Average attendance in 1972 ran at eleven cinema visits per person, plus three mobile cinema shows. The usual provisos must be made about statistics like these: totals and averages do not, for example, indicate the portion of the total population that formed the cinema-going public, nor, in the case of popular films, what proportion of the audience saw the film more than once. In the Cuban case, one must add that the two modes of exhibition—theaters and mobile cinemas—catered to different audiences, so the averages for each were actually higher. The significance of the figures for individual films is enormous. This size audience gave the filmmaker a degree of popular reach and cultural influence that had never previously been enjoyed by a Cuban artist in any field (except perhaps music). If this phenomenon is hardly unique to Cuba, the special conditions of the Revolution gave it particular force. ICAIC represented a public space that, under communism, had expanded, not contracted, and, as a popular communicator, the Cuban filmmaker enjoyed a social reach that was not only unprecedented, but probably only exceeded by Fidel Castro himself—a situation that made ICAIC the object of constant scrutiny by political watchdogs, but also lent the filmmaker unusual influence, with the result that Cuban cinema was politicized through and through. When the Soviet influence began to prevail, with the effect of somewhat constraining traditional forms of public debate, ICAIC retained its own voice, and became a vicarious surrogate for a public sphere diminished by ideological orthodoxy and technocratic dirigisme, balancing its output between affirmative films and those that reserved the right to critically question stereotypes and aporias.

In the 1970s, with the growth of both television and competing live attractions, the paying cinema audience began to decline, although mobile cinema spectatorship held up. But in 1977, the cinema audience had fallen to under 59 million. This audience was divided between the same number of films in the cinemas: ten or twelve new foreign films every month. In terms of its own productions, however, ICAIC managed to sustain the popularity that Cuban cinema achieved in its first ten years, with another five films reaching the same high ratings before the end of its second decade (Table 2). Three of these films were representative of the turn toward the popular genre movie that García Espinosa warned about at the beginning of the 1970s. The fourth, *Elpidio Valdés,* made by Juan Padrón, was ICAIC's first full-length animated cartoon, the tale of a hero of the nineteenth-century wars of liberation against Spain. This delightful picture is a highly effective demonstration that an animation factory like Disney's is not a prerequisite of producing a cartoon feature. Padrón had only a very small team to work with—three key animators and half a dozen assistants—but evolved a highly economic graphic style in a series of short cartoons over several years, pared down to the simplest elements, and in Elpidio, a character of strong popular appeal not only to children in Cuba but wherever the film was seen in Latin America.

The last of these films, *Retrato de Teresa* (Portrait of Teresa), a first feature by Pastor Vega, with Daisy Granados in the title role and a script by Ambrosio Fornet, was a piece of raw realism about the breakup of a marriage, which quickly proved to be ICAIC's most controversial movie in twenty years. Nevertheless, a number of observers expressed the feeling that Cuban cinema was in process of paying for its capacity to communicate to the detriment of its thematic and stylistic audacity. The English scholar John King would suggest there was "a deliberate shift to capture a more 'popular' audience, which in turn implies a more transparent style."[3] According to the German critic Peter Schumann, efforts directed toward the "cinematic literacy" that García Espinosa dreamed

Table 2. Top Cuban films by admission, 1972–79 (Cuba)

Film	Director	Year	Admissions (in millions)
El hombre de Maisinicú	Manuel Pérez	1973	1.9
Patty-Candela	Rogelio París	1976	1.1
El brigadista	Octavio Cortázar	1977	1.8
Elpidio Valdés	Juan Padrón	1979	1.9
Retrato de Teresa	Pastor Vega	1979	1.5

of did not bear much fruit, and rather than the pursuit of quality, ICAIC sadly preferred to follow the taste of the public, in pursuit of profitability."[4] The American Julianne Burton attributed the decline in formal experimentalism to the influence of government cultural policy in the early 1970s, with its emphasis on mass participation, youth, and ideological conformity.[5] In short, the 1970s tested ICAIC's viability in difficult economic circumstances and a changing political reality.

At the start of its second decade, the internal problems that mainly exercised ICAIC centered on questions of praxis in the change from the euphoria of the heroic years, which incorporated the guerrilla mentality of *cine militante,* to the industrial structure of production within the communist state. As García Espinosa reminded his listeners in 1974, "We don't, as intellectuals and artists, achieve proletarian consciousness simply by going along to factories and union meetings, filming the life and conditions of the workers, necessary as all these things are, unless our consciousness is subjected to the same determinants as those workers, and that means, through the experience of our own labor process."[6] This may sound like theoretical rhetoric, but the nature of the labor process and the relations of production were a subject of active discussion and even experiment within ICAIC, and ways of working were modified in response to collective discussion about the best interpretation of the socialist principles of productive relations. The abolition of capitalist relations of production, through the amalgamation into one enterprise of what are otherwise separate companies buying and selling each other's services, favored the streamlining of the production process. A particularly productive example was the creation of a special effects department that brought the processes of rostrum camera animation together with those of the optical camera that is conventionally attached to the laboratory.

This reorganization answered to economic necessity, since without it it would not have been possible to accomplish the necessary amount of work—but neither would the stylistic evolution of newsreel and documentary pioneered by Santiago Álvarez, with its integration of combined effects, have been possible otherwise.

In applying the procedures of works meetings and workers' councils (paralleled, of course, by the meetings of the Institute's party committee), ICAIC developed working methods that fostered a constant sharing of experience with real aesthetic benefits, because each production department felt supported and they consequently all worked well together. When the filmmakers went out to film this type of works meeting in other places, especially Sara Gómez in *De cierta manera* and Alea in *Hasta cierto punto,* they did so not like film crews shooting an industrial dispute in a liberal democracy, as foreigners to the scenes they were filming, but rather as participant observers in a social process that they shared with their subjects.

Another instance of streamlined practice concerns the role of music and the composer. On the one hand, with the creation of the Grupo Sonora Experimental at the end of the 1960s, and the reintegration of the composer with the performing group, ICAIC actively encouraged musical innovation. At the same time, the composer became more integrated into the editing process than happens in standard Hollywood practice, where the music for a film is not usually composed until the editing is almost complete, and a special music editor, working in the cutting room, prepares a music cue sheet for the composer with appropriate timings and visual cues. At ICAIC, there were no special music editors. Composers prepared cue sheets for themselves. But this is a great advantage from an aesthetic point of view, a blow against the segmentation of creative input. The composer who works through the film with the director and editor in the cutting room can develop a more organic approach to the music.

The same practice of debate brought directors and creative personnel together for internal screenings of films not only by ICAIC itself but also by Latin American comrades. Visiting filmmakers who participated in these screenings spoke of an intense and critical dialogue among equals.[7] According to García Espinosa, recalling the period thirty years later—when these debates no longer happened—the form they took was the sign and guarantee of ICAIC's health: the two main strands among the Institute's members, the Marxists and the libertarian, confronted each other, argued their piece, and learned to respect the other's positions. What emerged was a collective wisdom that avoided the extremes of both, and thrived on stylistic diversity.

On the screen, ICAIC succeeded in creating an identity for itself that reflected its encouragement of diversity. ICAIC as the institutional author of its films is the opposite of the commercial studios as the corporate authors of theirs. In Cuban cinemas there is neither a censorship certificate nor the announcement of the distribution company, no lions or gongs or globes. The institute has not even employed a fixed logo or trademark as producer or distributor, and signs on with "ICAIC presents" wherever the filmmaker decides to put it, and in whatever graphic form, which thus varies with every film. It presents itself, in other words, not as the entity that merchandises the film, or that classifies it, but as an author among the authors. At the same time, with the growing use of pretitle sequences, the opening scenes of a Cuban film often become a way of reasserting the primacy of the image over the signs of its authorship.

Not all the films that were made in the first decade were released. One reason is that in creating the space for the filmmakers to learn on the job, some of the films that went into production failed to run the course and were aborted. Countries with established film industries often rely on a combination of apprenticeship and film schools to develop new filmmakers, yet film industries all over the world still end up with disasters on their hands. This is no more than a consequence of the inherent risks of the medium, of the costliness of film production and the need to cut your losses when necessary. There can be no surprise if the same thing happened in ICAIC, where the urgency of the cultural needs of the Revolution made taking risks the only possible artistic policy. Accusations were made of censorship and autocracy, but in the early years it would sometimes have been both artistically and politically counterproductive to continue spending money on completing films that too clearly displayed their apprentice nature. It is not surprising if, as we've seen, some of those involved would quit ICAIC and Cuba.

Even after the departures of the 1960s it remained inevitable that conflict would sooner or later arise, if not within ICAIC itself, then between ICAIC and those fractions within the party incapable of distinguishing between art and propaganda. If this would sometimes make ICAIC cautious, then the problem intensified in the "gray years" of the 1970s, when the country turned in on itself and the party line was hardened. However, although this process suggests the "Sovietization" of the Cuban political system, it would be tendentious to describe it as Stalinism. The severity of the sanctions against the recalcitrant individual in Cuba hardly compared with the extremities of Stalin's, or even post-Stalinist rule; and in aesthetic matters, notions of socialist realism mostly remained anathema, and in ICAIC were followed only by a small minority. If there were heavy pressures toward political orthodoxy and compliance, the core of the problem was the persistence of a narrow and dogmatic paternalism within powerful sections of the ruling echelons. In the blinkered view of the party orthodox, the mass media, cinema included, were only to be seen as a means of supporting and strengthening the efficacy of social control. But from an artistic point of view, which was the position that ICAIC defended, this authoritarianism is not just mistaken but also precarious, because the medium itself has a contrary emancipatory potential—the emancipation of the imagination from all forms of mechanical, sclerotic, and sectarian thinking. ICAIC was therefore cast in the role of internal critic from the left.

In this situation, ICAIC's own antisectarianism was its strength. It welcomed independent-minded artists and intellectuals—the musicians in the Grupo Sonora Experimental, figures like the writer Jesús Díaz— and gave them the benefit of sharing a collective identity based on the combination of political engagement and artistic freedom. It was a point of principle that political engagement provided the grounds for the expressive richness of the artistic endeavor, but, as Jorge Fraga would tell a group of visitors from Britain, ICAIC was a collective with no norm to determine the way that the collective and the individuals within it were interlinked. Fraga himself began his career as a television cameraman, joined ICAIC in its founding year, began directing documentaries in 1960, and became head of production in 1978. The consensus view, he said, was that artistic creativity was a personal process within a collective one. Directors "know they have to look for ideas which will be cheap to do, and this is their responsibility, their share of the common problems." Ideas are progressed by discussion, "because when you just cut away the final results" you risk becoming a censor, "but if you work in the process from the start you're more constructive, you're part of it, trying to stimulate and seek solutions."[8]

If this is a difference that the unsympathetic observer quickly dismisses with the objection that if it isn't censorship, then it's self-censorship, it must be said that in the Cuban context, self-censorship was a volatile affair with its own special character, a game more than a regime. According to Fornet, referring to Fidel's formula of 1961, "The fact is that, in the context of a state of siege, aesthetic discourse, perhaps because of its own polysemic nature, delights in the license of this 'inside' where everything—or almost everything—is permitted." Nor are the limits ever fixed, because "the 'everything' permitted is not a permanent right but an arena of conflict that must be renegotiated every day, with no quarter granted to the bureaucracy and with the temptation of irresponsible whimsy firmly resisted."[9] In short, if some found the daily struggle too much and abandoned Cuba, there were others whose work was interrupted or held back who did not. Humberto Solás, for example, did not react this way over *Un día de noviembre,* nor did Manuel Octavio Gómez, when he was obliged to put aside the documentary he was shooting in Nuevitas, which he later incorporated into *Una mujer, un hombre, una ciudad.* On the contrary, both would find other ways of addressing the issues that concerned them. And the same is true for Sara Gómez, when she had to abandon a projected trilogy of documentaries that touched on the excesses of machismo and the persistence of racism, topics considered potentially divisive not only by the ideologically orthodox.

What these cases suggest is not a regime of inflexible orthodoxy but a space where the limits were not infrequently put to the test. For the filmmakers who did the testing, the problem was less a matter of Stalinist tendencies, real or imagined, than of the contradictions revealed in the Revolution's unfolding project of modernization, especially in the social domain, where great advances had been made but many traditional prejudices remained resistant to change. Officially, for example, machismo and racism belonged to the colonial and underdeveloped past, and the Revolution had condemned and reversed them: racism was gone forever, and as for machismo, it was on the way out. In reality, consciousness lagged behind. Women and blacks enjoyed real advances in legal rights, employment, education, and health care, yet active traces of patriarchy and prejudice persisted, obstinately contradicting the official ideology. Moreover, within ICAIC itself, black and women directors remained underrepresented (and the death of Sara Gómez deprived ICAIC of one of its three black directors of the 1970s). According to one commentator, writing at the end of the 1980s, it is ironic that of the four great Cuban films about women's emancipation, three were made by men—*Lucía* (1968), *Retrato de Teresa* (1979), and *Hasta cierto punto* (1983)—while the fourth, *De cierta manera* by Sara Gómez, was completed by men after her untimely death. This, says Jean Stubbs, reflects the state of the struggle within the film industry, where, despite substantial numbers of women working in production, the only women directors were in documentary and newsreel.[10] Despite significant exceptions, the dominant perspective on the Cuban screen thus remained masculine, even when it wasn't *machista*. At the same time, however, Cuban cinema provided a space for a small number of extraordinary actresses to create a series of strong female personae with few parallels elsewhere in Latin America (at least before the emergence of feminist directors like María Luisa Bemberg in Argentina)—in particular Idalia Anreus, Daisy Granados, and Mirta Ibarra. There is doubtless a certain significance in the fact that all three were married to the directors of the films in which they created many of their screen characters.

In racial terms, meanwhile, Cuban cinema was neither black nor white, but is better described as creole, a native category in which the Hispanic and African traits in Cuban culture are conjoined. Many members of ICAIC held to a position that disavowed any real difference between Cuban and Afro-Cuban culture, on the grounds that the former is already imbued with the latter, an attitude that goes back to the modernists of the 1920s and that finds expression not only in music, an eminently syncretistic medium in which the two influences inflect each other at every turn, but also in painters from Wilfredo Lam to Manuel Mendive. According to this view, black Cubans do not represent a distinct and separate cultural unity any more than whites; rather, authentic Cuban culture is infused with the African legacy. Moreover, the artistic imagination was also a way of transcending the color of the artist's skin. As the black director Sergio Giral attested in 1991, "One thing's been proven in Cuba, which is that not only blacks are capable of dealing with black themes, not only women can deal with the theme of women, and today the theme of gays is being dealt with by people who are not gay."[11] In this spirit, many aspects of Afro-Cuban culture readily found their way onto the screen, not only in a wealth of documentaries on cultural themes like music and dance, but also in a steady stream of feature films foregrounding the black experience, from Jorge Fraga's *La odisea de*

General José in 1968 to Sergio Giral's slave trilogy in the 1970s, with Alea's *La última cena* and *Cecilia* by Humberto Solás at the end of the decade—films made, except for Giral, by white directors, though the writers were sometimes black, as of course were the actors. The growing treatment of black thematics brought a much greater diversity of racial representation to the Cuban screen in the 1960s and 1970s than could be found at that time in European and Anglo-Saxon countries, and the emergence of black actors, like Miguel Benavides and Samuel Claxton, of great strength and dignity. On the other hand, unless the film explicitly concerned a black thematic, few principal roles were allotted to black actors, and whiteness remained the paradigm of the handsome and the beautiful, especially in the feminine domain.

It goes without saying that this is not what it feels like on the streets. Cuba is a more multiracial society than most, and in between those of pure descent, either Hispanic or African, is a large mulatto population, of mixed racial descent—from Chinese to Jewish—which creates a highly diverse range of features. This variety becomes a constant presence in Cuban cinema as the background of actuality in which the principals, not all of whom display dominant Hispanic features anyway, are generally seen. The vivid presence of this actuality in Cuban films works against the old dualistic cinematic codes, and actors like Idalia Anreus, Daysi Granados, José Rodríguez, and Luis Alberto García display a chameleon-like capacity, often aided by the cinematography, to become more black or more Hispanic in their gestures and looks according to the character's needs.

However, there was a catch in the unfolding political process. On the one hand, black people came to be widely seen, by themselves and others, as special beneficiaries of the new social order, to which they have mainly awarded unconditional loyalty. At the same time, racial prejudice was officially considered a negative legacy of the past. On the other hand, social attitudes are subject to uneven development and blackness was still identified by many people (of different ethnicities) with negative stereotypes, such as antisocial behavior and lack of family values and morality.[12] But because these were understood as vestiges of history, anyone who took a more critical view was in a potential double bind, since to foreground such problems was seen as unsettling to political consensus and unity.

This double bind was not limited to racial issues, but applied to any kind of problem that suggested social—and therefore political—weakness under siege. The ruling maxim became "hablar de nuestras contradicciones es darle armas al enemigo" (to talk of our contradictions is to offer arms to the enemy). There were certain topics, then, that by general consensus it was better not to touch on directly, for fear of provoking conflict. According to the director Juan Carlos Tabío, the artist in Cuba became subject to a debate that was both internal and external, and provided the meat for both censorship and self-censorship;[13] or, as Sergio Giral put it, "You exercise a form of self-censorship in not wanting to destroy the cake by sticking your fingers in it too much," especially if you felt a sense of political and social responsibility and wanted what you did to serve the revolutionary process.[14] The more orthodox Fraga explained the problem bluntly: "there are certain aims that in order to achieve them, the best thing to do is not make a public debate about it. There are other means."[15]

The danger in this kind of political climate, whether inside ICAIC or beyond, is that a wedge is driven between two types of language, the public and the private, political rhetoric and colloquial speech. In the latter, the former is impugned, especially through humor and irony, and dubbed with the slang term *teque*. If this linguistic split is manifest throughout civil society, it also has special consequences for artistic discourse, with its polysemic vocation, and perhaps for cinema in particular, a medium in which colloquial forms of speech are part of the fabric of the narrative, and *teque* becomes particularly alienating. But there were also filmmakers in Cuba who believed that cinema is precisely a medium where these publicly hidden topics can be brought into view. It is no accident that these directors were not much associated with the genre option, where representation becomes stylized, stereotyped, and loses its edge, but with the ideas of imperfect cinema.

However, it is not as if imperfect cinema ever became a doctrine or an orthodoxy, and ICAIC's feature output in the 1970s includes films of several different trends. Fornet has identified three fundamental tendencies.[16] The first he describes as the exploration of the limits of a quotidian dramaturgy with a strong charge of social critique; it is found in *Ustedes tienen la palabra* by Manuel Octavio Gómez (1973), and *De cierta manera* by Sara Gómez (1974); significantly, both were filmed on 16 mm to permit a more spontaneous visual style. Manuel Octavio Gómez will visit this terrain again with *Una mujer, un hombre, una ciudad* in

1977, and Pastor Vega, with his controversial *Retrato de Teresa* in 1979. Yet the truth is that this was not a strong current in Cuban fiction cinema of the 1970s, and the absence of contemporary subjects was conspicuous. It is not simply a product of the dogmatism of the five gray years that began the decade, however, since the absence of the contemporary is more marked in the second half of the 1970s. In any case, the Cuban critics Caballero and del Río maintain that ICAIC was not directly affected by the conformism of the time because films take a long time to make. (On the other hand, they also pass through three distinct stages of production—scripting, shooting, and editing—which permit major modifications to be made along the way; this entails the risks of censorship but also allows creative responses to political changes.) The question cannot therefore simply be put down to an inimical political climate, but indicates the problematic nature of contemporary reality on other, more existential levels, the difficulty in the new circumstances of finding the right kind of form for the treatment of the contemporary subject—in other words a problem as much aesthetic as political, because the two have become inseparable. Only one thing was certain: formulas don't work very well.

The second tendency is the elaboration of new forms of historical recovery, exemplified by Giral's *El otro Francisco,* and including a film by Humberto Solás from 1975, *Cantata de Chile,* as well as *Mella* by Enrique Pineda Barnet the following year. Sometimes these films retain the approach of imperfect cinema, but not always; the historical drama has a liability to pull in a different direction, toward cinema as spectacle, which Solás in particular takes up the challenge to tame in the epic *Cecilia* of 1981, a film fated, as we shall see, to provoke a crisis in ICAIC.

Furthest from imperfect cinema, the third tendency was the recourse to traditional genres, initially with the double aim of using their proven efficacy of communication and transforming them from inside (though it is questionable how far the latter was achieved). Here the first exemplars, both in 1973, are *El extraño caso de Rachel K.* by Óscar Valdés, and especially *El hombre de Maisinicú* by Manuel Pérez. Ideologically safer, with a populist aesthetic, it is which becomes the strongest tendency in the second half of the 1970s, with *Patty-Candela* by Rogelio París in 1976; Octavio Cortázar's *El brigadista* and *Río Negro* by Manuel Pérez in 1977; Enrique Pineda Barnet's *Aquella larga noche* and Manuel Herrera's *No hay sabado sin sol* in 1979—films that demonstrate a high level of competence in conventional narrative cinema (though the last two less so), but little to stretch the viewer's critical faculties.

These three tendencies are not hermetic categories, however, and several films cut across and combine them. Giral followed the deconstructionist *El otro Francisco* with conventional narrative treatments of the slavery theme in *Rancheador* and *Maluala*; Alea applies a linear narrative to the same theme but with very different effect in *La última cena,* which can hardly be considered a genre movie in the narrow sense (unless the genre is the historical allegory, which implies no particular narrative mode). All four films address the recovery of the history of slavery, offering allegories of national identity that addressed the present indirectly, by reexamining the historical legacy that perhaps more than any other was responsible for shaping both Cuban society and the Cuban character.

The most baroque piece of experimental cinema of the 1970s was undoubtedly *Cantata de Chile,* a film of impeccable revolutionary credentials and highly unconventional form, a poetic and musical tapestry (the music is by Leo Brouwer) that brings together *cine solidaridad, cine rescate,* and *cine militante.* The narrative form of the film goes back to Griffith's *Intolerance,* here interweaving four episodes in Chilean history (the Araucanian struggle against the Spanish colonizers; the nineteenth-century independence struggle; the strike of Iquique in 1907, which ended in a massacre; and the contemporary opposition to Pinochet) to become what Fornet calls a synchronic treatment of history, "the coexistence of different times in the same geographical space," and which he considers a notable innovation in the narrative structures of Cuban cinema.[17] Others took a different view, like Jorge Fraga, who found it "very militant," but also very rhetorical, adding that in Cuba it was a complete failure.[18]

Two other films fall outside the general pattern: *La tierra y el cielo* (Heaven and earth) by Manuel Octavio Gómez, dating from 1976, and Alea's *Los sobrevivientes* (The survivors) of 1978. The former, made with the Haitian community in Cuba, is the story of two young cane cutters of Haitian origin and followers of voodoo who join the rebels in the Sierra Maestra, in a plot that stages a confrontation between the human world of revolutionary struggle and the magical world of saint worship, a practice that in the Cuban form of Santería was still the subject of official disapproval. The latter is a Buñuelesque comedy of the absurd, which traces the degeneration of an upper-class Cuban family who lock themselves in their mansion when the Cuban Revolution comes to power, to sit out the bad times and preserve their class values, but who then proceed to regress from capitalism back to the condition of savagery. Neither is among the directors' strongest films.

Some commentators see the whole of the 1970s as a colorless time; for others, the gray years come to an end after the middle of the decade with the stage known as the "institutionalization" of the revolution, a political process that began with the first Communist Party congress in 1975 and the proclamation of a new one-party constitution a year later, followed before the year was out by the first elections in sixteen years. The powers of local government were now exercised by directly elected municipal assemblies; the delegates to these assemblies elected deputies to the National Assembly, which elected the members of the Council of State, whose president—Fidel Castro—was (and is) both head of state and head of government. Since delegates and deputies—generally party-approved—hold regular jobs, and the National Assembly meets only twice a year, political hegemony remained in the hands of the party apparatus. On the other hand, the new system aimed for a partial decentralization of the management of services and local activities that successfully devolved responsibility for local affairs to the level where they matter most closely, and this initially encouraged popular participation. (Direct elections to the National Assembly would be introduced fifteen years later, when the collapse of communism in Eastern Europe threatened political instability at home.) This decentralization had particular implications for the Film Institute. It meant that the management of the cinemas now came under the aegis of local government—except for a few showcase movie theaters owned by ICAIC—which rented its films from ICAIC's distribution arm.

The process of institutional reform reached the cultural sector in 1976, with the creation of the Ministry of Culture under Armando Hart, who, as minister of education at the beginning of the Revolution, had overseen the literacy campaign. Hart was a sympathetic cultural commissar, with a sympathetic view of cultural issues informed by a reading of Gramsci. Replacing the limited functions of the National Council for Culture (Consejo Nacional de Cultura), the new ministry divided the cultural infrastructure of the country into five vice ministries: music and spectacles; theater and dance; books; plastic arts and design; and film—thereby incorporating ICAIC, under the continuing direction of Alfredo Guevara, who now became a vice minister. (Meanwhile, Julio García Espinosa became vice minister for music and spectacles; the experimental film *Son o no son,* which he shot in 1978, was a direct result of this involvement.) Absent from the cultural domain, however, were radio and television, which, like the press, answered to the central committee through supervision by the party's ideological office. The result was a split between cinema and television with both cultural and ideological consequences. Fraga told his British visitors, "We don't have a relationship with [television] . . . in our opinion they have a very rigid mentality with a very popularistic approach to things and a tendency to standardise."[19] In theory, intercourse between the two domains was not impossible, but in practice there was little movement between them, by either directors and technicians or even actors; the separation underlined the tight control exercised over broadcasting as against the respect accorded to artistic values in the cinema. The problem would only become problematic for ICAIC at the beginning of the 1990s, when a merger was threatened. But if the members of ICAIC tended to enjoy the sense of privilege and distinction that this division sustained, then given their well-developed senses of irony and conscientiousness, neither did they refrain—following Alea's lead in *Hasta cierto punto* of 1983—from satirizing themselves for it.

If ICAIC suffered a symbolic loss of autonomy when it was brought under the culture ministry, the new arrangements had no immediate effect on the types of films that were made. In literary and intellectual spheres, on the other hand, the new climate brought welcome relief, as—according to one account—the "unspoken blacklisting of certain authors was dropped and publications began to open up to more controversial figures and writing."[20] There were other implications for ICAIC, however, that began to work themselves out behind the scenes. In the economic reforms that accompanied the institutionalization process, which aimed at linking wage increases to increased productivity, the Revolution was staging a partial retreat from the idealistic voluntarism associated with Che Guevara, in the hope that this would succeed in improving the efficiency and profitability of economic enterprise. ICAIC, of course, suffered many of the same problems that could be found in other sectors of production—limited financial and technical resources, a demand that exceeded production capacities—as well as problems

like a lack of wherewithal to develop new talent to which artistic enterprises are specially prone. The new salary system bought in at the end of
the 1970s, in accordance with national policy, and after due internal discussion, lumbered it with unnecessary complications: ICAIC had never
measured success by profitability. The new system required that wages
be adjusted by means of bonuses, linked to the productivity of the
enterprise and differentiated according to sector. ICAIC introduced incentives aimed to encourage directors and crews to get films made within
the time and budget allotted to them, with bonuses awarded by a committee of peers for high-quality results. The theory was that people were
rewarded for making films more quickly, more cheaply, and more efficiently, but without penalizing artistic quality. It was an awkward balancing act.

At the same time, in line with a general trend throughout the economy, the organization of the Institute grew progressively more complex.
Before 1975, it was run by a central committee directly overseeing four
departments (studios and labor; technical processes; finances; and artistic programming, which included production). By the early 1980s, it
had been reorganized into three enterprises, each comprising a number
of departments. The core of ICAIC was devoted to production and production services. A separate office was devoted to exhibition and associated activities (difusión), divided into the Cinemateca and first-run
theaters; the national distribution operation; international operations;
and a press and information center. A third section consisted in provincial service units for maintaining the cinemas up and down the country.[21] With astute programming and a small number of highly successful
films of its own, and leaving aside the necessary dollar expenditure on
film stock and the like, ICAIC managed to keep its head above water,
with average annual profits of around half a million pesos—a modest
but significant figure. On the other hand, it suffered a problematic imbalance. While the feature movie continued to be regarded as the paradigm of cinema and the pinnacle of the director's art, fiction production remained low. According to figures given by Fornet for the first
thirty years, average annual production during the 1970s amounted to 35
documentaries (including some feature-length), 52 newsreels, 7 animated cartoons, and only 3 features—the same as in the 1960s. Jorge
Fraga gave similar figures to the British visitors in 1983: "this year we
made 43 short documentaries, which for a country like us is OK. The

aim is do one a week, and more are not needed unless they are for TV or some other use, but for the cinema circuit, 52...is the maximum. But we want to do not less than one feature a month, and if we could, and if there were the demand, we would do one a week."[22] This, of course, was a pipe dream, a level of productivity quite beyond their means in an economic situation in which ICAIC could barely afford to strike enough prints for national distribution. The intention was for all new Cuban films to be shown for two weeks on the main circuit in Havana and the provinces, but there are fourteen of these in the country, and ICAIC could afford no more than six or eight prints, so country-wide release was staggered. In 1975, when Julio García Espinosa criticized the "aristocratic attitude" of those who disparaged commercial cinema and spoke of the need for a more quotidian form of dramaturgy that connected more strongly with popular experience, he was also thinking, says Fornet, of how to increase productivity.[23]

The year 1979 saw five feature films released. Manuel Herrera (who made the remarkable *Girón*) attempted a contemporary social comedy with *No hay sábado sin sol* (No Saturday without sun), the story of a young woman community worker faced with intransigence among peasant families who are supposed to be moving to new housing in the nearby town. For *Aquella larga noche* (That long night), Enrique Pineda Barnet returned to the 1950s, with a story of two women in the urban underground who were caught and tortured. Ironically, it suffers from the problem of evoking the films of revolutionary heroism of the early 1960s while not being a genre movie in the mold of *Patty-Candela* or *Río Negro*. Rather different was *Prisioneros desaparecidos* (Disappeared prisoners), a drama of solidarity with the victims of Pinochet's Chile, and directed by the exiled Chilean director Sergio Castilla, of special interest as one of the first of a wave of coproductions that ICAIC undertook during the 1980s with a range of Latin American directors (and with coproducers in both Latin America and Europe).

The two films that topped the box office in 1979 appealed to different audiences. Where *Elpidio Valdés* was a children's animation film, *Retrato de Teresa* (Portrait of Teresa) was made for their parents. A film about the breakdown of a marriage, it triggered huge public response, which was taken up across the mass media throughout the country. According to Julianne Burton, there were "weeks of heated debate in newspapers

and magazines, on radio, television and streetcorners." Half the adult
population of Havana, where the film was set, had seen the movie within
the first six weeks of its release, "and, apparently, few viewers declined
to take sides in the confrontation between 'sacred' family tradition and
women's need for self-realization."[24] Teresa, played with extraordinary
conviction by Daisy Granados, struggles against the intransigence of
her *machista* husband. A television repairman with a roving eye, Ramón
is played by Adolfo Llauradó, repeating the role of the uncomprehend-
ing husband in the third part of *Lucía*, to which *Teresa*, as Burton remarks, can thus be read as a sequel, a further stage in the struggle of the
Cuban woman to acquire autonomy. Teresa leads not a double but a
triple life: housewife and mother of three young children, with a day
job in a textile factory, she is also union cultural secretary and the main
mover behind the factory's amateur dance group—it is the time this
takes up that is the initial bone of marital contention. When the group is
selected for a national competition, the pressures mount, Ramón threatens
to leave, and she ends up throwing him out. As the filmmaker Mayra
Vilasís recalled, "The polemic embraced the broadest sectors of society.
The equalities of the Cuban woman became a theme of public discussion, outside the home. Teresa, as a worker, found a very important
interlocutor, a fundamental element of our society, the working-class
woman. From one day to the next, Teresa became the *image* of the Cuban
woman, typifying her conflicts."[25]

If Cuban audiences were shocked to see Teresa physically fighting off
Ramón, and if many of them cheered her on when she called him to account, their response was nourished by the film's representational quality, the stylistic objectivity of its new wave neorealism, and what the
German critic Peter Schumann aptly calls "the precision with which it
describes the typical situation of the Cuban woman."[26] Pastor Vega spoke
in an interview of his admiration for both Robert Flaherty's and the
Italian neorealists' ability to reveal drama in the simple observation of
daily life, in the spirit of which he sets up a linear narrative, filmed with
a controlled camera, free of subjective shots and cinematic tricks.[27] The
narrative moves back and forth between Teresa's life and Ramón's,
counterposing the wide range of social spaces through which they variously move—the Havana outdoors of the film's opening, the factory, the
home, the rehearsal hall, the TV repair workshop, the homes Ramón
visits on the job, streets, bars, and restaurants—to become, in Burton's

phrase, "a dynamic assembly of scenes and events in which the nominal subject is not always present, or, if present, is not always the primary focus."[28] Everywhere the film is full of detailed social observation. Not least, it offers almost casually, as Burton puts it, "a very studied cross section of kinds and classes of Cuban housing and family structure: the modest but cheerful bungalows of Teresa and Ramón's neighborhood, the modern high rise apartment blocks of Alamar, the elegant colonial patio of Teresa's mother's house, the decrepit shack of an inhospitable black man, the plush appointments and generous proportions of the nineteenth-century mansion where Ramón's girlfriend lives with her parents." An idea of the nuclear family prevails, but various versions of the extended family are also in evidence. And when Teresa throws Ramón out, he moves back in with his mother.

The film's rootedness in the immediate social reality is all the more gritty for the direct sound track and the eschewal of background music, except for a couple of highly romanticized scenes—above all, the family outing to the park, which paints an idyllic portrait of the family life that is threatened by parental disaccord. But these moments so imbue the film that, according to Burton, *Retrato de Teresa* not only leaves behind the kind of experiments in deconstruction of cinematic form that prevailed in Cuban cinema until the mid-1970s, but also evokes "the allure of the 'perfect cinema' of Hollywood-style production values and sunset-bathed television commercials."[29] What is true is that the camera has abandoned the agitated and nervous visual style, and the editing has relinquished the jerky, fast, almost syncopated cutting that characterized the effervescent cinema of the late 1960s. In this sense, Burton is perhaps correct when she calls *Retrato de Teresa* a turning point in Cuban cinema, a film that exemplified "the generic and stylistic shifts that would characterize Cuban filmmaking in the subsequent decade," although there is inevitably a certain degree of generalization in such a judgment.[30]

In the daytime scenes, Livio Delgado's light and airy cinematography is full of bright sun and pastel colors. Much of the film is shot in long takes, with the camera on a tripod and subtle use of the zoom; the dance rehearsals are filmed with a handheld camera, but far more controlled than is common practice in Cuban documentary of the same period. With equal propriety, the camera captures Teresa's early-morning routine—naturally, she is the first to get up—as she prepares her children's milk in the still-dark kitchen, wakes her husband, gets the children dressed, and makes breakfast, in a stark sequence that seems to echo the work of feminist filmmakers like Chantal Akerman (though Burton herself mentions Robert Benton's *Kramer vs. Kramer* of the same year) in which, unalleviated by subjectivizing close-ups, "the long takes and stationary camera placement accentuate the tedium of her kitchen tasks."[31] The cool, observational documentary quality of the camera is maintained when the couple come to blows, the camera retaining its distance, allowing us always to see them both fully in frame, and who is doing what to whom. Again, as Burton sums up, "The film's 'objectivity' and even realism of tone are never violated in the interest of communicating a more subjective kind of experience. . . . It is not that the heroine is elusive but that the filmmaker, in keeping with his quest for a documentary-style vision, chooses an unmitigatedly externalized mode of portrayal, preferring to expend more energy on social interaction than on inner being."[32]

Vega described the film's intentions in good ideological terms: "The enemy of Teresa and Ramón is the assembly of traditions engendered by the family structure of the bourgeoisie and the petite bourgeoisie which still survives in the depths of consciousness and which holds back the emergence and development of emotions and feelings of greater depth, richness, and value. Teresa struggles to stop being a wife and become a *compañera*." In this context, however, the film targets television as a site of false ideological reassurance, counterposing the real lifeworld with that of the TV set—which is symbolized in its offer of "schlocky" and inauthentic popular music (home-grown or imported) in place of the Afro-Cuban rhythms of Teresa's dance group. Not for nothing have the filmmakers given Ramón the job of a TV repairman, and not just because (as Burton points out) his work gives him entrée to people's homes, thus allowing the viewer significant glimpses of other domestic arrangements. The film sets television up as a source of distraction, fantasy, and the projection of a mendacious image of society. Early in the film (as Burton mentions), Teresa arrives home from a late rehearsal to find two women neighbors watching a melodrama on the TV, while Ramón sulks in the bedroom. In a later scene, Ramón, waiting for payment, is forced to watch with a mesmerized customer while an actress in early-nineteenth-century frills gushes over her erring lover's sagacity in winning her forgiveness by offering her a rose, a gesture Ramón will later repeat only to discover that what works on television fails to do so in real life.

Ramón is good at his job—just as he's a good father—but in what is possibly the most arresting moment in the film, the image he fixes so well takes its revenge, and television betrays him. On the night Teresa's dance group wins the competition and she and the group's choreographer Tomás are interviewed on television, Ramón is found playing dominoes at the neighborhood guard post. The TV set is malfunctioning and he gets asked to fix it just as the unctuous interviewer (played by the vintage Cuban TV presenter Germán Pinelli) turns to Teresa uttering *piropos* and joking about what a fine couple she and Tomás would make. For the first time in the film, Ramón watches the television he fixes, as the presenter offers his wife an orchid and a kiss on the hand, asks Teresa her husband's name, and turns to camera to pronounce "Ramón, con permiso" (With your permission, Ramón). If Ramón, as he silently turns away, is deflated, the viewer's sympathy for him is ambivalent and double-edged, thrown into relief by the disclosure of TV's own falsity of substance and tone.

Burton ends up feeling that the film strikes a potentially subversive chord against the dominant ideology of Cuban sexual politics, but remains within the problematic of *la pareja*, the (heterosexual) couple. She finds a telling disparity in the film's treatment of its protagonist and her husband, for it presents more details of Ramón's life than of Teresa's. In particular, we witness the inception, development, and decline of his extramarital affair, whereas Teresa's possible intimacy with Tomás remains an enigma. For Burton this is evidence of a certain ideological limitation in the film's attitude toward its subject, an ellipsis that replicates the social attitude the film purportedly criticizes, "that extra-marital sexual intimacy is tolerable, even encouraged, for men but inconceivable for women."[33] The issue is not academic since the denouement of the film hangs on the question. In Burton's own account,

> In their culminating exchange, which begins in a cafeteria and ends, pointedly, in front of a bridal shop, Teresa claims the right to be as unforgiving of his infidelity as he would be of hers. She has to ask three times what he would do if the tables were turned; from his obtuse point of view, she seems to be positing the inconceivable. Echoing the dual morality espoused earlier by Teresa's cousin, her mother, and his own,

Ramón insists, "It's not the same." Teresa repeats his phrase, transforming it into a question, before turning on her heel and walking out of the
cafeteria. Increasingly alarmed as the import of her suggestion begins
to dawn on him, Ramón chases her down the street and, in front of
mannequins in wedding gowns, demands, "Tell me the truth! What have
you done, Teresa?" In one final repetition, she reminds him firmly before
she disappears into the crowd, "Remember, it's not the same."

However, the ambiguity of this denouement brilliantly and deliberately
plays on the susceptibilities of the audience. As Vega explained, "If we'd
made it definite that she'd had an affair, Cuban viewers would simply
have said that she deserved what she got. . . . And we wanted people to
hear *all* of what Teresa says, not just what she says about sex."[34] It certainly
seems, from the film's success, that it was the right aesthetic calculation
to make.

The competition in *Retrato de Teresa* that is won by Teresa's group has
the purpose of finding a troupe of *aficionados* to perform at the World
Youth Festival, which was held in Cuba in 1978. It was partly the experience that ICAIC gained in organizing screenings as part of the Youth
Festival that decided it to launch an annual film festival of its own, and
Pastor Vega, on completing *Retrato de Teresa,* took up a new job as its
first director. The International Festival of the New Latin American Cinema, first held in December 1979, rapidly became the principal event of
the Latin American film calendar, drawing to Havana every December
the crop of the continent's directors, producers, critics, young tyros,
and aspirants. Since the trip was for many of them not an easy one, due
to Cuba's continuing isolation, their presence was a gesture of political as
well as cultural acknowledgment toward Cuba, which was fully in keeping with the politics of the film movement to which they all belonged.
With symbolic aplomb, the first Havana festival opened with the first
showing of the first newsreel by the new Nicaraguan Film Institute, the
creation of the Sandinista revolution six months earlier, which came
out of the laboratories in Havana only a few days before the festival.
Those in Latin America who didn't wish to display this kind of commitment to radical politics and a radical cinema didn't go to Havana,
which kept away the commercial operators in the big film industries of
Mexico, Brazil, and Argentina, even when the success of the festival began to draw contingents of prominent Hollywood names like Francis

Ford Coppola, Harry Belafonte, Jack Lemmon, and Robert De Niro—but then coming to Havana was a political statement for them too, which identified them as left liberals and suggested that not everybody in Hollywood supported Washington's blockade of the island.

The Havana Film Festival exemplified from the start the wider significance of cinema in sustaining the Cuban public sphere. As *Retrato de Teresa* fully confirmed, film in Cuba was a powerful medium capable of stimulating public debate around important issues, through which people were drawn into dialogue and spoke to the political leaders. This was a reflection not only of the film's immense popularity but also of ICAIC's role in focusing public attention. The Film Institute served as a model of a Gramscian kind for the organic integration of the intellectual into public creative endeavor, both socially useful and aesthetically legitimate, and attracted practically the whole artistic and intellectual community like moths to light (while television repelled them). The film festival turned this position to account first of all simply by taking place. A rupture in Cuba's isolation, bringing old friends and new to Havana on a regular basis, and sending out powerful signals of life, it represented a public opening up toward the outside world that served as an example beyond the sphere of cinema itself.

In the process, if the Havana festival gave the term *nuevo cine latinoamericano* official status, the festival brought Cuban cinema back into the fold where it belonged. From this perspective, its antecedents go back to the first meetings of Latin American filmmakers organized by a film club in Viña del Mar in Chile in 1967 and 1969. According to Vega, "since there were already strong and coherent signs of activity in Argentina, in Bolivia, in Brazil, in Cuba and other places, which were not connected, didn't know each other, hadn't seen each other's films, didn't know each other's theoretical positions or what they were investigating, when they met in Viña, it all took off." There were similar meetings in Venezuela, in Mérida at the University of the Andes, in 1968, Caracas in 1974, Mérida again in 1977, when the Committee of Latin American Film Makers was set up—small meetings which kept the coherence and communication of the movement alive, "but a festival was needed, a structure to allow people to meet, to see each other's works, reflect, discuss."[35]

Indeed, it was overdue. By the late 1970s, the disparate efforts of filmmakers in different countries amounted to a diverse movement with an impressive record and its own polemics and positions. Critical maga-

zines had appeared in several countries in which the filmmakers themselves were the leading contributors to a debate about the values and
uses of the film medium in which the political imperative was central.
Some of the earliest initiatives occurred in out-of-the-way places like
Cuzco in Peru, where a film club was set up in 1955 and Manuel Chambi
and others started making short documentaries on ethnographic and
sociocultural themes—the French film historian Sadoul called them the
Cuzco School; they were not unique. The 1950s saw the spread of film
societies throughout the continent, the proliferation of filmmaking
courses and contests, and the publication of magazines. It was in the
pages of such publications as *Hablemos de cine* in Peru and *Cine al día* in
Venezuela that the movement debated its values and sense of identity.

"Our cinema," said the Committee of Latin American Film Makers
in 1977, "is clandestine or semi-clandestine when circumstances and
repression require it to be. Our cinema is alternative to the cinemas
controlled by the transnationals and their local agents when its political
content or the particular conditions of a country demand it."[36] Theoretical grounding for this location was provided eight years earlier by
the Argentinian filmmakers Fernando Solanas and Octavio Getino, in a
manifesto titled *Towards a Third Cinema.* Just as García Espinosa in Cuba
had based his call for an imperfect cinema on his experience making
films, Solanas and Getino took their analysis from the experience of
making a mammoth three-part political documentary titled *La hora de
los hornos (The Hour of the Furnaces).* The title is a phrase from Martí
quoted by Che Guevara in the famous speech where he called for more
Vietnams: "It is the hour of the furnaces, all that need be seen is their
light."[37] Constrained by the conditions of military rule after the coup of
1966, but bolstered by the growth of organized resistance, the film was
shot clandestinely in conjunction with cadres of the Peronist movement. As one account puts it, it was made "in the interstices of the system
and against the system . . . independent in production, militant in politics, and experimental in language."[38]

Third cinema was thus conceived as a cinema of liberation "whose
moving force is to be found in the Third World countries" (though not
exclusively so—the films of the student movements in Paris, London,
and North America, they said, were also examples of third cinema).[39]
It is a defining moment within the cultural domain of the emergence
of a new global geography, a postcolonial imperative that began at the

Bandung Conference of 1955, the founding conference of the Non-Aligned Movement, where China promulgated the theory of the three worlds, a historical process that is the political converse of the economic globalization of multinational capitalism. First and second cinema correspond, however, not to the first and second worlds (the capitalist countries of the Western bloc, the socialist bloc led by the Soviet Union), but constitute a virtual geography of their own. First cinema is the model imposed by the American film industry, the Hollywood movie, wherever it is found—Los Angeles, Mexico City, or Bombay; second cinema Solanas and Getino identify with auteur cinema, which in turn is not just a European phenomenon, but is also found in places like Buenos Aires. Second cinema is politically reformist but incapable of achieving any profound change. It is especially impotent in the face of the kind of repression unleashed by neofascist forces like the Latin American military. The only alternative, they said, is a third cinema, films the system cannot assimilate, which "directly and explicitly set out to fight the system."[40] In this context, of course, Cuba represented a special case—the only Latin American country where third cinema was not an oppositional principle but the order of the day. But then it was also the only filmically free territory in Latin America, where cinema was not dominated and controlled by the Hollywood majors and their lackeys.

Brazilian Cinema Novo and a new generation of directors emerging in Mexico both questioned the formulas of the established industries in those countries, while the new cinema also took root in several others where state support for the first time created conditions for limited levels of production, like Venezuela. Chile, at the beginning of the 1970s, was another critical site for the new film movement, where militant filmmakers operated in parallel within the system and at its edges. Here, filmmakers came together during the 1960s to support the coalition of left-wing parties known as Popular Unity. The years leading up to the electoral victory of Salvador Allende in 1970 saw a new wave in both fiction and documentary. The film essays of the experimentalists of the 1950s turned into a cinema of urgency, which combined political campaign films with innovation in filmic technique and language to denounce the marginalism inherent in underdevelopment. The same spirit fed a crop of features that appeared in the late 1960s such as *Tres tristes tigres* by Raúl Ruiz, *Valparaíso mi amor* by Aldo Francia (the moving spirit behind the festival in Viña del Mar in 1967), and Miguel Littin's *El chacal de Nahueltoro.*

The attempts of a hard-strapped socialist government to place this activity on a more secure footing were cut short by the military coup of 1973. The most extraordinary film to emerge from the latter part of this period is probably Patricio Guzmán's three-part documentary *La batalla de Chile (The Battle of Chile),* a record of the months leading up to the coup. A fertile mixture of direct cinema observation and investigative reportage, the footage was smuggled out immediately after Allende's fall and eventually edited in Cuba at ICAIC. The result is a poignant work of historical testimony almost unique in the annals of cinema. Cuban cinema also gained the presence, among others, of the actor Nelson Villagra and the film editor Pedro Chaskel. The Chileans, supported by a strong international solidarity movement, became the leading practitioners of a cinema of exile that grew up in the 1970s on the margins and in the interstices of the world film industry (according to one count, they made 176 films in the ten years 1973–83, fifty-six of them features), which contributed a new genre to the history of world cinema as directors like Ruiz took the experience of exile as their subject matter, turning out a series of remarkable expositions of the struggle to understand the exile's misplaced identity. In 1982, Miguel Littin, director of *El chacal de Nahueltoro* and head of Chile Films under Allende, would contribute a coproduction between Cuba, Nicaragua, Mexico, and Costa Rica, *Alsino y el cóndor,* the first feature film to be shot in Nicaragua.

Imperfect cinema, third cinema—these are not the same as *nuevo cine latinoamericano* taken as a whole, but specific instances and national variants of the political vanguard of a broad movement. Indeed, the diversity of independent Latin American cinema was growing. Jorge Sanjinés in Bolivia took the road of indigenist cinema, while in Venezuela, Román Chalbaud evolved new politically edged forms of old Latin American genres. They and others achieved top box-office ratings in their own countries, outgrossing all but the biggest Hollywood hits, and sometimes even those. Only U.S. monopolization of international distribution prevented their reaching a wider international audience. Nevertheless, by the time ICAIC launched the Havana Film Festival in 1979, it seemed at last as if a critical, national, popular cinema was more than a dream in several countries.

From this perspective, if Havana became the projection of a cultural geography in the very process of inventing itself, at the same time it also had a very practical dimension, which answered to the problems ICAIC had to face as a distributor, both at home and abroad. In the early 1980s, Cuban films, the big successes included, were only 3 percent of national screenings. ICAIC brought in 140 foreign films a year. Some 35 percent came from the countries of Eastern Europe. In Western Europe, ICAIC faced difficulties, because, as Fraga explained, many European producers, being indirectly controlled by American companies, refrained from selling to it. "Sometimes we have to wait for up to five years until the rights come back to the producer and then we can buy them. The other problem is that sometimes it takes two years to buy a film, because no one is interested in selling for a thousand dollars; it takes time to persuade people to sell for this price." These were supplemented by a smattering of films from countries like Japan, and ten or twelve new American films each year, which were always popular, and slipped in already subtitled through means no one would ever disclose, rumored to be a back door in Spain.[41] The biggest problem was how to widen access to worthwhile Spanish-language films from Latin America. An agreement with Mexico (the only Latin American country never to break off relations with Cuba) allowed one Cuban film into Mexico for every three Mexican films shown in Cuba; even then, the Cuban films shown in Mexico only got small-scale distribution. The Havana Film Festival was therefore conceived as an offensive, which combined competition screenings, press conferences, seminars, and musical performances by the leading bands of the day, with an international distributors' market, though only of modest proportions. This, over the years, would continue to be the most difficult part of the festival's work.

The first Havana Film Festival confirmed the aesthetic diversity that tempered the unified politics of the gathering. The top fiction prize was shared by the Brazilian director Geraldo Sarno, for *Coronel Delmiro Gouveía*, and the Cuban Sergio Giral, for *Maluala*. Both films are historical reconstructions, the former a sober and closely observed study of an episode of the early years of the century in which an enlightened businessman gets in the way of the local oligarchy and ends up assassinated. The latter, by contrast, adopts a lyrical approach to enter the rather less well documented historical territory of escaped slaves and the *palenque,* opting for the slow-motioning of brutal and bloody violence in what some might think the inappropriate style of Sam Peckinpah. Meanwhile, the top documentary prize went to Guzmán's *Batalla de Chile*, edging out the Mexican Paul Leduc's *ABC del etnocidio: Notas sobre Mesquital*, and the Colombian Ciro Durán's *Gamin*, both of them also extraordinary films in a vintage year for Latin American documentary. The film by Leduc, an A to Z of indictments against the modernizing state, confirmed its director as the foremost experimental filmmaker in Mexico, while *Gamin* explores the world of the Bogotá street urchin in a provocative and interventionist version of direct cinema in which the filmmaker does not shrink back from filming the children apparently committing street robberies, although shooting was by arrangement with the police.[42]

As for Cuban cinema, from now on it would be judged in the direct and often highly challenging light of films coming from all over Latin America, and ICAIC won no fiction prize for the next two years, only regaining the top prize at the fifth festival in 1983 with Tomás Gutiérrez Alea's *Hasta cierto punto*. The Cuban documentary, meanwhile, not only held its own, but brought forward new talents, as a new generation of filmmakers, who made their first short documentaries in the mid-1970s, acquired full command of their talents. Paradoxically, the most politicized screen space in the whole of Latin America encouraged an art of documentary that sometimes took an apolitical, and frequently humorous, form. It was, said some, a sign of maturity in the film culture succored by the Institute that young directors should treat the cinema as a poetic medium that encouraged the expression of the director's personal vision. To consider a small but characteristic selection, the results can be seen in films like *Madera* (Wood, 1980) by Daniel Díaz Torres, a highly lyrical and brilliantly edited ten-minute study of an important natural resource and its uses, imbued with a gentle sense of humor and emphasizing the human values of the craftworker's care for the product. Humor was even more in evidence in Fernando Pérez's *4000 niños* (4,000 children, 1980), which—again without commentary—portrays four months of preparations for a huge gymnastic display on International Children's Day. Any description of this film, with its shots of wet patches left on the floor by impatient four-year-olds, can only make it sound twee; the trick is in its accomplished execution. But humor was also turned on social issues such as machismo. A ten-minute film in 1978 by Luis

Felipe Bernaza, *El piropo,* took a well-aimed swipe at the common habit of Cuban men of throwing "compliments" at women on the street—here the women answer back. In 1981, Rolando Díaz came up with a brilliant musical satire called *Controversia* (Controversy, 1981), again a mere ten minutes, whose title refers to both subject and form—a *controversia* being a traditional type of Cuban song in which two singers improvise an argument, which here becomes a comic dialogue between a male and a female singer about the battle of the sexes, appropriately set in the countryside among peasants on a collective farm. Bernaza meanwhile pursued another of the characteristic thematic spaces of documentary art for which the maturity of Cuban cinema provided more room than in its earlier, more urgent days, that of oral history. *Cayita: Leyenda y Gesta (Cayita: The Legend and the Face,* 1980) is an exemplary thirty-minute testimonial by the ninety-six-year-old teacher Cayita Araújo, who devoted her life to the popular struggle, and here touchingly recounts various anecdotes of the island's history from Martí to Castro.

The start of the 1980s saw a hike in the level of documentary production, from 35 in 1979, to 56 in 1980, and 50 in 1981, falling back to 41 in 1982, but still covering a wide thematic range. While subject to a certain political caution, these films generally showed a form of stylization that responded to the restrictions of filming on 35 mm for cinema release, and with the very low shooting ratios that were all that ICAIC could afford. As a result, most directors generally steered clear of the more investigative modes of documentary that elsewhere had developed apace during the 1970s, usually shooting for television on 16 mm with direct sound, while the newsreel, where investigation was high on the agenda, was limited in scope by its one-reel length, and a mode of address that allowed a degree of artistic license but under the jurisdiction of a suitable commentary. The documentarist Melchor Casals, who entered ICAIC in the mid-1960s and began directing in 1972, took a different approach in *Historia de una descarga* (Story of an unloading, 1981, with a commentary by Ambrosio Fornet), a thirty-minute reportage on inefficiency in the port of Cienfuegos that would not have been out of place in a current-affairs slot on television in Britain or the United States, but that is unusual to find in the cinema, probably anywhere. In a surprisingly frank interview for the time, Casals described the forms of self-censorship that came to operate in the Cuban documentary.[43] Shooting a series of films on the sugar industry in the province of Las Tunas, delighted by the access he had obtained to a remote part of the island, he got to the end of the third in the series and realized that "because I had been backed by the Party and the provincial officials, I was filming in a way that was not objective and true to reality," so he changed his approach for the fourth in the series. *Cumplimiento* (Fulfillment) criticized a factory that fulfilled its production quotas only by working straight through the rainy season, thus using up more fuel, producing more breakdowns in equipment, and failing to turn out the best-quality sugar. The people criticized in the film were unhappy, but it met with the approval of the Sugar Ministry, which asked for it to be shown at sugar mills across the country; it also taught Casals how to maneuver politically. "I knew people in the newsreel division who had been making films that were critical of certain enterprises, such as factories, and they couldn't get those films shown because the officials of these places would prevent it. I don't know what right these people had to prohibit the films' being shown, but they did." When a speech by a member of the politburo gave him the idea for a film about problems in the ports, he knew that in order to shoot what was happening he needed high-level support, and obtained it from a member of the party secretariat before starting. The film tracks a mysterious shipment of paper pulp that no one seems to want or need—it has arrived at the wrong port, there isn't the right equipment to unload it, a forklift truck is produced but it's too big to enter the door of the warehouse, the cargo will have to be left in the open exposed to the elements—to become an ironic and comic exposé of bureaucratic bungling and indifference. In offering a concrete representation of an instance of what official discourse usually describes as "domestic problems," by giving it a local habitation and a name— and doing so without falling back on rhetoric to make its point—this is a film that does more than simply bring a problem to public attention; here the mode of reportage creates a space in which the viewer ceases to be the passive recipient of ideological exhortation, but is invited by this tale of woe to consider their own relation to the structures of authority implicated in these events.

A comparable effect can be found in each of two feature-length documentaries, by the writer Jesús Díaz, *55 hermanos* (55 brothers and sisters) in 1978, and two years later, *En tierra de Sandino* (In the land of Sandino), both shot on 16 mm using the techniques of direct cinema, and with the same cameraman, Adriano Moreno. The first of these follows a brigade of sons and daughters of Cuban exiles returning to their country for the first time, on a highly charged three-week trip that ends with a meeting between the brigade and Fidel. A film originally intended as a twenty-minute reportage, it grew to feature length because the situation created its own demands and determined its own scope, and ICAIC was organized in a way that was capable of recognizing and responding when this happened. According to Díaz, the film constituted a process of mutual discovery by the filmmakers, on the one hand, and the members of the brigade, on the other. The *brigadistas,* said Díaz, had "a great need—they even say so in the film—to be recognized as Cubans. Well, then, how to be recognized if not firstly by communicating? They had a restless need to speak about Cuba, economics, politics, history, literature, cinema, and we were converted—like everyone else they came in touch with—into their interlocutors, and this produced a sense of communication, a friendship, a real brother-and-sisterliness." A film made under these conditions is obviously going to be exceptional, and it shows. It conveys a sense of energy that, as Díaz says, takes it beyond just a certain way of working, a certain skill, or a certain kind of manipulation.[44]

En tierra de Sandino applied the lessons learned to the complexities of the Sandinista revolution in Nicaragua, by going in search of what Díaz called "situations": events, or better, processes, that occur in front of the camera but create their own dynamic, developing and unfolding in unforeseeable ways. According to Diáz's own account, they arrived fourteen days after the fall of Somoza and immediately started shooting what was going on in the streets, the rejoicing, the speeches, the dancing. "After fifteen days I realized that if I continued to work in this way I would make a pretty film, and that was not what I wanted to do. Actually, I was more sure of the film I didn't want to make."[45] For almost the next four weeks, he went around everywhere he could looking for incidents and "clashes" to film, but inevitably got there too late, or the camera upset the participants. He finally struck lucky when he heard about a coffee plantation where the owner was refusing to pay his workers. The first day they arrived, the owner wasn't there; posing as a crew from a television station in Panama, they filmed an interview with the foreman and started trying to get the confidence of the workers, to whom they admitted that they were Cubans, hoping that there wasn't an informer among them. When the owner came back the next day, both he and his wife turned out to be far from camera shy, with extraordinary results. The end result is a film made up of just three sections, each of which consists of a "situation" of a different kind; this is not a three-act structure but a triangulation of the Nicaraguan revolution itself. Each section is a more or less self-contained narrative unit not unlike the movements of a symphony or sonata, which presents its own themes, textures, and rhythms, but related to the others through an underlying structural logic. The film's jubilant opening movement portrays a religious fiesta in the town of Masaya, lasting from morning to night, which takes on a political dimension with the flag of the Sandinista National Liberation Front sharing the honors with the banner of the town's patron saint. The last, the most reflective, is a record of the experience of a Cuban woman teacher in a countryside village. Between them, the most extended and extraordinary are the events at the coffee plantation, a "situation" with an internal dynamic that gives it the feeling of having been scripted, though it clearly wasn't, in which the camera was evidently the catalyst, but did little except film as judiciously as possible what began to unfold. "It is only under special conditions," says Díaz, "that an owner will talk to his workers and the workers will make demands for the first time in their lives. It is an extraordinary moment in history. In being able to film such a situation, it is rare that the people who are filming will have the confidence of both sides. It is also a strange moment because . . . which side will defeat the other has not yet been decided."[46] What emerges, as the workers grow in self-confidence and articulacy, and the foreman, the owner, and his wife become more ruffled and finally cornered, is a head-on collision in which, with the authority of the revolution behind them and the camera as their witness, the underprivileged become aware for the first time of their own strength.

In 1980, Octavio Cortázar, the director of the highly successful *El brigadista* of 1977, came out with *Guardafronteras* (Border guards), a revolutionary genre movie set in 1963, in which a squadron of young soldiers is sent to defend a cay off the coast of Las Villas, at the northern tip of the island. The scriptwriter, Luis Rogelio Nogueras, admitted that the intention of this immensely popular film—which outstripped *El brigadista* at the box office—was perfectly straightforward: "to contribute to the patriotic-military education of the youth."[47] The critic Carlos Galiano, who considers the script too predictable, attributed its success as a youth movie to various factors: a lot of action and a simple linear narrative, delivered by cinematography that pleasingly exploits the natural scenery of the location, and above all a young cast combining familiar faces from *El brigadista* with others who owed their popularity to the television program *Para bailar*.[48] This, he thought, made it not just a youth movie but a film belonging to the youth, but that is the kindest thing he says about it. It was certainly not the type of thing that foreign visitors to the Havana Film Festival, or the international jury, were looking to see.

Had ICAIC indeed lost its sense of direction? In place of a search for new forms of expression, says Peter Schumann, ICAIC had established a craft routine of well-made confectionery for the masses. Alfredo Guevara, he suggests, tried to overcome this situation by undertaking a historical superproduction aimed at the international market and costing the whole year's production budget. But Humberto Solás, who had made film history with *Lucía,* was unable to repeat the success, and the failure of *Cecilia* would become Alfredo Guevara's nemesis. Schumann, however, is rather too summary in his judgment that "This new drama on emancipation was unconvincing, it was too conventional and unfolded too slowly, without the fantasy of the same director's earlier films."[49] The truth is that no Cuban film ever prodded a raw nerve more insistently than this one, revealing in the process the dangers of interfering with certain types of cultural icon; for where Giral based the first film of his trilogy on an abolitionist novel that was now little read, and proceeded in a didactic fashion to deconstruct the confusions and contradictions of its well-meaning ideology, Solás took the best known of nineteenth-century Cuban novels, Cirilo Villaverde's *Cecilia Valdés,* and gave a revered classic a free adaptation that disconcerted both traditionalists and the popular audience. In the words of the Cuban critics Rufo Caballero and Joel del Río, writing a retrospective essay on Cuban cinema in 1995 under the title "No Adult Cinema without Systematic Heresy," "*Cecilia,* criticized for disrespect, fixation, and mannerism, implied a split in Cuban cinema, not only on account of its treatment of characters enveloped in myth, but also for raising questions about the artistic means of assuming the historical and the literary."[50] Significantly, the title of this extremely important essay refers back to a piece by Alfredo Guevara, "No es fácil la herejía" (Heresy isn't easy), dating from 1963, which argues passionately the artists' right to their own understanding, with all the risks that this entails.

Even with such low levels of feature production ICAIC had sustained a number of thematic trends in its output, and *Cecilia* was the latest in the line of historical recovery pursued during the 1970s in Giral's slave trilogy and *La última cena* by Alea. We are in the Havana of the 1830s, a culture of believers arraigned between two religious systems, Catholicism and Santería, the latter inhabited by African deities, the orishas, disguised as Catholic saints. The colonial capital is a social melting pot with a sizable population of freed slaves—many of them, like the character of Pimienta, making a living as musicians—and a growing *criollo* class of mixed extraction, whose economic progress and political designs are in process of challenging the hegemony of an aristocratic white population with strong ties to its Spanish forebears; Pimienta, as well as being Cecilia's spurned black lover, is a political conspirator. Cecilia, a beautiful and ambitious mulatta, falls prey to the attentions of the foppish and nihilistic Leonardo, heir to a slaver's fortune. Leonardo's mother disapproves of the liaison, and goes about arranging his marriage to Isabel, an heiress in her own right, but a modernizer and an abolitionist. The English, Isabel tells Leonardo, have come out against the slave trade—they want to sell machinery to the Caribbean instead. "What are you?" asks Leonardo in response to the lecture, "a woman or a book?" "I am a book," she replies, "but with many pages forbidden by the pope." Pimienta is trying to hide an aged maroon; Cecilia persuades Leonardo to give the man refuge in return for her becoming Leonardo's mistress, only to be tormented by jealousy when she hears of his betrothal to Isabel, who in turn is tormented by nightmares of a slave revolt at the plantation. When an informer warns Leonardo's mother that her son is harboring a runaway, she turns informer herself, denouncing the old man's whereabouts in exchange for her son's immunity, with the aim of saving him and his marriage while getting rid of Cecilia. Authority can be persuaded to protect its own children but the conspirators are not so easy to deal with. Under cover of festivities for Epiphany, Pimienta, believing Leonardo himself to have been the informer, dons the costume of the warlike Shangó and breaks into the cathedral where the wedding is taking place to exact his vengeance.

If this is a Cecilia Valdés seen through a prism that turns the white perspective of the classic novel inside out, there are different ways such an approach might be accomplished. Giral created an imaginary vision of the same history three different ways: first, through deconstruction in *El otro Francisco,* then using the outward form of a western in *Rancheador,* and lastly, in *Maluala,* by inserting the black subject into a realist historical drama. Alea, in *La última cena,* proposed an allegorical version of the same imaginary in the parody of a religious morality play, evoking both Brecht and Buñuel. In *Cecilia,* Solás presents a world in which historical materialism is crossed with psychoanalysis, and where economic determination meets a collective unconscious with its own interpretation of the historical world in terms of elemental human forces, in a reading that enables him to transform one kind of melodrama into another. The tone is set by a long and extraordinary opening sequence, reminiscent of the scene in *Los días de agua* by Manuel Octavio Gómez where two religious processions, one Catholic, one Yoruba, meet and fuse, only here there is no fusion, but an extended musical battle played out on the sound track. An old black woman recounts to her granddaughter a Cuban version of the legend of Oshún, goddess of love, who is sold as a slave in Africa and transformed into a beautiful mulatta in Cuba. In the view of Paolo Antonio Paranagua, the whole film is imbued with Santería and animism, and it is Solás himself who has placed the myths of Oshún and Shangó at the center of this version of a novel previously regarded as a classic piece of *costumbrista* (costume) literature.[51] In Solás's version, the narrative is permeated by the dualism of Cecilia-Oshún and Pimienta-Shangó, which shifts the balance between the characters and subverts the conventional reading.

The effects are peculiarly problematic for an audience for whom these are not just characters in a novel but have lives beyond the page, as idealized projections of national character types. *Cecilia Valdés* is not only a novel but also a zarzuela and a ballet. As Reynaldo González puts it, she became a myth unto herself, a literary figure who came to epitomize the Cuban feminine in a form often far removed from the anecdote in the novel but rooted in historical reality.[52] Indeed, Villaverde gave literary shape to an already-existing myth in the social world of his time: Cecilia is the *mulata blanconaza*—the mulatta woman who is able to pass for white—and the queen of the *pardos y morenos* (mulattos and blacks) of her neighborhood, possessed of a special beauty and vivaciousness supposedly born of her racial mix, whose feminine charm, being her only tool for social improvement, thereby condemns her to serve as a carnal attraction to rich, young white men. She is, of course, doubly positioned, an object of sexist manipulation and of racial prejudice. A femme fatale lacking the virtues that "society" required of its wives, her social career traverses the stages of the flirtatious, desire, passion, and jealousy, but she never escapes the condition of discrimination. In short, as the personification of Cuban feminine beauty, she represents, on the one hand, a tacit acknowledgment by all social classes of the blackness in Cuban blood, and, on the other, a figure of tragedy. Solás gives his Cecilia a knowing character that provoked unease, and the film was criticized for casting the no longer young Daisy Granados as Cecilia when the part called for a bewitching actress in her late teens or early twenties.

The effect on the figure of Leonardo is also crucial: in another element Solás has brought into his reading of the novel, Leonardo is caught up in an oedipal relationship with his mother that, in spite of the stylish acting of the Spanish actor Imanol Arias, constituted a particularly problematic redrawing of the character, by turning Leonardo from a regular macho into something like one of those pathological heroes whose emergence in the modern dramatic narrative was described, as Fredric Jameson reminds us, by Georg Lukács at the beginning of the century. It is as if Solás has confronted a potent cultural icon with its own recalcitrance by stripping the hero of his Romantic aura and reinserting him into the modern world, a move that provoked great anxiety in those attached to the original figure. Caballero and del Río, who consider it a film distinguished by unusual aesthetic skill and daring, regard its appearance as a decisive moment in the interrelation between Cuban cinema, criticism, the public, and the cultural apparatus of the state, in which questions were asked at every level of society about the "liberties and licence" that, according to its detractors, the film took with myth and history as well as its source.[53]

Solás was quite clear about what he was doing. We are in the territory mapped by Jameson in his discussion of third-world literature, in which the story of private individual destinies is to be read as an allegory of the embattled situation of the society they belong to, a form of national allegory that is already present in Villaverde's novel.[54] Jameson is concerned with discovering how to read such literature from outside, whereas Solás is approaching the issue from within, and in full knowledge of the allegorical power of his target, which is a moving one. Villaverde's novel, he explained, "is an active and living part of national folklore," and so are the zarzuela and the ballet, so inevitably it is hard to escape the tenor of tunes that can be heard every day—"the novel's romantic interpretation of nineteenth-century Cuba, the cultural stamp of the zarzuela that exalts certain republican sectors (similar to the way the music 'domesticates' the African legacy in [Cuban] culture), the mythification which, in spite of critical attention, is found in the ballet," and the film, he says, is meant as a rebellion against these various versions.[55] The result, according to Caballero and del Río, is that Solás splits open the drama in pursuit of a reflection on national identity and the weight it gives to the mulatta. Her inevitable tragedy is seen as an allegory of the challenges and destiny of the Cuban nation, while the much-discussed incest—between siblings in Villaverde, reformulated by Solás as a mother–son relationship—refers to the unnatural and essentially corrupt relations of metropolis and colony.

At the same time, what Solás intended was a critique of melodrama without renouncing the melodramatic. He calculated that this could be achieved through the big operatic gesture he first deployed in *Lucía* and further developed in *Cantata de Chile,* but here folded back into a single narrative. The operatic conception is reflected, on the one hand, in the music (by Leo Brouwer), and, on the other, in the cinematography (by Livio Delgado), with both of whom he had worked before on the previous films. The result is both highly controlled and highly stylized: the takes are long and agile, the pace is slow, at times ponderous, the emphasis is on an elaborate mise-en-scène modeled on Visconti and the Eisenstein of *Ivan the Terrible.* Most of all, the image is dark. The first several sequences, and much of the rest of the film, take place at night, outdoors and indoors, and when the film reaches the first daytime outdoor scene after more than half an hour, the sunlight is sepia-toned. Again, the film offended against the popular image of the world it represented, causing considerable irritation among many of its viewers, some of whom considered it veritably perverse.

Indubitably, the project suffered from the terms of the coproduction arrangements required to finance it, which required three different versions: for Spanish television, a serial of six hours; for the Cuban cinema screen, a four-hour version; and for international distribution, another version running almost three hours. The denouement in the full version runs forty-five minutes, in the shortest version, a mere ten. It is difficult for a film to retain its identity in such circumstances, and if the full version, for which Solás expresses his own preference, stands up as a superior piece of television, in the cinema the film failed to satisfy. As Paranagua chronicles, *Cecilia* was massacred by the critics.[56] In the weekly *Bohemia* it was panned for its "Visconti-esque mannerism" and an adaptation that failed to respect the "essence" of the novel. *Verde Olivo*—the magazine of the military—attacked its "excess": its constant high pitch, overabundance of symbolism, the artifice of certain of its situations, which escape comprehension and dilute the narrative discourse through excessive generalization. In the satirical magazine *El Caimán Barbudo*, the writer Eliseo Alberto regretted the "politicization" of the story, and the hysterical relationship between mother and son, "which seemed lacking in historical sense." The newspaper *Tribuna de La Habana* compared the whole enterprise to *The Fall of the House of Usher*, reproaching its "decadent mannerism," denouncing the supposed influence of German Expressionism and its "doubtful" baroque style. But the principal prosecutor was Mario Rodríguez Alemán in the newspaper *Trabajadores*, who wrote three damning pieces about the film. Rodríguez Alemán contests the Freudian treatment, which removes the film from what he calls "critical realism"; nor does he accept the transformation of Pimienta into Shangó, and he finds the ending "repulsive." He alleges that "the excessive religious charge," the predominance of the "sacred," the priority given to myth, oneiricism, mysticism, and "folklore," are contradictory elements, relegating the political and social connotations of Villaverde's original to the background. And he confirms our findings about the character of Leonardo in his complaint that Leonardo presents himself as a "pathological case."

His worst charge, however, is that the adaptation completely alters the original, an inadmissible move when the authorities are engaged in the effort to preserve the national patrimony. Moreover, not content with wilfully interfering with a cultural monument, ICAIC had contravened the orientation declared by the first party congress, by concentrating the resources of the Cuban film industry on a superproduction. Paranagua comments that the vocabulary deployed by the film's critics "reveals their resistance to the irruption of the unconscious and the imaginary," but this attack against *Cecilia* by an orthodox party critic should not be underestimated.[57] According to Caballero and del Río, there was a good deal of monolithic manipulation of opinion—of the kind that they note would occur again almost ten years later with *Alicia en el pueblo de Maravillas*—which tried to insist on the need to place conditions on the arbitrary freedom of creativity produced by the Revolution itself. The attack was to prove fatal not for Solás, but to Alfredo Guevara's leadership of ICAIC. The film had tied up so much of the Institute's production capacity, and overrun its shooting schedule by many months, throwing everybody else's production plans into disarray— though none of this became public at the time—that it caused considerable chagrin among other filmmakers (the high number of documentaries produced in 1980 and 1981 was intended to compensate). When *Cecilia* flopped, despite European coproduction funding, disarray among the filmmakers enabled Guevara's old enemies to mount a rearguard attack and edge him out of power. In 1982, Fidel sent his old friend to Paris as Cuba's ambassador to UNESCO, and replaced him with Julio García Espinosa. By not acceding to dogmatic advice about his successor, he allowed that the error of judgment, albeit an expensive miscalculation, was a personal one, and it did not impugn the Institute or place its autonomy in jeopardy.

García Espinosa takes an ironic view of the episode, ascribing the film's failure with the audience to the fact that it literally hit the wrong note. The zarzuela by Gonzalo Roig, dating from the 1930s, is something of a travesty of the novel but follows it in one respect. "The amorous triangle between the mulatta, the white, and the mestizo, which is the typical triangle of a melodrama, was also a little the drama of our history in the nineteenth century, at a moment when Cuba was about to embark on its independence struggle, and was looking to see if it were something more than black and white. The film does not respect this triangle—it polarizes it in other directions. The zarzuela sticks to it." The zarzuela was like a national hymn—every soprano of any quality had to sing it—and when the film didn't use the music of the zarzuela the public somehow felt cheated, which facilitated attacks on the film. *Cecilia* produced adverse reactions because there have always been sectors who saw ICAIC's political attitude as insufficiently orthodox in its relationship to the country's reality, because of its critical approach to that very reality. "These sectors have always been latent, and were mobilized by the kind of criticism *Cecilia* provoked."[58]

Nevertheless, with García Espinosa's appointment, everyone at ICAIC breathed a sigh of relief and got on with the job, which for Solás meant a new film.

CHAPTER SIXTEEN

Return of the Popular

Shortly before becoming Alfredo Guevara's successor as head of ICAIC, Julio García Espinosa returned to the concept of imperfect cinema:

> Just as we have to learn things even from the metropolis which is so much ahead of the underdeveloped countries, so we have to learn from their cinema too. But just as in our social aspirations we're looking for better means of human self-fulfillment, so we have to search for the appropriate cinema. For me, the societies of the great metropolis are marked by an economy of waste, and to this economy of waste there corresponds a culture of waste. Such a diabolical system has been created that people think that to make the most of their lives they have to be wasteful of things. And the question is how really to live a full life. So in the face of a culture of waste you have to search for a culture of true liberation. It's not possible to propose the idea of a New Economic Order without a new culture as well. Because in the underdeveloped world, suffering so much scarcity, people still often think that they have to achieve the same levels of consumption as the developed countries, and that's a lie. We cannot—the world cannot—aspire to such levels of consumption. Therefore the culture has to provide new ways of feeling and enjoying life, different from irrational consumption. This is the basis of imperfect cinema. Since we're creating a society which, although it's full of imperfections, will finally achieve a new kind of human productiveness, I suggested a cinema which although it has imperfections is essentially much more consistent with real human needs.[1]

When he took the helm at ICAIC, the obvious question arose: what would become of these fine ideas?

If an equally obvious place to look for signs of an answer was his own practice as a filmmaker, García Espinosa had directed nothing since *Tercer mundo, tercer guerra mundial* in 1970, except for an episode in a documentary on the sixtieth anniversary of the Soviet Revolution, and an experimental work called *Son o no son* that had not been released. Here he set out to interrogate some of the more intractable issues about popular culture that exercised him while serving as vice minister of culture in charge of music and spectacles. The title, *Son o no son,* is a pun: literally, "They are or they aren't," *son* is also the name of an Afro-Cuban song form—like the *rumba,* only slower. Titles and music come to an end. The camera moves in on a stage where a ham actor evokes, in satirical mistranslation, Hamlet's famous monologue. Not "To be or not to be" but "*Son* or not *son*. Whether 'tis nobler in the mind and all that, to suffer the outrage of so many bad songs and stupid soap operas, or what? But how to end them? *That* is the question." The bad taste is reminiscent of Mel Brooks—not so much bad taste as the parody of bad taste. *Son o no son* remained without a release (until many years later), although not because it was one of those films that were rumored in whispers abroad as instances of censorship, but because the director himself felt unsatisfied with it; perhaps it was *too* experimental. After its eventual public screening, Caballero and del Río suggested that it was not as if the film were bad, "but there were no current theoretical instruments or aesthetic criteria to understand it, and the solution was deafening silence."[2] It thus led a kind of underground existence as García Espinosa showed it to people who visited ICAIC, through which, in fact, it reached its intended audience. For *Son o no son* is essentially a polemical essay addressed to fellow practitioners of radical cinema in Latin America, those with whom Cuban cinema has always been in dialogue about culture, politics, and entertainment, in which everything about mass culture, film, theater, radio, television, and the rest is questioned, including the present phase of banality and distortion of national cultures. It is therefore a kind of laboratory experiment in imperfect cinema.

The film takes the form of a musical comedy show, in which song-and-dance numbers are interspersed with sketches, comic monologues, documentary inserts, and film clips. Mostly we are in the Tropicana nightclub, but in the daytime with no audience, watching rehearsals, and the banter of the artistes as they work up new routines. We also get sequences of television-style lectures about North American versus Latin American cinema, and about the characteristics of Afro-American music;

a letter to the Bolivian film director Jorge Sanjinés; a bad joke about Marshall McLuhan, and a conversation between a couple, voice-over as we drive through Havana, about the true values of popular culture. It is also an exemplar of *cine pobre,* of the lowest possible budget filmmaking: the mise-en-scène is designed to employ the simplest setups and minimum footage. The film is not carried by any visual richness but by its music and its ideas. Sometimes the mise-en-scène suffers from a lack of cuts. The musical numbers are mostly filmed to playback, in long shots of the dancers and singers with very little camera movement. But this not only gives the film a stagy look, it foregrounds the music and the singing without recourse to the spectacular staging and multiple camera angles of Hollywood; this is more like the minimalism of Jean-Marie Straub and Danielle Huillet. Intertextual references to other films and directors abound. While the director reads his letter to Sanjinés we see a clip from one of the Bolivian's documentary dramas about the violent repression of workers' struggles. The traveling shot through Havana, through the windshield of the car in which the couple are arguing, is a parody of Godard. The clip we see of a classic Hollywood musical— Shirley MacLaine in Bob Fosse's *Sweet Charity*—is a screen adaptation of a popular Broadway musical that was derived from Fellini's *Notti di Cabiria.* Near the end, the argument of the couple in the car is interrupted by the "Kanonen-Song" (Canon song) from Bertolt Brecht and Kurt Weill's *Threepenny Opera,* in a clip from the film version by Pabst, and the caption "A small homage to Bertolt Brecht who also shared these anxieties." All this makes for a highly self-reflexive film essay, full of self-interruptions and allusions that seem cousin to similar practices in European avant-garde cinema of the same period. Or are they? According to the director himself: "I wanted to make the ugliest film in the world, that is to say, to eliminate customary expectations like suspense, the primacy of the image, virtuosic mise-en-scène, beautiful photography, etc., and for the film to be sustained only through its dramaturgy. It became the intention to destroy the central nucleus of traditional or Aristotelian dramaturgy. It was and is an experimental film. From *Aventuras de Juan Quin Quin* till now, nothing else interests me."[3]

Except for the musical comedy format, it was all very different from the new film by Manuel Octavio Gómez, *Patakín,* which came out in the year of the handover. An ambitious attempt to make a popular musical—the first in Cuba since *Un día en el solar* by Eduardo Manet in

1965—this film occupies the same zone of Afro-Cuban culture and Santería as *Cecilia* but comes at it from a very different angle. Transposing
two figures out of Yoruba mythology (*patakín* means "fable" in Yoruba)
to contemporary Cuba—here Shangó is an irresistible lumpen layabout,
while his nemesis, Ogún, is a staid model worker—the tale takes the
form of a series of disasters followed by a floor show with the added attraction of Mr. Death making a cameo appearance as a boxing match
referee, while the score by Rembert Egües romps through a variety of
styles, from Broadway to cabaret to Soviet tractor music. Panned by the
critics (though not unsuccessful with the audience), it might have worked,
if not for two things. From one point of view, a kind of modest version
of *West Side Story,* from another it suffers precisely from the fact that it
isn't *West Side Story*—the music is pleasant but not nearly distinctive
and biting enough to make it work as a musical. And second, if only it
hadn't tried so hard to fit the Yoruba myth to official revolutionary ideology, in which the struggle between Shangó and Ogún is presented as
the expression of an ancestral struggle between ethical attitudes that
still remain valid, like honesty versus deceit, or seriousness versus superficiality. It is as if the film takes its own premises too seriously, afraid
to carry them beyond a certain limited level of permitted double entendre;
and in this respect it is marked by the political caution of the moment.

One film fell victim to this caution, when *Techo de vidrio* (Glass
roof), the first film by Sergio Giral to tackle a contemporary theme—
that of bureaucratic corruption—was withheld from exhibition "for
aesthetic reasons," according to Caballero and del Río. When it was released six years later, opinions diverged. *Revolución y cultura* wrote that
Giral had not escaped the triumphalist recipe of the old Soviet cinema,
at the moment that what was needed was to confront the contradictions appearing within socialism; for *El Caimán Barbudo,* the film was
neither better not worse than average, but it had one great merit, that of
proposing a reflection on ethics."[4] Part of the problem lay in the details of
the plot, in which a worker (played by Samuel Claxton), accused of supplying an engineer in the same factory with building materials, resorts to
old religious practices, while the two are treated unequally by the process
of justice, which allows the engineer's status in the hierarchy to protect
him. But the film lends itself to a double reading because the worker is
black and the engineer is white, thus suggesting the persistence of
racism in the interstices of the system. Caballero and del Río approve

the film's fundamental polemicism, its concern for "issues that are difficult or hidden by official discourse," but consider it overschematic, "flawed by being seen through tinted and reductive lenses that produce restricted and partial vision."[5]

For Rolando Pérez Betancourt, the merit of the film was that it assumed "the risk of the interpretation of problems and conflicts inherent to the era." These lines, however, by a leading film critic writing in the party newspaper *Granma*, are best read, in the spirit of Erving Goffman, symptomatically, where the words "inherent to the era" refer back to the political context at the moment when the film was made. In 1982, Castro began to attack misconduct such as the misuse of state funds by managers of enterprises, and illegitimate profits made by middlemen on the free farmers' markets that had been introduced two years earlier. It took four years before the farmers' markets were closed down and an offensive declared "against those who confuse income from work and speculation, or fiddlers who are little better than thieves, and indeed often are thieves."[6] Thus, by the time the film was released, what was problematic to represent on screen in 1982, despite borrowing Castro's authority, had acquired an official vocabulary: *corrupción, doble moral, falta de exigencia, amiguismo, desinterés*—corruption, double morals, lack of care, buddyism, indifference. Officially, these are code words for modes of behavior inherited from the time of the pseudorepublic and dependent capitalism, succored by petit bourgeois tendencies that contravened communist ideals and contradicted the image of *el hombre nuevo*, the new man of socialism. But there is also another interpretation—that they implied various forms of failure within the revolutionary project, identified with the economic, social, and political effects of the reform begun in the mid-1970s, which led to the growth of bureaucracy, privileges, and corruption, a fall in labor productivity, and eventually the development of a black market. Clearly, it was one thing for Castro to denounce what troubled him and another for a film to attempt to portray the same problems, especially when the thematic of racial representation added to the difficulty. Giral told this writer before the film was completed that he knew he was treading on delicate ground; the subsequent ban on the film came from high places above ICAIC, and in discussions with the party's ideological chiefs the film was found to suffer from aesthetic and dramatic weaknesses that made it difficult for ICAIC's defense of it to prevail.[7] Again, reading symptomatically, one supposes that all this is known to José Antonio Evora when he writes that this was a film that, despite its pamphleteering tone, answered to urgent social needs, and should be considered a pioneer of "a critical line that (in the director's own words) would open up channels for the 'disalienation' of self-censorship."[8]

The other new fiction film to appear in 1982 was the first feature by novelist and documentarist Jesús Díaz. At first sight, *Polvo rojo* (Red dust) is evidence of a trend in which the documentarist-turned-feature director must prove his spurs with a debut aimed at a popular audience, which in practice means a genre piece. Díaz chooses a historical drama, based on real events, the story of a small mining town in a third-world country at a time of revolution, where the plant is owned by North Americans; in short, Cuba 1959, and the town of Moa in Oriente. At first the North Americans believe they can reach an accommodation with the new regime, largely because they think the Cubans incapable of operating the plant for themselves; events force them to pull out all the same, leaving behind a single technician who comes under suspicion for his political ambivalence, but in the effort to get the plant started up again becomes more and more committed to the revolutionary process, even when his family decides to abandon the country. This thematic link with Díaz's earlier documentary, *55 hermanos* (55 brothers and sisters), gives the film its allegorical level: behind the public drama is the pathos of the equally political but private drama of the division of families. But this public-private drama is not over, and Díaz's film therefore takes on intertextual allusion to subsequent events such as the Mariel exodus of 1980.

Mariel was an ugly moment in the history of the Cuban Revolution, when a hundred thousand people crowded into embassy compounds and forced the Cuban government to let them leave, mostly, of course, to Miami. Early in 1979, Cuba had opened its doors for Miami Cubans to visit friends and family in Cuba; more than a hundred thousand of them came, bringing dollars, gifts, and tales of prosperity. The disdainful and ill-informed attitudes of the visitors often renewed the division of families rather than healing it, and the government was much criticized. A weak economy contributed to discontent, especially among underemployed young men who saw few prospects for self-improvement, and foreign embassies began receiving waves of applicants for visas to emigrate. Miami was the most popular destination, but Washington wasn't opening the doors. To force the situation, in April 1980 Castro declared them free to leave—through the small port of Mariel near Havana. By October, nearly 150,000 people had taken up the offer, of whom 120,000 headed for the States, where Jimmy Carter welcomed these new refugees from Communism "with an open heart and open arms." However, Washington was soon accusing Castro of taking his revenge by sending delinquents, criminals, and even the inmates of mental hospitals, all mixed in with the political refugees. Castro replied with a denial, describing the Marielitos as an antigovernment and "antisocial lumpen," and the only mentally ill people transported in the boatlift had been requested by family members already living in the United States. The truth, as this writer discovered from subsequent conversations in Havana, is that the situation had got out of control and there were incidents in which people turned on neighbors they distrusted and forced them to go; some of them were malcontents and petty criminals of one kind or another; others were gays.

In short, *Polvo rojo* is not simply a historical genre movie about the early days of the Revolution, but a film that addressed itself implicitly to one of the most upsetting legacies of the social disruption entailed by the unfolding political dynamic of the Revolution. When it was screened at a festival in the United States, the *Los Angeles Times* found it an impressive combination of the epic and the personal, although from a different perspective it relies too readily on the expectable characteristics of the genre, and the direction of the concluding scenes was fluffed. The director readily admitted it, adding that before making this film he had never been on a fiction film set, even as an observer.[9]

García Espinosa quickly brought fresh vision to ICAIC, pursuing a policy of low-budget production, and giving a new generation of directors a chance to prove themselves. In due course he would go further, and devolve the internal decision-making process to teams of directors working in groups. Initially, the recipe was straightforward: to increase the number of films being made and bring in new blood by abandoning costly productions, holding budgets down to 125,000 pesos and four weeks' shooting. As one of the first of these films, he approved a new script by Humberto Solás, a move designed to give reassurance that offenses committed by artistic license are not considered sanctionable.

The following year, Solás came back with *Amada,* and Alea came up with *Hasta cierto punto (Up to a Point),* a project started before the changeover at the top.

The film by Solás is another, but much more modest, historical drama. Havana, 1914: Amada, a young conservative woman from a declining aristocratic family, is in a lifeless marriage to a politician; tied to obsolete values, she falls passionately in love with her cousin Marcial, an anarchist poet who tries to shake her out of her traditionalism. Solás aims at a psychological study, replete with whispers, faces bathed in tears, and repeated close-ups, which "takes the temperature of an epoch of frustration" to become a strong indictment of patriarchal politics.[10] A professional stylistic exercise with skilled contributions from composer Leo Brouwer, cinematographer Livio Delgado, and Eslinda Núñez in the title role.

In *Hasta cierto punto,* on the other hand, center stage is given to the identity crisis of Cuban cinema itself, as Alea returns to the theme of the relationship of the intellectual to the Revolution that he first explored in *Memorias del subdesarrollo.* The new film contrasts the filmmakers' world with that of the Havana dockworkers, where Óscar, a scriptwriter, and Arturo, a director, are planning to make a film about machismo. In the course of their investigations, Óscar becomes embroiled in a fraught relationship with Lina, a checker at the docks and an unmarried mother; the relationship, which throws the theme of the proposed movie into ironic perspective, comes to nothing because the writer won't leave his wife. The film opens with one of the interviews that they videotape as part of their research, in which a black dockworker is saying, "I can't do it, because I've lived so long in the old society. . . . I'm 80 percent changed, but I can't make it 100 percent . . . because this business about equality between men and women is correct, but only up to a point *[hasta cierta punto].*" Alea adopts the phrase as the title of the film because it evokes *De cierta manera* and Sara Gómez, to whom this film "pays beautiful homage," as Jesús Díaz puts it: "one of the rare instances in history where the master had enough humility to publicly recognize his disciple."[11]

Like its predecessor, *Hasta cierto punto* is told in two modes: documentary (the video recordings of interviews and workers' meetings) and fiction (the rest of the scenario). Thanks to Alea's know-how and experience, says Díaz, the former never falls into didacticism, as it did in *De cierta manera.* In the earlier film, the documentary sequences serve broadly to the locate the protagonists within a certain cultural history elaborated by an ideologically orthodox commentary; here, without commentary, they locate them within a messy present. Where Gómez proposes a historicist analysis of social contradictions, within a classic Marxist teleology that leads to a utopian future, Alea offers a synchronic analysis, a cognitive mapping of the same territory but one that is necessarily much more open and incomplete, a quality that Zuzana Pick locates not just within the structure of the narrative but in the methodology employed in making the film, "an approach similar to documentary film-making whereby the result of research motivates narrative and formal choices."[12] She is not mistaken that this methodology implied a critique of the situation at ICAIC, where directors were trained in documentary, their scripts were criticized when they turned to fiction, and, ironically, scriptwriters were hired to turn them into formally correct shooting scripts. This, Alea seems to want to say, is no way to go about things.

The video footage in *Hasta cierto punto* was shot by Alea with a skeleton crew during the preproduction of the film, originally as part of their own research. But, as he told Enrique Colina in an interview, they quickly thought of the idea of incorporating this footage in the film itself as a form of documentary testimonial—a risky undertaking, said Alea, because of the surprises it would throw up (naturally, because a film that abandons a homogeneous narrative to incorporate a multiplicity of voices is necessarily more difficult to control, and indeed can hardly manage to do so according to traditional criteria of narrative coherence). They then began the main shoot without a completed script but only a provisional outline, which was built up "as we proceeded, as we were engaged in the investigation. We had to change the problematic various times. . . . Sometimes dramatic possibilities arose that corresponded to our ideas, but the themes would also escape our objectives."[13] Indeed, this process becomes part of the subject matter of the film in front of us on the screen. Not only do the video sequences constantly pull the viewer back into the "real world"—the primary world of the workers where the fictional characters are guests—but, as the scriptwriter remarks to his wife, "We went to a workers' assembly and very interesting things came up. Now I don't know how to put all these issues into a simple love story." This, too, then—the impossibility of making the film that we're watching—is the subject that the film presents to the viewer, in a quasi-

Brechtian fashion characterized by self-interruption and ironic self-reference, and the distantiation produced by the counterpoint of documentary and fiction. In short, notwithstanding the central role of the romance, the video interviews set the stage, as Pick describes it, for a critique of gender and class relations that highlights conflicts that the intended film within a film is unable, or perhaps refuses, to resolve.[14]

Other writers find parallels between the two films by teacher and disciple. Catherine Davies observes that both focus on a love affair between a man and a woman from different class backgrounds, though here it is the man who is middle-class and the woman who is working-class; in both, it is the female protagonist "who most clearly represents the revolution and pushes for change," while "the male ego, based on power and privilege, is seen to be under threat"; in both films, substantial scenes are located in places of work (a bus factory, the docks), with prominent scenes of workers' assemblies.[15] One of these assembles is where Óscar first spots Lina, as she makes a public protest about hazardous working conditions. Óscar, looking for someone to serve as a model for his film character, is dazzled by her forceful intervention, and a relationship develops between the bourgeois intellectual and the unmarried working-class mother with a boy of twelve, which produces a crisis in Óscar's marriage to his actress wife, Marián, who is slated to play the character based on his lover. The affair also changes Óscar's take on the script he is supposed to be writing. Setting out to corroborate his director's orthodox thesis that machismo is a vestige of prerevolutionary thinking, he begins to change his views. Arturo, who has observed the funny look in Óscar's face whenever Lina is around, suspects that the intentions of the script are threatened by Óscar's infatuation. Óscar and Arturo begin to disagree over the way the script is progressing, as the director resists his scriptwriter's growing grasp of the real milieu. When Óscar suggests that maybe the heroine should be an unmarried mother, Arturo parries "Like *Moscow Doesn't Believe in Tears*?" Óscar realizes the dangers of isolating machismo from its class context; in a muted showdown with his director, he protests that "it isn't enough to portray the macho as a man who beats his wife and won't let her go out to work: it's much more complicated." But Óscar has been seen with Lina, and Arturo believes the affair has distorted Óscar's judgment. The film falls through— at least for Óscar—while Lina, dissatisfied with her lack of prospects at the dock, does what she told Óscar when they first met that she was thinking of doing, and flies off to another life back in Santiago de Cuba where (like Sara Gómez) she grew up.

For Marvin D'Lugo, the most striking formal feature that Alea borrows from Gómez is the scenes of the workers' assemblies, which amount to "the staging of an on-screen audience within the film who comment on and assess the themes that shape the film's narrative."[16] These scenes have a special interest from a sociological point of view, for the participation of the workers themselves as actors in the film, and the intense documentary quality of the filming, turn them into primary evidence of the exercise of power in the workplace, and of the adaptation of such participation to the political climate of the day.[17] Workers' councils were formally set up in 1965 to rule on problems of violations of labor law and indiscipline—as occurs in *De cierta manera*. This function was eroded by changes introduced in the period of institutionalization in the late 1970s. By the time of *Hasta cierto punto,* workers' assemblies have become occasions where workers debate the problems of management in an economy that is showing serious signs of strain. When the workers in the film also appear in a series of spontaneous, unscripted interviews, the result is to enunciate a sense of collective identity and values that reminds D'Lugo of what Stanley Fish called an interpretive community. The effect is that of conjoining a Greek chorus and a Brechtian commentary that serves for the Cuban audience as a conduit between the film and the viewer, because the interpretive community on-screen (leaving aside the particular social sector of the individual audience member) is continuous with the one offscreen—a particularly useful form of triangulation that is also found in other Cuban films, like *Ustedes tienen la palabra.* But if these scenes embody the theme of the community's participation in the prosecution of revolutionary values, then it is not because they hold the key to the truth but because the community is both the site of the problem and the proper space of communicative dialogue about solutions, and this dialogue is what activates the film's textual complexity. What passes for a straightforward love story is continually subjected to a form of oblique scrutiny and indirect critique, through the agency of an interpretive community whose presence on-screen is doubled by its counterpart in front of the screen. The film acquires a divergent structure—a difficult balance between the inquiry on machismo and the love story—that Cuban critics found wanting, although Pick feels that the film's refusal to provide answers to the problems it presents is indeed counterbalanced by the way in which it activates a critical exchange between the screen and the viewer.

Is *Hasta cierto punto* a feminist film, or only a film about the crisis of masculinity? Davies thinks that Lina is too idealized, and her experience fails to match that of the vast majority of Cuban working mothers. Pick, on the other hand, believes that the film sets up a forceful paradox between the romantic imaginary and female desire in which Lina's character (powerfully played by Mirta Ibarra) acts out a subtle, yet powerful, resistance to machismo. For D'Lugo, Lina "functions as the catalyst for Oscar's confrontation with the confining patterns of his own consciousness"[18]—she tells him machismo is everywhere, not just among dockers; she criticizes the absence of women in a crew making a film about machismo; she warns him not to confuse her with the fictional character of his proposed movie. She goes to the theater to see a play he has written, a social comedy, which ends with the leading character refusing to finish according to the script, which she throws at the audience; Lina is not convinced by this Brechtian gesture. Her view of cinema is a popular one, and she's puzzled by what Óscar is looking for. "You spend all day handling sacks in the dock," she protests, "then in the movies you see the same thing? No one will go and see that film. When people go to the movies after work, they want to cut off *[desconectar]*, see nice entertaining things, right?" Although their relationship is portrayed with tenderness, says another writer, Jorge Ruffinelli, it is also a vicious circle. Alea-Óscar symbolizes Lina as a bird in flight, in the words of a Basque song that serves as an epigram for the film, and which Óscar plays Lina on a cassette: "I could clip her wings if I liked / Then she couldn't fly / and she'd be mine / but what I love is the bird." He, and the film, begin by positioning her as an alluring object of research and investigation, but she refuses to be pinned down and ends by escaping, belying the implicit machismo of the song playing the film out on the sound track by suggesting that he could not have clipped her wings if he'd wanted to after all. Here too there is an echo of *De cierta manera*, which similarly ends with a song with an ambiguous moral, and a certain dose of irony, as if Lina "were tearing up Oscar's script, and . . . Alea were tearing up his own script and . . . tossing it into the lap of the audience."[19]

Nevertheless, the ending has been criticized as too facile. For Davies, who finds the film wanting in comparison to *De cierta manera*, "The result is a sentimental romance, which goes nowhere, couched in an overview of Cuban society as experiencing stasis and paralysis at the levels of production, morality and art."[20] Díaz thinks that Alea privileges the love story to the detriment of the documentary. Pick takes a more complex view: on the one hand, "it is as if the sociological purpose of the issues raised in the videotaped segments is progressively eclipsed by traditional melodramatic convention," but a closer look suggests a pattern to the video footage with broader implications.[21] As the clips shift from talk about machismo, by way of collective voicing of labor issues, to reflections on individual consciousness and responsibility, the interviews broaden out beyond their function as an ironic counterpoint to the narrative, to evoke the larger community as the source and arbiter of the social meanings presented and contested within the film. This repositioning coincides with the dramatic portrayal of Óscar's machismo and Arturo's inability to shed his preconceived ideas, and amounts to a critique of both of them. Although clearly Alea's sympathy in the conflict between them is with his fictional scriptwriter, the film, as Ruffinelli puts it, criticizes the intellectual's vision of the workers and the schematic positivism of cinema, at least as conceived by Arturo.[22]

For Alea himself, the film is marked by the same concerns he had just written about in an essay on cinema called *The Viewer's Dialectic,* a kind of formal credo of an independent Marxist intellectual that represents Alea's version of imperfect cinema. The argument is a thoroughly materialist one—Alea never doubts that there is a physical reality that cinema promises to redeem, but this reality and its representation are both of them thoroughly problematic. The filmmaker, he says, "is immersed in a complex milieu, with a profound meaning which does not lie on the surface. If film-makers want to express their world coherently, and at the same time respond to the demands their world places on them, they should go out armed not just with a camera and their sensibility, but also with solid theoretical judgement."[23] The question was especially vigilant in Cuba: "The level of complexity at which the ideological struggle unfolds makes demands on film-makers to overcome completely not only the spontaneity of the first years of the revolutionary triumph but also the dangers inherent in a tendency to schematize" (18).

Alea engages in a theoretical debate because "Film not only entertains and informs, it also shapes taste, intellectual judgement and states of consciousness. If film-makers are fully to assume their own social and historical responsibilities, they will have to come face to face with the inevitable need to promote the theoretical development of their artistic practice" (37). To begin with, he disposes of the old form/content debate with the comment that the separation of form and content is simplistic; it is a bureaucratic idea to suppose that content is what fills up a form, and worst of all, it also construes the spectator as a passive receptor. The spectator, Alea insists, is neither an abstraction nor a passive monad but a social being who is historically and socially conditioned, who is cast, by definition, in an attitude of contemplation, a condition not only induced by the object being contemplated (the film) but by the position the subject occupies in relation to it. People can be actors or spectators in the face of the same phenomenon, and the task of a radical cinema is to waken them from their slumbering.

In fact, cinema offers the audience different modes of address, allows them various "levels of mediation," which carry them toward or away from reality. Cinema may produce a mythology, an illusory consciousness, populated only by imaginary beings, by ghosts that vanish as soon as the spectators are forced to face up to their own reality, to stop being spectators. Or else it can be demythifying, and send the spectators out into the street to become actors in their own lives. The different capacities of cinema are not mutually exclusive, just as emotion and intellect are not opposed; the question is how to engage the one in relation to the other. For illumination, Alea compares the twin stars of Marxist aesthetics in practice, Eisenstein and Brecht. Cinema, he finds, has certain resources highly akin to Brecht's notion of distantiation, the effect of estrangement or defamiliarization that is the precondition of discovering anything, as in Hegel's dictum, which Alea quotes, "The familiar, just because it is familiar, is not cognitively understood." Indeed, the art of montage, elucidated by Eisenstein, "constitutes a specifically cinematic mode of the estrangement effect," a resource for revealing new data about reality, a means of discovering truths "previously obscured by accommodation to daily life" (46). The meeting between the two is all the more significant because they approach the problem from opposite ends. Eisenstein directs his attention to the logic of emotions—working through the emotions toward intellect—whereas Brecht is concerned with the emotion of logic, with mobilizing the pleasure of intellectual recognition. Eisenstein's sense of *pathos* and Brecht's technique of *estrangement* are two moments of the same dialectical process, a movement between attraction and separation, which also constitute two moments in the relation of the spectator to the spectacle. Alea thinks the shift from one state to the other can happen several times as the spectacle unfolds, and is analogous to the experience of shifting from everyday reality to the theater or cinema and back again. This is the dialectic of the spectator, "this leaving everyday reality to submerge themselves into a fictional reality, an autonomous world in which they will recognise themselves, and after which they return enriched by the experience, is also a shift of alienation and de-alienation."

Perhaps *Hasta cierto punto* tries too hard to be a thesis film, which, as Alea himself admitted, "hasta cierto punto se logró" (is achieved up to a point).[24] The character of Arturo, he felt, emerged too weak, and he regretted the casting.[25] Yet the film, especially with Mario García Joya's highly mobile camera, has great fluidity, and the editing, by Miriam Talavera, gives it immense narrative economy—achieved precisely by cutting back and forth between different levels of reality and condensing the entire story into barely seventy minutes. Nevertheless, the impression it gives is not that it has been censored but simply truncated in some way, leaving untidy traces, to end without a climax, resolution, or catharsis. Instead, it exposes as a defense mechanism what Jameson, in the essay mentioned earlier, calls our "deep cultural conviction" that our private life experience is "somehow incommensurable with the abstractions of economic science and political dynamics." In that case, perhaps it is almost bound to frustrate, precisely to the extent that it begins to work on us. Given Alea's method, perhaps this was inevitable, and not at all a conventional mark of failure. The failure would have been for the film to confirm the split between public and private that permits the machismo to continue.

Jorge Fraga told his British visitors in 1983 that "All Cuban films of the last ten years have attracted full houses for the first two weeks, whether the film was liked or not. They have to see it for themselves; the films have a prestige of their own. Before the Revolution people didn't go to see a film because it was Cuban, and now they go because it is." But he thought that Cuban cinema had changed its image since the 1960s, with films like *La primera carga al machete* and *Memorias del subdesarrollo* giving way to titles such as *El hombre de Maisinicú* and *Retrato de Teresa*, which do not appear so "modern." What did this mean? That ICAIC was becoming "some sort of standardised production unit because of an excessive concern with public opinion? It's possible, I don't deny it." But he felt that the innovations of the 1960s had their own limitations. He claimed, for example, that *Lucía* was much less innovative from a dramaturgical point of view than *Teresa,* which shattered the conventions of its genre without any pyrotechnics. And even those films, such as *El hombre de Maisinicú,* that appear to borrow the format of Hollywood genres like the western, ended up quite different from Hollywood dramaturgy, through a form of treatment that brings to Fraga's mind the title of an essay by the Russian formalist Victor Shklovsky, "the dissimilarity of the similar."[26] Perhaps what Fraga is arguing here is a serious and plausible theoretical position, but not one that was fashionable at the time, and it therefore sounds more like a defense of populism. But it was not the same as the position held by García Espinosa, who, looking back years later, emphasized that for him the objective was not a populist but a popular cinema, which avoided pandering to anyone or anything because it was palpably engaged in a dialogue with popular culture, and thus also transcended the inherited separation of the popular from the elite, which, after all, would only be to fulfill the promise of cinema as the true democratic art form of the twentieth century.[27]

A special season of new films presented at the end of March 1984 to celebrate ICAIC's first twenty-five years already reflected the changes brought in by García Espinosa. There were half a dozen of them, three by established directors—Enrique Pineda Barnet, Pastor Vega, and Manuel Pérez—and three debuts, by Miguel Torres, Rolando Díaz, and Juan Carlos Tabío. In the case of the first group, none of the films are among their best. *Tiempo de amar* (Time to love) by Enrique Pineda Barnet is a love story set against the missile crisis of October 1962, of private sentiments in the midst of the country's mobilization, in the style, says Peter Schumann, of the French director Claude Lelouch. Equally unconvincing was *Habanera* by Pastor Vega, in which "a psychologist tries to realize her personal aims in an exquisite bourgeois milieu which has little or nothing to do with the reality of a Spartan society like Cuba." But, in Schumann's unkindest cut, Pérez's *La segunda hora de Esteban Zayas* (The second hour of Esteban Zayas)—the story of man marked by a sense of political failure who is pulled back into militant politics in the 1950s—"turns into the hour of truth for its director."[28] The Cuban critics did not think highly of the film either.

Of the three new feature directors, Miguel Torres, unusually, came from television. His film *Primero de enero* (First of January) is aptly described by Schumann as "a kind of epic song to the triumph of the Revolution" in which "Torres reconstructs history, using the style of the newsreel of the epoch, transforming the material in such a way that it becomes difficult to distinguish genuine historical footage from the reconstructions."[29] It was not a great hit with the public. Real success was reserved for the other two newcomers: both *Los pájaros tirándole a la escopeta* (Tables turned) by Rolando Díaz, and *Se permuta* (For exchange) by Juan Carlos Tabío, attracted huge audiences. In the list of most popular Cuban films compiled by ICAIC in 1988, they come second and fourth, respectively, with audiences of 2.8 million and 2.2 million (see Table 3). Both are comedies that propose a critical vision of daily reality. *Los pájaros* is a story of machismo in which the son forbids his mother to have a relationship with the man who is the father of the woman he himself is in love with. This creates of a set of complications that are resolved with the necessary dose of good humor about generational conflict. Comic complications are also the order of the day in *Se permuta*, in which a woman decides to move to what she considers a better neighborhood in order to get her daughter away from her suitor, a mere mechanic. The problem? How to get ahead in a society that professes everyone to be equal. The phenomenon of the house-buying chain is known in other countries—and there are other films about it—but in Havana, where no one is buying or selling, but only swapping, the intricacies of organizing a chain are of a different order. The film was very timely. The house swap, a spontaneous but piecemeal solution to Havana's housing problems, was neither legal nor illegal, but had developed to such a point that it provoked a public debate about the need for solutions. The year after the film appeared, the National Assembly approved a new housing law that allowed tenants to become house owners and let out rooms in certain circumstances.

In the process of following Gloria's endeavors, the film paints a multiple portrait of diverse personalities and attitudes within the society, ranging from an idealist architect to an opportunistic bureaucrat, to great comic effect, with the result, as Jesús Díaz puts it, that while bureaucracy is seen as an impersonal machine, the film celebrates the resourcefulness with which people solve their own problems.[30] The film bears allegiance to the comic world of Alea. Indeed, *Se permuta* started life as

Table 3. Top Cuban films by admission, 1980–87 (Cuba)

Film	Director	Year	Admissions (in millions)
Guardafronteras	Octavio Cortázar	1980	2.5
Polvo rojo	Jesús Díaz	1981	1.1
Se permuta	Juan Carlos Tabío	1983	2.2
Los pájaros tirándole a la escopeta	Rolando Díaz	1984	2.8
De tal pedro, tal astilla	Luis Felipe Bernaza	1985	1.8
Una novia para David	Orlando Rojas	1985	1.4
En tres y dos	Rolando Díaz	1985	1
Clandestinos	Fernando Pérez	1987	1.1

a stage play based on an idea of Alea's to use "a chain of house swaps as a pretext to reveal a cross section of our society"[31]—the same play of which we catch a glimpse in *Hasta cierto punto,* where its authorship is attributed to the character of Óscar. (Tabío was very much Alea's protégé and would later become his most selfless collaborator when he supported him in his illness by codirecting his two last films.) The film was a particular success for Rosa Fornés, an actress who had made many films in Mexico but here appeared in her first for ICAIC, re-creating her stage role on film.

If Tabío has the edge over Rolando Díaz when it comes to comic timing, these two films between them effectively reinvent the genre of social comedy pioneered by Alea and García Espinosa in the 1960s; they take up the earlier films' play upon revolutionary manners to reinsert it into a quite different social climate, where comedy becomes the most effective way of engaging in social criticism. Both are debut features that establish a new genre of sociocritical comedy that will grow stronger over the years, developing into one of the most effective strands in ICAIC's output (and in the 1990s, evolving a surrealistic strand). That both these films use generational conflict and amorous affairs as their basic material is not just because these topics commend themselves as a photogenic site for exploration, especially given the vitality of the popular sense of humor, but because they mark the parallel emergence of new generations. These films appeared at the moment when those born in the first few years of the Revolution were reaching their maturity. In

1984, more than half the population was born after 1959. They were not to experience the same forms of poverty, illiteracy, and discrimination that obtained before the overthrow of Batista. But the previous generation, who came of age in the 1960s, had enjoyed ready social promotion because of the lack of cadres (and the emigration of so many middle-class professionals); the next generation would find social advancement more difficult, especially as pockets of hidden unemployment placed a brake on prospects for the professional development of new blood.

ICAIC itself represented a peculiar variation on this theme. Those who are commonly thought of as the first generation of directors break down into several groups: the founders (including Guevara, Alea, García Espinosa, and Álvarez), who were then mostly in their thirties and had prior experience in film production (or, in the case of Álvarez, radio); a second group who debuted in the early 1960s (including Solás, Manuel Pérez, and Sergio Giral); and a younger group of apprentice directors who made their first films in the mid- to late 1960s (Tabío, Sara Gómez, Cortázar, and others). What unites this otherwise disparate collectivity is their shared experience of the heady, euphoric years of the 1960s. Those in the second group generally made their first features in the late 1960s or early 1970s; for those in the third group, the prospects were rather more patchy—ICAIC had reached the limits of its resources for large-scale production. On the other hand, production of shorts and newsreels allowed the recruitment of what became the second generation of directors, those who began to make films in the 1970s, whose graduation to features was delayed until the early 1980s. They were not in conflict with the generation that preceded them—on the contrary, they respected them highly—but their experience of the Revolution had already moved on. As a result, when they got their chance, they immediately opened up a new space, a new thematics that corresponded to a social reality reconfigured by the accelerated social development of the Revolution, within which attitudes and values change more rapidly than outside, and to judge from the films, successive generations get wise more quickly.

The new regime of García Espinosa was beginning to work. Out of 120 new feature films released in Cuba during 1984, as many as eight were Cuban, and they were seen by almost 20 percent of the total audience; the following year came another eight, including five debut features, three of which achieved audiences of one million or more (Table 3).

For Caballero and del Río, looking back, this renovation succeeded only up to a point. The number of films produced increased, and new directors entered the scene, but the majority by way of a decorous *opera prima* designed to appeal to the popular audience. García Espinosa, also looking back, defended his record. The promotion of new directors was urgent, so the first thing was to increase production. This meant some consternation for the public since these debut films, though generally superior to those of the 1960s, were often easy to criticize; but it opened the possibility to a greater pluralism. There was neither a single political line that feature production was required to follow nor a single artistic line, although comedies clearly had a special value in the circumstances of the period—they represented a popular current undervalued in comparison to straight drama, "but you could do more disturbing things with them."[32]

Meanwhile, among the new documentary directors who emerged in the 1980s were a number of women who developed a new optic of their own. Two films by Marisol Trujillo in 1983 stand at the beginning of this new trend, *Mujer ante el espejo* (Woman facing the mirror) and *Oración* (Prayer). In the former, the classical ballet dancer Charín observes the changes in her body brought about by pregnancy and then returns to the stage with a new self-image. The latter follows the model of Álvarez, a brilliant and disturbing experimental film essay using nothing but found footage to compose a montage to accompany a poem about Marilyn Monroe by the Nicaraguan poet-priest Ernesto Cardenal. Here, while the text speaks of Monroe as an innocent who dreamed of becoming a star and "only acted the script that we gave her," the image ranges disjunctively from clips of her films to scenes of warfare and mass protest that indict the hegemony of the empire. These and other short films by other directors, including Rebeca Chávez and Mayra Vilásis, achieve what Catherine Benamou calls "an expansion inward" of the testimonial documentary into the exploration of feminine subjectivity, even when the subjects are public figures like Rigoberta Menchú and Winnie Mandela, where the contrapuntal use of the female voice, archival images, and music drawn from different contexts "emphasizes the historical connection between the protagonists' evolving sense of identity and their national arenas of struggle, without losing sight of the affective influences on their inner-developing consciousness."[33]

Mention should also be made of other currents, with productions by entities that included the studios of the Armed Forces (ECTVFAR) and the television stations.[34] There were also the film-club activists who began to become organized at the end of the 1970s, although all this work remains outside the purview of the present study, except for the fact that one or two of the directors involved, notably Tomás Piard, would also make inroads in cinema (or television).

The changes at ICAIC under García Espinosa were not programmatic, nor do they suggest a smooth translation of the ideas of imperfect cinema from page to practice, but rather a principled policy to succor a pluralist space of respect for creative endeavor. The Havana Film Festival ensured that the results were now regularly exposed to a sympathetic international audience—the filmmakers of the new cinema movement in Latin America who brought their own films and watched them side by side. To mount the festival, ICAIC created a network of collaborators across the continent, who organized the selection of films and national contingents. Selection was officially open, and in many countries it was more a question of ensuring supply than choosing films that observed particular criteria. In practice, an unspoken code encouraged independent filmmakers and kept away producers who were politically reluctant to be seen in Cuba. As a result, most worthwhile production found its way to Havana, while purely commercial stuff, like Brazilian *porno-chanchada,* did not. By 1983, there were 160 distributors from thirty-one countries—in Latin America and elsewhere—in the market section of the festival, MECLA (Mercado de Cine Latinoamericano).

The festival included from the outset an accompanying program of meetings, seminars, and symposiums, on topics like the role of transnational capitalism in media and communications, or the functions of criticism. The intellectual agenda was encapsulated at the very first festival in a contribution by the North American political scientist Herbert Schiller, who analyzed the semantics of terms like the *free flow of information* and *underdevelopment.* The former, he explained, was used by the powerful to disguise the structures of control that in fact impede the free flow of information, and that operate at a global level through transnational corporations. Underdevelopment is more paradoxical. It is not a mark of underdevelopment, he said, to use simple and traditional means of communication. On the contrary, advanced technologies are not only extremely powerful, they induce a frightening degree of passivity in the public. Only communication as a collective and reciprocal social activity can be strong enough to combat the technological apparatus of the transnationals. This is an analysis that corroborates that of imperfect cinema, implicitly supporting the project of a new cinema based in quasi-artisanal modes of production, motivated by a profound desire for communicative action, and faced with the need to carve out space for itself both nationally and, if possible, internationally.[35]

García Espinosa saw the festival as a means of invading this international space on condition that the films were promoted more aggressively. The formula he applied included opening the festival up to television and video, and recruiting the presence of stars, mainly from Hollywood, who were known from private contacts to be sufficiently sympathetic toward Cuba to accept an invitation. (Their reward would be a meeting with the Comandante en Jefe; but then, every visitor from California strengthened Hollywood's growing disapproval of Washington policy toward Cuba.) A big push was made for the seventh edition of the festival in 1985, at which 100 features, 150 documentaries, and more than 400 videos were projected for some two thousand foreign delegates, who included Francis Ford Coppola, Jack Lemmon, Harry Belafonte, Robert De Niro, Christopher Walken, and Treat Williams. Behind the publicity operation, the delegates engaged in serious work. There were meetings of international committees of organizations like the Congreso Internacional de Cine Clubes and the Sindicatos y Uniones de Actores Latinoamericanos, and the creation of new ones. These included a new Fundación del Nuevo Cine Latinoamericano, one of whose tasks would be the establishment of a new international film school, located in Cuba, with support from the Cuban government, though its students would be drawn from the three continents of the tricontinental movement of the 1960s—Latin America, Africa, and Asia. The school was officially opened by Castro the following year, at San Antonio de los Baños near Havana, with Fernando Birri as its first director. The growing links would also bear fruit in the 1990s, in the support that Cuban filmmakers found in institutions like Robert Redford's Sundance Institute.

Fidel duly appeared at the closing session of the 1985 festival, and spoke about his liking for cinema—the speech was a short one, only forty-five minutes. He gave little away on the level of personal taste, claiming simply to be "one of those people who have been conquered by the New Latin American Cinema, and that's what it should be called—a conquest," but he spoke of the problems of cultural imperialism. "I can imagine how much our writers and thinkers suffer when they see what happens in our countries, with this alienating system that operates every day, at every hour of the day, through the screens. And where is the majority of what we see produced, what we enjoy or try to enjoy? Not in our own countries, not in Latin America." It was not only expensive high technology, from aircraft to computers, that the underdeveloped countries were forced to purchase, along with all sorts of equipment, merchandise, and industrial products, "but we also import our cinema, our television, our culture—or false culture! We experience complete decadence and don't realise the extent to which we are subjected to cultural colonisation."

For the first time, the Hollywood trade journal *Variety* was in attendance, and published reviews of the crop of new Cuban films on show at the festival. If they were not particularly impressed, neither was anyone else, except by the fact that ICAIC was presenting five new feature directors, some of whom enjoyed considerable success with Cuban audiences. *Una novia para David* (A girlfriend for David) by Orlando Rojas—which was seen by eight hundred thousand people in its first six weeks—is an affectionate, if visually dull, portrayal of life among college kids in Havana in the late 1960s. John King is unkind but not entirely incorrect to compare it with a sophomore movie like *Porky's* (dir. Bob Clark, 1981), as an example of a subgenre of raunchy, low-budget adolescent comedy. From Luis Felipe Bernaza, *De tal pedro, tal astilla* (A chip off the old block) is a fictional version of the same director's amusing documentary of 1980, *Pedro cero por ciento* (Pedro zero percent), about a dairy farmer on a small cattle ranch in the province of Sancti Spiritus, who has not let a single cow die in seven years. The fictional version has two rivals, driven by socialist emulation, vying for top place. Parodying Cervantes and Shakespeare at the same time, the film shows young people, members of rival families, who fall in love, to the great displeasure of their parents, who end up in physical confrontation. This film was even more popular, but, however funny, it represented a highly idealized version of the conditions in the Cuban countryside, a year before the farmers' markets, introduced in 1980, were closed down because of excessive profiteering.[36]

Something similar is true of *El corazón sobre la tierra* (Heart across the land), by Constante Diego, which, according to Caballero and del Río, was classed by certain critics as the height of supposed Cuban socialist realism. A father and son in Havana dream of starting a cooperative in the far-off Sierra Maestra mountains, but when the son is killed in action in Ethiopia, the father throws himself into the cause of the cooperative with maniacal devotion. While *Variety* found it a "predictable and quickly tiresome tract designed to demonstrate how even independent-minded roughnecks in the Cuban mountains can rally round the spirit of the revolution," for the Cuban critics, the film indicates the solidity of a social project whose dramatic representation however, is misjudged. *Jíbaro* (Wild dog) by Daniel Díaz Torres is set in the Escambray in the heroic early days of the Revolution, where wily old peasants play their part in the struggle against the counterrevolutionaries; the title is an obvious metaphor for the reactionary elements that need killing off. *Variety* called it "a didactic modern-day Western" filled with predictable action and sentiment, but it made a respectable, if duly conventional, debut.

More interesting was *Como la vida misma* (Like life itself) by Víctor Casaus, which marked the return to the Cuban cinema screen of Sergio Corrieri. Corrieri, anxious to avoid becoming a typecast star, had left the cinema to form a theater group in the Escambray, presenting to countryside audiences with no experience of theater, plays collectively written about their own concerns. The film is a fictionalized account of one of these productions, and thus presents a picture of the Escambray very different from that of the genre movies. The subject is not the economy of the countryside, however, but deficiencies in the education system admitted by the education minister, José Fernández, the same year the film came out, and indicated by the statistics on cheating, which went on in 34 percent of secondary schools.[37] We are in a high school, where an incident of cheating occurs, and the theater group decides to make it the theme of the play. The cast consists of actors both professional and nonprofessional, and of personages both real and fictional, in a mold now well established in Cuban cinema; but the lines are crossed, and some of the professional actors, including Corrieri, represent not fictional characters but themselves. *Variety* calls the film "an amiable comic drama . . . punctuated by sizeable helpings of lowbrow, but frequently funny, comedy," but finds what it calls the subplot about cheating uninvolving. This is to miss the point of a film that sets out to use the subplot to investigate the attitudes and beliefs of the new generation growing up within the Revolution. In the school, the disciplinary investigation of the incident runs parallel to the preparation of the production, until an improvisation onstage gets too close to the bone, and in a tense moment the culprit confesses. There is also a romantic subplot and Casaus breaks up the narrative with disparate elements like tape-recorded interviews—unfortunately, not always well integrated. He has, nonetheless, in attempting to emulate Alea, come up with a film that is not moralistic, but, much more important, interrogative, and in this respect more truly represents the self-questioning of imperfect cinema than the genre celebrations of revolutionary bravery.

A couple more things might be said of this film. First, it shows how Cuban cinema learned to attune its vocation for social criticism by taking public admissions of problems and inserting them into dramatic contexts. If the fate of *Techo de vidrio,* despite the problems raised by Fidel the same year it was made, suggests this was not always a strategy that succeeded, *Se permuta* fared better by picking on a problem that was already subject to wide comment, and, in making *Como la vida misma,* it does Casaus no harm when cheating is admitted by the minister in charge. Second, as a conceptually ambitious film, it shows that the demands of imperfect cinema are not an easy option; in fact, they might well make a successful debut feature more difficult. But the result is a film that flags up a social problem that would only intensify over the coming years, namely, the signs of malaise among the youth.

This left two new films by the brothers Rolando and Jesús Díaz. Rolando's *En tres y dos* is a baseball story that *Variety* called "an intelligent, sympathetic but poorly structured look at a top Cuban baseball star who is forced to confront his retirement from the sport," but it was put off by what it called "some unique digressions by way of vintage newsreel footage and contemporary interviews" with athletic legends like boxer Kid Chocolate and the runner Juantorena, and judged the film "somewhat confusing even for baseball fans." If these "digressions" are precisely the elements that differentiate the film from a Hollywood biopic, the Cuban critic Rolando Pérez Betancourt, himself a keen baseball fan who found the film at certain points very moving, suspected it was unintelligible for those who knew nothing about the sport. "Some comrades," he wrote, "have asked me if it's true that to see *En tres y dos* you need to know about the game. At the 1985 film festival, Gian Maria Volonté remarked that he'd seen the film, and he could tell it dealt with important matters, but not knowing baseball much of it was lost on him, and the same thing happened to the members of the jury."[38]

Much more to *Variety*'s liking was the other brother's *Lejanía*, "the first local feature to deal with the issue of Cuban exiles returning to the island for visits with relatives," and the most ambitious and controversial of the Cuban films "unspooled" at the 1985 festival. In the journal's inimitable language, "Although pic would be restricted by its nature to select and specialized houses, its creative virtues and US-related subject matter are such that it deserves some limited commercial playoff in addition to international fest slottings."[39] A man and his family are reunited with his mother and his cousin and childhood playmate. A Cuban exile (Verónica Lynn) returns to Havana from Miami with her niece (Isabel Santos) to visit the son she left behind (Jorge Trinchet) and his wife (Beatriz Valdés). Enclosed within the space of an apartment in the Havana district of Vedado, with its rooftop overlooking the city, and in the time span of a couple of days, a woman who abandoned her teenage son—because boys approaching military age were not allowed to leave—for the "good life" in the United States, returns trailing guilt and suitcases stuffed with gifts in a vain attempt to reclaim him. The trauma of families divided by the revolution, a theme that Jesús Díaz had tackled twice before, is here given a contemporary setting that entirely casts aside the dimensions of the epic to home in, like a play by Chekov, on half a dozen characters.

Díaz uses the spatial texture of the apartment to reveal the distances that separate his characters on various different levels—political, psychological, and cultural. Reinaldo's mother Susana, whom even *Variety* describes as "a middle-aged woman of deep-rooted bourgeois tastes," is puzzled by the bare furnishings; when she asks why the coffee isn't served in the cups she was given on her wedding, Reinaldo replies, "Who remembers that?" Aleida, his wife, tells her that after she left, Reinaldo sold off the contents bit by bit—clothes, furniture, decorations. As Susana effuses nostalgia for her former home—and for a Cuba that now only exists in her mind—the apartment becomes a symbolic mise-en-scène that Reinaldo has tried to empty of memories and where his mother now appears to him like a ghost—whom he addresses throughout her visitation, even after her objections, not as *tú* but with the formal *Usted*. *Variety* remarks that "the photographer Mario García Joya's very mobile lensing in the tight quarters is superior." Indeed, the camera circles the characters, follows them down corridors, peers through half-open doors, with a fluidity all the more astonishing when you know that this is a handheld camera without a steadycam. García Joya—"Mayito"—applied the wiliness of imperfect cinema to the skills of cinematography; a steadycam was an impossible luxury, so he devised a simple wooden pole with a crosspiece at the top of exactly the right height on which to rest the handheld camera when he was standing still; his camera assistant slid it into place when he wanted the camera to come to rest, and took it away when he wanted to move again. (A year or so later, shooting a coproduction in Colombia—Jorge Alí Triana's *Tiempo de morir*—without the luxury of camera tracks, he stripped down an old Deux Chevaux to make a dolly that could ride smoothly down a poorly maintained street.)

The intensely naturalistic feel achieved by the use of available light is intensified by the direct location sound; if the film never feels claustrophobic, this is largely because of the constant presence on the sound track of the world outside, mostly unobtrusive but unobscured by background music. Nearly all the music in the film, except for the theme song over the credits, is diegetic and acousmatic: it comes from the television, the radio, and the stereo that Susana has brought from Miami. It is the everyday music of the contemporary world of the film, which becomes an ironic intertext because it reveals the presence of the past in the cultural substrate in a manner that intertwines public and private memories. Thus cousin Ana, left alone for the first time with Reinaldo, turns on the television to discover a popular black entertainer she doesn't recognize singing an old-style ballad she doesn't know, but which in her present situation she finds intensely sad; it is the singer Omara Portuondo and the film's theme song, "Veinte años atrás" (Twenty years ago), about the separation of two lovers and the impossibility of rekindling their love: "I was the illusion in your life a long time ago, I represent the past, I cannot be consoled." (With gentle self-mockery, it is immediately followed by a snatch of Carlos Gardel singing his most famous tango and the very epitome of nostalgia: "Volver" [Return].) Configured in the song are both the unbridgeable separation of the exile from their country and the personal separation between the cousins; and if they start by fooling around like children, they end up in an embrace with distinctly erotic overtones. Indeed, when Aleida comes back later in the day to find a television set left on and a rumpled bed, she is prepared to think the worst, momentarily revealing the Cuban woman's constitutional suspicion of the Cuban man.

From time to time, the camera stays or comes to halt on blank surfaces: a blank page in a photograph album where the family photos ran out; the plain white wall; the TV screen that Susana impetuously turns off because it is showing "one of those propaganda films"—it is, in fact, a scene from Alea's *La última cena.* How should we read these blank frames? Susana has brought with her an 8 mm home movie of the family in Florida. They close the blinds and project the jerky and of course silent film on the wall. Brief images of a comfortable American suburbia peopled by a big happy family are followed by an old man silently mouthing the words that she has brought separately on tape—the father's last message to his son. Reinaldo left alone in the flat, rifles through the suitcases, tries on this or that, mockingly plugs a hair dryer into his ear in a shot in front of a mirror that pointedly evokes another of Alea's films, the scene of Sergio Corrieri in *Memorias del subdesarrollo* playing with the appurtenances his wife left behind when she left for the States— an allusion through which Díaz not only declares allegiance to Alea's type of cinema but lays claim to a history of representation in which the Cuban cinema viewer may discover the traces of what may not be openly spoken, but about which it is not possible to remain silent. Late at night, after a row with Aleida, Reinaldo listens to his father's tape. The cassette player, the blank television screen, and the seated listener are silhouetted against the blank wall, in a paradoxical image whose composition seems deliberately unpictorial, and both empty and full at the same time. It is as if memory itself is desynchronized.

"Western viewers," says *Variety,* "will be amazed by the diffidence with which Reinaldo is able to treat his mother, and perhaps a bit appalled at the manner in which American values are exclusively tied to material possessions." If so, they would be falling into a well-prepared trap. As Díaz explained to *Cine Cubano,* the gifts from Florida become an ethical touchstone by exposing the various attitudes of different members of the family, from gleeful acceptance to cutting rejection, thus confronting the viewer with the problem of which character to identify with.[40] As a narrative device, this works with any audience, but differently for Cuban viewers, as *Variety* seems to be aware, even if it balks at the central metaphor in which Susana offers Reinaldo a world of material riches in exchange for the emotional succor she took away from him. The perversion of motherly love in the service of the dehumanizing culture of consumerism becomes, in Cuba, a mark of perverse complicity with an ideology that places wasteful materialism above natural human feeling. The effect is to place at the center of the film a metaphor of the double-sided condition that divides the first world and the third, the two faces of deprivation, emotional in one, material in the other.

From Ana, however, Reinaldo learns that the loss he suffered may well be no less than hers, in being dragged away from her country, her culture. When the two of them emerge into the daylight for the first time, halfway through the film, onto the roof of the house with its panorama of the city, Ana's eyes become tearful as she recites for him a poem about exile by the Cuban-American poet Lourdes Casal (to whom Díaz has dedicated the film), recounting the feeling of being a stranger in the city where you live, and a foreigner when you go back to the city of your infancy: "Demasiado habanera para ser neoyorquina / Demasiada neoyorquina para ser— / Aun volver a ser—cualquier otra cosa" (Too much of an Habanera to be a New Yorker, too much a New Yorker to be, even go back to being, anything else). This quiet moment, the insertion of the voice of Otherness, is perhaps the heart of the film, a moment wrenched out of division, disruption, and hostility, which accomplishes the humanization of the estranged.

Díaz has claimed, with justice, that *Lejanía* is one of the few films of the day "that dares to treat a really complex and controversial subject, and, moreover, does it without *teque* [political rhetoric], without external abuse of the ideological, without even showing the work of the Revolution explicitly," that is to say, without falling back on the achievements of the Revolution as counters in the moral and emotional debate that the film represents.[41] This was to make many viewers on both sides of the divide quite uncomfortable. *Variety* commended Díaz "for tackling such a politically sensitive and tricky subject in such a forthright manner," but felt that he ended up "painting a devastating and exceedingly bleak picture of the possibilities of any reconciliation between mother and son, and, by extension, between the two countries." The reviewer also picked up on the problematic reception of the film in Cuba, reporting that, "ironically, Díaz has been attacked by certain quarters in his native country for trading as extensively as he does in ambiguities," or simply for suggesting that there are some Cubans ready to be seduced

by the supposedly superficial attractions of "decadent" American society. These include the figure of Reinaldo's uncle, Jacinto, a bureaucrat and
terrible opportunist, who, despite his revolutionary credentials, is presented as morally on a par with Susana. But others, instead of attacking
the film, ignored it. One review even drew attention to the phenomenon,
under the title "Algunos prefieren callarse" (Some prefer to keep quiet),
in parody of the Spanish title of *Some Like It Hot,* (Algunos prefieren
quemarse).

The fate of *Lejanía* raises the general problem of film criticism in Cuba.
This inevitably raises the question of the relation of ICAIC and its filmmakers to the critics, and the critics' relation to the press and the public.
This in turn brings us back to the question of ICAIC's role in the transformation of the public sphere in Cuba following the Revolution. By the
1970s, the relations between the various social actors had become distinctly asymmetrical. The filmmakers occupied a public space more privileged than the press, enjoying a direct popular appeal of their own, as
well as the soft regime of the Ministry of Culture compared to the supervision of the hard-liners in the ideological office of the central committee. The press was necessarily cautious, inclined toward ambivalence in
making judgments, sometimes even to reproof; the Institute found the
press frequently unhelpful.

Julianne Burton has suggested that ICAIC was always leery of professional critics and therefore decided early on to assume the critic's task
itself by creating the journal *Cine Cubano*.[42] If it is true that many Cuban
filmmakers believed the exercise of criticism to be a responsibility of
the filmmaker, not to be left to journalists and literati, the journal was
also an expression of the same imperative that guided the creation of
film magazines throughout Latin America wherever a nucleus of filmmakers committed to the new cinema movement took root: a magazine
was a declaration of existence, a claim for attention, an instrument in
the construction of an identity. Publications of this kind tend to share
with the films of the movement they belong to many of the same artisanal qualities, and are devoted more to championing a cause and dis-
seminating positions than traditional forms of critical reflection. *Cine
Cubano* set new standards in the service of propagation and the education of its readership, and showed its spirit in its own distinctive modern typography and design. Abroad, the magazine became a primary

source of information about Cuban and the new Latin American cinema in general. At home, the readership included the expanding circle of critics at a time when their numbers were growing, with more space to fill in a press transformed by the Revolution.

In this way *Cine Cubano* quickly took on its primary function, becoming a cross between a house magazine and a journal of record, with background material on new and upcoming films together with interviews with leading Cuban, Latin American, and other filmmakers and the like. The dominant discourse was that of the filmmakers, their intentions, desires, hopes, explanations, and theoretical formations, often of a sociological character. The newspapers were left with the job of reviewing new releases, with other journals carrying interviews and background pieces. No longer quite the same as what Brecht once called copywriting for the entertainment industry, nevertheless the predominant stance among many of the newspaper critics tended toward political conformism dressed up in sometimes florid aesthetic appraisal; there was little attempt to elucidate possible metaphorical and subtextual readings of the films, especially when these might reveal a critical angle. As well as publishing *Cine Cubano*, icaic's solution to this situation was to take on the task of animating a wider sense of film culture in the general audience, bypassing the critics and reaching out directly to the public through television, employing a couple of specialists for the purpose. Carlos Galiano, who also wrote reviews in *Granma*, hosted weekly screenings under the title *History of Cinema*, and Enrique Colina presented the prime-time *Twenty-Four Frames a Second*, one of the most popular programs on Cuban television, an intelligent viewer's guide to current and new cinema from around the world.

Colina turned filmmaker in the 1980s with a series of shorts whose humor made him one of the most distinctive experimentalists of the decade. As Paranagua puts it, he "succeeded in getting the most conventional kind of documentary, the didactic film, to implode with a dose of corrosive humour."[43] Colina's targets range from the misadventures of consumers in Cuba's counterconsumption society, to productivity and carelessness, by way of the irritating habits of one's neighbors. *Estética* (Aesthetics) satirizes the vagaries of popular taste, *Vecinos* exposes noisemakers. His style is one of tightly edited free association of observed scenes, interviews, film clips and apposite songs on the sound track. *Chapucerías* (Sloppy work), a critique of negligence in the fulfillment of work goals—"Please excuse the sloppy work, we've surpassed our work plan"—presents itself as a self-reflexive documentary that crosscuts the investigation with the editors at the editing table sloppily putting together this very film and even, at the end, trying to find a suitable conclusion. This is a mode of filmmaking that surpasses easy labeling. When is a documentary not a documentary? And yet not to be considered as fiction, because its characters are not invented—they are "gente con nombre y apellido," people with their own first and second name.

Burton, writing in the mid-1980s, blamed the principle articulated by García Espinosa in 1970—"imperfect cinema rejects whatever services criticism has to offer and considers the function of mediators and intermediaries anachronistic"—for holding *Cine Cubano* back, since "largely as a result of such attitudes" the magazine did not keep pace "with the explosion of theoretical and methodological inquiry in the field of film studies over the past two decades."[44] But then *Cine Cubano* was neither an academic journal nor ever intended to be, and the intellectual focus for such studies in Cuba lay elsewhere, catered for by critical journals like *Temas* and educational publishing houses that issued translations of Russian semiologists like Mikhail Bakhtin and Yuri Lotman, when they were still little known in Western Europe and North America. On the other hand, Burton is correct to say that while the presentation of cinema on television was remarkably sophisticated, its print counterpart remained "deplorably limited." In a word, the critical function did not recover from the conformism imposed on the media during the gray years of the early 1970s. The critic merely passed from a condition of crude ideological orthodoxy to a state of timidity, especially when confronted with a film that addressed a topic surrounded with taboos. Jesús Díaz was not wrong to complain that critics "who do not express an opinion are simply not fulfilling their function. It is disconcerting that there have sometimes been calls for cinema to treat the complex problems of our reality, our ideological struggle, and when this happens there's nothing, a culpable silence."[45]

The changes introduced in ICAIC by García Espinosa entered a new phase after the middle of the decade, in the search for a response to a situation of growing contradictions, both internally and externally. Cuba in the 1980s had not yet fully escaped the economic legacy of its past. It had not achieved the economic diversification for which Che Guevara and others had argued in the 1960s. Membership of the Soviet trading bloc, Comecon, brought huge advantages: for example, what the Soviet Union paid for Cuban sugar was way above the market price, an adjustment that the West called subsidy while the Communists called it a reversal of the unequal terms of trade imposed by the core capitalist countries on the third world. But, as the economist Carlos Tablada wrote in a book that won the Casa de las Américas prize in 1987, two nations can proceed to trade with each other in such a way that both benefit, even though one exploits and constantly robs the other; and thus the more developed socialist countries can contribute to the development of dependent countries while they also participate, to a greater or lesser degree, in their exploitation.[46] Remarks like this would have been impossible in public only a few years earlier. On this reading, a combination of Soviet-style economic centralization and the historic effects of underdevelopment—in short, continuing dependency on two or three principal cash crops (sugar, tobacco, and coffee)—effectively held back Cuba's further development. A fall in world sugar prices that began in 1982 had a serious impact on its economy. By the mid-1980s, the economy was slowing down seriously enough to occasion austerity measures. By the end of the decade, the ICAIC newsreel was reporting the terrible effects produced, for example, by breakdowns in public transport in Havana, or the city's housing crisis.

In Tablada's view, one kind of dependency turned into another, and produced new inefficiencies; these affected ICAIC in much the same way as everyone else. In 1987, while making a television documentary on the economic and political situation in Cuba, the present writer filmed a textile factory in Santiago de Cuba that was operating at only 43 percent of capacity, partly because of problems in the supply of raw materials, some of which came from the Soviet Union and East Germany.[47] At the same time, ICAIC was suffering holdups at the laboratories through lack of film stock from the same sources, which they used for work copies and prints. (For reasons of quality, features were shot on Eastman Kodak, officially unavailable because of the American blockade but obtainable in other countries through friends.) In a word, the economy was underproducing. Yet despite such problems, the same thing could be said of Cuba that, according to Eric Hobsbawm, was true of Soviet communism. For most Soviet citizens, the Brezhnev era was not one of stagnation, but the best times they, their parents, and their grandparents had ever known. The system "provided a guaranteed livelihood and comprehensive social security at a modest but real level, a socially and economically egalitarian society and at least one of the traditional aspirations of socialism, Paul Lafargue's 'Right to Idleness.'"[48] In short, the system adapted, and a certain form of underemployment became institutionalized. In the Cuban context, Hobsbawm's invocation of Marx's son-in-law, one of the founders of the French communist movement, is especially apt. As García Espinosa once pointed out to me with ironic patriotism, Lafargue was born in Santiago de Cuba—Marx once casually referred in a letter to his "mulatto blood"—and, from a Cuban point of view, was only articulating a very Cuban attitude.

In 1985, a passionate reformer, Mikhail Gorbachev, came to power as general secretary of the Soviet Communist Party, and with the new watchwords of *perestroika* and *glasnost,* restructuring and openness, the whole Soviet bloc was thrown into intense debate about an agenda for the transformation of the communist state that, as Hobsbawm reminds us, had in fact been brewing for a good while.[49] In Cuba, over the next few years, Soviet affairs were followed with a surprising passion that made the weekly *Moscow News* a best-seller, while audiences battled to get into the cinemas to see previously banned films like Tengiz Abuladze's *Repentance* of 1984. Amid this heady atmosphere, the imperative need at ICAIC was for some kind of internal reorganization to cope with an increase in production, since it was one thing for everyone to agree to restrict their budgets in order to get more films made, another to properly supervise their making. But the new ideological climate, in which the campaign of *rectificación* (rectification) that Castro launched at the end of 1986 was initially seen as the Cuban counterpart to *perestroika,* opened up a space that, in theory, extended the range of thinkable solutions beyond the orthodox, and in the case of ICAIC, did so in practice.

Perestroika and *rectificación* would turn out rather differently. Perestroika sought to address the need for fundamental economic and political transformations, in the process unleashing forces that would prove uncontrollable. Castro spoke merely of "rectifying errors and negative tendencies in all spheres of society" in a battle against economic inefficiency and the growth of social inequalities. García Espinosa treated perestroika and rectification in practical terms as the same, and took off to Moscow to investigate the approach of the new head of the Soviet film industry, Elem Klimov. The trip confirmed him in the conviction that Cuba had no cause to follow other models, but needed a home-made solution of its own. The ideal—a series of independent studios or production houses—was impossible with Cuba's lack of resources; on the other hand, ICAIC was too large to function as efficiently as it might. His answer was to devolve control over the production process to three "creative groups" *(grupos de creación)*, with their own programs of production, which they supervised themselves from beginning to end.

In his own account, the *grupos de creación* answered to several imperatives, including the lack of experienced executive producers, a role that in ICAIC was effectively fulfilled by the head of production. When he had occupied this position himself in the 1960s, at a time when ICAIC was only producing three or four features a year, he had also occupied the role of executive producer, but this could hardly be considered viable for a single person when there were eight or nine films a year to deal with. Moreover, times had changed, and it was no longer possible for a single person to exercise a "historical authority" in this way. In a capitalist film industry, the executive producer had the clear function of molding the film and controlling the budget in the interests of financial success. In Cuba, the aims were different. Instead of slavery to the market, the objective was "to try and conciliate quality and communication"; in other words, a question of a certain cultural politics. "Who," he asked, "should fulfill this function of being the trustees of ICAIC's politics if not the filmmakers themselves? Better filmmakers than functionaries."[50] Not only would the groups form a more democratic internal structure that guarded against arbitrary decisions being handed down from on high. At the same time, by giving each group control over its own production program, the arrangement would allow a more flexible approach to resourcing, and thus an expanded production program. Under the existing system, planning was governed by official work norms, which, rather like union rules under capitalism, would determine such considerations as the official size of the film crew, whether the director needed them or not; the new groups would be able to shift these norms around to suit the needs of the film. If production increased as a result, it would be to everyone's benefit.

Finally, and by no means least, the scheme benefited from allowing for association on the basis of personal allegiances. The three groups, which were set up in 1987, were headed by Manuel Pérez, Humberto Solás, and Tomás Gutiérrez Alea. They soon became known affectionately as *los rojos, los rosados,* and *los verdes* (reds, pinks, and greens), respectively—a joke with a strong dose of popular wisdom in it. Although the categories should not be applied too strictly to individuals, it is no accident if this color scheme suggests a triangulation to be found within ICAIC in the late 1980s, in both aesthetic predilection and political tendency, where red is the color of political orthodoxy and populism, pink of sexual libertarianism and visual stylistics, and green of radicalism and "imperfect cinema."

The dominant trends to begin with were the red and the pink. In *Clandestinos,* Fernando Pérez conformed to pattern for his effective debut feature with a genre exercise directed at the youth audience. Based on historical events but with fictional characters, with a well-crafted script by Jesús Díaz, the story concerns the life of a group of young people involved in the clandestine struggle against Batista in the 1950s. Solid, well paced, and atmospheric, it is described by the director as a love story in the context of the underground struggle—"it was not my intention to make a historical film, although we were inspired by real facts, but to deal with themes to be found throughout history like love and death." Solás, meanwhile, pursued the critique of historical spectacle with *Un hombre de éxito,* a film in which for the first time since *Un día de noviembre* he focused on a male rather than a female progatonist. A study in opportunism, a chronicle of the moral decline of the bourgeoisie over three decades from the 1930s to the eve of the Revolution, seen through the lives of two brothers separated by ideology and ambition, what most impressed the critics was the opulent mise-en-scène, which gave the film the impression of a superproduction and garnered much praise for ICAIC's art directors, set dressers, and costumiers, and especially Livio Delgado's cinematography, which, as Pérez Betancourt put it, "seems to leave nothing to chance."[51] There was much more talk about what the same critic called "those long shots which—through the architecture, decor, and the most varied details of the ambience—capture the whole personality of an epoch." If this calls forth comparison, as with previous films by Solás, with Visconti, the film is much more than a stylistic exercise. Solás is clearly more interested in the ambience than the politics, which is treated fairly schematically, and uses the Viscontiesque camera to scrutinize the pose the bourgeoisie constructs for itself in the privacy of its own domain. As a result, the film is less a political allegory than a commentary on historical complacence, although it also elicited comments about the way Solás was using history to make references to the present—if no one said exactly what this consisted of, it seemed obvious enough. In 1986, a vice minister had absconded to Spain with half a million dollars; to this, by the time the film was premiered, must be added the defection to the United States of an air force general, the arrest on corruption charges of the president of the civil aviation institute, and a couple more defections—a sequence of events that revealed the reappearance in the ruling echelons of phenomena that had disappeared in the first years of the revolution.[52]

An independence of spirit also fed the monthly newsreel, which pursued the public criticism of political issues more single-mindedly than either television or the press. There were newsreels on topics like food shortages, the high marriage and divorce rate, and religious practice. In José Padrón's investigation of the state of Havana's public transport system in Newsreel No. 1403 (*Transporte Popular* [Public transport], 1988), a bus driver complains of a report in *Granma* charging that drivers were lax, and often failed to turn up on time for duty, when the truth was that dozens of buses were standing idle in the depot for want of spare parts, or they could only take them out for half the length of their roster because the engines quickly overheated. A year later, Padrón reported on the city's housing crisis in *Los albergados* (Hostel-dwellers, Newsreel No. 1460, 1989), exposing the reality of a situation that most broadcasters and journalists preferred not to deal with. The camera takes us on a tour of hostels, which housed less than seven thousand of the more than sixty-five thousand Habaneros who officially qualified for hostel accommodation due to the deteriorated state of their dwellings. The commentary explains that the provision of adequate housing is a task beyond the capacity of the microbrigades, the voluntary construction teams composed of ordinary workers seconded from their own workplace that originated in the 1960s but were later run down. The camera takes direct testimony from a number of occupants: a worker lamenting the effects on family life when children live with their mothers while the men are housed separately; a schoolgirl who never brings her friends "home"; a young woman with a babe in arms who admits that she and her husband have to go out to find some secluded place to make love.

Shot with a mobile handheld camera, the director adopts the role of on-screen reporter questioning participants, and the commentary takes on a critical tone. In the space of eleven minutes, the traditional newsreel length of one 35 mm reel, these are individually crafted investigative documentary shorts in the best tradition created by Santiago Álvarez. In style, tone, and mode of address, they become essays in politically responsible personal authorship. *Los albergados* ends with an official admitting that at the present rate of construction, the problem will not be solved until the year 2001, whereupon the sound track, in ironic allusion to the film by Stanley Kubrick, brings in the famous opening measures of *Also Sprach Zarathustra* over a final montage of miserable dwellings. In another edition (*Río Almendares,* Newsreel No. 1435, 1990), Padrón interrogates the pollution along the Almendares River, which runs into the sea along Havana's northern coast, between Vedado and Miramar. Here the language of the commentary is unequivocal. Those mainly responsible for the fact that so many years after the Revolution there are people still living in shacks and shantytowns along the river are the technocratic managers of the 1970s who opposed the microbrigades with a neocapitalist concept of planning that failed to take account of the social needs of the majority of the people. A popular band performs a satirical song about the pollution of the Almendares, an informant reveals the insufficient capacity of the water purification works, bathers complain that the river mouth is so contaminated they can't go swimming, and the band patrolling the beach dressed in antipollution gear brings the film to an end in the style of a pop video.

Another element in García Espinosa's strategy was to continue the policy of international coproduction, mostly with Latin America, which began at the end of the 1970s with two films by exiled Chilean directors (Sergio Castilla's *Prisioneros desaparecidos* of 1979, and *La viuda de Montiel* by Miguel Littin in 1980), a policy that contributed significantly to the flow of new films. Between 1981 and 1987 there were as many as sixteen such projects, that is, more than a third of ICAIC's total production over the same period.[53] The directors included another Chilean, Patricio Guzmán, the Peruvians Federico García and Alberto Durant, the Colombian Jorge Alí Triana, and the veteran Argentinean Fernando Birri.[54] Generally the films were shot outside Cuba with Cuban personnel in the crew and postproduction in Cuba, although Guzmán and Birri shot on location outside Havana. In both cases, however, the place represented on screen was not Cuba but "somewhere in Latin America," and quite possibly the lack of specificity contributes to a kind of vagueness in the two films, which both aim for a kind of mythical and magical-that realist Latin American universalism that is less than fully convincing. The end of the decade also saw a new trend, with three international coproductions in 1988 directed by Cubans. Manuel Herrera's *Capablanca* had the USSR as partner; *Gallego* by Manuel Octavio Gómez was the first coproduction with Spain; and Alea's *Cartas del parque* (Letters from the park) was one of six adaptations by different Latin American directors of stories by Gabriel García Márquez made for European television. The first was a prosaic biography of the Cuban chess player. The second, based on a book by Miguel Barnet, and with excellent acting by Francisco Rabal, failed to live up to its promise; it was the director's last film (Gómez died in 1988). The last, a love story set in the Cuban town of Matanzas in 1913, caused consternation among critics who felt that Alea had somehow betrayed his principles by making an entirely apolitical film. Alea himself explained, "The story takes place in Matanzas City, a hundred kilometers east of Havana, in 1913. Two lovers enlist the services of the same scribe—each of their own accord, and without the other's knowledge—to transmit their feelings to their beloved in letters the scribe pens for them. However, little by little, the scribe's own feelings prevail, much against his will, and reveal an eternal truth: love cannot be tricked."[55]

Miguel Barnet's novel *Canción de Rachel* also provided the source for a film the following year, *La bella del Alhambra* (The belle of the Alhambra) directed by the writer's cousin Enrique Pineda Barnet, which brings to life the atmosphere of the Havana theater world of the 1920s in which a chorus girl dreams of becoming a star at the Alhambra; the cost of her ambition, however, which includes sleeping with the theater's owner, drives her lover to suicide. A celebration of a controversial period in Cuban musical culture, Pineda Barnet intended the film—a little too obviously perhaps—as an allegory on the republic, which prostituted itself to foreign capital in the name of higher aspirations. A melodrama that incorporates musical numbers but is not exactly a musical, *La bella del Alhambra* was both a popular and a critical success, especially for Beatriz Valdés as Rachel, who was praised for her combination of ingenuousness, frivolity, grace, timidity, and a certain eroticized malice.[56] It was also the first Cuban film to be nominated for an Oscar. Less successful films in the same year included Pastor Vega's *En el aire* (In the air), Luis Felipe Bernaza's *Vals de La Habana Vieja* (Waltz of Old

Havana), and *La vida en rosa* (A rosy life) by Rolando Díaz. Ironically, all three deal with contemporary subjects. The first takes a young university-trained journalist to confront the daily reality of a small radio station in the countryside; the second is a social comedy that satirizes the tradition of *los quince,* the coming-out party for fifteen-year-old girls; the third is an absurdist comedy, in which a group of young people encounter their future selves as old people, and are forced to confront the question of personal values. It's an interesting experiment. As Paranagua puts it, Díaz "imagined a dramaturgical solution diametrically opposed to the usual schema: instead of a retrospective narration using flashbacks, his young characters are projected into the future, seeing themselves as old, as they will become . . . unless they manage to change their destinies."[57] The film has magical moments but suffers from an unavoidable hole in the premise, the projection of a world emptied of history, in which nothing external has changed between the present day of the young people and that of their older selves, an inevitable lapse that unfortunately robs it of credibility. One other film of 1989 deserves mention: García Espinosa's *La inútil muerte de mi socio Manolo* (The useless death of my buddy Manolo), adapted from a play by Eugenio Hernández, is a two-hander about an encounter between two men, youthful friends in the heroic days of the Revolution who now have very different perspectives on life and politics. In pursuit as ever of radical low-budget efficacy, the film is shot in a studio, eschewing a naturalistic mise-en-scène in favor of an open set and a fluid camera, tightly framing the two actors, Mario Balmaseda and Pedro Renteria, who respond with performances of great intensity. A film that touches on private disillusionment, to hint at a more metaphorical malaise.

Caballero and del Río, looking back on the period, raise the question of whether Cuban cinema in the 1980s succumbed after all to the precepts of socialist realism. In a decade flanked by the events of Mariel and the collapse of European communism, they say, Cuban cinema opted for the illustration of a general catalog of social life in Cuba. There were workers' films (like *Hasta cierto punto*), youth movies (like *Una novia para David*), urban comedies *(Se permuta),* rural comedies *(De tal pedro, tal astilla),* dramas about professionals *(Habanera),* in short, the rule of a preconception, dear to socialist realism, that the work of art must be conceived in terms of an all-embracing generality; a generality, however, that impedes the visualization of significant and symptomatic detail in favor of a condescending amalgam of references, resulting in films whose only and doubtful success rests on occasional, shallow communication with the large public. Unfortunately, they say, this link with the public "dominates the aesthetic elaboration, subordinates the principle of authorship, [and] the films end up too contingent and hence pedestrian, of meager conceptual level, lifeless, skin-deep," when what was needed was a way of exposing "the entropy of certain totalitarian discourses." In spite of intermittent signs of the difficulties and contradictions within contemporary Cuban society, these films, they say, avoided taking risks, falling back on well-known but debatable features of *cubanidad*—expressions, jokes, prejudices—without demonstrating a genuinely critical point of view; they opted instead for vulgarity and "peripheric" folklorism. Some directors embarked on a problematizing cinema that was more clearly articulated, but where the treatment of difficult edges of reality was limited to sketching out a certain disfunctionality; the filmmakers boldly entered a terrain mined with years of silence, but the impulse gave way to a simple schematicism that crippled them, and kept them from achieving half of what they aimed at (here they include such titles as *Lejanía, Techo de vidrio,* and *En el aire*).

This article, published in 1995, marks a signal new departure in Cuban film criticism. Here for the first time in print are opinions that had been circulating orally for some time, raising serious questions about the direction and achievements of Cuban cinema in its most recent phase. We shall come back to the question of what made this critical development possible, but whatever the justice of this harsh critique, there were three films in the late 1980s that, for different reasons, stand out, free of these strictures. In 1986, Juan Padron's cartoon feature *Vampiros en la Habana* (Vampires in Havana) provided unalloyed delight. It is nicely described in *Variety*'s telegraphese: "amusing sendup of gangster and vampire pictures recalling something of the raunchy irreverent spirit if not the style of Fritz the Cat. Bubbling brew of a plot has leading vampire members of the international mafia converging on Havana, circa 1933, to try to lay their hands on a new invention called Vampisol, a potion that allows vampires to survive in sunlight. . . . Everything is played in delightfully broad caricature. Animation style is crude but witty, and director-writer-designer has slipped in lots of sly pokes at gangster and vampire mythology, the Machado dictatorship, tourists and morally slack musicians . . . , a lively, bawdy effort . . . , this is certainly not the

sort of film one expects to be produced by a state controlled film industry." (Of course, it depends who the one is, and which is the state.) To
which can be added the comments of a twelve-year-old girl, the daughter
of an American mother and a Cuban father, in a conversation with the
present writer after the film's premiere: "The European vampires want
the formula for the benefit of all the vampires in Europe, and the vampires in the United States want to destroy it so it won't ruin their business, which is underground beaches. That's why at the end, Pepito, the
hero, tells all the vampires what the formula is, so everybody can have
it. It was like the Europeans and the North Americans trying to get the
most out of Cuba, which is what really happened in history. And because the film is about vampires, I would say that Cuba was the blood,
and the Europeans and North Americans were the vampires trying to
suck the blood."

There was also nothing timid about Juan Carlos Tabío's *¡Plaff! o demasiado miedo a la vida* of 1988 *(Plaff!, or Too Much Fear of Life)*, an
anarchic comedy that caught the eye of foreign reviewers and was hailed
by *Variety* as "the best Cuban film this decade": "From the minute the
projector rolls," said the Hollywood journal, "it is obvious *Plaff!* is an
original venture." Others found it "a quirky, funny film . . . packed with
surprises . . . vigorously played by a cast led by the magnificent [Daisy]
Granados"; and "a raucous contemporary satire which lampoons all
things Cuban from the socialist bureaucracy to santería."[58] Not unex-
pectably, some Cuban critics found the film disconcerting, but audiences
loved it (John King reports that "the cinema where I saw the film in
Havana was in hilarious uproar throughout the screening"[59]). The ono-
matopoeic title refers to the sound of an egg hitting the wall of a house.
Concha (Daisy Granados), is a widow with a nervous disposition and a
follower of Santería, who shares her house with her athletic son and his
brainy, modern-minded wife Clarita (Thaïs Valdés). Concha, consumed
by resentment against her dead husband for his infidelities, unable to
get along with anyone, even Tomás, the patient widower who is courting
her, finds herself under attack: someone is pelting the house with eggs,
and the saints are of no help in finding the culprit. The mystery intensifies, as every time Concha thinks she knows who it is and confronts
them, another egg is thrown, driving her ever more distraught. A parallel plot has Clarita, a biochemist, in conflict with the shortsightedness
of the bureaucrats who run the laboratory where she works: she has

invented a new polymer that would save the country money, but that they fail to put into production because, as she complains, "it wasn't planned, so it can't be done." To make matters worse, her polymer is made with pig droppings, and when she wins a prize for innovation, jurisdiction is claimed by another organization, the IDIE, or Institute for the Development and Investigation of Excrement; this twist not only allows for some very funny lines but marks the introduction of the scatological into the Cuban film comedy.

As D'Lugo observes, *¡Plaff!* is a parody on those films that allegorize the nation through their female characters. In this comic reduction of the nation's problems to the conflict between mothers and daughters-in-law, Concha embodies the revolutionary values of the 1960s, Clarita is a representative of a younger generation that sees the waste and inefficiency of twenty years later as the result precisely of people like Concha, a variation on the theme of generational conflict entirely characteristic of the genre of critical social comedy to which this film belongs. Tabío uses this double structure to take potshots at jealous mothers-in-law, the superstitions of Santería, the Cuban housing shortage, attitudes to race, sex, family, bureaucracy—and the very process of filmmaking. The story is told inside out, starting, as it were, in the middle: an opening credit, announcing that the film has been finished in record time in order to have it ready for Filmmakers' Day, gives way to an upside-down image, whereupon the projectionist calls out that something is wrong with the first reel, he'll send it back to ICAIC, and begin with the second. Indeed, the whole film is plagued by technical "gaffes," including sloppy edits and overexposed shots; the camera crew is momentarily visible in a mirror, an actor is given a cue on-screen, a missing prop is tossed in, the director intervenes to address the viewers to explain why an important scene was not shot. These Brechtian self-interruptions make the film, as Catherine Davies has observed, a parodic homage to García Espinosa's "imperfect cinema," with Cuban filmmaking presented here "not as radical third cinema at the cutting edge but as bungling incompetence." The imperfections are perfectly controlled, like the eggs that splatter on walls at perfectly timed intervals, which drive the plot forward and constitute a game between the director and the spectator, in which the former assumes the right to play god and challenges the latter to second-guess the moment when the hidden hand will strike again. As Pérez Betancourt put it, the most dramatic moments are nonchalantly interrupted by devices that keep reminding the spectators that they're watching a film,[60] while Jesús Díaz finds that these devices are integrated into the film's structure in an organic manner that gives them narrative value and enriches Tabío's brilliant cinematographic treatment. This is particularly effective, Díaz believes, in delivering the film's critique of bureaucracy: "The mechanism that consists in doing violence to reality, whatever the price, characteristic of the voluntaristic Cuban bureaucracy and responsible for many deficiencies in our production, ends up also part of the film's plot, which thus carries a strong electric shock."[61] The extraordinary outcome deals the viewer a double blow. The comedy is revealed as a tragedy, as Concha succumbs to a heart attack, and the mystery of the eggs is uncovered: they have all been throwing them, unknown to each other, but with the same intention: to persuade Concha to marry Tomás, to go and live with him, and let the young couple have the house to themselves. But who threw the first egg and gave them all the idea? The answer is revealed by the missing first reel of the film, which has turned up during the projection to be tacked on at the end: it was Concha herself, who threw an egg at her son and Clarita before they got married at the beginning of reel two, in order to try and drive her away.

¡Plaff! is clearly a film in the tradition of imperfect cinema, in which at the same time one senses a new departure, a turn toward a new sense of ambiguity in the representation of the social process, which also finds expression in a growing susceptibility for the surreal. The film is rendered peculiarly disconcerting by its double set of interruptions, the surrealistic eggs and the technical mishaps, beginning with the interruption at the very start, which only demonstrates that you can launch into a story anywhere you like. The interpretive cues are ineluctably mixed. One critic suggests that the film loosely follows the narrative structure of the detective genre, with Concha's *madrina* (the *santera* she goes to for guidance) playing the role of the detective, while another complains of the disconcerting eclecticism of what he expected to be "an enjoyable comedy of customs."[62] The comedy is absurdist, while the cinematography is that of the new-wave realism of *Retrato de Teresa*, and the acting similarly is completely straight. As for Concha herself, Tabío has borrowed from certain films of Alea the trope of a central protagonist who repels identification; Concha is not at all a likable character, but a paranoid neurotic, consumed by resentment, hardly deserving of

¡Plaff! o demasiado miedo a la vida (Juan Carlos Tabío, 1988)

the spectator's sympathy even if she is a victim of machismo. He then wields the parallel narratives to establish a clear equivalence between Concha's fear of life and the dead hand of bureaucracy that threatens to suffocate her daughter-in-law. An early scene has Clarita criticizing Concha precisely for coldly following the rules in the shop where she works when they could be interpreted more liberally to help a customer; later, Concha's *madrina* explains that she cast a spell without a name: "This business of identity is very important. That's why we have passports, fingerprints, ID cards, and birth certificates. The saints have their bureaucracy too." Beneath our laughter, the noose is tightening, and when the circle closes at the end with the missing beginning, the film simply refuses to absolve the spectator.

Cuban critics compared *¡Plaff!* to Alea's *La muerte de un burócrata,* in consideration of both its principal satiric target and its comic style, with its allusions to the comedy classics. But *¡Plaff!* is more than *Burócrata* revisited, for here the equation of death and bureaucracy is much more chilling. For another thing, Tabío's film is equally indebted to the deconstructionism of García Espinosa's *Las aventuras de Juan Quin Quin*—

and is also more than *Juan Quin Quin* revisited, for *¡Plaff!*'s deconstruction of comedy serves not merely to subvert the ideology of the image on the screen, but to question the lifeworld outside the cinema that it is taken to represent. In short, *¡Plaff!* combines both models in a tragicomedy that implicates the spectator in a sadistic practical joke with tragic consequences. Despite its huge success with the Cuban public, it is not a comfortable film.

For the last of these films, Orlando Rojas chose a lifeworld very different from both *¡Plaff!* and his own first feature, *Una novia para David*— indeed, nothing in that first and rather lightweight genre movie prepares us for the complex subtleties of *Papeles secundarios* (Supporting roles), which are played out in the rarefied, dark, enclosed atmosphere of the theater. A company of actors is preparing a production of a modern Cuban classic, Carlos Felipe's *Requiem por Yarini*, a tragic love story set in a Havana brothel at the beginning of the century. Under the management of an aging star, Rosa, the company has lost its sense of direction. The company's female principal, Mirta, is at the point of abandoning the stage when Alejandro, a director condemned to years in the provinces for ideological misdemeanors who has finally been given the chance to redeem himself, offers her the lead. All of them face the challenge of a group of young actors who have just joined the company, and the unsettling effects of a visit by a government inspector. The inspector insists that "youth is in fashion"; the young actors question the relevance of a play dating from 1960 about the turn of the century to the lives of their own generation, yet they too belong to the same theatrical world of fragile egos, of self-dramatized fears, and anxieties over love and success, in which identity and character are suspended and intermingled, and which always exercises enormous vicarious fascination on the mere spectator. As Paranagua puts it, the microcosm presented by a theater group putting on a play immediately introduces a plurality of levels and the promise of metaphorical readings, especially when the play in question resonates with the underpinning plot—such that the games of power and seduction among the characters in the play are echoed among the actors who play them. Paranagua observes that Rojas "doesn't mind at all running the risk of overdoing it, obviously preferring to have too much rather than emptiness, banality and sloppiness." For Pérez Betancourt, this excess derives from the theatricality that is a basic premise of the mise-en-scène, allowing Rojas, on the one hand, to maintain, in the

Papeles secundarios (Orlando Rojas, 1989)

photography, the dialogue, and the montage, "a constant play with the art of suggestion," and, on the other, justifying passages of extended dialogue that make the film unquestionably demanding but reward the spectator's intelligence in a manner uncommon in Cuban cinema, and that give the film a certain European cast. (*Variety*, on the other hand, found the film a "rambling, talky pic," a "non-story" with a "tedious script.")[63]

For Davies, the doubling effects of the play within the film are several: the characters in the play, which dramatizes Afro-Cuban magic, function as incarnations of Yoruba spirits, with their own duplicities and constant doubling, which further blurs the boundaries between real and fictive identities, including sexual identity. Furthermore, the spectator must handle four frames of reference: the timelessness of Afro-Cuban myth; a social drama of 1910; the representation of the drama in 1960; and the contemporary reality of 1989 when it is being staged. In this way, the microcosm opens out to encompass the functions of allegory, and the result is an expressive density all the more vivid for what Paranagua calls the "rigorous and sophisticated aesthetics of the image."[64] The story unfolds in an ambiance of shadows, enclosed spaces, and constant rain. The camera pans along corridors past open doors giving glimpses of dressing rooms. Windows are forever being opened and closed again. Repeated images of water and light become symbols of promise and life both fulfilled and unfulfilled. When the group takes a break on the theater roof, the bitching and generational conflicts are momentarily dissolved under the purifying sunlight—but there is also water at hand to baptize the sinners, as Pérez Betancourt puts it.[65] Paranagua reserves special praise for the cinematography of Raúl Pérez Ureta, who succeeds "in totally overturning the lighting, the framing and the colours that have prevailed in Cuban cinema, proving that the insipidity of the images since the change-over to colour could not be blamed on the quality of the stock or other technical constraints."[66] Rojas himself comments that his intention was to break with what he called "the frontalism of the Cuban camera," a limiting tendency from a plastic point of view, to full-on, "objective," and plain composition, which went along with another recurrent problem of Cuban cinema, namely, "a certain rhetorical intention toward explication and information" to be found in its scripts. Instead, following a line that was half Solás and half Alea (the film could have been made, he claimed, by either of them), his purpose was "not to present a finished discourse where the spectator takes away prefabricated ideas accepted for what they are [but] quite the opposite, to offer them various points of view, various possibilities for rethinking history."[67]

This history is marked, as Caballero and del Río observe, by "dejected resignation in the face of arbitrary arrangements and mechanisms" of the kind that frustrated the generation of the 1970s, as a result of the particularly rigid politics of the decade—a history evoked by the story Mirtha recounts of her erstwhile lover, a young poet forced to abandon the country for writing "existential" poems that officialdom judged as decadent. As Paranagua puts it, this bravura piece of acting by Luisa Pérez Nieto "exposes a wound that is at the same time emotional and social" and one of the film's strongest political moments.[68] Rojas wishes to reclaim the space for an existential discourse, taking his motivation from human interiority and interrelations, not for the purpose of psychologizing the individual—he prefers to respect the secret intentions that are a constant in almost all the characters—but in order to reconnect the private and the political, and thus call into question phenomena like machismo, bureaucracy, double standards, the painful divisions of exile, the marginalization of youth. Parallel, then, to the intimate intro-spection of the film, there is another half-hidden discourse that weaves subtle allegories on power as a dark, frustrating, and discriminatory force.

The Cuban critics conclude: "The expressive richness, the dramatic study of color, the narrative fragmentation that refers to atomized lives, the disintegration (the result of cuts on movement, as unusual in Cuban cinema as it is common elsewhere in modern films), make *Papeles secun-darios* one of the peaks of Cuban cinema of the 1980s, unique in the high ambition with which it merges social investigation with a markedly metaphorical language and the expressive autonomy of filmic art, itself capable of signification." And they note that Rojas is responsible for a text called Por un cinema incómodo (For an uncomfortable cinema), a title that alludes to García Espinosa's essay of twenty years earlier, and stakes a claim to representing the same tradition.[69] Both the differences and possible correspondence between "the uncomfortable" according to Rojas and "the imperfect" according to García Espinosa represent, they believe, a tenacious vocation to which Cuban cinema still sometimes aspired in the 1980s.

CHAPTER SEVENTEEN

Wonderland

Perestroika began to destabilize the Cuban economy well before Castro declared the "Special Period in Times of Peace" in 1990, the year before the collapse of Soviet communism. In 1987, as perestroika brought unintended disruption in the USSR, Cuban imports from the Soviet Union, which had grown steadily for nearly three decades, suddenly went into reverse, and economic activity began to contract (*Miami Herald*, March 10, 1988). By the middle of 1988, diplomatic sources in Havana were suggesting that the differences between Gorbachev's perestroika and Castro's rectification were becoming deeply political, and foreign journalists reported that Castro was "out of step with his patrons in Moscow" (*Sunday Times*, June 26, 1988). It seemed a major ideological split was in the offing, as Havana's determination to remain a bastion of socialism clashed with the stark reality that Cuba's centrally planned economy was unable to cope with the decentralizing reforms going on in the Comecon countries. A year later, in his traditional speech at the annual celebration of July 26, Castro replied with defiance to Gorbachev's demands, during a visit to Cuba earlier in the year, that Cuba fall into line with economic reform to reduce its reliance on Soviet aid, instead characterizing the political and economic reforms inherent in perestroika as concessions to capitalist concepts of democracy and the free market (*Independent*, July 28, 1989). Knowing that new cuts in Soviet support were about to hit, he warned Cubans to brace themselves for more economic difficulties. He also expressed concern and astonishment that the opposition might win elections in Poland and Hungary, but conspicuously

made no mention of Cuba's own political upheaval, which had culmi-
nated two weeks earlier in the execution of four senior army officers for
corruption and drug smuggling. A month later, the Cuban government
placed a ban on two Soviet publications, *Sputnik* and *Moscow News*,
which *Granma* accused of becoming an apologia for bourgeois and capitalist values, "denying history," and "presenting a chaotic impression of
the present" (*Guardian,* August 5, 1989). By the end of the year, this
history-denying chaos was becoming fact, as communist power abdi-
cated or disappeared in Poland, Czechoslovakia, Hungary, Romania,
Bulgaria, and the German Democratic Republic. Would Cuba not be
next? In Miami, many supposed so, and even some in Havana.

According to French commentator Janette Habel, one of the reasons
Moscow News bothered the Cuban leadership was its coverage of the
new electoral experiences in Russia, but the ban "was as much due to
internal tensions as it was to differences with Moscow."[1] *Granma* justified it on grounds that included the damaging influence these examples
of glasnost exercised on ill-informed young people bent on mimicry of
the Soviet Union. It was precisely this kind of misplaced paternalism
that aggravated the youth, and provoked, among other things, the icon-
oclastic creations of the young plastic artists of the 1980s that began to
test the patience of the regime. These artists were certainly not imitating Moscow. Described by the American David Craven as a highly distinctive and rambunctious generation, they combined a "post-modernist
engagement with home-made kitsch" and "the Surrealist tradition of
disjunctive figuration and tense assemblages" with the critical assimilation of foreign idioms and a devotion to hybridization—an aesthetic
not unlike that which had been developing in a more populist form at
ICAIC.[2]

Some commentators speculated that the Special Period in Times of
Peace implied the sort of restrictions on freedom of expression associated with times of war, but this is simplistic. The evidence suggests a
battle between different tendencies and levels within the party. Although
Fidel had criticized the timidity of the press in 1986, the media remained firmly under the thumb of the party's ideological overseers, while
the cultural regime remained a liberal one. In testing the limits of this
liberalism, the young artists provoked a backlash among hard-liners,
whose position was strengthened as political tensions with the Soviet
Union mounted. In 1988, the same year Fidel appeared at the UNEAC

congress and asserted full liberty for artists in content as well as form, a number of shows were canceled or closed for various reasons that the artistic community interpreted as euphemisms for censorship. A few weeks after the ban on the Soviet publications in 1989, a series of exhibitions by young artists in the Castillo de la Fuerza was shut down after some portraits of Fidel by Eduardo Pon Juan and René Francisco caused offense. One of them depicted Castro speaking in the Plaza de la Revolución to a myriad of reflections of himself, another, titled *Suicide,* showed him on a shooting range again surrounded by mirrors. According to the art critic Gerardo Mosquera, writing in 1991, "It was the final cut, that show in 1989. From that time to today, the cultural arena has been closing.... The visual arts were the first to open critical issues in Cuban culture. They have been enclosing that space and encouraging the artists to go."[3] ICAIC would come under attack for displaying a similar parodistic irreverence in the film *Alicia en el pueblo de Maravillas* by Daniel Díaz Torres, and the Film Institute was precipitated, as we shall see, into the greatest crisis of its history when the film was attacked by the party faithful as counterrevolutionary, and banned.

If the collapse of communism was not even expected by right-wing capitalists, as if they too believed in Marx's principle that history is irreversible, in Cuba the effects were crushing. In November 1990, new measures were introduced against corruption and the growing black market; five hundred people were arrested over the next three months. In December, crowds of youths rioted in two towns near Havana. In Bejucal, they marched on the police station after police had wounded a drunken reveler. In Pinar del Río, a crowd surrounded the jail demanding the release of an arrested youth; two people were reportedly killed in the fray. This kind of disturbance was mild in comparison to the everyday violence of economic distress in other Latin American countries, but in Cuba it signaled a painful process of social readjustment that implied an attack on thirty years of socialist values. A few months later, visiting the location in Old Havana where Humberto Solás was shooting *El siglo de las luces,* I was engaged in conversation by one of the assistant directors whom I knew from previous visits as a friendly acquaintance, who expressed between takes the huge disillusion into which the recent events, both at home and abroad, had cast him and his friends. He would not predict what might happen—nobody would—but insisted simply that everyone had been living a dream, the beautiful dream of socialism, a dream that was now over.

The Cuban economy, disconnected from its lines of credit, its markets, and sources of supply, suffered a huge decline in foreign trade and buying power (the figures differ according to the sources consulted). To be thus stranded in a sea of international capitalism gave rise to intensified sensations of isolation and helplessness, and fear of new vulnerability to threats from Washington, the apparent victor of the Cold War. In the words of the Cuban political scientist Rafael Hernández, "To wake up in the post–Cold War world was for Cubans like waking up to an endless nightmare."[4] If the ruin of actually existing socialism produced disorientation, and what Hernández calls "a loss of historical references," in large sectors of the population, the result included loss of faith in the dogmatic discourse of the Communist Party and its scholastic catechisms that was shared by many artists and intellectuals. But there were also important sectors where the shock discovery that socialism was reversible nourished a spirit of resistance, and especially in the face of intensifying U.S. pressure, a conservative defense of the regime. As official rhetoric began to shift away from appeal to Marxism and back to the Cuban nationalist pantheon of Félix Varela and José Martí, where social justice can only be achieved through the country's authentic independence, these sentiments would mesh with a powerful sense of patriotism to prevent the body politic from disintegrating, but only on condition that the regime accepted the need for a degree of economic liberalization.

The dismantling of the Soviet bloc and the collapse of the Soviet Union left Cuba in a crisis of double isolation. As the supply of everyday goods shriveled and the country spiraled toward near-bankruptcy, the Special Period became one of electricity blackouts, severe gasoline rationing, huge cuts in public transport, and bicycles from China. Dollars, which were illegal tender but came into the country with tourists and visitors from the exile community in Miami, fueled a growing black market, as the exchange rate on the street rate rose to fifty and then 150 pesos to the dollar. At a political meeting in ICAIC, Alea presented a paper on the situation. A luxury hotel in the resort of Varadero, he had learned, one of the new mixed enterprises managed by a Spanish company, consumed no more than 40 percent of the quantity of goods supplied to a similar hotel at the same resort under Cuban administration. In other words, some 60 percent of the goods supplied to the Cuban hotel was disappearing into the subterranean economy.[5] On one level or another everyone was involved, since many everyday articles, from lightbulbs to toothpaste, could often not be obtained by other means except recourse to the "informal sector" of the economy. An ethos developed in which, because everyone did it, they also forgave each other for it. There was no other way to get by.

Filmmakers, artists, and intellectuals all felt the consequences along with everybody else. At ICAIC, although they managed to keep the annual film festival going, not only would they be forced to curtail production, but they also faced radical alteration in the economic regime that provided for their existence. In 1991, state companies involved in import/export were instructed to aim for financial autonomy in hard-currency dealings—in other words, no more subsidies. ICAIC's foreign income from distribution was never very great, but by dint of coproductions, the sale of services, and hire of personnel to foreign producers, which had all been growing during the 1980s, it was able to fulfill the new requirements and even bring in dollars. Yet now, the economic collapse of the country meant that home-based production without foreign participation would be drastically reduced, and filmmakers would become idle. The consequences included an erosion of the Institute's personnel as its members began to disperse, seeking work in other countries (although some found useful employment at the international film school at San Antonio de los Baños; in 1993, after leaving ICAIC, García Espinosa would shoot a feature on video with students at the school called El Plano [The shot] as a demonstration of how to make a virtually no-budget film).

The whole cultural sector suffered. Plastic artists were not only under political pressure to conform but lost the domestic market for their work that had opened up in the 1980s. With work piling up in their studios unsold, they quickly began to leave in such numbers that one commentator calls it a mass exodus by "a veritable roll call of the 80s generation"[6] (although they would soon be replaced by the next). Musicians, who continued to enjoy huge popularity while suffering the same privations as their audiences, took every opportunity for trips abroad. These opportunities were on the increase because the period coincided with the rediscovery of Cuban music by foreign audiences and promoters. By the mid-1990s, music had become Cuba's principal cultural export, far greater than film had ever been, embroiled in an ideologically ambiguous trade that inevitably transmitted certain stereotypes along with its apparently nonideological joie de vivre. Worst hit were the writers, when the publishing industry was brought to its knees through a collapse in the paper supply. The news reached the ears of the *Economist* in London, which reported that Cuba had been hit by "a paper shortage unparalleled in 32 years of revolution. With Soviet shipments no longer guaranteed and no hard currency to buy supplies elsewhere, printing has come to a standstill. An estimated $17m would be needed to maintain present levels of book production."[7] Two months later I found two friends in Havana who worked in academic publishing languishing at home without any work to do, and another friend, a writer, frustrated at the closure of the journals he wrote for. Only one of them was still in Cuba when I was next there in 1995, but the regime they left behind had not collapsed.

Despite the growing crisis, ICAIC completed three features in 1990. It is notable that in all of them the central characters are women, carrying the suggestion that the representation of women was now recognized as specially fertile ground for investigation, although only one of these films had a contemporary setting. *Hello Hemingway* by Fernando Pérez is a sequel to his earlier *Clandestinos,* another youth film set in the 1950s, but here portraying the frustrations of the time from the perspective of Larita, a talented girl from a poor background, struggling to win a scholarship to study in the United States, who happens to be a neighbor of the famous American writer. Hemingway, who is seldom there, and never more than glimpsed in the distance, is a mere cipher for Larita's longings; it is not the unapproachable figure of the writer but Larita's reading of *The Old Man and the Sea* that gives the film its resonance. She argues with her rebellious boyfriend and comes to realize that her background and lack of financial resources will prevent her dream of a scholarship coming true. In genre terms, this is a coming-of-age story that once again allegorizes the nation as a young woman seeking to take control of her destiny. It includes a memorable cameo appearance by José Manuel Rodríguez as the old bookseller who encourages Larita to read Hemingway's novella and explains to her its theme: "a man may be destroyed, but he cannot be defeated." An extremely modest film, which deftly recaptures the look of 1950s Havana in a few strokes, the tale is handled with a sensitivity and reserve that allow it to address the young audience of 1990 without preaching or condescension. For an older viewer, it offers the pleasure of a gentle rumination on the theme of the secret dialogue between writer and reader, who may even be neighbors, but always remain unknown to each other.

Sergio Giral had turned back to history for *Plácido* in 1986, based on events in Matanzas in 1844, when a mulatto poet, caught up by the racial, political, and human contradictions in which he lives, ends up being shot on trumped-up charges as the leader of a black conspiracy. Taken from a play by Gerardo Fulleda, the film was judged too histrionic, and failed to make its mark. *María Antonia,* this time taken from a play by Eugenio Hernández, proved a much greater success. María Antonia is a mulatta living in a Havana slum in the 1950s, in rebellion against both men and the Yoruba divinities, whose tumultuous relationship with a boxer and defiance of the *santeros* leads to tragedy. Deeply rooted in the Santería it portrayed, the play had been shelved after it first opened in 1967, until the period of dogmatism passed and it was rehabilitated; in some ways, therefore, it can be seen, despite the setting of the 1950s, as a contemporary story, a calling of attention to the superstition and violence that persisted in what official rhetoric continued to call the marginal sectors of society. On one level this is not a political tract, the female lead is not an allegorical figure, the film is not a social metaphor. Giral's intention, supported by music from the group Síntesis, was to reinstate certain elements found in the *rumbera* or "low-life" cinema of Latin America in the 1950s, through the story of a woman who cannot conquer her destiny, and in this way to present an existential melodrama.[8] The power of the film, as García Borrero puts it, lies in the conviction of its atmosphere and the credibility of the action. Paranagua goes further. For him, the film recovers the mythical dimension and gives it dramatic function: "Not only is machismo depicted without any blandishments, shown in all its brutality, but also its opposite and complement, *hembrismo.* A whole religious, moral, familial and sexual psychology is exposed with sweltering sensuality. Never before have Cuban screens cast such a raw light on the carnal relations between men and women. Giral's mise-en-scène convinces through its passionate fusion of social tragedy and popular mythology in an atmosphere dripping with eroticism." You have to see the film, says Paranagua, in an overheated cinema in Havana, to fully appreciate how directly it manages to touch a hidden side within its audience.[9] (Some would say not so hidden.) In the process, however, the film represents a challenge to the ideological orthodoxy that persists in considering this world as a marginal one, when it can also be said that its survival marks it as one of the most deeply characteristic features of Cuban popular culture.

Meanwhile, faced with a reduction in ICAIC's program of production owing to the economic crisis, the *grupo de creación* headed by Humberto Solás had come up with the idea of a compendium, a feature comprising five separate episodes around a theme summed up by the title, *Mujer transparente* (Transparent woman), an update on the progress of women in Cuban society in the form of five stories of representative women of different ages and social background, which would also serve as an outing in fiction for a new generation of directors (and many of the producers, scriptwriters, cinematographers, editors, and musicians working with them). The five directors, all experienced in documentary or as assistant directors in features, were Héctor Veitía, Mayra Segura, Mayra Vilasís, Mario Crespo, and Ana Rodríguez. Despite their varied styles and aesthetics, the films are unified by using the perspective of feminine interiority (all but one are narrated by the protagonist's voice-over) to ask a series of awkward questions, and cumulatively, and in some cases individually, they bring something new to Cuban cinema.

Veitía's *Isabel* is a middle-aged woman, totally eclipsed at home, who is promoted to a managerial position at work and rebels against the insensitivity of her husband and grown-up children, who cannot understand what the promotion means to her. Segura's *Adriana* attempts to enter the fantasy world of a lonely old woman through an imaginative treatment of image and sound, in the single setting of her lonely apartment. In *Julia,* with Mirta Ibarra in the title role, Vilasís presents a woman's recollections of a failed marriage. The visual economy of this short film, says Zuzana Pick, which simply intercuts Julia in the present, performing everyday actions, with images of her past, "is designed to emphasise privacy as the space in which interiority is given full expression." As the character's intense questioning of past and present plays itself out in the darkened apartment, the film articulates "the courageous resolve of a divorced woman" in "an affirmative image of retrospection and, despite its ambivalent ending, an empowering portrait of femininity."[10] Fourth, Crespo's *Zoe* presents two diametrically opposed characters, the eponymous art student, a nonconformist frustrated by the rigid framework in which she has to live and study, and the disciplined militant, whom she ironically calls "Battleship Potemkin," sent to investigate her absence from the university. Here another single setting—the garage-cum-studio where she lives—is used to observe gender and social differences close up, in a mise-en-scène that brings to the screen the milieu of the rebellious young artists of the late 1980s. It also, says García Borrero, anticipates what will become one of the great themes of the Cuban cinema of the 1990s, namely, tolerance of the other, the exploration of the possibility or impossibility of dialogue,[11] while Pick sums up: femininity in *Mujer transparente* is contradictory, contextualized by generation, social background, personal history, and introspection.

It was the last episode, however, that was for several critics the most successful. In *Laura*, Rodríguez presents a woman's uncertain emotions toward a childhood girlfriend who chose to leave the country and is now returning for a visit. The most obviously political of the five films, Laura's reminiscences of the two decades she has known her friend sketch out a history with which Cubans of more than one generation and both sexes could easily identify. Images of adolescence intercut with shots of Laura waiting for her friend in the hotel contrast the mutual estrangement of people in the lobby with private nostalgia, underlined by historical footage that references the backstory to the events of Mariel. Amid the tensions created by tourism, lost illusions, and wasted energies, the hotel lobby becomes a hostile space, where Laura is ignored by the desk clerk, thus making her feel an alien in her own country and provoking the question "Why do they treat those of us who stayed with such contempt?" The entire film serves as a question. The opening line— "Who are you, Polly Magoo?"—spoken over a black-and-white photo of a young woman in a miniskirt, sets off Laura's interior journey. "I look at myself in those photos," she says, "and I don't recognize myself." Later, over footage of the rallies that led up to the exodus from Mariel, she says, "You cannot see in black and white the most concrete feelings." In this way, through her own sense of nostalgia and loss, Laura's subjectivity speaks for the collectivity. For García Borrero, "A single sequence, which through masterly editing combines shots of those who left being abused by a noisy crowd, and the same people returning apparently to the adoration of the same crowds, stands as one of the most perturbing scenes in all Cuban cinema."[12]

The following year, the troubled milieu of Havana at the beginning of the decade is effectively captured in *Adorables mentiras* (Adorable lies), the debut feature of Gerardo Chijona, which pursues several concerns that first surfaced in the critical social comedies of the 1980s. To begin with, it revisits the same terrain treated straight in *Hasta cierto punto* and as comedy in *¡Plaff!*—that of Cuban cinema itself, which here becomes the object of an ironically narcissistic self-satire. A film extra and would-be screenwriter, Jorge Luis, meets beautiful Sissy at a film premiere. In order to impress her, he claims to be a director looking for a new actress. Harboring screen dreams of her own, she in turn invents a suitably glamorous identity with which to impress him. Both give false names, both neglect to mention that they're married—and a complicated romance ensues as each falls passionately in love with the assumed persona of the other. In short, an outrageous comedy with a showdown ending, made with help from Spanish TV and Robert Redford's Sundance Institute, which, according to one report, ran into censorship problems that delayed its release.[13] But why?

Take two: Jorge Luis, a film extra and would-be screenwriter, is struggling to maintain a wife and child while trying to write a script on spec for Arturo, an established director. Entranced by a woman he sees at the cinema, whom he fantasizes as Natassia Kinski, he boasts to her of being a prize-winning director of documentaries working on his first feature, by the name of Ricardo Girona (a play on the name of the film's director). Sissy, in turn, taking the name of Isabel, hides from him her marriage to García, a corrupt and middle-aged bureaucrat who saved her from a tarnished past. When Sissy finds herself falling in love with "Ricardo Girona," she turns for advice to her older friend Nancy—a figure from her shady past whom her husband has banished from his presence—while Jorge Luis's wife, Flora, distraught over his lack of attention to her, is encouraged by her neighbor Rita in the suspicion that he has "gone over" and is having a homosexual affair with Arturo. Rita supplements her income by selling bottles of vanilla on the street illegally. Nancy is a social(ist) disaster, a "loose woman" whose misery drives her to drink, the black market, and the brink of suicide. Before the film is over and the deception unmasked, García will be threatened with exposure for embezzlement of funds on a foreign trip. *Variety* called the film "A frank look at life in Cuba, where fantasy can be more appealing than the reality of scarce food and cramped apartments." Catherine Davies, more sympathetically, calls it a film about "broken dreams and lost illusions" and "the duplicity involved in sustaining the Cuban dream." It is given to the uneducated Nancy to articulate this element in the film's subtext with a comic seriousness that makes it all the more poignant. Recovering from a failed suicide bid, she complains to Sissy that she "can't even dream." "I've also had bad moments," Sissy replies, "but I don't kill myself." "It's different for you," says Nancy, "you belong to the Julio Iglesias generation, mine was the Beatles." Sissy objects, "They didn't even let you listen to them." "That doesn't matter," says Nancy, "I was able to dream . . . I could be a teacher, a doctor . . . You couldn't. Everything's laid out for you now. If you want to work on a hill and they say a hole, you end up in a hole. I used to dream, but I got it all wrong." Paranagua writes that Senel Paz's script makes a "link between a critique of individual hypocrisy in sexual and conjugal relations with double standards in social life": the bureaucrat's corruption is part of a chain of deceit that includes the apprentice intellectual and the prostitute eking out a living on the black market—a film, then, about dreams and illusions, which uses a story about conjugal hypocrisy to take a swipe at the pretensions of the cinema, and thereby to contrast the fantasy world of the screen with the intractability of real life.

The film has a lightweight tone, and a bright and agile appearance. The actors play straight, but at certain moments, aided by bursts of ironically sentimental music, it takes off self-consciously into the most soupy representation of romance, only to be brought back down to ground by sharply crosscutting to one of the parallel plot lines. The satire against the lost illusions of Cuban cinema is merciless, and prone to in-jokes. Jorge Luis, sitting in front of his beat-up old typewriter, daydreams of being Jean-Claude Carrière in front of an Apple Macintosh. When Sissy tells Nancy she has fallen in love with a film director, Nancy, a woman of the world, responds witheringly, "Oh, not that! There aren't many directors in Cuba. You think he'll just give you a part?" "No," says Sissy, "but he'll give me an audition." "Sure," Nancy replies, "I auditioned for Cecilia Valdés, for Marie Antoinette, and for that woman who eats her children. And the first thing they want is to see your tits." The script Jorge Luis is writing is set in the world of the cabaret, where Jorge Luis has pretensions "to film the tragedy behind the glitter," meanwhile taking Sissy-Isabel to dinner at the Tropicana. In a delicious moment, Nancy diffidently enters a church to go to confession; the priest is played by Santiago Álvarez. But behind the jokes lies a serious problem: the experience of different generations is indeed quite distinct. A first-time director in the Special Period, surrounded by signs of the collapse of the socialism, cannot make films with the same uncomplicated enthusiasm for the Revolution as twenty years earlier—even if some of the audience still wanted such films—and he is quite aware of it. However, this is far from saying that a film like this is directed against the revolution.

Like *Papeles secundarios,* the plot involves a series of doublings, which here center on the key scene in which Jorge Luis, who is genuinely writing a real script but pretending to be his alias, auditions Sissy, who is pretending to be Isabel, but who is really trying to act the part, a scene that, as it unfolds, teases and implicates the spectator with the passage from the acting of sexual attraction to the frisson of its real manifestation. (Isabel Santos claimed she had difficulties representing Sissy: "she has two facets: as she really is and as she seems to be. . . . I had to be two characters in the same scene.")[14] The crosscurrents set in play among the central group of protagonists—one man and three women—reminded some critics of the rising star of Spanish cinema, Pedro Almodóvar, and others of Woody Allen, but the most illuminating intertextual referents are to be found in Cuban cinema itself. *Adorables mentiras* deals in one of the most curious phenomena to emerge in Cuban cinema at this time: the doubling of characters between different films, that is to say, films that without being sequels in the conventional sense, employ the same actors playing comparable roles in different dramas, sometimes even with the same name, a form of intertextuality that carries the suggestion that the other films in which they have appeared represent their past and real secret lives. Thus Luis Alberto García (in the part of Jorge Luis) has played opposite both Isabel Santos (as Sissy) and Thaïs Valdés (as Flora) before: with the former as the ill-starred lovers of *Clandestinos,* and as the latter's husband in *¡Plaff!.* As Catherine Davies remarks, the

Cuban viewers would have been shocked to see him looking so thin and drawn (he lost thirty pounds to play the part in *Adorables mentiras*), but would sympathize—they would take it as a sign of the times.[15] They were also confronted, however, with his transformation from supportive husband to one who cheats on his wife, while Thaïs Valdés was no longer the confident and modern young woman of the former film, but a down-trodden housewife trying to make ends meet, while Isabel Santos had turned from an unsung heroine of the Revolution into a trendy, cropped-haired blonde, a woman so perfectly capable of masking her Cuban identity that the black-market money traders in the street mistake her for a tourist. Nor is Mirta Ibarra's Nancy—who will later reappear in Alea's *Fresa y chocolate*—the same self-confident liberated woman as Lina in *Hasta cierto punto*. But these changes, however brutal, are no more than those that the Cuban audience could observe within themselves, thereby strengthening the bond between character and spectator.

This phenomenon is neither a matter of typecasting, nor are these simply the expectable reincarnations of actors as different characters that can be found in any regular film industry and that underpin the star system. Perhaps because Cuban films are so few, the result of this recurrence is that these films begin to hinge together, as Davies puts it, like a national family saga. In these circumstances, Cuban film actors quickly come to embody ego-ideals that are independent of the characters they portray, but the stuff that gives these characters their density. Tabío said that *¡Plaff!* and the earlier *Se permuta* were "the same film told twice" because they presented the same characters.[16] When the same actors turn up again in *Adorables mentiras,* the audience perceives them as familiar friends and regards them as basically *buena gente,* good people, whom circumstances have induced to develop double standards in order to survive, thus identifying with characters who are false, involved in all sorts of role-playing, from whom at the same time they are distanced by the film's softened Brechtian alienation effects. The director of the film himself displays the same ambivalence toward his own characters when he sums up, "the film sticks its nose in several things, including the crisis of Cuban cinema—there's a scriptwriter with no talent, a stupid filmmaker, and a housewife who all want to change it—and all of them behave mendaciously. . . . I love them all." This last admission is crucial to the proper comprehension of what is going on here. It is also true of *¡Plaff!* and *Papeles secundarios* and other such films. The characters are not arraigned in order to judge them for their failings, but only in order to allow them to confess to them, and thereby to be collectively absolved.

Adorables mentiras was somewhat eclipsed when ICAIC was thrown into political crisis by the other new film of the year, when *Alicia en el pueblo de Maravillas* (Alice in Wondertown), directed by Daniel Díaz Torres, was banned in Cuba after winning an award at the Berlin Film Festival. The crisis was compounded by the announcement around the same time of a scheme to merge ICAIC with Cuban television and the film unit of the Armed Forces, as part of a general plan of rationalization of human and material resources by the state, in the face of the greater economic crisis that had befallen Cuba with the collapse of communism in Eastern Europe. At ICAIC, following unprecedented protests by the film directors, the situation was resolved by the end of the summer. The Institute survived, but the film remained banned, and the head of Institute, Julio García Espinosa, was replaced by the return of its founder, Alfredo Guevara. That we can still talk of Cuban cinema today, according to Enrique Colina in 1995, is due to strong protests by Cuban filmmakers against the suppression of this film, which was seen as an act of censorship directed not merely against the film itself but, because of the accompanying threat against the film institute, against the right to free artistic expression.[17]

First reports of the film, after its Berlin screening, suggested that it revisited the same terrain as *La muerte de un burócrata* by Tomás Gutiérrez Alea back in 1966, a black comedy about the sins of bureaucracy. Colina calls *Alicia* "a satirical parody of the misadventures of a Cuban Alice in an imaginary hell-town, where those guilty of lèse-majesté against Socialism redeem their sins. A surreal metaphor, absurd and exaggerated." Maravillas is a town lost in the crack between two provinces where a job as a community drama coach awaits the film's Alicia (Thaïs Valdés). Her friends advise her not to go—the place is notorious for its "microclimate" of strong winds and strangely colored overhanging clouds. In Maravillas, Alicia finds, nothing works properly and the people behave in the strangest ways. A restaurant has chained the cutlery to the table to prevent its being stolen, and some of the chains are too short. Indoors and outdoors, wild animals roam around freely because when the zoo was started, the animals came but the cages never arrived. People spy on each other. At the Sanatorium for Active Therapy and Neuro-biology, or SATAN for short, the patients drink sulphurous water and take mud baths; the whole town goes there.

This is a town where people are sent who have "problems." The exemplary worker caught distributing food from the back of his truck at an illegal beer shop, the bureaucrat involved in petty corruption. No one ever knows who sent them there, and to Alicia they all appear to be cowards. All this is communicated through vivid and at times quite hallucinatory images. The humor is black and scatological. A local *aficionado* has made a children's cartoon film in which a duck is shat on by a cow while a cheerful song pronounces "Destiny is a fatal voice where conformity lies hidden, its course cannot be changed." The children applaud and explain the moral: "Not all those who are covered with shit are bad, but if you *are* covered in shit it's best to keep cool." The animation, of course, is crude, but this is visually one of the most original Cuban films for many years: the farce has become a bad dream in which everyone is implicated.

In certain respects, *Alicia* also harks back to another Cuban comedy of the 1960s, Julio García Espinosa's *Las aventuras de Juan Quin Quin*. Like Espinosa's film, it has a didactic and post-Brechtian approach to the construction of the narrative, which is constantly interrupted by two kinds of interpolated sequence. First are a number of flashbacks that recount the stories of several of the characters Alicia meets in Maravillas; second are television programs that Alicia watches on the local TV station, and that beautifully satirize the bland inanities of official discourse. García Espinosa says he saw *Alicia* very much in terms of the motto of the opening title, a quote from Lewis Carroll: "For, you see, so many out-of-the-way things had happened lately, that Alice had begun to think that very few things indeed were really impossible." In short, a surreal allegory on the human being's adaptability, a tale of how, with the help of opportunists and frauds, a situation could reach such a point that people adapt to it as if it were all perfectly natural, and thus become accomplices of the absurd. A little too surrealist, he thought, but with some brilliant sequences. But he also considers the scandal that followed to be the result of a process of demonization that befell the film at the hands of certain people set on stirring things up, so that when it was finally screened, people went to see it looking for devils.[18]

Alicia had in fact been three years in the making, and the script, which dated from 1988, was read not only by the people at ICAIC but also by others outside.[19] Perhaps they supposed it to be another farcical social comedy, of a kind with which the Film Institute had recently been enjoying a run of popular successes (films like *Se permuta* and *¡Plaff!*), although one of those involved, Jesús Díaz, who collaborated on the script, said that they were clear about the kind of trouble they might be courting.[20] A complex film to shoot, *Alicia* was eight months in pre-production; filming was completed in February 1990, and postproduction at the end of the year. The country had changed considerably over this period. The Berlin Wall had fallen. Throughout Eastern Europe, Communism had collapsed. In Moscow, Gorbachev was hanging on by the skin of his teeth. Cuba was isolated as never before. What had doubtless always been a risky project now emerged as a gloating satire on the *cavernicola,* or caveman attitudes of the party orthodoxy, at the very moment when everything seemed to be collapsing around them.

It was also unusually scatological in its sense of humor, and the shit hit the proverbial fan immediately after the Berlin Film Festival success. According to García Espinosa, *Alicia* aroused the ire in particular of the then senior party ideologue, Carlos Aldana, who had a number of video copies made of the film so certain people could see it.[21] Copies of the copies soon began to proliferate and all sorts of rumors started circulating about hidden connotations in the film, the satirical targets of its characters, especially the suggestion that certain gestures that Reynaldo Miravalles incorporated into the character of the director of the sanatorium were reminiscent of Fidel Castro himself, and that the film was a direct attack on the Revolution.[22] The timing of the episode could hardly be worse. To confront the mounting economic crisis, the government had decided on a program of administrative rationalization intended to save management costs. The decision was taken to merge ICAIC with Cuban television and the film section of the Armed Forces. The politicians were quite unprepared for the response of the filmmakers, who immediately, including those who were party members, signed an unprecedented document declaring their total opposition to the plan. The unity of the Film Institute would force the government to back down.

Manuel Pérez subsequently gave an account of the events in an interview in the journal *La Gaceta de Cuba:*

Reynaldo Miravalles in *Alicia en el pueblo de Maravillas* (Daniel Díaz Torres, 1991)

> We got the news, if memory serves, on May 13, and it was published on the fourteenth. Obviously, we didn't agree with it and the very same night of the thirteenth we began to meet to see what we could do, and over the next few days we formed a committee of eighteen *compañeros* who took on the burden of writing letters and documents and calling meetings with the party leadership.[23]

This group included both party members and others.[24] All shared the feeling that there was more at issue than the economic situation in the country, which was the given reason for the merger plan, but that there had been a loss of political confidence in the film institute and its direction. Their task was therefore to defend both ICAIC's autonomy as a cultural institution and its position over culture and cinema. "I believe," says Pérez, "that we did this effectively and intelligently, without ignoring the country's problems or abandoning what we felt to be our principles." This maturity and unity, he adds, was achieved thanks to the existence and the work of the *grupos de creación*.[25]

García Espinosa defended the film in the highest councils of the party, and it finally opened in ten cinemas in Havana on June 13, only to be withdrawn after four days marked by disturbances in the cinemas.

The audience was packed with party militants, to keep as many others out as possible, and ideological insults were thrown at the screens. The newspaper *Granma* condemned the "exaggerated pessimism" of its political satire and resolutely rejected its "defeatism, hopelessness and bitterness."[26] The Film Institute responded with a further protest, which led to the creation of a commission composed of Carlos Aldana, the country's senior vice president, Carlos Rafael Rodríguez, and the original head of ICAIC, Alfredo Guevara. It was a very difficult moment, Pérez commented, to be defending the necessity of art and its critical role in a such a society. "To give you an idea of the context, one of the meetings with the party leadership had to be suspended because the news arrived of the coup d'état in the Soviet Union. That's to say that while we were debating, the last socialist country in Europe disappeared, and the whole world was waiting for Cuba to join the domino effect." The commission met twice with the whole of ICAIC and the exchange of opinions was said to be "very frank." The conflict was so entrenched, however, that it called for the return of Alfredo Guevara as the only person capable of bringing about a resolution.[27] The truth is that the politicians were hardly prepared for the unprecedented response of the filmmakers. This show of unity forced an equally unprecedented retreat. The commission never reported officially, but shortly afterwards García Espinosa stepped down, Alfredo Guevara took over again as ICAIC's head, and everyone went back to work. At the same time, Guevara became a member of the central committee of the Cuban Communist Party. There was no victimization of those who had signed the protest, but García Espinosa parted company with ICAIC and went to work at the Fundación para el Nuevo Cine Latinoamericano (Foundation for New Latin American Cinema). One other person involved, Jesús Díaz, who collaborated on the script, left Cuba around this time to teach in Berlin, and would never go back.[28]

While the *Alicia* affair was unfolding, Humberto Solás was at work on *El siglo de las luces*, completed the following year as crisis continued in the land (it would get worse before getting better). The film, an adaptation of the historical novel by Alejo Carpentier, takes us back to the Havana of the late eighteenth century and the time of the French Revolution, where the lives of three fictional young aristocrats, Sofía, Carlos, and Esteban, are fatefully touched by that of a historical personage, a French overseas adventurer and revolutionary living in Port-au-Prince by the name of Victor Hugues (or Hughes). The Frenchman brings them into contact with the spirit of the Enlightenment and the Revolution, whose aftermath draws them in, producing a series of events that carry us to Jacobin Paris with Esteban, to Spain, where he ends up in prison disillusioned, and then back to the Caribbean, where Hugues, as Robespierre's deputy in Guadaloupe, takes on an American invasion. (The episode was forgotten by historians; Carpentier wrote the novel after hearing about it in the 1950s.)[29] As for Sofía, who hopes for more from Hugues than he gives her, when the rupture between them comes, she takes off for Madrid to obtain Esteban's freedom, carrying the film into the territory of Goya's paintings of the horrors of the second and third of May.

A film no less ambitious than *Cecilia,* it was likewise an international coproduction made for television, and unfortunately suffered from the consequences. Conceived in terms of three episodes running five and a half hours, the cinema version, running 120 minutes, is structurally off balance, a problem aggravated by awkward dubbing of French into Spanish, thus leaving Livio Delgado's admirable cinematography as the dominant level of effect. Solás made what he calls a "personal translation" of the original, tailored to the limitations of his budget—a careful selection of locations, scenography, and costumes to evoke the symbolism of the epoch, with the recurrent presence of Masonic columns, guillotines, and scientific artifacts, dressed by Delgado alternately in long tracking shots, deep-focus wide shots, and big close-ups, replete with chiaroscuro, an enclosed atmosphere, and moments of intimacy. Since it is difficult to imagine a film about the French Revolution involving Cubans by a Cuban director not being intended as an allegory on the Cuban Revolution, it is not surprising that Solás calls this his "political testament."[30] Behind the historical imagery, the film operates on two levels. On the most direct level, it traces the link, harmonious or contradictory, between social liberation and individual comportment, with characters at the same time in and out of synchronization with social reality. Punctuating this narrative is a series of letters from Esteban to Sofía in which he traces his growing disillusion—letters that are neither in the novel nor in the original script, but which were added in postproduction. Here Esteban speaks of the "end of modernity, again the failure of the Enlightenment idea of utopia," and declares that "politics is an abomination, the obscene manipulation of history." On this second level, where the figure of Victor Hugues merges with Robespierre, there is an allegory on the present day that no one spoke about.

The following year, Alea returned to the screens with a film that was equally critical but made only the slightest allusion to Castro. *Fresa y chocolate* (Strawberry and chocolate) was based on a short story by Senel Paz, who also wrote the script; when the film was set to start shooting and Alea was diagnosed with cancer, Juan Carlos Tabío joined him as codirector. Tabío and Alea later explained how their codirection worked.[31] First of all, Tabío was familiar with the script, since they'd worked on it together in the *grupo de creación*. This enabled him to take over the preparation for the shoot while Titón was undergoing surgery. On the set, the problem of a possible dichotomy of styles was obviated by the active participation of the cinematographer Mayito. Titón would set up the shots in the morning and Tabío would complete them in the afternoon; the next morning Titón would see the rushes and reshoot anything that seemed to him necessary. The film thus remained essentially Titón's, in its vision and its realization, and Tabío thus became the most selfless of Titón's collaborators.

Near the beginning of *Fresa y chocolate,* Diego, a gay photographer and art critic, puts on a recording of Maria Callas to entertain his guest David, a university student and Young Communist militant whom he has just picked up. "God, what a voice!" he sighs. "Why can't this island produce a voice like that? We need another voice so badly, huh? We've had enough of María Remolá!" Never mind who that is, for the Cuban audience there is an obvious double entendre. We are back in the irreverent and rebellious world of the young artists of the late 1980s—although the film is nominally set in 1979, shortly after the fall of Somoza, and evidently filmed in contemporary Havana, where the buildings are reaching an advanced state of disrepair. This deliberate blurring of the historical moment (which is noted by several commentators) has the effect of intensifying the film's sense of contemporaneity. The students in the university common room watch a documentary about the overthrow of the Nicaragua dictator, which, according to the commentary, took place a few months earlier, but in the streets outside, a squealing pig being carried up a staircase to be slaughtered presents an image of the hardships of the Special Period. In the view of a critic writing in *La Gaceta de Cuba,* Jorge Yglesias, who traces a number of mixed historical signals throughout the film, "The confluence of times past with the present gives *Fresa y chocolate* its particular character and perhaps a more profound and inclusive dimension."[32]

If *Fresa y chocolate* caused a stir by making its central character, for the first time in Cuban cinema, a gay man, its phenomenal success—it ran in Havana for eight months—certainly suggests that it touched a deep nerve in the social body. As Ian Lumsden has written, "It unleashed a popular discourse about a culturally tabooed and politically repressed issue that went beyond the confines of the film itself.[33] It is not, however, a "gay" film in the regular sense at all, and not because the authors were straight. The tale of friendship between David, a young man of solid Marxist beliefs, and Diego, a homosexual poorly looked on by society, becomes the dramaturgical premise for something much more unfashionable, a hard-core political film, brimming with explicit dialogue about censorship, Marxism-Leninism, nationalism, aesthetics, and not least, sexuality. The narrative takes the form, as John Hess has observed, of a kind of Cuban bildungsroman—the education of an innocent in the ways of the world; in this case, the cultural, political, and sexual education of a patriotic young Cuban male growing up at any time since the Revolution (hence with broad appeal across the generations), but with a twist: sidestepping the conventional expectations of the genre, it is a cultured "bourgeois" homosexual—although their relationship remains unconsummated—who educates the ideologically challenged peasant student.[34]

If Diego (a flamboyant performance by Jorge Perugorría) flaunts his sexuality with outrageous good humor, he does so with a sense of political purpose. He is not a *loca* (a queen)—although he can quite well play the part—but in Hess's phrase, "a feminized lover of art and culture."[35] There is some debate among writers on the film about the precise location of Diego's sexuality within Cuban homosexual culture (and for some foreign viewers Perugorría overacts), but the crux is that to be gay for Diego is not just a question of sexuality; it is also to be in possession of a cultural tradition in which the father of Cuban nationalism, José Martí, rubs shoulders with the great Cuban writer Lezama Lima, whom he calls "a universal Cuban," whose novel *Paradiso* had been suppressed in Cuba because of its portrayal of homosexuality; who in turn rubs shoulders with John Donne and Cavafy, Oscar Wilde, Gide, and Lorca. Diego's sense of Cuban culture is all-inclusive and not at all chauvinistic. (Similarly, his musical tastes run from opera to the piano dances of the Cuban composers Cervantes and Lecuona.) His first criticism of the party is that what it tries to repress is imagination, and it can only think of art in terms of either propaganda or mere decoration. As he protests to his neighbor Nancy, "Art is not for sending messages, it's for feeling and thinking. Messages are for the radio." What he most opposes in "the system" is the regimentation of thought, as he declares in another scene to David:

> I also had dreams. When I was fourteen I joined the literacy campaign. Because I wanted to. I went to pick coffee in the hills, and studied to be a teacher. What happened? This head of mine thinks, and anyone who doesn't say "yes" to everything, they reject.

In short, Diego challenges David's assumption that because he's gay he couldn't be a revolutionary, and isn't patriotic—he defends the country "so that people know what's good about it. I don't want the Americans or anyone coming to tell us what we have to do"—just as he also dismisses the explanations of homosexuality that David draws from the political textbooks; and when David accuses him of always thinking about men, he replies, angrily, "I think about men when it's time to think about men! Like you think about women," which David finds he cannot answer.

Diego and David belong to different fractions within the society that appear to repel each other; they meet when Diego picks up David in the Coppelia, Havana's famous open-air ice-cream parlor, which lends the film its richly ironic title. Strawberry, in what Yglesias punningly calls "dogmatic-machista heraldry" *(la heráldica dogmático-machista)*, signifies "ideological weakness" and homosexuality, while chocolate signifies manhood and straight-thinking; on the other hand, says Yglesias, they are also complimentary, and the two flavors are often combined. The most significant historical detail in this scene comes from the books, including a novel by Mario Vargas Llosa, with which Diego provocatively tries to tempt David's interest: unobtainable editions of literature condemned as counterrevolutionary, which represent for David, a would-be writer, both the fear of and fascination with the Other that equally marks his attitude toward Diego himself. The mix of historical references continues when Diego returns to his *guarida* (den) and utters expressions that belong more to the present than to ten or fifteen years earlier, while the propaganda posters on the staircase of the house, Yglesias notes, belong to the 1980s. This word *guarida* introduces another history: according to Emilio Bejel, writing about the film in *Casa de las Américas,* the adoption of the word by homosexuals to refer to the places where they lived and met, goes back to the 1880s.[36] Indeed, Diego's *guarida,* cluttered with Cuban iconography spanning at least a century, recalls the descriptions of Julián del Casal (1863–93) as a bourgeois aesthete— the first Cuban poet to be stigmatized as a homosexual. As Hess describes the scene, "The first time David enters this space, he stands in awe. His eyes, in a clearly established point-of-view shot, lovingly scan the walls, covered with all manner of art (photos, paintings, clippings from periodicals, parts of colonial wrought-iron decorations, wooden cherubs and angels) and the shelves filled with books, magazines, sound tapes, small figures and other objets d'art"—and, in a corner, a large figure of a saint.[37] By bringing this forbidden world to the screen, *Fresa y chocolate* represents what Bejel calls a "coming out" of the Cuban homosexual subject, an emergence from private to public space, and from a negative definition and situation, oppressed and hidden, to greater acceptance, or at least less concealed, with consequences not just for gays but for Cuban society as a whole.

David (sensitively played by Vladimir Cruz) is fascinated by Diego and initially reluctant to get mixed up with him. He is given the excuse he needs to go and see him again by his university friend Miguel, a party activist to whom David mentions that Diego is preparing an exhibition of sculptures by the latter's friend Germán (who is indeed a *loca*) and with the possible support of an unnamed embassy; Miguel gives David the "mission" of spying on Diego, a mission he will soon become reluctant to fulfill. Catching sight of his reflection in a shopwindow as he saunters along the street gives him a start that pulls him out of his daydreams, as he asks himself what kind of *hijo de puta* behaves like that. If the shot evokes Sergio walking around Havana in *Memorias del subdesarrollo,* reminding the viewer of another would-be writer's ideological dilemma, it also shows Alea as a filmmaker in constant dialogue with himself and his world.

Germán's sculptures, which are currently housed in Diego's apartment, are pastiche saints in the satiric style of the late 1980s, including one of Karl Marx with a crown of thorns. This makes them, to Diego at least, semisacred objects, cousins to the saints that both he and Nancy keep in their rooms and whom they look upon to serve their interests. As Steve Wilkinson observes in another account of the film, the troubles Diego suffers at the hands of the authorities are not simply due to his open homosexuality, but follow from his insistence on writing to the authorities to complain when Germán's exhibition is threatened with a ban unless certain sculptures are withdrawn.[38] Germán, who complies, is promised a trip to Mexico in reward, while Diego loses his job and, at the end of the film, follows the only option left to him, to leave the country. (Germán argues with Diego, tells him he should be "realistic," that two or three works of art are not worth the trouble, before hysterically putting an end to the argument by smashing up the Karl Marx while crying, "It's mine! It's mine!" Diego's doppelgänger, his attitude would seem to confirm Wilkinson's argument that what the Cuban regime punishes is not homosexuality per se but noncompliance with authority; but it also shows the personal cost of his acquiescence, the loss of self-respect and mature identity in which the character momentarily regresses to the behavior of the frustrated child.)

Clearly, *Fresa y chocolate* is not just about the homophobia of the Cuban Communist Party, but also a critique of its aesthetic puritanism, and the suppression of artistic voices considered by authority as deviant. If the association of homosexuality with art and art with deviance is not something dreamed up by a new breed of communist hard-liners but, as elsewhere, has long existed within Cuban culture, the exiled Cuban writer René Vásquez Díaz believes it has something to do with a "subtle aspect of our machismo: books are not written with balls"— that's something done by *comemierdas* (i.e., "faggots").[39] Senel Paz encountered this attitude growing up in the 1960s: "I started to recite things in school assemblies. Everything was going well until some friends of my sister said one day that anyone who read poems in assembly or wrote plays was a *maricón*—a queer. I stopped doing those things."[40] In short, the Revolution, which was built on a strong dose of machismo, inherited a link between homophobia and cultural suspicion, which boiled over in the UMAP camps that David and Diego argue about in the film. Set up in 1965, and supposed by Cubanologists to have been modeled on the Soviet Gulag, these camps were filled by drafting gays and other social deviants, and, according to one account, their treatment was brutal enough that some of the officers were subsequently court-martialed. When numbers of intellectuals, artists, and academics were rounded up on account of their homosexuality, there were protests by organizations like UNEAC and ICAIC. Castro was persuaded that the situation was scandalous, and in 1967 the UMAPs were disbanded.[41] In the film, it is the young communist David who brings up the subject of the UMAPs in arguing with Diego about the fundamental ethics of the Revolution: "What I'm trying to say is that it's lamentable but understandable if mistakes are made like sending Pablito Milanés to the UMAP." This admission comes as a dramatic revelation not because the fact was unknown but because of the public nature of the forum in which it is here acknowledged, and not least by invoking the name of one of the leading singers of the Nueva Trova.

At this point, the film bears on the unwritten history of ICAIC itself, with its homophilic culture that no one ever talked about publicly, but that was common knowledge to anyone on familiar terms with the institute as a community—a silence that suggests that while open repression of gays was brought to an end, enough of a homophobic atmosphere persisted outside cultural institutions like ICAIC to keep it a hidden topic, and to ensure that Cuban cinema refrained from bringing gay subjects to the screen until very late in the day, and after many filmmakers elsewhere in Latin America. The first examples are the theme of homosexuality in *Adorables mentiras* and a secondary character in *La bella del Alhambra*. But now, after the *Alicia* affair, a film comes along that openly eschews self-censorship and has clearly not been censored. The force of the moment is underlined by Diego's defiant response to David's admission about the singer: "Not only him! What of all the *locas* who don't sing!" David presses his point: "The mistakes are not the Revolution. They're part of the Revolution, but not the whole of it, do you see?" But Diego has the last word: "And the bill, who should that go to? Who's going to answer for them?"

The introduction of Mirta Ibarra as Nancy from *Adorables mentiras* was the idea of Senel Paz. It not only creates a nexus between the two films but opens up the story on which *Fresa y chocolate* is based by doubling the prejudices and rejection directed to the homosexual with those directed at a fallen woman, who is now a black marketeer prone to suicidal depression, here attempting to kill herself again. Already known to the audience as a woman full of human warmth and a spirit of independence, struggling not to succumb to the abyss, Nancy has the effect of underlining David's innocence. David, who as yet knows nothing of

Nancy's past, arrives on the scene just as she is being carried down to the ambulance; Diego pulls him along, knowing that as a good revolutionary he will be ready to give his blood at the hospital, an act that will afterwards serve to draw him closer to her suffering. When Diego tells David she has done it five times before, the spectator who remembers *Adorables mentiras* may also recall Nancy's bitterness, which she shares in that film with Sissy: "When they say there's no prostitution here, I want to hide under the bed and stay there. It's my fault they're lying. That's why they hate me. I wasn't meant to be a whore. I was meant to be an agronomist." But this comic-pathetic confession is ambiguous, and in neither film do we ever see Nancy turning tricks—she is not the kind of prostitute catering to the tourist trade, known as the *jinetera*, who reemerged in the 1990s, but a woman who claims the same sexual freedom as men, and pays the price of sexual liberation in a *machista* society: she is made to *feel* like a whore. Bejel describes her as "an example of what Marxism calls the lumpen, because she doesn't work, enjoys promiscuity, and lives from illegal dollar trading," and the film claims a space for this lumpen too.[42] As Ibarra puts it, her character is something of an "everywoman" who "personifies the crisis of the country."[43]

There are several ways of mapping the relationships between the various characters. Hess notes that the film establishes clear oppositions between two pairs, one male, the other female.[44] On the one hand are Miguel, the Communist macho, and Diego, the cultured gay who has lost his illusions about the revolution. On the other are Nancy and Vivian, David's girlfriend from the opening sequence, who throws him over to marry an older and more successful man because she wants to "live well" and "begin a family immediately." David's trajectory carries him from Miguel to Diego and from Vivian to Nancy. But these two pairs can also be mapped across the genders: Miguel and Vivian are conformists who accept their prescribed conventional sex roles—thus representing not revolutionary values but the continuance of small-minded conservative values within the Revolution. On the other hand, Diego and Nancy are outsiders, nonconformists, and, in their different ways, rebels. They are also "warm, loving, sensitive, eclectic in their tastes ... who see the Revolution in terms of the personal and their lost ideals."[45] And in the middle, between them all, is David.

Nancy's presence transforms a story of male bonding into a triangle, in which David becomes an object of desire for both Diego and herself.

David is thus the central figure in two triangles, Miguel-David-Diego, and Diego-David-Nancy, not to mention a third, Vivian-David-Nancy. David is a disputed object body and soul. Miguel tries to hold David to a closed and homophobic posture, while Diego aspires to convert him to a broader cultural vision that includes the acceptance of homosexuality. As Diego protests to David, the last thing he wants to do is leave: "I form part of this country whatever they like and I have the right to do things for it. I'm not going away! Let them burn my ass! *Coño*, without me there's a piece of earth missing." The only terrain that allows any mediation between these positions is the discourse of patriotism and nationhood, where in the end David will recognize the natural justice of Diego's inclusive and eclectic vision of Cuban culture and nationhood. At the same time, David is also desired sexually by both Diego and Nancy, a rivalry in which heterosexuality is victorious, thus framing the gay theme within a hetero narrative—as some critics outside Cuba have charged—in which a neurotic woman "rescues" David from the fate of a homosexual relationship.[46] Worse still, she does so only after Diego has renounced his own claims. As Bejel puts it, Diego is the one who cedes, even suggesting to Nancy that she "initiate" David sexually.[47] This initially offends her, because it implies she's a simple *puta;* nevertheless, it coincides with her desire, and Nancy prays to her Santa Bárbara that David should find her attractive. Consummation takes place in Diego's own bed.

This turns of events represents a problem for several writers, including Hess, who believes that the oppositions of sexuality that Alea sets up are in the end normalized by David's heterosexual initiation, and "the film's clichéd melodrama, whatever the director's intent, reproduces Cuba's homophobic and sexist ideologies."[48] Bejel, too, considers that the plot "falls back too easily on the well-tried 'happy ending' of heterosexual lovers, the man happily finding the woman he needs, leaving the homosexual alone and unhappy."[49] This is not to say that nothing fundamental has changed, that when David and Diego finally hug each other on the eve of Diego's departure—a hug that also embraces the spectator in a powerful release of sympathetic human feeling—it makes no larger difference. Moreover, the closure of this ending is far from complete, since both David and Diego are left in quite different situations from where they started. While Diego leaves to face a wholly uncertain future, it is difficult to believe that David's relationship with Nancy, a woman many years his senior, a black marketeer and a religious believer, can possibly last. As Hess puts it: "It is hard to imagine how such contradictory people might live in Cuba, how David might remain a member of the Communist Party while also remaining true to Nancy." Worse still, he has been attacked by Miguel, who calls him a *maricón* and threatens political consequences: "such serious charges would certainly have damaged if not destroyed a young man like David's career, especially in 1979 when the film is set."[50] (One can imagine just such a mistake as the reason why Alejandro, in *Papeles secundarios,* was banished to the provinces.)

The hug embodies a shift in values that can be located in the difference between Miguel's loss and Diego's symbolic gain. As Bejel sees it, "From the symbolic point of view, what is in play is a conception of nationality in transition—Nancy and Diego both symbolize elements in Cuban society that the film suggests should be integrated into a 'new' conception of the nation." In short, Diego has not "lost" David, because he has given him an anti-*machista* vision of society; and, in ceding place to Nancy, Diego himself passes to another value system that allows this act of "altruism." Thus, Bejel locates this allegory of the nation, which, like other classic examples of national allegory is based on the symbolic representation of doomed or frustrated desire, in the triangulations between the characters. "If we conceive *Fresa y chocolate* as a national allegory in which the desires of sexual attraction or friendship serve as symbolic acts in the problematic of a historical subtext, then we shall be in a better position to understand the importance of the triangular relations in this work—the conflicts between the characters are symbolic representations of political and ideological struggles in the society (using the term 'symbolic representation' in [Fredric] Jameson's sense, and not in the sense of a 'mimetic representation' of so-called 'reality.'"[51] On this reading, if the symbolism of the struggle in the triangle of Miguel-David-Diego is obvious, that of Diego-David-Nancy is not so clear. How to interpret Nancy's role in this national allegory? The "happy ending" is a stratagem that hides other possible interpretations. When David gives blood to help save Nancy's life, as Diego has done before him, they both establish a relation of gift giving toward Nancy that contributes to her well-being. Can Nancy be seen as the part of the nation that asks to be saved from suicide? Could one say that Diego and David must ally themselves in order that this salvation can be achieved? But this alliance is not fulfilled—Diego and David end up separating, and Diego's exile is a truncated and impossible solution.

Fresa y chocolate took top prize at both the Havana Film Festival in 1993 and in Berlin in 1994, and was bought by Miramax for distribution in the United States, allowing Hollywood to pay homage to Alea, who was ill with cancer, and at the same time send a message of solidarity to the beleaguered Cuban filmmakers by nominating it for an Oscar as Best Foreign Film. In many ways a breakthrough film, it played very differently, however, to audiences at home and abroad. In Cuba, its runaway popularity gave it the largest-ever audience for a Cuban film in the shortest period of time, provoking a commotion that took on the dimensions of a sociological phenomenon.[52] (The building where it was filmed now houses a *paladar,* one of the private restaurants permitted under the economic liberalization of the mid-1990s.) Alea told a Spanish journalist when the film opened in Madrid that he was taken by surprise, "but realized that people reacted like that because they had the need to hear these things out loud, not just whispered in corridors and cafés. It's a film that says aloud what many people think but don't dare utter. I think that seeing it becomes a huge liberation for the spectator, whom it allows to openly share these ideas."[53] There can be no better description of the role that Cuban cinema plays as a surrogate public sphere. A film cannot replace the need for public speech, but it can feed it. In this case, the effect is powerful enough to be remarked by a foreign observer. "Both homosexuals and homosexual oppression," says Lumsden, "became visible in a totally new way," which gives him the impression that "the release of the film was also a concession by the regime that its homophobic policies have been counterproductive."[54]

However, *Fresa y chocolate* was not (and not intended as) a campaigning film, but as an intervention in a national debate that by the time the film was made had already begun to change significantly. As another foreign observer reports, life for gays had improved long before the film was made. The government had reviewed the issue in the mid-1980s, and in 1988 repealed public ostentation laws that had been in force since 1938—long before the Revolution. Police were ordered to stop harassing people for their appearance; the law now only prohibited homosexual acts that were violent, coercive, or with underage persons. According to a report in 1988 by the National Lawyers Guild (of America), based on interviews with gay men and lesbians: "They are not fearful of being identified as homosexual and have many more opportunities for employment. Continued homophobia is blamed on societal values and not on official policy."[55] Four years later, as Alea started work on the film, a play by Senel Paz based on the same story opened in Havana, where it ran for two months, and Fidel Castro declared he was "absolutely opposed to all forms of oppression, contempt, scorn, or discrimination with regard to homosexuals."[56] What Alea did was seize the moment to test the sincerity of this mood of liberalism by fixing it in the eye. In the view of Reynaldo González, who accepts that it could not have been shown without approval, *Fresa y chocolate* goes much further than any official ideology and digs deeper than any Cuban film before it: it "points an accusing finger at intolerance in its broadest form" and provokes reflections that go much beyond the anguish of a particular marginalized community; in short, it was a highly liberating film.[57]

Outside Cuba, the film repeated the achievement of *Memorias del subdesarrollo* twenty-five years earlier, which was to center attention on Cuba by breaking the stereotypes to which the island was subjected in the media at large, an effect that inevitably elicits varied and contradictory responses conditioned by the proclivities of different audiences. At the showcase Berlin Film Festival, according to the Spanish film critic Ángel Fernández-Santos, "this poor film, made for threepence, surpassed the opulent films of the West in aesthetic and moral richness."[58] On the other hand, some critics noted that it had none of the Brechtian distancing devices of earlier films like *Memorias . . .* or *Hasta cierto punto,* with the implication that Alea was sliding back into the conventions of European art cinema, although the same had been said of *La última cena.* As for the United States, Hess reported that "my small town video store has eight copies and I found the sound track at Tower Records," while Siskel and Ebert gave it "Two Thumbs Up." Here, where it was perceived as an emotional melodrama in which patriarchy takes a severe beating although it sneaks back in at the end, "conventional stereotypes, such as the hooker with a heart of gold and the cultured gay man, contribute[d] much to the film's popularity."[59]

These differences only confirm the paradox of the screen as a representational space—that the image itself is one thing, but how it is read depends in critical ways on the space between the screen and the viewer's eyes, and thus, in common parlance, where he or she is coming from. Observing these discrepancies, Hess reminds us that in certain societies audiences become adept at reading subtleties in conventional and stereo-typed representations when these are the only kind permitted, as in much of Eastern European cinema in the 1960s and 1970s, or Brazilian "Tropicalism" in the same period. Here local audiences see certain films as resistant and progressive, while in other countries the stereotypes seems to weaken their element of social critique.[60] Alea knows that even though the film is a coproduction and therefore addressed to an inter-national audience, the foreign viewer can hardly have the same invest-ment in it, emotionally, ideologically, and politically, as the primary audi-ence at home—a difference complicated in this case by the subject matter, since discourses of sexuality have evolved rather differently within Cuba and beyond.

However, for one small group, dispersed but vocal, *Fresa y chocolate* revived a ten-year-old controversy around a documentary, *Improper Con-duct*, by Alea's youthful collaborator Néstor Almendros, which indicted the Cuban regime as homophobic, sexist, racist, and totalitarian. Alea had anticipated this response. *Fresa y chocolate* was in preparation when he heard of the death of Almendros, with whom he made his first films on 8 mm back in the 1940s. He considered *Improper Conduct*, which consists of a series of interviews about the repression of homosexuals in the 1960s, some honest, some grossly exaggerated, "a very crude and schematic simplification of reality, very manipulative, like a piece of so-cialist realism in reverse," and agreed that "since one could hardly make a film on the theme of homosexuality in Cuba without thinking of what Néstor had done, *Fresa y chocolate* was in a way a reply to *Conducta im-propia*."[61] (Lumsden—a North American gay—considers Almendros's film "particularly misleading in its use of emotive analogies to Pinochet's Chile, Nazi Germany, and Stalin's Russia.")[62] In short, when a protest letter was sent to Jack Valenti, president of the Motion Picture Associa-tion of America (MPAA), signed by such luminaries as Cabrera Infante and Andy García, charging *Fresa y chocolate* with being an apologia for the Cuban regime and attempting to impede Alea's Oscar nomination, the answer had already be sent.

In order to shoot *Fresa y chocolate*, Tabío had interrupted the editing of his own film, *El elefante y la bicicleta (The Elephant and the Bicycle)*, which came out in 1994, and probably suffered as a result of the inter-ruption. A pity, says the Cuban critic Julio César Aguillera, that a film with such a good dramaturgical idea dissolves into a complicated succession of gags and uneven subplots that fail to establish solid links between them.[63] Made to celebrate the centenary of cinema, a recent writer on political cinema, Mike Wayne, sees it as "an extended, self-reflexive meditation on cinema and society," adding that it seems like a humorous commentary on Alea's *The Viewer's Dialectic:* a projectionist brings cinema to a symbolic island called La Fe (Faith) for the first time in the year 1925.[64] Taking its title from the pre-credits sequence, in which a classroom full of children unwittingly evoke Hamlet's conversation with Polonius about the shapes to be seen in a certain cloud—camel, weasel, or whale, or, in this case, elephant or bicycle—the film is full of allusions to the history of cinema from a decidedly Latin American perspective.

The projectionist has brought a single film, which recounts the legend of Robin Hood. The audience is completely entranced, as they begin to see themselves as the characters on the screen—who are played by the same actors as various characters on the island. They clamor to see the film again and again, confusing the events on the screen with events in their lives. The second night the film is screened the story shifts to a Latin American location—the outlaws become native Indians, the authorities are transformed into the white Spanish colonizers—and the film has acquired a sound track. It is next reconfigured as a tale of the Mexican Revolution, then becomes a story of the Brazilian *sertão* in homage to Glauber Rocha, the characters always undergoing wondrous transformations as the erstwhile Robin Hood turns up as the bandit Corisco from *Antonio das Mortes,* or Friar Tuck turns into a revolutionary priest urging his comrades to change themselves in order to change the world. In the world of La Fe, which, of course, represents Cuba itself, the arrival of the Revolution occasions an homage to Eisenstein's *October.*

In a study of the dialectics of third cinema, Mike Wayne sees the film in terms of Alea's argument that the spectacle of cinema ought to function like an interruption of normal life in which "real life is transfigured into reel life in such a way as to make the audience reconsider their values," a process metaphorically configured here in the parallels between the characters on the island and in the films they watch, and their confusion over the events in their own lives and those that occur in the films—a confusion that comes from the spectator's act of identification with the screen world. Alea's aesthetic is about the capacity of cinema to make this a productive identification that feeds the need for social change. The last of the film within the film's cinematic transformations is a projection of the dilemma of Cuba in the 1990s as the triumph of the revolution is celebrated in a parody of the Soviet musical—whereupon the projector breaks down. When the projectionist manages to solve the problem by adapting the damaged part from a printing machine, the audience returns to the cinema anxious to see how the film ends. As the screen lights up, what they see is a frontal shot of an audience looking directly at camera, out into the audience watching them. Again themselves. Up on the screen, some of the audience in the film within the film stir restlessly and declare themselves bored with looking at these people who are looking at them. But Doña Illuminada, the symbolically named blind teacher from the classroom at the very beginning, tells them to wait, declaring that "she wants to see what they [the watching audience] do!" This, concludes Wayne, "is precisely what we, the real audience, demand of the characters: we go to the cinema to see what *they* do."[65] Obviously this ending has a different effect when seen in Cuba, by an audience that has recognized itself on the screen, than it does, say, late at night on British television, where it functions as little more than an amusing existential conundrum.

With the huge success of *Fresa y chocolate* abroad, Alea was soon at work on his last film, *Guantanamera,* another Spanish coproduction, again selflessly codirected by Juan Carlos Tabío. The eponymous song of the title is an old favorite. Back in the 1930s, it was the theme tune of the popular singer Joseito Fernández, when he had a weekly radio program and used it to improvise a witty commentary on current events. Here it fulfills the function of a kind of Greek—or Brechtian—chorus, punctuating the journey of a corpse from one end of the island to the other in a cross between a black comedy and a road movie. The humor of death is another of Alea's favorite themes.

The corpse in question is the aunt of the provincial funeral director in her home town of Guantánamo, where she dies while on a visit, but since she has long lived in Havana she must now be taken back there for burial. Her nephew uses the occasion to prove his management skills, according to his theory that the only way to keep the funeral services within their quota of gasoline in such a situation is to organize a relay from one provincial capital to the next. The narrative skillfully intertwines the mishaps along the way with the affairs of a truck driver (Jorge

Perugorría) and his involvement with the bureaucrat's wife (Mirta Ibarra). But at the heart of the film, its real protagonist, is an almost silent character, the old musician who was once the aunt's lover, whom she hasn't seen since their youth, and in whose arms she dies at the start of the film. He, as the cortège makes its way across the island, keeps seeing the image of his lover as a young girl in a photograph, who first materializes in front of his eyes standing beneath a placard with the old revolutionary slogan, *¡Revolución o Muerte!,* stationed under the word *death.* This was not the only political allusion that offended the orthodox, for the corpse inevitably followed the same route as the guerrilla army back in 1958 on its march to Havana and the triumph of the Revolution.

This time the party orthodox were prepared, and when it opened in Havana a few days before the 1995 film festival, to immediate popular approval, it was disparaged by critics for not achieving the same sublimity as Alea's success of the 1960s, *La muerte de un burócrata.* Some even complained that it was out of date before it was made, citing the scene of illicit dollar trading, which they claimed was a falsification of reality since the dollar had been legalized, an objection made in bad faith because legalization of the dollar was only introduced after the film had been shot. The public took a different view, taking it as a wistful film but not one of resignation and negativity, and *Guantanamera* justifiably scored a popular success. It is also a valedictory film, not to be lightly dismissed, by a dying director involved in a personal dialogue with his audience. Alea's cinema is always one of individual exorcism, played out in different keys, on themes that are chosen because they coincided with popular experience. Sergio in *Memorias,* for example, can be seen as his own alter ego, but the popular appeal of the film came from the fact that what intellectuals in Latin America call the *desgarramiento,* the rupture, the breakdown of the familiar vocabulary of existence in the face of revolutionary change, is not a monopoly of theirs; everyone is confronted with the same problem of the need for the personal reconstruction of values. Something similar is true here. In *Guantanamera,* Alea seized the moment in order to exorcise his private experience one last time, to joke about death in the teeth of it. But while the private subject of the film is his own approaching end, he turns it into a dance with another, more symbolic death. In the film's most beautiful sequence, as the countryside is drenched in tropical rain, a voice-off recounts the legend of the Afro-Cuban deity Iku: Olofi it was who gave life to man and woman, but he forgot to create death. People grew old but didn't die, and they kept following the old laws. The young cried out to Olofi, who began to feel old himself, and unable to deal with the problem, so he called on Iku to find a solution. Iku caused it to rain for thirty days and nights. Only the young, who were able to climb the trees and the mountains, survived, and then, when the flood cleared and they came down, they saw that the earth was clean and beautiful, and gave thanks to Olofi for bringing an end to immortality. The metaphor is crystal clear: it is an allegory on the irony that the same man who brought Cuba to Revolution may now be forced to see it off. But spoken wistfully, the dialogue with death turns into a dialogue with a dream of life: a legend talking of mortality that at the same time celebrates the vigor of the young. Alea died a few months after the film's Havana premiere.

García Espinosa chose a less explicit approach for *Reina y Rey* (Queen and king, 1994). An homage to neorealism, this is a latter-day Cuban version of Vittorio De Sica's *Umberto D.* of 1952, the story of an old woman and her dog in the Havana of the Special Period. Reina, desperate to feed Rey, eventually bows to the inevitable and takes him to the dog pound, only shrinking back at the last moment from abandoning him to a miserable end; but then he runs away, to forage with other strays on the city's rubbish tips, perhaps even to be eaten by other starving dogs. Reina is left alone in the house where she was once the servant of a family who abandoned Cuba for Miami, who now return on a visit. They try to persuade her to go back with them to the States and her job as their servant, and cannot understand why she declines the offer. A simple and sentimental tale, Colina considers the attempt to transplant postwar Rome to the Special Period to be a case of nostalgia.[66] The most striking images in the film are those of Havana itself. Even without seeing the worst dilapidation, these images of the dog pound, the rubbish tip, and the railway sidings (where Reina takes a seat in an old railway carriage and enjoys a moment of private fantasy) amount to a quite novel representation of the city, of its interstitial spaces of abandonment, a visual figuration common enough in the case of other cities and other cinemas but not seen in Cuban cinema until recently. In fact, Havana has often been a character in its own right in Cuban cinema. In films like *Memorias del subdesarrollo* of 1967, *Hasta cierto punto* in the early 1970s, *Retrato de Teresa* and *Se permuta* (House for swap) ten or a dozen years later, the city becomes, in all its social and architectural diversity, the visual inscription of the Revolution, and the Revolution, in a phrase this writer has heard used in conversation more than once, is "like a mirror in which you see your own reflection." But in several films of the mid-1990s, the city's appearance has become instantly haunting. In *Madagascar* (1994) and *La ola* (The wave, 1995), for example, photographed by Raúl Pérez Ureta and Santiago Yanez, respectively, the city becomes a landscape of existential crisis, disappointment, and internal spiritual exile, and its limpid cinematography emerges as the most sentient aspect of Cuban cinema in the 1990s.

By the middle of the decade there were significant signs of economic change. As well as legalization of the dollar in 1993, which halted inflation in the black market, a series of staggered reforms to the system began in 1992 with a new constitution, which, among other things, modified the concept of property, allowing for certain kinds of small-scale private ownership and large-scale mixed enterprises with foreign companies. A year later, land ownership passed to agricultural cooperatives, and self-employment was permitted. Markets were introduced in 1994 for agricultural produce and industrial and artisanal products, and the following year saw a new law on foreign investment, extending the entry of foreign capital into all sectors of the economy except for public health, education, and the Armed Forces, subject to various controls. The object was to stimulate economic growth by inviting foreign investment in modernization, especially in key dollar-earning sectors such as tourism. In whatever way these moves were construed abroad, at home it was widely understood that there was no intention of abandoning socialist principles, or of sacrificing the egalitarian gains of the Revolution on the altar of capitalism and the free market. A transition was beginning, but not one that was intended to lead to the abdication of socialist power. Nevertheless, it meant that the state had decided to adjust its behavior toward the economy and accept a transformation of the social environment, an alteration in the relations between State and society that was argued by some to constitute the creation of an apparently contradictory animal, a socialist civil society.

In this new situation, the problem for the filmmakers who were once in the vanguard of revolutionary culture was ICAIC's own internal loss of dynamic. The Institute was now held back by the inbuilt delay mechanism of production, the long wait between the original conception of a film and getting it to the screen, exacerbated by the economic crisis. In 1996, the Institute failed to complete any new feature films, and although new productions were already in the pipeline, there was a growing sense that the Institute was simply lurching from one crisis to another, more protracted, and potentially more fatal. A disillusion that, as in the country at large, only added to the difficulties. Between 1981 and 1990, ICAIC had earned approximately $7.7 million in hard currency, of which $5.9 million came from film sales and distribution, mainly in Western Europe, and the remaining $1.8 million—just under a quarter—from service fees. In 1993, the proportions had changed, with service-fee revenues of $454,000 coming out roughly equal to earnings from international sales and distribution.[67] Reduced levels of production made it unlikely that this trend could be reversed, and with the shift to self-financing, these earnings were not sufficient to sustain ICAIC as a significant producer. The only quick answer in these conditions was to try and build on the international success of *Fresa y chocolate* and *Guantanamera*, and further pursue international coproductions with commercial partners in the attempt to ensure survival. The risk was evident, and not only financial. The expectations of these mainly European coproducers were inevitably different from the Latin Americans with whom ICAIC worked during the 1980s, and did not necessarily concur with a filmmaking tradition predicated on engagement with national cultural values and social critique. What they sought from ICAIC, with some exceptions, were films that exploited the island's exotic image, providing local color as a background for low-budget genre movies, supported by a range of services such as the provision of highly qualified technical staff and experienced character actors. The fear was that directors who wanted to take advantage of such a situation would have to learn to adapt their sensibilities accordingly. One commentator quotes the opinion of Pastor Vega: "Have I changed anything in the way I conceive my work? Absolutely. Before one thought only about the Cuban public. Now you have to think about 'marketing' and 'profits' and all that." Another director, Orlando Rojas, thought that while Cuban directors were now beginning to think about commercial success, "as yet there are not a lot of mercenaries," but people were becoming more realistic "and this would give rise to another kind of film."[68]

The dangers were illustrated by a couple of films by Spanish directors that came out in 1998. *Cuarteto de la Habana* (Havana quartet), directed by Fernando Colomo, had Cuba's two best-known actresses, Mirta Ibarra and Daisy Granados, as its stars. A comedy with a clever script and splendid acting, especially from Mirta Ibarra as Lita, the film presents a touristic image of Havana, while playing on the "double morality" that characterizes daily life in Havana in the 1990s. The plot is highly contrived. The Spanish actor Ernesto Alterio plays a young jazz musician who lives with his grandmother in Madrid, who when she dies discovers a video that purports to be a message from his mother in Havana. Arriving in Cuba, he finds that his supposed sister is engaged to the steward on the Spanish flight that took him there, and her mother, Lita, is busy fleecing the Spaniard in order to buy things like a new refrigerator for the very large house in which they live. Needless to say, sister and mother turn out not to be who he thought them to be. The film tries to be fair by poking fun at both Cubans and tourists, but in the end leaves a bad taste. Less offensive was *Mambí*, directed by the Ríos brothers from a workmanlike script by Ambrosio Fornet, which tells the story of the Cuban war of liberation against Spain in 1896–98 from the point of view of a conscripted Spanish soldier who has family in Havana (and, of course, falls in love with a Cuban woman). In Spain, the film offended against the orthodox version of history; elsewhere, it would be found too orthodox a genre movie to make any ripples.

At all events, the need for hard currency became so pressing that it strengthened the authority of ICAIC's production office, whose approval now became a sine qua non, whereas previously the department had functioned in the service of productions that were undertaken on the basis of cultural and aesthetic criteria. Inevitably, the situation led to considerable resentment and even suspicion of mismanagement. As the film critic Luciano Castilla wrote in 1999, "It is a puzzle how income from the supply of services to these coproductions is reinvested in national cinema."[69] Other effects included the departure for foreign shores of more ICAIC personnel and several actors, and a generalized feeling that Alfredo Guevara himself, ICAIC's founder and chief ideologue, had finally been defeated by the turn of events, and had lost the sense of conviction with which he had once inspired the Institute.

Ironically, in another sign of changing times, there has also been a gradual but definite growth in *aficionado* filmmaking, which by the end of the 1990s would largely employ video. The cine-club movement dates back to the end of the 1970s, and began to make an appearance at the film festival in the mid-1980s, a development that lies outside the purview of the present study. Juan Antonio García Borrero suggests that an evaluation of this "other" cinema might serve to explain "mutations in the communicative codes of certain official productions" in the 1990s; perhaps, he says, some of the elements in recent films that people find disconcerting come from the transculturation of the newest directors in their move from *aficionado* to professional filmmaking.[70] The films in question include Arturo Sotto's *Pon tu pensamiento en mí* (Turn your thoughts to me, 1995) and *La ola* (1995) by Enrique Álvarez, whose first shorts were made as member of the Taller de Cine de la Asociación Hermanos Saíz. For the most part, for example, in the work of Tomás Piard, who has also made films with ICAIC and television, the approaches cultivated by the *aficionado* movement have been visually symbolic, metaphorical, and aestheticist, rather than politically programmatic. However, in 1997 one of these independent videos turned a Hi8 camera on ICAIC itself. *Secuencias inconclusas*, directed by a young graduate of the Instituto Superior del Arte, Amanda Chávez, and dedicated to the memory of Tomás Gutiérrez Alea, begins with an extract from *Memorias del subdesarrollo* that in the context acquires a new resonance: "Here everything's always the same... then suddenly it looks like a city of cardboard... today everything looks different. Have I changed, or has the city?"

Neither the film nor those who appear in it pull any punches. The clips from *Memorias* lead into a series of commentaries by ICAIC directors. Orlando Rojas considers that the scandal of *Alicia* has left a negative mark in Cuban film culture, a wound that has not yet been healed. *Alicia*'s director Daniel Díaz Torres admits that many people at different political levels in the country continue to find the film uncomfortable, but believes it remains possible to continue making a Cuban cinema, a national cinema, belonging to the Revolution but in touch with the complexities of reality and its contradictions. According to Pastor Vega, however, you have to add to the economic and social problems that make up the Special Period a certain inertia, and even apathy in the ICAIC administration, which left ICAIC at this moment at its lowest ever ebb, in terms of both production and risk taking, a sense of experiment and search. Where every film can become a problem, the polemical is of little interest. For Juan Carlos Tabío, the main difficulties are of a financial order, and coproductions help. Fernando Pérez finds that the first problem is "that when you're suddenly forced to go out and find your own finance, it needs a mentality for which the Cuban film-maker is ill prepared; and the rules are unclear, as decisions about what goes into production become more centralized, when before they were made by the directors in their creative groups."

García Espinosa explains the danger of coproductions: they distort the whole character of the film, which now has to be shaped by commercial opportunity—an actor from this or that country, a story that justifies the partner's participation—which overrides aesthetic judgment and cultural authenticity. The actor Luis Alberto García accepts that coproductions provide material support and an opening to a market that was previously unavailable, but cannot believe they offer a solution for a genuinely Cuban cinema, which is of no interest to foreign capital. Humberto Solás wonders why it isn't possible to use some of the funds brought in by coproduction to support small-scale but entirely local productions, "but I'm not an economist, I don't understand all that." Orlando Rojas doubts that these banal subproducts bring in much money, which is why there is little investment in national productions, but everyone wants to work on them, because they help people make a living. In other words, people prefer to work on a French serial or a Canadian or Italian picture, because officially or unofficially they get a part of their salary in foreign currency. National films are disadvantaged. The system is not healthy.

The situation leaves actors particularly exposed. Beatriz Valdés asks why economic chaos should have to mean that foreign producers pay thousands of dollars for Cuban actors whose share of this income is abysmally low, "because we're talking exploitation here." Adolfo Llaurado reports that people are scandalized when he tells them he earns 340 Cuban pesos a month, the same as thirty years earlier. "Thirty years ago that was quite a lot, today it's about seven dollars a month ... but still, I'll go on living on my seven dollars, and not do anything I don't want to do; I'd rather do something for free and not be corrupted." Jorge Perugorría protests that ICAIC has no right to include the actors in its sales package to foreign producers, "French, Italian, Spanish, who pay three million dollars to make a film here and we're included as if we're ICAIC's property." (Three years later, some of these problems were being resolved, at least as far as entitlement to dollar payments is concerned.)

The community is denuded by emigration. Luis Alberto García laments how he meets up with a group of friends only to find that half the old bunch are no longer there; "fifteen has been reduced to seven, some have left for good, others have gone on an international mission for fifteen or twenty years." It is not, he says, just economic, "because a director who leaves is not just going off to earn more money, he's going because he wants to make a film, like a cinematographer who hasn't shot a film in four or five years will go to Ecuador or the Straits of Magellan to shoot a picture, in order to be behind a camera, because that's his life." Among those who remain, these conditions take their toll in destroying the sense of a community of filmmakers with a shared vision. Fernando Pérez feels he can no longer claim to represent his generation "because many of them aren't making films—or can't." There is a policy of encouraging young directors, but one of them, Arturo Soto, admits that the circumstances require concessions and it isn't his responsibility as a representative of the youth that concerns him but supplying the market. Here an undercurrent emerges that goes beyond García Borrero's comments on a new aesthetic among younger directors, for this is an individualist attitude that no one in ICAIC has expressed before. Perrugoría wants to know how ICAIC can let go of its heritage like this: "after so many years of sacrifice and so much work by so many people for so many years, I don't know what they're thinking or even if there's anyone in ICAIC asking these questions."

Secuencias inconclusas is a sad and shocking picture of a dispirited group of filmmakers trying to keep hold of a dream, and it was not surprisingly withheld from screening at the Havana Film Festival, restricting it to a small circulation on video. Nevertheless, it also represents a certain defiance in the face of the odds, and a determination not to go under.

One of the paradoxes of Cuba in the 1990s was the creation of an annual Workshop on Film Criticism (Taller Nacional de Crítica Cinematográfica) at the very moment, in 1993, when the exercise of the profession reached its nadir, the moment when publications disappeared due to the paper shortage—even *Cine Cubano* was suspended—and a lack of new releases anyway robbed the critics of their daily bread and butter. Since then, year by year, critics from one end of the island to the other have assembled every March in Camagüey, which García Borrero, the moving force behind this initiative, dubs "the symbolic city," to discuss a range of issues such as the virtues and limitations of film criticism in Cuba, the character of Cuban cinema in the 1990s, and in 1995, the centenary of cinema. The following years brought discussion on issues of postmodernism, the carnivalesque, and otherness; the relationship between filmmakers and critics; between film criticism and criticism in the other arts; and in 1999, questions of new technologies and the horizon of audience expectations. According to García Borrero, introducing the eighth workshop in 2000, there have been several observable results. The practice of film criticism in Cuba has acquired greater cohesion; this includes the reconfiguration of the national critical map through recognition of the role of film critics working in the provinces. At the same time, contacts have been improved between national and international critics and institutions, and between Cuban critics and filmmakers. Further, the analytical arsenal of the film critic has expanded, and links have been forged between film criticism and that of other arts. The event has also helped to stimulate the promotion of film culture at the very moment it came under threat because of the contraction of activity. García Borrero cites the examples of film events in other provincial cities including Ciego de Ávila, Las Turnas, Santa Clara, and Cienfuegos, while in Camagüey itself (the country's third-largest city) the screenings accompanying the Workshop now attracted an audience of some sixty thousand.[71]

He also mentions that the Workshop has served to preserve the critical memory of the period by publishing its proceedings at a moment when it seemed that criticism had become an oral activity, but there is a rider to this. The critics at the Round Table at the eighth workshop in 2000 did not all agree that the conditions for the practice of their craft had entirely improved, but several of them noted an increase in the number and variety of texts published since the middle of the decade, when the publishing industry began to recover. What seems to have happened is that film criticism has moved from the newspapers to the journals, and at the same time changed its orientation, since, as one of them points out, the daily or weekly column that reviews new films becomes a fairly pointless activity when irregularities in publication produce a gap between the release of a new film and the publication of the review, and anyway the number of new releases is minimal.[72] If this new criticism ironically appeared just as the island's film culture entered into crisis, then through its tenor and terms of reference it also stakes out a place in the wider transformation going on in the political culture in the same period. It is more analytical, its discourse is less tied to mechanical models of Marxism and more cognizant of the theories of postmodernism in the West; above all, it operates with a knowledge of cinema that is up to date and impressively wide-ranging. This indicates not only the efficacy of video in breaking through the blockade, but also a shift in outlook, in which Cuban cinema is increasingly seen within a global perspective that places Latin American films alongside the latest from Hollywood, China, Iran, or England without privileging any of them. This a world in which the old idea of the New Latin American Cinema has been superseded by a new reality, which in Cuba takes on a double significance, for, in passing through the crisis of the 1990s to survive without any strings attaching it to a foreign power, Cuba has entered a new global space in which the authenticity of national cultures is everywhere both asserted and called into question.

In certain respects, however, the new criticism is not entirely new. One of the first examples is an article already cited in these pages, "No Adult Cinema without Systematic Heresy," by Rufo Caballero and Joel del Río, which appeared in the journal *Temas* in 1995. The significance of the piece is not that what it says has never been uttered before, but rather that such opinions are here appearing for the first time in print. *Temas,* a publication financed by the ministry of culture, was established precisely in order to provide a forum for critical debate across a wide range of subjects around the social sciences, and, together with *La Gaceta de Cuba,* published by UNEAC, has played a crucial role in the gestation of the new film criticism. The critic is now daring to write what many have been thinking and feeling already for some time, at the same time developing ideas in new directions. What has happened is that the boundaries between different types of speech, dating back to the 1970s, are being redrawn, and what could not be said directly in public discourse but circulated in public through interpersonal speech is now beginning to appear in print, albeit in small-circulation publications. This is not say that the official discourse has been taken over by new thinking, but rather that it has lost its exclusive hold over the spaces of public debate, where discussion has become more porous.

The foreign observer, like the writer of these lines, who returns to Cuba in the late 1990s, also discovers that conversation is no longer hemmed in by tacit understanding about what can and cannot be said. On the contrary, interlocutors who would once have guarded their words, not wishing to be overheard by the wrong person, or sometimes simply not to hear themselves say such things, now speak freely what is on their minds. As Rafael Hernández puts it, what was previously perceived as a deviation from the norm, inconsistent with prevailing values, and suspect as being bourgeois in origin, is no longer automatically rejected as offensive to good habits, and has even become paradigmatic for certain groups.[73] While Hernández is speaking here of economic activity, like living off a dollar income and indulging in consumerist behavior, that the same is true of the world of ideas is demonstrated by the very article where the comment is made, which appeared in the journal *Nueva Sociedad* in 1998. A commentary of a kind that it would have been difficult to publish a few years previously, this article also serves, as the work of a party intellectual, to indicate a certain space of polemic that has opened up within the party itself, which perhaps represents a new political realism. But political reality in Cuba remains paradoxical and one must be careful not to draw the wrong conclusions. Hernández, for example, believes it difficult to assess the real extent of this eroded consensus because of its very characteristics, which occlude the extent of its penetration into the deepest structures of social psychology. But in political terms, he says, there is little sign either of the consensus breaking up "or of the emergence of a public consciousness favorable to the collapse of the established order."[74] Foreign observers find this puzzling to the extent that they assume Cuba must be undergoing a transition of the same kind as occurred in Eastern Europe, to liberal democracy, and they attribute the lack of progress to continuing political control. They do not consider the possibility that the "lack of public desire for the collapse of the established order" is a positive choice, the legitimate sentiment of a majority that does not wish to see the even greater damage to their lives that such a disruption would bring: a form of existential patience in the face of acute frustration.

The new criticism is certainly informed by a sense of political realism. At the dawn of the new century, one of the most striking examples is an essay by Désirée Díaz published in *La Gaceta de Cuba* in 2000, "The Ulysses Syndrome: The Journey in Cuban Cinema in the 90s." Here, in examining the figure of the journey to be found in several different guises in a number of Cuban films of the preceeding decade,

Díaz places these films and their symbolism in the context of recent critical thinking on migration and diaspora, identity and displacement, and the imagined communities of nationhood. Cuba, which has suffered intensely from the effects of migration, now finds itself in a world of global displacements of populations and the formation of new diasporas, especially in the hegemonic countries of the North, which destabilize the concepts of identity, tradition, and cultural belonging. These questions take on a particular cast in Cuba, a country that has been split into fractured moieties by successive waves of emigration over the preceding four decades, each of which claims a monopoly on patriotism. Departing Cuba, says Díaz, has long been seen as a dramatic act associated with feelings of rupture, repudiation, and loss that leave their mark on every level—the individual, the family, the island, the nation—but that are all too frequently suppressed by the drastic postures of official discourse in both the emigrant and immigrant countries. Again, this essay and its subject are part of a the same ideological alteration. In Cuba, simply to speak of the nation as an imagined community already marks a signal shift in critical discourse, and if the stereotype of the counter-revolutionary *gusano* massed in Miami is weakened through the introduction of the term *diaspora,* the films of the 1990s similarly show a marked tendency to rethink the metaphorical, existential, and even ontological character of Cuba's isolation and insularity.

Díáz's thesis is that Cuban cinema in the 1990s sought to question the traditional view that stigmatized the émigré, and to develop a more subtle and flexible attitude toward the issue in place of dogmatism and belligerence. The phenomenon of migration comes to be inscribed in these films in a number of forms—as departure, return, internal exile, or nostalgia. The journey, real or metaphorical, is represented fundamentally in two ways: "as a circumstance that creates a rupture and a loss—often magnified—or, more conceptually, as the transition between two moments." It is also the sign of a process of search.[75] If very few films before the 1990s confronted the disjuncture caused by emigration—*Lejanía* by Jesús Díaz is the obvious exception, and it was largely ignored or belittled by the critics—Désirée Díaz sees the theme as a recurring preoccupation of the last decade of the century. Indeed, it is already present in three films from the early 1990s that she doesn't mention, *Mujer transparente, Fresa y chocolate,* and *Reina y Rey.* It then comes up in a pair of films by Fernando Pérez, *Madagascar* (1994) and *La vida es silbar* (1998), two films by new directors, *La ola* by Enrique Álvarez (1995) and *Amor vertical* by Arturo Sotto (1997), and again, more allegorically, in *Lista de espera* by Juan Carlos Tabío (2000).

La ola centers on a pair of young lovers enduring the summer of 1994, searching out isolated corners of the city in order to make love, whose only real difference is that she wishes to leave and he prefers to stay. In every other respect, says Díaz, the two of them are interchangeable, mutually complementary representatives of a generation shorn of ideological preoccupations that is condemned to a waiting game. The film represents, she says, "an ontological search that coincides... with the localization of real spaces attuned to personal realization" in which the sea and the waves present a defining question: for one of them to cross the waters would constitute a definitive separation, a loss for both of them. It all sounds rather rarefied, and it is, with the consequence that the most impressive thing about the film is the cinematography of Santiago Yanez, which presents a vision of Havana far from the typical colorful crowded city of popular imagination, but full of longing, or what might be called nostalgia for an unknown future.

Sotto, like Álvarez, again poses the problem of emigration in terms of the existential dilemma of departure and the rupture it necessarily implies, although they differ in both their treatment of the theme and their aesthetics. *Amor vertical* was Sotto's second feature. A graduate of the film school of San Antonio de los Baños, he won a first prize at the Havana Film Festival in 1992 for a fictional short, *Talco para lo negro* (Talcum for the black man), and quickly went on to make his first feature. *Pon tu pensamiento en mí* is an unlikely religious allegory about a troupe of itinerant players in an unidentified Latin American country in an unspecified time, one of whom appears to perform miracles on the stage, though he only has two tricks up his sleeve, one with bread and one with fish. Full of intertextual allusions to other films on the same allegory such as *Jesus of Montreal,* and officially promoted as an extraordinary debut, it proved a damp squib. Sotto has defended the lack of temporal and geographical specificity as the product of the exigencies of production in Cuba in a particularly problematic moment,[76] but the film was too abstract and too obvious at the same time: the people believe the actor is the new savior, he denies it, but the people need something to believe in—so what? *Amor vertical,* which followed two years later, is not much more convincing, but rather funnier. A surreal sociocritical comedy about frustrated love, which this time pays explicit homage to Buñuel and Fellini, it takes its title from a comic sequence in which a couple take advantage of a power cut to make love in an elevator. Díaz, however, cites an unforgettable scene that portrays a different kind of conjoining, that of a pair of Siamese twins who need an operation to separate them that is only available in the United States, but they have opposing political views and cannot agree to go. When one says, "I've told you that living in the island is a very expensive dignity," the other replies, "You don't realize that Miami is a cardboard city." The symbolic pair literally embody a metaphor of the nation, the girls forcibly united by natural conditions, wanting to separate and follow different paths, who represent the polarization suffered by everyone faced with the disjuncture of departure: they are two, yet they are one, and express the duality by which Cuba is now constituted. To have the operation in Havana, it is likely one of them will die—which will it be? Here the twins become a sign of the death that follows separation: "not physical death, as may occur in the film, but emotional, cultural, and moral (the nation may die when it separates, when one part goes and the other remains, or what amounts to the same, when one part stays put without its other half)."[77]

In *Madagascar* the journey is imaginary and internal—and condensed into fifty minutes of cinematic poetry. Evoking the model of one of the finest of all Cuban films, *Lucía* of 1968, in which Humberto Solás told the stories of three women at three different historical moments, Pérez paints a wistful portrait of three generations of women living under the same roof in contemporary Cuba. Laura (Zaida Castellanos), a physics lecturer, twice divorced, tells her doctor that she has problems dreaming: she dreams what she lives, the same thing twenty-four hours a day, and she would like to dream something else; Laurita (Laura de la Uz), her daughter, daydreams of going to Madagascar, quits school, and discovers religion; her boyfriend, a silent and irreverent painter, plays Monopoly with her grandmother (Elena Bolaños), who delights in putting the little red hotels on her property.

Originally intended as one of a trilogy of short dramas, Pérez returns to the same territory as his previous film, *Hello Hemingway,* but this time turns out a narrative experiment that seems intent on upsetting stereotypes, whether those of a girl's coming-of-age story, or the allegory of the nation as woman. In this purportedly ordinary Cuban family,

Amor vertical (Arturo Sotto, 1997)

where it happens that men are marginal or wholly absent, the grandmother, as Anne Marie Stock points out, is not a repository of traditional wisdom. At the beginning of the film, Laurita is rebellious and
consumed by the angst of growing up, reads the poetry of Rimbaud,
and turns to religion. By the end, she has become the model daughter,
returns to school, passes her exams, talks to people. But at the same
time, she swaps positions with her mother, who finds it increasingly
difficult to keep up her engagement with an inert reality in which she
can no longer discover her past. When Laura gets out an old newspaper
clipping with a photograph of a political rally, which she inspects with a
magnifying glass, the close-up image becomes an undifferentiated mass
of dots as she asks herself out loud, "Where am I, *Dios mío,* where am
I?" "What remains of the young woman in that public square in the
1960s," observes Stock, "are memories inextricable from her yearnings
of today and her hopes for the future."[78] The mother ends up asking the
daughter, "Do you have your bags packed? We're going to Madagascar."

Why Madagascar? Because, of course, it is like a mirror image of Cuba,
a poor island separated from a nearby continent, somewhere practically
impossible to get to. But Madagascar, as Stock puts it, is "more a state of
mind than a place, internal rather than external, intangible . . . emotional
and spiritual" (27). It is not an accident that Laurita reads Rimbaud and

conceives an imaginary journey as a means of escape. She looks out toward the sea and says, "I'm going to Madagascar. It's not stupid, it's what I don't know." In another scene, she stands on one of Havana's flat roofs, chanting "Madagascar, Madagascar, Madagascar," arms outstretched, body forming a cross, or perhaps an embrace, or as if she were about to launch herself in flight over the city. Here (and elsewhere) the film departs from representational realism as the camera moves back to reveal similar figures on similar roofs, T-shaped forms interrupting the uniform urban skyline, like a series of antennae receiving and transmitting, "a blend of multiple voices all chanting in unison."

From the beginning, the film presents a series of images that evoke states of transition or movement toward an unknown or unreal destination. In the opening sequence, which is unlike anything previously seen in Cuban cinema, a series of shots of torsos in movement are revealed as a sea of cyclists on their way to work "in a haunting shadowy blue dawn." What we see here, says Stock, is not people reaching their destination but only their effort to keep moving. During the film, the family moves, riding on a truck loaded with furniture and chattels through the city. "Piled boxes, crated furniture, squeaking pulleys, and empty rooms" underline their state of migrancy (25). At the end, mother and daughter are left pushing their bikes through a tunnel; the picture cuts to a train clacking along the tracks past dilapidated buildings in a stark industrial landscape, while the sound track has the legendary Omara Portuondo singing about the impossibility of living separately. The old-style love song becomes an existential lament. Frustration, lack of communication between the generations, silence about the degeneration of the Revolution, Havana here is a city of disillusion, disappointment, discouragement, bathed in a strange, timeless beauty, and of meditation on the entanglement of the lost promises of youth and revolutionary hopes.

The urge for the outside that nourishes Laurita is what Elpidio in *La vida es silbar* resists, in another film that serves as a barometer of the thwarted aspirations of present-day Cuban life. A much more elaborate and symbolically coded film, again beautifully shot by Raúl Pérez Ureta, this is a touching and slyly critical social comedy with absurdist elements and surreal imagery, like the mysterious figure of Bebe, a face that always appears underwater, who narrates the film and sometimes intervenes to alter the details—is she telling or inventing it? Bebe is the link between

Madagascar (Fernando Pérez, 1994)

the parallel stories of three characters who never meet but share a common yearning for an elusive happiness. Mariana is a ballerina about to dance her first *Giselle* (a role identified in Cuba with the legendary Alicia Alonso); in her desperate anxiety to succeed, she promises God to give up sex. Julia, who works in an old people's home, suffers from a strange illness, which her psychiatrist explains is not unusual, in fact many Habaneros suffer from it—they collapse in a faint on hearing certain words pronounced in their hearing. In her case the word is *sex*, but his diagnosis is hilariously demonstrated as she flees from the hospital in disbelief, and, chasing after her, people around them fall to the ground as he calls out words like *free, double morality, opportunism,* and *fear of the truth.* Elpidio, surname Valdés, who calls his mother Cuba, is a would-be musician who lives off his wits. A composite figure with the same name as the hero of Cuba's popular cartoon series, a nineteenth-century freedom fighter for the island's independence, he is also the symbolic son of Santa Bárbara and the Afro-Cuban deity Shangó; virile and strong, he worships a Santa Bárbara he keeps at home. The outside world is represented by Chrissy, the foreigner arriving in Cuba on a research mission, literally descending from the skies in a balloon, who becomes Elpidio's lover. Chrissy, according to the director, represents "another way of thinking and seeing life," but cannot tempt Elpidio to go with her when she leaves.[79] As they float over the city in Chrissy's balloon, she offers to take him off to her own world, to discover other sensations, other feelings. "This is freedom!" she says. "Do you know freedom?" and Elpidio answers, "I don't know, I feel dizzy." Here the journey is seen as a need to flee from precarious circumstances while emotional attachments prevent it. As the bicycle-taxi driver puts it, pondering a snail, "Snails are almost perfect, because they're the only ones who can live abroad without feeling nostalgia for home." Elpidio rejects the temptation to escape because of the atavistic influence of the earth mother, the love of a country that transcends the political patriotism that is owed to the state, but his desire will not be quelled by compliance. He ends up addressing his island mother, "I'm not going to change now, but I can't live without you either. If you want to accept me as I am, let my music take me to you." It is possible to critique this film—though without disparaging its poetics—as itself an attempt to escape reality, to soften the anxieties and disillusion of the unending Special Period with a symbolic fantasy about spirituality, and this indeed is in part what the Cuban audience felt about it. The most ambiguous of its symbols is the promise that is made in the film of a happier future in the year 2020, which is, at one and the same time, less than a lifetime hence but impossibly far into the future.

In Tabío's *Lista de espera* (Waiting list) of 2000, the journey is again forbidden and impossible, because there are no buses to allow them to get away. Díaz offers a striking interpretation that sees the film as the inverse of *Alicia*. In *Alicia* a young drama teacher is sent to a town lost in the middle of the country that embodies the worst of real socialism. She struggles to change their demented ways but meets with incomprehension, and finally has to make her escape. In *Lista de espera* a group of people are stuck in a bus station at the edge of a town that could also be called Maravillas, yet faced with the impossibility of achieving their objective, they band together and spend their time doing the bus station up, painting it, installing a library, cooking a collective meal of celebration. Next morning they wake up to realize they've been caught up in a collective dream. As Díaz sees it, in *Alicia* the protagonist wants at first to remain and take on the whole world, then decides she has to leave. In

Lista de espera the characters start by wanting to leave but end up not wanting to abandon the place they have constructed together. But this is progress: "In *Alicia*, at the beginning of the decade, there are no solutions available and anxiety for change is nothing more than a fanciful idea, while *Lista de espera* reverses this ending, and the compulsion to go somewhere else is no longer so urgent."[80]

Lead actor Vladimir Cruz calls the film "a sort of metaphor on the construction of paradise or utopia, which is rather like the history of Cuba over the last few years."[81] His character is an engineer who loves his profession but earns a miserable salary that hardly amounts to a living. His only remedy is to give up his job and join his family in Oriente breeding pigs in order to make some money. In the bus station, he meets a young professional woman, but she is going to Havana to marry a Spaniard. This love story satisfies the conventional demands of the genre, but the thrust of the film is the fragility of the utopian dream.

In fine, *Lista de espera* is a film in the mold of a Buñuelesque comedy in the style of Alea that could perhaps have been made at any time in the last twenty years, but it is also a film that leaves a critical question hanging in the air. As Cruz puts it, "We Cubans have turned postponement into an art; we are the inventors of the art of knowing how to wait. What we have constructed, rather than the dream, is the waiting room to the dream." And this, indeed, is the very question that faces Cuba at the dawn of the new century—the imperative to make sense of the waiting room to a dream.

Notes

Preface

1. Juan Antonio García Borrero, *Guía crítica del cine cubano de ficción* (1910/ 1998) (Havana: Editorial Arte y Literatura, 2001).

Introduction

1. The present account is based on the printed version of the original speech and conversations in Havana in December 1998.

2. Manuel Vásquez Montalbán, *Y Dios entró en La Habana* (Madrid: El País/ Águilar, 1998), 684.

3. The interview was published later in the year. See Alfredo Guevara, *Revolución es lucidez* (Havana: Ediciones ICAIC, 1998), 53.

4. Conversation in Havana, December 1998.

5. Vásquez Montalbán, *Y Dios entró en La Habana,* 353.

6. Fidel Castro, "Words to the Intellectuals," in Lee Baxandall, ed., *Radical Perspectives in the Arts* (Harmondsworth: Penguin, 1972), 276.

7. Quoted in Vásquez Montalbán, *Y Dios entró en La Habana,* 331.

8. Conversation with Tomás Gutiérrez Alea.

9. Quoted in David Craven, "The Visual Arts since the Cuban Revolution," *Third Text* 20 (1992): 91–92.

10. John Hess, "No más Habermas," *Screen* 40:2 (1999): 203–7. See also http:// www.igc.org/jhess/cuba-screen.html.

11. Oscar Quiros, "Critical Mass of Cuban Cinema: Art as the Vanguard of Society," *Screen* 37:3 (1996): 279–93; Catherine Davies, "Modernity, Masculinity and Imperfect Cinema in Cuba," *Screen* 38:4 (winter 1997): 345–59.

12. Davies, "Modernity, Masculinity," 358; and see Julia Lesage, "One Way or Another: Dialectical, Revolutionary, Feminist," *Jump Cut* 20 (May 1979): 20–23.

13. E. Ann Kaplan, *Women and Film: Both Sides of the Camera* (London: Routledge, 1983), 190; and Julio García Espinosa, *For an Imperfect Cinema,* in Michael

Chanan, ed., *Twenty-Five Years of the New Latin American Cinema* (London: British Film Institute/Channel 4, 1983).

14. Quiros, "Critical Mass of Cuban Cinema." 286, 289.

15. See entry for *Amada* in Juan Antonio García Borrero, *Guía crítica del cine cubano de ficción* (1910/1998) (Havana: Editorial Arte y Literatura, 2001).

16. Fredric Jameson, "Third World Literature in the Era of Multinational Capitalism," *Social Text* 15 (fall 1986).

17. Hess, "No más Habermas."

18. See Quiros, "Critical Mass of Cuban Cinema." On Julio García Espinosa's *Por un cine imperfecto,* see chapter 13.

19. Walter Benjamin, "The Work of Art in the Age of Mechanical Reproduction," in *Illuminations,* ed. Hannah Arendt (New York: Schocken Paperback, 1969), 242.

20. The only exception I would make is a series of three films by an English filmmaker, the late Marc Karlin.

21. See Rafael Hernández, *Mirar a Cuba: Ensayos sobre cultura y sociedad civil* (Havana: Editorial Letras Cubanas, 1999), 128–29.

22. Conversation in Havana, December 1998.

1. For the First Time

1. Throughout the book, quotations from films have been made either from dialogue scripts provided by ICAIC or, as in this case, by direct transcription from the film on a viewing machine. Some of the dialogue scripts were supplied in English translation; otherwise all translations are my own. This also applies to all foreign-language texts unless an English translation is cited.

2. Maksim Gorki, "You Don't Believe Your Eyes," *World Film News* (March 1938).

3. Antonio Banfi, *Filosofía del arte* (Havana: Ediciones ICAIC, 1967), 72.

4. Figures compiled from the *Anuario Cinematográfico y Radial Cubano,* the prerevolutionary film trade annual; Francisco Mota, "12 aspectos económicos de la cinematografía cubana," *Lunes de Revolución,* February 6, 1961; Armando Hart, *Del trabajo cultural* (Havana: Editorial de Ciencias Sociales, 1978), 338.

5. Néstor García Canclini, *Arte popular y sociedad en América Latina* (Mexico City: Editorial Grijalbo, 1977), 247–48; 16 mm exhibition figures supplied by ICAIC, 1983.

6. Mayra Vilasis, interview with Octavio Cortázar, "El documental, Cortázar, El brigadista," *Cine Cubano* 93: 76.

7. Fernando Birri in *New Cinema of Latin America, I—Cinema of the Humble,* dir. Michael Chanan, 1983. See also Fernando Birri, "Cinema y subdesarrollo," *Cine Cubano* 42–44: 13.

8. Interview with Ruy Guerra, "El cine brasileño y la experiencia del Cinema Nuovo," *Octubre* (Mexico) 2–3 (January 1975): 46.

2. Back to the Beginning

1. Philip S. Foner, *The Spanish-Cuban-American War and the Birth of American Imperialism* (New York: Monthly Review Press, 1972), 1:167–68.

2. H. Wayne Morgan, *America's Road to Empire: The War with Spain and Overseas Expansion* (New York: John Wiley and Sons, 1965), 13.

3. Albert E. Smith, *Two Reels and a Crank* (New York: Doubleday, 1952), 55. Subsequent references are given in the text.

4. Sara Calvo and Alejandro Armangol, *El racismo en el cine*, Serie Literatura y Arte (Havana: Departamento de Actividades Culturales Universidad de la Habana, 1978), 27 n. 16.

5. Susan Sontag, *On Photography* (New York: Farrar, Straus and Giroux, 1977), 54–55.

6. For details in this paragraph and what follows, see Aurelio de los Reyes, *Los orígenes del cine en México (1896–1900)* (Mexico City: UNAM Cuadernos de Cine, 1973), 178; Arturo Agramonte, *Cronología del cine cubano* (Havana: Ediciones ICAIC, 1966); articles in the *Anuario Cinematográfico y Radial Cubano*; and Rolando Díaz Rodríguez and Lázaro Buria Pérez, "Un caso de colonización cinematográfica," *Caimán Barbudo* 85 (December 1975).

7. Quoted in Foner, *The Spanish-Cuban-American War*, 2:562.

8. Ibid., 669.

9. J. M. Valdés Rodríguez, "Algo en torno al cine y la República Cubana," Part II, *El Mundo*, April 19, 1960.

10. Sontag, *On Photography*, 64.

3. The Nineteenth-Century Heritage

1. Francisco López Segrera, "La economía y la política en la república neocolonial (1902–1933)," in *La república neocolonial, Anuario de estudios cubanos* 1 (Havana: Editorial de Ciencias Sociales, 1975), 130–32.

2. José Carlos Mariátegui, *Siete ensayos de interpretación de la realidad peruana*, (Havana: Casa de las Américas, 1975), 21.

3. Quoted in Andre Gunder Frank, *Capitalism and Underdevelopment in Latin America* (London: Penguin, 1971), 115.

4. Ambrosio Fornet, "Literatura y mercado en la Cuba colonial (1830–60)," *Casa de las Américas* 84: 48.

5. Alejo Carpentier, *La música en Cuba* (1946), 90. On nineteenth-century musical culture in Europe, see William Weber, *Music and the Middle Classes*, (Croom Helm, 1975).

6. Quoted in Gordon Brotherstone, *Latin American Poetry* (Cambridge: Cambridge University Press, 1975), 56.

7. Quoted in Françoise Perus, *Literatura y sociedad en America Latina: el modernismo* (Havana: Casa de las Américas 1976), 99.

8. Jean Franco, *The Modern Culture of Latin America* (London: Penguin, 1970), 31.

9. Cited in Arturo Agramonte, *Cronología del cine cubano* (Havana: Ediciones ICAIC, 1966), 32.

10. J. M. Valdés Rodríguez, "Algo en torno al cine y la República Cubana," Part III, *El Mundo*, April 21, 1960.

11. Ibid., 33.

4. Melodrama and White Horses

1. Rolando Díaz Rodríguez and Lázaro Buria Pérez, "Un caso de colonización cinematográfica," *Caimán Barbudo* 85 (December 1975): 6–7.

2. See Francisco Mota, "12 aspectos económicos de la cinematografía cubana, *Lunes de Revolución,* February 6, 1961.

3. José Agustín Mahieu, *Breve historia del cine argentino* (Buenos Aires: Editorial Universitaria, 1966), 5.

4. Pierre Bachlin, *Histoire économique du cinéma* (Paris: La Nouvelle Édition, 1947), 21.

5. William Martson Seabury, *The Public and the Motion Picture Industry* (New York: Macmillan, 1926), 39.

6. Bachlin, *Histoire économique du cinéma,* 127.

7. *Report on Market for Cinematograph Films in Cuba* (furnished by His Majesty's Consul-General in Havana, March 13, 1923), typewritten copy, Library of the British Film Institute.

8. Seabury, *The Public and the Motion Picture Industry,* 283.

9. Quoted in Arturo Agramonte, *Cronología dol cine cubano* (Havana: Ediciones ICAIC, 1966), 42.

10. "Distributing the Product" in J. P. Kennedy, ed., *The Story of the Film* (London: A. W. Shaw & Co., 1927), 225–26.

11. Thomas Guback, *The International Film Industry* (Bloomington: Indiana University Press, 1969), 7–8.

12. Ibid., 3.

13. *World Trade in Commodities,* November 1947, Motion Pictures and Equipment (report by Byron White, U.S. embassy, Havana), 3.

14. E. Bradford Burns, Introduction, in Beatriz Reyes Nevares, *The Mexican Cinema: Interviews with Thirteen Directors* (Albuquerque: University of New Mexico Press, 1976), xii.

15. Eduardo Colina and Daniel Díaz Torres, "Ideología del melodrama en el viejo cine latinoamericano," *Cine Cubano* 73–75: 15.

16. Jorge Ayala Blanco, *La aventura del cine mexicano* (Mexico City: Ediciones Era, 1968), 48.

17. Colina and Díaz Torres, "Ideología del melodrama en el viejo cine latinoamericano."

18. See Emilio García Riera, *Historia documental del cine mexicano,* vol. 1 (Mexico City: Ediciones Era, 1969).

19. Agramonte, *Cronología del cine cubano,* 65.

20. Raimond del Castillo, "Cuban Cinema," *Sight and Sound* (September 1947).

21. Emilio García Riera, *El cine mexicano* (Mexico City: 1963), Ediciones Era, 28.

22. Quoted by Colina and Díaz Torres, "Ideología del melodrama en el viejo cine latinoamericano," 15 n. 12.

23. Ayala Blanco, *La aventura del cine mexicano,* 156.

24. García Riera, *Historia documental del cine mexicano,* 51.

25. J. M. Valdés Rodríguez, "Algo en torno al cine y la República Cubana," Part III, *El Mundo,* April 21, 1960.

26. "Cuban to Back Film Production Setup," *Variety,* February 11, 1953.

27. Óscar Pino Santos, "Las posibilidades de una industria cinematográfica en Cuba: Consideraciones," *Carteles*, November 30, 1958.

28. Francisco Mota, "12 aspectos económicos de la cinematografiá cubana," *Lunes de Revolución*, February 6, 1961.

29. "Cuba Tax in New Vexation," *Variety*, January 27, 1954.

5. Amateurs and Militants

1. Néstor Almendros, "The Cinema in Cuba," *Film Culture* 2:3 (1956).

2. Néstor Almendros, *Días de una cámara* (Barcelona: Seix Barral, 1982), 44ff. (English: *The Man with a Camera* [London: Faber and Faber, 1985].)

3. Alfredo Guevara, "Una nueva etapa del cine en Cuba," *Cine Cubano* 3.

4. "Postwar Market Potentialities for Motion Picture Equipment in Cuba," by Nathan D. Golden, Motion Picture Unit Chief, *Industrial Reference Service*, vol. 3, Part III, no. 7 (August 1945).

5. See Anthony Sampson, *The Sovereign State: The Secret History of ITT* (London: Coronet, 1974).

6. See Rolando Díaz Rodríguez and Lázaro Buria Pérez, "Un caso de colonización cinematográfica," *Caimán Barbudo* 87 (February 1975).

7. Figures extrapolated from Warren Dygart, *Radio as an Advertising Medium* (New York: McGraw-Hill, 1939), 231–33.

8. Alejo Carpentier, *La música en Cuba* (1946), 1.

9. See Rachael Low, *Films of Comment and Persuasion of the 1930s (The History of the British Film 1929–1939)* (London: Allen and Unwin, 1979), 128–30.

10. Miguel Torres, "Respuesta," *Cine Cubano* 54–55: 19.

11. "Motion Pictures and Equipment," *World Trade in Commodities* (November 1947): 4.

12. Conversation with Tomás Gutiérrez Alea, Havana, January 1980.

13. For this and the next citation, see the appropriate entries in Georges Sadoul, *Dictionary of Films*, trans. and ed. P. Morris (Berkeley and Los Angeles: University of California Press, 1972).

14. Julio Antonio Mella, "Octubre," *Tren Blindado* (Mexico, 1928), reprinted in *Cine Cubano* 54–55: 111–12.

15. J. M. Valdés Rodríguez, "Hollywood: Sales Agent of American Imperialism," *Experimental Cinema* 4.

16. See Max Henríquez Urea, *Panorama histórico de la literatura cubana*, vol. 2 (Havana: Editorial Arte y Literatura, 1979), 421.

17. Cf. Robin Blackburn, "Class Forces in the Cuban Revolution: A Reply to Peter Binns and Mike Gonzalez," *International Socialism*, series 2, no. 9.

18. Quoted in Jean Franco, *The Modern Culture of Latin America* (Harmondsworth: Penguin, 1970), 134.

19. See Zoila Gómez, *Amadeo Roldán* (Havana: Editorial Arte y Literatura, 1977), 63.

20. Arturo Agramonte, *Cronología del cine cubano* (Havana: Ediciones ICAIC, 1966), 156.

21. Conversation with Tomás Gutiérrez Alea, Havana, January 1981.

22. See Valdés Rodríguez, "Hollywood."

23. Conversation with Alfredo Guevara, Havana, September 1979.

24. Agramonte, *Cronología del cine cubano,* 80–81, 86–87.

25. See Rolando E. Bonachea and Nelson P. Valdés, *Revolutionary Struggle 1947–1958: Selected Works of Fidel Castro,* vol. 1 (Cambridge: MIT Press, 1972), 24–25.

26. Agramonte, *Cronología del cine cubano,* 159.

27. José Antonio Gronzález, "Apuntes para la historia de un cine sin historia," *Cine Cubano* 86–88.

28. Harold Gramatges, "La música en defensa del hombre," *Revolución y Cultura* 52–54 (1976–77).

29. José Antonio Portuondo, *Itinerario estético de la Revolución Cubana* (Havana: Editorial Letras Cubanas, 1979).

30. Agramonte, 160–62.

31. Conversation with Manuel Pérez, Havana, January 1980.

32. Conversation with Julio García Espinosa, Havana, January 1981.

33. Conversation with Julio García Espinosa, Havana, January 1980.

34. Fulgencio Batista, *Piedras y Leyes* (Mexico City: Ediciones Botas, 1961), 73, 80.

35. Lionel Martin, *The Early Fidel: The Roots of Castro's Communism* (Secaucus, N.J.: Lyle Stuart, 1978), 227.

36. See Bonachea and Valdés, *Revolutionary Struggle 1947–1958,* Introduction.

37. Marshall McLuhan, *Understanding Media* (London: Signet, 1966), 24.

38. Quoted in Herbert Schiller, *Mass Communications and American Empire* (Boston: Beacon Press, 1971), 1.

39. See Bonachea and Valdés, *Revolutionary Struggle 1947–1958,* 109.

40. Che Guevara to Nuestro Tiempo, January 27, 1959, in *Œuvres révolutionnaires 1959–1967* (Paris: Maspero, 1968), 25.

6. The Coming of Socialism

1. Jean-Paul Sartre, *On Cuba,* (London: Ballantine Books, 1961), 62.

2. Sergio Carbo, "El segundo movimiento," *Anuario Cinematográfico y Radial Cubano,* 1959.

3. Editorial, *Anuario Cinematográfico y Radial Cubano,* 1959.

4. Edward Boorstein, *The Economic Transformation of Cuba* (New York: Monthly Review Press, 1969), 53.

5. Leo Huberman and Paul Sweezy, *Cuba: Anatomy of a Revolution* (New York: Monthly Review Press, 1968), 85–86.

6. Richard M. Nixon, *Six Crises* (New York: Pocket Books, 1962), 379.

7. Conversation with Julio García Espinosa, Havana, January 1980.

8. *Cine Cubano* 95: 13.

9. Carlos Franqui, *Family Portrait with Fidel* (London: Jonathan Cape, 1983), 9, 10.

10. Conversation with Alfredo Guevara, Havana, January 1980.

11. Ambrosio Fornet, *El intelectual y la sociedad,* Colección Mínima No. 28 (Mexico City: Siglo Veintiuno Editores, 1969), 49.

12. See Tariq Ali in Carl Gardner, ed., *Media, Politics and Culture* (London: Macmillan, 1979), 152.

13. Conversation with Julio García Espinosa, Havana, January 1980. (During

research for this book, I sought to obtain an interview with Guillermo Cabrera Infante, who lives in London, but received no response.)

14. Alfredo Guevara, "Revisando nuestro trabajo," *Cine Cubano* 2: 12.

15. Sartre, *On Cuba*, 142.

16. Ibid., 152.

17. Ibid., 149.

18. Fornet, *El intelectual y la sociedad*, 48.

19. Tad Szulc and Karl E. Mayer, in Boorstein, *The Economic Transformation of Cuba*, 29.

20. *Financial Times*, May 13, 1961; *Times*, January 6, 1965.

21. Conversation with Enrique Pineda Barnet, Havana, January 1980.

22. Néstor Almendros, *Días de un cámara* (Barcelona: Seix Barral, 1982), 47.

23. Ugo Ulive, "Crónica del cine cubano," *Cine al día* 12 (March 1971): 9.

24. Guevara, "Revisando nuestro trabajo," 14.

25. Boorstein, *The Economic Transformation of Cuba*, 81–84.

26. This and subsequent quotations by Alfredo Guevara are from a conversation in Havana, January 1980.

27. See Robin Blackburn, "Class Forces in the Cuban Revolution: A Reply to Peter Binns and Mike Gonzalez," *International Socialism*, series 2, no. 9.

28. Nicholas Wollaston, *Red Rumba*, Readers Union edition (1964).

29. Guillermo Cabrera Infante, "Notes from the Bearded Crocodile," *London Review of Books*, June 4–17, 1981.

30. Pedro Pérez Sarduy, "An Infant in English Breeches: What Really Happened in Cuba," *Red Letters* 15 (1983): 25.

31. Serge Daney, "Sur Salador" in "Travail, lecture, jouissance," *Cahiers du Cinéma* 222.

32. Alfredo Guevara, "Una nueva etapa del cine en Cuba," *Cine Cubano* 3.

33. Michèle Firk, "Naissance d'un cinéma," *Positif* 53 (June 1963): 15.

34. Fidel Castro, "Words to the Intellectuals," in Lee Baxandall, ed., *Radical Perspectives in the Arts* (London: Penguin, 1972).

35. Franqui, *Family Portrait with Fidel*, 130–34.

36. In Fornet, *El intelectual y la sociedad*, 92.

37. Ibid.

38. Julio García Espinosa, "Respuesta," *Cine Cubano* 54–55: 11–12.

7. The First Feature Films

1. Eduardo Heras León, "Historias de la revolución y el joven rebelde," *Pensamiento Crítico* 42 (July 1970): 128–34; reprinted in *Cine y Revolución en Cuba* (Barcelona: Editorial Fontamara, 1975).

2. "Resultados de una discusión crítica," *Cine al día* 12 (March 1971).

3. See Paulo Freire, *Cultural Action for Freedom* (Harmondsworth: Penguin Education, 1972).

4. Julianne Burton, "Individual Fulfillment and Collective Achievement, an Interview with T. G. Alea," *Cineaste* 8:1 (1977).

5. Ibid.

8. Beyond Neorealism

1. Alfredo Guevara, "Realidades y perspectivas de un nuevo cine," *Cine Cubano* 1.

2. Conversation with Sergio Giral, Havana, January 1980.

3. Conversation with Humberto Solás, Havana, January 1980.

4. Tomás Gutiérrez Alea, "12 notas para 'Las 12 Sillas,'" *Cine Cubano* 6 (1962): 15–19.

5. Conversation with Alfredo Guevara, Havana, September 1979; see also remarks by Julio García Espinosa in Augusto M. Torres and Manuel Pérez Estremera, "Breve historia del cine cubano," *Hablemos de cine* (Peru) 69, reprinted in the same authors' *Nuevo Cine Latinoamericano* (Barcelona: Editorial Anagrama, n.d.).

6. Julio García Espinosa, *Cine Cubano* 54–55: 12.

7. Quoted in Ugo Ulive, "Crónica del cine cubano," *Cine al día* 12 (March 1971).

8. Néstor García Canclini, *Arte popular y sociedad en América Latin* (Mexico City: Editorial Grijalbo, 1977), 196.

9. Ernesto Cardenal, *En Cuba.* (Mexico City: Ediciones Era, 1977), 164.

10. Interview with Claude Julien, *Le Monde,* March 22, 1963.

11. K. S. Karol, *Guerrillas in Power: The Course of the Cuban Revolution,* trans. Arnold Pomerans (London: Jonathan Cape, 1971), 241. Karol, a left-wing critic of the Cuban Revolution, was heavily criticized by the Cubans when his book was first published in France. As far as its discussion of cultural affairs is concerned, it is certainly in places inaccurate.

12. Alfredo Guevara, "Sobre un debate entre cineastas cubanos," *Cine Cubano* 14–15.

13. Tomás Gutiérrez Alea, "Notas sobre una discusión de un documento sobre una discusión (de otro documento)," and Julio García Espinosa, "Galgos y Podencos," both in *La Gaceta de Cuba* 29 (November 5, 1963).

14. Ulive, "Crónica del cine cubano."

15. Adolfo Sánchez Vásquez, *Art and Society: Essays in Marxist Aesthetics* (London: Merlin Press, 1973).

16. Julio García Espinosa, "Antecendentes para un estudio del cine cubano," interview in *Primer Plano* (Ediciones Universitarias de Valparaiso) 1:2 (autumn 1972).

17. "Discussion with Jorge Fraga Recorded in Havana," *Undercut* 12 (summer 1984).

18. Ibid.

19. Julianne Burton, "Individual Fulfillment and Collective Achievement, an Interview with T. G. Alea," *Cineaste* 8:1 (1977).

20. Conversation with Alfredo Guevara, Havana, September 1979.

21. Karol, *Guerrillas in Power,* 394.

22. Torres and Pérez Estremera, "Breve historia del cine cubano."

23. Conversation with Jorge Fraga, Havana, January 1980.

24. Raúl Molina, "En días como aquéllas," *La Gaceta de Cuba* 50 (April–May 1966).

9. The Documentary in the Revolution

1. Quoted in Alan Lovell and Jim Hillier, *Studies in Documentary,* Cinema One Series No. 21 (London: Secker and Warburg, 1972), 138.

2. Tomás Gutiérrez Alea, "Free Cinema," *Cine Cubano* 4.

3. Quoted in Louis Marcorelles, *Living Cinema*, trans. Isabel Quigley (London: Allen and Unwin, 1973), 47.

4. Walter Benjamin, "The Work of Art in the Age of Mechanical Reproduction," in *Illuminations*, trans. Harry Zohn (New York: Schocken Books, 1969), 232–33.

5. Dziga Vertov, "Writings," *Film Culture* 25 (1962), 55, 57.

6. Mick Eaton, ed., *Anthropology—Reality—Cinema: The Films of Jean Rouch* (London: British Film Institute, 1979), 42.

7. Lucien Goldmann, "Thoughts on *Chronique d'un été*," in ibid., 66.

8. Régis Debray, *Prison Writings*, trans. Rosemary Sheed (London: Penguin, 1975), 176–79.

9. See K. S. Karol, *Guerrillas in Power: The Course of the Cuban Revolution*, trans. Arnold Pomerans (London: Jonathan Cape, 1971), 7.

10. Conversation with Richard Leacock, Paris, April 1980.

11. Chris Marker, *L'avant-scène du cinéma* 6 (1961).

12. Alfredo Guevara, "Revisando nuestro trabajo," *Cine Cubano* 2: 14.

13. Quoted in Marcorelles, *Living Cinema*, 19.

14. "Joris Ivens en Cuba," *Cine Cubano* 3: 21.

15. This and other details are from a conversation with Joris Ivens, Paris, spring 1980.

16. *Cine Cubano* 3: 22.

17. José Massip, "Crónicas de un viaje: Una lección de cine," *Cine Cubano* 3: 24.

18. Joris Ivens, *The Camera and I* (Berlin: Seven Seas Publishers, 1969), 56–57.

19. Tom Waugh, "Joris Ivens' Work in Cuba," *Jump Cut* 22: 28.

20. Richard Fagen, *The Transformation of Political Culture in Cuba* (Stanford, Calif.: Stanford University Press, 1969), 62.

21. Mario Tejada, "Introducción al cine documental cubano," *Hablamos de Cine* (Peru) 64: 30.

22. Mario Piedra, "El documental cubano a mil caracteres por minuto," *Cine Cubano* 108 (1984).

23. Fernando Solanas and Octavio Getino, "Hacia un tercer cine," *Tricontinental* 13 (October 1969), translated in Michael Chanan, ed., *Twenty-Five Years of the New Latin American Cinema* (London: British Film Institute/Channel 4, 1983).

24. Interview with Jorge Silva and Marta Rodríguez by Andrés Caicedo and Luis Ospina, *Ojo al cine* 1 (1974).

25. "Cine y subdesarrollo, entrevista a Fernando Birri," *Cine Cubano* 42–44 (1963).

26. Paulo Freire, *Cultural Action for Freedom* (Harmondsworth: Penguin Education, 1972), 52ff.

27. Interview with Eduardo Maldonado by Andrés de Luna and Susana Charand, *Otro Cine* 6 (1976).

28. Víctor Casaus, "El genero testimonio en el cine cubano," paper presented to seminar on the New Cinema and Literature, Second Havana Festival, 1980; in *Cine Cubano* 101 (1982).

29. Pastor Vega, "El documental didáctico y la táctica," *Pensamiento Crítico* 42 (1970): 99.

30. Jorge Fraga, Estrella Pantin, and Julio García Espinosa, "El cine didáctico," *Cine Cubano* 69–70, translated as "Towards a Definition of the Didactic Documentary," in Zuzana Pick, ed., *Latin American Film Makers and the Third Cinema* (London: Carleton University Film Studies Program, 1978), 200.

31. Raúl Beceyro, *Cine y política* (Caracas, 1976), Dirección General de Cultura, 27.

32. Pierre Francastel, "Espace et Illusion," *Revue Internationale de Filmologie* 2:5 (1951).

33. Fredric Jameson, *The Prison-House of Language* (Princeton: Princeton University Press, 1972), 32–33.

34. Interview with Jorge Silva and Marta Rodríguez by Andrés Caicedo and Luis Ospina.

10. The Revolution in the Documentary

1. Quoted in Hans Ehrmann, "Cuba's Films," *Variety*, April 26, 1967.

2. Conversation with Santiago Álvarez, Havana, January 1980.

3. Bertram Silverman, ed., *Man and Socialism in Cuba*, (New York: Atheneum, 1971), 17.

4. Ibid., 7.

5. "Santiago Álvarez habla de su cine," *Hablemos de Cine* (Peru) 54: 39.

6. Quoted in Miguel Orodea, "Álvarez and Vertov," in M. Chanan, ed., *Santiago Álvarez*, BFI Dossier no. 2 (London: British Film Institute, 1980), 24.

7. Ibid., 25.

8. Conversation with Santiago Álvarez.

9. "Santiago Álvarez habla de su cine," 39.

10. Conversation with Santiago Álvarez.

11. Leo Brouwer speaking in *New Cinema of Latin America, Part II*, "The Long Road," dir. Michael Chanan, 1983.

12. Fidel Castro, speech of October 18, 1967, in Che Guevara, *Reminiscences of the Cuban Revolutionary War* (Harmondsworth: Penguin, 1969).

13. Román Karmen, *No pasarán!,* (Moscow: Editorial Progreso, 1976), 368.

14. Stuart Hood, "Murder on the Way," *New Statesman*, April 18, 1980.

15. Manuel López Oliva, "Imágenes de LBJ," *El Mundo*, December 13, 1968.

16. In *Hablemos de Cine* 54.

17. Hood, "Murder on the Way."

11. The Current of Experimentalism

1. Personal communication from Steve Wilkinson, 2001.

2. The episode has a sequel. Cuba had withdrawn from international copyright agreements on the grounds that culture was the patrimony of the people and from a third-world point of view, copyright mainly served the interests of the transnational corporations that collected most of it. Like so many others, Korda accepted this position, and in any case there was no remedy until Cuba rejoined the international copyright convention in the 1990s. Furthermore, that he was not particularly concerned about author's rights can also be understood on the same principle that a composer who hears his song being whistled in the street would hardly attempt to sue the whistler for breaching his rights. He was happy enough that the image served to sustain Che's memory. However, angered when the photo appeared in a Smirnoff advertisement in the United Kingdom in 1999—Che never drank—he

decided to take action, and the Cuba Solidarity Campaign in London helped him sue Smirnoff's advertising agency, Lowe Lintas, and the picture library Rex Features for infringement. By happy coincidence, he received the news of an out-of-court settlement on his seventy-second birthday, during a visit to London for an exhibition of Cuban photography; he immediately handed over an undisclosed sum for damages to buy much-needed medicine for Cuban children.

3. See Rolando E. Bonachea and Nelson P. Valdés, *Revolutionary Struggle 1947–1958: Selected Works of Fidel Castro*, vol. 1 (Cambridge: MIT Press, 1972), 141.

4. "David: Método o Actitud?" *Hablemos de Cine* 54.

5. Ibid.

6. José Massip, "David es el comienzo," *Cine Cubano* 45–46 (1967).

7. Conversation with Tomás Gutiérrez Alea, Havana, June 1984.

8. Ibid.

9. Cf. B. Ruby Rich, "Madcap Comedy Cuban Style," *Jump Cut* 22.

10. See Bernardo Callejas, "La muerte de un burócrata," *Granma*, July 28, 1966, and Desiderio Navarro, "La muerte de un burócrata," *Adelante* (Camagüey), August 23, 1966.

11. In Mario Rodríguez Alemán.

12. Conversation with Tomás Gutiérrez Alea, Havana, January 1980.

13. Rich, "Madcap Comedy Cuban Style."

14. Callejas, "La muerte de un burócrata."

15. Conversation with Tomás Gutiérrez Alea, Havana, January 1980.

16. "Resultados de una discusión crítica," *Cine al día* 12 (March 1971).

17. Pablo Martínez, "Entrevista con Humberto Solás," *Hablemos de Cine* 54.

18. *Vanguardia* (Santa Clara), December 26, 1967.

19. *Verde Olivo*, October 1, 1967.

20. "Julio García Espinosa en dos tiempos," *Hablemos de Cine* 54.

21. See Julio García Espinosa, "A propósito de Aventuras de Juan Quin Quin," *Cine y Revolución en Cuba* (Barcelona: Editorial Fontamara, 1975), 157–60.

22. Anna Marie Taylor, "Imperfect Cinema, Brecht and *The Adventures of Juan Quin Quin*," *Jump Cut* 20.

23. See "Fotonovelas: la realidad entre paréntesis," in Michèle Mattelart, *La cultura de la opresión femenina* (Mexico City: Ediciones Era, 1977); see also Fellini's first solo film as director, *Lo Sceicco Bianco*.

24. García Espinosa, "A propósito de Avenfuras de Juan Quin Quin."

25. Conversation with Julio García Espinosa, Havana, January 1980.

26. In James Hogg, ed., *Psychology and the Visual Arts* (London: Penguin, 1969), 114; see also Anton Ehrenzweig, *The Psychoanalysis of Artistic Vision and Hearing* (London: Routledge and Kegan Paul, 1953), especially chapter 2.

27. Bell Gale Chevigny, "Running the Blockade: Six Cuban Writers," *Socialist Review* 59 (1981): 92.

28. Quoted in Herbert Schiller, *Mass Communications and American Empire* (Boston: Beacon Press, 1971), 106.

29. Conversation with Alfredo Guevara, Havana, January 1980.

30. Alonso Águilar, "The Intellectuals and the Revolution," *Monthly Review* 19:10 (March 1968). Participants from Britain, who numbered twenty-three, included Arnold Wesker, Nathaniel Tarn, David Mercer, Adrian Mitchell, Ralph Milliband, Eric Hobsbawm, David Cooper, and Irving Teitelbaum. Bertrand Russell, like Sartre and

Ernst Fischer, sent a message of support. The U.S. delegation included Jules Feiffer, David Dellinger, Barbara Dane, and Irwin Silber. Among others from Europe—including sixty-six from France, twenty-seven from Spain, and twenty-five from Italy—were Michel Leiris, Jorge Semprun, Hans Magnus Enzensberger, and Rossana Rossanda. From Latin America and the Caribbean, apart from the host country, there were seventy-five. The Antilleans included C. L. R. James, Aimé Césaire, John La Rose, Andrew Salkey, René Depestre; the continental Latins, Mario Benedetti, Julio Cortázar, Adolfo Sánchez Vásquez, and others.

31. Andrew Salkey, *Havana Journal* (Harmondsworth: Penguin, 1971), 110.

32. Ibid., 118ff.

33. See Ambrosio Fornet, *El intellectual y la sociedad,* Colección Mínima no. 28 (Mexico City: Siglo Veintiuno Editores, 1969).

34. Adolfo Sánchez Vásquez, "Vanguardia artística y vanguardia política," in *Literatura y arte nuevo en Cuba* (Barcelona: Editorial Laia, 1977).

35. Che Guevara, "Socialism and Man in Cuba" and other works (Havana: Instituto del Libro, 1968).

36. Second Declaration of Havana, February 4, 1962, in *Fidel Castro Speaks* (Harmondsworth: Penguin, 1972), 127.

37. Fidel Castro, speech of September 28, 1967, *Granma Weekly Review,* October 8, 1967.

38. Fidel Castro, speech of January 12, 1968, *Granma Weekly Review,* January 21, 1968.

12. Four Films

1. "Entrevista con Jorge Fraga con la participación de Manuel Octavio Gómez," *Hablemos de Cine* 54.

2. The letter from Máximo Gómez is to his wife, dated July 27, 1896.

3. See Néstor García Miranda, "La odisea del General José de Jorge Fraga," *Hablemos de Cine* 54.

4. Che Guevara, *The Bolivian Diaries of Che Guevara* (London: Bertrand Russell Peace Foundation, n.d.), 136.

5. García Miranda, "La odisea del General José de Jorge Fraga."

6. Marta Alvear, "Interview with Humberto Solás," *Jump Cut* 19.

7. Teresa Fernández Coca, "Interview with Humberto Solás," *Granma,* October 23, 1968.

8. Anna Marie Taylor, "Lucía," *Film Quarterly* 28:2 (winter 1974–75); John Mraz, "Lucía: History and Film in Revolutionary Cuba," *Film and History* 5:1 (1975).

9. Steven Kovacs, "Lucia: Style and Meaning in Revolutionary Film," *Monthly Review* 27:2 (1975): 34.

10. Isaac León Frias, "Lucía," *Hablemos de Cine* 54.

11. Fernández Coca interview.

12. Taylor, "Lucia."

13. Peter Biskind, "Lucia—Struggles with History," *Jump Cut* 2 (1974).

14. "Resultados de una discusión crítica," *Cine al día* 12 (March 1971).

15. Daniel Díaz Torres, "Lucía," *Granma Weekly Review,* October 20, 1968.

16. Puri Faget, "Lucía, un punto de partida," *El Mundo* (Havana), October 15, 1968.

17. Glauber Rocha, "The Aesthetics of Violence," *Revista Civilizaçao Brasileira* 3 (1965); translated in Michael Chanan, ed., *Twenty-Five Years of the New Latin American Cinema* (London: British Film Institute/Channel 4, 1983).

18. See Manuel Octavio Gómez, "Entrevista con Jorge Fraga."

19. John Mraz, "Lucia: Visual Style and Historical Portrayal," *Jump Cut* 19.

20. Michael Myerson, ed., *Memories of Underdevelopment: The Revolutionary Films of Cuba* (New York: Grossman, 1973), 118.

21. *Ibid.*, 43.

22. Tomás Gutiérrez Alea, "Memorias del subdesarrollo, notas de trabajo," *Hablemos de Cine* 54.

23. See the citation of Vincent Canby's review in *Granma*, "Elogian críticos norteamericanos filme cubano," June 13, 1973.

24. See Julianne Burton, "Interview with Alea," *Cineaste* 8:1: 59.

25. Myerson, *Memories of Underdevelopment*, 34.

26. Ibid., 36.

27. Ibid., 34–35.

28. See Pastor Vega, "Medida torpe y arbitraria de los imperialistas yanquis," *Granma,* January 22, 1974.

29. Ibid.

30. Burton, "Interview with Alea."

31. Conversation with Tomás Gutiérrez Alea, Havana, January 1980.

32. Interview with Manuel Octavio Gómez, *Hablemos de Cine* 54.

13. Imperfect Cinema and the Seventies

1. First published in *Cine Cubano* 42–44 (1967); translated in Michael Chanan, ed., *Twenty-Five Years of the New Latin American Cinema* (London: British Film Institute/Channel 4, 1983).

2. Julio García Espinosa, "Meditations on Imperfect Cinema . . . Fifteen Years Later," trans. Michael Chanan, *Screen* 26:3–4 (1985): 93.

3. Rigoberto López, "Hablar de Sara, de cierta manera," *Cine Cubano* 93: 110–11.

4. Juan M. Bullitta, in *Hablemos de Cine* 54.

5. *Granma*, April 14, 1972.

6. Stuart Hood, "Murder on the Way," *New Statesman,* April 18, 1980.

7. Arthur MacEwan, *Revolution and Economic Development in Cuba* (London: Macmillan, 1981), 117.

8. Jorge Edwards, *Persona Non Grata*, trans. Colin Harding (London: Bodley Head, 1976), 229.

9. Ambrosio Fornet, "Trente and de cinéma dans la Révolution," in Paulo Antonio Paranagua, ed., *Le Cinéma cubain* (Paris: Centre Georges Pompidou, 1990), 91.

10. Ambrosio Fornet, Introduction, in Antonio Fornet, ed., *Bridging Enigma: Cubans on Cuba*, Special Issue of *South Atlantic Quarterly* 96:1 (winter 1997): 11.

11. Rufo Caballero and Joel del Río, "No hay cine adulto sin herejía sistemática," *Temas* 3 (1995).

12. Quoted in María Teresa Linares, *La música popular* (Havana: Instituto del Libro, 1970), 18.

13. Enrique Colina and Daniel Díaz Torres, "Ideología del melodrama en el riejo cine latinoamericano," *Cine Cubano* 73–75.

14. During a viewing of the film with Tomás Gutiérrez Alea in Havana, July 1984.

15. Alejo Carpentier, *Music in Cuba,* ed. Timothy Brennan, trans. Alan West-Durán (Minneapolis: University of Minnesota Press, 2001), 79.

16. George Lamming, *The Pleasures of Exile* (London: Michael Joseph, 1960), 99.

17. Julianne Burton, "Marginal Cinemas and Mainstream Critical Theory," *Screen* 26:3–4 (1985): 14.

18. Philip French, "Crucified in Cuba," *Observer,* March 11, 1979.

19. Dennis West, "Slavery and Cinema in Cuba: The Case of Gutiérrez Alea's 'The Last Supper,'" *Western Journal of Black Studies* 3:2 (summer 1979).

14. One Way or Another

1. Julio García Espinosa, in *Rencontres Internationales pour un Nouveau Cinéma, Cahiers* No. 3, Montreal, 1975, 25.

2. "Discussion with Jorge Fraga," *Undercut* 12 (summer 1984).

3. Ambrosio Fornet, "Trente ans de cinéma dans la Révolution," in Paulo Antonio Paranagua, ed., *Le Cinéma cubain* (Paris: Centre Georges Pompidou, 1990), 95–96.

4. John Hess, "The Personal Is Political in Cuba," *Jump Cut* 20: 15.

5. Interview in *Romances,* April 1974.

6. Conversation with Tomás Gutiérrez Alea, Havana, June 1984.

7. Quoted in Rigoberto López, "Hablar de Sara, de cierta manera," *Cine Cubano* 93.

8. Ibid.

9. Julia Lesage, "One Way or Another: The Revolution in Action," *Jump Cut* 19 (December 1978): 33.

10. Annette Kuhn, *Women's Pictures, Feminism and Cinema* (London: Routledge and Kegan Paul, 1982), 163.

11. E. Ann Kaplan, *Women and Film: Both Sides of the Camera* (London: Methuen, 1983), 193.

12. Conversation with Jorge Sotolongo, Oberhausen, 1981.

15. Reconnecting

1. Ambrosio Fornet in *New Cinema of Latin America,* Part I, "Cinema of the Humble," dir. Michael Chanan, 1983.

2. Figures taken from Ambrosio Fornet, "Trente ans de cinéma dans la Révolution," in Paulo Antonio Paranagua, ed., *Le Cinéma cubain,* (Paris: Centre Georges Pompidou, 1990), 105.

3. John King, *Magical Reels* (London: Verso, 1990), 159.

4. Peter B. Schumann, *Historia del cine latinoamericano* (Buenos Aires: Legasa, 1986), 175.

5. Julianne Burton, "Film and Revolution in Cuba: The First Twenty-Five Years," in Michael T. Martin, ed., *The New Latin American Cinema,* vol. 2, *Studies of National Cinemas* (Detroit: Wayne State University Press, 1997), 133.

6. Julio García Espinosa, *Rencontres Internationales pour un Nouveau Cinéma, Cahiers* No. 3, Montreal, 1975, 25.

7. Here I can add my own personal testimony, dating from 1983, when I was invited to show a pair of documentaries I made for Channel 4 (United Kingdom) on the New Latin American Cinema to one of these internal ICAIC screenings. What could have been a rather unnerving experience, especially because ICAIC itself was featured in the films, became a memorable one precisely because of the open and inclusive spirit of the gathering.

8. "Discussion with Jorge Fraga," *Undercut* (London Film-makers Co-op) 12 (summer 1984): 7.

9. Ambrosio Fornet, "Introduction," in Ambrosio Fornet, ed., *Bridging Enigma: Cubans on Cuba,* Special Issue of *South Atlantic Quarterly* 96:1 (winter 1997): 11–12.

10. Jean Stubbs, *Cuba: The Test of Time* (London: Latin American Bureau, 1989), 81.

11. Sergio Giral, "Images and Icons," in Pedro Pérez Sarduy and Jean Stubbs, eds., *Afrocuba: An Anthology of Cuban Writing on Race, Politics and Culture* (London: Ocean/Latin American Bureau, 1993), 268.

12. See Alejandro de la Fuente and Laurence Glasco, "Are Blacks 'Getting Out of Control'? Racial Attitudes, Revolution, and Political Transition in Cuba," in Miguel Ángel Centeno and Mauricio Font, *Toward a New Cuba?* (Boulder, Colo.: Lynne Rienner, 1998).

13. Juan Carlos Tabío, in the entry for *¡Plaff!* in Juan Antonio García Borrero, *Guía crítica del cine cubano de ficción* (1910/1998) (Havana: Editorial Arte y Literatura, 2001).

14. Giral, "Images and Icons," 266.

15. Jorge Fraga, *Underout* 12 (summer 1984).

16. Fornet, in "Trente ans de cinéma dans la Révolution," 92.

17. Ibid., 93.

18. Fraga, 11.

19. Ibid., 10.

20. Stubbs, *Cuba,* 19.

21. For details, see diagrams in Julianne Burton, in Paulo Antonio Paranagua, ed., *Le Cinéma cubain* (Paris: Centre Georges Pompidou, 1990), 134–36.

22. Fraga, 10.

23. Fornet "Trente ans de cinéma dans la Révolution," 99.

24. Julianne Burton, "Seeing, Being, Being Seen: Portrait of Teresa, or Contradictions of Sexual Politics in Contemporary Cuba," *Social Text* 4 (1991): 82.

25. Quoted in King, *Magical Reeds,* 159.

26. Schumann, *Historia del cine latinoamericano,* 174.

27. Pat Aufderheide and Carlos Galiano, "Retrato de Teresa: Hacer por medio de la ficción un reportaje de la vida actual en nuestra sociedad," *Granma,* July 24, 1979.

28. Julianne Burton, "Portrait(s) of Teresa: Gender Politics and the Reluctant Revival of Melodrama in Cuba Film," in Diane Carson, Linda Dittmar, and Janice R. Welsch, eds., *Multiple Voices in Feminist Film Criticism* (Minneapolis: University of Minnesota Press, 1994), 307.

29. Ibid., 317.

30. Ibid., 305.

31. Burton, "Seeing, Being, Being Seen," 91.

32. Ibid., 93–94.

33. Ibid., 86.

34. Publicity material distributed by Unifilm, New York.

35. Pastor Vega, in *New Cinema of Latin America,* Part II, "The Long Road," dir. Michael Chanan, 1983.

36. Quoted in Michael Chanan, ed., *Twenty-Five Years of the New Cinema in Latin America* (London: British Film Institute/Channel 4, 1983), 2.

37. "Mensaje a los pueblos del mundo a través de la Tricontinental" (1967), in *Ernesto Che Guevara: Obras (1957–1967),* 2d ed. (Havana: Casa de las Américas, 1977), 2:584.

38. Robert Stam, "The Hour of the Furnaces and the Two Avant-Gardes," in Coco Fusco, ed., *Reviewing Histories: Selections from New Latin American Cinema* (Buffalo: Hallwalls, 1987), 91–92.

39. For a history of the concept of third cinema, see Michael Chanan, "The Changing Geography of Third Cinema," *Screen* 38:4 (1997).

40. Fernando Solanas and Octavio Getino, "Towards a Third Cinema," (1969), in Chanan, *Twenty-Five Years of the New Cinema in Latin America.*

41. Fraga, 12.

42. Conversation with Ciro Durán, Havana, December 1979.

43. Interview with Melchor Casals in Susan Fanshel, *A Decade of Cuban Documentary Film* (New York: Young Filmmakers Foundation, 1982), 21–22.

44. Interview with Jesús Díaz in Fanshel, *A Decade of Cuban Documentary Film,* 17.

45. Ibid.

46. Ibid., 18.

47. Entry for *Guardafronteras* in García Borrero, *Guía crítica del cine cubano de ficción.*

48. Ibid.

49. Schumann, *Historia del cine latinoamericano,* 175.

50. Rufo Caballero and Joel del Río, "No hay cine adulto sin herejía sistemática," *Temas,* 3 (1995).

51. Paolo Antonio Paranagua, in Paranagua, *La Cinéma cubain,* 142.

52. Reynaldo González, "A White Problem: Reinterpreting 'Cecilia Valdés,'" in Pedro Pérez Sarduy and Jean Stubbs, eds., *Afrocuba: An Anthology of Cuban Writing on Race, Politics and Culture* (London: Ocean/Latin American Bureau, 1993), 205–7.

53. Caballero and del Río, "No hay cine adulto sin herejía sistemática."

54. Fredric Jameson, "Third World Literature in the Era of Multinational Capitalism," *Social Text* 15 (1986): 69.

55. Humberto Solás, in the entry for *Cecilia Valdés* in García Borrero, *Guía crítica del cine cubano de ficción.*

56. See Paranagua, *Le Cinéma cubain,* 141–51.

57. Ibid., 147.

58. Conversation with Julio García Espinosa, Boston, April 16, 1997.

16. Return of the Popular

1. Julio García Espinosa in *New Cinema of Latin America,* Part I, dir. Michael Chanan.

2. Rufo Caballero and Joel del Río, "No hay cine adulto sin herejía sistemática," *Temas* 3 (1995).

3. Conversation with Julio García Espinosa, Boston, April 16, 1997.

4. Ambrosio Fornet quoting Arturo Arias Polo, *Revolución y cultura* (December 1988): 71, and Lourdes Pasalodos, *Caimán Barbudo* (November 1988): 31, in Paulo Antonio Paranagua, *Le Cinéma cubain* (Paris: Centre Georges Pompidou, 1990), 96.

5. Caballero and del Río, "No hay cine adulto sin herejía sistemática."

6. Janette Habel, *Cuba: The Revolution in Peril*, trans. Jon Barnes (London: Verso, 1991), 59–60.

7. Conversations with Sergio Giral and Tomás Gutiérrez Alea, Havana, 1981–82.

8. See the entry for the film in Juan Antonio García Borrero, *Guía crítica del cine cubano de ficción* (1910/1998) (Havana: Editorial Arte y Literatura, 2001).

9. Conversation with Jesús Díaz, Madrid, April 1996.

10. See the entry for the film in García Borrero, *Guía crítica del cine cubano de ficción.*

11. Jesús Díaz, "Les défis de la contemporanéité: notes sur le cinéma de fiction cubain," in Paranagua, *Le Cinéma cubain*, 118.

12. Zuzana Pick, *The New Latin American Cinema: A Continental Project* (Austin: University of Texas Press, 1993), 50.

13. Interview by Enrique Colina in *Tomás Gutiérrez Alea poesía y revolución* (Filmoteca Canaria, 1994), 184; see also *New Cinema of Latin America*, Part II, "The Long Road," dir. Michael Chanan, 1984.

14. Pick, *The New Latin American Cinema*, 51–52.

15. Catherine Davies, *Screen* 38:4 (1997): 350.

16. Marvin D'Lugo, "'Transparent Women': Gender and Nation in Cuban Cinema," in Michael T. Martin, ed., *The New Latin American Cinema*, vol. 2, *Studies of National Cinemas* (Detroit: Wayne State University Press, 1997), 157.

17. See Habel, *Cuba*, 81–85.

18. D'Lugo, "'Transparent Women,'" 159.

19. J. R. Macbean, "A Dialogue with Tomás Gutiérrez Alea on the Dialectics of the Spectator in *Hasta Cierto Punto*," *Film Quarterly* 38:22–29 (1985).

20. Davies, 349.

21. Pick, *The New Latin American Cinema*, 51.

22. Jorge Ruffinelli, *Casa de las Américas* 203: 11.

23. Tomás Gutiérrez Alea, *The Viewer's Dialectic* (Havana: Editorial José Martí, 1988), 17. Subsequent references are given in the text.

24. Testimony of Juan Carlos Tabío in the entry for the film in García Borrero, *Guía crítica del cine cubano de ficción.*

25. Personal communication.

26. Jorge Fraga, *Undercut* 12 (summer 1984): 11.

27. Julio García Espinosa speaking at UNEAC, December 2000.

28. Peter B. Schumann, *Historia del cine latinoamericano* (Buenos Aires: Legasa, 1986), 177.

29. Ibid.

30. My interpretation of Jesús Diáz's observations in Parangua, *Le Cinéma cubain*, 115.

31. Tabío, in the entry for the film in García Borrero, *Guía crítica del cine cubano de ficción.*

32. Conversation with Julio García Espinosa, April 16, 1997.

33. Catherine Benamou, "Cuban Cinema: On the Threshold of Gender," in Diana Robin and Ira Jaffe, eds., *Redirecting the Gaze: Gender, Theory, and Cinema in the Third World* (Albany: State University of New York Press, 1999), 85–86.

34. See Juan Antonio García Borrero, "El cine cubano sumegido," *Antenas, Tercera Época* 1 (July–September 1999): 40–46.

35. Michael Chanan, "Report on Havana Film Festival," *Framework* 12 (1980).

36. See Habel, *Cuba,* 39–43.

37. Ibid., 69.

38. Rolando Pérez Betancourt, *Rollo crítico* (Havana: Editorial Pablode la Torriete, 1990), 245.

39. *Variety,* January 1, 1986, 18.

40. "Es una apuesta, no sé si habré perdido," interview with Jesús Díaz, *Cine Cubano* 113.

41. See the entry for the film in García Borrero, *Guía crítica del cine cubano de ficción.*

42. Julianne Burton, "Film and Revolution in Cuba: The First Twenty-Five Years," in Peter Steven, ed., *Jump Cut: Hollywood, Politics, and Counter Cinema* (Toronto: Between the Lines, 1985), 356.

43. Paulo Antonio Parangua, "Letter from Cuba to an Unfaithful Europe: The Political Position of the Cuban Cinema," *Framework* 38/39 (1992): 13.

44. Burton, "Film and Revolution in Cuba," 356.

45. See the entry for the film in García Borrero, *Guía crítica del cine cubano de ficción.*

46. Quoted in Habel, *Cuba,* 153–54.

47. *Cuba from Inside,* dir. Michael Chanan, Channel 4, 1986.

48. Eric Hobsbawm, *The Age of Extremes: The Short Twentieth Century 1914–1991,* (London: Michael Joseph, 1994), 478.

49. Ibid., 476.

50. Conversation with Julio García Espinosa recorded in Boston, April 16, 1997.

51. Pérez Betancourt, *Rollo crítico,* 250.

52. See Habel, *Cuba,* 59.

53. Fornet, in Parangua, *Le Cinéma cubain,* 104 n. 69.

54. The titles included another film by Littin, shot in Nicaragua, *Alsino y el Condor* (1982); Guzmán's *La rosa de los vientos* (1983); Alberto Durant's *Los ojos del pero* (1981) and *Malabrigo* (1986); Federico García's *Túpac Amaru* (1984); Jorge Alí Triana's *Tiempo de morir* (1985); and Birri's *Un señor muy viejo con unas alas enormes* (1988).

55. Personal communication.

56. Eduardo López Morales, quoted in the entry for the film in García Borrero, *Guía crítica del cine cubano de ficción.*

57. Parangua, "Letter from Cuba to an Unfaithful Europe," 12.

58. "Cuban Cinema in the Revolution (Pacifique Cinemateque)": http://www.cinematheque.bc.ca/previous/ja98cuba.html.

59. John King, *Magical Reels* (London: Verso, 1990), 163.

60. See Pérez Betancourt, *Rollo crítico,* 258.

61. Jesús Díaz, in Parangua, *Le Cinéma cubain,* 115.

62. See Mario Naito, entry for the film in García Borrero, *Guía crítica del cine cubano de ficción,* and Catherine Davies, "Recent Cuban Fiction Films: Identification, Interpretation, Disorder," *Bulletin of Latin American Research* 15:2 (1996): 191.

63. Quoted in Davies, "Recent Cuban Fiction Films," 186.

64. Parangua, "Letter from Cuba to an Unfaithful Europe," 10.

65. Pérez Betancourt, *Rollo crítico*, 268.

66. Paranagua, "Letter from Cuba to an Unfaithful Europe," 12.

67. Quoted in the entry for the film in García Borrero, *Guía crítica del cine cubano de ficción*.

68. Paranagua, "Letter from Cuba to an Unfaithful Europe," 9.

69. Orlando Rojas, "Por un cine incómodo," *Cine Cubano* 130.

17. Wonderland

1. Janette Habel, 191.

2. David Craven, "The Visual Arts since the Cuban Revolution," *Third Text* 20 (1992): 91.

3. Jay Murphy, "The Young and Restless in Havana," *Third Text* 20 (1992): 116.

4. Rafael Hernández, *Mirar a Cuba* (Havana: Editorial Letras Cubana, 1999), 96–97.

5. Unpublished discussion paper by Tomás Gutiérrez Alea, read to ICAIC in 1991.

6. Murphy, "The Young and Restless in Havana," 117.

7. "When the Books Run Out," *Economist,* February 9, 1991.

8. See the entry for the film in Juan Antonio García Borrero, *Guía crítica del cine cubano de ficción* (1910/1998) (Havana: Editorial Arte y Literatura, 2001), and Sergio Giral interviewed in Pedro Pérez Sarduy and Jean Stubbs, eds., *Afrocuba: An Anthology of Cuban Writing on Race, Politics and Culture* (London: Ocean/Latin American Bureau, 1993), 269.

9. Paulo Antonio Paranagua, "Letter from Cuba to an Unfaithful Europe: The Political Position of the Cuban Cinema," *Framework* 38/39 (1992): 16.

10. Zuzana Pick, *The New Latin American Cinema: A Continental Project* (Austin: University of Texas Press, 1993), 79.

11. See the entry for the film in García Borrero, *Guía crítica del cine cubano de ficción*.

12. See the entry for the film in ibid.

13. See "Cuban Cinema in the Revolution (Pacifique Cinemateque)": http://www.cinematheque.bc.ca/previous/ja98cuba.html.

14. Quoted in Catherine Davies, *Screen* 38:4 (1997): 182.

15. Ibid.

16. See the entry for ¡*Plaff!* in García Borrero, *Guía crítica del cine cubano de ficción*.

17. Enrique Colina, "El cine cubano: Dentro y fuera de la pantalla," unpublished manuscript, 1995.

18. Conversation with Julio García Espinosa, Boston, April 16, 1997.

19. Conversation with Daniel Díaz Torres, Havana, December 1995.

20. Conversation with Jesús Díaz, Madrid, April 1996.

21. Conversation with Julio García Espinosa, Boston, April 16, 1997. Aldana lost his job a year later in a leadership shake-up.

22. Castro himself may have seen the film in April. I happened to be on a visit to Cuba while these events were unfolding, and on asking to see the film was told

apologetically that this was unfortunately not possible, because the only available copy was at that moment being viewed in "high places."

23. Arturo Arango, "Manuel Pérez o el ejercicio de la memoria," *La Gaceta de Cuba,* September–October 1997.

24. The group included Santiago Álvarez, Titón (Tomás Gutiérrez Alea), Ambrosio Fornet, Senel Paz, Juan Carlos Tabío, Pastor Vega, Juan Padrón, Mario Rivas, Rebeca Chávez, Enrique Colina, Jorge Luis Sánchez, Daniel Díaz Torres, Fernando Pérez, Orlando Rojas, Rolando Díaz, Guillermo Centeno, Humberto Solás. Interview with Manuel Pérez, Havana, January 1980.

25. Interview with Manuel Pérez, Havana, January 1980.

26. Quoted in Paulo Antonio Paranagua, "Cuban Cinema's Political Challenges," in Michael T. Martin, ed., *New Latin American Cinema,* vol. 2, *Studies of National Cinemas* (Detroit: Wayne State University Press, 1997), 167.

27. Interview with Manuel Pérez. Havana, January 1980.

28. A leading figure among Cuba's writers and filmmakers, and, like García Espinosa, a (onetime) member of the party, Díaz left Cuba to teach in Berlin and then moved to Madrid. There he edited a cultural journal promoting dialogue of the left between Cuba and its émigrés, an activity the regime he left behind dislikes but does not impede beyond trying to dissuade contributors. He died in 2002.

29. See the entry for the film in García Borrero, *Guía crítica del cine cubano de ficción.*

30. Conversation with Humberto Solás, Havana, December 1998.

31. Interview with Juan Carlos Tabío, *Cineaste*; interview with Tomás Gutiérrez Alea by the author.

32. Jorge Yglesias, "La espera del futuro," *La Gaceta de Cuba* 4 (July–August 1994).

33. Ian Lumsden, *Machos, Maricones, and Gays: Cuba and Homosexuality* (Philadelphia: Temple University Press, 1996), 194.

34. See John Hess, "Melodrama, Sex, and the Cuban Revolution," *Jump Cut* 41: 120.

35. Ibid., 124.

36. Emilio Bejel, "*Fresa y chocolate* o la salida de la *guarida,*" *Casa de las Américas* 35:196 (June–September 1994): 10–22.

37. Hess, "Melodrama, Sex, and the Cuban Revolution," 121.

38. Stephen Wilkinson, "Homosexuality and the Repression of Intellectuals in *Fresa y chocolate* and *Máscaras,*" *Bulletin of Latin American Research* 18, no. 1 (1999): 17–33.

39. Quoted in ibid., 19.

40. Senel Paz (1995), 7–8.

41. See Wilkinson, n. 1, citing Jorge Domínguez, *Order and Revolution* (Cambridge: Harvard University Press, 1978), 357.

42. Bejel "*Fresa y chocolate* o la salida de la *guarida,*" 17.

43. Mirta Ibarra, "'Strawberry' at the New York Film Festival: Interview with Mirta Ibarra," *Cuba Update* (November–December 1994): 34–35.

44. Hess, "Melodrama, Sex, and the Cuban Revolution," 121.

45. Ibid., 122.

46. See Paul Julian Smith, *Vision Machines: Cinema, Literature, and Sexuality in Spain and Cuba, 1983–1993* (New York: Verso, 1996).

47. Bejel, "*Fresa y chocolate* o la salida de la *guarida,*" 16.

48. Hess, "Melodrama, Sex, and the Cuban Revolution," 119.

49. Bejel, "*Fresa y chocolate* o la salida de la *guarida*," 18.

50. Hess, "Melodrama, Sex, and the Cuban Revolution," 120.

51. Bejel, "*Fresa y chocolate* o la salida de la *guarida*," 15.

52. Interview with Tomás Gutiérrez Alea by Dennis West, *Cineaste* 22:1–2: 20.

53. Interview in *El Mundo,* April 30, 1994, section "Cinelandia," 2.

54. Lumsden, *Machos, Maricones, and Gays,*" 194.

55. Quoted in Hess, "Melodrama, Sex, and the Cuban Revolution," 120.

56. Ibid.

57. Quoted in ibid.

58. *El País,* April 29, 1994, 38.

59. John Hess, "The Revolution Will Be Melodramatized: Strawberry and Chocolate as Teacherly and Readerly Text," photocopied paper, 1996.

60. Ibid.

61. Interview with Tomás Gutiérrez Alea by Michael Chanan, *Encuentro de la cultura cubana* 1 (1996): 71.

62. Lumsden, *Machos, Maricones, and Gays,* 69.

63. Julio César Aguillera in García Borrero, *Guía crítica del cine cubano de ficción.*

64. Mike Wayne, *Political Film: The Dialectics of Third Cinema* (London: Pluto, 2001) 151.

65. Ibid., 156.

66. Colina, "El cine cubano."

67. These figures are drawn from Roxana Pollo, "Puede ser este un año favorable para la economía del cine cubano," *Granma,* May 1994, quoted in Diane Soles, "The Cuban Film Industry: Between a Rock and Hard Place," *Global Development Studies* 1:3–4 (winter 1998–spring 1999): 104–5 and 111.

68. Soles, "The Cuban Film Industry," 112, 113 (retranslated from the Spanish quotations in the footnotes on these pages).

69. Luciano Castillo, "Lágrimas para un melodrama: hacia dónde va nuestro cine," *Antenas, Tercera Época* 1 (July–September 1999): 12.

70. Juan Antonio García Borrero, "El cine cubano sumegido," *Antenas, Tercera Época* 1 (July–September 1999): 40–46.

71. See Juan Antonio García Borrero, "Los Talleres de Crítica Cinematográfica: Estrategias desde el margen," in Juan Antonio García Borrero, ed., *La ciudad simbólica: Memorias del 8vo Taller de Crítica Cinematográfica de Camagüey* (Camagüey: Editorial Ácana, 2000), 5–12.

72. Mario Naito in García Borrero, *La ciudad simbólica,* 123.

73. Hernández, *Mirar a Cuba,* 101.

74. Ibid., 109.

75. Désirée Díaz, *La Gaceta de Cuba* (2000): 38.

76. Ivette Leyva, "Arturo Sotto: Yo sólo quiero saber, *La Gaceta de Cuba,* (January–February 1999): 29.

77. Díaz, 38.

78. Anne Marie Stock, "Migrancy and the Latin American Cinemascape: Towards a Post-National Critical Praxis," in *Revista Canadiense de Estudio Hispánicos* 20:1 (1995): 25. Subsequent references are given in the text.

79. Quoted in Díaz, 39.

80. Ibid., 40.

81. Vladimir Cruz, *Cine Cubano* 148, 44.

Distribution Information

The following organizations distribute Cuban films in the United States and Europe.

Center for Cuban Studies
124 West Twenty-Third Street
New York, NY 10011
(212) 242-0559
(212) 242-1937 FAX
www.cubaupdate.org

Cinema Guild
130 Madison Avenue, 2d Floor
New York, NY 10016-6242
(212) 685-6242
(212) 685-4717 FAX
www.cinemaguild.com

Miramax
99 Hudson Street, 5th Floor
New York, NY 10013
(212) 941-3800
(212) 941-3949 FAX
www.miramax.com

New Yorker Films
85 Fifth Avenue, 11th Floor
New York, NY 10013
(212) 645-4600
(212) 645-3030 FAX
www.NewYorkerFilms.com

Index of Film Titles

Following the Index of Film Titles is an Index of Names.

Index of Names

Preceding the Index of Names is an Index of Film Titles.

Michael Chanan is professor of cultural and media studies at the University of the West of England, Bristol. He has written, edited, and translated books and articles on film and music, including *The Dream That Kicks,* on the invention and early years of cinema in Britain, *Musica Practica* and *From Handel to Hendrix* on the social history of music, and *Repeated Takes,* a history of recording. He is also a documentary filmmaker and taught filmmaking for many years in London.